The Encyclopedia of
ITALIAN COOKING
1001 AUTHENTIC RECIPES

The Encyclopedia of
ITALIAN COOKING
1001 AUTHENTIC RECIPES

Reader's Digest

THE READER'S DIGEST ASSOCIATION, INC.
PLEASANTVILLE, NEW YORK / MONTREAL

A READER'S DIGEST BOOK

This edition first published
in the US and Canada by Reader's Digest

Copyright © McRae Books Srl 2001

This book was conceived, edited and designed by
McRae Books Srl
Via de' Rustici, 5,
50122 Florence, Italy
info@mcraebooks.com

LIBRARY OF CONGRESS CATALOGING IN PUBLICATION DATA

The encyclopedia of Italian cooking : 1,001 authentic recipes.
   p. cm.
   Includes index.
   ISBN 0-7621-0340-X
   1. Cookery, Italian. I. Reader's Digest Association.
TX723 .E533 2001
641.5945–dc21   2001019984

Project Director: Anne McRae
Design Director: Marco Nardi
Text: Carla Bardi, Rosalba Gioffrè, Mariapaola Dettore, Sara Vignozzi, Elisabetta Lotti, Leonardo Castellucci
Photography: Marco Lanza, Walter Mericchi
Set Design: Rosalba Gioffrè
Layout: Giovanni Mattioli, Laura Ottina, Paola Baldanzi
Translation from the Italian: Christine Sawyer
Editing: Susan Kelly, Paige Weber, Holly Willis, Loredana Agosta

READER'S DIGEST PROJECT STAFF
Editorial Director: Fred DuBose
Editorial Manager: Christine R. Guido

Contributing Editor: Susan McQuillan
Contributing Project Designer: Jane Wilson

READER'S DIGEST ILLUSTRATED REFERENCE BOOKS

Editor-in-Chief: Christopher Cavanaugh
Art Director: Joan Mazzeo
Director, Trade Publishing: Christopher T. Reggio
Editorial Director, Trade: Susan Randol
Senior Design Director, Trade: Elizabeth L. Tunnicliffe

Color separations: R.A.F., Fotolito Toscana, and Litocolor, Florence, Italy
Printed and bound in Italy, by Arte Grafica, Verona

1 3 5 7 9 10 8 6 4 2

CONTENTS

INTRODUCTION

Each of Italy's 20 regions has its own special local foods and wines.

In the western alpine region of Valle d'Aosta, creamy Fontina cheese fondue is served on winter evenings.

In Italy, food is a central part of life. Cooking, or even just talking about food and cooking, is something we Italians indulge in on a daily basis. And everyone (including people who have never entered a kitchen!) is an expert, with strong opinions and well-rounded advice to give. Food is associated with family meals and celebrations, but also with village feast days, festivities for patron saints, harvest feasts, and religious celebrations of every sort. Every occasion has its own special dish or menu.

What many foreigners don't realize about Italian cooking is how regional it is. For example, most dishes in the northern regions are based on butter, whereas in the south they are oil-based. Rice and polenta are more traditional in the north than in the south, where dried pasta is the staple first course. The regions themselves all have specialties; agnolotti are the delicious filled pasta of Piedmont, while tortellini are typical of Emilia in central Italy. The pastry cooks of Sicily are renowned for the range and quality of their cakes and desserts, while other regions of Italy, such as Lazio, have only a limited number of traditional sweets. Tuscany is famous for its Florentine steak, traditionally served so lightly cooked that the inside is hardly warmed. Not surprisingly, it was banned in April of 2001 for several months because of the mad cow disease scare. Even within the regions, there are many variations. The beautiful medieval town of Siena, in Tuscany, is celebrated for its *panforte* and a range of local cookies. Although only 40 miles away, Florentines would look askance at anyone who thought that these sweets came from their hometown. Some dishes even vary from village to village, just as recipes change from family to family....

In this book, we have sought out more than 1,001 traditional dishes from every region of Italy. Most are classic recipes that have been adapted for modern use. They are all ranked from 1 (easy) to 3 (complicated); you will find that almost all are either easy or fairly easy (2). And this is the beauty of Italian cooking – the ease with which most mouthwatering dishes can be prepared, even by novice cooks.

There are just a few basic rules to remember when preparing Italian food to achieve perfect results. Unlike many other cuisines, Italian cooking does not rely heavily on sauces that camouflage or change the basic flavor of the foods being served. Where sauces are used, they are simple, fresh,

The recipes in this book are divided into chapters arranged more or less in the order that they would be served in during a large formal meal. Use them to plan a family lunch or a dinner party for friends. Begin the meal with one or more antipasti *(appetizers)*. Follow this with a primo piatto *(pasta, rice, polenta, gnocchi or crepes)*, then a meat or egg dish served with a salad or vegetable. Finish with a pudding or some ice cream.

Even when you are not planning a large complicated meal, you will find that there are recipes here for every occasion, from breakfast and brunch, through lunch and afternoon tea, to dinner and late night snacks. Good luck and Buon appetito!

and usually intended to draw out or highlight the taste of the ingredients in the dish itself. Which means that the basic ingredients must be of the best possible quality. Don't skimp when buying olive oil, for example. All your best efforts will be in vain if you don't use high-quality extra-virgin oil.

Although it is difficult to imagine Italian cooking today without the tomato, it was only brought to Europe by explorers returning home in the 16th century. Before that time, many pasta dishes were served with spices and sweetened with sugar.

Secondly, be inventive – we are all artists in Italy, or at least in our own kitchens! You may want to follow a recipe to the letter the first time you make it, and then try out variations once you have the basic idea. While every effort has been made to suggest ingredients that you will be able to find easily, don't fuss if you don't have every single one of them. Adapt the recipe to use what you do have in your garden or refrigerator. If you don't like some ingredients, just leave them out. How many of my American friends will not eat anchovies, so I simply don't use them when they are my guests. Don't insist that "this is the way you make this dish." Italian cooking isn't like that.

Carla Bardi, Editor

Sauces abound in Italian cooking. In this chapter we have identified 39 of the most common and versatile sauces. We have also included some classic pasta sauces here, such as pesto and Bolognese meat sauce. Many more pasta sauces can be found in the chapter on pasta. Each recipe in this section has a serving suggestion at the end of the method.

SAUCES

SALSA VERDE
Green sauce

¹/₂	cup fresh white bread crumbs
3–4	tablespoons red wine vinegar
1	hard-boiled egg yolk
3	tablespoons finely chopped parsley
1–2	cloves garlic, finely chopped
1	salted anchovy, rinsed and boned, or 2–3 anchovy fillets (optional)
¹/₂	cup extra-virgin olive oil
	salt and freshly ground white pepper to taste

Soak the bread crumbs for a few minutes in the vinegar (diluted with a little cold water, if it is very strong) and then squeeze out excess moisture. • Place the egg yolk in a bowl and mash with a fork. Add the parsley, garlic, anchovy, and bread crumbs and mix well. • Trickle in sufficient oil to make a fairly thick sauce while stirring continuously. Season to taste with salt (if using anchovies, the sauce may already be salty enough) and white pepper. • The sauce can also be made in a blender. In that case, place all the ingredients in the blender (the parsley and garlic will not need to be chopped), and process for 2–3 minutes. • Leave to stand for at least 30 minutes, preferably 1 hour, before serving. Stir carefully and serve with boiled meats and fish.
Serves: 4 · Prep: 15–20 min. + 30 min. to stand · Level: 1

◄ Bell pepper sauce (see recipe, page 15)
▲ Green sauce

SALSA ROSSA PIEMONTESE
Piedmontese tomato sauce

☞ This sauce can be prepared in advance and reheated just before serving. Stored in an airtight container, it will keep in the refrigerator for several days.

1¼ lb ripe tomatoes
1 small onion, coarsely chopped
1 tender stalk celery, coarsely chopped
1 small carrot, coarsely chopped
2 cloves garlic, finely chopped
1 tablespoon finely chopped parsley
1 fresh hot chile, thinly sliced
¼ cup extra-virgin olive oil
1 teaspoon hot mustard
1 tablespoon red wine vinegar
   salt to taste

Blanch the tomatoes for 1 minute in boiling water, then slip the skins off with your fingers. Cut the tomatoes in half and remove the seeds. Set aside to drain for 15 minutes in a colander, cut side downward. • Chop the tomatoes and place them in a saucepan with the onion, celery, carrot, garlic, parsley, and chile. Cook over low heat, uncovered, for 1½ hours, stirring frequently. • Sieve the contents of the saucepan (or reduce them to a purée in a food processor), then blend in the oil, mustard, and vinegar. Season with salt and serve hot. • To give the sauce an agreeable sweet-sour taste, add an extra ½ cup vinegar and 1 tablespoon of sugar after the other ingredients have cooked for 1 hour. • Serve with boiled meats.

Serves: 4 · Prep: 25 min. · Cooking: 1½ hrs · Level: 1

Honey sauce

SALSA PICCANTE AL POMODORO
Spicy tomato sauce

½ cup extra-virgin olive oil
10 whole cloves garlic
1½ lb peeled and chopped fresh or canned tomatoes
   salt to taste
2–4 hot chilies, dried or fresh, crumbled or sliced

Heat the oil in a small, heavy-bottomed pan over low heat. • Add the garlic and tomatoes. Sprinkle with salt, add the chilies and cook, partially covered, for at least 1 hour. • Serve hot or warm with boiled, braised, or grilled meats.

Serves: 8–10 · Prep: 5 min. · Cooking: 1 hr · Level: 1

SALSA AL BURRO E PARMIGIANO
Butter and Parmesan sauce

¾ cup butter
1½ cups freshly grated Parmesan cheese

Melt the butter in a heavy-bottomed pan over low heat and stir in half the Parmesan. • Sprinkle the remaining Parmesan over the dish you intend to serve it with and pour the sauce over the top. • Serve with boiled or baked vegetables, dried and fresh pasta, or potato gnocchi.

Serves: 4 · Cooking: 5 min. · Level: 1

SALSA AL BURRO E SALVIA
Butter and sage sauce

¾ cup butter
10 fresh sage leaves

Cook the butter and sage in a heavy-bottomed pan over very low heat until the butter turns

light gold. • Serve hot with boiled vegetables, dried and fresh pasta, or potato gnocchi.

Serves: 4 · Prep: 5 min. · Cooking: 5 min. · Level: 1

SALSA AL BURRO E ROSMARINO
Butter and rosemary sauce

¾ cup butter
5 twigs fresh rosemary

Cook the butter and rosemary in a heavy-bottomed pan over very low heat until the butter turns light gold. • Remove the rosemary and serve hot with dried and fresh pasta or potato gnocchi.

Serves: 4 · Prep: 5 min. · Cooking: 5 min. · Level: 1

SALSA DI MIELE
Honey sauce

12 shelled walnut halves
¾ cup mild, liquid honey
2 tablespoons mustard
1–2 tablespoons boiling water

Pound the walnuts finely using a mortar and pestle, or chop in a food processor. • Mix the honey and mustard in a small bowl. Add the water and then the walnuts. Stir well. • Serve warm or at room temperature with boiled meats or slices of Pecorino cheese.

Serves: 4 · Prep: 10 min. · Level: 1

SALSA ACCIUGATA
Anchovy sauce

10 salted anchovy fillets, crumbled
¾ cup butter

Rinse the anchovies thoroughly to remove extra salt. • Place the anchovies in a heavy-bottomed pan over medium-low heat. Mash with a fork. Add the butter and cook, stirring frequently, until creamy. • Serve hot with poached or baked fish.

Serves: 6 · Prep: 10 min. · Cooking: 5 min. · Level: 1

SALSA DI PEPERONI
Bell pepper sauce

☞ This sauce becomes even tastier if served the day after it is made.

- 3 large bell peppers
- 2 cloves garlic, finely chopped
- 3 tablespoons finely chopped parsley
- 1 medium onion, finely chopped
- 1 tablespoon sugar
- 1 tablespoon white wine vinegar
- 1/4 cup extra-virgin olive oil
  salt to taste

Clean the bell peppers, removing the core and seeds. Rinse and chop very finely. • Combine with the garlic, parsley, and onion and place in a heavy-bottomed saucepan. Cover with cold water and simmer for 30 minutes. • Add the sugar, vinegar, and olive oil. Season with salt and cook for another 5–10 minutes, or until the sauce is thick. • Serve at room temperature with boiled meats, poached or baked fish, baked vegetables, or boiled rice.

Serves: 4–6 · Prep: 10 min. · Cooking: 40 min. · Level: 1

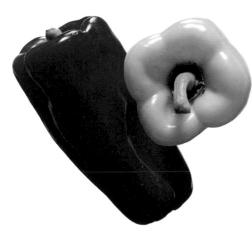

SALSA ALLE CIPOLLE
Onion sauce

- 6 large white onions, thinly sliced
- 1/3 cup extra-virgin olive oil
  salt and freshly ground black pepper to taste
- 1 cup Beef stock (see recipe, page 105)

Place the onions in a heavy-bottomed pan with the oil over low heat. Season with a little salt (use less than normal because the very slow cooking enhances the taste of the salt). Add a grinding of pepper and cover. • Cook gently over low heat for at least 3

Onion sauce

hours. The onions must not burn, but should slowly melt. Stir frequently, adding stock as necessary to keep the sauce moist. • When cooked, the sauce should be creamy and golden. • Serve with baked vegetables or roast meats.

Serves: 6 · Prep: 15 min. · Cooking: 3 hrs · Level: 1

SALSA ALLE OLIVE NERE
Black olive sauce

- 20 large black olives, pitted and chopped
- 1/4 cup finely chopped parsley
- 1 teaspoon capers, chopped
- 1 clove garlic, finely chopped
- 1 hard-boiled egg yolk
- 1 teaspoon white vinegar
  freshly ground black pepper to taste

Mix the olives, parsley, capers, and garlic in a small bowl until blended. Add the egg yolk, vinegar, and pepper and mix until creamy. • Serve with poached fish.

Serves: 4 · Prep: 10 min. · Level: 1

SALSA DEL POVR'OM
Poor man's sauce

- 3 tablespoons butter
- 1–2 cloves garlic, peeled and lightly crushed
- 1 teaspoon all-purpose flour
- 2 tablespoons red wine vinegar
  salt and freshly ground white pepper to taste
- 2 whole eggs + 1 extra yolk

Melt the butter in a small saucepan over low heat. Add the garlic and cook very slowly until pale gold (take care not to burn the garlic because it will give the sauce a bitter flavor). • Mix the flour and vinegar in a bowl and season with salt and pepper. Add the whole eggs and the extra yolk and beat lightly with a fork, making sure they don't become frothy. • Remove the garlic from the butter and add the egg mixture gradually while stirring continuously over very low heat. Cook until the mixture is smooth and creamy. • Serve warm or at room temperature with boiled asparagus, or other boiled vegetables and meats.

Serves: 4 · Prep: 5 min. · Cooking: 7–9 min. · Level: 1

SALSA DI FAVE
Fava bean sauce

- 8 oz fava beans, podded
- 2 cloves garlic, chopped
- 6 leaves fresh mint
- 3 oz fresh Pecorino cheese
- 2 hard-boiled egg yolks
- 1/4 cup extra-virgin olive oil
  salt and freshly ground black pepper to taste

Chop the beans, garlic, mint, cheese, and egg yolks in a food processor. Add the oil gradually and mix until smooth and creamy. • Serve with boiled, baked, or grilled vegetables.

Serves: 4 · Prep: 5 min. · Level: 1

MAIONESE
Mayonnaise

- 2 egg yolks
- 2 tablespoons lemon juice or vinegar
- 2 tablespoons water
- 1 teaspoon sugar
- 1 teaspoon dry mustard
- ½ teaspoon salt
  freshly ground black pepper to taste (optional)
- 1 cup extra-virgin olive oil

In a small saucepan, stir together the egg yolks, lemon juice or vinegar, water, sugar, mustard, salt, and pepper, if using, until thoroughly blended. • Cook over very low heat, stirring constantly, until the mixture bubbles in 1 or 2 places. Remove from heat. Let stand for 5 minutes. • Pour into blender container. Cover and blend at very high speed. While blending, very slowly add the oil. Blend until thick and smooth. Occasionally, turn off the blender and scrape down the sides of the container with a rubber spatula. • Cover and refrigerate for up to 3 days.

Serves: 4 · Prep: 15 min. · Level: 2

MAIONESE CON LA SENAPE
Mustard mayonnaise

- 1 quantity Mayonnaise, made with lemon juice (see preceding recipe)
- 2 teaspoons hot mustard
- ¼ cup heavy cream

Prepare the mayonnaise as explained above, then stir in the mustard followed by the cream. • Serve with hard boiled eggs or boiled, grilled, or baked vegetables.

Serves: 4 · Prep: 15 min. · Level: 2

SALSA DI CAPPERI
Caper sauce

- 4 oz pickled capers, drained
- 4 anchovy fillets
- 2 cloves garlic, finely chopped
- ¼ cup extra-virgin olive oil
  juice of 1 lemon

Rinse the capers and chop finely. Carefully rinse the anchovies and crumble. • Combine the capers and anchovies in a bowl with the garlic and gradually stir in the oil. Pour in the lemon juice and mix well. • Serve with poached fish or hard-boiled eggs.

Serves: 4 · Prep: 5 min. · Level: 1

AGLIATA
Garlic mayonnaise

- 1 quantity Mayonnaise, made with lemon juice (see recipe, left)
- 2 cloves garlic, very finely chopped
- 1 tablespoon extra-virgin olive oil

Prepare the mayonnaise. • When the mayonnaise is ready, stir in the garlic, extra oil, and pepper. Leave to stand for at least 1 hour before serving. • Serve with boiled meats and fish.

Serves: 4 · Prep: 15 min. · Level: 2

SALSA ALLO YOGURT E TONNO
Yogurt and tuna sauce

- 1 cup plain yogurt
- 3 tablespoons capers packed in salt, rinsed and dried
- 4 oz canned tuna fish
  salt and freshly ground black pepper to taste

Place the yogurt, capers, tuna, salt, and pepper in a blender and mix until smooth and creamy. • This delicate sauce is delicious with poached fish.

Serves: 4 · Prep: 10 min. · Level: 1

SALSA BESCIAMELLA
Béchamel sauce

☞ Béchamel sauce is a basic ingredient in many recipes. It is quick and easy to prepare and should be used as soon as it is made.

- 2 cups milk
- ¼ cup butter
- ½ cup all-purpose flour
  salt to taste

Heat the milk in a saucepan until it is almost boiling. • In a heavy-bottomed saucepan, melt the butter with the flour over low heat, stirring rapidly with a wooden spoon. Cook for about 1 minute. • Remove from heat and add half the hot milk, stirring constantly. Return to low heat and stir until the sauce starts to thicken. • Add the rest of the milk gradually and continue stirring until it comes to a boil. • Season with salt and continue stirring until the béchamel is the right thickness. • If any lumps form, beat the sauce rapidly with a whisk until they dissolve.

Serves: 4 · Prep: 5 min. · Cooking: 7–8 min. · Level: 1

SALSA MOSTARDA
Fruit mustard sauce

2¹/₂	lb mixed fruit (white grapes, apples, pears, apricots, cherries, etc.)
	juice and peel of 1 lemon
¹/₂	cup honey
1¹/₂	cups dry white wine
¹/₃	cup mustard powder

Wash and peel the fruit. Cut into fairly large pieces, leaving the grapes and cherries whole. • Put the fruit in a heavy-bottomed saucepan and cover with water. Place over medium heat. Add the lemon juice and peel and 2 tablespoons of honey. • In a separate saucepan, simmer the wine with the remaining honey over medium-low heat. • After 10 minutes add the mustard to the wine and honey. Stir thoroughly and cook until thick. • Pour the mustard and wine mixture over the fruit and mix carefully. • Serve at room temperature with boiled and roast meats.

Serves: 12 · Prep: 15 min. · Cooking: 1 hr · Level: 1

◄ Fruit mustard sauce

Basic tomato sauce

RAGÙ AL POMODORO
Tomato meat sauce

☞ This is a basic tomato ragù. Very versatile, it goes perfectly with any type of pasta, but can also be served on polenta, rice, or vegetables.

- ¼ cup butter
- ½ cup diced pancetta
- 1 onion, 1 carrot, 1 stalk celery, all finely chopped
- 10 oz ground beef
- 5 oz lean ground pork
- 1 cup dry red wine
- 1¼ cups Beef stock (see recipe, page 105)
- 1 tablespoon tomato paste
- 15 oz peeled and chopped fresh or canned tomatoes
  salt and freshly ground black pepper to taste

In a heavy-bottomed saucepan, melt the butter until it bubbles. Add the pancetta, onion, carrot, and celery and sauté over low heat for 10 minutes. • Add the beef and pork and cook for 5 minutes more, stirring frequently. • Pour in half the wine and, when it has partially evaporated, add a third of the stock. • Simmer until the liquid has reduced, then add the tomato paste and a little more wine and stock. •

After 10–15 minutes, add the tomatoes, salt, and pepper. • Continue cooking over low heat, gradually stirring in the remaining wine and stock. When cooked, the sauce should be fairly thick. This will take about 2 hours in all.

Serves: 4 · Prep: 10 min. · Cooking: 2 hrs · Level: 1

SUGO FINTO
False meat sauce

- ½ cup diced pancetta
- 1 cup finely chopped parsley
- 1 large onion, 2 carrots, 2 stalks celery, 2 cloves garlic, all finely chopped
- 2 tablespoons extra-virgin olive oil
- ¼ cup butter
- 6 tomatoes, peeled and chopped
  salt and freshly ground black pepper to taste

Put the pancetta, parsley, onion, carrots, celery, and garlic in a skillet with the oil and butter. Cook over medium-high heat for 5 minutes. • Add the tomatoes and season with salt and pepper. • Simmer over medium-low heat for about 25 minutes.

Serves: 4 · Prep: 10 min. · Cooking: 30 min. · Level: 1

POMAROLA
Basic tomato sauce

☞ This recipe makes a fairly large quantity. Freeze it or store in the refrigerator in an airtight container.

- 4 lb fresh or canned tomatoes
- 1 large onion, 1 large carrot, 1 stalk celery, 1 clove garlic, coarsely chopped
- 1 tablespoon finely chopped parsley
- 8 fresh basil leaves, torn
- ¼ cup extra-virgin olive oil
- 1 teaspoon sugar
  salt and freshly ground black pepper to taste

Sauté the onion, carrot, celery and garlic in a skillet with the oil for 5 minutes. • Add the tomatoes, parsley, basil, salt, pepper, and sugar. Cover and cook over low heat for about 45 minutes, or until the tomato and oil begin to separate. • For a smoother sauce, press the mixture through a food mill. • Serve with all kinds of fresh and dried pasta, and potato gnocchi.

Serves: 8 · Prep: 15 min. · Cooking: 50 min. · Level: 1

SALSA AL POMODORO
Simple tomato sauce

☞ Oil-based tomato sauce is a classic topping for all dried pasta. It is also good with gnocchi, polenta, rice, and boiled or baked vegetables.

- 2 cloves garlic, finely chopped
- ¼ cup extra-virgin olive oil
- 6 fresh basil leaves, torn
- 2 lb peeled and chopped fresh or canned tomatoes
  salt and freshly ground black pepper to taste

Put the garlic and oil in a large skillet and sauté over medium heat until the garlic is golden brown. Add the basil and tomatoes. Season with salt and pepper, and simmer for about 15–20 minutes, or until the oil begins to separate from the tomato.

Serves: 4 · Prep: 15 min. · Cooking: 20 min. · Level: 1

SALSA DI BURRO E POMODORO
Tomato and butter sauce

☞ Another versatile sauce that can be served with all types of pasta, gnocchi, crêpes, and boiled or baked vegetables.

- 3 cloves garlic, finely chopped
- 1 large onion, finely chopped
- ¼ cup butter
- ¼ cup extra-virgin olive oil
- 1½ lb peeled and chopped fresh or canned tomatoes
  salt and freshly ground black pepper to taste
- 12 fresh basil leaves, torn

Combine the garlic and onion in a skillet with the butter and oil. Sauté over medium heat until the onion is transparent. • Add the tomatoes and season with salt and pepper. Simmer over medium-low heat for about 25 minutes. • Add the basil just before removing from heat.

Serves: 4 · Prep: 10 min. · Cooking: 30 · Level: 1

RAGÙ DI CARNE ALLA BOLOGNESE
Bolognese meat sauce

☞ This classic meat sauce is famous all over the world as a pasta sauce. It is very good with pasta, but can also be served on gnocchi, polenta, and potatoes, as well as in a variety of baked dishes. The secret of a successful ragù lies in the cooking; it should be simmered over low heat for at least 2½ hours. This ragù can be made ahead of time and kept in the refrigerator for up to 3 days. It also freezes well.

- ½ cup diced pancetta
- 1 medium onion, 1 stalk celery, 1 carrot, all finely chopped
- ¼ cup butter
- 10 oz ground beef
- 4 oz ground pork
- 4 oz Italian pork sausage, peeled and crumbled
- 1 freshly ground clove
  pinch of cinnamon
- 1 teaspoon freshly ground black pepper
- 1 (15 oz) can peeled and chopped tomatoes
- 1 cup whole milk
  salt to taste

Combine the pancetta, onion, celery, and carrot in a sauté pan with the butter and cook over medium heat until the onion turns pale gold. • Add the beef, pork, and sausage and cook until browned. Sprinkle with the clove, cinnamon, and pepper. Stir in the tomatoes and cook over medium heat for 15 minutes. • Add the milk and season with salt. Turn the heat down to low and simmer for at least 2½ hours, stirring frequently.

Serves: 4 · Prep: 30 min. · Cooking: 3 hrs · Level: 1

RAGÙ ALLA NAPOLETANA
Neapolitan meat sauce

☞ This sauce comes from the exuberant southern city of Naples. The meat is cooked in one large piece and served as a second course after the pasta.

- 2 lb lean beef (rump)
- ¼ cup lard, diced
- ¼ cup extra-virgin olive oil
- 2 large onions, finely chopped

Neapolitan meat sauce

- 2 carrots, finely chopped
- 1 stalk celery, finely chopped
- 1 cup dry red wine
  salt to taste
- 1 (15 oz) can peeled and chopped tomatoes

Place the beef in a heavy-bottomed pan with the lard and oil. Add the onion, carrot, and celery and sauté over medium heat until the vegetables are transparent. • Pour in the wine and cook until it evaporates. Season with salt, partially cover, and cook over low heat for 30 minutes. • Add the tomatoes and cook for another 2 hours. • Remove the piece of beef and serve the sauce with pasta.

Serves: 6 · Prep: 30 min. · Cooking: 2½ hrs · Level: 1

SUGO DI PESCE
Fish sauce

☞ Many different sorts of fish will work in this sauce. Ask your fish vendor for the same type of fish that are suitable for making soup.

- 1½ lb assorted fresh fish, such as cod, sea bass, halibut, and red snapper, gutted
- 2 tablespoons fresh rosemary leaves
- 1 onion, finely chopped
- 1 clove garlic, finely chopped
- ½ cup extra-virgin olive oil
  salt and freshly ground black pepper to taste

Place the fish in a large pot of water with the rosemary and bring to a boil. Cook for 15 minutes. Take the fish out, remove the skin and bones, and crumble the cooked meat. Strain the liquid and discard the rosemary leaves. • Sauté the onion and garlic in a large skillet with the oil until light gold in color. Add the fish meat and 3 cups of the stock in which it was cooked. Season with salt and pepper and simmer over low heat for about 30–35 minutes. • Serve with pasta.

Serves: 4 · Prep: 15 min. · Cooking: 50 min. · Level: 2

SUGO DI SALSICCE
Sausage meat sauce

- 1 oz dried porcini mushrooms
- 1 large onion, finely chopped
- 1 clove garlic, finely chopped
- 1/2 cup diced pancetta
- 2 tablespoons extra-virgin olive oil
- 10 oz Italian pork sausage, peeled and crumbled
- 1 (15 oz) can peeled and chopped tomatoes
  salt and freshly ground black pepper to taste

Soak the mushrooms in a bowl of warm water for 20 minutes. Rinse well and chop coarsely. • Put the onion, garlic, pancetta, and oil in a skillet and sauté over medium heat until the onion is transparent. Add the sausage and sauté for 5 more minutes. • Add the tomatoes and mushrooms, season with salt and pepper, and simmer over medium-low heat for about 20 minutes, stirring frequently. • Serve with pasta, gnocchi, rice, polenta, or boiled or baked vegetables.

Serves: 4 · Prep: 25 min. · Cooking: 30 min. · Level: 1

SALSA DI NOCI
Walnut sauce

- 2 slices day-old bread (crusts removed)
- 1/4 cup white wine vinegar
- 30 blanched walnuts
  small bunch of parsley
- 1/3 cup extra-virgin olive oil
  salt and freshly ground black pepper to taste

Crumble the bread and moisten it with the vinegar. • Chop the walnuts and parsley in a food processor. Add the bread and mix, while gradually adding the olive oil. Season with salt and pepper. Serve with poached fish, poultry, and baked vegetables.

Serves: 4 · Prep: 10 min. · Level: 1

INTINGOLO DI FUNGHI PORCINI
Italian mushroom sauce

☞ Fresh porcini mushrooms are hard to find outside of Italy and France, but are widely available in their dried form. If you can't get fresh porcini, combine a small amount of soaked, dried porcini with fresh white mushrooms. The dried porcini have such a strong taste they will flavor the dish almost as well as the fresh ones.

- 14 oz coarsely chopped fresh porcini mushrooms (or 12 oz white mushrooms and 1 oz dried porcini)
- 2 cloves garlic, finely chopped
  sprig of fresh rosemary, finely chopped
- 2 tablespoons butter
- 1/4 cup extra-virgin olive oil
  salt and freshly ground black pepper to taste

If using dried porcini, soak them in 1 cup of warm water for about 20 minutes. Drain and squeeze out the excess water. Chop coarsely. • Put the garlic and rosemary in a large skillet with the butter and oil and sauté over medium heat for 4–5 minutes. Add the mushrooms and season with salt and pepper. Cover and cook over medium-low heat for about 15 minutes, or until the mushrooms are very tender.

Serves: 4 · Prep: 15 min. + time to soak the mushrooms · Cooking: 20 min. · Level: 1

SALSA AL PECORINO
Pecorino cheese sauce

  small bunch of parsley
- 20 basil leaves
- 2 tablespoons pine nuts
- 1 hard-boiled egg
- 4 oz aged Pecorino cheese
- 1/3 cup extra-virgin olive oil
  salt and freshly ground black pepper to taste

In a blender or food processor, blend the parsley, basil, and pine nuts. • Add the

hard-boiled egg, Pecorino, and olive oil. Mix well. • Serve with poultry or fish.

Serves: 4 · Prep: 5 min. · Level: 1

INTINGOLO DI FEGATINI
Chicken liver sauce

- 1/3 cup extra-virgin olive oil
- 1 large onion, finely chopped
- 1 large carrot, finely chopped
- 1 stalk celery, finely chopped
- 8 chicken livers, cleaned and coarsely chopped
- 1/3 cup dry red or white wine
- 1 tablespoon tomato paste
- 1 cup shelled peas
  salt and freshly ground white pepper to taste

Heat the oil in a small skillet and sauté the onion, carrot, and celery over medium-low heat for 6–7 minutes. • Add the chicken livers and cook for 2–3 minutes. • Pour in the wine and after another 2–3 minutes, add the tomato paste diluted in 2/3 cup of water. Mix well, and add the peas. • Cook for another 15–20 minutes. • Serve with fresh pasta, boiled rice, or polenta.

Serves: 4 · Prep: 15 min. · Cooking: 30 min. · Level: 1

SALSA AI PINOLI
Pine nut sauce

- 2 slices day-old bread
- 1/4 cup white wine vinegar
- 2 tablespoons cider vinegar
- 2 teaspoons sugar
- 1 1/2 cups pine nuts
- 1/2 cup extra-virgin olive oil

Crumble the bread into small pieces and moisten it with the vinegars. • In a blender or food processor, finely chop the bread, sugar, and pine nuts, gradually adding the olive oil a little at a time. Serve with fish and poultry.

Serves: 4 · Prep: 5 min. · Level: 1

SALSA AL PEPE
Pepper sauce

- 2 slices of day-old bread
- 1/4 cup cider vinegar
- 2 tablespoons black pepper corns
- 2 tablespoons red pepper corns
- 2 tablespoons pink pepper corns
- 1/2 cup extra-virgin olive oil

Crumble the bread and moisten it with the vinegar. • In a food processor, grind the pepper corns. Then add the bread and oil. Process until the sauce is well mixed. • Serve with roasted meats.

Serves: 4 · Prep: 5 min. · Level: 1

SALSA DI AGRESTO
Grape juice sauce

- 1 cup grape juice
- 2 slices day-old bread
- 1 large onion
  zest of 1 orange
  salt and freshly ground black pepper to taste
- 1/2 cup extra-virgin olive oil

Boil the grape juice until about two-thirds of it has evaporated, removing the foam that forms on top. • Soak the bread in the hot juice. • In a food processor or blender, finely chop the onion and orange zest. Add the soaked bread and continue to mix. Transfer to a small bowl, and gradually add the oil while whipping the

mixture by hand with a fork. • Serve with meat, poultry, or game.

Serves: 4 · Prep: 10 min. · Level: 1

SALSA AL DRAGONCELLO
Tarragon sauce

☞ This sauce will keep in the refrigerator for 2–3 days if covered with a thin coat of olive oil.

- 2 tablespoons parsley
- 2 tablespoons tarragon
- 2 cloves garlic
- 2 tablespoons bread crumbs soaked in vinegar
- 1/4 cup extra-virgin olive oil

In a blender or food processor, chop the ingredients together, then gradually pour in the olive oil. • Serve with boiled meats or fish.

Serves: 4 · Prep: 5 min. · Level: 1

Pesto comes from the Liguria region in northern Italy and is named for its capital city, Genoa. Traditionally, it is served with *trenette*, a local egg-based pasta similar to fettuccine. It is also good with dried pasta, and is delicious with potato gnocchi or instead of meat sauce in lasagne.

PESTO ALLA GENOVESE
Genoese basil sauce

- 2 cups fresh basil leaves
- 2 tablespoons pine nuts
- 2 cloves garlic
- 1/2 cup extra-virgin olive oil
  salt to taste
- 2 tablespoons freshly grated Parmesan cheese
- 2 tablespoons freshly grated Pecorino cheese
- 2 tablespoons of water from the pasta pot
  pat of butter for serving

Combine the basil, pine nuts, garlic, olive oil, and salt in a food processor and chop until smooth. Place the mixture in a large serving bowl and stir in the cheeses. • Add the water and butter and stir well. Serve at room temperature.

Serves: 4 · Prep: 10 minutes · Level: 1

PESTO TOSCANO
Tuscan-style pesto

- 30 shelled walnuts
- 1 cup fresh basil leaves
- 1 clove garlic
- 1 medium bread roll
- 1 cup Beef stock (see recipe, page 105)
  salt to taste
  juice of 1 lemon
- 2 tablespoons extra-virgin olive oil

Put the walnuts, basil, and garlic in a food processor and chop to a cream. Transfer to a mixing bowl. • Remove the crust from the bread roll and soak the inside in the stock. Squeeze well and add to the walnut mixture. Add the salt, lemon juice, and oil (you may need slightly more or slightly less oil depending on how much the walnuts absorb), and mix well. • Serve with pasta, gnocchi, or vegetables.

Serves: 4 · Prep: 10 min. · Level: 1

Genoese basil sauce with trofie pasta

BREAD & FOCACCIA

Every region of Italy has its own special range of breads and crusty focaccia. The variety is stunning, and villages just a few miles apart will have quite different recipes and traditions.

FOCACCIA RIPIENA
Filled focaccia

1	quantity Basic focaccia dough (see recipe, page 25)
1	lb ripe tomatoes, sliced
14	oz fresh Mozzarella cheese, sliced
12	leaves fresh basil, torn
	salt and freshly ground black pepper to taste

Wine: a young, dry red (Chianti dei Colli Fiorentini)

Prepare the focaccia as explained on pages 24–25. • When the rising time has elapsed (about 1½ hours), transfer the dough to a lightly floured work surface and knead for 2–3 minutes. • Place the dough in an oiled 12 x 16-inch dish and, using your hands, spread it evenly to about ½ inch thick. • Drizzle with the remaining oil and sprinkle with the coarse salt. • Bake in a preheated oven at 450°F for about 20 minutes. • When cooked, slice the focaccia open down the middle. • Cover half with the tomatoes, Mozzarella, and basil. Season with salt and pepper. Cover with the other half, then cut into 4 or 6 sandwiches.

Makes: 1 focaccia, 12 inches in diameter · Prep: 20 min. · Rising time: about 1½ hrs · Cooking: 20 min. · Level: 1

◄ Selection of typical Italian breads
➤ Filled focaccia

MAKING BREAD AND FOCACCIA

In Italy, fresh yeast is widely available in supermarkets, or can be bought from local bakeries. However, active dry yeast can be used with the same success in all the recipes in this book.

➤ Basic focaccia and Rosemary focaccia
▽ Basic white loaves and Basic olive oil bread (see recipes, page 26)

To prepare the yeast you will need a small bowl, a wooden spoon, warm water, and a little sugar. Exact quantities are given in each recipe.

1

1 Put the fresh or active dry yeast in a small bowl. If using fresh yeast, crumble it with your fingertips.

2

2 Add the sugar and half the warm water and stir with a fork until the yeast has dissolved.

3

3 Set the mixture aside for about 10 minutes. It will look creamy when ready. Stir again before proceeding to make the dough.

The dough

To prepare the dough you will need a bowl, flour, salt, the yeast mixture, a wooden spoon, and the remaining water. Some recipes use slightly different ingredients.

1 Place the flour in a mixing bowl and sprinkle with the salt. Make a hollow in the center and pour in the yeast mixture, the remaining water, and any other ingredients listed in the recipe. Use a wooden spoon to stir the mixture. Stir well until the flour has almost all been absorbed.

2 The dough will be a rough and shaggy ball in the bottom of the bowl. Sprinkle a work surface, preferably made of wood, with a little flour. Note that the flour used to prepare the work surface is not included in the quantities given in the recipes. You will need about half a cup extra for this. Use a spatula (or your hands) to transfer the dough to the work surface. Curl your fingers around the dough and press it together to form a compact ball.

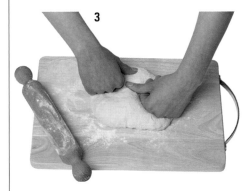

3 Press down on the dough with your knuckles to spread it a little. Take the far end of the dough, fold it a short distance toward you, then push it away again with the heel of your palm. Flexing your wrist, fold it toward you again, give it a quarter turn, then push it away. Repeat these motions, gently and with the lightest possible touch, for about 8–10 minutes. When the dough is firm and no longer sticks to your hands or the work surface, lift it up and bang it down hard against the work surface a couple of times. This will develop the gluten. When ready, the dough should be smooth and elastic. It should show definite air bubbles beneath the surface and should spring back if you flatten it with your palm.

4 When the dough is kneaded, place it in a large clean bowl and cover with a cloth. Most of the breads in this book have two rising times, while the pizzas are left to rise just once. The dough should double in volume during rising. To test whether it has risen sufficiently, poke your finger gently into the dough; if the impression remains, then the dough is ready. The rising times given in each recipe are approximate; remember that yeast is a living ingredient and is affected by air temperature and humidity, among other things. Some days it will take longer to rise than others.

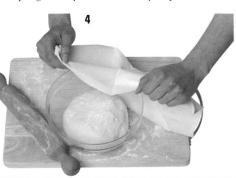

FOCACCIA ALL'OLIO
Basic focaccia

- ½ oz fresh yeast
  or 1 (¼ oz) package active dry yeast
- 1 teaspoon sugar
- 1 cup warm water
- 3¼ cups unbleached white flour
- 1 teaspoon fine salt
- ⅓ cup extra-virgin olive oil
- 1 heaped teaspoon coarse sea salt

Prepare the yeast as explained on page 24. • Put the flour in a large bowl with the fine salt, yeast mixture, half the oil, and the remaining water, and prepare the dough as shown on these pages. • When the rising time has elapsed (about 1½ hours), transfer the dough to a lightly floured work surface and knead for 2–3 minutes. • Place the dough on an oiled baking sheet and, using your hands, spread it into a circular shape about 12 inches in diameter and ½ inch thick. Dimple the surface with your fingertips, drizzle with the remaining oil, and sprinkle with the coarse salt. • Bake in a preheated oven at 425°F for about 20 minutes. The focaccia should be pale golden brown. The bottoms of the dimples will be slightly darker.

Makes: 1 focaccia, 12 inches in diameter · Prep: 20 min. · Rising time: about 1½ hrs · Cooking: 20 min. · Level: 1

Garbanzo bean flatbread

CECINA
Garbanzo bean flatbread

4¹/₂ cups garbanzo bean flour
4¹/₂ pints water
³/₄ cup extra-virgin olive oil
    salt and freshly ground black pepper to taste

Put the garbanzo bean flour in a large mixing bowl and, using a wooden spoon or a balloon whisk, gradually stir in enough water to form a thick pouring batter with no lumps. • Beat in the oil and a generous pinch of salt. • When the batter is smooth, pour it into a nonstick roasting pan or similar ovenproof dish, filling to a depth of about ¹/₄ inch. • Bake in a preheated oven at 400°F for 10 minutes. A thin crust should form on the surface. • Transfer the flatbread to a heated serving dish, sprinkle with freshly ground pepper, and serve hot.

Serves: 6 · Prep: 5 min. · Cooking: 10 min. · Level: 1

PANINI AL PARMIGIANO CON LE NOCI
Walnut and Parmesan rolls

1 oz fresh yeast or 2 (¹/₄ oz) packages active dry yeast
1 teaspoon sugar
1¹/₃ cups warm water
4¹/₄ cups unbleached white flour
1 cup freshly grated Parmesan cheese
1¹/₄ cups shelled walnuts, coarsely chopped
1–2 teaspoons salt
    freshly ground black pepper to taste
2 tablespoons lard (or 3 tablespoons extra-virgin olive oil)

Prepare the yeast mixture as shown on page 24. • Put the flour, Parmesan, walnuts, salt, and pepper in a large bowl. Mix well and add the lard (or oil), yeast mixture, and remaining water, and prepare the dough as shown on page 25. • When the rising time has elapsed (about 1 hour), transfer the dough to a lightly floured work surface and knead for 2–3 minutes. • Divide into 8–10 equal portions and shape into rolls. • Place on two oiled baking sheets, keeping them well spaced (they will double in size as they rise). • Cover with a cloth and leave to rise for 1 hour. • Bake in a preheated oven at 400°F for 25–30 minutes.

Makes: about 2¹/₂ lb of bread · Prep: 40 min. · Rising time: about 2 hrs · Cooking: 25–30 min. · Level: 2

PANE BIANCO
Basic white loaves or rolls

☞ Until quite recently, almost all the breads in Italy were made with unbleached, white flour. This is a basic recipe for a versatile white bread. To freeze, wrap the loaves or rolls tightly in foil and place in the freezer. When serving frozen bread, don't let it thaw. Place it directly in a preheated oven at 325°F for 15–25 minutes (less time for rolls than for the larger loaves).

1 oz fresh yeast or 2 (¹/₄ oz) packages active dry yeast
1 teaspoon sugar
1¹/₂ cups warm water
6¹/₂ cups unbleached white flour
2–3 teaspoons salt

Prepare the yeast mixture as shown on page 24. • Put the flour in a large bowl with the yeast mixture, salt, and remaining water, and proceed as shown on page 25. • When the rising time has elapsed (about 1¹/₄ hours), transfer the dough to a lightly floured work surface. Knead for several minutes. • Place the dough on an oiled baking sheet, and shape it into a long oval loaf. • Sprinkle the surface with flour and, using a serrated knife, cut several diagonal slashes about ¹/₂-inch deep in the top. • For a large, ring-shaped loaf, about 12 inches in diameter, gently flatten the dough and make a hole in the middle with your fingers. Carefully enlarge the hole, shaping the dough into a ring. • For rolls, divide the dough into 8 equal portions and shape them into rolls.

The dough will double in size during rising, so position the rolls at least 1¹/₂ inches apart. • Cover with a cloth and leave to rise for about 40 minutes. • Bake in a preheated oven at 400°F. Large loaves will need about 40 minutes, the ring-shaped loaf about 30 minutes, and the rolls 20–25 minutes.

Makes: about 2 lb of bread · Prep: 30 min. · Rising time: 2 hrs · Cooking: 20–40 min. · Level: 2

PANE ALL'OLIO
Basic olive oil bread

1 oz fresh yeast or 2 (¹/₄ oz) packages active dry yeast
1 teaspoon sugar
1¹/₄ cups warm water
6 cups unbleached white flour
2–3 teaspoons salt
5 tablespoons extra-virgin olive oil

Proceed as for white bread (see previous recipe), adding the oil to the yeast mixture at the beginning. Instead of kneading, mix the soft, sticky dough in the bowl with a wooden spoon. • When the rising time has elapsed (about 1¹/₂ hours), mix the dough again for a few minutes. • Use a spatula to transfer it to an oiled baking pan about 12 inches in diameter. Cover with a cloth and leave to rise for 30 minutes. • Bake in a preheated oven at 400° for about 35 minutes.

Makes: about 2 lb of bread · Prep: 30 min. · Rising time: about 2 hrs · Cooking: 35 min. · Level: 2

PANINI ALLE NOCCIOLE
Hazelnut rolls

    1   oz fresh yeast or 2 (¼ oz) packages active dry yeast
    1   teaspoon sugar
 1¼   cups warm water
 2¼   cups whole-wheat flour
    3   cups unbleached white flour
    1   cup roasted hazelnuts, shelled and coarsely chopped
 1–2 teaspoons salt
   ¼   cup extra-virgin olive oil

Prepare the yeast mixture as shown on page 24. • Put both flours in a large bowl with the hazelnuts, mix well, and sprinkle with the salt. Pour in the yeast mixture, 3 tablespoons of the oil, and the remaining water, and prepare the dough as shown on page 25. • When the rising time has elapsed (about 1 hour), transfer the dough to a lightly floured work surface and knead for 2–3 minutes. • Divide the dough into 14–18 equal portions and shape into long rolls. • Transfer to two oiled baking sheets, keeping the rolls well spaced (they will double in size as they rise). Cover with a cloth and leave to rise for 1 hour. • Cook in a preheated oven at 425°F for about 25 minutes.

Makes: about 14–18 rolls · Prep: 30 min. · Rising time: about 2 hrs · Cooking: 30 min. · Level: 2

PANE ALLO STRUTTO
Lard bread

    1   oz fresh yeast or 2 (¼ oz) packages active dry yeast
    1   teaspoon sugar
 1¼   cups warm water
    3   oz lard
    6   cups unbleached white flour
 2–3 teaspoons salt

Prepare the yeast mixture as shown on page 24. • Melt the lard in a small saucepan over low heat, then set aside. • Put the flour in a large bowl with the lard, yeast mixture, salt, and remaining water, and prepare the dough as shown on page 25. • When the rising time has elapsed (about 1½ hours), transfer the dough to a lightly floured work surface. Knead for 4–5 minutes. • Divide the dough into 4 equal portions and shape them into loaves about 12 inches long. Pick each loaf up and twist it slightly, making sure it does not become too long. The loaves should have a slight spiral shape. • Place the loaves on two oiled baking sheets, keeping them well spaced (they will double in size as they rise). • Cover with a cloth and leave to rise for 30 minutes. • Bake in a preheated oven at 425°F for 30–35 minutes.

Makes: about 2 lb of bread · Prep: 30 min. · Rising time: about 2 hrs · Cooking: 30–35 min. · Level: 2

PANINI AI CECI
Garbanzo bean rolls

    1   oz fresh yeast or 2 (¼ oz) packages active dry yeast
    1   teaspoon sugar
    1   cup warm water
    8   oz canned garbanzo beans
    6   cups unbleached white flour
 2–3 teaspoons salt
   ⅓   cup extra-virgin olive oil

Prepare the yeast mixture as shown on page 24. • Drain the garbanzo beans and purée in a food processor with the remaining water. • Put the flour in a large bowl with the salt, yeast mixture, garbanzo bean purée, and ¼ cup of the oil, and prepare the dough as shown on page 25. • When the rising time has elapsed (about 1½ hours), transfer the dough to a lightly floured work surface. Knead for 2 minutes. • Divide the dough into 16–20 equal portions and shape into round rolls. • Smear a few drops of the remaining oil over the top of each roll with your fingers. • Use a serrated knife to cut a ¼-inch deep cross in the surface of each roll. • Transfer to two oiled baking sheets, keeping the rolls well spaced (they will double in size as they rise). Cover with a cloth and leave to rise for 1 hour. • Bake in a preheated oven at 425°F for 18–20 minutes.

Makes: about 16–20 rolls · Prep: 30 min. · Rising time: about 2½ hrs · Cooking: 18–20 min. · Level: 2

PANE DI SEGALE AL FINOCCHIO
Rye bread with fennel seeds

    1   oz fresh yeast or 2 (¼ oz) packages active dry yeast
    1   teaspoon sugar
 1½   cups warm water
    4   cups rye flour
    1   cup unbleached white flour
 1½   tablespoons fennel seeds
 1–2 teaspoons salt
    2   tablespoons extra-virgin olive oil

Prepare the yeast mixture as shown on page 24. • Put both flours in a large bowl with the fennel seeds, salt, yeast mixture, oil, and the remaining water, and prepare the dough as shown on page 25. • When the rising time has elapsed (about 2 hours), transfer the dough to a lightly floured work surface and knead for 2–3 minutes. • Divide the dough into 4–6 equal portions and shape into oval loaves. • Transfer to two oiled baking sheets. Cover with a cloth and leave to rise for 1 hour. • Bake in a preheated oven at 425°F for 25 minutes.

Makes: about 2 lb of bread · Prep: 30 min. · Rising time: 2–3 hrs · Cooking: 25 min. · Level: 2

Garbanzo bean rolls

Delicious Romagnol flatbread, known in Italian as *piadina*, comes from the Adriatic coast in the area around Rimini. Its origins can be traced back almost 3,000 years, to Etruscan times. Be sure to serve the piadina straight from the pan (it becomes heavy as it cools) or reheat it before bringing it to the table. Serve the flatbread with a green salad, a platter of deli meats, such as salami, mortadella, prosciutto, and ham, and soft, fresh cheeses, like Caprino or Stracchino. In Rimini, piadina is served with the local Squaquarone cheese (shown below). Most Italians drink a glass of the local red Sangiovese wine with their piadina, but the people of Rimini recommend a glass of light, white Trebbiano. Try them both!

PIADINA
Romagna-style flatbread

- 4 cups unbleached white flour
- 1 teaspoon baking soda
- ½ teaspoon salt
- ⅓ cup lard, at room temperature, thinly sliced
- ½ cup warm water

Put the flour, baking soda, and salt in a large bowl. Make a hollow in the center and add the lard and water. Mix well, then transfer to a lightly floured work surface. • Knead until the dough is smooth and elastic. Return to the bowl. Cover with a cloth and set aside for about 30 minutes. • Divide into pieces about the size of an egg. Sprinkle with flour and roll into ⅛-inch thick disks about 6 inches in diameter. Prick well with a fork. • Cook one at a time in a very hot griddle or cast-iron pan, without adding any fat. After 2–3 minutes turn the flatbread and cook for 2–3 minutes more. • Stack the flatbread up on a plate and serve hot with deli meats and fresh, soft cheeses.

Makes: about 10 piadina · Prep: 15 min. + 30 min. to rest · Cooking: 30 min. · Level: 1

⋏ Squaquarone cheese
⋗ Piadina filled with ham and cheese

PANINI AL SESAMO
Sesame seed rolls

    1   oz fresh yeast or 2 (¹/₄ oz) packages active dry yeast
    1   teaspoon sugar
  1¹/₄ cups warm water
  3¹/₂ cups unbleached white flour
  2¹/₂ cups whole-wheat flour
    5   heaped tablespoons sesame seeds
  2–3   teaspoons salt
    1   egg white

Prepare the yeast mixture as shown on page 24. • Combine both flours in a large bowl with half the sesame seeds. Mix carefully and sprinkle with salt. Add the yeast mixture and remaining water, and prepare the dough as shown on page 25. • When the rising time has elapsed (about 1 hour), transfer the dough to a lightly floured work surface and knead for 2–3 minutes. • Divide the dough into 8–10 equal portions. • Arrange the rolls on two oiled baking sheets, keeping them well spaced (they will double in size as they rise). • Lightly beat the egg white with a teaspoon of water and brush the surface of rolls with the mixture. Sprinkle with the remaining sesame seeds. • Cover with a cloth and leave to rise for 1 hour. • Bake in a preheated oven at 400°F for 30 minutes.

Makes: about 2 lb of bread · Prep: 30 min. · Rising time: about 2 hrs · Cooking: 35–40 min. · Level: 2

PANE ALLE ERBE
Herb bread

    1   oz fresh yeast or 2 (¹/₄ oz) packages active dry yeast
    1   teaspoon sugar
  1¹/₄ cups warm water
    4   cups whole-wheat flour
    1   cup unbleached white flour
    1   tablespoon finely chopped fresh oregano
    1   tablespoon finely chopped fresh marjoram
  2–3   teaspoons salt

Prepare the yeast mixture as shown on page 24. • Combine both flours in a large bowl with the oregano and marjoram, yeast mixture, salt, and remaining water, and prepare the dough as shown on page 25. • When the rising time has elapsed (about 1¹/₂ hours), transfer the dough to a lightly floured work surface. Knead for several minutes. • Divide the dough into 4–6 equal portions and shape each into a

loaf about 14 inches long. • Place the loaves on two oiled baking sheets. Pull the ends of each loaf round and join them to make circular loaves, or leave them straight, as preferred. • Use a serrated knife to make a ¹/₂-inch deep incision along the top of each loaf. • Cover with a cloth and leave to rise for 30–40 minutes. • Bake in a preheated oven at 425°F for about 30 minutes.

Makes: about 2 lb of bread · Prep: 30 min. · Rising time: about 2 hrs · Cooking: 35 min. · Level: 2

PANE DI MAIS
Italian corn bread

  1¹/₂ oz fresh yeast or 3 (¹/₄ oz) packages active dry yeast
    1   teaspoon sugar
    1   cup warm milk
  2¹/₂ cups unbleached white flour
  2¹/₂ cups finely ground cornmeal
  2–3   teaspoons salt
    1   egg, lightly beaten

Prepare the yeast mixture as shown on page 24, using half the milk instead of water. • Combine the flour and cornmeal in a large bowl with the salt, egg, yeast mixture, and remaining milk, and prepare the dough as shown on page 25. • When the rising time has elapsed (about 1 hour), transfer the dough to a lightly floured work surface and knead for 2–3 minutes. • Divide the dough in half and shape into two round loaves. Sprinkle with flour and transfer to an oiled baking sheet. • Cover with a cloth and leave to rise for about 30 minutes. • Bake in a preheated oven at 425°F for about 25 minutes.

Makes: about 1¹/₂ lb bread · Prep: 30 min. Rising time: 1¹/₂ hrs · Cooking: 25 min. · Level: 2

PANE AL PARMIGIANO
Parmesan bread

    1   oz fresh yeast
        or 2 (¹/₄ oz) packages active dry yeast
    1   teaspoon sugar
  1¹/₄ cups warm water
    6   cups unbleached white flour
    3   cups freshly grated Parmesan cheese
        freshly ground black pepper to taste
    2   teaspoons salt
    1   egg, lightly beaten

Prepare the yeast mixture as shown on page 24. • Put the flour in a large bowl

with 2¹/₂ cups of Parmesan and the pepper. Mix well, sprinkle with salt, and add the yeast mixture and remaining water. Prepare the dough as shown on page 25. • When the rising time has elapsed (about 1 hour), transfer the dough to a lightly floured work surface and knead for 2 minutes. • Divide the dough into 4 equal portions and shape each into a roll about 16 inches long. Brush each roll with the egg. Sprinkle the rolls with the remaining Parmesan. • Fold each roll in two, twisting each part carefully to make a false braid. • Transfer to two oiled baking sheets. • Cover with a cloth and set aside to rise for about 1 hour. • Bake in a preheated oven at 400°F for 30 minutes.

Makes: about 2 lb of bread · Prep: 30 min. · Rising time: about 2 hrs · Cooking: 30 min. · Level: 2

PANE CON PATATE
Potato bread

☞ This soft, delicate bread is perfect for the table and also makes very good sandwiches.

    1   oz fresh yeast or 2 (¹/₄ oz) packages active dry yeast
    1   teaspoon sugar
    1   cup warm water
    5   oz boiled potatoes, still warm
    2   tablespoons extra-virgin olive oil
    4   cups unbleached white flour
  2–3   teaspoons salt

Prepare the yeast mixture as shown on page 24. • Mash the potatoes and transfer to a large bowl. Stir in the oil, flour, salt, yeast mixture, and remaining water, and prepare the dough as shown on page 25. • When the rising time has elapsed (about 1¹/₄ hours), transfer the dough (which will be quite soft) to a lightly floured work surface and knead for 1 minute. • Divide the dough into 2 equal portions and shape each one into an oval loaf. • Place the loaves on an oiled baking sheet, keeping them well spaced (they will double in size as they rise). Cover with a cloth and leave to rise for about 45 minutes. • Bake in a preheated oven at 400°F for 30–35 minutes.

Makes: about 2 lb of bread · Prep: 30 min. · Rising time: about 2 hrs · Cooking: 30–35 min. · Level: 2

PANE SARACENO
Buckwheat loaves

1¼ oz fresh yeast or 2½ (¼ oz) packages active dry yeast
1 teaspoon sugar
1½ cups warm water
4 cups buckwheat flour
1¼ cups unbleached white flour
2 teaspoons salt
¼ cup extra-virgin olive oil

Prepare the yeast mixture as shown on page 24. • Put the flours in a large bowl with the salt, yeast mixture, oil, and remaining water, and prepare the dough as shown on page 25. • When the rising time has elapsed (about 1 hour), transfer the dough to a lightly floured work surface and knead for 2–3 minutes. • Divide the dough in 4 equal portions and shape into round loaves. Sprinkle with flour and use a serrated knife to cut a ½-inch deep cross in the surface of each. • Transfer to two oiled baking sheets. Cover with a cloth and leave to rise for 1 hour. • Bake in a preheated oven at 400°F for 30–35 minutes.

Makes: about 2 lb of bread · Prep: 30 min. · Rising time: about 2 hrs · Cooking: 30–35 min. · Level: 2

FITASCETTA
Ring focaccia with red onions

1 oz fresh yeast or 2 (¼ oz) packages active dry yeast
1 teaspoon sugar
1 cup warm water
3 cups unbleached white flour
1–2 teaspoons salt
1 lb red onions
2 tablespoons butter

Prepare the yeast mixture as shown on page 24. • Put the flour in a large bowl with the salt, yeast mixture, and remaining water, and prepare the dough as shown on page 25. The dough should be rather soft; if it is difficult to knead, leave it in the bowl and mix for several minutes with a wooden spoon. • While the dough is rising, peel and slice the onions. Cook over medium-low heat with the butter and 1–2 tablespoons of water for 30 minutes. Remove from heat and leave to cool. • When the rising time has elapsed (about 1 hour), transfer the dough to a lightly floured work surface and knead for 2–3

PAN DI RAMERINO
Sweet rosemary rolls

☞ This is an old Florentine recipe. These rolls were traditionally eaten at Easter, when the local bakers set up stalls at church doors.

2 tablespoons fresh rosemary leaves
5 tablespoons extra-virgin olive oil
½ oz fresh yeast or 1 (¼ oz) package active dry yeast
2 tablespoons superfine sugar
¾ cup warm water
4 cups unbleached white flour
1 teaspoon salt
½ cup seedless raisins

Cook 1½ tablespoons of rosemary in ¼ cup of oil in a small pan over low heat for 10 minutes. Remove from heat, discard the rosemary, and set the oil aside to cool. • Prepare the yeast mixture as shown on page 24. • Put the flour in a large bowl with the salt, rosemary oil, yeast mixture, sugar, and remaining water, and prepare the dough as shown on page 25. • Rinse the raisins, drain, and pat dry with paper towels. • When the rising time has elapsed (about 1 hour), transfer the dough to a lightly floured work surface and knead for 2–3 minutes. Incorporate the raisins and remaining rosemary into the dough as you knead. • Divide the dough in 6–8 equal portions, drizzle with the remaining oil, and shape into oval rolls. • Place on an oiled baking sheet, keeping them well spaced (they will double in size as they rise). Use a serrated

knife to cut a cross into the surface of each roll. • Cover with a cloth and leave to rise for 30 minutes. • Bake in a preheated oven at 400°F for 20 minutes.

Makes: about 1¼ lb bread · Prep: 30 min. · Rising time: 1½ hrs · Cooking: 20 min. · Level: 2

PANE INTEGRALE
Whole-wheat loaves

1 oz fresh yeast or 2 (¼ oz) packages active dry yeast
1 teaspoon sugar
1¼ cups warm water
3½ cups whole-wheat flour
2 cups unbleached white flour
2 teaspoons salt

Prepare the yeast mixture as shown on page 24. • Put both flours in a large bowl with the yeast mixture, salt, and remaining water, and prepare the dough as shown on page 25. • When the rising time has elapsed (2 hours), transfer the dough to a lightly floured work surface and knead for 5 minutes. • Divide the dough into two equal portions and shape each one into a long loaf. Sprinkle with flour and use a serrated knife to cut diagonal slashes about ¼ inch deep along the top of each loaf. Repeat, making slashes in the other direction to create a grid pattern. • Cover with a cloth and leave to rise for 1½ hours. • Bake in a preheated oven at 400°F for 40 minutes.

Makes: about 2 lb of bread · Prep: 30 min. · Rising time: 3–4 hrs · Cooking: 40 min. · Level: 2

minutes. • Shape into a loaf about 3 feet long. • Transfer the loaf to an oiled baking sheet, and shape it into a ring, joining the two ends together, and leaving a large hole in the center. • Cover with a cloth and set aside to rise for 30 minutes. • When the second rising time has elapsed, flatten the dough a little with your hands and spread the onions on top. Sprinkle with salt. • Bake in a preheated oven at 400°F for about 30 minutes.

Makes: 1 large round focaccia · Prep: 30 min. · Rising time: about 1½ hrs · Cooking: 30 min. · Level: 1

FOCACCIA AL ROSMARINO
Rosemary focaccia

1   quantity Basic focaccia dough (see recipe, page 25)
1   tablespoon finely chopped fresh rosemary leaves

Prepare the focaccia as described on page 25. • Incorporate the rosemary into the dough as you knead after the second rising. • Alternatively, instead of chopping the rosemary leaves, sprinkle them whole over the surface of the dough when spread.

Makes: 1 focaccia, 12 inches in diameter · Prep: 20 min. · Rising time: about 1½ hrs · Cooking: 20 min. · Level: 1

FOCACCIA CON CIPOLLA
Onion focaccia

1   quantity Basic focaccia dough (see recipe, page 25)
1   large white onion

Prepare the focaccia as described on page 25. • Cook the onion in a pot of boiling, salted water for 3–4 minutes. Drain well, cut into fairly thick slices, and spread over the focaccia before sprinkling with the salt and drizzling with the oil.

Makes: 1 focaccia, 12 inches in diameter · Prep: 20 min. · Rising time: 1½ hrs · Cooking: 20 min. · Level: 1

FOCACCIA CON OLIVE
Focaccia with green or black olives

1   quantity Basic focaccia dough (see recipe, page 25)
1   cup pitted green or black olives, pitted and coarsely chopped

Prepare the focaccia as described on page 25. • Incorporate the olives into the dough as you knead after the second rising.

Makes: 1 focaccia, 12 inches in diameter · Prep: 20 min. · Rising time: about 1½ hrs · Cooking: 20 min. · Level: 1

FOCACCIA ALLA SALVIA
Sage focaccia

1   quantity Basic focaccia dough (see recipe, page 25)
2   tablespoons coarsely chopped fresh sage leaves

Prepare the focaccia as described on page 25. • Incorporate the sage into the dough as you knead after the second rising. • Alternatively, sauté the sage in 1 tablespoon of olive oil over medium heat for 1 minute. In this case, reduce the amount of oil added to the flour by 1 tablespoon.

Makes: 1 focaccia, 12 inches in diameter · Prep: 20 min. · Rising time: about 1½ hrs · Cooking: 20 min. · Level: 1

FOCACCIA ESTIVA
Summertime focaccia

1   oz fresh yeast or 2 (¼ oz) packages active dry yeast
1   teaspoon sugar
⅔   cup warm water
4   cups unbleached flour
1   teaspoon salt
½   cup extra-virgin olive oil
2   tablespoons white wine
1   lb green bell peppers, sliced
1   lb finely chopped onion
1   lb tomatoes, chopped
      salt and freshly ground black pepper to taste
3   tablespoons finely chopped parsley

Prepare the yeast as explained on page 24. • Put the flour in a large bowl with the salt, yeast mixture, 2 tablespoons of the oil, the remaining water, and the wine. Prepare the dough as shown on page 25. • When the rising time has elapsed (about 1½ hours), transfer the dough to a lightly floured work surface and knead for 2–3 minutes. • Place the dough in an oiled 12 x 16-inch pan and, using your hands, spread it evenly to about ½ inch thick. • Prick well with a fork. • Sprinkle with the bell peppers, onions, tomatoes, salt, pepper, and parsley. Drizzle with the remaining oil. • Bake in a preheated oven at 400°F for 25–30 minutes.

Makes: 1 rectangular focaccia, 12 x 16 inches · Prep: 20 min. · Rising time: about 1½ hrs · Cooking: 25–30 min. · Level: 1

FOCACCIA AL FORMAGGIO
Cheese focaccia

1   quantity Basic focaccia dough (see recipe, page 25)
8   oz Fontina cheese, cut in thin slices

Prepare the focaccia as described on page 25. • When the focaccia is ready to bake, arrange the slices of cheese on top and place in the oven.

Makes: 1 focaccia, 12 inches in diameter · Prep: 20 min. · Rising time: about 1½ hrs · Cooking: 20–25 min. · Level: 1

Summertime focaccia

Sesame, onion, and plain grissini

FOCACCIA CON PATATE
Focaccia with potatoes

- ½ oz fresh yeast or 1 (¼ oz) package active dry yeast
- 1 teaspoon sugar
- 5 tablespoons warm water
- 8 oz boiled potatoes, still warm
- 2 cups unbleached white flour
- 1–2 teaspoons fine salt
- 3–4 tablespoons extra-virgin olive oil
- 1 level teaspoon coarse salt

Prepare the yeast as explained on page 24. Use all the water to dissolve the yeast. • Mash the boiled potatoes while still hot. • Combine the potatoes in a large bowl with the flour, salt, yeast mixture, and 1 tablespoon of oil, and prepare the dough as shown on page 25. The dough will be too soft to knead by hand; leave it in the bowl and mix vigorously with a wooden spoon for 2–3 minutes. Set aside to rise. • When the rising time has elapsed (about 1 hour), mix again for 1 minute. • Transfer to an oiled nonstick baking pan 12 inches in diameter. Spread the dough with your hands. Cover with a cloth and leave to rise for 30 minutes. • Sprinkle with the coarse salt. Dimple the surface with your fingertips, and drizzle with the remaining oil. • Bake in a preheated oven at 400°F for 20–25 minutes.

Makes: 1 focaccia, 12 inches in diameter · Prep: 30 min. · Rising time: about 1½ hrs · Cooking: 20–25 min. · Level: 1

FOCACCIA NERA
Whole-wheat focaccia

- 1 oz fresh yeast or 2 (¼ oz) packages active dry yeast
- 1 teaspoon sugar
- 1 cup warm water
- 1 cup unbleached white flour
- 2 cups whole-wheat flour
- 1–2 teaspoons salt
- 5 tablespoons extra-virgin olive oil
- ½ cup pitted black olives, thinly sliced
- 1–2 fresh green chilies, thinly sliced

Prepare the yeast as explained on page 24. • Combine both flours in a large bowl with the salt, yeast mixture, 3 tablespoons of oil, and the remaining water, and prepare the dough as shown on page 25. • When the rising time has elapsed (about 1½ hours), transfer the dough to a lightly floured work surface and knead for 2–3 minutes. • Place the dough on an oiled baking sheet and spread it into a disk about 12 inches in diameter and ½ inch thick. Sprinkle with the olives and chilies, pressing them lightly into the dough with your fingertips. Drizzle with the remaining oil. • Bake in a preheated oven at 425°F for 25 minutes.

Makes: 1 focaccia, 12 inches in diameter · Prep: 30 min. · Rising time: about 1½ hrs · Cooking: 25 min. · Level: 1

TARALLUCCI
Breadrings

☞ Tarallucci are a specialty of southern Italy. These small, ring crackers can be seasoned with fennel seeds, chilies, or lard. They make perfect appetizers and snacks.

- 4 cups unbleached white flour
- 2 teaspoons salt
- 5 tablespoons extra-virgin olive oil
- 1 cup dry white wine

Combine the flour in a large bowl with the salt, oil, and wine. Mix well with a fork until all the flour has been absorbed. • Transfer the dough to a lightly floured work surface. Knead as shown on page 25 until the dough is soft, smooth, and elastic. • Return to the bowl and set aside for 20 minutes. • Divide the dough into 8–10 equal portions and shape each one into a long "sausage" about the thickness of your little finger. The dough will be very elastic and tend to contract; wet your hands so that you can work more easily. • Divide each sausage into segments about 3 inches long. Using your fingers and thumb, pinch the ends of each segment together to form a ring. Place the breadrings on paper towels. • Bring a high-sided pot containing about 3 quarts of salted water to the boil. Add the tarallucci (not more than 20 at a time), and boil until they rise to the surface. Scoop them out with a slotted spoon and place them on three or four oiled baking sheets. • Cover with lightly oiled foil and set aside to dry for about 30 minutes. • Bake in a preheated oven at 425°F for 20–25.

Makes: about 65 breadrings · Prep: 1 hr · Cooking: 35 min. · Level: 2

GRISSINI
Breadsticks

☞ Grissini are a specialty of Turin. They can be plain or flavored. Try sprinkling them with sesame seeds just before baking or adding 1 lightly sautéed onion to the dough.

- ³/₄ oz fresh yeast or 1¹/₂ (¹/₄ oz) packages active dry yeast
- 1 teaspoon sugar
- ³/₄ cup warm water
- 3¹/₂ cups unbleached white flour
- 1 teaspoon salt

Prepare the yeast as explained on page 24. • Combine the flour in a bowl with the salt, yeast mixture, and remaining water and prepare the dough as shown on page 25. • When the rising time has elapsed (about 1 hour), transfer the dough to a lightly floured work surface and knead for 2–3 minutes. • Divide the dough into portions about the size of an egg, then shape them into sticks about the thickness of your little finger. • Sprinkle with flour and transfer to three oiled baking sheets, keeping them a finger's width apart. • Cover with a cloth and set aside to rise for 1 hour. • Bake in a preheated oven at 450°F for 5 minutes. When cooked, the breadsticks will be well-browned but not too dark. Leave to cool before removing from the sheets.

Makes: about 1 lb breadsticks · Prep: 30 min. · Rising time: about 2 hrs · Cooking: 5 min. · Level: 2

FOCACCIA CON FORMAGGIO FRESCO
Focaccia filled with fresh cheese

- ¹/₂ oz fresh yeast or 1 (¹/₄ oz) package active dry yeast
- 1 teaspoon sugar
- ²/₃ cup warm water
- 2¹/₂ cups unbleached white flour
- 1 teaspoon salt
- 10 oz fresh, creamy cheese (Robiola, Mascarpone, Crescenza)
- ¹/₃ cup extra-virgin olive oil

Prepare the yeast as explained on page 24. • Combine the flour in a large bowl with the salt, yeast mixture, 2 tablespoons of oil, and the remaining water, and prepare the dough as shown on page 25. • When the rising time has elapsed (about 1¹/₂ hours), transfer the dough to a lightly floured work surface and knead for 2–3 minutes. • Divide into two portions, one slightly larger than the other, and roll them out. The larger

Raisin bread

portion should be about 14 inches in diameter, the smaller about 13 inches. • Transfer the larger one to an oiled baking sheet. Spread with the cheese, leaving a 1-inch border around the edge. • Cover with the smaller piece of dough. Fold back the edges of the larger sheet and press with your fingers to seal. Prick holes in the surface with a fork and brush with the remaining oil. • Bake in a preheated oven at 500°F for 15 minutes.

Makes: 1 focaccia, 13 inches in diameter · Prep: 30 min. · Rising time: about 1¹/₂ hrs · Cooking: 15 min. · Level: 2

PANE CON L'UVA
Raisin bread

☞ This is a very old recipe, common to many parts of Italy. The raisins and sugar make it slightly sweet. Try serving it with Mascarpone or other mild, creamy cheeses. It makes a wonderful afternoon tea or snack.

- 1 oz fresh yeast or 2 (¹/₄ oz) packages active dry yeast
- 2 tablespoons sugar
- ²/₃ cup warm water
- 3 cups unbleached white flour
- 3 tablespoons butter, at room temperature, chopped
- 1¹/₃ cups dark raisins
- 1 teaspoon salt

Prepare the yeast as explained on page 24. • Put the flour in a bowl, add the remaining sugar, the salt, yeast mixture, and the remaining water and mix well. Prepare the dough as shown on page 25. • Soak the raisins in 2 cups of warm water. After 15–20 minutes drain, dry, and lightly sprinkle with flour. • When the rising time has elapsed (about 1 hour), transfer the dough to a lightly floured work surface and knead well. Incorporate the raisins and butter into the dough as you knead. • Divide the dough into 7–8 equal portions, sprinkle with flour, and shape into long rolls. • Place on an oiled baking sheet, keeping them well spaced (their volume will double as they rise). Cover with a cloth and leave to rise for 30 minutes. • Bake in a preheated oven at 400°F for 20 minutes.

Makes: about 1³/₄ lb of bread · Prep: 30 min. · Rising time: 1¹/₂ hrs · Cooking: 20 min. · Level: 1

PIZZA & CALZONES

Along with pasta and high fashion, pizza is one of Italy's most successful exports. Don't be put off by the thought of preparing the dough. It is surprisingly easy to make. Here we have given the classic recipes, but you can vary the toppings to suit your tastes.

PIZZA CON LE MELANZANE
Eggplant pizza

- 1 quantity pizza dough (see recipe, page 37)
- 1 eggplant, about 12 oz
- 1/4 cup extra-virgin olive oil
  salt to taste
- 2 cloves garlic, finely chopped
- 2 tablespoons finely chopped parsley
- 8 oz drained and chopped canned tomatoes
- 6 oz Mozzarella cheese, diced
- 8 leaves fresh basil, torn

Wine: a dry rosé (Colli Altotiberini Rosato)

Prepare the dough. • Chop the eggplant into 1/2-inch thick slices and brush them lightly with half the oil. • Grill for about 5 minutes in a hot grill pan, turning frequently until the flesh is cooked. Sprinkle with salt, garlic, and parsley. Set aside. • When the rising time has elapsed, knead the dough on a lightly floured work surface for 1 minute. • Roll the dough to the desired thickness and transfer to an oiled baking sheet. • Spread the tomatoes over the top and sprinkle with the Mozzarella. Drizzle with 1 tablespoon of oil. • Bake in a preheated oven at 500°F for 10–15 minutes. • Take the pizza out of the oven and cover with the slices of eggplant, then cook for 5 more minutes. • When cooked, sprinkle with the basil, drizzle with the remaining oil, and serve hot.

Serves: 1–2 · Prep: 40 min. · Rising time: 1 hr · Cooking: 20 min. · Level: 1

◄ Pizza with water buffalo Mozzarella, cherry tomatoes, and zucchini flowers (see recipe, page 41)
⩘ Eggplant pizza

MAKING PIZZA AND CALZONES

Making pizza at home is fun, and simple. It also fits in well with busy schedules since the dough can be prepared ahead of time, and many toppings only take a few minutes to prepare. Most children love to eat pizza; they will also enjoy helping to knead the dough and sprinkling it with cheese and herbs for the toppings.

Pizza Margherita with black olives

Thickness of the dough

Some people like thick, doughy pizza crusts while others prefer them to be thin and crisp. In Italy, the thick, bread-like crusts are typical of pizzas made in Sicily and the south. Further north, crusts are thinner. Some pizzerias in Florence serve pizzas with such thin crusts that if you roll the topping up in them it is more like eating a crêpe than a pizza. Try several thicknesses, and decide which one you and your family prefer.

Making Pizza and Calzones

The ingredients given in the basic pizza dough recipe will make about 12 oz of dough. This is enough to make one round pizza, sufficient for one or two people.

IMPASTO PER PIZZA
Pizza dough

¼	oz fresh yeast
	or ½ (¼ oz) package active dry yeast
⅔	cup warm water
3	cups unbleached white flour
1	teaspoon fine salt

Prepare the yeast and dough as shown on pages 24–25. • When the rising time has elapsed, knead the dough for 1 minute on a lightly floured work surface. • If you are making more than one pizza, divide the dough into the number of pizzas you wish to make. • Roll each piece of dough into a ball and flatten a little with your hands. • Use your hands or a rolling pin to shape the pizza.

1 To shape the pizza with a rolling pin, open the dough out into a circular shape of the desired thickness. To finish, use your fingertips to make a rim around the edge of the pizza so that the topping won't drip out during cooking. Transfer the dough to an oiled baking sheet.

2 To shape the pizza by hand, place the dough in the pizza pan and push it outward with the palms of your hands and fingertips, opening it out into a circular shape. Press the dough out, stretching it as you go, until it is the required thickness.

3 When the pizza dough has been shaped and is in the pizza pan or on the baking sheet, set it aside for 10 minutes before adding the topping. This will give the dough time to regain some volume and will make the crust lighter and more appetizing.

4–5 To make calzones, proceed as for pizza, giving the dough a round shape. Place the topping on one half of the disk only, leaving a 1-inch border around the edge. Fold the other half over the filling and press the edges together with your fingertips to seal.

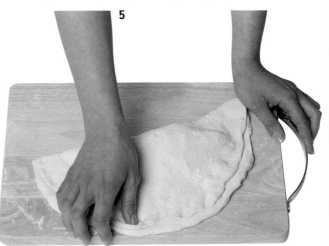

PIZZA MARGHERITA
Pizza Margherita

☞ This is one of the classics; for many it is synonymous with pizza. It was first made in Naples in 1889 for Queen Margherita of Italy.

- 1 quantity Pizza dough (see recipe, page 37)
- 8 oz drained and chopped canned tomatoes
- 6 oz Mozzarella cheese, thinly sliced
  salt to taste
- 2 tablespoons freshly grated Parmesan cheese
- 3 tablespoons extra-virgin olive oil
- 10 leaves fresh basil, torn

Wine: a dry white (Alto Adige Chardonnay)

Prepare the dough. • When the rising time has elapsed, knead the dough on a lightly floured work surface for 1 minute. • Roll the dough to the desired thickness and transfer to an oiled pizza pan. • Spread the tomatoes over the top, cover with the Mozzarella, and sprinkle with salt and Parmesan. Drizzle with 1 tablespoon of oil. • Bake in a preheated oven at 500°F for 15–20 minutes. • When cooked, sprinkle with the basil leaves, drizzle with the remaining oil, and serve.

Serves: 1–2 · Prep: 30 min. · Rising time: about 1 hr · Cooking: 15–20 min. · Level: 1

PIZZA CON AGLIO
Garlic pizza

☞ Try this pizza with 6 oz of diced Mozzarella cheese added halfway through the cooking time.

- 1 quantity Pizza dough (see recipe, page 37)
- 4–6 cloves garlic, thinly sliced
- 2 teaspoons dried oregano
  salt and freshly ground black pepper to taste
- ¼ cup extra-virgin olive oil

Wine: a dry white (Colli Albani)

Prepare the dough. • When the rising time has elapsed, knead the dough for 1 minute on a lightly floured work surface. • Roll the dough to the desired thickness and transfer to an oiled baking sheet. • Sprinkle the garlic and oregano over the top, season with salt and pepper, and drizzle with 1 tablespoon of oil. • Bake in a preheated oven at 500°F for 10 minutes. • When cooked, drizzle with the remaining oil and serve.

Serves: 1–2 · Prep: 30 min. · Rising time: about 1 hr · Cooking: 10 min. · Level: 1

PIZZA CON LE ACCIUGHE
Anchovy pizza

- 1 quantity Pizza dough (see recipe, page 37)
- 6 oz canned anchovies
- ¼ cup extra-virgin olive oil
- 2 cloves garlic, thinly sliced
- 1 teaspoon dried oregano
  salt and freshly ground black pepper to taste

Wine: a dry white (Pomino)

Prepare the dough. • Rinse the anchovies under cold running water to remove salt. Scrape the skin off each anchovy, then carefully remove the dorsal fin and the tiny bones attached to it. Split each anchovy in two with a sharp knife and remove the spine. • When the rising time has elapsed, knead the dough for 1 minute on a lightly floured work surface. • Roll the dough to the desired thickness and transfer to an oiled pizza pan. • Brush the dough with a little oil and arrange the anchovies on top. Sprinkle with the garlic, oregano, salt, and pepper. Drizzle with 1 tablespoon of oil. • Bake in a preheated oven at 500°F for 12–15 minutes. • When cooked, drizzle with the remaining oil and serve.

Serves: 1–2 · Prep: 30 min. · Rising time: about 1 hr · Cooking: 12–15 min. · Level: 1

PIZZA SICILIANA
Sicilian pizza

- 1 quantity Pizza dough (see recipe, page 37)
- 12 oz drained and chopped canned tomatoes
- 6 leaves fresh basil, torn
- 3 oz black olives
- 1 small onion, thinly sliced
- 2 oz freshly grated Pecorino cheese
- 1 teaspoon oregano
- 6 anchovy fillets, crumbled
- 2 tablespoons extra-virgin olive oil

Wine: a dry rosé (Etna Rosato)

Prepare the dough. • When the rising time has elapsed, knead the dough for 1 minute on a lightly floured work surface. • Roll the dough to the desired thickness and transfer to an oiled baking sheet. • Spread the tomatoes over the top, and sprinkle with the basil, olives, and onion, followed by the Pecorino and oregano. Finish with the anchovies and drizzle with 1 tablespoon of oil. • Bake in a preheated oven at 500°F for about 30 minutes. • When cooked, drizzle with the remaining oil and serve.

Serves: 1–2 · Prep: 30 min. · Rising time: about 1 hr · Cooking: 30 min. · Level: 1

PIZZA BIANCA
White pizza

- 1 quantity Pizza dough (see recipe, page 37)
- 1 tablespoon lard or olive oil
- 4 oz Mozzarella cheese, diced
- 2 oz Parmesan cheese, in flakes
  freshly ground black or white pepper to taste
- 6 leaves fresh basil, torn

Wine: a dry white (Orvieto Classico)

Prepare the dough. • When the rising time has elapsed, knead the dough for 1 minute on a lightly floured work surface. • Roll the dough to the desired thickness and transfer to an oiled baking sheet. • Spread with the lard, arrange the Pecorino on top, and sprinkle with pepper. • Bake in a preheated oven at 500°F for 10–15 minutes. • When cooked, sprinkle with the basil and serve.

Serves: 1–2 · Prep: 20 min. · Rising time: about 1 hr · Cooking: 10–15 min. · Level: 1

PIZZA QUATTRO STAGIONI
Four-seasons pizza

- 1 quantity Pizza dough (see recipe, page 37)
- 12 oz mussels, in shell
- 5 oz white mushrooms
- 3 tablespoons extra-virgin olive oil
  salt to taste
- 8 oz drained and chopped canned tomatoes
- 3 oz artichokes preserved in oil, drained and halved
- 3 oz pitted black olives
- 2–3 anchovy fillets, chopped
- 1 clove garlic, thinly sliced

Wine: a dry red (Chianti)

Prepare the dough. • Soak the mussels in a large bowl of water for 1 hour to purge them of sand. Pull off their beards, scrub, and rinse well in abundant cold water. • Clean the mushrooms, rinse well and slice. Sauté in 1 tablespoon of oil over medium-high heat for 3–4 minutes. Season with salt and set aside. • Place the mussels in a large skillet over high heat. Stir frequently until they open. Discard the shells of all but 3 or 4 mussels. Strain the liquid the mussels have produced and set aside with the mussels in a bowl. • When the rising time has elapsed, knead the dough for 1 minute on a lightly floured work surface. • Roll the dough to the desired thickness and transfer to an oiled baking sheet. • Spread the tomatoes evenly on top and sprinkle with salt. • Imagine the pizza divided into 4 equal parts: garnish one quarter with the mushrooms, one with the artichokes, one with the olives and anchovies, and one with the garlic. • Bake in a preheated oven at 500°F for 15–20 minutes. • When cooked, arrange the mussels on the part garnished with tomato and garlic. Drizzle the pizza with the remaining oil and serve.

Serves: 1–2 · Prep: 40 min. + 1 hr to soak mussels · Rising time: about 1 hr · Cooking: 15–20 min. · Level: 1

Pizza with Gorgonzola and pineapple

PIZZA CON GORGONZOLA E ANANAS
Pizza with Gorgonzola and pineapple

1   quantity Pizza dough (see recipe, page 37)
4   oz Gorgonzola cheese, diced
2   tablespoons freshly grated Parmesan cheese
3   tablespoons extra-virgin olive oil
4   oz Mozzarella cheese, diced
2   cloves garlic, finely chopped
4   oz canned pineapple rings
    freshly ground black pepper to taste (optional)

Wine: a dry white (Pinot Bianco)

Prepare the dough. • When the rising time has elapsed, knead the dough for 1 minute on a lightly floured work surface. • Roll the dough to the desired thickness and transfer to an oiled baking sheet. • Spread with the Gorgonzola, sprinkle with the Parmesan, and drizzle with 2 tablespoons of the oil. • Bake in a preheated oven at 500°F for 10 minutes. • Take the pizza out of the oven and arrange the pineapple rings on top. Sprinkle with the Mozzarella and garlic, drizzle with the remaining oil, and finish with a generous grinding of pepper, if using. • Cook for 5–10 more minutes. Serve hot.

Serves: 1–2 · Prep: 25 min. · Rising time: about 1 hr · Cooking: 25 min. · Level: 1

PIZZA AI CARCIOFI
Pizza with artichokes

1   quantity Pizza dough (see recipe, page 37)
3   large artichokes
    juice of 1 lemon
5   tablespoons extra-virgin olive oil
    salt and freshly ground black pepper to taste
4   oz Mozzarella cheese, diced

Wine: a dry white (Bianco di Pitigliano)

Prepare the dough. • Trim the artichoke stems, discard the tough outer leaves, and trim the tops. Cut in half and remove any fuzzy choke. Place in a bowl of cold water with the lemon juice for 10 minutes. • Drain the artichokes, pat dry with paper towels, and slice thinly. • Transfer to a skillet with 2 tablespoons of the oil and sauté over medium heat for 5 minutes. Season with salt. • When the rising time has elapsed, knead the dough for 1 minute on a lightly floured work surface. • Roll the dough to the desired thickness and transfer to an oiled baking sheet. • Brush the pizza with 1 tablespoon of oil and spread with the slices of artichoke. Season with salt and pepper and sprinkle the Mozzarella on top. Drizzle with the remaining oil. • Bake in a preheated oven at 500°F for 15–20

minutes. • When cooked, drizzle with the remaining oil, and serve.

Serves: 1–2 · Prep: 30 min. · Rising time: about 1 hr · Cooking: 15–20 min. · Level: 1

PIZZA ALLA RUCOLA IN BIANCO
Pizza with arugula and Mozzarella

1   quantity Pizza dough (see recipe, page 37)
2   tablespoons extra-virgin olive oil
    salt to taste
5   oz Mozzarella cheese, sliced or diced
3   oz prosciutto, thinly sliced
1   bunch arugula, washed, dried, and coarsely chopped

Wine: a dry white (Vernaccia di San Gimignano)

Prepare the dough. • When the rising time has elapsed, knead the dough for 1 minute on a lightly floured work surface. • Roll the dough to the desired thickness and transfer to an oiled pizza pan. • Brush with half the oil and sprinkle with salt. • Bake in a preheated oven at 450°F. After 6–8 minutes, sprinkle with the Mozzarella. Bake for 6–8 minutes more. • When baked, garnish with the prosciutto and arugula, drizzle with the remaining oil, and serve.

Serves: 1–2 · Prep: 30 min. · Rising time: about 1 hr · Cooking: 15–18 min. · Level: 1

Pizza Margherita with garlic, arugula, and Parmesan

PIZZA NAPOLETANA
Neapolitan pizza

1 quantity Pizza dough (see recipe, page 37)
8 oz drained and chopped canned tomatoes
7 oz Mozzarella cheese, thinly sliced
6 anchovy fillets, crumbled or whole
1 tablespoon capers
3 tablespoons extra-virgin olive oil
1 heaped teaspoon oregano

Wine: a dry red (Salice Salentino Rosso)

Prepare the dough. • When the rising time has elapsed, knead the dough for 1 minute on a lightly floured work surface. • Roll the dough to the desired thickness and transfer to an oiled pizza pan. • Spread the tomatoes over the top, then add the Mozzarella, anchovies, and capers. Drizzle with 1 tablespoon of oil. • Bake in a preheated oven at 500°F for 15–20 minutes. • Sprinkle with the oregano and drizzle with the remaining oil when cooked.

Serves: 1–2 · Prep: 30 min. · Rising time: about 1 hr · Cooking: 15–20 min. · Level: 1

PIZZA PICCANTE AL POMODORO
Spicy tomato pizza

1 quantity Pizza dough (see recipe, page 37)
12 oz ripe tomatoes
1/4 cup freshly grated Parmesan cheese
1 tablespoon finely chopped basil
1/2 teaspoon red pepper flakes
 salt and freshly ground black pepper to taste
1/4 cup extra-virgin olive oil

Wine: a dry white (Frascati)

Prepare the dough. • Chop the tomatoes coarsely and place in a colander to drain for 10 minutes. • When the rising time has elapsed, knead the dough for 1 minute on a lightly floured work surface. • Roll the dough to the desired thickness and transfer to an oiled pizza pan. • Spread the tomatoes over the top, sprinkle with the Parmesan, basil, pepper flakes, salt, and pepper, and drizzle with half the oil. • Bake in a preheated oven at 500°F for 10–15 minutes. • When cooked, drizzle with the remaining oil and serve.

Serves: 1–2 · Prep: 20 min. · Rising time: about 1 hr · Cooking: 10–15 min. · Level: 1

PIZZA MARINARA
Tomato and garlic pizza

☞ Light and simple, *la Marinara* is one of the most traditional pizza toppings in Italy.

1 quantity Pizza dough (see recipe, page 37)
12 oz drained and chopped canned tomatoes
2 cloves garlic, thinly sliced
1 teaspoon dried oregano
 salt to taste
1/4 cup extra-virgin olive oil
6 leaves fresh basil, torn

Wine: a dry rosé (Biferno Rosato)

Prepare the dough. • When the rising time has elapsed, knead the dough for 1 minute on a lightly floured work surface. • Roll the dough to the desired thickness and transfer to an oiled pizza pan. • Spread the tomatoes and garlic over the top. Sprinkle with the oregano and salt and drizzle with 1 tablespoon of the oil. • Bake in a preheated oven at 500°F for 15–20 minutes. • When cooked, sprinkle with the basil leaves and drizzle with the remaining oil.

Serves: 1–2 · Prep: 40 min. · Rising time: about 1 hr · Cooking: 15–20 min. · Level: 1

PIZZA MARGHERITA ESTIVA
Pizza Magherita with garlic, arugula, and Parmesan flakes

1 Pizza Margherita (see recipe, page 38)
3 cloves garlic, sliced
1 small bunch arugula, coarsely chopped
2 oz Parmesan cheese, flaked

Wine: a dry white (Vermentino di Sardegna)

Prepare the pizza, following the instructions on page 38. Add the garlic to the Margherita pizza together with the Mozzarella • Bake in a preheated oven at 500°F for 15–20 minutes. • When cooked, sprinkle with the arugula and Parmesan. Drizzle with the remaining oil and serve hot.

Serves: 1–2 · Prep: 40 min. · Rising time: about 1 hr · Cooking: 20–25 min. · Level: 1

PIZZA CON PEPERONI E CAPPERI
Bell pepper, onion, and caper pizza

- 1 quantity Pizza dough (see recipe, page 37)
- 2 small onions, sliced
- 3 tablespoons extra-virgin olive oil
- 12 oz bell peppers, mixed colors, cut in strips
- 8 oz canned tomatoes
- 2 tablespoons capers
  salt to taste
- 4 oz Mozzarella cheese, diced
- 1/2 cup freshly grated Parmesan cheese
- 1 tablespoon finely chopped parsley (optional)

Wine: a dry rosé (Lagrein Rosato)

Prepare the dough. • Sauté the onion with 2 tablespoons of oil for 3 minutes over medium heat. Add the bell peppers, tomatoes, and capers. Season with salt and cook for 10 minutes. • When the rising time has elapsed, knead the dough for 1 minute on a lightly floured work surface. • Roll the dough to the desired thickness and transfer to an oiled pizza pan. • Spread with the bell pepper mixture, sprinkle with the cheeses, drizzle with the remaining oil, and sprinkle with the parsley, if using. • Bake in a preheated oven at 500°F for 15–20 minutes.

Serves: 1–2 · Prep: 40 min. · Rising time: about 1 hr · Cooking: 15–20 min. · Level: 1

PIZZA ALL'ANDREA
Andrea's Pizza

- 1 quantity Pizza dough (see recipe, page 37)
- 1/3 cup extra-virgin olive oil
- 2 large onions, finely sliced
- 1 lb fresh or canned tomatoes, peeled and chopped
  salt and freshly ground black pepper to taste
- 4 leaves basil, torn
- 8 anchovy fillets
- 2 tablespoons black olives

Wine: a dry white (Vermentino di Imperia)

Prepare the dough, incorporating 2 tablespoons of the oil into the dough. • When the rising time has elapsed, knead the dough for 1 minute on a lightly floured work surface. • Roll the dough to the desired thickness and transfer to an oiled pizza pan. Leave a raised border around the outer edge. • Place the remaining oil in a pan over low heat and lightly sauté the onion, add the tomatoes, a little salt, a dash of freshly ground black pepper and the basil. Cook over low heat until the sauce has reduced. Add the anchovies, remove from the heat and stir well. • Pour

Andrea's Pizza

the sauce over the dough, scatter with olives, and bake in a preheated oven at 400° F about 30 minutes, or until the dough is cooked and golden.

Serves: 1–2 · Prep: 20 min. · Rising time: about 1 hr · Cooking: 30 min. · Level: 1

PIZZA CAPRICCIOSA
Pizza with mixed topping

- 1 quantity Pizza dough (see recipe, page 37)
- 8 oz drained and chopped canned tomatoes
- 2 oz ham, cut in strips
- 4 anchovy fillets, crumbled
- 6 oz Mozzarella cheese, diced
- 2 oz artichokes in oil, drained and cut in half
- 2 oz button mushrooms preserved in oil, cut in half
- 2 oz black olives
- 2 cloves garlic, sliced
- 1 teaspoon dried oregano
- 3 tablespoons extra-virgin olive oil

Wine: a dry red (Montecarlo Rosso)

Prepare the dough. • When the rising time has elapsed, knead the dough for 1 minute on a lightly floured work surface. • Roll the dough to the desired thickness and transfer to an oiled pizza pan. •

Spread the tomatoes over the top, then add the ham, anchovies, Mozzarella, artichokes, mushrooms, olives, and garlic. Sprinkle with oregano and drizzle with 1 tablespoon of oil. • Bake in a preheated oven at 500°F for 15–20 minutes. • When cooked, drizzle with the remaining oil and serve.

Serves: 1–2 · Prep: 30 min. · Rising time: about 1 hr · Cooking: 15–20 min. · Level: 1

PIZZA AI FIORI DI ZUCCA
Pizza with water buffalo Mozzarella, cherry tomatoes, and zucchini flowers

- 1 White pizza (see recipe, page 38)
- 6 oz water buffalo Mozzarella cheese
- 4–6 large zucchini flowers, rinsed and dried
- 8–10 cherry tomatoes, cut in half

Wine: a dry white (Isonzo Chardonnay)

Prepare the White pizza, but omit both the ordinary Mozzarella and Parmesan cheeses. Use the water buffalo Mozzarella in their place. • About 5 minutes before the pizza is cooked, add the zucchini flowers and tomatoes. Serve hot.

Serves: 1–2 · Prep: 20 min. · Rising time: about 1 hr · Cooking: 15 min. · Level: 1

Pizza with four-cheese topping

Mix well. • When the rising time has elapsed, knead the dough for 1 minute on a lightly floured work surface. • Roll the dough to the desired thickness and transfer to an oiled pizza pan. • Spread the topping evenly over the pizza and bake in a preheated oven at 450°F for 15–20 minutes.

Serves: 1–2 · Prep: 45 min. · Rising time: about 1 hr · Cooking: 15–20 min. · Level: 1

PIZZA AI QUATTRO FORMAGGI
Pizza with four-cheese topping

1	quantity Pizza dough (see recipe, page 37)
4	oz Mozzarella cheese, diced
1/4	cup freshly grated Parmesan cheese
4	oz Gorgonzola cheese, diced
2	oz Emmental cheese, thinly sliced
1	tablespoon extra-virgin olive oil

Wine: a dry red (Pignoletto)

Prepare the dough. • When the rising time has elapsed, knead the dough for 1 minute on a lightly floured work surface. • Roll the dough to the desired thickness and transfer to an oiled pizza pan. • Spread the surface with the cheeses and drizzle with the oil. • Bake in a preheated oven at 500°F for 15–20 minutes. • Serve hot.

Serves: 1–2 · Prep: 30 min. · Rising time: about 1 hr · Cooking: 15–20 min. · Level: 1

PIZZA AI DUE FORMAGGI
Pizza with Mozzarella and Gorgonzola cheese

1	quantity Pizza dough (see recipe, page 37)
4	oz Mozzarella cheese, diced
6	oz Gorgonzola cheese, diced
2	tablespoons finely chopped chives
2	cloves garlic, finely chopped
1–2	tablespoons heavy cream
1	tablespoon extra-virgin olive oil freshly ground black pepper to taste

Wine: a dry white (Elba Bianco)

Prepare the dough. • Put the Mozzarella, Gorgonzola, chives, garlic, cream, and oil in a bowl and mix thoroughly. • When the rising time has elapsed, knead the dough for 1 minute on a lightly floured work surface. • Roll the dough to the desired thickness and transfer to an oiled pizza pan. • Spread the cheese mixture over the top and bake in a preheated oven at 500°F for 10–15 minutes. Season with pepper and serve.

Serves: 1–2 · Prep: 30 min. · Rising time: about 1 hr · Cooking: 10–15 min. · Level: 1

PIZZA AI FUNGHI
Mushroom pizza

1	quantity Pizza dough (see recipe, page 37)
10	oz white mushrooms
3	tablespoons extra-virgin olive oil
1	tablespoon finely chopped thyme
1	small clove garlic, finely chopped salt and freshly ground black pepper to taste

Wine: a dry red (Grignolino)

Prepare the dough. • Rinse the mushrooms under cold running water. Pat dry and slice thinly. • Sauté the mushrooms with 1 tablespoon of oil over high heat for 2–3 minutes. Drain off any excess liquid and stir in the thyme and garlic. Set aside. • When the rising time has elapsed, knead the dough for 1 minute on a lightly floured work surface. • Roll the dough to the desired thickness and transfer to an oiled pizza pan. • Spread the mushrooms over the top and sprinkle with a little salt and pepper. Drizzle with the remaining oil and bake in a preheated oven at 500°F for 10–20 minutes.

Serves: 1–2 · Prep: 30 min. · Rising time: about 1 hr · Cooking: 15–20 min. · Level: 1

PIZZA CON PANCETTA E PORRI
Pizza with pancetta and leek topping

1	quantity Pizza dough (see recipe, page 37)
1/2	cup diced pancetta
2	tablespoons extra-virgin olive oil
12	oz leeks, cleaned and thinly sliced salt and freshly ground black pepper to taste
1	egg
2	tablespoons heavy cream
1/2	cup freshly grated Parmesan cheese
2	oz Gruyère cheese, very thinly sliced

Wine: a dry white (Pinot Grigio Briganze)

Prepare the dough. • Sauté the pancetta in a skillet over high heat for 2–3 minutes. Add the oil and leeks and sauté for 10 more minutes over medium heat. Season with salt and pepper and set aside to cool. • Beat the egg with the cream in a bowl. Add the leek and pancetta mixture and the two cheeses.

PIZZA ALLA ROMANA
Roman-style pizza

1	quantity Pizza dough (see recipe, page 37)
8	oz drained and chopped canned tomatoes
4	oz Mozzarella cheese, diced
1/2	cup freshly grated Pecorino romano cheese
4	anchovy fillets, crumbled salt and freshly ground black pepper to taste
1/4	cup extra-virgin olive oil
5–6	leaves fresh basil, torn

Wine: a dry white (Frascati)

Prepare the dough. • When the rising time has elapsed, knead the dough for 1 minute on a lightly floured work surface. • Roll the dough to the desired thickness and transfer to an oiled pizza pan. • Spread the tomatoes over the top and sprinkle with the Mozzarella, Pecorino romano, and anchovies. Season with salt and pepper and drizzle with 1 tablespoon of oil. • Bake in a preheated oven at 500°F for 15–20 minutes. • When cooked, sprinkle with the basil leaves, drizzle with the remaining oil and serve.

Serves: 1–2 · Prep: 30 min. · Rising time: about 1 hr · Cooking: 15–20 min. · Level: 1

PIZZA ISOLANA
Pizza with Pecorino cheese, black olives, and anchovies

   1   quantity Pizza dough (see recipe, page 37)
       salt to taste
   5   tablespoons extra-virgin olive oil
   1   medium onion, thinly sliced
  12   anchovy fillets, very coarsely chopped or torn
       into small pieces
   5   oz aged Pecorino cheese, thinly sliced
  10   black olives, pitted and coarsely chopped
   2   large tomatoes, skinned and diced (optional)
   1   teaspoon oregano

Wine: a dry red (Rosso di Donnafugata)

Prepare the dough. • When the rising time has elapsed, knead the dough for 1 minute on a lightly floured work surface. • Roll the dough to the desired thickness and transfer to an oiled pizza pan. • Press the surface of the dough with your fingertips to make little dimples in it. • Sprinkle with a little salt and half the oil. Top with the ingredients in the following order: onion, anchovies, cheese, olives, tomatoes, if using, and oregano. Drizzle with the remaining oil. • Bake in a preheated oven at 425°F for 20–25 minutes.

Serves: 1–2 min. · Prep: 25 min. · Rising time: about 1 hr · Cooking: 20–25 min. · Level: 1

PIZZA MEDITERRANEA
Mediterranean pizza

   1   quantity Pizza dough
       (see recipe, page 37)
   1   lb fresh tomatoes
  1/4 cup extra-virgin olive oil
   1   clove garlic, sliced
       salt and freshly ground black pepper to taste
   8   oz tuna in oil, drained and in chunks
   6   anchovy fillets (optional)
   2   oz black olives
   1   teaspoon dried oregano
   1   tablespoon capers
   4   oz Mozzarella cheese,
       diced (optional)

Wine: a dry white
(Corvo di Salaparuta)

Prepare the dough. • Blanch the tomatoes in boiling water for 1 minute, then slip off the skins. Cut them in two and remove the seeds. Set aside in a colander for 10 minutes to drain. • Transfer the tomatoes to a skillet with 1–2 tablespoons of the oil, the garlic, and salt to taste. Sauté for 4–5 minutes, then set aside. • When the rising time has elapsed, knead the dough for 1 minute on a lightly floured work surface. • Roll the dough to the desired thickness and transfer to an oiled pizza pan. • Spread the tomato mixture over the top, then add the tuna, anchovies, olives, oregano, and capers. • Bake in a preheated oven at 500°F for 15–20 minutes. • If using the Mozzarella, sprinkle the cheese over the pizza after it has been in the oven for 8–10 minutes. • When cooked, drizzle with the remaining oil, and serve.

Serves: 1–2 min. · Prep: 35 min. · Rising time: about 1 hr · Cooking: 15–20 min. · Level: 1

PIZZA AL PROSCIUTTO
Ham pizza

   1   quantity Pizza dough (see recipe, page 37)
   4   oz sliced ham, each slice torn in 2–3 pieces
   6   oz Mozzarella cheese, diced
       freshly ground black pepper or 1/2 teaspoon
       crushed red pepper flakes (optional)
   2   tablespoons extra-virgin olive oil

Wine: a dry red (Carmignano)

Prepare the dough. • When the rising time has elapsed, knead the dough for 1 minute on a lightly floured work surface. • Roll the dough to the desired thickness and transfer to an oiled pizza pan. • Brush with a little oil and arrange the ham on top. Sprinkle with the Mozzarella and the pepper or pepper flakes, if using. Drizzle with 1 tablespoon of oil. • Bake in a preheated oven at 500°F for 15–20 minutes. • When cooked, drizzle with the remaining oil and serve.

Serves: 1–2 · Prep: 30 min. · Rising time: about 1 hr · Cooking: 15–20 min. · Level: 1

PIZZA CON LE OLIVE NERE
Pizza with black olives

   1   quantity Pizza dough (see recipe, page 37)
   8   oz drained and chopped canned tomatoes
  8–12 black olives
  2–3   teaspoons capers
   3   tablespoons extra-virgin olive oil

Wine: a dry rosé (Brindisi Rosato)

Prepare the dough. • When the rising time has elapsed, knead the dough for 1 minute on a lightly floured work surface. • Roll the dough to the desired thickness and transfer to an oiled pizza pan. • Spread with the tomatoes and garnish with the olives and capers. Drizzle with 1 tablespoon of oil. • Bake in a preheated oven at 500°F for 15–20 minutes. • When cooked, drizzle with the remaining oil, and serve.

Serves 1–2 · Prep: 30 min. · Rising time: about 1 hr · Cooking: 15–20 min. · Level: 1

Pizza with black olives

Egg calzones

seal. Brush the calzones with 1 tablespoon of oil and arrange them on lightly oiled baking sheets. • Mix the tomatoes with salt and 2 tablespoons of oil. Spread over the calzoni. • Bake in a preheated oven at 450°F for 20–25 minutes. The calzones should be puffed and golden brown.

Serves: 4–6 · Prep: 35 min. · Rising time: about 1 hr · Cooking: 20–25 min. · Level: 1

CALZONE BISMARCK
Egg calzones

    4   Ham calzones (see preceding recipe)
    4   eggs

Wine: a dry red (Rosso Conero)

Prepare the dough. • Proceed as for Ham calzones, adding 1 raw egg to each calzone together with the ham.

Serves: 4–6 · Prep: 40 min. · Rising time: about 1 hr · Cooking: 20–25 min. · Level: 1

CALZONE ALLA NAPOLETANA
Neapolitan calzones

    3   quantities Pizza dough (see recipe, page 37)
    8   oz soft Ricotta cheese
  1/3   cup freshly grated Pecorino romano
        (or Parmesan) cheese
    2   eggs
    8   oz Mozzarella cheese, diced
    4   oz Neapolitan salami, diced
        salt to taste
    2   tablespoons extra-virgin olive oil

Wine: a dry red (Ischia)

Prepare the dough. • Mix the Ricotta, Pecorino (or Parmesan), and eggs in a bowl. Add the Mozzarella, salami, and salt to taste. Mix well and set aside. • When the rising time has elapsed, knead the dough briefly on a floured work surface, then divide into 4 equal portions. • Roll the dough into disks about 9 inches in diameter. • Spread the filling on half of each disk, leaving a 1-inch border around the edge. Fold the other half of the dough over the top, pressing down on the edges to seal. Brush the calzones with the oil and arrange on lightly oiled baking sheets. • Bake in a preheated oven at 450°F for 25 minutes. The calzones should be puffed and golden brown.

Serves: 4–6 · Prep: 35 min. · Rising time: about1 hr · Cooking: 25 min. · Level: 1

PIZZA ALLA RUCOLA CON POMODORO
Pizza with arugula, tomato, and Mozzarella cheese

    1   quantity Pizza dough (see recipe, page 37)
    8   oz drained and chopped canned tomatoes
    5   oz Mozzarella cheese, sliced
    2   tablespoons extra-virgin olive oil
    1   small bunch arugula, coarsely chopped
        freshly ground black pepper to taste

Wine: a young, dry red (Carmignano)

Prepare the dough. • When the rising time has elapsed, knead the dough for 1 minute on a lightly floured work surface. • Roll the dough to the desired thickness and transfer to an oiled pizza pan. • Spread the tomatoes over the top and bake in a preheated oven at 500°F for 10 minutes. • Take the pizza out of the oven, cover with the Mozzarella and drizzle with half the oil. Return to the oven and cook for 6–8 minutes more. • When cooked, garnish with the arugula and black pepper. Drizzle with the remaining oil and serve.

Serves: 1–2 · Prep: 30 min. · Rising time: about 1 hr · Cooking: 15–20 min. · Level: 1

SCACCIA DI RICOTTA
Sicilian calzones with Ricotta and sausage

    3   quantities Pizza dough (see recipe, page 37)
 1 1/2 lb Ricotta cheese
   14   oz fresh, spicy Italian sausage meat
  1/4   cup extra-virgin olive oil
        salt and freshly ground black pepper to taste

Wine: a dry red (Rosso di Donnafugata)

Prepare the dough. • When the rising time has elapsed, knead the dough for 1 minute on a lightly floured work surface. • Divide the dough into 4 portions and roll each one into a rectangular sheet 1/4 inch thick. • Spread a quarter of the Ricotta over one half of each rectangle, leaving a narrow border around the edge. • Place a quarter of the sausage meat on top of the Ricotta and sprinkle with a little pepper, salt, and oil. • Fold the uncovered half of each rectangle over the filling and pinch the edges together, then fold them back over to form a narrow rolled edge. • Bake in a preheated oven at 450°F for 20 minutes, or until golden brown.

Serves: 4–6 · Prep: 25 min. · Rising time: about 1 hr · Cooking: 20 min. · Level: 1

CALZONE CON PROSCIUTTO
Ham calzones

    3   quantities Pizza dough (see recipe, page 37)
    8   oz fresh Ricotta cheese
    8   oz Mozzarella cheese, diced
    8   oz ham, thinly sliced
  1/4   cup extra-virgin olive oil
    4   oz drained and chopped canned tomatoes
        salt to taste

Wine: a dry white (Orvieto Classico)

Prepare the dough. • When the rising time has elapsed, knead the dough briefly on a lightly floured work surface, then divide into 4 equal portions. • Roll or stretch the dough into disks, about 9 inches in diameter. • Spread half of each disk with the Ricotta, then sprinkle with the Mozzarella and ham, leaving a 1-inch border around the edge for sealing. Fold the other half of the dough over the top, pressing down carefully on the edges to

CALZONE AL PROSCIUTTO COTTO
Calzones with ham and cheese

- 3 quantities Pizza dough (see recipe, page 37)
- 1 cup ham, coarsely chopped
- 6 oz Provolone cheese, diced
- 6 oz Ricotta salata cheese, grated
- 6 oz Mozzarella cheese, diced
- 2 tablespoons finely chopped parsley
- 2 tablespoons extra-virgin olive oil

Wine: a dry rosé (Chiaretto di Bardolino)

Prepare the dough. • Combine the ham, cheeses, and parsley in a bowl. Set aside. • When the rising time has elapsed, knead the dough for 1 minute on a lightly floured work surface, then divide into 4 equal portions. • Roll or stretch the dough into disks, about 9 inches in diameter. • Spread the filling on one half of each disk, leaving a 1-inch border around the edge. Fold the other half of the dough over the top, pressing down carefully on the edges to seal. • Brush the calzones with the oil, and arrange them on lightly oiled baking sheets. • Bake in a preheated oven at 450°F for 20–25 minutes.

Serves: 4–6 · Prep: 35 min. · Rising time: about 1 hr · Cooking: 20–25 min. · Level: 1

CALZONE ALLE MELANZANE
Eggplant calzones

- 3 quantities Pizza dough (see recipe, page 37)
- 2¹/₂ cups eggplant, diced
- ¹/₄ cup extra-virgin olive oil
- 3 tablespoons finely chopped fresh marjoram
- 1 clove garlic, finely chopped
  salt to taste
- 12 oz drained and chopped canned tomatoes
- 2 teaspoons finely chopped parsley
- 6 leaves fresh basil, torn
- 6 oz Pecorino cheese, diced

Wine: a dry white (Corvo di Salaparuta)

Prepare the dough. • Fry the eggplant in 3 tablespoons of oil in a large skillet over medium heat. After 8–10 minutes, add the marjoram, garlic, salt, and, if necessary, a little more oil. Cook for 2–3 minutes more. • Add the tomatoes, parsley, basil, and Pecorino. Stir for 1 minute then remove from heat. • When the rising time has elapsed, knead the dough for 1 minute on a lightly floured work surface. Divide into 4 equal portions. • Roll or stretch the

dough into disks, about 9 inches in diameter. • Spread the filling on one half of each disk, leaving a 1-inch border around the edge for sealing. Fold the other half of the dough over the top, pressing down carefully on the edges to seal. Brush the calzones with the remaining oil and bake in a preheated oven at 450°F for 20–25 minutes. Serve hot.

Serves: 4–6 · Prep: 40 min. · Rising time: about 1 hr · Cooking: 20–25 min. · Level: 1

CALZONE ALLA CIPOLLA
Onion calzones

- 3 quantities Pizza dough (see recipe, page 37)
- 1¹/₄ lb onions, sliced
- ¹/₄ cup extra-virgin olive oil
- 12 oz drained and chopped canned tomatoes
- 7 oz black olives, pitted and halved
- 8 anchovy fillets, crumbled
- 2 tablespoons capers
- 8 leaves fresh basil, torn
  salt to taste
- 6 oz Pecorino cheese, diced

Wine: a dry red (Rosso dell'Oltrepò Pavese)

Prepare the dough. • Sauté the onions in 2 tablespoons of oil in a large skillet for 5 minutes. Add the tomatoes, olives, anchovies, capers, basil, and salt. Mix and cook over medium heat for 3–4 minutes more. Remove from heat. • When the mixture is cool, add the Pecorino. • When the rising time has elapsed, knead the dough on a lightly floured work surface, then divide into 4 equal portions. • Roll or stretch the dough into disks about 9 inches in diameter. • Spread the filling on one half of each disk, leaving a 1-inch border

Fried pizzas

around the edge for sealing. Fold the other half of the dough over the top, pressing down carefully on the edges to seal. • Brush the calzones with the remaining oil, and arrange them on lightly oiled baking sheets. • Bake in a preheated oven at 450°F for 25 minutes. Serve hot.

Serves: 4–6 · Prep: 35 min. · Rising time: about 1 hr · Cooking: 25 min. · Level: 1

PIZZE FRITTE
Fried pizzas

- 3 quantities Pizza dough (see recipe, page 37)
- 14 oz Mozzarella cheese, sliced
- 6 tomatoes, sliced
- 8 anchovy fillets, chopped
- 2 tablespoons finely chopped parsley
  salt and freshly ground black pepper to taste
- 2 cups oil, for frying

Wine: a dry rosé (Cirò Rosato)

Prepare the dough. • When the rising time has elapsed, knead the dough briefly on a lightly floured work surface, then divide into 6 equal portions. • Roll or stretch the dough into disks, about 9 inches in diameter. • Cover half of each disk with slices of Mozzarella and tomato, leaving a 1-inch border around the edge for sealing. Sprinkle with anchovy, parsley, salt, and pepper. Fold the other half of the dough over the top, pressing down carefully on the edges to seal. • Heat the oil to very hot in a skillet and fry the pizzas two at a time until deep golden brown. Serve hot.

Serves: 4–6 · Prep: 35 min. · Rising time: about 1 hr · Cooking: 20–25 min. · Level: 1

SAVORY PIES

This chapter covers a tantalizing array of egg, meat, and vegetable pies. Many have a bread or pastry base and some also have a "lid." These quiche-like dishes are very popular in Italy, where they are served as appetizers or snacks. They also make wonderful picnic food.

TORTA SALATA VESUVIANA
Neapolitan bread with tomatoes and Mozzarella cheese

²/₃	oz fresh yeast or 1¹/₂ (¹/₄ oz) packages active dry yeast
2	teaspoons sugar
¹/₄	cup lukewarm milk (or water)
2	cups unbleached white flour
1	heaped teaspoon salt
²/₃	cup butter, at room temperature, thinly sliced
4	eggs, lightly beaten
14	oz ripe tomatoes
2	tablespoons extra-virgin olive oil
10	oz Mozzarella cheese, sliced
	salt and freshly ground black pepper to taste
8–10	leaves fresh basil, torn
5	oz prosciutto, sliced and cut in strips
¹/₂	cup freshly grated Parmesan cheese
1	egg, beaten
2	tablespoons butter

Wine: a dry white (Pinot Grigio)

Crumble the yeast into a bowl and add the sugar. Mix with the milk (or water) and set aside for 5 minutes. • Put the flour in a mixing bowl, sprinkle with salt and make a hollow in the middle. Fill with the yeast mixture, butter, and eggs. Mix with a wooden spoon until the flour absorbs most of the ingredients. • Transfer to a lightly floured work surface. Use a soft spatula to remove all the mixture from the bowl. • Knead for several minutes until the dough becomes soft and elastic. • Place in a bowl, cover with a cloth, and leave to rise in a warm, sheltered place for 2 hours. • Place the tomatoes in boiling water for 1 minute, then peel, cut in half, and remove the seeds. • Sauté the tomatoes in the oil over high heat for 3–4 minutes. Shake the pan from time to time to move and turn the tomatoes, rather than stirring them. • Butter and flour a 9-inch springform pan. • When the rising time has elapsed (about 2 hours), transfer the dough to a lightly floured work surface and tap lightly with your fingers so that it contracts a little. • Break off about a third of the dough and set aside. • Place the rest in the springform pan and spread by hand to line the base and sides of the pan. • Cover with half the Mozzarella, followed by the tomatoes. Sprinkle with salt and pepper, scatter with the basil, and cover with the prosciutto and remaining Mozzarella. • Sprinkle with the Parmesan and, if liked, more pepper. • Roll the remaining dough into a disk as large as the springform pan. Brush the edges of the dough with half the beaten egg. Cover the filling with the sheet and seal the edges of the two sheets by pressing them together lightly with your fingers. • Leave to rise for about 1 hour. • Brush the surface of the dish with the remaining egg and bake in a preheated oven at 400°F for 25–30 minutes. • Serve hot.

Makes: 1 filled bread, 9 inches in diameter · Prep: 45 min. · Rising time: 3 hrs · Cooking: 30 min. · Level: 2

◄ Neapolitan bread with tomatoes and Mozzarella cheese

MAKING PASTRY

Most of the recipes in this chapter have a pastry base. Making plain pastry at home is simple and quick. We have given three basic recipes for pastry here. They can all be used in most of the recipes in this chapter. A good recipe for puff pastry is included in the Cakes chapter of this book.

Making plain pastry

PASTAFROLLA SALATA
Plain pastry

    2   cups all-purpose flour
    1½ teaspoons salt
    1   egg yolk
    ½   cup butter, at room temperature, thinly sliced
    1–2 tablespoons water

Place the flour and salt in a mound on a clean work surface. Make a hollow in the center and fill with the egg, butter, and water. Mix the ingredients with a fork, mashing the butter as you work. • After 2–3 minutes the dough will have absorbed almost all the flour. It should be quite crumbly. • Transfer to a lightly floured work surface and shape into a soft compact ball, kneading as little as possible. • Place in a 9-inch springform pan or pie plate and flatten a little. Using the heels of your palms and your fingertips, spread the dough so that it covers the base of the pan evenly and three-quarters of the sides. Use a fork to shape the sides and bring to the same height. • Cover with plastic wrap and place in the refrigerator for at least 30 minutes. • This pastry can be made a few hours ahead, or even the day before.

For: a 9-inch springform pan or pie plate · Prep: 10 min. + at least 30 min. to chill

PASTA ALLA RICOTTA
Ricotta pastry

    1¾ cups all-purpose flour
    1½ teaspoons salt
    ¼   cup butter
    4   oz soft Ricotta cheese

Proceed as explained for plain pastry (above). Add the Ricotta when the flour and butter are almost mixed.

For: a 9-inch springform pan or pie plate · Prep: 10 min. + 30 min. to chill

---

Making short crust pastry

    2   cups unbleached white flour
    1½ teaspoons salt
    ¼   cup butter, at room temperature, thinly sliced
    5–6 tablespoons cold water

1 Place the flour and salt in a mound on a clean work surface. Make a hollow in the center and fill with the butter and water. Mix the ingredients with your hands, working the butter into the flour. • When the ingredients are roughly mixed, transfer to a lightly floured work surface and knead until the dough is soft, smooth, and elastic. • Flatten the dough with a rolling pin and shape it into a rectangle. Fold the shorter sides of the rectangle inward, one over the other. Roll the dough into another rectangle, working in the opposite direction to the folds. Fold the shorter sides of the rectangle inward again. Repeat the two steps once more. • Roll the dough into a rectangle or circle, depending on the pan or pie plate you are using. The dough should be about ¼ inch thick. • Line the base and sides of the pan or pie plate, cover with plastic.

For: a 9-inch springform pan or pie plate · Prep: 15 min. + 30 min. to chill

CROSTATA DI SPINACI
Spinach pie

- 1 quantity Plain pastry (see recipe, page 49)
- 1½ lb spinach, cooked, squeezed dry and chopped
- 8 oz Ricotta cheese
- ⅓ cup freshly grated Parmesan cheese
- 2 eggs, beaten
- ⅔ cup heavy cream
  - salt and freshly ground black pepper to taste
  - pinch of nutmeg
- 2 tablespoons bread crumbs
- 2 tablespoons butter

Prepare the pastry base. • Mix the spinach and Ricotta in a bowl. Add the Parmesan, eggs, cream, salt, pepper, and nutmeg. Mix well. • Remove the pastry base from the refrigerator and discard the plastic wrap. • Spread with the topping and sprinkle with the bread crumbs. • Arrange pats of butter on top and bake in a preheated oven at 350°F for 40 minutes. • Serve hot or at room temperature.

Makes: 1 pie, 9 inches in diameter · Prep: 30 min. + 40 min. for the pastry · Cooking: 40 min. · Level: 2

ERBAZZONE EMILIANO
Swiss chard pie

- 2½ lb Swiss chard, spinach beet, or spinach leaves
- 1¼ cups chopped pancetta
- 2 tablespoons finely chopped parsley
- 1 clove garlic, finely chopped
- 6 scallions, finely chopped
- 2 tablespoons butter
- ¾ cup freshly grated Parmesan cheese
  - salt and freshly ground pepper to taste
- 3 cups all-purpose flour
- ¼ cup melted lard
  - warm water for the dough

Wine: a dry white (Pomposa Bianco)

Rinse the Swiss chard or spinach leaves under cold running, but do not dry. Cook for a few minutes with just the water left clinging to the leaves. Squeeze out as much moisture as possible and chop coarsely. • Sauté the pancetta, parsley, garlic, and scallions in a skillet with 1 tablespoon of butter for 3–5 minutes. • Set 1 tablespoon of this mixture aside. Leave the rest in the skillet and add the Swiss chard or spinach, Parmesan, salt, and pepper. Stir well. • Sift the flour and

salt into a mixing bowl. Pour in the lard and stir it into the flour, adding a little warm water at intervals, to form a workable dough. • Transfer to a lightly floured work surface and knead the dough until smooth and elastic. • Divide it into two parts, one larger than the other, and roll out into two thin disks. Use the larger one to line a 10-inch pie pan greased with the remaining butter. It should overlap the edges a little. • Fill with the vegetable mixture. Cover with the other disk, sealing the edges well. • Spread the reserved fried mixture over the top. Bake in a preheated oven at 400°F for 30 minutes.

Makes: 1 pie, 10 inches in diameter · Prep: 30 min. · Cooking: 35 min. · Level: 2

TORTA DI CARCIOFI
Artichoke pie

- 1 quantity Plain pastry (see recipe, page 49)
- 12 artichokes
- 1 lb frozen spinach
- 1 onion, finely chopped
- 6 tablespoons extra-virgin olive oil
- 2 eggs, beaten
- ¼ cup freshly grated Parmesan cheese
- ¾ cup whole milk
  - salt and freshly ground black pepper to taste
- 1 tablespoon finely chopped fresh marjoram

Wine: a dry white (Tocai)

Prepare the pastry base. • Trim the artichoke stems, discard the tough outer leaves, and trim the tops. Cut in half and remove any fuzzy choke. Slice in thin wedges. • Boil the spinach in a little salted water for 5–7 minutes. Chop coarsely. • Sauté the onion in the oil in a large skillet for 5 minutes. Add the artichokes and cook for 10 minutes, stirring frequently. • Remove from the heat and add the spinach, eggs, Parmesan, milk, salt, pepper, and marjoram, and mix well. • Remove the pastry base from the refrigerator and discard the plastic wrap. • Spread with the filling. • Bake in a preheated oven at 400°F for 25–30 minutes.

Makes: 1 pie, 9 inches in diameter · Prep: 30 min. + 40 min. for the pastry · Cooking: 25–30 min. · Level: 2

This delicious pie from Liguria was traditionally made with 33 sheets of pastry, reflecting Christ's age when he died. Nowadays, this number is usually reduced, as in the following version.

TORTA PASQUALINA
Easter pie

- 4 cups unbleached white flour
- 2 teaspoons salt
- 1 cup extra-virgin olive oil
- 1 cup water
- 2 lb fresh Swiss chard
- 2 tablespoons onion, finely chopped
- 1 clove garlic, finely chopped (optional)
- 1 tablespoon finely chopped parsley
- 1 heaped teaspoon marjoram, fresh
- 7 oz soft Ricotta cheese
- 5 tablespoons heavy cream
- 1 heaped tablespoon flour
- 8 eggs
  - salt and freshly ground black pepper to taste
- ½ cup freshly grated Parmesan cheese
- 2 tablespoons butter

Wine: a dry white (Colli di Luni)

Put the flour and salt in a mixing bowl. Add ½ cup oil and water and stir with a wooden spoon until the flour has been absorbed. • Transfer the mixture to a lightly floured work surface and knead until the dough is smooth and elastic. • Divide into 15 portions, 14 of the same size and one slightly larger. Cover with a damp cloth and set aside for 30 minutes. • Trim the Swiss chard, rinse well, and cook for 5–7 minutes in a little salted, boiling water. Drain, squeeze, and coarsely chop. • Sauté the onion, garlic, and parsley in 3 tablespoons of oil for 2 minutes over medium heat. • Add the Swiss chard and cook, stirring frequently, for about 5 minutes. Turn off the heat, add the marjoram, stir well, and set aside to cool. • Combine the Ricotta, cream, the second measure of flour, and 2 eggs in a bowl, season with salt and pepper, and mix well. • Roll out the larger piece of dough on a lightly floured work surface to obtain a very thin disk large enough to cover the base of a 12-inch springform pan. •

Oil the pan and line the base and sides with the dough, leaving a little to overlap at the top. The dough should be very thin, almost transparent. Brush with oil. • Prepare another 6 sheets of dough, large enough to cover the base and three-quarters of the sides of the springform pan. Place them in the pan one by one, brushing their surfaces with oil, except for the last one. • Spread the Swiss chard evenly over the top sheet and sprinkle with half of the Parmesan. Drizzle with 2 tablespoons of the oil and cover with the Ricotta mixture. • Use the back of a spoon to make 6 fairly deep hollows evenly spaced in the filling. Place a pat of butter in each hollow, then break an egg into each, taking care to keep the yolks intact. Season with salt and pepper, drizzle each egg with a few drops of olive oil, and sprinkle with the remaining Parmesan. • Use the remaining dough to make another 6 sheets about the same size as the springform pan. Place them over the filling one by one, brushing their surfaces with oil. • Fold back the edges of the first sheet to seal the sheets inside. Brush the surface with oil and prick with a fork. • Bake in a preheated oven at 375°F for 50 minutes. • Set aside to cool before removing from the pan. Serve at room temperature.

Makes: 1 pie, about 10 inches in diameter · Prep: 3½ hrs · Cooking: 50 min. · Level 3

Easter pie

TORTA DI PORRI E BROCCOLI
Leek and broccoli pie

- 1 quantity Plain pastry (see recipe, page 49)
- 2 medium leeks
- 2 tablespoons extra-virgin olive oil
- 1¼ cups pancetta, cut in strips
- 1 lb broccoli
- 3 eggs + 2 yolks
- 1½ cups milk
- 1 cup heavy cream
- 1 cup freshly grated Parmesan cheese
  salt and freshly ground black pepper to taste

Wine: a dry white (Sauvignon)

Prepare the pastry base. • Cut the root and the green tops off the leeks and chop the white parts into thin wheels. • Put the leeks in a skillet with the oil, cover, and cook for 15 minutes. Remove from heat and set aside. • Dry the oil in the skillet with paper towels and sauté the pancetta until crisp and brown. Set aside. • Divide the broccoli into florets with ½-inch stems and cook in a pot of salted, boiling water for 7–10 minutes, or until they are cooked but still crunchy. • Remove the pastry base from the refrigerator and discard the plastic wrap. • Cover the base with a sheet of foil, pressing it down carefully so that it adheres to the pastry. Fill with pie weights or dried beans. • Bake in a preheated oven at 350°F for 15 minutes. • Take the pan out of the oven and, using the palm of a gloved hand, carefully press the base down

so that it contracts a little. • Remove the foil and beans and return the base to the oven for 5 minutes more. • In the meantime, beat the eggs in a bowl and add the milk, cream, Parmesan, salt, and pepper. Beat with a whisk until frothy. • Put the leeks and broccoli in the baked pie shell, sprinkle the pancetta over the top, and pour the eggs and cheese over the top. • Bake in a preheated oven at 350°F for about 35 minutes.

Makes: 1 pie, 9 inches in diameter · Prep: 20 min. + 40 min. for the pastry · Cooking: 1 hr · Level: 2

CROSTATA DI PISELLI
Pea pie

- 1 quantity Plain or Ricotta pastry (see recipes, page 49)
- 1¼ cups fresh or frozen peas
- 3 tablespoons butter
  salt and freshly ground black pepper to taste
- 1 tablespoon flour
- 1 cup hot milk
- 1 egg white
- ⅔ cup ham, coarsely chopped
- ¼ cup freshly grated Parmesan cheese

Wine: a dry white (Chardonnay di Franciacorta)

Prepare the pastry base. • Parboil the peas for 5–10 minutes (depending on their size) in a pot of salted, boiling water. Drain and place in a small, heavy-bottomed saucepan with 2 tablespoons of melted butter. Sauté over medium-low heat for about 5 minutes, or until the peas are

tender. Season with salt. • Remove the pastry base from the refrigerator and discard the plastic wrap. Cover the base with a sheet of foil, pressing it down carefully so that it adheres to the pastry. • Bake in a preheated oven at 350°F for 15 minutes. • Take the pan out of the oven and, using the palm of a gloved hand, carefully press the base down so that it contracts a little. • Discard the foil and return the base to the oven for 5 minutes more. • In the meantime, melt the remaining butter in a small saucepan. Add the flour and cook over low heat for 2 minutes, stirring constantly. Add the milk, a little at a time, stirring continuously. In 4–5 minutes you will obtain a smooth, rather thick Béchamel. • Beat the egg white until stiff and combine with the peas, Béchamel, ham, Parmesan, salt, and pepper. • Mix well and pour into the pastry base. • Bake in a preheated oven at 350°F for 30 minutes, or until the surface is light gold.

Makes: 1 pie, 9 inches in diameter · Prep: 10 min. + 40 min. for the pastry · Cooking: 40 min. · Level: 2

CROSTATA DI PORRI
Leek pie

- 1 quantity Short crust pastry (see recipe, page 49)
- 2 lb leeks
- ¼ cup butter
  salt and freshly ground black pepper to taste
- 1 tablespoon flour
- 1 cup hot milk
- 1 egg white
- ¼ cup freshly grated Gruyère cheese
- 2 tablespoons freshly grated Parmesan cheese

Wine: a dry red (Sangue di Giuda)

Prepare the pastry base. • Clean the leeks and slice thinly, using the white part and only the start of the green. • Sauté the leeks in a large sauté pan in 3 tablespoons of butter over medium-low heat for 15–20 minutes. Season with salt and pepper and set aside to cool. • In the meantime, melt the remaining butter in a small saucepan. Add the flour and cook over low heat for 2 minutes, stirring

Swiss chard pie

Zucchini pie

continuously. Add the milk, a little at a time, stirring continuously. In 4–5 minutes you will obtain a smooth Béchamel; it should be rather dense, so do not use too much milk. • Beat the egg white until stiff and combine with the leeks, Béchamel, Gruyère, salt, and pepper. Mix well. • Remove the pastry base from the refrigerator and discard the plastic wrap. • Pour the leek mixture over the top and sprinkle with the Parmesan. Bake in a preheated oven at 350°F for 40 minutes. Serve hot.

Makes: 1 pie, 9 inches in diameter · Prep: 40 min. · Cooking: 40 min. + 40 min. for the pastry · Level: 2

CROSTATA DI ZUCCHINE
Zucchini pie

- 1 quantity Plain pastry (see recipe, page 49)
- 1 oz dried mushrooms
- 1 cup smoked pancetta (or bacon), sliced
- 3 tablespoons extra-virgin olive oil
- 6 medium zucchini, sliced
  salt and freshly ground black pepper to taste
- 3½ oz Pecorino romano cheese, flaked
- 3 tablespoons freshly grated Parmesan cheese
- 2 eggs
- 1 tablespoon marjoram
- 1 tablespoon bread crumbs

Prepare the pastry base. • Soak the mushrooms in a little lukewarm water for 15 minutes. Drain and chop coarsely. • Remove the rind from the pancetta and sauté over medium-high heat for 3–4 minutes. Set aside, discarding the fat that the pancetta produces. • Heat the oil in the same sauté pan and cook the zucchini and mushrooms over medium heat for 10–15 minutes, stirring frequently. Season with salt and pepper and set aside to cool. • Lightly beat the eggs in a mixing bowl, add the two cheeses, marjoram, zucchini, and pancetta. • Remove the pastry base from the refrigerator and discard the plastic wrap. • Spread the topping over the base and sprinkle with the bread crumbs. • Bake in a preheated oven at 350°F for 35–40 minutes.

Makes: 1 pie, 9 inches in diameter · Prep: 20 min.+ 40 min. for the pastry · Cooking: 35–40 min. · Level: 2

TORTA DI ZUCCHINE E FAGIOLINI
Zucchini and green bean pie

- 10 oz zucchini
- 8 oz green beans
- 1 teaspoon salt
- ⅔ cup butter
- 4 eggs
- ⅔ cup sugar
- 2½ cups all-purpose flour
- ⅔ cup pine nuts
- 2 teaspoons baking powder
  butter to grease the cake pan

Wine: a dry red (Sangiovese di Romagna)

Cook the zucchini and beans in a pot of salted, boiling water for 10 minutes. Drain and cut the zucchini into wheels and the beans into pieces. Dry on a cotton dishcloth. • Melt the butter and place in a bowl with two whole eggs, two yolks, and the sugar. Beat vigorously for 2 minutes with a whisk or fork. Stir in the flour, zucchini, beans, pine nuts, and baking powder. • Beat the remaining egg whites to stiff peaks and carefully fold into the mixture. • Grease a 10 x 6-inch cake pan with butter and pour in the mixture. • Bake in a preheated oven at 350°F for 1 hour. • Remove from the pan when cool and cut into ½-inch thick slices to serve.

Serves: 4 · Prep: 15 min. · Cooking: 1¼ hr · Level: 1

TORTA DI ASPARAGI
Asparagus pie

☞ This pie is delicious with asparagus. But when asparagus is out of season, substitute with 1¾ lb of green beans or 1¾ lb of mushrooms. If using green beans or mushrooms, add 2 cloves of finely chopped garlic and 2 tablespoons of finely chopped parsley for extra flavor.

- 1 quantity Plain pastry (see recipe, page 49)
- 3 lb fresh asparagus
- 3 tablespoons butter
- 4 eggs
- ½ cup freshly grated Parmesan cheese
- 8 oz soft Ricotta cheese
- 2 tablespoons extra-virgin olive oil
  salt and freshly ground black pepper to taste

Wine: a dry white (Galestro)

Prepare the pastry base. • Steam the asparagus, drain, and discard all but the green tips. Divide the tips into 2–3 strips and sauté for a few minutes in the butter. • Beat the eggs in a bowl and stir in the cheeses and oil. Season with salt and pepper. • Remove the pastry base from the refrigerator and proceed as in the previous recipe for Onion pie.

Makes: 1 pie, 9 inches in diameter · Prep: 1 hr · Cooking: 30 min. · Level: 2

Broccoli and leek pie

CROSTATA DI CIPOLLE
Onion pie

- 1 quantity Plain pastry (see recipe, page 49)
  salt and freshly ground black pepper to taste
- 2 lb onions, sliced
- 1/4 cup butter
- 1 egg
- 1 cup milk
- 1 tablespoon all-purpose flour

Wine: a dry white (Pinot Bianco)

Prepare the pastry base. • Sauté the onions in the butter over low heat for 25–30 minutes, stirring frequently. When cooked, the onions should be soft and golden brown. • Lightly beat the egg in a bowl, and add the milk and the flour, mixing well so that no lumps form. Season with salt and pepper. • Remove the pastry base from the refrigerator and discard the plastic wrap. • Cover the base with a sheet of foil, pressing it down carefully so that it adheres to the pastry. •

Bake in a preheated oven at 350°F for 15 minutes. • Take the springform pan out of the oven and, using the palm of a gloved hand, carefully press the base down so that it contracts a little. • Discard the foil and return the pie to the oven for 5 minutes more. • Take the base out again, spread evenly with the onion mixture and pour the egg and milk mixture over the top. • Bake 20 minutes more. Serve hot.

Makes: 1 pie, 9 inches in diameter · Prep: 10 min. + 40 min. for the pastry · Cooking: 50 min. · Level: 2

TORTA DI SCAROLA
Filled bread with Batavian endive

☞ This is a traditional dish for Christmas Eve from Campania, in the south.

- 1/2 oz fresh yeast or 1 (1/4 oz) package active dry yeast
- 1 teaspoon sugar
- 1 cup lukewarm water
- 3 cups unbleached white flour
- 2 teaspoons salt
- 2 1/2 lb Belgian endives, cleaned and washed
- 1 clove garlic, cut in half

- 1/2 cup extra-virgin olive oil
- 2 tablespoons capers
- 4 oz pitted black olives
- 8 anchovy fillets, chopped
- 1 scant tablespoon lard or butter
  salt to taste
- 2 tablespoons raisins, rinsed in warm water (optional)

Wine: a dry white (Greco di Tufo)

Prepare the yeast and then the dough as shown on pages 24–25. • Blanch the Belgian endive in boiling water to cover for 2–3 minutes. Drain, squeeze out the excess moisture, and chop coarsely. • Sauté the garlic in 5 tablespoons of the oil until it turns light gold. Discard the garlic. • Add the endive, capers, and olives and sauté over medium heat for 7–8 minutes. • Turn off the heat and add the anchovies. Stir well and set aside to cool. • When the rising time has elapsed (about 1 1/2 hours), knead the dough for 1 minute on a lightly floured work surface. • Break off about a third of the dough and set aside. • Roll the rest into a disk about 12 inches in diameter. • Grease a 9-inch springform pan with the lard and line the base and sides with the dough. • Taste the filling and season with salt if necessary. Spread the base with the filling and, if liked, sprinkle with the raisins. • Roll the remaining dough into a disk as large as the springform pan and cover the filling. Seal the dish by folding the edges of the first sheet of dough over the second to make a border. Brush the surface with the remaining oil, and leave to rise for 30 minutes. • Bake in a preheated oven at 400°F for about 30 minutes.

Makes: 1 filled bread, 9 inches in diameter · Prep: 45 min. · Rising time: about 2 hrs · Cooking: 30 min. · Level: 2

TORTA DI VERDURE MISTE
Mixed vegetable pie

- 2 red bell peppers
- 4 zucchini
- 4 large carrots
  salt and freshly ground black pepper to taste
- 3 tablespoons extra-virgin olive oil
- 2 tablespoons butter
- 1/2 cup white wine
- 1 roll frozen flaky pastry, thawed

Wine: a dry white (Est! Est!! Est!!! di Montefiascone)

Cut the bell peppers in thin strips, the zucchini in wheels, and the carrots in ribbons. • Sauté the bell peppers and a pinch of salt in the oil in a skillet over high heat for 10 minutes. Take the bell peppers out and set aside. • Use the same oil to sauté the zucchini with a pinch of salt. Remove from the skillet and set aside. • Use a paper towel to eliminate the oil in the skillet. Put the butter, carrots, wine, and a pinch of salt in the skillet and cook until the liquid has evaporated and the carrots are soft. Set the carrots aside. • On a clean, lightly floured work bench, roll out the pastry dough and line a greased 10-inch quiche pan with borders at least 1 inch high. Prick the dough with a fork. • Cover the pie crust with a sheet of foil, weigh it down with pie weights or dried beans, and bake in a preheated oven at 375°F for 35 minutes. • Remove the foil and beans and bake for 10 minutes more. • Garnish with the vegetables and serve.

Serves 6 · Prep: 20 min. · Cooking: 1 hr · Level: 1

TORTA DI UOVA E PANCETTA
Pancetta and egg pie

- ¹/₂ quantity Plain pastry (see recipe, page 49)
- 8   slices smoked pancetta (or bacon)
- 6   eggs
- ¹/₂ tablespoon dried oregano
       salt and freshly ground black pepper to taste

Wine: a dry rosé (Viganello Rosato)

Prepare the pastry. • Dice the pancetta into bite-sized pieces and sauté in a skillet for 5 minutes. • Roll out the pastry, and use it to line a 10-inch springform pan or quiche dish. • Place about half the pancetta pieces on the pastry and break the eggs over the top. Stab each yolk with a knife so that they run a little. Sprinkle with the oregano. Season with salt and pepper. • Arrange the remaining pancetta on top. • Bake at 400°F for about 40 minutes, or until the pastry is golden brown. • Serve hot or at room temperature.

Serves: 4 · Prep: 10 min. + time to make the pastry · Cooking: 40 min. · Level: 1

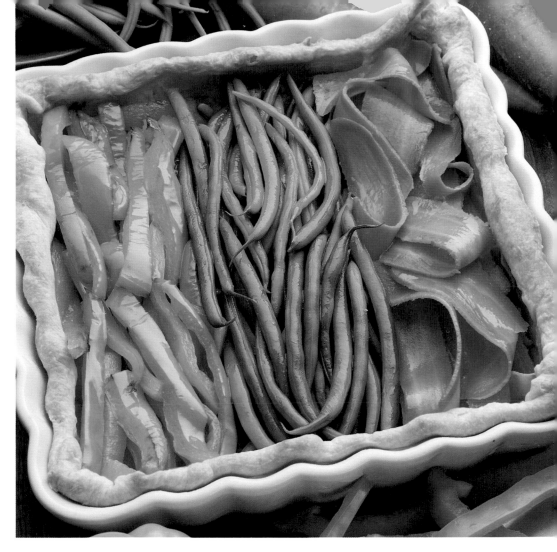

Mixed vegetable pie

TORTA DI ZUCCA E PATATE
Potato and pumpkin pie

- 1   lb pumpkin
- 1   lb potatoes
- ¹/₄ cup butter
- 4   eggs, separated
- 1   cup freshly grated Parmesan cheese
       salt and freshly ground black pepper to taste
- 2   tablespoons bread crumbs
- 12 oz Mozzarella cheese, sliced

Wine: a dry red (Nebbiolo)

Peel the pumpkin and cut it in slices. Place the slices on a baking sheet. Cover with aluminum foil and bake in a preheated oven at 300°F for about 25 minutes, or until soft. • Boil the potatoes in their skins for about 25 minutes. Drain and peel. • Mash the potatoes and pumpkin together. • Add half the butter, then the egg yolks and Parmesan cheese. Mix well, and season with salt and pepper. • Beat the egg whites to stiff peaks and fold them into the

mixture. • Grease an ovenproof dish with butter and sprinkle with the bread crumbs. • Spread half the mixture over the bottom of the dish and cover with the Mozzarella. Cover with the rest of the mixture. • Use a spoon to level, sprinkle with Parmesan cheese, dot with the remaining butter, and bake in a preheated oven at 350°F for 50 minutes. • Serve hot.

Serves: 4 · Prep: 20 min. · Cooking: 1¹/₄ hrs · Level: 1

TORTINO DI CARCIOFI
Italian artichoke omelet

16 frozen artichoke hearts, thawed
1/2 cup all-purpose flour
1/2 cup extra-virgin olive oil
5 large fresh eggs
salt and freshly ground black pepper to taste

Wine: a light, dry white (Soave)

Coat the artichoke hearts with flour, shaking off any excess. • Heat all but 2 tablespoons of the oil in a large skillet over high heat until very hot. • Sauté the artichokes for about 8 minutes, turning them several times to cook evenly. When they are lightly browned, drain on paper towels. • Discard the oil used for frying and replace with the remaining oil. Arrange the artichokes in the skillet and return to a moderately high heat. • Beat the eggs lightly with the salt and pepper then pour over the artichokes. Cook for 4–5 minutes. • Turn the omelet carefully and cook for 4 minutes more. It should be firm and lightly browned on both sides. • Turn out onto a heated serving dish and serve.

Serves: 4 · Prep: 10 min. · Cooking: 15 min. · Level: 1

Italian artichoke omelet

TORTA DI RISO CON LA ZUCCA
Rice and pumpkin pie

2 cups water
1³/₄ cups milk
salt and freshly ground black pepper to taste
1¹/₂ cups uncooked short-grain rice
piece of pumpkin weighing about 1 lb
1/2 cup freshly grated Parmesan cheese
4 oz fresh Ricotta cheese
1 egg
2¹/₂ tablespoons butter
2 cups all-purpose flour
2 tablespoons extra-virgin olive oil
fine, dry bread crumbs
oil for brushing

Wine: a dry rosé (Trentino Lagrein Rosato)

Bring the water, milk, and a pinch of salt to the boil. Add the rice. Cook for 10 minutes then drain. • Peel the pumpkin. Remove the seeds and grate the flesh finely into a clean cloth. Gather up the cloth and twist it tightly to squeeze the moisture out. • Mix the pumpkin with the rice, then add the Parmesan, Ricotta, egg, 1¹/₂ tablespoons butter, salt, and pepper. • Sift the flour into a bowl, pour in the oil and a little water, and

mix, adding more water a little at a time, to form an easily worked dough. • Knead the dough until smooth and elastic, then roll it out into a thin sheet. • Cut out two disks of pastry, one larger than the other, to fit a 10-inch pie pan. Use the bigger one to line the bottom of the pan greased with the remaining butter and sprinkled with the bread crumbs. • Fill with the rice and pumpkin mixture and cover with the other disk of pastry, pinching the edges to seal. Brush the surface with the oil and prick several times with a fork. • Bake in a preheated oven at 350°F for about 45 minutes.

Serves: 6–8 · Prep: 30 min. · Cooking: 45 min. · Level: 2

PIZZA ALLA BARESE
Tomato, olive, and onion filled bread

1/2 oz fresh yeast or 1 (¹/₄ oz) package active dry yeast
1 teaspoon sugar
1 cup lukewarm water
3 cups unbleached white flour
2 teaspoons salt
1 lb ripe tomatoes
7 tablespoons extra-virgin olive oil
1 medium onion, sliced

3 oz pitted black olives, cut in 4 lengthwise
salt and freshly ground black pepper to taste
6 oz Ricotta salata cheese, in flakes

Use the first 5 ingredients to prepare the yeast and then the dough as shown on pages 24–25. • Blanch the tomatoes in boiling water for 1 minute and slip off their skins. Divide into segments and remove as many seeds as possible. • Heat half the oil in a skillet and sauté the onion for 1 minute. Add the tomatoes and cook over high heat for 3–4 minutes, stirring as little as possible to avoid crushing the tomatoes. Remove from heat. • Add the olives to the tomato mixture. Season with salt and pepper. • When the rising time has elapsed (about 1¹/₂ hours), knead the dough on a lightly floured work surface for 1 minute. • Break off a third of the dough and set aside. Roll the rest into a disk about 12 inches in diameter. • Oil a 9-inch springform pan and line the base and sides with the dough. • Spread with the tomato mixture and sprinkle with the Ricotta. • Roll the remaining dough into a disk as large as the springform pan and cover the filling. Seal the dish by folding the edges of the first sheet of dough over the second to make a border. Brush the surface with the oil and leave to rise for 30 minutes. • Bake in a preheated oven at 400°F for about 30 minutes. • Serve hot or lukewarm.

Makes: 1 filled bread, 9 inches in diameter · Prep: 40 min. · Rising time: about 2 hrs · Cooking: 30 min. · Level: 2

PITTA ALLA CALABRESE
Calabrian-style filled bread

- ½ oz fresh yeast or 1 (¼ oz) package active dry yeast
- 1 teaspoon sugar
- 1 cup lukewarm water
- 3 cups unbleached white flour
- 1–2 teaspoons salt
- 10 oz drained and chopped canned tomatoes
- 1 clove garlic, finely chopped
- 3–4 tablespoons extra-virgin olive oil
- 8 oz tuna preserved in oil, drained and chopped
- 3 oz pitted black olives, cut in quarters
- 8 anchovy fillets, crumbled
- 1 tablespoon capers
  salt and freshly ground black pepper to taste
- ¼ cup lard (or butter), at room temperature
- 1 egg yolk

Wine: a dry red (Savuto)

Use the first 5 ingredients to prepare the yeast and then the dough as shown on pages 24–25. • For the filling, combine the tomatoes, garlic, and 2 tablespoons of oil in a saucepan. Cook over medium-low heat for 8–10 minutes, stirring frequently. Remove from heat and leave to cool. • Add the tuna, olives, anchovies, and capers. Mix well and taste before seasoning with salt and pepper. • When the rising time has elapsed (about 1½ hours), knead the dough on a lightly floured work surface for 1 minute. Flatten the dough and spread with the lard. Add the egg yolk and knead again. • Break off about a third of the dough and set aside. • Roll the rest into a disk about 12 inches in diameter. • Oil a 9-inch springform pan and line the bottom and sides with the dough. • Spread with the filling. • Roll the remaining dough into a disk as large as the springform pan and use it to cover the filling. Seal the dish by folding the edges of the first sheet of dough over the top sheet to make a border. • Brush the surface with oil and leave to rise for about 30 minutes. • Bake in a preheated oven at 400°F for about 30 minutes, or until the top is nicely browned. • Serve hot.

Makes: 1 filled bread, 9 inches in diameter · Prep: 40 min. · Rising time: about 2 hrs · Cooking: 30 min. · Level: 2

TORTA DI AGRIGENTO
Agrigento-style country pie

☞ This hearty dish comes from Agrigento, in Sicily, which is also famous for the spectacular ancient Greek ruins in the Valley of the Temples.

- ½ oz fresh yeast or 1 (¼ oz) package active dry yeast
- 1 teaspoon sugar
- 1 cup lukewarm water
- 3 cups unbleached white flour
- 2 teaspoons salt
- 2 lb raw spinach, trimmed, washed, and cooked
- 1 cauliflower, trimmed, cut into florets, and cooked
- ½ cup extra-virgin olive oil
- 6 oz semi-mature spicy Provolone cheese, diced
- 6 oz tuna in oil, drained and flaked
- 12 black olives, pitted and coarsely chopped

Wine: a dry white (Alcamo)

Use the first 5 ingredients to prepare the yeast and then the dough as shown on pages 24–25. • Drain the cooked spinach well and squeeze out excess moisture. • Sauté the spinach and cauliflower in 2 tablespoons of the oil. • When the rising time has elapsed (about 1 hour), knead the dough on a lightly floured work surface for 1 minute. Break off a third of the dough and set aside. • Roll the rest into a disk about ⅛ inch thick to line the bottom and sides of an oiled 9-inch springform pan, slightly overlapping the edges. • Spread with the spinach and cover with the cauliflower, cheese, tuna, and olives. • Roll the remaining dough into a disk as large as the springform pan and

use it to cover the filling. Seal the dish by folding the edges of the first sheet of dough over the top sheet to make a border. Brush the surface with the remaining oil and prick with a fork. • Bake in a preheated oven at 400°F for 30–35 minutes or until the crust is golden brown. • Serve very hot.

Makes: 1 filled bread, 9 inches in diameter · Prep: 1 hr · Rising time: 1 hr · Cooking: 30–35 min. · Level: 2

SCACCIATA
Pecorino, tomato, and anchovy filled bread

- ½ oz fresh yeast or 1 (¼ oz) package active dry yeast
- 1 teaspoon sugar
- 1 cup lukewarm water
- 3 cups unbleached white flour
- 2 teaspoons salt
- 1 tablespoon lard or butter, in thin slices
- 10 oz ripe tomatoes
- 10 oz Pecorino cheese, sliced
  salt and freshly ground black pepper to taste
- 8 anchovy fillets, crumbled
- 2 tablespoons onion, finely chopped
- 1 tablespoon extra-virgin olive oil

Wine: a dry rosé (Etna Rosato)

Use the first 6 ingredients to prepare the yeast and then the dough as shown on pages 24–25, incorporating the lard while kneading the dough. • Blanch the tomatoes in boiling water for 1 minute, then peel. Cut them in two, remove the seeds, and cut in half again. • When the rising time has elapsed (about 1½ hours), knead the dough for 1 minute on a lightly floured work surface. • Break off about a third of the dough and set aside. • Roll the rest into a disk about 12 inches in diameter. • Oil a 9-inch springform pan and line the base and sides with the dough. • Cover with the cheese, followed by the tomatoes. Sprinkle with salt and pepper. Add the anchovies and onion. • Roll the remaining dough into a disk as large as the pan and cover the filling. Seal the dish by folding the edges of the first sheet of dough over the second to make a border. Prick the surface with a fork and brush with the oil. Set aside to rise for about 30 minutes. • Bake in a preheated oven at 400°F for 30 minutes.

Makes: 1 filled bread, about 9 inches in diameter · Prep: 35 min. · Rising time: 2 hrs · Cooking: 30 min. · Level: 2

Ricotta and sausage filled bread

PITTA RUSTICA
Cheese, ham, and salami filled bread

- ½ oz fresh yeast or 1 (¼ oz) package active dry yeast
- 1 teaspoon sugar
- 1 cup lukewarm water
- 3 cups unbleached white flour
- 2 teaspoons salt
- 7 oz Ricotta cheese
- 4 oz Provolone cheese, diced
- 3 oz freshly grated Pecorino cheese
- 2½ oz ham, diced
- 2 oz salami, diced
- 1 egg
  salt and freshly ground black pepper to taste
- ¼ cup lard (or butter)
- 2 tablespoons extra-virgin olive oil

Wine: a dry white (Galestro)

Use the first 5 ingredients to prepare the yeast and then the dough as shown on pages 24–25. • Combine the Ricotta, Provolone, Pecorino, ham, salami, egg, salt, and pepper in a bowl, and mix well. • When the rising time has elapsed (about 1½ hours), knead the dough for 1 minute on a lightly floured work surface. • Flatten the dough, sprinkle with the lard, and knead again. • Break off about a third of the dough and set aside. • Roll the rest into a disk about 12 inches in diameter. • Oil a 9-inch springform pan and line the base and sides with the dough. • Spread with the filling. • Roll the remaining dough into a disk as large as the springform pan and cover the filling. Seal the dish by folding the edges of the first sheet of dough over the second to make a border. Brush the surface with the oil and leave to rise for 30 minutes. • Bake in a preheated oven at 400°F for about 25 minutes.

Makes: 1 filled bread, 9 inches in diameter · Prep: 35 min. · Rising time: about 2 hrs · Cooking: 25 min. · Level: 2

PITTA ALLA REGGINA
Ricotta and sausage filled bread

- ½ oz fresh yeast or 1 (¼ oz) package active dry yeast
- 1 teaspoon sugar
- 1 cup lukewarm water
- 3 cups unbleached white flour
- 3 tablespoons extra-virgin olive oil
- 2 teaspoons salt
- 8 oz soft Ricotta cheese
- 4 oz cooked Italian sausage, diced
- 3¼ cups freshly grated Pecorino cheese
- 1 tablespoon finely chopped parsley
  salt and freshly ground black pepper to taste
- 1 tablespoon lard or butter
- 2 hard-boiled eggs, sliced

Use the first 6 ingredients to prepare the yeast and then the dough as shown on pages 24–25 (add the oil to the flour). • Mix the Ricotta, sausage, Pecorino, parsley, salt, and pepper in a bowl. • When the rising time has elapsed (about 1¾ hours), knead the dough on a lightly floured work surface for 1 minute. • Break off about a third of the dough and set aside. • Roll the rest into a disk about 12 inches in diameter. Grease a 9-inch springform pan with a little of the lard and line the base and sides with the dough. • Spread with half the filling, followed by a layer of egg. Cover with the rest of the filling. • Roll the remaining dough into a disk as large as the springform pan and cover the filling. Seal the dish by folding the edges of the first sheet of dough over the second to make a border. Prick the surface with a fork and dot with the remaining lard. Cover the pan with a cloth and set aside in a warm place for 15 minutes. • Bake in a preheated oven at 400°F for about 30 minutes.

Makes: 1 filled bread, 9 inches in diameter · Prep: 40 min. · Rising time: about 2 hrs · Cooking: 30 min. · Level: 2

CROSTATA AL FORMAGGIO
Egg and cheese pie

- 1 quantity Ricotta pastry (see recipe, page 49)
- 3 eggs, lightly beaten
  salt and freshly ground black pepper
- 4 oz freshly grated Emmenthal cheese
- ⅔ cup light cream
- 4 oz bacon, cooked and coarsely chopped

Wine: a dry white (Soave Classico)

Prepare the Ricotta pastry base. • Combine the eggs in a bowl with salt and pepper to taste. Add the Emmenthal and cream. • Remove the pastry base from the refrigerator and discard the plastic wrap.

Sprinkle the speck over the base, then pour the egg mixture over the top. • Bake in a preheated oven at 350°F for 30–35 minutes. Raise the oven temperature a little for the last 5 minutes, so that the top will turn golden brown.

Makes: 1 pie, 9 inches in diameter; Preparation: 10' + 40' for the pastry; Cooking: 30–35'; Level: 2

CROSTATA DI RICOTTA
Ricotta pie

- 1 quantity Special or Plain pastry (see recipes, page 49)
- 10 oz Ricotta cheese
- 2 eggs, beaten
- 2 oz ham, chopped
- 3 oz mortadella, chopped
- 2 oz freshly grated Provolone cheese
- 2 tablespoons light cream
  salt and freshly ground black pepper to taste

Prepare the pastry base. • Combine the Ricotta, eggs, ham, mortadella, Provolone, cream, salt, and pepper in a mixing bowl. • Remove the pastry base from the refrigerator and discard the plastic wrap. • Spread the base evenly with the filling and bake in a preheated oven at 375°F for about 40 minutes, or until the top is golden brown.

Makes: 1 pie, 9 inches in diameter · Prep: 30 min. + 1 hr for the pastry · Cooking: 40 min. · Level: 2

TORTA DI GAMBERI
Shrimp pie

- 1 quantity Plain pastry (see recipe, page 49)
- 1½ lb shrimp
- 2 cloves garlic, finely chopped
- 3 tablespoons butter
- 2 tablespoons brandy
  salt and freshly ground black pepper to taste
- 3 eggs
- 2 tablespoons all-purpose flour
- ¼ cup finely chopped parsley
- 1 cup heavy cream

Wine: a dry white (Traminer Aromatico)

Prepare the pastry base. • Shell the shrimp and remove the dark intestinal veins. Chop off the heads, and rinse well in cold running water. • Sauté over medium-high heat for 5 minutes in a skillet with the garlic and butter. • Pour in the brandy and cook for 2 minutes more, stirring all the time. Season with salt and pepper and remove from the heat. • In a bowl,

Egg and cheese pie

combine the eggs, flour, salt, and pepper, and mix until smooth. • Add the parsley, cream, shrimp, and the liquid they produced while cooking. • Remove the pastry base from the refrigerator and discard the plastic wrap. Pour the filling mixture over the base and bake in a preheated oven at 400°F for 40 minutes. • Serve hot or at room temperature.

Makes: 1 pie, 9 inches in diameter · Prep: 30 min. + 40 min. for the pastry · Cooking: 50 min. · Level: 2

TORTA AL FORMAGGIO
Cheese flatbread

☞ An Easter specialty from Umbria, this cheese flatbread is traditionally served piping hot with sliced ham, prosciutto, salami, mortadella, and other deli meats.

- ⅔ oz fresh yeast or 1½ (¼ oz) packages active dry yeast
- 3½ tablespoons warm water
- 1 teaspoon sugar
- 3 eggs + 1 yolk, beaten
- ⅓ cup extra-virgin olive oil
- 2½ cups unbleached white flour
- 2 teaspoons salt
- 4 oz freshly grated mature Pecorino cheese
- 3 oz fresh Pecorino cheese, diced
- ½ teaspoon white pepper

Mix the yeast with the water, add the sugar and set aside for 10 minutes. • Combine the eggs with the oil in a bowl. • Put the flour into a bowl, sprinkle with salt, and make a hollow in the center. Stir in the yeast and egg mixtures until the flour absorbs all the ingredients. The dough will be soft and sticky. • Mix for 6–8 minutes with a wooden spoon. Cover with a cloth and leave to rise for 2 hours. • When the rising time has elapsed, add the two cheeses and pepper and mix again for 3–4 minutes. • Oil and flour a 10-inch springform pan. Fill with the dough and leave to rise for 2 hours. • Bake in a preheated oven at 375°F for 40 minutes.

Makes: 1 flatbread, 10 inches in diameter · Prep: 40 min. · Rising time: about 4 hrs · Cooking: 40 min. · Level: 1

FRIED DISHES

Fried foods are delicious and not especially bad for you if prepared with care and eaten in moderation (see pages 62–63 for tips for successful frying). In Italy, vegetables are often fried and served as a side dish with meat. In Emilia-Romagna, in central Italy, some of the most delicious appetizers are made of fried batter, served with platters of fresh creamy cheeses, ham, salami, and local deli meats.

SALVIA FRITTA
Fried fresh sage leaves

☞ These crisp little fritters are also good with sugar. For the sweet version, sprinkle with 2 tablespoons of sugar instead of salt before serving.

- 40 large fresh sage leaves
- 2 tablespoons all-purpose flour
- 1 large egg, beaten until foamy with a pinch of salt
- 1½ cups fine dry bread crumbs
- 2 cups oil, for frying
  salt to taste

Wine: a dry or sweet sparkling white (Asti Spumante)

Rinse the sage leaves under cold running water, then pat dry with paper towels.

• Dredge the leaves in the flour. Dip in the egg, and coat well with the bread crumbs. • Heat the oil to very hot (test by dropping a leaf into the oil; if ready, it will sizzle sharply) and add half the leaves. They will turn golden brown almost immediately. Turn them once, then scoop them out with a slotted spoon. Drain on paper towels. Cook the remaining leaves. • Sprinkle with salt and serve as an appetizer or snack.

Serves: 4 · Prep: 10 min. · Cooking: instant frying at 350°F · Level: 1

◄ Mixed fried vegetables (see recipe, page 69)
► Fried fresh sage leaves

HOW TO FRY VEGETABLES *The Basics*

Frying food successfully is an art. Correctly fried foods are nutty-flavored and succulent within, and crisp, golden brown on the outside. There are two ways of frying food – deep-frying, where the food is immersed in a fryer or deep pot of oil, and pan-frying, where the food is placed in about ½ inch of oil, and turned to cook on all sides. In Italy, olive oil is considered the healthiest oil for frying. Because it is expensive, most people pan-fry their food. Peanut oil is a viable alternative, but sunflower, maize, and other seed oils are not recommended.

Fried onion rings

Frying vegetables

Foods that will form a crust in the oil, such as potatoes or small fish, can be fried without batter. However, most foods are better when fried in batter because it forms a protective crust around them as soon as they are put in the oil.

BATTER

1 cup all-purpose flour
  pinch of salt
1 egg, separated
1 tablespoon extra-virgin olive oil
  cold water

1 Sift the flour and salt into a bowl. Make a hollow in the center and add the egg yolk and oil. Use a whisk to stir the mixture as you add enough water to from a thick, but fluid, batter with no lumps. Set aside for 30 minutes to rest. Just before frying, beat the egg white until stiff and stir it into the batter. The water can be replaced with milk, which will make a soft sweet batter, or beer, which puffs up during frying and is crisper.

2 Put enough oil (1–2 cups) in a 12-inch skillet to reach a depth of about ½ inch. Place over medium-high heat and heat to frying point (see page 62). Dip the food you wish to fry in the batter, shake off any excess, and place a few pieces in the pan. Don't put too many pieces in at once. This will lower the temperature of the oil, increasing cooking time and causing the food to absorb more oil.

3 When you add the food to the pan, turn the heat up to high for about 10 seconds so that the oil quickly regains its ideal temperature.

4 When the food is golden brown on one side, use a slotted spoon to turn it over and fry until golden brown on the other side.

5 Remove the fried food one piece at a time with a slotted spoon. Place on paper towels or kitchen paper to drain. Never use the same oil more than once. During cooking, keep the oil clean; if you leave even tiny pieces of batter or food in the pan, they will burn and their acrid flavor will contaminate the taste of what you fry next. Keep the oil topped up to the same level during cooking.

Fried artichokes

POMODORI CROCCANTI
Fried tomatoes

- 8 large green tomatoes
- 1¼ cups all-purpose flour
- 5 eggs, beaten to a foam
- ⅓ cup beer
- 2 cups fine dry bread crumbs
- 2 cups oil, for frying
  salt to taste

Wine: a dry white (Greco di Tufo)

Rinse the tomatoes and cut in ½-inch thick slices. • Place three bowls side by side and fill the first with the flour, the second with the beaten eggs and beer, and the last with bread crumbs. • Dredge the tomatoes in the flour, coat well, and shake off any excess. Place in a single layer on paper towels. • Dip the slices in the egg, drain, and pass to the bowl of bread crumbs. Dip in egg again, then return to the bread crumbs. • Heat the oil to frying point (see page 62) in a 12-inch skillet. • Fry the tomatoes in batches for about 10 minutes, turning frequently, until golden brown. Fry all the tomatoes in the same way. • Drain on paper towels. Sprinkle with salt and serve hot.

Serves: 4 · Prep: 10 min. · Cooking: 30 min. · Level: 1

ANELLI DI CIPOLLA FRITTI
Fried onion rings

- 1 quantity batter (see recipe, page 63)
- 6 medium red or white onions
- 2 egg whites, beaten to stiff peaks
- 2 cups oil, for frying
  salt to taste

Wine: a dry red (Barbera dei Colli Bolognesi)

Prepare the batter. • Peel the onions and cut in ¼-inch thick slices. Separate the rings and place on a clean cloth to dry. • Fold the extra egg whites into the batter. •Heat the oil to frying point (see page 62) in a 12-inch skillet. • Dip the rings in the batter, shake off any excess, and fry in batches until golden brown. Turn once or twice during cooking with tongs or a fork. • Drain on paper towels. Sprinkle with salt and serve hot.

Serves: 4 · Prep: 20 min. + 1 hr for the batter · Cooking: 20 min. · Level: 1

CARCIOFI FRITTI
Fried artichokes

- 8 large artichokes
  juice of 1 lemon
- 2 cups oil, for frying
  salt to taste

Wine: a dry rosé (Chiaretto Bardolino)

Clean the artichokes by trimming the tops and stalk (leave about 1½ inches of stalk attached). Remove all the tough outer leaves so that only the pale, inner leaves and heart remain. Soak the cleaned artichokes in a bowl of cold water with the lemon juice. • Drain well, and bang each artichoke down on the bench so that the leaves open out like flowers. • Heat the oil to frying point (see page 62) in a 12-inch skillet. Add the artichokes and fry for about 15 minutes. When they are tender, turn up the heat for 2–3 minutes. They should turn golden brown. • Drain on paper towels, sprinkle with salt, and serve hot.

Serves: 4 · Prep: 20 min. · Cooking: 15 min. · Level: 1

CAVOLFIORE FRITTO CON TIMO
Fried cauliflower with herb marinade

- 1 cauliflower (about 1 lb), divided in florets
  salt and freshly ground black pepper to taste
- 4 eggs, lightly beaten
- ⅓ cup beer
- 1 cup all-purpose flour
- 2 cups oil, for frying
- 1 cup white wine vinegar
- 1 small onion, finely chopped
- 2 tablespoons finely chopped fresh thyme

Wine: a light, sparkling red (Lambrusco Grasparossa)

Blanch the cauliflower florets in a pot of salted, boiling water for 4 minutes. Drain, and place on a clean dishcloth to dry. • Combine the eggs with the beer. • Place the flour in a bowl, dredge the florets, and shake off any excess. • Heat the oil to frying point (see page 62) in a 12-inch skillet. • Dip 8–10 florets in the egg mixture and fry for about 10 minutes, turning frequently, until golden brown all over. Drain on paper towels. Repeat until all the florets are fried. Sprinkle with salt. • Put the vinegar in a small saucepan with the onion. Boil for 5–6 minutes, add the thyme, and remove

from heat. Pour into a serving bowl. •
Serve the cauliflower hot as an appetizer,
with the sauce passed separately.

Serves: 4 · Prep: 15 min. · Cooking: 40 min. · Level: 1

FUNGHI FRITTI
Fried mushrooms

1¼	lb fresh large white mushrooms
2	quantities batter (see recipe, page 63)
3	cups oil, for frying
	salt to taste

Wine: a dry red (Rosso di Montalcino)

Trim the roots from the mushrooms and
peel the bottom of the stem if discolored
or moldy. • Detach the stems from the
caps and rinse under cold running water.
Dry on paper towels. • Cut the stems and
caps in slices about ¼-inch thick. • Dip
the mushrooms in the batter, and shake off
any excess. • Heat the oil to frying point (see
page 62) in a 12-inch skillet. • Fry the
mushrooms in batches until golden
brown. • Drain on paper towels, sprinkle
with salt, and serve hot.

Serves: 4 · Prep: 15 min. · Cooking: 25 min. Level: 1

ZUCCA FRITTA CON PINOLI
Fried pumpkin with pine nuts

2	lb peeled pumpkin
1	cup all-purpose flour
2	cups oil, for frying
3	cloves garlic, sliced
30	fresh mint leaves
16	anchovy fillets
	salt and freshly ground black pepper to taste
3	tablespoons extra-virgin olive oil
2	tablespoons apple vinegar
⅔	cup pine nuts, sautéed in a little oil for 2–3 minutes

Wine: a dry white (Sauvignon)

Cut the pumpkin into cubes about 1 inch
square. Dredge in the flour. • Heat the oil
to frying point (see page 62) in a 12-inch
skillet. • Fry the pumpkin in batches for
7–8 minutes. Drain on paper towels. •
Place on a serving dish and sprinkle with
the garlic, half the mint, the anchovy
fillets, salt, and pepper. Dress with the
olive oil and vinegar, and mix carefully.
Set aside to marinate for at least 3 hours.
• Add the pine nuts and remaining mint
just before serving.

Serves: 4 · Prep: 20 min. · Cooking: 30 min. · Level: 1

Fried mixed meat, vegetables, and bread

FRITTO MISTO
Mixed meat, vegetables, and bread

☞ This is a fairly filling dish; served with a
green salad to refresh the palate, it is a meal in
itself. Vary the types of meat and vegetables used
according to taste.

1	calf's brain, weighing about 1 lb (optional)
1	lb calf's liver, cut in slices ½ inch thick
4–6	artichokes
	juice of 1 lemon
4–8	slices firm-textured bread
¼	cup milk
2–3	cups oil, for frying
1¼	cups all-purpose flour
3	eggs, beaten
	salt to taste

Wine: a dry red (Sangiovese d'Aprilia)

If using, wash the calf's brains thoroughly
under cold running water, then soak in a
bowl of cold water for 10 minutes. • Place
in a pot of cold water and bring to the
boil. Cook for 20 minutes. Remove all the
brown parts and cut the brain into 6
pieces. • Cut the calf's liver into cubes
about 1½ inches square. • Clean the
artichokes by trimming the tops and stalk
(leave about ¼ inch of stalk attached).
Remove all the tough outer leaves so that
only the pale, inner part remains. Cut
each artichoke into quarters. As you clean
the artichokes, place them in a large bowl
of cold water with the lemon juice (which
will stop them from discoloring). Drain
well and pat dry. • Place the bread on a
plate and drizzle with the milk. The slices
should be damp, but not soggy. • Heat the
oil to frying point (see page 62) in a 12-inch
skillet. • Dip the meats, artichokes, and
bread in the flour, then in the egg. Fry
them in batches, turning frequently, until
golden brown all over. Drain on paper
towels. Don't try to fry too much at once.
The pieces of meat and artichokes should
not touch one another when in the skillet.
• Sprinkle with salt and serve hot.

Serves: 4 · Prep: 20 min. · Cooking: 45 min. · Level: 2

Filled rice balls, Roman-style

mixture should be fairly liquid. • Grease the bottom of a cast-iron or iron pan no larger than 8 inches in diameter with a little olive oil. Place over high heat. • When the oil is very hot, add 2–3 tablespoons of the mixture to cover the bottom of the pan in a thin layer. Flip after about 1 minute, or when the mixture is well set, and cook on the other side. • Repeat the process until all the mixture is used up. Stack the ciacci on a plate resting on a pot of boiling water to keep them warm. • Serve hot.

Serves: 4 · Prep: 3–4 min. · Cooking: 15 min. · Level: 1

ZUCCHINE FRITTE
Fried zucchini

8	large zucchini
1	cup all-purpose flour
2	eggs, beaten until foamy
2	cups oil, for frying
	salt to taste

Wine: a dry white (Frascati)

Rinse the zucchini under cold running water and trim the ends. Slice thinly lengthwise. • Place the flour in a bowl and dredge the slices, then dip in the beaten egg. • Heat the oil to frying point (see page 62) in a 12-inch skillet. Fry the zucchini in batches until golden brown all over. • Drain on paper towels, sprinkle with salt, and serve hot as an appetizer or side dish.

Serves: 4 · Prep: 10 min. · Cooking: 15–20 min. · Level: 1

FIORI DI ZUCCA FARCITI
Stuffed fried zucchini flowers

20	fresh zucchini flowers
6	anchovy fillets, crumbled
2	cups fine dry bread crumbs
1	tablespoon finely chopped parsley
3	eggs
	salt and freshly ground black pepper to taste
3/4	cup all-purpose flour
1–2	cups olive oil, for frying

Wine: a dry, fruity white (Colli Albani Secco)

Rinse the flowers carefully under cold running water. Trim the stalks and dry the flowers carefully with paper towels. • Mix the anchovies with the bread crumbs in a bowl. Add the parsley, 1 egg, and salt and pepper to taste (since the anchovies are already salty, you may not need much salt). Mix well. • Use this mixture to carefully stuff the

SUPPLÌ ALLA ROMANA
Filled rice balls, Roman-style

1/4	cup dried porcini mushrooms
2	cups cold water
5	large, very ripe tomatoes, peeled
1/2	cup butter, chopped
	salt to taste
2	cups short-grain rice (preferably Italian semifino or fino)
1/2	cup freshly grated Parmesan cheese
2	eggs
1	small onion, finely chopped
1	stalk celery, finely chopped
5	oz ground beef
4	chicken livers, finely chopped
1/2	cup finely chopped prosciutto
1/2	cup fresh or frozen peas
31/2	oz Mozzarella cheese, diced in 1/2-inch cubes
2	cups fine dry bread crumbs
2	cups olive oil, for frying

Wine: a dry white (Albana di Romagna Secco)

Place the mushrooms in a small bowl and cover with warm water. Leave to soften for about 20 minutes. • Put the cold water, 4 chopped tomatoes, three-quarters of the butter, and salt in a large saucepan. Bring to a boil and add the rice. Stir frequently and cook until the rice is tender. • Remove from heat and stir in the Parmesan and the eggs. Spread the mixture out on a large plate to cool. • In the meantime, drain the mushrooms and chop coarsely. Heat the remaining butter in a small skillet and sauté the mushrooms with the onion, celery, beef, chicken livers, prosciutto, and peas for 4–5 minutes over medium heat. • Add the remaining chopped tomato and season with salt to taste. Cover and cook over a low heat

for about 20 minutes, or until the sauce has reduced. Stir frequently so that the sauce doesn't stick. • Use a tablespoon to scoop up some rice and shape it into a ball about the size of an egg. Make a hollow in the ball of rice and fill with the meat sauce and one or two cubes of Mozzarella. Seal with a little more rice. Roll the filled rice ball in the bread crumbs and set it aside on a plate. Repeat until all the rice, meat sauce, and cheese have been used. • Heat the oil to frying point (see page 62) in a 12-inch skillet. Fry the rice balls until crisp and golden brown all over. • Drain on paper towels and serve immediately.

Serves: 4 · Prep: 20 min. · Cooking: 1 hr · Level: 2

CIACCI
Chestnut flour fritters

11/4	cups chestnut flour
11/2	cups water
1	teaspoon salt
1/2	cup extra-virgin olive oil

Wine: a dry, sparkling red (Lambrusco di Sorbara)

Mix the flour with the water and salt using a whisk to prevent lumps from forming. The

flowers. • Beat the remaining eggs and place them in a shallow bowl. Place the flour in a shallow bowl and dip the stuffed flowers first in the flour, then in the egg. • Heat the oil to frying point (see page 62) in a 12-inch skillet. Fry the flowers in batches of 5 or 6 at a time. Turn them so that they brown all over. Drain on paper towels. Repeat until all the flowers are cooked. Sprinkle with a little salt, if liked. • Serve hot.

Serves: 4 · Prep: 10 min. · Cooking: 15 min. · Level: 1

FRITTATINE ALL'ACETO BALSAMICO
Fritters in balsamic vinegar

4	large onions, thinly sliced
¼	cup extra-virgin olive oil
4	eggs
	salt to taste
½	cup freshly grated Parmesan cheese
½	cup fine dry bread crumbs
1	cup oil, for frying
	balsamic vinegar

Wine: a dry white (Riesling Italico)

Sauté the onions in the extra-virgin oil until light golden brown. • Beat the eggs and salt in a bowl, then stir in the Parmesan and bread crumbs. • Add the onions and mix well. Set aside for at least 30 minutes. • Heat the oil to frying point (see page 62) in a 12-inch skillet. Fry spoonfuls of the mixture until golden brown. • Drain the fritters on paper towels. Drizzle with balsamic vinegar to taste and serve.

Serves: 4 · Prep: 15 min. + 30 min. to stand · Cooking: 15 min. · Level:1

CARDUNI FRITTI
Crumbed fried cardoons

☞ If cardoons are unavailable, replace with 1 large bunch of celery. In this case, there will be no need to soak the stalks in water and lemon juice and the boiling time will be reduced to about 10 minutes.

4–6	cardoons
½	lemon
2½	tablespoons all-purpose flour
1	egg, lightly beaten
	salt and freshly ground black pepper to taste
½	cup fine dry bread crumbs
2	cups oil, for frying

Wine: a dry rosé (Etna Rosato)

Discard the tough outer stalks of the cardoons. Remove the strings from the inner stalks, and rub with lemon to prevent them turning black. • Cut the stalks into pieces about 4 inches long and boil in plenty of salted water for 20–30 minutes, or until tender. Test by piercing with a fork. • Drain well. Coat with flour, dip in the egg seasoned with salt and pepper, and roll in the bread crumbs. • Heat the oil to frying point (see page 62) in a 12-inch skillet. Fry until golden brown. Drain on paper towels and serve hot.

Serves: 4 · Prep: 10 min. · Cooking: 30–40 min. · Level: 1

FRITTELLE DI PATATE
Potato patties

1¼	lb potatoes
2	eggs, beaten until foamy
2	tablespoons all-purpose flour
	salt and freshly ground black pepper to taste
2	cups oil, for frying

Wine: a dry rosé (Lagrein Rosato)

Peel the potatoes and grate into julienne strips. Rinse them in plenty of cold water, drain well, and spread on a cotton dish cloth to dry. • Place the eggs, flour, salt, and pepper in a bowl, add the potatoes, and mix well. • Heat the oil to frying point (see page 62) in a 12-inch skillet. Place 6–8 tablespoonfuls of the mixture in the oil. Brown on one side then turn carefully and fry until brown on the other. • Scoop the patties out with a slotted spoon and drain on paper towels. • Serve hot.

Serves: 4 · Prep: 15 min. · Cooking: 15–20 min. · Level: 1

ASPARAGI FRITTI
Fried asparagus

☞ Use only very thin stalks of asparagus for this exquisite dish.

1	lb asparagus
1	cup all-purpose flour
3	eggs, beaten until foamy
1	cup oil, for frying
	salt to taste

Wine: a dry white (Pinot Grigio)

Rinse the asparagus under cold running water and steam over a little lightly salted water for about 5 minutes, or until just cooked (this will depend on the thickness of the stalks). • Drain well and pat dry with paper towels. Trim the tough bottom part off the stalks. • Dredge the asparagus carefully in the flour and dip in the egg. • Heat the oil to frying point (see page 62) in a 12-inch skillet. Fry the asparagus in batches until golden brown. Drain on paper towels, sprinkle with salt, and serve hot.

Serves: 4 · Prep: 10 min. · Cooking: 25 min. · Level: 1

Fritters in balsamic vinegar

FRITTO MISTO DI VERDURE
Mixed fried vegetables

☞ In Italy, a platter of crisp fried vegetables will often be served as a side dish with roast, fried, or grilled meats. The vegetables will vary according to the season. This recipe is for summer vegetables. In winter, you can replace them with artichoke wedges, carrots and potatoes cut in sticks, sliced fennel, and florets of cauliflower or broccoli. The procedure is the same except that the fennel and broccoli must be lightly cooked first in salted, boiling water and dried on paper towels before flouring.

- 6 medium zucchini
- 2 large eggplants
- 12 large zucchini flowers
- 2 cups all-purpose flour
- 4 eggs, beaten until foamy
- 1/3 cup beer
- 3 cups oil, for frying
  salt to taste

Wine: a dry white (Galestro)

Cut the zucchini in half crosswise, and cut each half in quarters lengthwise. Cut the eggplants in 1/4-inch thick slices and cut each slice in halves or quarters (depending on how big they are). • Trim the stems of the zucchini flowers and wash carefully. Place on paper towels to dry. • Put the flour in a large bowl next to another containing the eggs and beer. • Heat the oil to frying point (see page 62) in a 12-inch skillet. • Flour the vegetables, shake off any excess and dip in the egg. Shake off excess egg and fry. • Begin frying a few pieces at a time; if there are too many in the skillet at once they will stick to one another. • Turn the vegetables as they cook. When the pieces are golden brown, scoop them up with a slotted spoon and drain on paper towels. Repeat until all the vegetables are cooked. • Sprinkle with salt and serve hot.

Serves: 4 · Prep: 20 min. · Cooking: 50 min. · Level: 1

CROCCHETTE DI SPINACI
Spinach croquettes

- 3 lb boiling potatoes
- 1 lb fresh or 12 oz frozen spinach
- 1 egg + 1 yolk, beaten
  salt and freshly ground black pepper to taste
- 1/2 cup freshly grated Parmesan cheese
- 5 oz Taleggio or Fontina cheese, cut in 1/4-inch cubes
- 2 cups fine dry bread crumbs
- 2 cups oil, for frying

Wine: a dry white (Pinot Bianco)

Cook the potatoes in their skins in a pot of salted, boiling water for about 25 minutes.

Drain, slip the skins off with your fingers, and mash until smooth. • Cook the spinach in a pot of salted, boiling water until tender (3–4 minutes if frozen, 8–10 minutes if fresh). Drain, cool under cold running water, squeeze out excess moisture, and chop finely. • Combine with the potatoes and mix well. • Put the eggs in a bowl with the salt, pepper, potatoes, spinach, and Parmesan and blend with a fork until smooth. • Place a tablespoonful of the mixture in the palm of your hand. Press a cube of cheese into the center and close the mixture round it in an oblong croquette. The cheese must be completely covered. Roll in the bread crumbs. • Heat the oil to frying point (see page 62) in a 12-inch skillet. • Fry the croquettes about 5–6 at a time, turning them in the oil so that they turn golden brown all over. Remove with a slotted spoon and drain on paper towels. Repeat until all the croquettes are cooked. • Serve hot as appetizers, or with a mixed salad as a main course.

Serves: 4–6 min. · Prep: 30 min. · Cooking: 1 hr · Level: 1

CROCCHETTE DI POMODORO
Tomato croquettes

☞ Make these unusual croquettes during the summer months when tomatoes are plentiful and full of flavor.

- 1 lb ripe tomatoes
- 9 oz Ricotta cheese, crumbled
- 2 eggs, beaten until foamy + 2 yolks
- 2 tablespoons finely chopped parsley
  nutmeg to taste
  salt and freshly ground black pepper to taste
- 1 cup all-purpose flour
- 1 cup dry bread crumbs
- 2 cups oil, for frying

Wine: a light, dry rosé (Rosato di Bolgheri)

Blanch the tomatoes for 1 minute in boiling water, then slip off the skins. Squeeze out as many of the seeds as possible, chop coarsely, and set in a colander to drain. • Place the Ricotta and egg yolks in a bowl and mix to a smooth paste. • Add the tomatoes, parsley, nutmeg, salt, and pepper and mix well. • Prepare 3 separate bowls: one with the flour, one with the beaten egg, and one with the bread crumbs. • Mold the

Tomato croquettes

mixture into croquettes of about 2 inches long and 1 inch thick. The mixture should be firm; if it is too runny, add 1–2 of tablespoons dry bread crumbs or freshly grated Parmesan cheese. • Roll the croquettes in the flour, dip them in the egg, and roll in the bread crumbs. • Heat the oil to frying point (see page 62) in a 12-inch skillet. Fry the croquettes in batches for about 10 minutes, or until golden brown. Turn with tongs or a fork during cooking so that they brown evenly all over. • Use a slotted spoon to scoop them out and drain on paper towels. • Serve hot.

Serves: 4 · Prep: 20 min. · Cooking: 40 min. · Level: 2

POLPETTINE DI LESSO E PATATE
Boiled meat and potato meatballs

- 2 large potatoes, boiled
- 14 oz boiled brisket or chuck
- 1–2 eggs
- 1 tablespoon finely chopped parsley
- 1 clove garlic, finely chopped
  salt and freshly ground black pepper to taste
- 1 cup dry bread crumbs
- 1/2 cup oil, for frying

Wine: a dry rosé (Rosé Antinori)

Mash the potatoes with a potato masher until smooth. Do not use a food processor because the mixture will become too sticky and the meatballs will be difficult to fry. Transfer the mixture to a bowl. • In the meantime, grind the boiled meat in a food processor and add to the bowl with the potatoes. • Stir in one egg, the parsley, and garlic. Season with salt and pepper and mix well. The mixture should be quite dense, but if it is too dry, add the other egg. • Shape the mixture into oblong croquettes, and roll them in bread crumbs. • Heat the oil to frying point (see page 62) in a 12-inch skillet. Fry the croquettes in batches until

golden brown. • Drain on paper towels. Sprinkle with salt and serve hot.

Serves: 4 · Prep: 25 min. · Cooking: 20–25 min. · Level: 1

PANELLE
Garbanzo bean fritters

- 2 1/2 cups garbanzo bean flour
- 1 quart cold water
- 1 teaspoon salt
- 1 tablespoon finely chopped parsley
- 1 cup oil, for frying

Wine: a dry white (Greco di Tufo)

Mix the flour, water, and salt in a food processor. The mixture will be fairly thick. • Transfer to a heavy-bottomed saucepan and cook over low heat for 30 minutes, stirring constantly. • Add the parsley. • Transfer the dough to a lightly oiled work surface and spread with a spatula until it is about 1/4-inch thick. • Leave to cool, then cut into diamond shapes or squares. •Heat the oil to frying point (see page 62) in a 12-inch skillet. Fry the dough in batches until golden brown on both sides. Drain on paper towels, sprinkle with salt and serve hot.

Serves: 4 · Prep: 10 min. · Cooking: 40 min. · Level: 1

CRESCENTINE
Savory fritters

- 3 cups all-purpose flour
- 1 teaspoon salt
- 1/2 cup extra-virgin olive oil
- 1/2 cup warm milk
- 2 cups oil, for frying

Wine: a dry red (Sangiovese)

Combine the flour and salt in a bowl and pour in the oil and milk. Mix well. • Transfer to a lightly floured work surface and knead until the dough is soft and smooth. • Cover with a cloth and set aside for 30 minutes. • Roll the dough out to about 1/2-inch thick. Cut in strips 2 inches wide and roll each strip to about 1/8 inch thick. • Cut into diamond-shapes with sides 3 inches long and place on clean paper towels. • Heat the oil to frying point (see page 62) in a 12-inch skillet. Fry the fritters 5–6 at a time. They will swell up and may even flip over in the pan. Cook for about 1 minute, or until they are golden brown. • Drain on paper towels and serve hot.

Serves: 4 · Prep: 10 min. + 30 min. to rest · Cooking: 15 min. · Level: 2

PANDORATO RIPIENO
Fried Mozzarella sandwiches

4	large, thin slices of firm-textured bread
	freshly ground black pepper to taste
12	oz Mozzarella cheese, sliced
4	anchovy fillets, crumbled (optional)
1	cup milk
1	cup all-purpose flour
2	eggs
	pinch of salt
1–2	cups oil, for frying

Wine: a dry white (Orvieto)

Remove the crusts from the bread and cut each slice in halves or quarters. Sprinkle with pepper. • Cover half the bread with the mozzarella slices and the anchovies, if using. Place the remaining slices of bread over the top to make little sandwiches. • Dip the sandwiches briefly into the milk, then sprinkle well with flour. Arrange the sandwiches on a large plate. • Beat the eggs with the salt and pour over the sandwiches. Leave for about 1 hour, or until the egg is completely absorbed. • Heat the oil to frying point (see page 62) in a 12-inch skillet. Fry the sandwiches a few at a time until they are deep golden brown all over. Drain well and place on paper towels. • Serve hot.

Serves: 4 · Prep: 10 min. + 1 hr to rest · Cooking: 15 min. · Level: 2

CHIZZE
Parmesan fritters

2¹/₂	cups all-purpose flour
1	teaspoon salt
2	tablespoons lard
2	tablespoons butter
1	cup lukewarm water
5	oz Parmesan cheese, thinly sliced
1–2	cups oil, for frying

Wine: a dry red (Gutturnio)

Put the flour in a bowl, add the salt, lard, and butter, and mix well with a fork. Add the water gradually, and, when all the flour has been absorbed, transfer the mixture to a lightly floured work surface. • Knead until the dough is smooth and elastic. • Roll out to about ¹/₈-inch thick and cut into 3-inch squares. Place a slice of Parmesan on one half of each square and fold the dough over the top to form a triangle. Moisten the edges with a few drops of

water and seal by pressing down with your fingertips. • Heat the oil to frying point (see page 62) in a 12-inch skillet. Fry the fritters 3 or 4 at a time until golden brown. Drain on paper towels. • Serve hot or at room temperature.

Serves: 4 · Prep: 30 min. · Cooking: 20 min. · Level: 2

PALLINE DI PARMIGIANO
Parmesan puffs

1¹/₄	cups water
1	teaspoon salt
¹/₄	cup butter
1¹/₄	cups all-purpose flour, sifted
4	eggs
1	cup freshly grated Parmesan cheese
¹/₂	cup coarsely grated Emmental cheese
2	cups oil, for frying

Wine: a dry red (Sangiovese)

Place the water, salt, and butter in a saucepan over medium heat and bring to the boil. • Stir in the flour, remove from the heat, and mix vigorously with a wooden spoon. • When the mixture is smooth, return to the heat and cook until the batter comes away from the sides of the pan. Set aside to cool. • Add the eggs one at a time, mixing each one in before adding the next. • Stir in the cheeses and mix well. • Mold the mixture into marble-size balls. • Heat the oil to frying point (see page 62) in a 12-inch skillet. Fry the puffs in batches until golden brown all over. • Drain on paper towels, sprinkle with salt, and serve hot.

Serves: 6 · Prep: 20 min. · Cooking: 20 min. · Level: 2

TORTA FRITTA
Fried bread dough

1	oz fresh yeast or 2 (¹/₄ oz) packages active dry yeast
	about ¹/₂ cup lukewarm water
2¹/₂	cups unbleached white flour
2	tablespoons lard (or butter), thinly sliced
1	teaspoon salt
1–2	cups oil for frying

Wine: a dry red (Colli di Parma)

Prepare the yeast as explained on page 24. • Put the flour in a bowl and sprinkle with salt. Make a hollow in the flour and fill with the lard. • Pour in the yeast mixture and the remaining water and mix the ingredients with a fork. • Transfer the dough to a lightly floured work surface and knead until soft and smooth. • Shape the dough into a ball, cover with a cloth and set aside to rise (it should double in volume). • Roll the risen dough out to about ¹/₂-inch thick. Cut into diamond shapes with sides 2 inches long and place on clean paper towels. • Heat the oil to frying point (see page 62) in a 12-inch skillet. • Fry the dough in batches until golden brown. Drain on paper towels, sprinkle with salt, and serve hot.

Serves: 4 · Prep: 30 min. · Rising time: 1¹/₂ hrs · Cooking: 15–20 min. · Level: 2

PANZEROTTI GHIOTTI
Fritters with Ricotta and ham filling

¹/₂	oz fresh yeast or 1 (¹/₄ oz) packages active dry yeast
1	teaspoon sugar
²/₃	cup lukewarm water
3	cups unbleached white flour
1	teaspoon salt
7	oz fresh Ricotta cheese
5	oz ham, coarsely chopped
	freshly ground black pepper to taste
1–2	cups oil, for frying

Wine: a dry red (Chianti Classico)

Prepare the dough as explained on page 24. • Mix the Ricotta, ham, and pepper together in a bowl. • When the rising time has elapsed (1 hour), transfer the dough to a lightly floured work surface and knead for 1 minute. • Shape into a long thin loaf and divide into 10–12 portions. • Roll the dough into disks about 3 inches in diameter. • Place a heaped teaspoon of filling on one half of each and spread a little. Fold the dough over the top to form crescent shapes. Moisten the edges with a few drops of water and seal by pressing down with your fingertips. • Heat the oil to frying point (see page 62) in a 12-inch skillet. Fry the panzerotti 5–6 at a time until golden brown. Drain on paper towels. • Serve hot.

Serves: 4 · Prep: 10 min. · Rising time: 1 hr · Cooking: 15 min. · Level: 1

PANZEROTTI AL FORMAGGIO
Fritters with cheese filling

- ½ oz fresh yeast or 1 (¼ oz) packages active dry yeast
- 1 teaspoon sugar
- ⅔ cup lukewarm water
- 3 cups unbleached white flour
- 1 teaspoon salt
- 3 oz fresh Ricotta cheese
- 3 oz freshly grated Provolone cheese
- 3 oz Mozzarella cheese, diced
- 1 scant tablespoon milk
- 1 teaspoon finely chopped parsley
- 1–2 cups oil, for frying

Wine: a smooth, dry red (Merlot)

Use the first 5 ingredients to prepare a dough as explained on pages 24–25. • Mix the Ricotta, Provolone, Mozzarella, milk, and parsley together in a bowl. • When the rising time has elapsed (1 hour), transfer the dough to a lightly floured work surface and knead for 1 minute. • Shape into a long thin loaf and divide into 10–12 portions. • Roll the dough into disks about 3 inches in diameter. • Place a heaped teaspoon of filling on one half of each and spread a little. Fold the dough over the top to form crescent shapes. Moisten the edges with a few drops of water and seal by pressing down with your fingertips. • Heat the oil to frying point (see page 62) in a 12-inch skillet. Fry the panzerotti 5–6 at a time until brown. Drain on paper towels. • Serve hot.

Serves: 4 min. · Prep: 15 min. · Rising time: 1 hr · Cooking: 15 min. · Level: 1

PANZEROTTI CON POMODORO E MOZZARELLA
Mozzarella and tomato fritters

- ½ oz fresh yeast or 1 (¼ oz) packages active dry yeast
- 1 teaspoon sugar
- ⅔ cup lukewarm water
- 3 cups unbleached white flour
- 1 teaspoon salt
- 2 cups oil, for frying
- 12 oz diced tomatoes
- 10 oz Mozzarella cheese, sliced
  salt and freshly ground black pepper to taste

Wine: a dry red (Chianti Classico)

Use the first 5 ingredients to prepare a dough as explained on pages 24–25. • Place the tomatoes in a heavy-bottomed saucepan over medium heat, with no added seasoning. Cook for 8–10 minutes until they reduce a little. • When the rising

Fritters with cheese filling

time has elapsed, shape the dough into panzerotti as explained on page 71. • Place a teaspoonful of tomato filling on each, cover with a slice of mozzarella and sprinkle with salt and pepper. Moisten the edges with 2–3 drops of water and seal by pressing down with your fingertips. • Heat the oil to frying point (see page 62) in a 12-inch skillet. Fry the panzerotti 5–6 at a time until brown. • Drain on paper towels to absorb excess oil. • Serve hot.

Serves: 4 · Prep: 25–30 min. · Rising time: 1 hr · Cooking: 25 min. · Level: 1

PANZEROTTI AL FORMAGGIO PICCANTE
Fritters with spicy ham and cheese filling

- ½ oz fresh yeast or 1 (¼ oz) packages active dry yeast
- 1 teaspoon sugar
- ⅔ cup lukewarm water
- 3 cups unbleached white flour
- 1 teaspoon salt
- 1 cup ham, coarsely chopped
- 1 oz freshly grated Parmesan cheese
- 3 oz Emmental cheese, diced
- 1 tablespoon heavy cream
- 1 teaspoon crushed red pepper flakes
- 1–2 cups oil, for frying

Wine: a dry rosé (Merlot)

Use the first 5 ingredients to prepare a dough as explained on pages 24–25. • Mix the ham, Parmesan, Emmental, cream, and pepper flakes together in a bowl. • When the rising time has elapsed (1 hour), transfer the dough to a lightly floured work surface and knead for 1 minute. • Shape into a long thin loaf and divide into 10–12 portions. • Roll the dough into disks about 3 inches in diameter. • Place a heaped teaspoon of filling on one half of each and spread a little. Fold the dough over the top to form crescent shapes. Moisten the edges with a few drops of water and seal by pressing down with your fingertips. • Heat the oil to frying point (see page 62) in a 12-inch skillet. Fry the panzerotti 5–6 at a time until golden brown. Drain on paper towels. • Serve hot.

Serves: 4 · Prep: 10 min. · Rising time: 1 hr · Cooking: 15 min. · Level: 1

Fried mortadella

MORTADELLA FRITTA
Fried mortadella

☞ This recipe comes from Emilia, which is the home of mortadella. It makes a very hearty appetizer.

- 4 ¼-inch thick, large slices mortadella
- 1 cup warm milk
- ¾ cup all-purpose flour
- 1 egg
  salt and freshly ground black pepper to taste
  pinch of nutmeg
- ¾ cup fine dry bread crumbs
- 1 cup oil, for frying

Wine: a dry lightly sparkling red (Lambrusco Grasparossa di Castelvetro)

Cut the Mortadella slices into quarters and place in a small bowl. Pour in the milk and set aside for 2 hours. • Drain the Mortadella. Dry with paper towels and coat with flour. • Lightly beat the egg and season with salt, pepper, and nutmeg. • Dip the mortadella in the egg and then coat with the bread crumbs. • Heat the oil to frying point (see page 62) in a 12-inch skillet. Fry the mortadella a few slices at a time until golden brown. • Drain on paper towels and serve hot.

Serves: 4–6 · Prep: 15 min. + 2 hrs to soak · Cooking: 10 min. · Level: 1

FAGOTTINI DI SPINACI
Spinach fritters

- 1 quantity Plain pastry (see recipe, page 49)
- 1½ lb fresh spinach
  salt and freshly ground black pepper to taste
- 2 eggs + 1 yolk
- 8 oz Ricotta cheese, drained and crumbled
- 6 oz diced Mozzarella cheese
- 1 cup freshly grated Parmesan cheese
- 2 cups oil, for frying

Wine: a light, dry red (Chianti dei Colli Aretini)

Prepare the pastry dough. • Cook the spinach in a pot of salted, boiling water for 8–10 minutes, or until tender. Drain, cool under cold running water, squeeze out excess moisture, and chop finely. • Beat the 2 eggs in a bowl and add the Ricotta, Mozzarella, Parmesan, salt, and pepper, and mix well. • Add the spinach and mix well. • Roll the pastry dough out on a clean, floured work bench until very thin. Cut into squares of about 4 inches. • Place a little filling at the center of each and fold in half. Beat the

PIZZELLE
Neapolitan fritters with tomato sauce

☞ These fritters come from the beautiful southern city of Naples, where they are served as appetizers or snacks.

- ½ oz fresh yeast or 1 (¼ oz) package active dry yeast
- ⅔ cup lukewarm water
- 3 cups unbleached white flour
- 1 teaspoon salt
- 1 (15 oz) can drained and chopped tomatoes
- 2 cloves garlic, finely chopped
- 1 teaspoon oregano
  salt and freshly ground black pepper to taste
- 2 tablespoons extra-virgin olive oil
- 1–2 cups oil, for frying

Wine: a dry red (Cilento Rosso)

Use the first 4 ingredients to prepare a dough as explained on pages 24–25. • When the rising time has elapsed (about 1 hour), knead the dough on a floured work surface for 2–3 minutes. Divide into 10–12 portions. Shape into balls, cover with a cloth and set aside to rise for about 1 hour. • Place the tomatoes in a heavy-bottomed saucepan with the garlic, oregano, salt, pepper, and oil. Cook over medium heat for about 15 minutes, or until the sauce has reduced. • When the second rising time has elapsed, use your hands or a rolling pin to flatten the dough into disks about 3 inches in diameter. • Heat the oil to frying point (see page 62) in a 12-inch skillet. Fry the fritters 2–3 at a time until golden brown. Turn the fritters halfway through cooking. They will be ready in about 2 minutes. • Drain on paper towels. • Arrange the fritters on a heated serving

dish and cover each one with a tablespoon of the hot tomato sauce. • Serve hot.

Serves: 4 · Prep: 30 min. · Rising time: 2 hrs · Cooking: 20 min. · Level: 1

FRITTO ALLA GARISENDA
Fried bread with cheese and prosciutto

- 24 slices day-old white bread
- 4 oz prosciutto, thinly sliced
- 6 oz Parmesan or Gruyère cheese, sliced
- 1 white truffle (optional)
- ½ cup cold milk
- 3 eggs, beaten to a foam
- 1¼ cups fine dry bread crumbs
- ½ cup butter

Wine: a dry red (Gutturnio)

Remove the crusts from the bread. Use a pastry cutter or the rim of a small glass to cut out disks about 2 inches in diameter. • Make sandwiches with pairs of disks, filling each with a slice of prosciutto and cheese (trimmed to a slightly smaller size than the bread disks). • If using truffle, place shavings between the prosciutto and cheese. • Press the layers to make them stick together. • Dip quickly in the milk, then in the egg, then coat with bread crumbs. Dip the sandwiches into the egg again, and finish with another coating of bread crumbs. • Check that the edges of the sandwiches are firmly sealed and well coated with egg and bread crumbs. • Heat the butter in a large skillet and fry the sandwiches, turning once, until they are golden brown. • Drain on paper towels and serve hot.

Serves: 6 · Prep: 25 min. · Cooking: 20 min. · Level: 1

remaining egg yolk and brush the edges of each square before pressing firmly to seal. • Heat the oil to frying point (see page 62) in a 12-inch skillet. Fry the fritters in batches of 3–4 for about 10 minutes, or until golden brown. Turn using tongs or two spoons. • Serve hot.

Serves: 4 · Prep: 30 min. · Cooking: 50 min. · Level: 1

FRITTELLE DI BIANCHETTI
Whitebait fritters

1¼	lb whitebait, washed and dried in a dishcloth
4	cloves garlic, finely chopped
¼	cup finely chopped parsley
¼	cup freshly grated Parmesan cheese
2	eggs, beaten to a foam
1	tablespoon fine dry bread crumbs
	salt to taste
2	cups oil, for frying

Wine: a dry white (Bianco Vergine Valdichiana)

Put the whitebait in a bowl and add the garlic, parsley, Parmesan, egg, bread crumbs, and salt. Mix thoroughly and, using a spoon and your hands, form the mixture into fritters. • Heat the oil to frying point (see page 62) in a 12-inch skillet. Fry the fritters in batches until golden brown. Drain on paper towels. • Sprinkle with salt and serve hot.

Serves: 4 · Prep: 20 min. · Cooking: 15 min. · Level: 2

CRISPEDDI
Anchovy fritters with oregano

½	oz fresh yeast or 1 (¼ oz) packages active dry yeast
½	cup lukewarm water
2½	cups unbleached white flour
1	teaspoon salt
1	tablespoon butter, chopped
7	oz anchovy fillets
2	teaspoons dried oregano
2	cups oil, for frying

Wine: a dry white (Orvieto Classico)

Use the first 5 ingredients to prepare a dough as explained on pages 24–25. • Wash the anchovies thoroughly under cold running water and pat dry with paper towels. • When the rising time has elapsed (about 1 hour), place the dough on a lightly floured work surface and knead for 1 minute. Divide into egg-sized portions and shape into long rolls. • Cut

them open lengthwise and place an anchovy fillet and a sprinkling of oregano in each. Close up the dough and place the rolls on a clean cloth. • Cover with another cloth and leave to rise for 30 minutes. • Heat the oil to frying point (see page 62) in a 12-inch skillet. • Fry the rolls 2 or 3 at a time until lightly browned. Drain on paper towels. • Serve hot.

Serves: 4 · Prep: 30 min. · Rising time: 1½ hr · Cooking: 10 min. · Level: 1

FRITTATINE DI COZZE
Mussel fritters

1½	lb mussels, in shell
½	cup dry white wine
¾	cup cold water
2	tablespoons butter
	pinch of salt
1	cup all-purpose flour
4	eggs
2	tablespoons finely chopped parsley
¼	cup freshly grated Parmesan cheese
2	cups oil, for frying

Wine: a dry white (Zagarolo)

Soak the mussels in a large bowl of water for 1 hour. Pull off their beards, scrub, and rinse well in plenty of cold water. • Put the mussels in a large skillet over high heat, sprinkle with the wine, and cover. • When all the shells are open (discard any that do not open), pick the mussels out of their shells. • Bring the water, butter, and salt to a boil in a small pot, add the flour, and remove from heat. Beat with a wooden spoon until the mixture is thick and well mixed. • Return to medium heat and stir until the mixture sticks to the sides and bottom of the pot. • Let cool. Transfer to a bowl, stir in the eggs one by one, and add the parsley, Parmesan, and mussels. • Heat the oil to very hot. Use a spoon to add small quantities of the mussel batter into the oil. The fritters will swell and turn golden brown. • Drain on paper towels, sprinkle with salt, and serve.

Serves: 4–6 · Prep: 30 min. + 1 hr to soak mussels · Cooking: 30 min. · Level: 2

FRITTO DI POLENTA E MOZZARELLA
Fried polenta and Mozzarella cheese

½	quantity cold Basic polenta (see recipe, page 184)
8	oz Mozzarella cheese
	freshly ground white pepper to taste
2	cups oil, for frying

Wine: a dry white (Elba Bianco)

Chop the polenta and the Mozzarella into cubes about 1 inch square. • Grind the pepper over the Mozzarella. • Place a cube of Mozzarella between two cubes of polenta and join with a wooden toothpick. • Heat the oil to frying point (see page 62) in a 12-inch skillet. Add the polenta and cheese and fry until light golden brown. Turn them often as they cook. • Drain on paper towels, sprinkle with a little salt, and serve hot.

Serves: 6 · Prep: 10 min. · Cooking: 15 min. · Level: 1

Mussel fritters

The Italian food that is so popular today is based on la cucina povera, *or peasant cuisine. Until recently, if served at all, appetizers consisted of a few slices of ham or salami. Nowadays, soaring living standards in Italy have led to the invention of a host of mouthwatering* antipasti.

APPETIZERS

PANZANELLA
Tuscan bread salad

☞ Panzanella is a typical Tuscan salad. Like many of that region's famous dishes, it is based on bread. Ingredients vary according to which town or village you are eating in, so feel free to enrich the salad by adding diced carrots, fennel, celery, hard-boiled eggs, capers, or Pecorino cheese.

1   lb dense grain, day-old bread
5   medium tomatoes
2   red onions
1   cucumber
12 leaves fresh basil, torn
    salt and freshly ground black pepper to taste
1/3 cup extra-virgin olive oil
1   tablespoon red wine vinegar

Wine: a dry red (Chianti dei Colli Fiorentini)

Soak the bread in a bowl of cold water for 15 minutes. • Squeeze out as much water as possible, then crumble the almost dry bread into a large salad bowl. • Slice the tomatoes and remove as many seeds as possible. Peel the onions and cucumber and slice thinly. • Combine the tomatoes, cucumber, basil, and onions in the bowl with the bread. Season with salt, pepper, and 1/4 cup of oil. Toss briefly. • Chill in the refrigerator for 15 minutes. • Just before serving, add the vinegar and remaining oil and toss again.

Serves: 4 · Prep: 5 min. + 30 min. to soak and chill · Level: 1

◄ Mixed deli meats
➤ Tuscan bread salad

BRUSCHETTA

Bruschetta is a classic Roman appetizer, although many regions of Italy have similar dishes. It is difficult to recreate the authentic taste abroad because Roman bread is white, very compact, and unsalted. Use firm-textured bread that is not too fresh; yesterday's leftover loaf is ideal. Toast in the oven rather than in the toaster. The bread should be as dry as possible.

Toasted bread with garlic, salt, and oil

Bruschetta

Toasted bread with garlic, salt, and oil

    6   large, thick slices of white, unsalted bread
    3   cloves garlic
        salt and freshly ground black pepper to taste
    ⅓   cup extra-virgin olive oil

Serves: 6 · Prep: 5 min. · Cooking: 10 min. · Level: 1

1 Toast the bread in a preheated oven at 350°F until golden brown on both sides.

2 Peel the garlic and rub each slice of toast with half a clove.

3 Sprinkle each slice with salt and pepper.

4 Drizzle each slice with oil and serve.

Bruschetta con pomodori

Fresh tomato bruschetta

☞ This dish can be prepared ahead of time. Keep the toasted bread and tomato mixture separate until just before serving, otherwise the dish will become soggy and unappetizing.

    6   slices Bruschetta (see recipe, this page)
    3   large ripe tomatoes
    ¼   cup extra-virgin olive oil
    1   teaspoon oregano (optional)
        salt and freshly ground black pepper to taste
    8   fresh basil leaves, torn

Wine: a dry white (Orvieto Classico)
Serves: 6 · Prep: 10 min. · Cooking: 10 min. · Level: 1

1 Prepare the bruschetta. • Dice the tomatoes into bite-size chunks. Place them in a bowl and mix with the oil, oregano, salt, and pepper.

2 Spoon the tomato mixture over the bruschetta.

3 Arrange the basil on top and serve.

Bruschetta con fagioli
Bruschetta with white beans

- 4 slices Bruschetta
- 1 (15 oz) can white beans, drained
  salt and freshly ground black pepper to taste
- 1 tablespoon extra-virgin olive oil

Wine: a dry red (Chianti Rufina)

*Serves: 4 · Prep: 10 min. · Cooking: 10 min. ·
Level: 1*

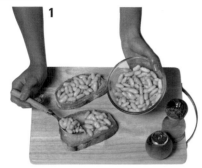

1 Prepare the bruschetta. • Heat the beans in a small saucepan. Taste for salt; season if necessary. • Spoon the hot beans over the bruschetta.

2 Drizzle each slice with oil.

3 Season with a generous grinding of pepper and serve hot.

BRUSCHETTE CON FRUTTI DI MARE
Seafood bruschetta

- 8 oz mussels, in shell
- 8 oz clams, in shell
- 2 tablespoons extra-virgin olive oil
- 2 cloves garlic
- 2 tablespoons finely chopped parsley
- 1 cup dry white wine
- 7 oz small squid
- 8 oz shrimp
- 1 red bell pepper
- 1 scallion, finely chopped
- ½ tablespoon butter
- 1 teaspoon saffron, dissolved in ½ cup lukewarm milk
  salt and freshly ground black pepper to taste
- 8 slices Bruschetta

Wine: a dry white (Pinot Grigio di Aquileia)

Soak the mussels and clams in a large bowl of cold water for 1 hour. • Pull the beards off the mussels and scrub well. Rinse under cold running water. Drain well. • Sauté half the oil, garlic, and parsley in a large skillet for 2–3 minutes. • Add the mussels and clams and pour in half the wine. • Cover the pan and place over medium-high heat for 5–10 minutes. Shake the pan often until the shells are all open. • Strain the liquid they have produced and set aside. Discard any shells that haven't opened. • Detach the mussels and clams from their shells and set aside. • Clean the squid as explained on page 200. Rinse well in cold running water. • Shell the shrimp and remove the dark intestinal veins. Chop off the heads, and rinse thoroughly in cold running water. • Carefully wash the bell pepper, cut in half, remove the seeds and core, and dice. • Sauté the scallion in a skillet with the butter and the remaining oil. Add the bell pepper and sauté briefly, stirring continuously with a wooden spoon. • Add the remaining wine and continue cooking over high heat. • When the wine has evaporated, add the mussel liquid and the saffron and milk. Season with salt and pepper. • Cook over high heat for a few minutes until the sauce is thick. Add the mussels, clams, shrimp, and squid and cook for 3 minutes more, mixing often. • Sprinkle with the remaining parsley. • Prepare the bruschetta. • Spoon the seafood over the bruschetta and serve hot.

*Serves: 4 · Prep: 30 min. + 1 hr to soak the shellfish ·
Cooking: 20 min. · Level: 2*

Seafood bruschetta

CROSTONI AL FORMAGGIO
Four-cheese crostini

☞ Cheese on toast is always delicious. Vary the cheeses in this recipe according to personal tastes and what you have in the refrigerator.

- 4 oz Caprino cheese
- ½ cup freshly grated Parmesan cheese
- 4 oz Gorgonzola cheese, diced
- 4 oz Fontina cheese, freshly grated
- 2 tablespoons extra-virgin olive oil
   salt and freshly ground black pepper to taste
   pinch each of oregano and marjoram
- 8 large slices firm-textured bread

Wine: a dry white (Greco di Tufo)

Mix the cheeses in a bowl with the oil. Season with salt, oregano, and marjoram. • Mash with a fork and stir until well mixed. If the mixture is too thick, add more oil. • Spread on the bread. Grind a little pepper over the top. Arrange the slices of bread on a baking sheet. • Bake in a preheated oven at 375°F for 10 minutes, or until the cheese is golden brown.

Serves: 4 · Prep: 10 min. · Cooking: 10 min. · Level: 1

CROSTINI CON I FUNGHI
Mushroom crostini

☞ In Italy, porcini are used in this recipe. If you can't get them, try other wild mushrooms, such as shiitake, chanterelles, or morels.

- 1¼ lb fresh porcini or other wild mushrooms
- 2 tablespoons butter
- ¼ cup extra-virgin olive oil
- ½ onion, finely chopped
- 2 cloves garlic, finely chopped
- 1 tablespoon finely chopped parsley
- ½ cup Vegetable stock (see recipe, page 104)
   salt and freshly ground black pepper to taste
- 1 long loaf firm-textured Italian or French bread, (about 3 inches in diameter) cut in ½-inch thick slices and toasted

Wine: a dry white (Colli Euganei Pinot Bianco)

Rinse the mushrooms carefully under cold running water and dry with paper towels. Use a knife to remove any dirt from the stems. • Separate the stems from the caps and dice the firm, unblemished parts of the stems. Chop the caps coarsely. • Heat the butter and oil in a skillet over medium heat and sauté the onion, garlic, and parsley for 4–5 minutes. • Add the mushrooms, season with salt and pepper, and cook for 5 minutes, stirring continuously. • Stir in enough stock to keep the mixture moist and cook until the mushrooms are tender but not too mushy. • Spread each toast with the mushroom mixture and serve.

Serves: 4–6 · Prep: 20 min. · Cooking: 20 min. · Level: 1

CROSTINI DI FUNGHI TARTUFATI
Mushroom and truffle crostini

☞ If fresh truffles are unavailable, truffle paste is a good substitute.

- 12 oz fresh mushrooms (porcini, or white cultivated mushrooms, or a mixture of the two)
- ¼ cup butter
- 1 tablespoon brandy
- 1 cup light cream
- 4 oz semi-soft melting cheese (Stracchino, Robiola)
- 1 small white truffle, fresh if possible, grated
- 12 large slices firm-textured bread, cut in half and toasted

Wine: a dry red (Nebbiolo)

Rinse the mushrooms carefully under cold running water and dry with paper towels. Use a knife to remove any dirt from the stems. Chop coarsely. • Melt the butter in a skillet over medium heat and add the mushrooms. Cook, stirring at intervals, until they are tender. • Sprinkle with the brandy and cook until it has evaporated. • Heat the cream separately in a small saucepan over low heat. Stir in the cheese. • When the cheese is completely blended with the cream, remove from heat and stir in the mushrooms and truffle. • Spread on the toast and serve hot.

Serves: 6 · Prep: 30 min. · Cooking: 20 min. · Level: 1

CROSTONI CON ASPARAGI E ARANCIA
Asparagus and orange crostoni

- 3 lb fresh asparagus
- 1 orange
- 12 slices firm-textured bread, toasted
- 3 egg yolks
- ⅔ cup butter, cut in small pieces
   salt to taste

Wine: a dry white (Vernaccia di San Gimignano)

Rinse the asparagus, trim the stalks, and cook in a pot of salted, boiling water for 8–10 minutes. • Drain well and cut off all but the most tender part of the stalks and tips. • Squeeze the orange and set the juice aside. Cut half the rind into thin strips. Blanch in a pot of boiling water for a few seconds. Drain well and dry carefully. • Place the asparagus on the toast. • Put a large pan of water over medium heat. • Combine the egg yolks with a few pieces of butter, a pinch of salt, and 1 tablespoon of water in a small pot. Beat well with a whisk. • Put the small pot in the larger one filled with water, keeping the heat low so the water doesn't boil. As soon as the butter begins to melt, add the rest a little at a time, so that it is gradually absorbed, whisking all the time and taking care that the sauce never boils. • When the sauce is creamy, add another pinch of salt and, very gradually, the orange juice, stirring carefully all the time. • Remove from heat and stir in the orange rind. • Spoon the sauce over the crostoni and serve.

Serves: 6–8 · Prep: 30 min. · Cooking: 30 min. · Level: 2

CROSTINI SICILIANI
Sicilian-style crostini

- 8 slices firm-textured bread
- 1 cup oil, for frying
- 2 tablespoons vinegar
- 1 teaspoon each sugar, capers, pine nuts, raisins, diced candied lemon peel
- 2 ripe tomatoes, diced

Wine: a dry red (Rosso di Donnafugata)

Trim the crusts from the bread and cut each slice in half. • Heat the oil in a skillet and fry the bread until golden brown on both sides. Drain on paper towels. • Bring the vinegar, sugar, and 2 tablespoons of water to the boil, then add the capers, pine nuts, raisins, lemon peel, and tomatoes. • Cook for 5 minutes, stirring with care. • Spread the fried bread with this mixture and serve.

Serves: 4 · Prep: 10 min. · Cooking: 10 min. · Level: 1

CROSTINI AL MISTO DI PESCE
Seafood crostini

- 8 oz squid
- 7 oz mussels, in shell
- 7 oz clams, in shell
- 1/3 cup extra-virgin olive oil
- 4 cloves garlic, finely chopped
- 1/3 cup finely chopped parsley
- 3 1/2 oz shrimp, peeled and cooked
- 4 small tomatoes, skinned and finely chopped
  salt and freshly ground black pepper to taste
- 1 baguette (French loaf), cut into 1/2-inch thick slices and toasted

Wine: a dry white (Capalbia Bianco)

Clean the squid as shown on page 200 and cut into small pieces using kitchen scissors. • Soak the mussels and clams in cold water for 1 hour. Place in a large skillet over medium-high heat for 8–10 minutes until they open. • Extract all the mollusks from the shells and discard the shells, placing the mollusks in a covered tureen. • Heat the oil in the skillet and sauté the garlic and parsley for 5 minutes. • Add the shrimp and squid and cook for 12 minutes. Add the tomatoes and cook for 5 more minutes.

• Add the clams and mussels, season with salt and pepper, and cook for 2 minutes. • Transfer the mixture to a food processor and blend to a purée. • Spread the fish mixture on the toast and serve.

Serves: 4 · Prep: 20 min. + 1 hr to soak shellfish · Cooking: 25 min. · Level: 2

CROSTONI DEL BUONGIORNO
Crostoni with ham, eggs, and mushrooms

- 6 oz white mushrooms
- 1/4 cup butter
- 1 teaspoon finely chopped fresh thyme
- 4 oz ham
  salt and freshly ground black pepper to taste
- 4 eggs
- 4–6 slices firm-textured bread, toasted
- 2 tablespoons finely chopped parsley

Wine: a dry white (Pinot Grigio)

Rinse the mushrooms carefully under cold running water and dry with paper towels. Use a knife to remove any dirt from the stems. • Slice the mushrooms and sauté in a skillet with half the butter and the thyme for 10 minutes. • Add the ham and season with salt. Mix well and remove from heat. • Melt the remaining butter in a saucepan over medium-low heat, break in the eggs, and let them set slightly before breaking them up with a fork. Cook, stirring continuously, until the eggs are cooked but still soft. Season with salt. •

Arrange the toast on a serving dish and cover each slice with the egg mixture, followed by the mushroom mixture. • Sprinkle with the parsley and pepper and serve.

Serves: 4 · Prep: 10 min. · Cooking: 15 min. · Level: 1

CROSTONI CON MOZZARELLA
Mozzarella and tomato crostoni

- 2 cloves garlic, finely chopped
- 1/4 cup extra-virgin olive oil
- 1 (15 oz) can peeled and chopped tomatoes
- 6 leaves fresh basil, torn
- 1 teaspoon dried oregano
  salt to taste
- 4 large slices firm-textured bread
- 6 oz Mozzarella cheese, thinly sliced

Wine: a dry white (Bianco Pisano do san Thorpè)

Sauté the garlic in half the oil until pale gold. • Add the tomatoes, basil, half the oregano, and salt, and simmer for 30 minutes. • Cut the slices of bread in half, cover with the Mozzarella, and place in an oiled baking dish. Sprinkle with the remaining oregano, drizzle with the remaining oil, and bake in a preheated oven at 400°F until the Mozzarella is lightly browned. • Remove from the oven and spread with the tomato sauce. • Serve hot.

Serves: 4 · Prep: 15 min. · Cooking: 45 min. · Level: 1

Asparagus and orange crostoni

Tuna crostini with pickles

Process the tuna, cocktail onions, pickled vegetables (except a few to garnish), and mayonnaise in a food processor until smooth. • Spread on the bread, garnish with the reserved vegetables, and serve.

Serves: 4 · Prep: 10 min. · Level: 1

CROSTINI CON GAMBERETTI
Shrimp crostini

- 1¼ lb shrimp
- 3 tablespoons chopped capers (+ a few whole to garnish)
- 2 tablespoons butter, at room temperature
- 1 tablespoon mustard
- 3 tablespoons tomato paste
  salt to taste
- 1 baguette (French loaf), cut into ½-inch thick slices and toasted

Wine: a dry white (Bianco di Custoza)

Clean and peel the shrimp as shown on page 200. • Cook the shrimp in boiling water for 2 minutes. Drain and chop in a food processor, reserving a few whole shrimp for garnish. • Put the shrimp mixture in a large bowl, add the chopped capers, butter, mustard, and tomato paste. Season with salt and mix well. • Spread the shrimp mixture on the toast and transfer to a serving platter. • Garnish with the reserved whole capers and shrimp.

Serves: 4 · Prep: 15 min. · Cooking: 2 min. · Level: 1

CROSTINI DI GAMBERI
Shrimp crostini with ketchup

- 1 lb small shrimp
- 1 quantity Mayonnaise (see recipe, page 16)
- ⅓ cup catsup
- 1 lemon, thinly sliced, then each slice quartered (reserve a few drops of the juice from slicing)
- 8 slices whole-wheat bread, cut in half and toasted
- 1 tablespoon finely chopped parsley

Wine: a dry white (Valle d'Aosta Bianco)

Cook the shrimp in boiling water for 2 minutes. If they are very tiny, 1 minute will be enough. Drain and cool slightly, then peel and set aside. • Mix the mayonnaise, catsup, and the reserved lemon juice in a serving dish large enough to hold the shrimp. • Add the shrimp to the sauce and mix gently. • Spread the shrimp mixture on the toast. Garnish each crostini with a sprinkling of parsley and a piece of lemon. Serve at once.

Serves: 4 · Prep: 30 min. · Cooking: 2 min. · Level: 1

CROSTINI CON I MOLLUSCHI
Mixed shellfish crostini

- 2 lb mussels, in shell
- 2 lb clams, in shell
- 2 lb razor clams, in shell
- 3 cloves garlic, minced
- ⅓ cup finely chopped parsley
  salt and freshly ground pepper to taste
- 10 walnuts, chopped
- 1 cup milk
- 1 cup light cream
- 2 eggs
- 1 baguette (French loaf), cut into ½-inch thick slices
- 2 cups oil, for frying
  juice of ½ lemon

Wine: a dry white (Albana di Romagna)

Soak the mussels and clams in a bowl of cold water for 1 hour to purge them of sand. Scrub the beards off the mussels under cold running water. • Place the shellfish in a large skillet over high heat and, as they open, transfer to a bowl. Discard any shells that have not opened. • Extract the mollusks from the shells, discarding the shells, and chop coarsely with a large knife. • Place in a bowl with the garlic and parsley, season with salt and a generous grinding of pepper and mix well. • In a medium bowl, combine the walnuts, milk, and cream. • Break the eggs into a small bowl, add a pinch of salt, and beat with a fork. • Remove the crusts from the bread and dip them first in the walnut mixture then in the beaten egg.• Heat the oil in a large skillet over high heat and fry the bread until pale golden brown on both sides. Drain on paper towels. • Cover with the shellfish mixture and sprinkle with the lemon juice. • Serve immediately.

Serves: 6 · Prep: 1 hr · Cooking: 20 min. · Level: 2

CROSTINI AL TONNO CON SOTTACETI
Tuna crostini with pickles

- 1 cup canned tuna, drained
- 2½ oz cocktail onions
- 2½ oz mixed pickled vegetables, drained
- 1 quantity Mayonnaise (see recipe, page 16)
- 1 baguette (French loaf), cut into ¼-inch thick slices

Wine: a dry white (Trebbiano di Aprilia)

CROSTONI ALLE VONGOLE
Crostoni with clams

- 2 lb clams, in shell
- 2/3 cup extra-virgin olive oil
- 2 cloves garlic, finely chopped + 1 whole clove garlic
- 1/2 cup dry white wine
- 3 tablespoons finely chopped parsley
- 2 dried red chilies, crumbled
- 5 tomatoes, skinned, seeded, and finely chopped
  salt to taste
- 16 slices firm-textured white bread about 1/2 inch thick

Wine: a dry white (Bianco di Capri)

Soak the clams in a bowl of cold water for 1 hour to purge them of sand. • Place the clams, 3 tablespoons of oil, and the whole clove of garlic in a large skillet over medium-high heat. • When the oil is sizzling, pour in the wine, cover, and heat until the clams have opened, about 5–7 minutes. • Turn off heat and remove the clams from the skillet, discarding any that have not opened. • Extract the clams from the open shells and place in a dish. Cover with a plate so they do not dry out too much. • Heat the remaining oil in the skillet over medium heat and sauté the garlic, parsley, and chilies for 1–2 minutes. • Add the tomatoes and cook for about 15 minutes, or until the sauce has reduced. • Add the clams at the last minute, stir well and remove from heat immediately. • Toast the bread in a preheated oven at 425°F for about 5 minutes, or until crisp and pale golden brown. • Cover with the clam mixture and serve.

Serves: 8 · Prep: 50 min. · Cooking: 20 min. · Level: 2

CROSTINI CON SALSICCIA
Crostini with sausage meat topping

- 8 oz fresh Italian sausages, skinned
- 8 oz fresh Stracchino cheese
  freshly ground black pepper to taste
- 1 long loaf firm-textured white bread, (about 3 inches in diameter) cut in 1/2-inch thick slices and toasted

Wine: a dry red (Chianti dei Colli Aretini)

Mix the sausage meat in a bowl with the cheese and pepper. • Spread each toast with the mixture and place in a large, shallow ovenproof dish. • Bake in a preheated oven at 400°F for 5 minutes, or

Crostoni with clams

until the topping is bubbling. • Serve hot.

Serves: 6 · Prep: 10 min. · Cooking: 5 min. · Level: 1

CROSTINI CON ACCIUGA E UOVO SODO
Anchovy and hard-boiled egg crostini

- 1/3 cup butter, at room temperature
- 1 oz anchovy paste
- 1 baguette (French loaf), cut into 1/2-inch thick slices
- 3 hard-boiled eggs, sliced
- 2 tablespoons capers

Wine: a dry, fruity white (Chardonnay)

Mix the butter with the anchovy paste until smooth and creamy. • Spread the bread with a thin layer of this mixture, top with slices of hard-boiled egg, and garnish with capers. • If not serving immediately, keep refrigerated for up to 1 hour.

Serves: 6 · Prep: 25 min. · Cooking: 10 min. · Level: 1

CROSTONI CON UOVA E CAROTE
Crostoni with eggs and carrots

- 1/4 cup butter
- 2 twigs fresh rosemary
- 8 oz carrots, scraped and sliced in very thin wheels
- 2 large eggs
- 2 tablespoons finely chopped parsley
- 3 tablespoons heavy cream
  pinch of nutmeg
  salt and freshly ground black pepper to taste
- 8 slices firm-textured white bread, about 1/2 inch thick
- 2 oz Emmental cheese, grated

Wine: a dry white (Verdicchio di Matelica)

Melt 2 tablespoons of butter in a large skillet over medium heat. Add the rosemary and cook until the butter begins to darken. • Discard the rosemary and add the carrots. Cover and cook over low heat for 10 minutes. • Beat the eggs with the parsley, cream, nutmeg, salt, and pepper. When the carrots are tender, pour the egg mixture into the skillet and stir until the eggs begin to harden. • Toast the bread in a preheated oven at 425°F for about 5 minutes, or until crisp and pale golden brown. • Cover with the carrot mixture, sprinkle with the cheese, and bake in a preheated oven at 400°F for 5 minutes, or until the cheese has melted. Serve hot.

Serves: 4 · Prep: 10 min. · Cooking: 5 min. · Level: 1

These mouthwatering crostini are served in homes and trattorias all over Tuscany. The soft liver pâté topping is surprisingly easy to make. Normally served on toasted bread, it is also very good on fried polenta crostini (see recipe, facing page). I have given the traditional recipe which calls for milt (calf's spleen). If preferred, omit the milt and double the quantity of chicken livers.

CROSTINI TOSCANI
Tuscan-style crostini

6½	oz calf's milt (optional, see above)
8	oz chicken livers
4	anchovy fillets
1	tablespoon capers
3	tablespoons butter
1	onion, finely chopped
½	cup dry white wine
¼	cup extra-virgin olive oil
	salt and freshly ground black pepper to taste
½	cup Beef stock (see recipe, page 105)
1	long loaf firm-textured white bread, (about 3 inches in diameter) cut in ½-inch thick slices and toasted

Wine: a young, fruity red (Chianti Montalbano)

Skin the calf's milt and cut into small pieces. • Trim any connective tissue and discolored parts from the chicken livers and chop into small pieces. • Finely chop the anchovy fillets and capers together. • Melt two-thirds of the butter in a skillet over medium heat, add the onion and sauté until tender. • Add the chicken livers and calf's milt, if using, and cook for 5 minutes, stirring frequently. • Season with salt and pepper. Add the wine and cook for 15 minutes, stirring frequently. If the mixture dries out, moisten with the stock. • Remove the skillet from the heat and set aside to cool a little. • Place the liver mixture on a chopping board and chop finely. • Heat the oil in the skillet over medium heat and add the liver mixture, anchovies, and capers. Stir well, add the remaining butter, and cook for 3–4 more minutes. • Spread this deliciously rich, savory mixture on the toasts and keep warm in the oven until just before serving.

Serves: 6–8 · Prep: 35 min. · Cooking: 30 min. · Level: 1

Tuscan-style crostini

CROSTINI RUSTICI
Country-style liver crostini

- ¼ cup extra-virgin olive oil
- 1 stalk celery, 1 carrot, 1 onion, 1 clove garlic, all coarsely chopped
- 2 tablespoons finely chopped parsley
- 4 chicken livers
- ½ cup dry white wine
- 3 tablespoons coarsely chopped capers
- 2 anchovy fillets, chopped
  salt and freshly ground black pepper to taste
- 4–8 slices firm-textured bread

Wine: a dry red (Sangiovese di Romagna)

Heat the oil in a skillet over medium heat and sauté the celery, carrot, onion, garlic, and parsley for 4–5 minutes. • Remove the bile and connective tissue from the chicken livers. Chop coarsely. • Add the chicken livers to the skillet and sauté for 4–5 minutes. • Pour in the wine and cook over low heat for 20 minutes. If the mixture drys out too much add a little more wine. • Stir in the capers and cook for 2–3 minutes. • Add the anchovies and season with salt and pepper. Remove from heat. • Toast the bread and spread with the liver mixture. Serve at room temperature.

Serves: 4 · Prep: 15 min. · Cooking: 30 min. · Level: 2

CROSTINI DI POLENTA FRITTA
Fried polenta crostini

☞ Fried or baked polenta crostini are a good way to use up leftover polenta. They can be served as they are or with a variety of toppings. Ideally, the polenta should be made at least 12 hours in advance; it needs time to firm up before frying or baking.

- 1 quantity cold Basic polenta (see recipe, page 184)
- 2 cups oil, for frying

Wine: a dry red (Rosso Piceno)

Prepare the polenta. • Turn the cooked polenta out onto a platter or board and leave to cool for at least 12 hours. • Cut the polenta in ½-inch slices. • Heat the oil until hot but not smoking and fry the polenta slices a few at a time for 6–8 minutes, or until golden brown on both sides. • Serve hot.

Serves: 8 · Prep: 15 · Cooking: 20 · Level: 2

CROSTONI DI POLENTA AI FORMAGGI
Fried polenta with mixed cheeses

- 6–8 oz mixed Italian cheeses, such as Gorgonzola, Fontina, Asiago, and Taleggio
- ½ cup extra-virgin olive oil
- 8–12 slices cold Basic polenta (see recipe, page 184), cut about ¾-inch thick and 3 inches long
- 6 sage leaves or 2 sprigs rosemary
  freshly ground white or black pepper to taste (optional)

Wine: a dry red (Sangiovese di Romagna)

Remove the crusts from the cheese and chop into pieces if soft, or in thin slices if hard. • Heat the oil in a large skillet until hot but not smoking. Add the sliced polenta and the sage or rosemary. Fry over high heat for 3 minutes, or until one side is golden brown. Turn the slices over and cover the cooked side with the cheese, leaving a small border around the edges. • Cook for another 3 minutes, or until the slices of polenta are browned and crisp on the underside and the cheese has melted. • Serve hot, with a grinding of pepper, if liked.

Serves: 4 · Prep: 10 min. · Cooking: 10 min. · Level: 1

CROSTINI DI POLENTA CON CIPOLLE
Baked polenta with onions

- ¾ cup extra-virgin olive oil
- 1 lb red or white onions, thinly sliced
  salt and freshly ground black pepper to taste
- 8–12 slices cold Basic polenta (see recipe, page 184), cut about ¾ inch thick and 3 inches long

Wine: a dry white (Vermentino di Gallura)

Heat ¼ cup of oil in a skillet and sauté the onions until light golden brown. Season with salt and pepper. • Bake the slices of polenta in a preheated oven at 350°F for 5–10 minutes until they are dry and crisp. Better still, grill over a barbecue or wood fire for 5 minutes until they are lightly browned. • Spread the onion mixture on the polenta slices and serve.

Serves: 4 · Prep: 10 min. · Cooking: 15 min. · Level: 1

CROSTINI DI POLENTA CON FUNGHI
Fried polenta crostini with mushrooms

- 1 quantity Italian mushroom sauce (see recipe, page 20)
- 1 quantity Fried polenta crostini (see recipe, this page)

Wine: a dry rosé (Lagrein Rosato)

Prepare the mushroom sauce. • Prepare the fried polenta crostini. • Spread the crostini with the mushroom sauce and serve.

Serves: 8 · Prep: 35 · Cooking: 30 min. · Level: 2

CROSTINI DI POLENTA CON SALSA AL POMODORO
Fried polenta crostini with tomato sauce

- 1 quantity Tomato and butter sauce (see recipe, page 18)
- 1 quantity Fried polenta crostini (see recipe, this page)

Wine: a light, dry white (Frascati)

Prepare the tomato and butter sauce. • Prepare the fried polenta crostini. • Spread the crostini with the tomato and butter sauce, and serve.

Serves: 8 · Prep: 20 min. · Cooking: 30 min. · Level: 2

Baked polenta with onions

Boat-shaped shells with herb mayonnaise

BARCHETTE
Boat-shaped shells

☞ These small pastry shells are called *barchette* ("little boats") in Italian because of their shape. If you don't have boat-shaped molds, use any small cake mold.

2   cups all-purpose flour
²/₃   cup butter
2–3   tablespoons cold water
         pinch of salt

Sift the flour in a large mixing bowl. Rub in the butter using your fingertips until the mixture is the same texture as coarse meal. • Make a well in the center and add the water and salt. Mix until the dough is soft and smooth. • Shape into a ball, wrap in waxed paper, and chill in the refrigerator for 30 minutes. • Flour a clean work surface and roll the dough out to about ⅛ inch thick. • Line the molds with the dough and prick the bottoms with a fork. Cover with pieces of waxed paper and fill with pie weights or dried beans. • Bake the shells in a preheated oven at 350°F for 12–15 minutes. • Remove the waxed paper and weights or beans, invert the molds and set aside to cool. Fill the shells with mayonnaise, soft fresh cheeses, Onion sauce (see recipe, page 15), or invent new fillings.

Serves: 6 · Prep: 15 min. + 30 min. to chill · Cooking: 15 min. · Level: 1

OLIVE ALL'ASCOLANA
Stuffed fried olives

☞ This dish comes from the Marches region in central Italy. It makes rather a filling appetizer, so be sure to follow with something light.

¼   cup extra-virgin olive oil
5   oz beef, coarsely chopped
5   oz pork, coarsely chopped
3   tablespoons tomato paste
3½   oz chicken livers, coarsely chopped
2   slices firm-textured, day-old bread
4   eggs
¾   cup freshly grated Parmesan cheese
         salt and freshly ground black pepper to taste
         pinch of nutmeg
60   giant green olives, pitted
1   cup all-purpose flour
3   cups fine dry bread crumbs
2   cups oil, for frying
1   lemon, sliced, and small sprigs of parsley, to garnish

Wine: a dry rosé (Rosato di Bolgheri)

Heat the oil in a skillet and sauté the beef and pork for 5 minutes. Add the tomato paste and cook for 10 minutes. • Add the chicken livers and cook for 5 minutes more. • Remove from heat, chop the meat very finely, and return to the skillet. • Soak the bread roll in cold water, squeeze out excess moisture, and crumble. • Add the bread, two eggs, the Parmesan, salt, pepper, and nutmeg to the meat mixture. • Mix well with a fork, then use the mixture to stuff the olives. • Heat the oil in a skillet until very hot, but not smoking. • Arrange three bowls, the first with the flour, the second with 2 beaten eggs, and the third with the bread crumbs. • Dredge the olives in the flour, dip in the egg, then roll in the bread crumbs. Remove excess crumbs by rolling the olives in your hands. • Heat the oil in a large skillet until hot but not smoking, and fry the olives in small batches until crisp and golden brown. Remove from the skillet with a slotted spoon and drain on paper towels. • Garnish with the lemon and parsley. Serve hot.

Serves: 6 · Prep: 30 min. · Cooking: 40 min. · Level: 2

BARCHETTE CON MAIONESE E ERBE
Boat-shaped shells with herb mayonnaise

1   quantity Boat-shaped shells (see recipe, this page)
1   quantity Mayonnaise (see recipe, page 16)
2   hard-boiled eggs, peeled and chopped
2   tablespoons each finely chopped parsley and marjoram

Wine: a light, dry white (Trebbiano di Romagna)

Prepare the shells. • Prepare the mayonnaise. • Place the eggs in a bowl and mix with the parsley, marjoram, and mayonnaise. • Fill the shells with the sauce. • Serve at once before the shells become soggy.

Serves: 4 · Prep: 10 min. + time to make the shells and mayonnaise · Level: 1

BARCHETTE CON FORMAGGIO
Boat-shaped shells with cheese

1   quantity Boat-shaped shells (see recipe, this page)
1   quantity Béchamel sauce (see recipe, page 16)
1   clove garlic, minced
5   oz Gruyère cheese, freshly grated
7   oz Mozzarella cheese, chopped
1   tablespoon each finely chopped thyme and basil

Wine: a dry white (Est! Est!! Est!!!)

Prepare the shells. • Make a thick béchamel sauce. • Add the garlic and cheeses to the béchamel sauce, and stir over very low heat until they have melted. • Stir the herbs into the cheese sauce and fill the shells with it. Bake in a preheated oven at 350°F for 5 minutes, or until the cheese is light golden brown. • Serve hot or at room temperature.

Serves: 6 · Prep: 10 min. + time to make the shells · Cooking: 15 min. · Level: 1

CETRIOLI IN AGRODOLCE
Sweet and sour cucumbers

- 1 lb cucumbers
- 1 large green bell pepper
- 8 oz white onions, thinly sliced
   salt to taste
- 3/4 cup white wine vinegar
- 1/4 cup brown sugar
- 1 tablespoon grated lemon zest
- 1 teaspoon mustard powder
- 1/2 teaspoon nutmeg

Wine: a light, dry white (Colli Albani Secco)

Peel the cucumbers and chop into small cubes. • Clean the bell pepper, removing the core and seeds, and cut into small squares. • Put the cucumber, bell pepper, and onions in a bowl and sprinkle with the salt. Set aside for 4 hours. • Drain and dry with paper towels. • Combine the vinegar, sugar, lemon zest, mustard powder, and nutmeg in a saucepan and bring to the boil, stirring continuously. • Boil gently for 5 minutes, then add the vegetables. Simmer for 10 more minutes. • Remove from heat and set aside to cool. • Chill in the refrigerator for 4 hours before serving.

Serves: 6 · Prep: 20 min.+ 4 hrs to marinate and 4 hrs to chill · Cooking: 15 min. · Level: 1

OLIVE CONDITE
Piquant green olives

☞ This fiery dish comes from Sicily. For best results, use high quality green olives packed in brine. Serve with a basket of freshly baked bread to help offset some of the fire in the dressing.

- 60 large green olives, pitted
- 4 cloves garlic, finely chopped
- 1 tablespoon finely chopped parsley
- 1 tablespoon coarsely chopped fresh mint
   pinch of oregano
- 1 teaspoon red pepper flakes
- 1/4 cup extra-virgin olive oil

Wine: a dry white (Etna Bianco)

Rinse the olives in cold water and pat dry with paper towels. • Lightly crush the olives with a meat-pounding mallet. • Place the olives and garlic in a serving dish. Add the parsley, mint, oregano, pepper flakes, and oil. Mix well and cover. • Set aside in a cool place (not the refrigerator) for 2 hours before serving.

Serves: 6 · Prep: 10 min. + 2 hrs to marinate · Level: 1

ZUCCHINE CRUDE PICCANTI
Zucchini with spicy mayonnaise

- 6 large zucchini
- 1/3 cup white wine vinegar
   salt and freshly ground black pepper to taste
- 1 quantity Mustard mayonnaise (see recipe, page 16)
- 2 tablespoons finely chopped chives

Wine: a dry rosé (Lagrein Rosato)

Rinse the zucchini, trim the ends, and slice thinly lengthwise. • Place in a bowl, add the vinegar, and sprinkle with salt. Mix well and leave to marinate for at least 2 hours. • Prepare the mustard mayonnaise. • Drain the zucchini, squeezing them gently to remove as much vinegar as possible. • Mix the zucchini with the mayonnaise and place in a serving dish. • Sprinkle with the chives and serve.

Serves: 6 · Prep: 20 min. + 2 hrs to marinate · Level: 1

PEPERONI ARROSTITI ALL'ACCIUGA
Broiled bell peppers with anchovies

- 4 medium yellow and red bell peppers
   salt to taste
- 3 cloves garlic, thinly sliced
- 1/4 cup extra-virgin olive oil
- 8 anchovy fillets

Wine: a dry white (Greco di Tufo)

Place the bell peppers whole under the broiler at fairly high heat, giving them quarter turns until their skins scorch and blacken. This will take about 20 minutes. When the peppers are black all over, wrap them in foil (not too tightly) and set aside for 10 minutes. When unwrapped, the skins will peel away easily. • Cut the bell peppers in half lengthwise and discard the stalks, seeds, and the pulpy inner core. Rinse under cold running water to get rid of any remaining burnt skin. • Slice the bell peppers lengthwise into strips about 1¼ inches wide and then place in a colander, sprinkling each layer with a little salt. Leave to drain for at least 1 hour. This will make the bell peppers easier to digest. • Place the garlic in a small saucepan with the oil and cook over very low heat for 3–5 minutes; do not let the garlic color. • Add the anchovies and crush them with a fork until they dissolve in the oil. Cook for 2 more minutes. • Place the bell peppers in a serving dish and drizzle with the anchovy dressing. • Serve at room temperature.

Serves: 4 · Prep: 25 min. + 1 hr to rest · Cooking: 25 min. · Level: 1

Piquant green olives

Fava beans with Pecorino cheese

set aside in a small covered bowl so they do not dry out too much. • Wash the celery, remove any stringy fibers, and cut into 2½-inch pieces. Cut a sliver off the bottom of each piece so they will sit firmly on the plate without rolling over. • Fill the celery with the cheese mixture, top with pieces of shrimp, and serve.

Serves: 4 · Prep: 30 min. · Cooking: 2 min. · Level: 2

POMODORI CON SALSA VERDE
Tomatoes with green sauce and mayonnaise

1   quantity Green sauce (see recipe, page 13)
½   cup Mayonnaise (see recipe, page 16)
4–8   large ripe salad tomatoes

Wine: a dry, lightly sparkling red (Freisa d'Asti)

Prepare the green sauce and the mayonnaise. • Cut the tomatoes in half horizontally. Remove the seeds (but not the fleshy divisions between the seed chambers), and place upside down in a colander to drain for 5–10 minutes. • Mix the green sauce and mayonnaise in a bowl then fill each tomato half with the sauce. Arrange the tomatoes on a serving dish and serve.

Serves: 4 · Prep: 15 min. + time to make the sauces · Level: 1

CIPOLLINE IN AGRODOLCE
Sweet and sour baby onions

1   lb white baby onions
¼   cup prosciutto, coarsely chopped
1   tablespoon extra-virgin olive oil
    salt and freshly ground black pepper to taste
1   tablespoon sugar
3   tablespoons white wine vinegar
    scant ½ cup cold water

Wine: a light, dry white (Colli Albani)

Clean the onions and place in a bowl of cold water. • Sauté the prosciutto in the oil. • Drain the onions and add to the pan. Season with salt and pepper and add the sugar. Pour in the vinegar and water. • Cook over medium-low heat until the onions are tender and the cooking juices have almost all been absorbed. • Serve hot or at room temperature.

Serves: 4 · Prep: 10 min. · Cooking: 35 min. · Level: 1

FAVE CON PECORINO
Fava beans with Pecorino cheese

☞ This appetizer heralds the approach of spring in central Italy. As soon as the first tender fava beans appear in the markets, this dish is served in homes and restaurants throughout Tuscany, Umbria, the Marches, and Lazio.

3   lb raw, young fava beans in their pods
12   oz Pecorino cheese

Wine: a light, dry red (Carmignano Rosso)

Rinse the beans thoroughly under cold running water. Dry well with paper towels. Discard any tough or withered looking pods, or any with ugly spots or marks. • Slice the cheese into large dice or wedges. • Arrange the beans and cheese on an attractive platter and serve.

Serves: 6–8 · Prep: 5 min. · Level: 1

POMODORINI CON RICOTTA
Cherry tomatoes with Ricotta cheese

16   cherry tomatoes
½   tablespoon extra-virgin olive oil
1   small clove garlic, finely chopped
    salt and freshly ground black pepper to taste
8   oz fresh Ricotta cheese
8   fresh basil leaves, torn in half

Wine: a dry white (Vermentino di Gallura)

Wash the tomatoes and dry with paper towels. • Use a sharp knife to slice off a

"lid." Set the lids aside. • Using a small teaspoon, carefully remove the pulp and reserve. Leave the tomatoes upside down to drain for 15 minutes. • In a bowl, mix the oil, garlic, salt, pepper, cheese, and enough of the tomato pulp to make a smooth cream. Don't add all the tomato at once as it may make the cream too liquid. • Stuff the tomatoes with the filling. Place half a basil leaf on each and cover with a "lid." Chill in the refrigerator for about 30 minutes before serving.

Serves: 4 · Prep: 10 min. + 30 min. to chill · Level: 1

COSTE DI SEDANO CON GAMBERI
Celery and shrimp barquettes

1   lb medium shrimp
10   oz Mascarpone cheese
    juice of 1 lemon wedge
1   tablespoon capers, chopped
1   tablespoon chives, chopped
2   teaspoons mustard
5   stalks celery, large but tender

Wine: a dry white (Lambrusco Reggiano)

Bring a pan of salted water to a boil. Add the shrimp, and cook for 2 minutes. Drain and allow to cool. • Put the Mascarpone in a large bowl and add the lemon juice, capers, chives, and mustard. Mix well and refrigerate. • Peel the shrimp, cut into two or three pieces, depending on size, and

BAGNA CAÔDA
Raw vegetables with anchovy dip

☞ This dip recipe comes from Piedmont, where it is served hot on the table in an earthenware pot over a warming apparatus with a selection of raw vegetables. It is also good with cooked vegetables, roast bell peppers, and as a sauce for fresh pasta and potato gnocchi.

- 6 cloves garlic, very finely chopped
- 1/4 cup butter
- 1 tablespoon cold water
- 20 anchovy fillets, finely chopped
- 1 cup extra-virgin olive oil
  platter of well-washed and chopped or sliced raw vegetables, including artichokes, carrots, celery, zucchini, bell peppers, radishes, spring onions, and chicory

Put the garlic in a small pot with 1 tablespoon of butter and the water. Simmer over very low heat and gradually stir in the remaining butter. Take care that the butter and garlic do not brown. • Add the anchovy fillets and the oil a little at a time. Mix well until the anchovies have dissolved in the sauce. Serve hot with the vegetables.

Serves: 4–6 · Prep: 10 min. · Cooking: 15 min. Level: 1

PERE CON GORGONZOLA
Pears with Gorgonzola cheese

- 4 large eating pears
  juice of 2 lemons
- 5 oz Gorgonzola cheese
- 2 tablespoons light cream
- 1/4 cup extra-virgin olive oil
- 1 tablespoon finely chopped mint, plus sprigs
  salt and freshly ground white pepper to taste

Wine: a dry white (Pinot Grigio)

Wash the pears, dry well, and remove the cores with a corer. • Brush the cavities with the juice of 1 lemon. • Put the Gorgonzola and cream in a bowl and mix until smooth and creamy. • Stuff the pears with the mixture, pressing it down so that the cavities are completely filled. • Chill in the cold part of the refrigerator for 1 hour. • Combine the oil, remaining lemon juice, chopped mint, salt, and pepper in a bowl and whisk until well mixed. • Use a sharp knife to cut the pears into thin round slices. • Arrange the rounds on a serving dish and spoon the sauce over the top. • Garnish with sprigs of mint and serve.

Serves: 4 · Prep: 25 min. + 1 hr to chill · Level: 1

PECORINO ALLA SICILIANA
Hot Pecorino cheese appetizer

- 1/4 cup extra-virgin olive oil
- 2–3 cloves garlic, slightly crushed
- 4 slices fresh Pecorino cheese, at least 1/2 in thick
- 2 tablespoons Italian red wine vinegar
- 1 tablespoon finely chopped fresh oregano
  freshly ground black pepper to taste

Wine: a dry red (Sciacca)

Heat the oil in a large skillet. Add the garlic and sauté over a low heat until pale golden brown. • Place the cheese slices in the skillet in a single layer, increase the heat and cook, turning several times with a spatula. • Sprinkle with the vinegar, oregano, and pepper. Cover and cook for 2 more minutes. • Serve hot.

Serves: 4 · Prep: 2 min. · Cooking: 6–7 min. · Level: 1

COSTE DI SEDANO FARCITE
Stuffed celery stalks

- 8 oz Gorgonzola cheese
- 4 oz Mascarpone cheese
- 1/4 cup milk
- 2 cloves garlic, finely chopped
- 1 tablespoon extra-virgin olive oil
  salt and freshly ground black pepper to taste
- 10 large tender stalks celery
- 1 tablespoon finely chopped parsley
- 1 tablespoon finely chopped chives

Wine: a dry white (Orvieto Classico)

Melt the Gorgonzola in a heavy-bottomed saucepan over very low heat. • Remove from heat and add the Mascarpone and enough milk to obtain a dense, creamy mixture. • Add the garlic, oil, salt, and pepper. Mix until smooth. • Cover and chill in the refrigerator for 1 hour. • Trim the celery stalks and remove any stringy fibers. Cut into pieces about 3 inches long. • Fill with the cheese mixture, sprinkle with the parsley and chives, and serve.

Serves: 6 · Prep: 15 min. + 1 hr to chill · Level: 1

PALLE DI GORGONZOLA E SEDANO
Gorgonzola balls with celery

- 3 tablespoons butter, melted
- 6 oz Gorgonzola cheese
- 4 oz Ricotta cheese
- 1 tablespoon extra-virgin olive oil
  juice of 1 lemon
  freshly ground white pepper to taste
- 8 large stalks celery

Wine: a light, dry white (Soave Classico)

Combine the butter, Gorgonzola, and Ricotta in a bowl and mix well. • Gradually stir in the oil, lemon juice, and pepper, until the mixture is dense and creamy. • Shape the cheese mixture into marble-sized balls. Place in a dish, cover with aluminum foil and chill in the refrigerator for 1 hour. • Wash and dry the celery and cut into sticks about 2 inches long and 1/4-inch wide. • Unwrap the cheese balls and serve with the celery.

Serves: 4 · Prep: 20 min. + 1 hr to chill · Level: 1

Stuffed celery stalks

PALLINE DI CAPRINO E FRUTTA
Caprino cheese and fruit salad

- 6 oz Caprino cheese
- 2 oz finely chopped mixed fresh herbs (parsley, chives, mint, thyme, marjoram, tarragon, dill, basil)
- 1 small cantaloupe, about 14 oz
- 1 cucumber, peeled
  juice of 1 orange
  salt and freshly ground black pepper to taste
- 1/4 cup extra-virgin olive oil
- 14 cherry tomatoes
- 8 small round radishes
- 6 oz purple grapes
  fresh spinach leaves

Wine: a dry rosé (Oltrepò Pavese Rosato)

Shape the Caprino into marble-size balls with your hands. Roll the balls in a dish with the chopped herbs until they are well coated. Set aside. • Use a small melon baller to make marble-sized balls from the cantaloupe and cucumber. • Sprinkle the cantaloupe balls with 1 tablespoon of orange juice and dust with black pepper. • Drizzle the cucumber balls with salt and 1 tablespoon of oil. • Wash, dry, and remove the stems from the tomatoes. • Wash, dry, and trim the radishes, cutting off roots and leaves. • Wash and dry the grapes (peel, if preferred). • Line a large serving bowl with the spinach leaves. • Arrange the cheese, vegetables, and fruit on top. • Drizzle with the remaining oil and orange juice just before serving.

Serves: 4–6 · Prep: 25 min. · Level: 1

RICOTTA ALLE ERBE
Ricotta cheese with mixed herbs

☞ Fresh, delicate Ricotta cheese makes an excellent base for other flavors. Serve with fresh bread or a platter of raw vegetables.

- 12 oz very fresh Ricotta cheese
- 12 basil leaves, torn
- 1 tablespoon finely chopped parsley
- 1 tablespoon each finely chopped thyme and chives
- 2 bay leaves
- 1 teaspoon fennel seeds
  salt and freshly ground black pepper to taste

Wine: a light, dry red (Isonzo Merlot)

Combine the Ricotta, basil, parsley, thyme, and chives in a bowl and mix well. • Add the bay leaves, fennel, salt, and pepper, and mix again. • Chill in the refrigerator for 1 hour. • Remove the bay leaves and garnish with sprigs of parsley. • Serve cold.

Serves: 4 · Prep: 10 min. + 1 hr to chill · Level: 1

TORTA DI CRÊPES
Filled crêpes

- 12 freshly made Crêpes (see recipe, page 185)
- 1 cup arugula
- 1 quantity Mayonnaise (see recipe, page 16)
- 2 large carrots, peeled and grated
- 2 tablespoons finely chopped parsley, plus 8 sprigs
- 4 oz Caprino cheese
- 4 hard-boiled eggs, thinly sliced
- 4 oz salami, thinly sliced

Wine: a dry red (Grignolino del Monferrato Casalese)

Prepare the crêpes. • Rinse the arugula under cold running water, drain, and dry well. Chop coarsely. • Place a crêpe on a serving dish, spread with mayonnaise and sprinkle with carrot and parsley. • Cover with a second crêpe, spread with Caprino and sprinkle with arugula. • Cover with a third crêpe, spread with mayonnaise and cover with slices of egg. • Cover with a fourth crêpe, spread with Caprino and cover with slices of salami. • Repeat this sequence until all the ingredients are used up. • Garnish the top with mayonnaise and sprigs of parsley and serve immediately.

Serves: 4–6 · Prep: 10 min. + 30 min. to rest · Cooking: 20 min. · Level: 1

GELATO DI PARMIGIANO
Parmesan cheese ice cream

☞ This unusual appetizer is delicious when served with slices of Parma ham.

- 2 cups light cream
- 3 cups freshly grated Parmesan cheese
  pinch of salt
  pinch of white or chile pepper

Wine: a dry or medium, lightly sparkling red (Lambrusco di Sorbara)

Mix the cream with the Parmesan, salt, and pepper in the top of a double boiler or in a heatproof bowl. Cook over simmering water until the cheese is melted. Remove from heat and set aside to cool. • Pour through a sieve to strain. • Pour the resulting liquid into an ice cream maker and proceed as though making ordinary ice cream. • If you don't have an ice cream maker, pour the liquid into a freezerproof container and freeze, stirring at intervals as the mixture thickens. • After 3 hours in the freezer, take the mixture out and transfer to a food processor. Blend until smooth, then return to the freezer. Repeat this process after another 3 hours' freezing. • Serve with an ice cream scoop or a tablespoon.

Serves: 6 · Prep: 15 min. + 6 hrs to freeze · Level: 1

Ricotta cheese with mixed herbs

Cheese fondue is made throughout the European alps. This recipe comes from the Italian side, in Valle d'Aosta and Piedmont in the northwest. It should be made in the top half of a double boiler so that the ingredients never boil. To serve, transfer to a fondue pot over a low flame so that the cheese stays deliciously warm as your guests dip their pieces of bread or polenta. The gourmet version of this fondue is served with a sprinkling of wafer-thin slices of white truffles from the Alba region in Piedmont.

FONDUTA PIEMONTESE
Piedmontese cheese fondue

- 1 lb (weight without crust) Fontina cheese
- 1¼ cups whole milk
- 3 tablespoons butter
- 5–6 egg yolks
  salt and freshly ground white pepper to taste
  toasted bread or baked or fried polenta,
  cut in cubes

Wine: a dry, full-bodied red (Barbera d'Asti)

Slice the cheese thinly and place in a bowl with enough milk to cover. Leave to stand for 2–4 hours. • Half-fill a saucepan or the bottom pan of a double boiler with water and bring to a very gentle boil. Place a heatproof bowl or the top pan of the double boiler containing the butter over the top and leave to melt. • Drain the milk off from the cheese, reserving the milk. Add the cheese to the melted butter, together with ¼ cup of the milk. • Stir continuously with a whisk or wooden spoon over the simmering water until the cheese has melted and threads start to form. At no point should the mixture be allowed to boil. • Adding one at a time, stir 5 egg yolks into the cheese, incorporating each of them very thoroughly. The mixture should now be glossy and smooth. If it still looks a little grainy, add the final, sixth egg yolk and stir well for 1 minute. • Season with salt and pepper to taste. • Transfer the mixture to a fondue pot and place at the center of the table. Give each guest a fondue fork for dipping the pieces of bread and polenta into the sauce.

Serves: 4 · Prep: 10 min. + 2–4 hrs to stand · Cooking: 10 min. · Level: 2

Piedmontese cheese fondue

Cheese, pear, and walnut molds

SFORMATINI DI FORMAGGIO, PERE E NOCI

Cheese, pear, and walnut molds

- 6 oz Ricotta cheese
- 8 oz each Mascarpone and Gorgonzola cheese
- 2 cups walnuts, shelled and finely chopped
  freshly ground black pepper to taste
- 2 tablespoons brandy
- 4 large sweet pears
- 1 tablespoon butter
- 2 tablespoons finely chopped chives

Wine: a dry white (Fiano di Avellino)

Combine the cheeses in a bowl, mix, then add the walnuts, pepper, and brandy. • Rinse the pears under cold running water, peel, core, and chop the pulp finely. Carefully stir the pulp into the cheese mixture. • Butter six small molds, and fill with the mixture. Chill in the refrigerator for at least 1 hour. • Invert the molds onto serving plates, garnish with the chives, and serve.

Serves: 6 · Prep: 15 min. + 1 hr to chill · Level: 1

CREMA DI PEPERONI

Striped bell pepper cream

- 12 oz each of red, yellow, and green bell peppers
- ½ cup extra-virgin olive oil
- 1 medium onion, finely chopped
- 1½ cups heavy cream
  salt and freshly ground white pepper to taste
- 1 oz gelatin
- 3 cups whole milk
- 6 egg yolks

Wine: a dry white (Greco di Tufo)

Rinse the bell peppers under cold running water and dry well. Cut in half and remove the seeds, filaments, and cores. Cut into small pieces, keeping the colors separate. • Place 2 tablespoons of oil in three separate saucepans, divide the onion in three parts, and sauté a part in each. • When the onion is transparent, add salt, pepper, 2 tablespoons of water, and bell peppers, keeping the colors separate in each pan. • Cover each pan and cook over medium heat for about 30 minutes, or until the bell peppers are soft and well-cooked. • Remove the pans from heat and

let the mixtures cool. • Purée the contents of each pan separately in a food processor. • Soften the gelatin in a little water. • Heat the milk in a large saucepan, without letting it boil. • Beat the egg yolks in a large bowl and add the hot milk a little at a time, stirring continuously. Season with salt and pepper. • Return the milk mixture to the saucepan and heat to boiling, stirring frequently. Stir in the gelatin. • Remove from the heat and beat with a fork until the gelatin has dissolved. • Pour equal parts of the mixture into three different bowls and set aside to cool. • Add one color of bell pepper purée to each and stir. • Whip the cream to stiff peaks and fold in equal parts to each of the three bowls. • Moisten a rectangular mold with water and pour in the yellow mixture. Place the mold in the refrigerator for 10 minutes. • Remove and pour in the red mixture. Return the mold to the refrigerator for 10 more minutes. • Remove again and add the green mixture. • Refrigerate for at least 2 hours. • Dip the mold for a second in hot water and invert the cream on a serving dish. Cut the cream in slices ½-inch thick and serve.

Serves: 4 Prep: 50 min. + 2 hrs to chill · Cooking: 30 min. · Level: 3

SFORMATO DI SEMOLINO

Semolina mold with meat sauce

- 1 quantity Bolognese meat sauce (see recipe, page 19)
- 3 cups whole milk
  salt and freshly ground black pepper to taste
- 1 cup semolina
  pinch of nutmeg
- ½ cup butter
- ¼ cup freshly grated Parmesan cheese
- 2 egg yolks
- 2 tablespoons bread crumbs
- 4 oz Fontina cheese, thinly sliced

Wine: a dry, full-bodied red (Barbera d'Asti)

Prepare the meat sauce. • Heat the milk and a pinch of salt in a large saucepan. • As the milk begins to boil, stir in the semolina. Cook for 10 minutes over low heat, stirring all the time. • Remove from the heat and add the nutmeg, half the butter, the Parmesan, and 2 egg yolks. • Butter a 12-inch pudding mold and sprinkle with bread crumbs. Line the sides and the bottom with the semolina mixture. • Scatter with the Fontina and spread with about one-third of the meat sauce. Fill with the remaining semolina. • Bake in a preheated oven at 400°F for 15–20 minutes. • When cooked, remove from the oven and invert into a casserole. • Return to the oven for a few minutes to brown the top. • Spoon the remaining sauce over the top and serve hot.

Serves: 4 · Prep: 15 min. + time to make the meat sauce · Cooking: 30 min. · Level: 2

INSALATA CAPRICCIOSA
Mixed ham and tongue salad

1/2	cup lean ham
1/2	cup cooked pickled ox tongue
1/2	cup mushrooms preserved in oil
1	large stalk celeriac
	juice of 1/2 lemon
1	cup Mayonnaise (see recipe, page 16)
	pickled vegetables for garnish (optional)

Wine: a young, dry red (Barbera d'Asti)

Slice the ham and tongue into thin strips. • Slice the mushrooms thinly. • Peel the celeriac and cut into julienne strips, sprinkling with lemon juice to prevent discoloration. • Place these four ingredients in a large bowl and mix with the mayonnaise. • Transfer to a serving dish and garnish, if liked, with a selection of pickled vegetables.

Serves: 4 · Prep: 15 min. · Level: 1

CANNOLI DI PROSCIUTTO COTTO
Ham rolls with Ricotta cheese

5	oz fresh Ricotta cheese
1	tablespoon finely chopped parsley
1	tablespoon finely chopped chives
2	teaspoons spicy mustard
	salt and freshly ground black pepper to taste
1/2	cup heavy cream
12	slices ham
4	slices sandwich bread

Wine: a dry white (Soave Superiore Classico)

Place the Ricotta in a mixing bowl and stir in the parsley, chives, and mustard. Season with salt and pepper and mix well. • Beat the cream to stiff peaks and carefully stir into the Ricotta mixture. • Spread one-twelfth of the mixture on a slice of ham and roll it up.

Baked Parmesan puffs

Repeat until all the rolls are made. • Toast the bread and cut each slice into four triangles. • Arrange the rolls on a round serving dish, separating each one with a quarter-slice of toast. • Serve immediately, before the toast becomes soggy.

Serves: 6 · Prep: 15 min. · Level: 1

BIGNÉ AL PARMIGIANO
Baked Parmesan puffs

3/4	cup almonds
2/3	cup cold water
1/4	cup butter
1	cup all-purpose flour, sifted, plus 2 tablespoons for dusting the baking sheet
	salt to taste
3/4	cup freshly grated Parmesan cheese
	pinch of paprika
2	eggs

Wine: a dry, sparkling white (Prosecco)

Blanch and peel the almonds, by placing them in a bowl and pour boiling water over the top so they are barely covered.

Leave for 1 minute. Drain and rinse under cold water. Pat dry and slip off the skins. Chop finely. • Combine the water with 3 tablespoons of butter in a small saucepan. Place over medium heat. When the water starts to boil, remove the pan from the heat and incorporate the flour and salt, stirring constantly with a wooden spoon. • Return the saucepan to the heat and cook until the dough is thick, stirring all the time. • Remove from the heat and stir in the Parmesan and paprika. Set aside to cool. • Add the eggs to the dough one at a time. • Beat the dough vigorously. Transfer to a pastry bag with a smooth tube about 1/4-inch in diameter. • Butter a baking sheet and dust with flour. • Place marble-size balls of dough on the baking sheet and sprinkle with the almonds, making sure they stick to the puffs. • Bake in a preheated oven at 400°F for 15–20 minutes. The puffs will swell as they bake. • Serve cool.

Serves: 4 · Prep: 10 min. · Cooking: 30 min. · Level: 2

with boiling water and a bouillon cube. • Butter a medium-sized mold, line with waxed paper, and fill with the mixture. Put the mold in a large pan of boiling water and leave it for at least 30 minutes. The pâté will finish cooking bain-marie. • Garnish with the parsley and serve.

Serves: 6 · Prep: 25 min. · Cooking: 40 min. · Level: 2

Prosciutto with cantaloupe

FRITTATA ALLA CIOCIARA
Frosinone omelet

- 6 large eggs
- 2 tablespoons pancetta, diced
- 2 tablespoons Mozzarella cheese, diced
- 1 tablespoon shallots, finely chopped
  salt and freshly ground black pepper to taste
- 1/4 cup butter

Wine: a dry rosé (Viganello Rosato)

Combine the eggs, pancetta, Mozzarella, shallots, salt, and pepper in a mixing bowl. • Heat two-thirds of the butter in a skillet over medium heat until light gold. Pour in the egg mixture and stir for a few seconds. Cook until golden brown underneath. Turn the half-cooked omelet out onto a large plate. • Add the remaining butter to the skillet. When it turns gold, return the omelet to the skillet with the other side down and cook until golden brown. • When the egg is cooked (dry, but not overcooked), slip the omelet onto a heated dish and serve at once.

Serves: 2–4 · Prep: 5 min. · Cooking: 10 min. · Level: 1

FRITTATA DI MENTA
Mint omelet

- 6 eggs
- 1/2 cup bread crumbs
- 1 1/4 cups freshly grated Pecorino cheese
- 12 mint leaves, finely chopped
- 2 tablespoons finely chopped parsley
  salt and freshly ground black pepper to taste
- 1/4 cup extra-virgin olive oil

Wine: a dry white (Bianco di Pitigliano)

Beat the eggs until foamy, then add the bread crumbs, Pecorino, mint, parsley, salt, and pepper. Heat the oil in a deep-sided skillet until very hot. • Pour in the egg mixture. Spread it out over the bottom and cook until the underside turns golden brown. • Flip the omelet and cook the other side. • Serve hot.

Serves: 4 · Prep: 10 min. · Cooking: 10 min. · Level: 1

PÂTÉ LOMBARDO
Lombardy pâté

- 5 chicken livers
- 1 lb calf's liver, coarsely chopped
- 1/4 cup butter
- 1 clove garlic, finely chopped
- 2 tablespoons finely chopped parsley +
  sprigs to garnish
  salt and freshly ground black pepper to taste
- 1 cup Marsala wine
- 1 1/2 cups fine dry bread crumbs
- 2 eggs + 2 yolks
- 1 cup freshly grated Parmesan cheese

Wine: a dry red (Oltrepò Pavese)

Remove the bile and connective tissue from the chicken livers and chop coarsely. • Sauté the chicken and calf's liver together in the butter with the garlic and parsley for a few minutes. Season with salt and pepper. • When the liver starts to dry out, add the Marsala and continue cooking for 5–10 minutes, or until the liver is cooked. • Remove the liver and add the bread crumbs to the juices in the pan. Mix well and remove from heat. • Chop the liver with the bread crumbs in a food processor. • Combine the eggs and yolks, liver mixture, and Parmesan in a bowl and stir well. The mixture should be fairly stiff. If it is too dry or firm, soften with a tablespoon or two of stock made

TORTINO DI CARCIOFI
Italian artichoke omelet

- 16 frozen artichoke hearts, thawed
- 1/2 cup all-purpose flour
- 1/2 cup extra-virgin olive oil
- 5 large fresh eggs
  salt and freshly ground black pepper to taste

Wine: a light, dry white (Soave)

Coat the artichoke hearts with flour, shaking off any excess. • Heat all but 2 tablespoons of the oil in a large skillet over high heat until very hot. • Sauté the artichokes for about 8 minutes, turning them several times to cook evenly. When they are lightly browned, drain on paper towels. • Discard the oil used for frying and replace with the remaining oil. Arrange the artichokes in the skillet and return to a moderately high heat. • Beat the eggs lightly with the salt and pepper then pour over the artichokes. Cook for 4–5 minutes. • Turn the omelet carefully and cook for 4 minutes more. It should be firm and lightly browned on both sides. • Turn out onto a heated serving dish and serve.

Serves: 4 · Prep: 10 min. · Cooking: 15 min. · Level: 1

PROSCIUTTO CON MELONE
Prosciutto with cantaloupe

- 16 slices prosciutto (preferably top-quality Parma ham)
- 1 medium cantaloupe

Wine: a light, dry white (Colli Piacentini Pinot Grigio)

Slice the cantaloupe into 8 wedges and remove the skin. • Place the ham slices in the center of a large serving dish. Arrange the melon slices around them and serve.

Serves: 6 · Prep: 10 min. · Level: 1

Italian omelets differ from their French counterparts by being more substantial. I have included them among appetizers since this is how they were traditionally served. Nowadays, they are also served, with salad, as a light lunch or dinner. This is the classic recipe for zucchini omelet; many different types of vegetable can be substituted. Try, for example, replacing the zucchini with 8 baby artichokes, or two medium onions.

TORTINO DI ZUCCHINI
Italian zucchini omelet

3	large zucchini
1/2	cup all-purpose flour
1/2	cup extra-virgin olive oil
6	large fresh eggs
	salt and freshly ground black pepper to taste

Wine: a young, dry white (Bianco Vergine Valdichiana)

Rinse the zucchini under cold running water and dry with paper towels • Slice the zucchini into thin wheels and coat with flour, shaking off any excess. • Heat all but 2 tablespoons of the oil in a large skillet over high heat until very hot. • Sauté the zucchini for about 8 minutes, turning them several times so that they cook evenly. When they are lightly browned, drain on paper towels. • Discard the oil and replace with the remaining oil. Arrange the zucchini in a single layer in the skillet and return to medium-high heat. • Beat the eggs lightly with the salt and pepper, then pour over the zucchini. Cook for 4–5 minutes. • Turn the omelet carefully and cook for 4 minutes more. It should be firm and lightly browned on both sides. • Turn out onto a heated serving dish and serve hot.

Serves: 4 · Prep: 10 min. · Cooking: 15 min. · Level: 1

Italian zucchini omelet

Crabmeat omelet

with the salt and pepper in a mixing bowl then add the prepared crabmeat and mix well. • Heat the remaining oil in the skillet used to fry the crabmeat, and pour in the egg mixture. Cook for 4–5 minutes. • Turn the omelet carefully and cook for 4 minutes more. It should be firm and lightly browned on both sides. • Turn out onto a heated serving dish and serve hot.

Serves: 4 · Prep: 10 min. · Cooking: 15 min. · Level: 1

ACCIUGHE MARINATE ALL'ACETO
Anchovies marinated in vinegar

1	lb fresh anchovies, rinsed and dried
2	cups white wine vinegar
1/3	cup water
	salt to taste
1	tablespoon black peppercorns
2	cloves garlic, sliced
4	bay leaves
2	dried red chilies, crumbled
1/4	cup extra-virgin olive oil

Wine: a dry white (Albana di Romagna Secco)

Clean and bone the anchovies following the instructions on page 201. Arrange them in a single layer in a deep, rectangular dish and cover with the mixed vinegar and water. Add salt and marinate in a cool place for 4 hours. The anchovies will "cook" in the vinegar and turn white. • Drain the anchovies thoroughly and wash the dish. • Arrange them once again in a single layer, if possible, in the dish. • Sprinkle with the peppercorns, garlic, bay leaves, chili, and salt. Drizzle with the oil. • Set aside for 2 hours before serving.

Serves: 4 · Prep: 25 min. + 4 hrs to marinate + 2 hrs to stand · Level: 2

UOVA NEL PRATO
Eggs with mayonnaise

1 1/2	quantities Mayonnaise (see recipe, page 16)
6	hard-boiled eggs, peeled
3	red plum tomatoes
1/4	cup finely chopped parsley
1/4	red and 1/4 yellow bell pepper, cut in small pieces
6	pickled gherkins, sliced

Wine: a dry, aromatic white (Muller Thurgau)

Prepare the mayonnaise and spread two-thirds of it over the bottom of a serving dish. • Cut a slice off the bottom of each egg so they will stand upright. Arrange the eggs in the mayonnaise. • Cut the plum tomatoes in half, remove the pulp and seeds, and place a tomato half on each egg. • Dot the tomato caps with the remaining mayonnaise, to look like the spots on mushrooms. • Garnish the mayonnaise in the serving dish with the parsley, pieces of bell pepper, and pickled gherkin. • Chill in the refrigerator for 30 minutes before serving.

Serves: 4 · Prep: 15 min. + 30 min. to chill · Level: 1

SALAME E FICHI FRESCHI
Salami and fresh figs

1	lb fresh green or black figs
10	oz Tuscan salami, thinly sliced
6	fresh fig leaves (optional)

Wine: a dry, aromatic white (Malvasia del Collio)

Wash the figs thoroughly under cold running water, then pat dry with paper towels. • Remove the rind from the salami. • If using, place the fig leaves on a large serving dish and arrange the salami and figs on top.

Serves: 4–6 · Prep: 5 min. · Level: 1

FRITTATA AL GRANCHIO
Crabmeat omelet

1/2	cup all-purpose flour
14	oz crabmeat, diced
1/2	cup extra-virgin olive oil
8	eggs
	salt and freshly ground black pepper to taste

Wine: a dry white (Traminer del Collio)

Lightly flour the crab meat. Heat 1/4 cup of oil in a medium skillet and fry the crabmeat for 4–5 minutes. • Beat the eggs

UOVA SODE CON PEPERONI
Eggs with tomato and bell pepper sauce

1	green and 1 red bell pepper, cleaned and finely chopped
2	white onions, finely chopped
2	cloves garlic, finely chopped
2	tablespoons finely chopped parsley
2	tablespoons finely chopped fresh basil
	salt and freshly ground black pepper to taste
3	tablespoons extra-virgin olive oil
4	large ripe tomatoes, peeled and coarsely chopped
1	tablespoon vinegar
1/2	tablespoon sugar
6	hard-boiled eggs, peeled

Wine: a dry white (Montecarlo Bianco)

Combine the bell peppers, onion, garlic, parsley, and basil in a skillet with a pinch of salt and the oil and sauté over medium heat. • Add the tomatoes to the skillet and cook over medium heat until the sauce is thick and smooth. • Add the vinegar and sugar, and mix well. Season with salt and pepper. • Remove from heat and set aside to cool. • Cut the hard-boiled eggs in half lengthwise. Remove the yolks, mash, and add to the tomato and bell pepper sauce. Mix well. • Fill the eggs with the bell pepper mixture and arrange them on a serving dish. Pour any extra sauce over the top. • Chill the eggs in the refrigerator for 30 minutes before serving.

Serves: 4–6 · Prep: 40 min. + 30 min. to chill · Cooking: 20 · Level: 1

UOVA BRUSCHE
Eggs rustic-style

- 8 basil leaves, finely chopped
- 3 tablespoons finely chopped parsley
- 2 tablespoons capers, finely chopped
- 5 oz green olives, pitted and finely chopped
- 1 cup freshly grated Parmesan cheese
- 1 cup fine dry bread crumbs
- 3/4 cup dry white wine
   freshly ground black pepper to taste
- 1/4 cup extra-virgin olive oil
- 12 hard-boiled eggs, sliced in half lengthwise

Wine: a dry white (Orvieto Classico)

Mix the basil, parsley, capers, and olives together in a bowl. Stir in the Parmesan and bread crumbs. Gradually stir in the wine. • Add the pepper and gradually stir in the oil. The mixture should be thick but still fluid. • Place the eggs on a platter with the yolks facing up. Pour the mixture over the eggs and serve.

Serves: 6 · Prep: 10 min. · Level: 1

GRANSEOLA ALLA VENEZIANA
Venetian-style crab

☞ The spider crab is the most highly prized of those found in Venice's lagoons. Other types of crab can also be used for this recipe.

- 6 medium spider crabs
   juice of 1 lemon
- 2 tablespoons extra-virgin olive oil
- 2 tablespoons finely chopped parsley
   salt and freshly ground white pepper to taste

Wine: a dry, aromatic white (Bianco di Custoza)

Eggs rustic-style

Clean the crabs by brushing them with a stiff brush under cold running water, then rinse well. • Cook the crabs for 7–10 minutes in salted, boiling water. Insert the tip of a strong knife in the underside, just under the eyes, and lever out the central section of the undershell. Keep the colored, top portions of the shells as serving dishes. • Take all the flesh out of the shells, discarding the grayish, feathery lungs, and reserving the coral (eggs). Cut the white flesh into small pieces. • Use special pincers or a nutcracker to break the hard shell of the legs and claws and take out all the flesh. • Beat the lemon juice, oil, parsley, a generous grinding of pepper, and salt in a bowl to make a dressing. • Wash and dry the empty shells, then arrange them upside down on a serving dish. Fill with the crab meat. Top with the coral as a garnish, sprinkle with the dressing, and serve.

Serves: 6 · Prep: 20 · Cooking: 7–10 min. · Level: 1

COPPINI DI LIMONE AL TONNO
Lemon cups with tuna and mayonnaise

- 4 lemons
- 8 oz tuna, packed in oil
- 2 tablespoons capers
- 8 pickled gherkins
- 2 hard-boiled egg yolks
   extra-virgin olive oil
- 1 quantity Mayonnaise (see recipe, page 16)
   salt to taste
   pickled gherkins, olives, and bell peppers, to garnish

Wine: a dry white (Bianco di Pitigliano)

Cut the lemons in half crosswise. Squeeze out the juice and reserve. • Using a sharp knife, scoop out the insides without piercing the rind. • Chop the tuna fish, capers, pickled gherkins, and egg yolks in a food processor until smooth. • Transfer the mixture to a bowl and add the oil, mayonnaise, salt, and lemon juice. Mix well and fill the lemon cups. • Arrange on a serving dish and garnish with slices of pickled gherkin, olives, and bell pepper.

Serves: 4 · Prep: 20 min. · Level: 1

TROTA IN CARPIONE
Marinated trout

☞ This recipe is also used for other freshwater fish (fillets of tench, carp, barbel), as well as for very small, whole fish which need much shorter cooking times.

- 16 small freshwater trout fillets
- 1/4 cup butter
- 20 fresh sage leaves
    small sprig fresh thyme
- 2/3 cup white wine vinegar
- 2/3 cup dry white wine
- 1–2 bay leaves
- 6 lightly crushed juniper berries
- 1 large onion, sliced about 1/8 inch thick
    salt to taste

Wine: a dry white (Cortese di Gavi)

Clean the fish as shown on page 201. Rinse well inside and out and dry with paper towels. • Place the butter, 5 sage leaves, and thyme in a large skillet over fairly high heat. The butter will foam gently as it heats; as soon as this foam has subsided, it is hot enough to add the trout. • Fry the trout for 5–6 minutes on one side, then turn them over and fry for another 5–6 minutes, or until they are tender. • While the fish are cooking, make the marinade. Bring the vinegar and wine to a boil with the bay leaves, juniper berries, remaining sage leaves, onion, and salt in a saucepan. Simmer over medium heat for 3–4 minutes. Turn off the heat. • As soon as the trout are done, transfer to a fairly deep dish just large enough to contain them in a single layer. Sprinkle with the hot marinade. Leave to cool at room temperature. • When cold, cover the dish with a piece of plastic wrap or foil. Refrigerate for at least 24 hours before serving. • Prepared in this way, the fish will keep for 5–6 days.

Serves: 4 · Prep: 20 min. + 24 hrs to marinate · Cooking: 10–15 min. · Level: 1

PESCIOLINI IN SAOR
Venetian-style marinated fish

☞ In Italy, tiny sole, hake, eel, red mullet, and sardines are used in this recipe. Sprats, whitebait, and baby sardines can be used instead.

- 2 lb baby fish (see above)
- 2 cups all-purpose flour
- 2 cups oil, for frying
    salt to taste
- 1/2 cup extra-virgin olive oil
- 1 lb white onions, very thinly sliced
- 2 cups red wine vinegar

Wine: a light, dry white (Soave Classico)

Rinse the fish under cold running water and dry well. Lightly coat with flour. • Heat the oil in a large skillet until hot but not smoking and fry the fish in batches until pale golden brown. Remove with a slotted spoon and drain on paper towels. Sprinkle with a little salt. • Discard the frying oil and pour the extra-virgin olive oil into the same skillet. Add the onions and cook over medium heat until very tender. • Add the vinegar and season with salt. Simmer for 10 minutes more. Remove from heat. • Arrange the fish and onions in layers in a shallow dish. Pour the vinegar over the top and leave to cool. • Cover with plastic wrap and refrigerate for 2 days before serving.

Serves: 6 · Prep: 30 min. · Cooking: 40 min. + 2 days to marinate · Level: 2

CANOCCHIE
Shrimp with olive oil and lemon juice

☞ The traditional Venetian recipe uses mantis shrimp, which is only found in the Adriatic Sea. Other types of medium or large shrimp can be used in its place.

- 2 lb medium or large raw shrimp, unshelled
- 2 tablespoons extra-virgin olive oil
    juice of 1 lemon
- 2 tablespoons finely chopped parsley
    salt and freshly ground black pepper

Wine: a light, dry white (Breganze Pinot Bianco)

Rinse the shrimp well under cold running water. Bring a large saucepan three-quarters full of salted water to a boil. Add all the shrimp at the same time. As soon as the water returns to a boil, drain the shrimp and spread out on a platter to cool. • Use sharp, pointed scissors to snip away the upper shells covering their backs. Do not remove the heads or tails. • Arrange the shrimp on a large platter. Drizzle with the oil and lemon juice. Sprinkle with the parsley, salt, and pepper, and serve.

Serves: 6 · Prep: 20 min. · Cooking: 5 min. · Level: 2

CORNETTI DI SALMONE CON INSALATA RUSSA
Smoked salmon cones with potato salad

- 7 oz potatoes
- 1 medium carrot
- 2 oz green beans
- 1 quantity Mayonnaise (see recipe, page 16)
- 3/4 cup frozen peas, thawed
- 2 tablespoons capers
- 2 tablespoons diced pickled gherkins
    salt and freshly ground black pepper to taste
- 8 slices smoked salmon (about 8 oz)
- 2 hard-boiled eggs, peeled and sliced
    sprigs of parsley, to garnish

Wine: a dry white (Riesling dell'Alto Adige)

Wash and peel the potatoes and cut into small cubes. Scrape the carrots and cut into small cubes. Snap the ends off the green beans and cut in small pieces. • Boil the potatoes, carrots, and green beans in a pot of salted, boiling water for 15–20 minutes. •

Venetian-style marinated fish

Octopus salad

Drain the vegetables and set aside to cool. • Prepare the mayonnaise. • When cold, combine the cooked vegetables in a pot with the peas, capers, pickled gherkins, and pepper. Add the mayonnaise, reserving some for the garnish, and mix well. • Arrange the slices of smoked salmon on a serving platter and put a spoonful of potato salad on the center of each slice. • Roll the salmon up around the salad into a cone. • Garnish with the remaining mayonnaise, hard-boiled eggs, and parsley. • Serve cold.

Serves: 4 · Prep: 40 min. · Cooking: 20 min. · Level: 1

INSALATA DI POLPO
Octopus salad

2	lb octopus
1	cup white wine vinegar
1	carrot
1	stalk celery
1	small onion
1	clove garlic
5	sprigs parsley
	salt and freshly ground black pepper to taste
¼	cup extra-virgin olive oil
	juice of 1 lemon
½	teaspoon crushed red pepper flakes

Wine: a dry white (Bianco del Vesuvio)

Clean the octopus as explained on page 200. • Place the octopus in a large pot of cold water with the vinegar, carrot, celery, onion, garlic, parsley, and salt. Cover and bring to a boil over high heat. Lower the heat and simmer for 1 hour. • Remove from the heat and leave to cool for at least 2 hours in the cooking water. This is very important because it makes the octopus meat tender. • Skin the octopus (it will come away easily together with the suckers – a few of the latter can be added to the salad). Cut the body in rings and the tentacles in small pieces. • Transfer to a serving dish and season with oil, lemon juice, salt, pepper, and pepper flakes. • Toss well and serve.

Serves: 6 · Prep: 30 min.+ 2 hrs to soften · Cooking: 1 hr · Level: 2

INSALATA DI MARE
Seafood salad

1	lb squid
14	oz cuttlefish
	salt and freshly ground black pepper to taste
14	oz shrimp, unshelled
14	oz clams, in shell
14	oz mussels, in shell
¼	cup extra-virgin olive oil
2	tablespoons finely chopped parsley
2	cloves garlic, finely chopped
1	teaspoon crushed red pepper flakes (optional)
	juice of ½ lemon

Wine: a dry white (Greco di Tufo)

Clean the squid as explained on page 200. • To clean the cuttlefish, cut each one lengthwise and remove the internal bone and the stomach. Discard the internal ink sac. • Place the cuttlefish in a pot with 5 pints of cold water and 1 tablespoon of salt and bring to a boil over high heat. • When the cuttlefish have been simmering for 5 minutes, add the squid and cook for 25 more minutes. • Drain and set aside to cool. • Chop the tentacles in small pieces and then slice the bodies in rings. Transfer to a salad bowl. • Bring 6 cups of water and 1 tablespoon of salt to a boil. Rinse the shrimp thoroughly and add to the pot. Cook for 2 minutes. Drain and set aside to cool. • Shell the shrimp and add to the salad bowl. • Soak the clams and mussels in a large bowl of water for 1 hour to purge them of sand. Pull the beards off the mussels. Scrub well and rinse in plenty of cold water. • Place the shellfish in a large skillet with 2 tablespoons of the oil and cook over medium heat until they are all open. Discard any that have not opened. • Discard the shells and add the mussels and clams to the salad bowl. • Mix the parsley, garlic, red pepper flakes, if using, lemon juice, the remaining oil, salt, and pepper in a bowl. Pour over the salad and toss well. • Place in the refrigerator for 30 minutes before serving.

Serves: 8 · Prep: 1 hr + 30 min. to chill · Cooking: 40 min. · Level: 2

SFORMATI DI GAMBERI
Shrimp molds

1½ lb shrimp
1¼ cups whole milk
3 eggs
bunch of chives, finely chopped
salt and freshly ground black pepper to taste
1 tablespoon butter

Wine: a dry white (Orvieto Classico)

Shell the shrimp and remove the dark intestinal veins. Chop off the heads, and rinse thoroughly in cold running water. Dry well and chop into small pieces. • Combine the milk, eggs, chives, salt, and pepper in a bowl and beat with a fork until well mixed. • Add the shrimp and pour the mixture into six 4-inch buttered molds. • Place a large pan filled with water in the oven and heat to 350°F. Place the molds in the water and cook bain-marie for 30 minutes. • Serve warm or cold.

Serves: 6 · Prep: 40 min. · Cooking: 30 min. · Level: 2

VOL-AU-VENT AI GAMBERI
Shrimp vol-au-vents

2 oz shrimp tails
3 tablespoons butter
3 tablespoons flour
1 cup milk
few drops lemon juice
1 tablespoon finely chopped chives
1 teaspoon paprika
salt and freshly ground black pepper to taste
24 small vol-au-vent shells

Wine: a dry white (Malvasia di Casorzo d'Asti)

Bring a small saucepan of salted water to a boil. Add the shrimp and cook for 1 minute. Drain, allow to cool, peel, and coarsely chop. • Melt the butter in a saucepan over low heat, add the flour and cook for 2 minutes, stirring continuously. • Remove from heat and pour in the milk all at once. Return to a slightly higher heat and cook until boiling and thickened. • Remove from heat, and stir in the shrimp, lemon juice, chives, paprika, salt, and pepper. • Fill the vol-au-vent shells with the mixture, and arrange them on a lightly greased baking sheet. • Bake in a preheated oven at 400°F for about 10 minutes. • Serve at room temperature.

Serves: 6 · Prep: 25 min. · Cooking: 22 min. · Level: 2

COCKTAIL DI GAMBERI ALL'ARANCIA
Orange-flavored shrimp cocktail

1¼ lb shrimp tails
1 quantity Mayonnaise (see recipe, page 16)
¼ cup catsup
4 drops hot pepper sauce
1 large orange
6 large unblemished lettuce leaves

Wine: a dry white (Sauvignon delle Venezie)

Fill a large pan with salted water and bring to a boil. Add the shrimp and cook for 2 minutes. Drain and set aside to cool. • In a serving bowl, mix the mayonnaise, catsup, and pepper sauce. • Peel the upper layer of the orange (orange part only) and cut into fine julienne strips. • Squeeze the orange to obtain ½ cup of juice. • Peel the shrimp and mix into the sauce. • Place a lettuce leaf in each of 6 glass or china ramekins. • Divide the shrimp cocktail equally between the ramekins and garnish with a few strips of orange peel. Chill in the refrigerator for 5 minutes before serving.

Serves: 6 · Prep: 35 min. · Cooking: 2 min. · Level: 2

CALAMARI FRITTI ALLE MANDORLE
Deep-fried calamari with almonds

½ cup all-purpose flour
salt and freshly ground black pepper to taste
2 eggs, beaten
2 cups fine dry bread crumbs
½ cup almonds, finely chopped
4 cups oil, for frying
14 oz calamari bodies, cut in ¼-inch wide rings
8 sprigs parsley, to garnish
1 lemon, sliced, to garnish

Wine: a dry white (Colli Euganei bianco)

Place the flour, salt, and pepper in a bowl. Put the eggs in another bowl, and the bread crumbs and the almonds in another. • Roll the calamari in the flour, shaking off any excess. Dip in the egg and roll in the bread crumbs and almonds. • Heat the oil in a skillet until hot but not smoking, and fry the calamari in batches. Remove with a slotted spoon as they turn golden brown (about 5 minutes) and drain on paper towels. Do not cook for longer or they will become tough. • Garnish with the parsley and lemon and serve.

Serves: 4 · Prep: 15 min. · Cooking: 20 min. · Level: 2

PESCE FINTO
False fish

☞ Children, even those who won't normally eat fish, usually like this dish. When preparing it for youngsters, place the capers strategically to represent the eyes, fins, and scales.

1½ lb potatoes
8 oz tuna, packed in oil
2 cloves garlic, finely chopped
3 tablespoons finely chopped parsley
salt to taste
1 quantity Mayonnaise (see recipe, page 16).
1 tablespoon capers, to garnish

Wine: a dry white (Orvieto Classico)

Cook the potatoes in their skins in a large pan of salted, boiling water for 25 minutes, or until tender • Drain, and slip the skins off with your fingers. Mash well. • When the potatoes are lukewarm, add the tuna, garlic, and parsley. Season with salt and mix well. • Spoon the mixture onto a large serving platter and mold it into a fish shape. Cover with mayonnaise and decorate with capers. • Chill in the refrigerator for 30 minutes before serving.

Serves: 4 · Prep: 20 min. · Cooking: 25 min. · Level: 1

MOUSSE DI TONNO
Tuna mousse

12 oz tuna, packed in oil
8 oz Mascarpone cheese
3 oz pickled onions, well drained and finely chopped
1 tablespoon finely chopped parsley
salt and freshly ground black pepper to taste
1 tablespoon butter
2 cups arugula
12 black olives, pitted and chopped

Wine: a dry white (Locorotondo)

Chop the tuna in a food processor for 1–2 minutes. • Transfer to a bowl and stir in the Mascarpone. Add the pickled onions and parsley and mix well. Season with salt and pepper. • Lightly butter an 8-inch pudding mold and line with aluminum foil. Fill with the tuna mixture and chill in the refrigerator for 6 hours. • Wash and dry the arugula and arrange on a serving dish. Invert the mousse onto the bed of arugula. Garnish with the olives and serve.

Serves: 4 · Prep: 15 min. + 6 hrs to chill · Level: 1

Deep-fried calamari with almonds

Spicy calamari with parsley

CALAMARI AL PREZZEMOLO
Spicy calamari with parsley

- 2 cloves garlic and 1 bunch parsley, finely chopped
- 2 dried red chiles, crumbled
- ¼ cup extra-virgin olive oil
- 8 calamari, cleaned (see page 200)
- ½ cup dry white wine
- 8 slices toasted bread

Wine: a dry white (Chardonnay)

In a large skillet, sauté the garlic, parsley, and chiles in the oil for 2 minutes. • Add the calamari and cook over high heat for 8 minutes. • Pour in the wine and cook until the calamari are tender. • Stir in the parsley and mix well. • Put the toast in a serving dish and spoon the calamari and their sauce over the top. Serve hot or warm.

Serves: 6 · Prep: 10 min. · Cooking: 20 min. · Level: 1

COZZE GRATINATE AL FORNO
Baked mussels

- 2 lb mussels, in shell
- 2 tablespoons finely chopped parsley
- 2 cloves garlic, finely chopped
- 1¾ cups fine dry bread crumbs
- 3 tablespoons extra-virgin olive oil
  salt and freshly ground black pepper to taste
- 1 tablespoon butter
  juice of 1 small lemon

Wine: a dry white (Colli di Luni Bianco)

Soak the mussels in a large bowl of water for 1 hour. Pull off their beards, scrub, and rinse under cold running water. • Place in a skillet, cover, and cook over medium heat until they are open. Discard any that have not opened. Reserve the cooking liquid. • Mix the parsley and garlic together in a bowl with the bread crumbs, 1 tablespoon of oil, salt, and pepper. Strain the cooking liquid and add 3 tablespoons to the bread mixture. Mix well. • Place the mussels in a buttered ovenproof dish. Fill each one with some of the mixture and drizzle with the remaining oil and lemon juice. • Bake in a preheated oven at 400°F for 15–20 minutes, or until the bread crumbs are golden brown. • Serve hot.

Serves: 4 · Prep: 30 min. + 1 hr to soak mussels · Cooking: 15 min. · Level: 1

COZZE IMPAZZITE
Spicy mussels

- 1½ lb mussels, in shell
- ¼ cup finely chopped parsley
- 1 clove garlic, finely chopped
- 2 tablespoons extra-virgin olive oil
  salt to taste
- 2 teaspoons freshly ground black pepper
- 6 slices Bruschetta (see recipe, page 76)

Wine: a dry white (Corvo di Salaparuta)

Soak the mussels in a large bowl of water for 1 hour. Pull off their beards, scrub, and rinse in cold running water. • Sauté the parsley and garlic in a skillet with the oil for 4–5 minutes. Season with salt. • Add the mussels and cook over medium heat until they are open. Discard any that do not open. • Add the pepper and cook for 2 minutes more, stirring all the time. • Prepare the bruschetta and place a slice in each serving dish. Cover with mussels and spoon some of the sauce from the skillet over each one. • Serve hot.

Serves: 6 · Prep: 10 min. + 1 hr to soak mussels · Cooking: 10 min. · Level: 1

VONGOLE CON PANNA FRESCA
Clams in cream sauce

- 4 lb clams, in shell
- 1 cup dry white wine
- 1 medium onion, finely chopped
- 2 cloves garlic, finely chopped
- ¼ cup butter
- 2 tablespoons all-purpose flour
  salt and freshly ground black pepper to taste
- 1¼ cups light cream
- 1 egg, beaten
- 1 tablespoon finely chopped parsley
  juice of ½ lemon

Wine: a dry white (Roero Arneis)

Soak the clams in a large bowl of water for 1 hour. Rinse well in cold water. • Place in a skillet with the wine, cover, and cook over high heat until they open. Discard any that do not open. Set aside in a warm place. • Strain the liquid left in the skillet and reserve. • In the same skillet, sauté the onion and garlic in the butter until soft. Add the flour and mix well. • Gradually add the clam liquid and mix until thick and creamy. Season with salt and pepper. • Beat the cream, egg, parsley, and lemon juice together and add to the sauce. Mix well and pour over the clams. • Serve hot.

Serves: 6 · Prep: 30 min. + 1 hr to soak clams · Cooking: 15 min. · Level: 1

VONGOLE IN BIANCO
Clams with garlic and white wine

- 2 lb very fresh clams, in shell
- ½ cup extra-virgin olive oil
- 2 cloves garlic, peeled and lightly crushed
- 1 cup dry white wine
- 2 tablespoons finely chopped parsley
  freshly ground black pepper to taste

Wine: a dry white (Breganze Pinot Grigio)

Soak the clams in a large bowl of water for 1 hour to purge them of sand. Rinse well in cold running water. • Place in a skillet with the oil and garlic, cover, and cook over high heat until they open. Discard any that have not opened. • Add the wine, parsley, and pepper, then cook for 5 minutes more. Serve hot.

Serves: 6 · Prep: 20 min. + 1 hr to soak clams · Cooking: 15 min. · Level: 1

CAPE SANTE CON FUNGHI
Baked scallops with mushrooms

☞ Scallops are always attractive when served in their shells. However, since scallops are almost always shucked immediately after harvest, you normally won't be able to buy them in their shells. Ask your fish vendor for shells.

- 12 oz fresh button mushrooms
- 1 small onion, finely chopped
- 1 clove garlic, finely chopped
- ¼ cup butter
- ½ tablespoon finely chopped fresh thyme
- ¼ cup chopped ham
  salt and freshly ground black pepper to taste
- 1 quantity Béchamel sauce (see recipe, page 16)
- 6 large sea scallops, about 1 lb
- ¼ cup freshly grated Parmesan cheese

Wine: a dry white (Gavi di Gavi)

Trim the mushrooms, wash carefully, and pat dry with paper towels. Chop coarsely. • Sauté the onion and garlic in 3 tablespoons of butter until soft. Add the thyme, ham, and mushrooms. Season with salt and pepper and cook for 10 minutes. • Prepare the béchamel sauce. • Use the remaining butter to grease the scallop shells or a baking pan large enough to hold the scallops in a single layer. • Chop the scallop meat coarsely

Venetian-style scallops

and place in the shells or baking pan. • Stir the mushroom mixture into the béchamel sauce and spoon over the scallops. • Sprinkle with the Parmesan and bake in a preheated oven at 400°F for 10–15 minutes. • Serve hot.

Serves: 6 · Prep: 15 min. · Cooking: 30 min. · Level: 2

CAPE SANTE ALLA VENETA
Venetian-style scallops

- 4 large sea scallops, about ¾ lb
- 2 tablespoons finely chopped parsley
- 1 clove garlic, finely chopped
- ¼ cup extra-virgin olive oil
  salt and freshly ground black pepper to taste
  juice of 1 lemon

Wine: a dry white (Breganze Pinot Grigio)

In a large skillet, sauté the parsley and garlic with the scallops in the oil over high heat for 4–5 minutes, or until the scallops are just tender. Do not overcook the scallops. Season with salt and pepper. • Spoon the mixture into 4–8 scallop shells

or into 4 individual serving dishes. Drizzle with the lemon juice and serve.

Serves: 6 · Prep: 10 min. · Cooking: 10–15 min. · Level: 1

ANTIPASTO DI PESCE
Fish appetizer

- ½ quantity Mayonnaise (see recipe, page 16)
- 14 oz boiled fish fillets (hake, sea bream, sea bass)
- 3 boiled potatoes, peeled and diced
- 1 tablespoon finely chopped parsley
- 1 tablespoon capers
  salt and freshly ground black pepper to taste
- 4 curved inner leaves from a lettuce heart
  lemon and sprigs of parsley, to garnish

Wine: a dry white (Verduzzo Friulano)

Prepare the mayonnaise. • Chop the boiled fish and mix with the diced potatoes. • Add the parsley, capers, mayonnaise, salt, and pepper. Mix carefully. • Spoon the mixture into the lettuce leaves. Chill in the refrigerator for 30 minutes before serving. Garnish with slices of lemon and sprigs of parsley.

Serves: 4 · Prep: 15 min. + 30 mins to chill · Level: 1

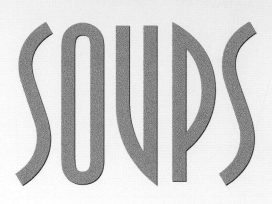

SOUPS

There is nothing more heartening on a cold winter's evening than a bowl of hot soup. Not surprisingly, many of the best soups come from northern Italy where the winters, while not unpleasantly long, can be gelid. Most of the traditional recipes are quite hearty and are based on rice, pasta, or legumes. Homemade stock is a basic ingredient in most soups, so we have included four basic recipes for stock in this chapter.

MACCO DI FAVE
Fava bean soup

☞ This recipe comes from Calabria, in the south. Its origins date back at least 2000 years to Roman times, when soups made from legumes or grains were an important part of the diet. The name comes from the Italian word *maccare*, which means "to crush."

1½ cups dry fava beans
¼   cup extra-virgin olive oil
1   lb peeled and chopped fresh or canned tomatoes
1   large onion, thinly sliced
3   celery stalks, finely chopped
2¼   quarts cold water
     salt and freshly ground black pepper to taste
¼   cup freshly grated Pecorino cheese (optional)

Wine: a dry red (San Severo Rosso)

Soak the fava beans in enough cold water to cover for 12 hours. • Drain the fava beans and combine with 2 tablespoons of the oil, the tomatoes, onion, and celery in a heavy-bottomed pan or earthenware pot. Add the water. • Partially cover and cook over low heat for 3 hours, stirring frequently and mashing the fava beans with a fork. They should be soft and mushy. • When cooked, add salt, pepper, and the remaining oil. • Sprinkle with the Pecorino, if using, and serve hot.

Serves: 4 · Prep: 15 min. + 12 hrs to soak the fava beans · Cooking: 3 hrs · Level: 1

◁ Roman cauliflower soup
(see recipe, page 114)
◣ Fava bean soup

PREPARING STOCK

Stock is widely used in Italian cooking and, while you can always substitute a bouillon cube and boiling water in any of the recipes where it is required, the best results will be achieved using homemade stock. Stock is easy to make and freezes well, so make it in large quantities and freeze to be used when needed.

Chicken stock

BRODO DI POLLO
Chicken stock

☞ If possible, use free-range chickens when making stock; they will take slightly longer to cook but the stock will be much tastier. In Italy, capons are sometimes used to make a "sweeter" stock, suitable for tortellini, agnolotti, or other pasta shapes traditionally served in hot stock.

1	chicken, cleaned, about 4 lb
2	celery stalks, 2 medium carrots, cut in half
1	large onion, stuck with 4 cloves (optional)
4	black peppercorns
	salt to taste
4	quarts cold water

Place the chicken in a large pot with the celery, carrots, onion, and peppercorns. Cover with the water and simmer for 3 hours over low heat. • Filter the stock, discarding the vegetables. The chicken can be served hot or cold with a sauce (try *Spicy tomato*–see recipe, page 14; *Bell pepper*–see recipe, page 15; *Grape juice*–see recipe, page 21). • To remove the fat, in part or completely, let the stock cool, then refrigerate for about 2 hours. The fat will solidify on the top and can be lifted off.

Makes: about 3 quarts · Prep: 10 min. · Cooking: 3 hrs · Level: 1

BRODO DI VERDURE
Vegetable stock

☞ Vegetable stock is deliciously light and refreshing. Vegetarians can use it in recipes that call for chicken, beef, or fish stock.

1/4	cup extra-virgin olive oil (or butter)
2	onions, 2 carrots, 2 leeks, 2 stalks celery, with leaves, all cut in half
4	tomatoes, cut in half
6	sprigs parsley
8	black peppercorns
2	cloves
1	bay leaf
4	quarts cold water
	salt to taste

Heat the oil (or butter) in a large, heavy-bottomed pan and sauté the onions, carrots, leeks, celery, tomatoes, parsley, peppercorns, cloves, and bay leaf over low heat for 8–10 minutes. • Pour in the water, season lightly with salt, and simmer for 1 hour over low heat, skimming off any foam as it forms. • Filter the stock when ready. • The vegetables can either be discarded or puréed in a food processor then combined with 2–4 cups of the stock to make a light, nourishing soup.

Makes: about 3 quarts · Prep: · 15 min. · Cooking: 1¼ hrs · Level: 1

BRODO DI PESCE
Fish stock

☞ Fish stock makes an appetizing change from beef stock as the basis for pasta soups.

1¼	lb assorted fresh fish, such as hake, sea bass, sea bream, and red snapper, cleaned and gutted
2	stalks celery
1	carrot
1	medium onion
4	ripe tomatoes
4	cloves garlic
2	tablespoons coarsely chopped parsley
2	quarts cold water
	salt to taste

Place the fish, vegetables, garlic, and parsley in a large pot with the water. Bring to the boil. • Partially cover and simmer over low heat for 1 hour. Season with salt and simmer for 15 more minutes. • Filter the stock into a bowl, discarding the vegetables and fish. When cool, place in the refrigerator.

Makes: about 1½ quarts · Prep: 15 min. · Cooking: 1¼ hrs · Level: 1

Making stock

BRODO DI CARNE
Beef stock

- 2 lb beef
- 2 lb meat bones
- 1 large carrot
- 1 large onion
- 1 stalk celery
- 1 whole clove
- 2 bay leaves
- 1 clove garlic
- 5 sprigs parsley
- 1 leek
- 2 very ripe tomatoes
- 4 quarts cold water
  salt and freshly ground
  black pepper to taste

Makes: about 3 quarts · Preparation: 15 min. ·
Cooking: 3 hrs · Level: 1

☞ Beef stock is the most commonly used stock in Italian cooking. It is used in countless recipes, from soups, to risotto and pasta recipes, to sauces and meat dishes. It will keep in the refrigerator for up to 3 days. To freeze stock, pour it into small containers (ice-cube trays or small plastic bowls are ideal), unmold it as soon as it is solid, and place in plastic bags. This way, if a recipe calls for small quantities of stock you will not waste the rest.

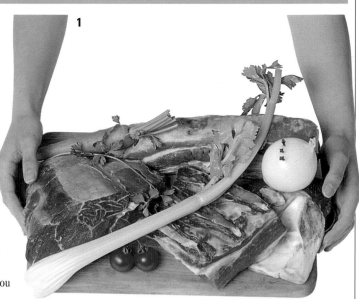

1 Rinse and peel or scrape the vegetables. If using cloves, stick them into the onion. Use very ripe tomatoes. Add the leaves of the celery stalk too.

2 Place a large pot containing the water over low heat and add the meat and bones. The water should come slowly to the boil and barely move throughout the cooking time.

3 Add the vegetables, herbs, and spices. Season with salt and pepper. Add just a little salt at the beginning; you can always add more during cooking.

4 Skim the stock during cooking to remove the scum that will rise to the surface at first abundantly and then tapering off. Cook the stock for 3 hours over very low heat.

5 Filter the stock into a bowl, discarding the vegetables. (The meat can be served with a favorite sauce–see the recipes in the Sauces chapter, pages 12–21). When the stock is completely cool, place in the refrigerator. If you wish to remove the fat, it will solidify on the top and can be lifted off and discarded.

Tuscan vegetable and bread soup

RIBOLLITA
Tuscan vegetable and bread soup

☞ Ribollita is a peasant dish from Tuscany. This is the basic recipe, to which you can add seasonal vegetables, including new potatoes, French beans, zucchini, peas, or whatever else you have on hand.

- 4 cherry tomatoes, pricked with a fork
- 1 lb fresh cannellini beans or 1¼ cups dry cannellini beans, soaked for 12 hours in cold water
- 2 cloves garlic
- 4 leaves fresh sage
   salt and freshly ground black pepper to taste
- 2 tablespoons finely chopped parsley
- 1 small sprig fresh thyme
- 1 onion, thinly sliced
- 1 leek, thinly sliced
- 2 medium carrots, diced
- 8 oz Swiss chard, shredded
- ½ small Savoy cabbage, shredded
- 1 (15 oz) can Italian tomatoes, coarsely chopped
- ¾ cup extra-virgin olive oil
- 5 cups Beef stock (see recipe, page 105)
- 10 oz firm-textured white or brown bread, sliced about ½-inch thick

Wine: a young, dry red (Chianti dei Colli Fiorentini)

Place the cherry tomatoes in a large, heavy-bottomed pan with the beans, garlic, and sage. Cover with cold water. If using fresh beans, season with salt. If using dry beans, wait to add salt until they are almost cooked or they will be tough. • Bring slowly to a boil, cover, and simmer for about 25 minutes for fresh beans or about 1 hour for dry beans. • Discard the garlic and sage and purée half the beans in a food processor. • Put the parsley, thyme, onion, leek, carrots, Swiss chard, cabbage, tomatoes, and ¼ cup of oil in a large, heavy-bottomed saucepan. Sauté over medium heat for a few minutes. • Add the puréed beans and the whole beans, and about two-thirds of the stock. Taste for salt. Cover and simmer for 1½ hours, adding more stock if the soup becomes too thick. • Heat another large, heavy-bottomed saucepan and add a ladle or two of the soup and a slice of bread. Keep adding more soup and bread until all the bread and soup are in the pan. Drizzle with ¼ cup of oil and sprinkle with pepper. Cover and leave to stand for 2–3 hours. • Return to heat and bring slowly to a boil. Simmer very gently for 20 minutes without stirring. Alternatively, reheat the soup in a preheated oven at 425°F for 10 minutes. •

Drizzle with the remaining oil and serve hot or at room temperature.

Serves: 6–8 · Prep: 45 min. + 2–3 hrs to stand · Cooking: 2–3 hrs · Level: 1

ZUPPA DI FAVE
Fava bean minestrone

- 1¾ cups dried fava beans
   salt and freshly ground black pepper to taste
- ¼ cup extra-virgin olive oil
- ¼ cup pancetta, diced
- 1 medium onion, finely chopped
- 1 stalk celery, finely chopped
- 1 carrot, finely chopped
- 2 tablespoons finely chopped parsley
- 15 oz peeled and chopped fresh or canned tomatoes
- 4 oz prosciutto, diced
- 1 cup boiling water
- 2 large, thick slices firm-textured day-old bread

Wine: a dry rosé (Rosato di Castel del Monte)

Soak the fava beans in enough cold water to cover for 12 hours. • Drain the beans and cook in a pot of unsalted water for 1 hour, or until tender. When cooked, season with salt. • Heat the oil in a large, heavy-bottomed pot and sauté the pancetta, onion, celery, carrot, and parsley until soft. • Add the tomatoes and cook over medium heat for 15 minutes. • Add the prosciutto and cook for 2–3 minutes. • Season with salt and pepper, then add the beans and boiling water. Cook for 10 minutes, stirring frequently. • Toast the bread and place a half slice in the bottom of 4 individual soup plates. Ladle the soup over the top and serve hot.

Serves: 4 · Prep: 10 min. + 12 hrs to soak the beans · Cooking: 1½ hrs · Level: 1

ZUPPA DI LENTICCHIE
Lentil soup

- 1¾ cups dry lentils
- 1 large onion, finely chopped
- 2 medium carrots, diced
- 2 stalks celery, thinly sliced
- 1 bay leaf
- 2 cloves garlic, finely chopped
- 4 fresh sage leaves, finely chopped
- 2 tablespoons finely chopped fresh rosemary
   salt and freshly ground white or black pepper to taste
- ¼ cup extra-virgin olive oil

Wine: a dry red (Chianti dei Colli Aretini)

Soak the lentils in enough cold water to cover for 3 hours. • Drain the lentils and place in a saucepan with the onion, carrots, celery, bay leaf, and garlic. Add enough cold water to cover to about 2 inches above the level of the lentils. • Cover and cook over low heat for 45 minutes. • Discard the bay leaf, add the sage and rosemary, and cook, still covered and over low heat, for 5–10 minutes more. • The lentils should be very soft. Season with salt and pepper, drizzle with oil, and serve.

Serves: 4 · Prep: 10 min. + 3 hrs to soak the lentils · Cooking: 50 min. · Level: 1

ZUPPA DI VINO BIANCO
White wine soup

3	cups dry white wine (Sauvignon or Pinot Grigio)
2	tablespoons sugar
1/2	teaspoon cinnamon
1/2	teaspoon nutmeg
1/4	cup butter
3	tablespoons all-purpose flour
3	cups milk
	salt and freshly ground black pepper to taste
6	egg yolks
1/4	cup freshly grated Parmesan cheese

Wine: a dry white (Sauvignon or Pinot Grigio)

Bring the wine to the boil and stir in the sugar, cinnamon, and nutmeg. • Melt the butter in a large, heavy-bottomed pan and stir in the flour. Gradually add the milk and stir to make a creamy sauce. Season with salt and pepper. • Pour the hot wine into the sauce and stir until smooth. • Stir the egg yolks in just before removing from heat. Sprinkle with the Parmesan and serve.

Serves: 4 · Prep: 10 min. · Cooking: 20 min. · Level: 1

MINESTRONE LOMBARDO
Lombardy-style minestrone

1	cup diced pancetta
3	cloves garlic, finely chopped
1	onion, coarsely chopped
4	stalks celery, sliced
2	tablespoons parsley, coarsely chopped
3	sage leaves, coarsely chopped
1	tablespoon finely chopped fresh rosemary leaves
1	potato, 2 carrots, 2 zucchini, 2 tomatoes, all diced
1	cup fresh red kidney beans
6	pints boiling water
1/2	Savoy cabbage, coarsely chopped
1/2	cup shelled peas
	salt and freshly ground black pepper
3/4	cup short-grain rice
1/4	cup freshly grated Parmesan cheese

Wine: a dry rosé (Biferno Rosato)

Put the pancetta, garlic, onion, celery, parsley, sage, rosemary, potato, carrots, zucchini, tomatoes, and beans in a large pot. Add the water, cover, and simmer over low heat for 1 1/4 hours. • Add the cabbage and peas. Cook for 25 more minutes. • Season with salt and pepper. Add the rice and cook for 20 minutes. • Sprinkle with the Parmesan and serve.

Serves: 4 · Prep: 30 min. · Cooking: 2 hrs · Level: 1

ZUPPA DI ORZO
Pearl barley soup

1	large carrot, diced
1	large zucchini, diced
1	large potato, diced
1	leek (white part only), thinly sliced
2	small celery hearts, sliced
1	medium onion, thinly sliced
1	oz spinach, coarsely chopped
2	tablespoons finely chopped parsley
1/2	cup pancetta, diced
5	cups boiling Beef stock (see recipe, page 105)
1	cup pearl barley
	salt and freshly ground black pepper to taste
1/4	cup extra-virgin olive oil

Wine: a light, dry red (Bardolino)

Put the vegetables, pancetta, and stock in a large pot over medium heat and bring to the boil. • Rinse the pearl barley under cold running water and add to the boiling stock. Cover the pot, and simmer for 1 hour, stirring occasionally. • When the barley is tender, season with salt and pepper and remove from heat. Drizzle with the oil, cover, and set aside for 5 minutes before serving.

Serves: 4 · Prep: 20 min. · Cooking: 1 hr · Level: 1

MINESTRA DI RISO E SPINACI
Spinach and rice soup

1	lb fresh spinach leaves, trimmed
2	tablespoons butter
	salt and freshly ground white pepper to taste
6	cups Beef stock (see recipe, page 105)
1	cup short-grain white rice
1	egg
1/4	cup freshly grated Parmesan cheese

Wine: a dry red (Grignolino del Monferrato Casalese)

Rinse the spinach under cold running water. Transfer to a large saucepan. Cover tightly and cook over medium heat for 2–3 minutes with just the water left clinging to the leaves. • Remove from heat, squeeze out as much moisture as possible, and chop coarsely. • Melt the butter in the same saucepan, then add the spinach and a little salt. Sauté over medium heat for 3 minutes. Set aside. • Bring the stock to a boil in a large saucepan. Add the rice and cook for 15 minutes, or until tender. • Add the spinach. • Beat the egg lightly in a bowl with salt and pepper. Add the Parmesan, then pour this mixture into the hot soup while beating with a whisk. • Leave to stand for 30 seconds before serving.

Serves: 4 · Prep: 10 min. · Cooking: 25 min. · Level: 1

Lombardy-style minestrone

ZUPPA CON UOVA E PARMIGIANO
Egg and Parmesan cheese soup

- 1/2   cup butter
- 8   thick slices firm-textured bread
- 4   large fresh eggs
- 1/4   cup freshly grated Parmesan cheese
      freshly ground black pepper to taste
- 6   cups boiling Beef stock (see recipe, page 105)

Heat the butter in a skillet and fry the bread until crisp and golden brown on both sides. • Place two slices in each of four preheated, individual soup bowls. • Break an egg carefully over the fried bread, making sure the yolks remain whole. Sprinkle with the cheese and a generous grinding of pepper. Pour the stock into each bowl, being careful not to pour it directly onto the eggs. • Let stand for 1–2 minutes to allow the eggs to cook.

Serves: 4 · Prep: 10 min. · Cooking: 5 min. · Level: 1

ZUPPA DI FARRO E VERDURE
Spelt and vegetable soup

- 1   cup dry cannellini or white kidney beans
- 1 1/2   cups spelt
- 4   cloves garlic, 2 bruised and 2 finely chopped
- 4   fresh sage leaves
      salt and freshly ground black pepper to taste
- 1/3   cup extra-virgin olive oil
- 1/2   cup diced pancetta
- 1   onion, sliced
- 1   stalk celery, sliced
- 1   carrot, diced
- 7   cups boiling Beef stock (see recipe, page 105)
- 6   peeled and chopped tomatoes
- 8   oz spinach or Swiss chard, washed and shredded

Wine: a dry, aromatic red (Elba Rosso)

Soak the beans for 12 hours in enough cold water to cover. • Place the drained, soaked beans in a large saucepan and cover with cold water. Place over medium heat and add the bruised garlic and sage. Bring to the boil, then simmer for about 50 minutes, or until the beans are tender. • Discard the garlic and sage and season with salt. • Drain the beans, reserving the cooking liquid. Place half the beans in a food processor and chop until smooth. • Heat 1/4 cup of the oil in a heavy-bottomed saucepan and sauté the chopped garlic and pancetta for 2–3 minutes. Add the onion, celery, and carrot and sauté until soft. • Pour in the stock, add the tomatoes and spinach or Swiss chard, and season with salt and pepper. Stir well, cover, and simmer over medium heat for 30 minutes. • Add the spelt to the pan. Cook for 20 minutes, then add the two bean mixtures. Adjust the seasoning and simmer for 20 more minutes. • Drizzle with the remaining oil and serve hot.

Serves: 4 · Prep: 20 min. · Cooking: 1 3/4 hrs · Level: 1

MINESTRONE TORINESE
Piedmontese minestrone

- 1 1/2   cups fresh red kidney beans
- 1/2   small Savoy cabbage
- 2   medium potatoes, diced
- 2   medium carrots, diced
- 2   celery stalks, sliced
- 1   cup short-grain white rice
- 1/2   cup pork fat
- 2   cloves garlic, finely chopped
- 2   tablespoons finely chopped parsley
- 6   leaves fresh basil, torn
      salt and freshly ground black pepper to taste
- 1/4   cup freshly grated Parmesan cheese

Wine: a dry red (Dolcetto d'Asti)

Put the beans in a large pot with enough cold water to cover by about 2 inches. • Cover and simmer over low heat for 30 minutes. • Cut the cabbage in 1/4-inch strips, discarding the core. • Add the cabbage, potatoes, carrots, and celery to the pot, stir, and cook for 30 minutes more. • If needed, add a little boiling water. • Add the rice and, after 15 minutes, the pork fat, garlic, parsley, and basil. Stir well. • Season with salt and pepper. • Remove from heat and let stand for a few minutes while the rice finishes cooking. • Serve with the Parmesan passed separately.

Serves: 4 · Prep: 20 min. · Cooking: 1 1/4 hrs · Level: 1

ACQUA COTTA MAREMMANA
Tuscan-style "cooked water"

- 15   oz peeled and chopped fresh or canned tomatoes
- 1/4   cup extra-virgin olive oil
- 2   onions, thinly sliced
- 2   stalks celery, finely chopped
- 10   basil leaves, torn
      salt and freshly ground black pepper to taste
- 6   cups boiling Beef stock (see recipe, page 105)
- 4–8   eggs
- 4–8   slices firm-textured bread, toasted
- 1/4   cup freshly grated Pecorino cheese

Wine: a dry white (Colli di Luni Bianco)

Plunge the tomatoes into boiling water for 10 seconds, then into cold water. Slip off the

Spelt has been cultivated in Italy for centuries. The Latins, who occupied Lazio before the rise of Rome, grew spelt. They used it to make *puls*, a type of porridge that was their staple food. Under the Romans, wheat began to be imported from Egypt and it replaced spelt for the wealthy. But the poor continued to eat spelt; this was the cereal the Roman emperors distributed to the poor to stop them from revolting. Spelt was grown throughout medieval and Renaissance times, but went out of fashion during the 19th and 20th centuries. Recently, as we have begun to rediscover our regional traditions and to look for healthy alternatives to processed foods, spelt has made a comeback. This recipe, slightly modified for modern tastes, comes from Lazio.

MINESTRA DI FARRO
Spelt soup

- 1/2 cup diced pancetta
- 1 onion, finely chopped
- 2 cloves garlic, finely chopped
- 1 tablespoon finely chopped parsley
- 1 tablespoon finely chopped marjoram
- 6 fresh basil leaves, torn
- 2 tomatoes, peeled and chopped
- 3 tablespoons extra-virgin olive oil
- 8 cups cold water
- 2 cups spelt (if spelt is not available, substitute with the same quantity of pearl barley) salt and freshly ground black pepper to taste
- 1/4 cup freshly grated Pecorino cheese

Wine: a dry white (Bianco di Pitigliano)

Sauté the pancetta, onion, garlic, parsley, marjoram, and basil in 1 tablespoon of the oil a heavy-bottomed saucepan for 4–5 minutes. • Add the tomatoes, then pour in the water and bring to the boil. • Add the spelt and season with salt and pepper. Cook, stirring frequently, for about 30 minutes, or until the spelt is tender. • Sprinkle with the Pecorino and drizzle with the remaining oil. • Serve hot.

Serves: 4 · Prep: 20 min. · Cooking: 35 min. Level: 1

skins and cut in half horizontally. Squeeze out some of the seeds and chop the flesh. • Heat the oil in a large, heavy-bottomed saucepan, add the onions and sauté over medium heat until soft. • Add the tomatoes, celery, and basil, and cook for 20 minutes. • Season with salt and pepper, add the stock, and cook for 20 more minutes. • Turn the heat down to low. Break the eggs carefully into the soup, not too close together and taking care not to break the yolks. After 2–3 minutes the eggs will have set but still be soft. • Put the bread in individual soup bowls and ladle the soup with one or two eggs into each one. Sprinkle with the Pecorino and serve.

Serves: 4 · Prep: 15 min. · Cooking: 45 min. · Level: 2

ZUPPA DI RAPE
Turnip soup

- 2 lb turnips, cleaned, cut in half vertically, and sliced
- 1/2 cup diced lean pancetta
- 1/4 cup lard, finely chopped
- 2 cloves garlic, finely chopped
- 2 quarts boiling Beef stock (see recipe, page 105) salt and freshly ground black pepper to taste
- 4–8 slices toasted bread
- 1/2 cup freshly grated Parmesan cheese

Wine: a light, dry white (Soave Classico)

Put the turnips, pancetta, lard, and garlic in a heavy-bottomed saucepan. Add the stock, cover, and simmer over low heat for 30 minutes. • Season with salt and pepper. • Arrange the toast in individual soup bowls, sprinkle with half the cheese, and ladle the soup over the top. • Sprinkle with the remaining cheese and serve hot.

Serves: 4 · Prep: 10 min. · Cooking: 30 min. · Level: 1

ZUPPA DI FUNGHI
Mushroom soup

- 1 oz dried porcini mushrooms
- 1 tablespoon finely chopped parsley
- 2 cloves garlic, finely chopped
- 1/4 cup extra-virgin olive oil
- 1 1/2 lb white mushrooms, cleaned and thinly sliced
- 1/2 cup dry white wine
- 6 cups boiling Vegetable stock (see recipe, page 104)
- 1 tablespoon all-purpose flour salt and freshly ground black pepper to taste
- 4 slices firm-textured bread, toasted

Wine: a light, dry rosé (Colli Altotiberini Rosato)

Soak the dried mushrooms in 1 cup of warm water for 30 minutes. Drain and chop finely. •

Strain the mushroom water and reserve. • In a large, heavy-bottomed saucepan, sauté the parsley and garlic in half the oil over medium heat. • Add the porcini mushrooms, and after a couple of minutes, the fresh mushrooms. Sauté for 5 minutes. • Pour in the wine, and after a couple of minutes begin gradually adding the stock and mushroom water (reserving 1/4 cup). • Simmer for about 25 minutes. • Heat the remaining oil in a small pan over low heat. Add the flour and brown slightly, stirring carefully. • Remove the small pan from heat and add the remaining mushroom liquid, mixing well so that no lumps form. • Pour this mixture into the soup. Cook for 2–3 minutes, stirring continuously. Season with salt and pepper. • Put the bread in individual soup bowls, ladle the soup over the top, and serve.

Serves: 4 · Prep: 40 min. · Cooking: 35–40 min. · Level: 1

ZUPPA DI CIPOLLE
Onion soup with toast

- 2 lb onions, thinly sliced
- 2 stalks celery, finely chopped
- 1 small carrot, finely chopped
- 1/2 cup extra-virgin olive oil salt and freshly ground black pepper to taste
- 6 cups boiling Beef stock (see recipe, page 105)
- 4 slices firm-textured bread, toasted
- 1/4 cup freshly grated Pecorino cheese

Wine: a dry, aromatic white (Tocai di Lison)

Place the onions, celery, and carrot in the oil in a deep, heavy-bottomed saucepan. Sauté over low heat for about 20 minutes. Season with salt and pepper. • Cook for 20 more minutes, stirring often and adding ladlefuls of stock until it is all in the pan. • Place the toast in individual soup bowls and ladle the soup over the top. Sprinkle with the Pecorino and serve.

Serves: 4 · Prep: 15 min. · Cooking: 40 min. · Level: 1

MINESTRA DI ZUCCHINE
Zucchini soup

- 1/4 cup extra-virgin olive oil
- 2 spring onions, finely chopped
- 8 zucchini, cleaned and diced
  salt and freshly ground black pepper to taste
- 6 cups boiling Beef stock (see recipe, page 105)
- 2 eggs, lightly beaten
- 1 tablespoon finely chopped parsley
- 1 tablespoon finely chopped basil
- 1/4 cup freshly grated Parmesan cheese
- 4 slices dense-grain bread, toasted and cut in cubes

Wine: a dry rosé (Lagrein Rosato)

Heat the oil in a heavy-bottomed saucepan and sauté the spring onions for 2–3 minutes. Add the zucchini and sauté for 5 more minutes. Season with salt and pepper. • Add the stock and cook over medium-low heat for 10 minutes, or until the zucchini are tender. • Add the eggs, parsley and basil and stir rapidly. Serve hot, with the toasted bread passed separately.

Serves: 4 · Prep: 10 min. · Cooking: 20 min. · Level: 1

ZUPPA DI CECI
Garbanzo bean soup

- 8 oz Swiss chard
- 1/4 cup extra-virgin olive oil
- 1 onion, finely chopped
- 2 cloves garlic, lightly crushed
- 4 anchovy fillets
- 1 3/4 cups dry garbanzo beans, soaked for 12 hours in cold water
- 3 plum tomatoes, peeled and chopped
  salt and freshly ground black pepper to taste
- 2 1/4 quarts boiling water
- 4–8 slices firm-textured bread, toasted
- 1/4 cup freshly grated Pecorino cheese

Wine: a light, dry red (Morellino di Scansano)

About 2 1/2 hours before you intend to serve the soup, rinse the chard under cold running water. Transfer to a large saucepan. Cover tightly and cook over medium heat for 5 minutes with just the water left clinging to the leaves. Set aside. • Heat the oil in a large, heavy-bottomed pan or earthenware pot. Add the onion and garlic and sauté until the onion is soft. • Add the anchovies, mashing them with a fork until they dissolve. • Add the garbanzo beans, Swiss chard with its cooking liquid, and the tomatoes to the pot. Season with salt and pepper, stir, and add the boiling water. •

Cover the pot and simmer over medium heat for at least 2 hours. The garbanzo beans should be very tender. • Arrange the toast in individual soup bowls and ladle the soup over the top. • Sprinkle with the cheese and serve.

Serves: 4 · Prep: 30 min. · Cooking: 2 1/2 hrs · Level: 2

PASTA E CECI
Pasta and garbanzo bean soup

- 1 2/3 cups dry garbanzo beans, soaked for 12 hours in cold water
- 4 cloves garlic, peeled and lightly crushed
- 2 sprigs rosemary
- 1/3 cup extra-virgin olive oil
- 1/4 cup tomato purée
- 1 cup boiling Beef stock (see recipe, page 105)
- 8 oz small soup pasta
  salt and freshly ground black pepper to taste

Wine: a light, dry red (Freisa d'Asti)

Place the beans in a saucepan, cover with cold water, add 2 cloves of garlic, and a sprig of rosemary. Partially cover, and simmer for 1 hour, or until the garbanzo beans are very tender. Season with salt and remove from heat. • Drain, reserving the cooking water. • Purée three-quarters of the garbanzo beans in a food processor, leaving the remainder whole. • Heat half the oil in a large heavy-bottomed saucepan and sauté the remaining garlic and rosemary sprig for 3 minutes. • Add the tomato purée and cook over medium heat

for 2 minutes. • Add the puréed and whole garbanzo beans and the reserved cooking liquid and bring to the boil. If the soup is very thick, dilute with a little hot stock. • Add the pasta and cook until the pasta is *al dente*. Season with salt and pepper. Drizzle with the remaining oil and serve.

Serves: 4 · Prep: 20 min. · Cooking: 1 1/4 hrs · Level: 1

PASTA E FAGIOLI ALLA VENEZIANA
Venetian-style pasta and beans

- 1 1/2 cups dry cranberry or borlotti beans, soaked for 12 hours in cold water
- 2 tablespoons extra-virgin olive oil
- 1 onion, finely chopped
- 1 clove garlic, finely chopped
- 1 carrot, finely chopped
- 1 stalk celery, finely chopped
- 1 sprig fresh rosemary, finely chopped
- 3/4 cup finely chopped pancetta
- 8 oz dry tagliatelle pasta, broken into short lengths
  salt and freshly ground black pepper to taste

Wine: a dry rosé (Lison Pramaggiore Merlot Rosato)

Place the beans in a saucepan with enough fresh unsalted cold water to cover. Boil gently for just under 2 hours, or until very tender. Do not drain. • Remove one-third of the beans with a slotted spoon and purée in a food processor. • Return the purée to the pan and stir. • Heat the oil in a skillet and sauté the onion, garlic, carrot, celery, and rosemary with the pancetta until lightly browned. • Stir this mixture into the beans.

Zucchini soup

Season with salt. Bring the beans back to the boil, add the pasta, cook for 5 minutes, then remove from heat. • Leave to stand for 20 minutes. Reheat and serve with a little extra pepper and oil.

Serves: 6 · Prep: 35 min. · Cooking: 2 hrs · Level: 1

MINESTRA DI RISO E FAGIOLI
Rice and bean soup

☞ Cannellini or white beans are not available fresh throughout the year, and soaking and cooking dried beans requires time and forethought. This recipe for a typically Tuscan soup is based on canned beans.

- 3 tablespoons extra-virgin olive oil
- ¼ cup finely chopped lean pancetta
- 1 medium onion, finely chopped
- 1 stalk celery, finely chopped
- 2 cloves garlic, finely chopped
- 1 tablespoon finely chopped parsley
- 6 basil leaves, torn
- ¼ teaspoon crushed red pepper flakes
- 1 sage leaf, finely chopped
- 3 medium tomatoes
- 2 (15 oz) cans white beans, drained
- 6 cups boiling Beef stock (see recipe, page 105)
- 1 cup short-grain white rice
  salt to taste

Wine: a dry red (Rosso delle Colline Lucchesi)

Put the oil, pancetta, onion, celery, garlic, parsley, basil, pepper flakes, and sage in a large pot, preferably earthenware. Sauté over low heat for 7–8 minutes. • In the meantime, plunge the tomatoes into boiling water for 1 minute, then into cold. Slip off the skins and cut in half horizontally. Squeeze lightly to remove as many of the seeds as possible. Chop the flesh coarsely and stir into the pot. • Cover, and simmer for 15 minutes, stirring occasionally. • Add the beans and stock and cook for 5 minutes more. • Add the rice and cook for 15 minutes, or until tender. If necessary, add a little more boiling stock or water. Season with salt and serve hot.

Serves: 4 · Prep: 25 min. · Cooking: 45 min. · Level: 1

MALMARITATI
Fresh pasta and bean soup

- ½ quantity Pasta dough (see recipe, page 124)
- 1½ cups dry borlotti or red kidney beans, soaked for 12 hours in cold water
- 1 small onion, peeled
- 1 carrot, peeled
- 2 stalks celery, trimmed
  salt to taste
- 1 clove garlic, peeled and lightly crushed
- ½ cup extra-virgin olive oil
- 1 tablespoon finely chopped parsley
- 8 oz fresh or canned tomatoes, sieved
- ½ cup freshly grated Parmesan cheese

Wine: a light, dry red (Merlot di Grave del Friuli)

Prepare the pasta dough. Shape into a ball and set aside to rest for 1 hour, wrapped in plastic wrap. • Roll out the dough into a thin sheet. Cut into uneven diamond shapes by first cutting it diagonally into strips, then cutting in the opposite direction. Set aside. • Place the beans in a deep saucepan with enough cold water to cover. Add the onion, carrot, and celery, but no salt at this stage. Bring to a boil and simmer gently for about 1½ hours. • When the beans are very tender, purée half in a food processor, then season with salt. Set the remaining beans and cooking liquid aside. • In a large, heavy-bottomed pan, sauté the garlic in half the oil. Discard when it starts to color. • Add the parsley and tomatoes to the flavored oil. Cook, uncovered, until the mixture reduces by

half. • Add the bean purée, the whole beans, and the cooking liquid. Bring to the boil, then add the pasta. It will take 3–4 minutes to cook. • Sprinkle with the Parmesan and drizzle with the remaining oil just before serving.

Serves: 4 · Prep: 30 min. + time to make the pasta · Cooking: 2 hrs · Level: 2

CREMA DI ASPARAGI
Cream of asparagus soup

- 2 lb asparagus
- ¼ cup butter
- 1 cup all-purpose flour
- 2 cups whole milk
- 3 cups Beef stock (see recipe, page 105)
  salt and freshly ground white pepper to taste
- 3 egg yolks
- ¾ cup freshly grated Parmesan cheese
- ½ cup light cream

Wine: a dry white (Breganze Vespaiolo)

Trim the tough parts off the asparagus stalks. • Melt half the butter in a heavy-bottomed pan and add the flour, stirring all the time. • Pour in the milk, then the stock. • Bring to the boil and add the asparagus. Season with salt and pepper. • Cook for 15 minutes. • Chop in a food processor until smooth, then return to heat. • Mix the egg yolks, remaining butter, Parmesan, and cream together in a bowl. • Pour the mixture into the asparagus, and stir until thick and creamy. • Serve hot.

Serves: 4 · Prep: 10 min. · Cooking: 20–25 min. · Level: 1

Cream of asparagus soup

RISI E BISI
Rice and pea soup

- ¼ cup butter
- 3 tablespoons extra-virgin olive oil
- 1 onion, finely chopped
- 1 tablespoon finely chopped parsley
- ½ clove garlic, finely chopped
- 2½ cups shelled baby peas
- 6 cups boiling Beef stock (see recipe, page 105)
- 1¼ cups short-grain white rice
  salt to taste
- ¼ cup freshly grated Parmesan cheese

Wine: a dry white (Pinot Bianco dei Colli Euganei)

Melt half the butter with the oil in a heavy-bottomed saucepan. Add the onion and sauté until soft. • Add the parsley and garlic and sauté for 2–3 minutes. • Add the peas and a ladleful of the stock. Cover and cook over low heat for 8–10 minutes. • Stir in the remaining stock. Add the rice and cook for 13 minutes, or until the rice is almost tender. • Season with salt. Add the remaining butter and finish cooking. This will take another 2–3 minutes, depending on the rice. • Sprinkle with the Parmesan, mix well, and serve.

Serves: 4 · Prep: 10 min. · Cooking: 30 min. · Level: 1

MINESTRA DI RISO E VERDURE
Rice and vegetable soup

- ¼ cup butter
- 2 medium potatoes, diced
- 2 small leeks (white part only), sliced
- 8 oz spinach, coarsely chopped
- 7 cups boiling Beef stock (see recipe, page 105)
- ¾ cup short-grain white rice
  salt to taste
- ¼ cup freshly grated Parmesan cheese

Wine: a dry white (Tocai di Lison)

Melt the butter in a large saucepan over low heat and add the potato, leeks, and spinach. Sauté for 5 minutes, stirring continuously. • Add the stock and simmer, covered, for 10 more minutes. • Add the rice and cook for 15 minutes, or until tender. Season with salt, sprinkle with the Parmesan, and serve hot.

Serves: 4 · Prep: 20 min. · Cooking: 30 min. · Level: 1

RISO E LATTE
Milk and rice soup

- 2 quarts whole milk
- 2 cups water
  salt to taste

- 1½ cups short-grain white rice
- 2 tablespoons butter
- ½ cup freshly grated Parmesan cheese
- 1 tablespoon finely chopped parsley

Wine: a dry white (Cori Bianco)

Put the milk and water in a large saucepan with ½ teaspoon salt and bring to the boil. • Add the rice, reduce the heat and cook for about 15 minutes. The cooking time depends on the quality of the rice, so taste after 15 minutes to see if it is ready. Add more salt, if necessary. • Turn off the heat and add the butter. • Cover and let stand for 3 minutes. Sprinkle with the Parmesan and parsley and serve.

Serves: 4 · Prep: 5 min. · Cooking: 35 min. · Level: 1

CREMA DI PISELLI
Cream of pea soup

- 1 medium onion, finely chopped
- 2 tablespoons butter
- 3 cups fresh peas, shelled
- 6 cups boiling Beef stock (see recipe, page 105)
- ½ quantity Béchamel sauce (see recipe, page 16)
  salt to taste

Wine: a dry white (Colli Albani)

In a large, heavy-bottomed saucepan, sauté the onion in the butter until soft. • Stir in the peas and cook for 2 minutes. • Add 4 cups of stock and cook for 20 minutes. • Prepare the béchamel sauce and set aside. • Purée the cooked peas in a food processor and return the purée to the pot. • Add the béchamel sauce into the mixture and stir well. If the soup seems too thick, add some of the remaining stock. Season with salt, if necessary. • Reheat for 2–3 minutes and serve.

Serves: 4 · Prep: 10 min. · Cooking: 25 min. · Level: 1

MINESTRA DI PATATE E RISO
Potato and rice soup

- ½ cup finely chopped pancetta
- 1 medium onion, finely chopped
- 1 tablespoon finely chopped fresh rosemary leaves

- 2 medium potatoes, peeled and diced
- 6 cups boiling Beef stock (see recipe, page 105)
- 1 cup short-grain white rice
  salt to taste
- 1 tablespoon coarsely chopped parsley
- ¼ cup freshly grated Parmesan cheese

Wine: a dry white (Pinot Bianco dei Colli Berici)

Sauté the pancetta, onion, and rosemary in a large, heavy-bottomed saucepan for 5 minutes. • Add the potatoes and the stock. As soon as it begins to boil, add the rice. Cook for 15 minutes, or until the rice and potatoes are tender. • Season with salt and stir in the parsley. Sprinkle with the Parmesan and serve hot.

Serves: 4 · Prep: 20 min. · Cooking: 25 min. · Level: 1

MINESTRA DI PREZZEMOLO E RISO
Parsley and rice soup

- 6 cups Beef stock (see recipe, page 105)
- 1 cup short-grain white rice
- ¼ cup finely chopped parsley
- 2 tablespoons butter
  salt and freshly ground black pepper to taste
- ½ cup freshly grated Parmesan cheese

Wine: a dry white (Pomino Bianco)

Bring the stock to the boil and add the rice. • Cook for 15 minutes, or until the rice is tender. • Add the parsley and butter just before removing from heat. • Season with salt, sprinkle with the Parmesan, and serve.

Serves: 4 · Prep: 5 min. · Cooking: 20 min. · Level: 1

CREMA DI ZUCCA
Cream of pumpkin soup

- 2 lb pumpkin, peeled and cut in pieces
- 10 oz each of carrots and leeks, diced
- 2 stalks celery, coarsely chopped
- 5 cups boiling Beef stock (see recipe, page 105)
- ½ cup light cream
  salt and freshly ground white pepper to taste
- ½ cup freshly grated Parmesan cheese

Wine: a light, dry red (Bardolino)

Combine the pumpkin, carrot, leeks, celery, and stock in a large, heavy-bottomed pot. Cover and simmer for 25 minutes, stirring occasionally. • Chop the vegetables in a food processor with a little of the stock until smooth. Return to the pot and reheat for 1–2 minutes. • Stir in the cream and season with salt and pepper. • Let stand for 1 minute, sprinkle with the Parmesan, and serve.

Serves: 4 · Prep: 20 min. · Cooking: 30 min. · Level: 1

This is one of three famous Tuscan dishes based on bread. The other two are *Ribollita* (Tuscan vegetable and bread soup; see recipe, page 106) and *Panzanella* (Tuscan bread salad; see recipe, page 75). These recipes can all be traced to the peasant tradition that underlies all Italian regional cooking. In the past, bread was a staple food for Tuscan peasants, who could not afford more expensive dishes. Nor could they afford to waste any bread, so what wasn't eaten within a day or two of being baked was made into soup or salad.

PAPPA AL POMODORO
Tuscan tomato bread soup

2	lb firm ripe tomatoes
1/2	cup extra-virgin olive oil
3	cloves garlic, finely chopped
2	bay leaves
1	lb firm-textured bread, 2 days old, cut in 1-inch cubes
	salt and freshly ground black pepper to taste
8–10	fresh basil leaves, torn

Wine: a light, dry red (Chianti dei Colli Aretini)

Plunge the tomatoes into a pan of boiling water for 1 minute, then into cold water. Peel and cut them in half horizontally. Squeeze gently to remove the seeds, then chop the flesh into small pieces. • Heat half the oil in a heavy-bottomed saucepan and sauté the garlic and bay leaves for 2–3 minutes. • Add the bread and cook over medium-low heat for 3–4 minutes, stirring frequently. • Stir in the tomatoes and, using a ladle, add about 2 cups of water. Season with salt and pepper. • Cook for 15 minutes, stirring often. If the soup becomes too thick, add a little more water (it should be about the same consistency as porridge). • Drizzle with the remaining oil, sprinkle with the basil, and serve.

Serves: 4 · Prep: 15 min. · Cooking: 25 min. · Level: 1

Tuscan tomato bread soup

ZUPPA DI BROCCOLI
Roman cauliflower soup

☞ Roman cauliflower is a beautiful emerald green and the florets are pointed rather than rounded as in white cauliflower. If you can't find it in your local market, use broccoflower in its place.

1 Roman cauliflower, about 2 lb
4 thick slices firm-textured bread
2 cloves garlic
1/2 cup extra-virgin olive oil
2 tablespoons lemon juice
   salt and freshly ground white pepper to taste

Wine: a dry white (Savuto)

Separate the florets from the core of the cauliflower, keeping the tender inner leaves. Rinse thoroughly and boil for 8–10 minutes in a pot of salted, boiling water. • Toast the bread, rub the slices with the garlic, and place them in individual soup bowls. When the cauliflower is cooked, pour a half ladleful of the cooking water over each slice. • Arrange the florets and leaves, well drained, on the toasted bread. Drizzle with the oil and lemon juice, and season with salt and pepper. Serve hot.

Serves: 4 · Prep: 10 min. · Cooking: 10 min. · Level: 1

PANADA
Venetian bread soup

1 lb day-old white bread
6 cups boiling Beef stock (see recipe, page 105)
   pinch of cinnamon
1/4 cup extra-virgin olive oil
1 cup freshly grated Parmesan cheese
   salt to taste

Wine: a light, dry white (Verduzzo del Piave)

Slice the bread and place in a heavy-bottomed saucepan. Pour in enough stock to cover it. Sprinkle with the cinnamon and 2 tablespoons of oil, then leave to stand for 40 minutes. • Place over a gentle heat and stir frequently until the mixture is smooth. This will take about 40 minutes. • Sprinkle with the Parmesan and season with salt. Stir well, drizzle with the remaining oil, and serve.

Serves: 4 · Prep: 5 min. + 40 min. to stand · Cooking: 40 min. · Level: 1

CRESPELLE IN BRODO
Crêpes in chicken stock

3 eggs
1 1/4 cups freshly grated Parmesan cheese
1 tablespoon finely chopped parsley
   salt to taste
   pinch of nutmeg
2/3 cup whole milk
2/3 cup all-purpose flour
1/4 cup butter
5 cups boiling Chicken stock (see recipe, page 104)

Wine: a dry white (Bianco del Collio)

Beat the eggs in a bowl with 2 tablespoons of the cheese, the parsley, salt, nutmeg, and one-third of the milk. • Gradually stir in the flour and the remaining milk. The batter should be fairly liquid. • Heat 1 tablespoon of butter in a skillet about 6–7 inches in diameter and add a ladleful of batter. Tip the skillet and rotate, so that the batter spreads evenly into a very thin crêpe. After 1 minute, flip the crêpe and

cook for 1 minute on the other side. • Slip it onto a plate and repeat, adding a dab of butter to the skillet each time, until all the batter has been used. Stack the crêpes up in a pile. • Sprinkle each crêpe with Parmesan, then roll them up loosely, and slice into ribbons. Divide equally among 4 individual soup bowls, and pour the boiling stock over the top. Serve hot.

Serves: 4 · Prep: 10 min. · Cooking: 30 min. · Level: 2

ZUPPA MITUNN
Bread and cheese soup

8 slices firm-textured white bread
2 cloves garlic, peeled
12 oz Gruyère cheese, thinly sliced
   salt and freshly ground black pepper to taste
5 cups boiling Beef stock (see recipe, page 105)

Wine: a dry red (Dolcetto d'Asti)

Toast the bread, then rub with the garlic. • Place the toast in a deep casserole in layers, alternating with slices of Gruyère. Sprinkle with salt and pepper. • Pour in enough stock to cover the top layer of toast. • Bake in a preheated oven at 400°F for 15 minutes. The toast should absorb all the stock during cooking. • Serve hot.

Serves: 4 · Prep: 15 min. · Cooking: 15 min. · Level: 1

CANEDERLI
Bread dumpling soup

1 1/4 cups whole milk
8 oz firm-textured bread, chopped
2 eggs
3 oz fresh Italian pork sausage meat
1/3 cup pancetta, finely chopped
3 oz prosciutto, finely chopped
1 tablespoon finely chopped onion
2 tablespoons finely chopped parsley
1/2 cup all-purpose flour
   salt to taste
5 cups boiling Beef stock (see recipe, page 105)

Wine: a dry rosé (Alezio Rosato)

Put 3/4 cup of milk in a large bowl with the bread and set aside for at least 30 minutes, mixing once or twice. The bread should be soft but not too wet. If necessary, add the remaining milk. • Squeeze out the excess milk and put the bread back in the bowl, discarding the milk first. • Gradually add the eggs, sausage, pancetta, prosciutto, onion, half the parsley, and 3 tablespoons of flour, stirring

Crêpes in chicken stock

continuously until the mixture is firm but elastic. If necessary, add more flour. • Shape the mixture into dumplings about 2 inches in diameter and dust with flour. • Place the stock in a fairly deep pot and drop the dumplings in. Turn the heat up to high so the stock returns to the boil, then lower slightly and simmer for 15 minutes. • Remove the dumplings with a slotted spoon. Place in a tureen, and cover with the stock. Sprinkle with the remaining parsley and serve.

Serves: 4 · Prep: 45 min. · Cooking: 15 min. · Level: 2

MINESTRA PASQUALE
Sicilian Easter soup

8	oz ground lean beef or pork
3	eggs
1/3	cup freshly grated Pecorino cheese
1	clove garlic, finely chopped
1	tablespoon finely chopped parsley
	pinch of nutmeg
	salt to taste
5	cups boiling Beef stock (see recipe, page 105)
8	oz soft fresh Ricotta cheese
1/3	cup fine dry bread crumbs
1	tablespoon seedless golden raisins

Wine: a dry white (Bianco di Donnafugata)

Place the meat in a mixing bowl and add 1 egg, the Pecorino, garlic, parsley, nutmeg, and salt. Mix well and shape into marble-sized meatballs. • Drop the meatballs into the boiling stock and cook for 4–5 minutes. • Beat the remaining eggs and combine with the Ricotta, bread crumbs, and raisins. Season with salt and mix until smooth. • Pour the egg mixture into the hot stock and stir with a fork for 1–2 minutes over medium heat, until the egg sets in tiny shreds. • Serve immediately.

Serves: 4 · Prep: 10 min. · Cooking: 5–7 min. · Level: 1

STRACCIATELLA ALLA ROMANA
Beef stock with egg, Roman style

5	eggs
	salt to taste
	pinch of nutmeg
1/2	cup freshly grated Parmesan cheese
7	cups boiling Beef stock (see recipe, page 105)

Wine: a dry white (Terlano)

Beat the eggs with a pinch each of salt and nutmeg. Add half the Parmesan and beat well. • Pour the egg mixture into the boiling stock. Beat with a fork for 1–2 minutes over medium heat until the egg sets in tiny shreds. • Sprinkle with the remaining Parmesan and serve.

Serves: 4 · Prep: 5 min. · Cooking: 30 min. · Level: 1

PASSATELLI
Cheese dumpling soup

1	cup freshly grated Parmesan cheese
1¼	cups fine dry bread crumbs
3	eggs
1	oz beef marrow or, if preferred, butter
	pinch of nutmeg
	finely grated zest of 1 lemon
	salt to taste
2	cups boiling Beef stock (see recipe, page 105)

Wine: a dry, fruity white (Colli Piacentini Chardonnay)

Combine the Parmesan with the bread crumbs and eggs in a mixing bowl. • Soften the beef marrow by heating gently in a small saucepan, then combine with the bread crumbs. • Add the nutmeg, lemon zest, and salt and set aside for 30 minutes. • Press the mixture through a food mill, fitted with the disk with the largest holes, to produce short, cylindrical dumplings, about 1½ inches long. Cut them off with the tip of a sharp knife as they are squeezed out of the mill. Let the little dumplings fall directly into a saucepan with the boiling stock and simmer until they bob up to the surface. • Remove from heat. Leave to stand for a few minutes before serving.

Serves: 4 · Prep: 25 min. + 30 min. to rest · Cooking: 4–5 min. · Level: 1

MINESTRA DI RISO E ZUCCA
Rice and pumpkin soup

3	lb pumpkin, peeled, seeded, and cut in 1-inch cubes
2	cups milk
	salt to taste
1	large onion, finely chopped
1/3	cup butter
6	cups boiling Beef stock (see recipe, page 105)
1	cup short-grain white rice
1/3	cup freshly grated Parmesan cheese

Wine: a dry white (Bianco di Donnafugata)

Put the pumpkin in a saucepan with the milk and salt and cook for 10 minutes, or until the pumpkin is tender. • Purée the pumpkin in a food processor. • Place the purée in a heavy-bottomed pan over very low heat and cook for about 5 minutes, stirring continuously with a wooden spoon. Remove from heat. • In a large heavy-bottomed pan, sauté the onion in the butter until soft. • Add the pumpkin mixture and mix well. • Pour the stock into the pumpkin mixture, and when it returns to the boil, add the rice. Check the seasoning and cook for about 15 minutes, or until the rice is tender. • Sprinkle with the Parmesan and serve hot.

Serves: 6 · Prep: 10 min. · Cooking: 30 min. · Level: 1

Rice and pumpkin soup

Tortellini in beef stock

This classic recipe comes from Bologna. There are many variations on the filling for the tortellini. We have given another one on page 154. Since making tortellini is time-consuming and requires practice, you may prefer to buy freshly made tortellini from a good delicatessen or specialty store.

TORTELLINI IN BRODO
Tortellini in beef stock

1	quantity pasta dough (see recipe, page 124)
2	tablespoons butter
4	oz lean pork, coarsely chopped
4	oz Mortadella
3	oz prosciutto
1	egg
1³/₄	cups freshly grated Parmesan cheese
	pinch of freshly grated nutmeg
	salt and freshly ground black pepper to taste
7	cups boiling Beef stock (see recipe, page 105)

Wine: a dry, sparkling red (Lambrusco Grasparossa)

Prepare the pasta dough. Shape the dough into a ball and set aside to rest for 1 hour, wrapped in plastic wrap. • Melt the butter in a skillet and sauté the pork. When browned, chop finely in a food processor together with the Mortadella and prosciutto. • Transfer the meat mixture to a bowl and mix with the egg, Parmesan, nutmeg, salt, and pepper. (The filling can be prepared a day in advance). • Prepare the tortellini as explained on page 125. Spread the freshly made pasta out on a clean cloth to dry for about 2 hours. • Add the tortellini to the stock and simmer gently for 2–3 minutes. • Serve in individual soup bowls, allowing about a tablespoon of stock for each tortellino.

Serves: 4 · Prep: 1 hr + 3 hrs to rest · Cooking: 3 hrs · Level: 3

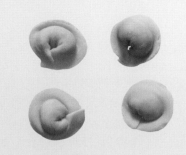

TORTELLINI DI MAGRO
Romagnol stuffed pasta

1	quantity Pasta dough (see recipe, page 124)
6	oz fresh, white soft cheese (Stracchino or Crescenza)
6	oz soft Ricotta cheese
³/₄	cup freshly grated Parmesan cheese
2	eggs
	pinch of nutmeg
	salt to taste
7	cups boiling Beef stock (see recipe, page 105)

Wine: a young, dry red (Rubicone Sangiovese)

Prepare the pasta dough. Shape the dough into a ball and set aside to rest for 1 hour, wrapped in plastic wrap. • Mix the cheeses in a bowl with the eggs, nutmeg, and salt. • • Prepare the tortellini as shown on page 125. • Add the tortellini to the boiling stock and simmer until the sealed edges of the pasta are *al dente*. • Ladle the tortellini and stock into individual soup bowls and serve hot.

Serves: 4 · Prep: 1 hr + time to make the pasta · Cooking: 3–5 min. · Level: 3

DADOLINI IN BRODO
Dice in beef or chicken stock

3	large eggs
2	tablespoons melted butter
³/₄	cup freshly grated Parmesan cheese
	salt to taste
	pinch of nutmeg
³/₄	cup all-purpose flour
7	cups Beef or Chicken stock (see recipes, pages 104–5)

Wine: a dry white (Verduzzo)

Combine the eggs, butter, Parmesan, salt, and nutmeg in a bowl. Mix well with a

fork, then gradually stir the flour into the mixture, making sure that no lumps form. • Pour into a lightly buttered square or rectangular ovenproof dish large enough to contain the mixture in a layer ³/₄-inch deep. • Bake in a preheated oven at 300°F for 1 hour. • Cut into squares when cool. Add to the tureen and pour the boiling stock over the top. • Serve immediately.

Serves: 4 · Prep: 10 min. · Cooking: 1 hr · Level: 1

AGNOLOTTI IN BRODO
Agnolotti in beef stock

☞ Agnolotti are a special pasta from Piedmont. Traditionally, they are served in steaming hot beef stock, but are also very good with other pasta sauces. See the recipes included in the pasta chapter on page 154. There are many variations on the classic recipe.

1	quantity Pasta dough (see recipe, page 124)
2	stalks celery, finely chopped
1	small onion, finely chopped
2	cloves garlic, finely chopped
1	carrot, finely chopped
¹/₄	cup butter
5	oz lean pork
5	oz lean veal
4	oz calf's liver
2	bay leaves
1	cup dry red wine
2	eggs
¹/₄	cup freshly grated Parmesan cheese
	pinch of nutmeg
	salt and freshly ground black pepper to taste
1	quantity Beef stock (see recipe, page 105)

Wine: a light dry red (Grignolino del Monferrato Casalese)

Prepare the pasta dough. • In a heavy-bottomed saucepan, sauté the celery, onion, garlic, and carrot in the butter until soft. • Add the pork, veal, liver, and bay leaves and sauté for 3–4 minutes. • Pour in the wine and simmer over low heat until the meat is cooked. • Transfer the mixture to a food processor and chop finely. Set aside for 10 minutes to cool. • Stir in the eggs, Parmesan, and nutmeg, and season with salt and pepper. • Prepare the agnolotti as explained on page 125. • Add the agnolotti carefully to the boiling stock and cook until the pasta around the sealed edges is cooked *al dente*. • Ladle the stock and agnolotti into individual soup dishes and serve hot.

Serves: 4 · Prep: 10 min. + time to make the pasta · Cooking: 6–8 min. · Level: 3

ZUPPA DI VALPELLINE
Valpelline soup

☞ This delicious soup comes from a village called Valpelline in the Valle d'Aosta, in the northwest. It calls for pan juices from a roast. If you do not have these on hand, substitute with ½ cup of beef stock.

1   medium Savoy cabbage
2   tablespoons salt pork
10 slices dense-grain, home-style bread, toasted
½   cup pan juices from a roast
6   oz prosciutto, finely chopped
    pinch of nutmeg
    pinch of ground cloves
    pinch of ground cinnamon
7   oz Fontina cheese, cut in thin slivers
6   cups boiling Beef stock (see recipe, page 105)
2   tablespoons butter, chopped

Wine: a dry white (Cori Bianco)

Clean the cabbage and cut in quarters, discarding the core so that the leaves are no longer attached. • Melt the salt pork in a heavy-bottomed saucepan over low heat, add the cabbage leaves, cover and cook for 10–15 minutes, stirring occasionally. • Lightly brown the bread in a preheated oven at 300°F for 15 minutes. • Arrange a layer of toasted bread in a large ovenproof baking dish and drizzle with 2 tablespoons of pan juices. Cover with one-third of the prosciutto and one-third of the cabbage. Season with a sprinkling of the spices and arrange one-third of the Fontina on top. Repeat the layering procedure twice. Before adding the last layer of Fontina,

pour in as much stock as required to just cover the layers. • Arrange the remaining Fontina on top and dot with the butter. • Place the dish in a preheated oven at 300°F and gradually increase the temperature (in 15 minutes it should reach 400°F). Cook for 30–40 minutes. • Serve hot.

Serves: 4 · Prep: 20 min. · Cooking: 1 hr · Level: 2

PASTA RIPIENA ALLA BRISIGHELLESE
Pasta filled with fresh cheese

½   quantity pasta dough (see recipe, page 124)
6   oz mild, fresh cheese (Squaquaron, Crescenza, Robiola, or Ricotta)
1   cup freshly grated Parmesan cheese
2   eggs
    salt to taste
7   cups boiling Beef stock (see recipe, page 105)

Wine: a young, dry red (Rubicone Sangiovese)

Prepare the pasta dough. Shape the dough into a ball and set aside to rest for about 1 hour, wrapped in plastic wrap. • Mix the fresh white cheese in a bowl with the Parmesan, eggs, and a pinch of salt. • Roll out the pasta dough into a very thin sheet. Cover one half with the cheese mixture, spreading it out evenly. • Fold the other half of the dough over the top and roll lightly with a rolling pin to ensure that the layers stick firmly together. • Use a fluted pastry wheel to cut into ³⁄₄-inch squares. • Add the pasta carefully to the boiling stock and cook until the edges of the pasta are cooked *al dente*. • Serve very hot.

Serves: 4 · Prep: 45 min. + time to make the pasta · Cooking: 10 min. · Level: 3

ZUPPA MARICONDA
Dumplings in chicken stock

7   oz day-old bread, without the crust, cut into pieces
1¼ cups whole milk
¼   cup butter
3   eggs
⅓   cup freshly grated Parmesan cheese
    pinch of nutmeg
    salt and freshly ground white pepper to taste
7   cups Chicken stock (see recipe, page 104)

Wine: a dry white (Pinot Bianco di Grave del Friuli)

Place the bread in a bowl with the milk to soften. After 15 minutes, drain and squeeze out most (but not all) of the milk. • Melt the butter in a skillet. Add the bread and let it dry out over low heat, mixing well. This will take 2–3 minutes. The bread should stay soft because it will have absorbed the butter. • Transfer to a bowl and add the eggs, Parmesan, nutmeg, salt, and pepper to taste. Mix well to obtain a smooth mixture. • Cover with plastic wrap or a plate and place in the refrigerator for 1 hour. • Take teaspoonfuls of the mixture to make small dumplings, about the size of a large marble, and line them up on a clean work surface. • Bring the stock to the boil in a fairly deep pot and add the dumplings. • Lower the heat as soon as the stock returns to the boil. When the dumplings are cooked they will rise to the surface. • Serve hot (with extra grated Parmesan, if liked).

Serves: 4 · Prep: 40 min. + 1 hr to chill · Cooking: 5–7 min. · Level: 2

SEMOLINO IN BRODO
Semolina in beef stock

½   cup coarse-grain semolina
7   cups boiling Beef stock (see recipe, page 105)
    salt to taste
2   tablespoons butter
1   cup freshly grated Parmesan cheese

Wine: a dry white (Colli Euganei Bianco)

Sift the semolina slowly into the boiling stock, stirring with a whisk to prevent lumps from forming. • Simmer for 20 minutes, stirring occasionally. • Season with salt. • Add the butter 1 minute before serving and stir again. • Sprinkle with the Parmesan and serve.

Serves: 4 · Prep: 5 min. · Cooking: 20 min. · Level: 1

BRODETTO DELL'ADRIATICO
Adriatic fish soup

- 3 lb mixed fish and seafood–squid, goatfish (red mullet), scorpionfish, sole, silver mullet (golden gray mullet), smooth hound or shark
- 1 cup extra-virgin olive oil
- 5 cloves garlic, 4 finely chopped + 1 whole clove
- 3 white onions, finely chopped
- ¼ cup finely chopped parsley
- 8 oz peeled and chopped fresh or canned tomatoes
- ½ cup white wine vinegar
  salt and freshly ground black pepper to taste
- 4 slices firm-textured white bread

Wine: a dry white (Bianco di Greco)

Clean and prepare the fish as shown on pages 200–01. • Pour the oil into a large, preferably earthenware, flameproof pan and sauté the garlic, onions, and parsley until soft. This will take about 10 minutes. To prevent the mixture from over-browning, you can add 3–4 tablespoons water while cooking. • Add the tomatoes, vinegar, and about 1½ cups water. Season with salt and pepper, cover, and cook over low heat for 30 minutes. • Carefully add the fish, check the seasoning, cover again, and cook over very low heat for another 30 minutes. Meanwhile, toast the bread and rub with the whole clove of garlic. • Place a slice of toast in each of 4 individual soup bowls and ladle the soup on top to serve.

Serves: 4 · Prep: 40 min. · Cooking: 1¼ hrs · Level: 2

ZUPPA DI POVERACCE
Clam soup

- 2¾ lb small clams, in shell
- 3 cloves garlic, peeled and crushed
- ½ cup extra-virgin olive oil
- 10 oz peeled and chopped fresh or canned tomatoes
  salt and freshly ground black pepper to taste
- ½ cup dry white wine
- 4 thick slices firm-textured bread, toasted
- 3 tablespoons finely chopped parsley

Wine: a dry white (Albana di Romagna)

Soak the clams in cold water for 1 hour to purge them of sand. • Rinse the clams in plenty of cold water, discarding any that are already open. • Sauté the garlic in the oil in a large heavy-bottomed saucepan for 1–2 minutes. Add the tomatoes and season with salt and pepper. Simmer for 10 minutes. • Add the clams. Cover and cook for a few minutes, until they have all opened (discard any that do not open). • Pour in the wine and simmer for 10 minutes more. • Arrange the toasted bread in individual soup bowls and ladle the clam soup over the top. Sprinkle with the parsley and serve.

Serves: 4 · Prep: 30 min. + 1 hr to soak · Cooking: 25 min. · Level: 1

ZUPPA DI MOSCARDINI
Baby octopus soup

- 4 medium tomatoes, ripe and firm
- 2 tablespoons finely chopped parsley
- 2 cloves garlic, finely chopped
- ¼ cup extra-virgin olive oil
- 1½ lb baby octopus, cleaned, rinsed, and cut in pieces
- ½ cup dry white wine
- ¼ teaspoon crushed red pepper flakes
  salt to taste
- 4–8 slices toasted bread

Wine: a dry white (Vernaccia di San Gimignano)

Plunge the tomatoes into boiling water for 1 minute, then into cold. Slip off the skins, and chop coarsely. • In a heavy-bottomed saucepan, sauté the parsley and garlic in the oil for 2–3 minutes. • Add the octopus and cook for 3 minutes over medium heat, stirring continuously. • Pour in the wine and cook until it has evaporated. Add the tomatoes, pepper flakes, and a little salt. • Stir well and cover the pot – the octopus produce a lot of liquid which has to be kept from evaporating. Cook for 30 minutes, stirring frequently. • Arrange the toast in a large tureen. Taste the soup for salt, then pour it over slices of toast. Serve hot.

Serves: 4 · Prep: 20 min. · Cooking: 40 min. · Level: 2

ZUPPA DI POLPETTI E MOSCARDINI
Baby octopus and squid soup

☞ To clean the octopus and squid, follow the instructions on page 200.

- 2 cloves garlic, peeled but whole
- ⅓ cup extra-virgin olive oil
- 1 onion, finely chopped
- 1 lb baby octopus, cleaned and coarsely chopped
- 8 oz baby squid, cleaned and coarsely chopped
  salt and freshly black ground pepper to taste
- ½ cup dry white wine
- 1 tablespoon finely chopped fresh marjoram
- ½ cup boiling water
- 8 oz tomatoes, peeled and coarsely chopped
- 4 slices dense-grain white bread

Wine: a dry white (Cori Bianco)

In a large, heavy-bottomed saucepan, sauté the garlic in the oil over medium heat for 2 minutes, then discard the garlic. • Add the onion and sauté for 5 minutes. Stir in the octopus and squid. • Season with salt and pepper and cook for 8 minutes, stirring frequently. Pour in the wine and cook until it has evaporated. • Add the marjoram, parsley, water, and tomatoes; cover and cook for 20 minutes over low heat. • Toast the bread and place one slice in each of 4 individual soup bowls. • Ladle the soup over the top and serve hot.

Serves: 4 · Prep: 30 min. · Cooking: 30 min. · Level: 2

CACCIUCCO
Tuscan fish soup

☞ This classic Tuscan soup is similar to *Bouillabaisse*, which is made in Provence, in southern France.

- 8 oz octopus, cut into bite-sized pieces
- 8 oz white fish fillets, cut into bite-sized pieces
- 8 oz squid, cut into bite-sized pieces
- 14 oz mussels, in shell
- 14 oz clams, in shell
  salt to taste
- ½ onion
- 1 stalk celery and 1 carrot, both cut in half
- 1 bunch parsley
- 5 basil leaves
- 1 bay leaf
- 8 oz hake
- 8 oz red mullet
- 8 oz monkfish (with the head if possible)
- ⅓ cup extra-virgin olive oil
- 6 cloves garlic, 5 finely chopped + 1 whole clove
- ½ cup finely chopped parsley
- 1 red chile, chopped
- 1 cup dry white wine
- 14 oz plum tomatoes, skinned and diced
- 3¾ cups Fish stock (see recipe, page 105)
- 4 medium shrimp or saltwater crayfish
- 7 oz smooth dogfish or shark
- 4 slices coarse white bread

Wine: a dry white (Ansonica Costa dell'Argentario)

Clean the octopus and squid as explained on page 200. • Soak the mussels and clams in cold water for 1 hour. Place in a skillet over high heat and cook until they are all open. Discard any that have not opened. Set aside the prepared fish and mollusks. • Half fill a medium pan with water, and add the onion, celery, carrot, parsley, basil, bay leaf, and 1 teaspoon of salt. Place over medium heat, cover, and bring to the boil. • Add the hake, red mullet, and monkfish head and bring to the boil again. Lower the heat, partially cover the pan and cook for 20 minutes. Turn off the heat. • Drain the stock through a colander into a tureen, discard the monkfish head, onion, celery, carrot,

parsley, basil, and bay leaf. • Push the fish through a food mill and set aside in a bowl. • Pour the oil into a large skillet and sauté the chopped garlic and parsley over medium heat for 5 minutes. Add the chile, squid, and octopus. • Cook for 10 minutes, or until reduced. • Pour in the wine and cook for 4 minutes. Lower the heat, add the diced tomatoes, stir, and check the seasoning. • Cook, covered, for about 20 minutes then add the creamed fish mixture, stock, the whole shrimp or saltwater crayfish, the smooth dogfish or shark and monkfish, its central bone removed, cut into four pieces, mussels, and clams. Cook for 10 minutes. • Toast the bread and rub the slices with the clove of garlic. • Place a piece of toast in each of 4 individual soup bowls and ladle the soup over the top. Serve hot or warm.

Serves: 4 · Prep: 50 min. · Cooking: 1¼ hrs · Level: 2

ZUPPA DI ACCIUGHE
Fresh anchovy soup

- ¼ cup extra-virgin olive oil
- ½ small onion, ½ celery stalk, ½ small carrot, all finely chopped
- ½ tablespoon finely chopped parsley
- 2 cloves garlic, finely chopped
- ¼ teaspoon crushed red pepper flakes
- 2 large tomatoes
- 2 lb fresh anchovies, without their heads, split, cleaned, and boned
- 1 cup dry white wine
- 2 cups salted, boiling water
  salt to taste
- 8 slices dense-grain bread, toasted

Wine: a dry white (Pigato di Albenga)

Combine the oil, onion, celery, carrot, parsley, garlic, and pepper flakes in a heavy-bottomed saucepan and sauté for 6–7 minutes. • Plunge the tomatoes into a pot of boiling water for 1 minute and then into cold. Drain and peel. • Cut them in half horizontally, and squeeze to remove some of the seeds. Chop coarsely. • Add to the pan and continue cooking for about 10 minutes. • Add the anchovies, pour in the wine, and stir carefully. • Simmer for 5–8 minutes over low heat, adding the boiling water a little at a time. • Pour the soup into individual soup bowls over the slices of toasted bread and serve.

Serves: 4 · Prep: 30 min. · Cooking: 25 min. · Level: 2

Tuscan fish soup

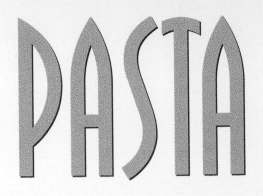
Pasta, the flagship of Italian cooking, is delicious, versatile, economical and easy to prepare. What's more, it is good for your health. A word about quantity: in Italy we allow 4 oz per person and serve it in a judicious amount of sauce. No matter the size of your serving, don't cancel out the delicate flavor of the pasta itself by drowning it in too much sauce!

PASTA

PENNE STRASCICATE
Tuscan-style penne

1	medium onion, finely chopped
1	small carrot, finely chopped
1	small stalk celery, finely chopped
2	tablespoons finely chopped parsley
1/3	cup extra-virgin olive oil
12	oz ground lean beef
1/2	cup full-bodied, dry red wine
1	(15 oz) can tomatoes, coarsely chopped
	salt and freshly ground black pepper to taste
1	cup Beef stock (see recipe, page 105)
1	lb penne pasta
1	cup freshly grated Parmesan cheese

Wine: a young, dry red (Chianti dei Colli Senesi)

In a large skillet, sauté the onion, carrot, celery, and parsley in the oil for 5 minutes. • Add the meat, and use a fork or wooden spoon to break up any lumps that form as it cooks. • When browned, pour in the wine and stir for 5 minutes. • Add the tomatoes, salt, and pepper, stir well and simmer for 5 minutes. • Add 2–3 tablespoons of the stock, cover and simmer for 40 minutes, stirring in stock at intervals to keep the sauce moist. • Cook the pasta in a large pan of salted, boiling water until *al dente*. Drain the pasta and add to the skillet with the meat sauce. Toss well, remove from heat, and leave for 2 minutes. • Stir in the Parmesan and serve.

Serves: 4 · Prep: 5 min. · Cooking: 15 min. · Level 1

◁ Spaghetti with tomato sauce
(see recipe, page 127)
▷ Tuscan-style penne

TYPES OF PASTA

The huge number of pasta varieties and shapes can be divided into two main groups—dry, factory-made pasta, and fresh pasta. Many types of fresh pasta can be made at home.

Dry, factory-made pasta

This group includes such familiar shapes as spaghetti, penne, and macaroni. This page shows all the dry, factory-made pasta shapes used in this book. Where the English name is different from the Italian, it is included in parenthesis.

Fresh pasta

Most types of fresh pasta are made with flour, eggs, and salt. Many are cut into noodle shapes of varying width, from tiny capellini to pappardelle. Lasagne is cut in sheets about 3x12 inches. Fresh pasta dough can also be used to make stuffed pasta shapes, including tortellini, ravioli, agnolotti, and many others. See pages 124–125 for instructions on how to make fresh pasta at home.

There are also many regional fresh pasta types, such as pici, bigoli, and pizzoccheri. Instructions for making these pasta types are included in the recipes.

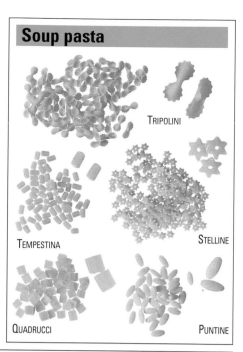

Soup pasta

TRIPOLINI

TEMPESTINA

STELLINE

QUADRUCCI

PUNTINE

Dry pasta

FARFALLE (Bow ties)

RUOTE (Wheels)

MALLOREDDUS (Sardinian gnocchi)

ELICHE (Spirals)

FUSILLI

RIGATONI

PENNE LISCE (Smooth penne)

CANNELLONI

MACCHERONI (Macaroni)

PENNE RIGATE (Ridged penne)

SPAGHETTINI

SPAGHETTI

LINGUINE

BUCATINI

ZITI

LASAGNE

MALTAGLIATI

PAGLIA E FIENO

PAPPARDELLE

GARGANELLI

ORECCHIETTE

TAGLIATELLE

RAVIOLI

PICI

FETTUCCINE

AGNOLOTTI

PIZZOCCHERI

TORTELLI

TAGLIOLINI

TORTELLINI

CAPPELLACCI

BIGOLI

TORTELLONI

CAPELLINI
(Angel hair)

MAKING FRESH PASTA

Making fresh pasta at home is a rewarding experience. Getting it right may take a little time, but it is well worth the effort. If you don't have time to make your own pasta, commercially-made fresh pasta can be substituted in all of the recipes in this chapter.

Making the pasta dough

PLAIN PASTA DOUGH

3	cups all-purpose flour
3	medium eggs
½	teaspoon salt

Serves: 4 · Prep: 20 min. + 2 hrs to rest · Level: 2

SPINACH PASTA DOUGH

Proceed as for Plain pasta dough, working the spinach into the flour with the eggs.

2	cups all-purpose flour
1	cup cooked spinach, finely chopped
2	large eggs
½	teaspoon salt

Serves: 4 · Prep: 20 min. + 2 hrs to rest · Level: 2

1 Sift the flour and salt into a mound on a clean work surface. Make a hollow in the center and break the eggs into it one by one.

2 Using a fork, gradually mix the eggs into the flour. Be careful not to break the wall of flour of the eggs will run. Continue until all the flour has been incorporated.

3 At a certain point the dough will be too thick to mix with a fork. Use your hands to shape the pasta into a ball. It should be smooth and not too sticky.

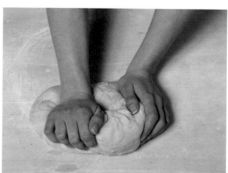

4 Knead the dough by pushing downward and forward on the ball of pasta with the heel of your palm. Fold the dough in half, give it a quarter-turn, and repeat the process. Knead for about 10 minutes.

5 Set the kneaded pasta aside for 15–20 minutes to rest. To roll the pasta by hand, flour a clean work surface and place a rolling pin on the top of the ball. Push outward from the center.

6 When the dough is about ¼ thick, curl the far edge of the dough around the pin and gently stretch it as you roll it onto the pin. Unroll and repeat until the dough is almost transparent.

7 To cut the pasta by hand, fold the sheet of dough loosely into a flat roll. Use a sharp knife to cut the roll into ⅛-inch slices for tagliolini, ¼-inch slices for fettuccine, ⅓-inch slices for tagliatelle, or ¾-inch slices for pappardelle. Unravel the strips of pasta and lay them on a clean cloth. To make lasagne, cut the dough into 3x12-inch sheets. To make maltagliati, roll the dough in strips about 2 inches wide and cut into diamond shapes. Paglia e fieno pasta for 4 servings is made with half quantities each of plain fettuccine and spinach fettuccine.

Using the pasta machine

1 To roll the dough using a pasta machine, divide it into several pieces and flatten them by hand. Set the machine with its rollers at the widest, and run each piece of pasta through the machine. Reduce the rollers' width by one notch and repeat. Continue until all the pasta has gone through the machine at the thinnest setting.

2 Cut the pieces of rolled pasta into sheets about 12 inches long. Attach the cutters to the pasta machine and set it at the widths given for the various types of pasta. Lay the cut pasta out on clean cloths to dry for 2 hours before use.

Making stuffed pasta

TO MAKE AGNOLOTTI, RAVIOLI, OR TORTELLI

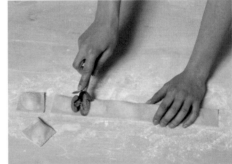

1 Cut the rolled dough into sheets about 4 inches wide. Place teaspoonfuls of filling at intervals of about 2 inches down the center.

2 Moisten the edges of the dough with a little water and fold it over to seal. Press down lightly between the mounds of filling.

3 Use a sharp knife or wheel cutter (the latter will give your pasta fluted edges) to cut between the mounds. If using a wheel cutter, roll it around the other sides so that they are attractively fluted too. Lay the stuffed pasta out on clean cloths for 2 hours before use.

TO MAKE TORTELLINI

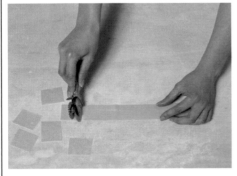

1 Cut the rolled dough into sheets about 2 inches wide. Cut them in squares.

2 Place teaspoonfuls of the filling mixture at the center of each. Moisten the edges of the pasta with a little water and fold over into a triangular shape.

3 Fold the top of the triangle over and pull the edges around to meet. Pinch the edges together and seal them. Lay the stuffed pasta out on clean cloths for 2 hours before use.

Spaghettini with garlic, oil, and chile

SPAGHETTI ALLA CARRETTIERA

Spaghetti with onion, garlic, and bread crumbs

☞ According to legend, this classic Roman dish is named for the *carrettieri* (cart-drivers) who once brought the famous Castelli Romani wines from the Alban Hills into Rome. There are many variations; I have included two of my favorites.

- 1   large onion, finely chopped
- 2   cloves garlic, finely chopped
- 2   tablespoons finely chopped parsley
- 1/2   cup diced pancetta
- 1/3   cup extra-virgin olive oil
     salt and freshly ground black pepper to taste
- 1/4   cup fine dry bread crumbs, toasted in a hot oven
- 1/2   teaspoon extra-virgin olive oil
- 1   lb spaghetti

Wine: a dry white (Velletri)

Sauté the onion, garlic, parsley, and pancetta in a skillet with 1/3 cup of oil over medium heat until the onion and garlic are soft. Season lightly with salt and pepper. Remove from heat. • Mix the bread crumbs with 1/2 teaspoon of oil. • Cook the spaghetti in a large pot of salted, boiling water until *al dente*. Drain well and place in a heated serving dish. Toss with the sauce and bread crumbs. Serve hot.

Serves: 4 · Prep: 10 min. · Cooking: 15 min. · Level: 1

SPAGHETTI ALLA CARRETTIERA ROSSA

Spaghetti with onion, garlic, tomato, and bread crumbs

Wine: a dry red (Savuto Rosso)

Proceed as in the preceding recipe, but add 6 large peeled and diced tomatoes and 1 teaspoon crushed red pepper flakes to the onion and garlic mixture after it has changed color. • Cook over medium heat for 10–15 minutes until the tomatoes have reduced.

Serves: 4 · Prep: 10 min. · Cooking: 15 min. · Level: 1

SPAGHETTI CON PANGRATTATO

Spaghetti with toasted bread crumbs

- 4   whole cloves garlic, lightly crushed
- 1/2   cup extra-virgin olive oil
- 10   anchovy fillets
- 2   tablespoons finely chopped parsley
- 1   lb peeled and chopped fresh or canned tomatoes
     salt to taste
- 1   lb spaghetti
- 1/3   cup fine dry bread crumbs, toasted in a hot oven

Wine: a dry white (Alcamo)

In a large skillet, sauté the garlic in the oil until it starts to color, then remove and discard. • Add the anchovies, crushing them with a fork so that they dissolve in the flavored oil. • Add the parsley and tomatoes. Simmer over low heat for 15–20 minutes. Season with salt. • Cook the pasta in a large pot of salted, boiling water until *al dente*. Drain, add to the sauce and toss well. • Place in a heated serving dish, sprinkle with the bread crumbs, and serve.

Serves: 4 · Prep: 10 min. · Cooking: 25 min. · Level: 1

SPAGHETTINI CON AGLIO OLIO E PEPERONCINO

Spaghettini with garlic, oil, and chile

- 1   lb spaghettini (thin spaghetti)
- 4   cloves garlic, finely chopped
- 2   tablespoons finely chopped parsley
- 1   dried red chile, crumbled
- 1/2   cup extra-virgin olive oil
     salt to taste

Wine: a dry white (Bianco di Velletri)

Cook the spaghettini in a large pot of salted, boiling water until *al dente*. • While the pasta is cooking, sauté the garlic, parsley, and chile in the oil in a small skillet over low heat until the garlic begins to change color. • Remove from heat and add 2 tablespoons of the cooking water from the pasta pot. Season with salt. • Drain the pasta and place in a heated serving dish. • Pour the sauce over the top and toss well. Serve hot.

Serves: 4 · Prep: 3 min. · Cooking: 10 min. · Level: 1

SPAGHETTI CACIO E PEPE

Spaghetti with Pecorino cheese and pepper

- 1   lb spaghetti
- 1 1/4   cups freshly grated Pecorino cheese
     freshly ground black pepper to taste

Wine: a young, dry red (Frascati Novello)

Cook the spaghetti in a large pot of salted, boiling water until *al dente*. • Drain the pasta when it is cooked, leaving just a little more water than usual. (This will melt the cheese and prevent the pasta from sticking together.) • Place the spaghetti in a heated serving dish. Sprinkle with the Pecorino and a generous grinding of pepper. Toss for 1–2 minutes and serve.

Serves: 4 · Prep: 5 min. · Cooking: 10 min. · Level: 1

SPAGHETTI CON OLIVE NERE
Spaghetti with black olives

1	lb peeled and chopped fresh or canned tomatoes
2	cloves garlic, finely chopped
5	tablespoons extra-virgin olive oil
1¼	cups black olives, pitted and coarsely chopped
2	teaspoons oregano
½	teaspoon crushed red pepper flakes
	salt to taste
1	lb spaghetti

Wine: a dry white (Greco di Tufo)

Place the tomatoes in a heavy-bottomed saucepan. Add the garlic and simmer over low heat for 15 minutes. • Add the oil, olives, oregano, and pepper flakes and cook for 2 minutes more. Season with salt. • Cook the spaghetti in a large pot of salted, boiling water until *al dente*. • Drain and add to the tomato mixture. Toss well and serve. Cheese is not served with this dish.

Serves: 4 · Prep: 10 min. · Cooking: 20 min. · Level: 1

SPAGHETTI AL POMODORO
Spaghetti with tomato sauce

1	lb spaghetti
1	quantity Basic tomato sauce

Wine: a dry white (Bianco di Velletri)

Prepare the tomato sauce. • Cook the spaghetti in a large pot of salted, boiling water until *al dente*. Drain well and place in a heated serving dish. • Pour the sauce over the top and toss well. Serve hot.

Serves: 4 · Prep: 3 min + time to make the sauce. · Cooking: 12 min. · Level: 1

SPAGHETTI AI POMODORI CRUDI
Spaghetti with fresh tomatoes and lemon

1	lb spaghetti
1½	lb ripe tomatoes
1	clove garlic
20	fresh basil leaves
	salt and freshly ground black pepper to taste
	freshly squeezed juice of 1 large lemon
½	cup extra-virgin olive oil

Wine: a dry white (Roero Arneis)

Spaghetti with raw tomatoes and lemon

Cook the spaghetti in a large pot of salted, boiling water until *al dente*. • While the pasta is cooking, peel the tomatoes, cut them in half, and squeeze out as many seeds as possible. Chop coarsely and place in a bowl. • Finely chop the garlic and basil together. Add to the tomatoes and season with salt and pepper (the salt will help the basil to keep its bright green color. • Pour in the lemon juice and oil and mix well. • Drain the pasta and place in a heated serving dish. Pour the sauce over the top and toss vigorously. • Serve hot.

Serves: 4 · Prep: 10 min. · Cooking: 12 min. · Level: 1

SPAGHETTI ALLA PUTTANESCA
Spicy spaghetti with olives and capers

1	lb ripe tomatoes
1¾	cups black olives
2	tablespoons extra-virgin olive oil
2	cloves garlic, peeled but whole
½	teaspoon crushed red pepper flakes
4	anchovy fillets (optional)
2	tablespoons capers
	salt and freshly ground black pepper to taste
1	lb spaghetti

Wine: a dry white (Frascati)

Peel the tomatoes and dice them. Pit and chop about three-quarters of the olives. • Heat the oil in a skillet and sauté the garlic with the pepper flakes. Discard the garlic when it has turned light gold. Add the anchovies, if using, and stir well in the oil until they dissolve. • Add the olives and capers, then the tomatoes. Season with salt and pepper (the anchovies and olives are both quite salty, so be sure to taste the sauce before seasoning). Cook over a medium-low heat for about 15 minutes, or until the sauce reduces. • Cook the spaghetti in a large pot of salted, boiling water until *al dente*. • Drain the pasta and place in a heated serving dish. Pour the sauce over the top, toss well, and serve.

Serves: 4 · Prep: 10 min. · Cooking: 25 min. · Level: 1

PASTA ALLA NORMA
Sicilian-style pasta

☞ This recipe comes from Catania and is named after Bellini's masterpiece, the opera *Norma*.

- 3 medium eggplants
  coarse sea salt
- 4 oz Ricotta salata or semi-hard Pecorino cheese
- 1½ lb fresh tomatoes, skinned and chopped
- 2 cloves garlic, finely chopped
- ¼ cup extra-virgin olive oil
- 1 lb spaghetti
- 1 cup oil, for frying
- 6 fresh basil leaves, torn
  salt and freshly ground black pepper to taste

Wine: a young rosé (Etna Rosato)

Cut the eggplants into ¼-inch thick slices. Sprinkle with the coarse sea salt and place on a slanted chopping board. Leave for at least 1 hour, then rinse thoroughly and dry on paper towels. • Use a fork to break the Ricotta into fairly small, crumbly pieces (or chop the Pecorino into small pieces with a knife). • In a large skillet, sauté the garlic in the oil until soft. Add the tomatoes and simmer for 30 minutes, stirring occasionally. • Sieve the thick tomato sauce and return to the skillet. Keep warm over very low heat. • Heat the frying oil to very hot in another skillet. Fry the slices of eggplant in batches until tender. Drain on paper towels. • Cook the spaghetti in a large pot of salted, boiling water until *al dente*. Drain well and place in a heated serving dish. • Add the tomato sauce and basil and half the cheese. • Toss well and place in four individual serving dishes. • Chop the eggplant into large squares. Top each portion with a quarter of the eggplant and the remaining Ricotta or Pecorino.

Serves: 4 · Prep: 15 min. + 1 hr to degorge the eggplants · Cooking: 35 min. · Level: 2

SPAGHETTI AI POMODORINI
Spaghetti with cherry tomatoes

- 2¼ lb cherry tomatoes
- 2 cloves of garlic, peeled but whole
- ½ teaspoon crushed red pepper flakes
  pinch of oregano
- 4 fresh basil leaves, torn
- ⅓ cup extra-virgin olive oil
  salt to taste
- 1 lb spaghetti

Wine: a dry rosé (Salice Salentino Rosato)

Wash and dry the tomatoes, cut each one in half, and place in a bowl with the garlic, pepper flakes, oregano, and basil. • Heat the oil in a large skillet over high heat and add the contents of the bowl. Cook for 5–6 minutes, gently stirring with a wooden spoon at frequent intervals. Season with salt and remove from heat. Do not overcook the tomatoes: they should still be firm and retain their skins at this stage. • Cook the spaghetti in a large pot of salted, boiling water for about 8–10 minutes. • Drain the spaghetti and add to the tomato mixture in the skillet. Cook for about 5 minutes more over high heat, stirring well, so that the tomato sauce is absorbed by the pasta as it finishes cooking. • Serve at once.

Serves: 4 · Prep: 15 min. · Cooking: 15 min. · Level: 1

LINGUINE AI GAMBERETTI E ZUCCHINE
Linguine with shrimp and zucchini

- 14 oz shrimp, shelled
- 4 small zucchini
- ⅓ cup extra-virgin olive oil
- 1 scallion, chopped
  salt and freshly ground pepper to taste
- 1 lb linguine pasta

Wine: a dry white (Parrina Bianco)

Chop half the shrimp and place in a covered bowl. • Wash the zucchini and cut into julienne strips. • Heat the oil in a large skillet and sauté the scallion for 3 minutes over medium heat. Add the zucchini and cook for 7 minutes. • Stir in the shrimp, season with salt and pepper, and cook for 5 minutes, adding a little of the water from the pasta if necessary. Turn off the heat. • Meanwhile, cook the linguine in a large pot of salted, boiling water until *al dente*. Drain and place in the skillet with the shrimp and zucchini sauce. • Toss well over high heat and serve.

Serves: 4 · Prep: 15 min. · Cooking: 15 min. · Level: 1

Spaghetti with cherry tomatoes

Spaghetti with smoked pancetta and egg

LINGUINE CON POMODORI SECCHI
Linguine with tomato and caper sauce

- ³/₄ lb very ripe fresh tomatoes
  salt to taste
- 4 oz dried tomatoes, finely chopped
- 1 lb linguine pasta
- ¼ cup capers
- 1 clove garlic, peeled but whole
- ⅓ cup extra-virgin olive oil
- ½ teaspoon crushed red pepper flakes

Wine: a dry rosé (Cirò Rosato Superiore)

Cut the fresh tomatoes in half or in quarters and squeeze them gently to remove the seeds. Sprinkle lightly with salt and leave to drain for 10 minutes. Sieve the tomatoes to remove the skins and any remaining seeds. • Put the oil in a heavy-bottomed saucepan over low heat. Add the dried tomatoes and cook over low heat for a few minutes before adding the sieved tomatoes, capers, garlic, and pepper flakes. Season with salt. Simmer for 20 minutes. • Cook the spaghetti in a large pot of salted, boiling water until *al dente*. Drain and place in a heated serving dish. Toss with the tomato sauce and serve.

Serves: 4 · Prep: 20 min. · Cooking: 35 min. · Level: 1

LINGUINE CON FAGIOLINI E PESTO
Linguine with green beans and basil sauce

- 1½ lb green beans, cleaned and cut into lengths
- 3 medium new potatoes, peeled and diced
- 1 quantity Genoese basil sauce (see recipe, page 21)
- 1 lb linguine pasta
- ¼ cup butter
- ¼ cup freshly grated Pecorino cheese
- ¼ cup freshly grated Parmesan cheese

Wine: a dry white (Riesling Sylvaner dell'Alto Adige)

Cook the beans and potatoes in a large pot of salted, boiling water until tender. Take

them out with a slotted spoon and use the same water to cook the pasta. • While the pasta is cooking, prepare the basil sauce. Add 2 tablespoons of boiling water from the pasta pot to make the basil sauce slightly more liquid. • When the pasta is cooked *al dente*, drain and place in a heated serving dish. Toss with the basil sauce, butter, and vegetables. Sprinkle with the cheeses, and serve hot.

Serves: 4 · Prep: 15 min. · Cooking: 25 min. · Level: 1

SPAGHETTI ALLA CARBONARA
Spaghetti with smoked pancetta and egg

☞ *La carbonara* is a classic Roman sauce. The trick is to toss the pasta very quickly with the egg and serve as soon as possible.

- 1 lb spaghetti
- 2 cloves garlic, lightly crushed but whole
- ¼ cup extra-virgin olive oil
- 6 oz diced smoked pancetta (or bacon)
- 4 fresh eggs
- ⅓ cup freshly grated Parmesan cheese
- ⅓ cup freshly grated Pecorino cheese
  salt and freshly ground black pepper to taste

Wine: a dry white (Pinot Grigio d'Isonzo)

Cook the spaghetti in a large pot of salted, boiling water until al dente. • Sauté the oil, garlic, and pancetta in a skillet over medium heat until the pancetta is golden brown but not crisp. Remove the skillet from heat and discard the garlic. • In a mixing bowl beat the eggs, Parmesan, Pecorino, and salt until well mixed. Set aside. • Drain the pasta and place in a heated serving dish. Add the egg mixture and toss. • Return the skillet with the

pancetta to high heat for 1 minute. Pour the hot oil and pancetta over the pasta and egg, and toss well. Grind a generous amount of black pepper over the top and serve.

Serves: 4 · Prep: 5 min. · Cooking: 15 min. · Level: 1

LINGUINE CON LE FAVE
Linguine with fava beans

- 3 lb fava beans, in their pods
- 2 cloves garlic
- 3 sprigs fresh rosemary
- ¼ cup butter
- ¼ cup extra-virgin olive oil
- 1 large onion, finely chopped
- 1½ cups Beef stock (see recipe, page 105)
  salt and freshly ground black pepper to taste
- 1 lb linguine pasta
- ⅓ cup freshly grated Parmesan cheese

Wine: a light, dry white (Verdicchio)

Pod the beans and set aside in a bowl of cold water. • Cut the cloves of garlic in two and place in a skillet with the rosemary, half the butter, and the oil. Sauté until the garlic begins to change color. • Remove the garlic and rosemary. Lower the heat to medium, add the onion, and sauté until soft. • Drain the fava beans and add to the skillet with the stock. Season with salt and pepper. • Cook over medium-low heat for about 20 minutes, or until the beans are tender, stirring from time to time. • Cook the linguine in a large pot of salted, boiling water until *al dente*. Drain and place in a heated serving dish. • Pour the sauce over the pasta and toss well with the Parmesan and the remaining butter. Serve hot.

Serves: 4 · Prep: 15 min. · Cooking: 30 min. · Level: 1

CAPELLINI OLIO E LIMONE
Angel hair with oil and lemon sauce

- 1 medium onion, finely chopped
- 1 cup extra-virgin olive oil
- 1 lb angel hair pasta
  juice of 3 lemons
  salt and freshly ground black pepper to taste
- 1 cup freshly grated Parmesan cheese

Wine: a dry white (Frascati)

Sauté the onion in the oil in a large skillet over medium heat until the onion turns pale gold. • Cook the pasta in a large pot of salted, boiling water until *al dente*. • Drain well and place in the pan with the onion. Toss the pasta briefly over medium heat and place in a heated serving dish. Add the lemon juice, salt, pepper, and Parmesan. Toss well and serve.

Serves: 4 · Prep: 5 min. · Cooking: 5 min. · Level: 1

BUCATINI CON CAPPERI E OLIVE
Bucatini with capers and olives

- 1 lb bucatini pasta
- 1/4 cup extra-virgin olive oil
- 2 cloves garlic, finely chopped
- 3 tablespoons finely chopped parsley
- 1 cup pitted and chopped black olives
- 3 tablespoons capers
- 1/3 cup freshly grated Pecorino cheese

Wine: a dry white (Bianco Vergine Valdichiana)

Cook the bucatini in a large pot of salted, boiling water until *al dente*. • In a large skillet, sauté the garlic and parsley in the oil over medium heat until the garlic starts to color. • Stir the olives and capers into the sauce and cook over low heat for 2–3 minutes. • Drain the pasta and place in the skillet. • Toss with the capers and olives over medium-high heat for 2 minutes. • Place in a heated serving dish and sprinkle with the Pecorino. • Serve hot.

Serves: 4 · Prep: 10 min. · Cooking: 15 min. · Level: 1

ZITI CON CAVOLFIORE
Ziti with cauliflower, raisins, and pine nuts

☞ To transform this recipe into a hearty winter dish, transfer the cooked pasta and cauliflower to an ovenproof dish and sprinkle with the Pecorino. Bake in a preheated oven at 425°F for 10 minutes, or until the cheese is brown.

- 1 small cauliflower, about 1 lb
  salt to taste
- 1 lb ziti pasta
- 1 medium onion, thinly sliced
- 1/3 cup extra-virgin olive oil
- 4 anchovy fillets
- 3 tablespoons small seedless white raisins
- 3 tablespoons pine nuts
- 1/4 teaspoon saffron, dissolved in 3 tablespoons hot water
  freshly ground black pepper
- 1/2 cup freshly grated Pecorino cheese

Wine: a dry white (Alcamo)

Boil the cauliflower in a large pot of salted water until just tender. Remove the cauliflower with a slotted spoon, reserving the water. Divide the cauliflower into small florets. • Bring the water back to the boil and add the pasta. • Meanwhile, sauté the onion for 1–2 minutes in the oil in a large, heavy-bottomed saucepan. Add the anchovies, raisins, pine nuts, and saffron. Stir for 2–3 minutes, then add the cauliflower and continue cooking over very low heat, stirring occasionally. • When the pasta is cooked *al dente*, drain and add to the cauliflower mixture. • Mix carefully, then place in a heated serving dish and sprinkle generously with pepper. • Sprinkle with the Pecorino and serve hot.

Serves: 4 · Prep: 15 min. · Cooking: 40 min. · Level: 1

BUCATINI CON PARMIGIANA DI ZUCCHINE
Bucatini with zucchini, basil, and tomatoes

- 1 small onion, finely chopped
- 2 tablespoons extra-virgin olive oil
- 2 1/4 lb peeled and chopped canned tomatoes,
- 4 fresh basil leaves, torn
  salt and pepper to taste
- 5 long zucchini, cut lengthwise in pieces about 2 x 1 inch
- 1/2 cup oil, for frying
- 1 lb bucatini pasta
- 1 3/4 cups freshly grated Parmesan cheese

Wine: a light, dry rosé (Castel del Monte Rosato)

Sauté the onion in a large, heavy-bottomed saucepan in the oil until soft. • Add the tomatoes and basil. Season with salt and pepper. Cover and simmer for 20 minutes. • Heat the frying oil in a skillet until very hot. Fry the zucchini in batches in the oil until light golden brown. Remove with a slotted spoon and drain on paper towels.

• Sprinkle lightly with salt and add to the tomato sauce. Cook gently for 10 minutes. Remove from heat. • Cook the bucatini in a large pan of salted, boiling water until *al dente*. Drain well, return to the saucepan, and add half the tomato and zucchini sauce. Stir well, then place in 4 individual serving dishes. Spoon equal amounts of the remaining tomato and zucchini sauce over each portion and sprinkle with the Parmesan. Serve at once.

Serves: 4 · Prep: 10 min. · Cooking: 35 min. · Level: 1

BUCATINI ALL'AMATRICIANA
Bucatini with pancetta and spicy tomato sauce

- 6 oz diced pancetta
- 2 tablespoons extra-virgin olive oil
- 1 onion, finely chopped
- 2 (15 oz) cans chopped tomatoes
- 1 teaspoon crushed red pepper flakes
  salt to taste
- 1 lb bucatini pasta
- 1/2 cup freshly grated Pecorino cheese

Wine: a dry rosé (Sangiovese di Aprilia)

Sauté the pancetta in a skillet with the oil for 2–3 minutes. Add the onion and cook until soft. • Stir in the tomatoes and pepper flakes. Season with salt and cook over medium-low heat for about 20 minutes, or until the tomatoes have begun to separate from the oil. • Cook the bucatini in a large pot of salted, boiling water until *al dente*. Drain well and place in a heated serving dish. • Toss with the sauce and Pecorino and serve immediately.

Serves: 4 · Prep: 5 min. · Cooking: 30 min. · Level: 1

SPAGHETTI AL TONNO
Spaghetti with tuna and tomato sauce

- 1 lb spaghetti
- 2 cloves garlic, finely chopped
- 3 tablespoons finely chopped parsley
- 1/2 cup extra-virgin olive oil
- 6 small tomatoes, sliced
  salt to taste
- 8 oz tuna, packed in oil, flaked

Wine: a dry white (Pinot Bianco)

Cook the spaghetti in a large pot of salted, boiling water until *al dente*. • Sauté the garlic and parsley in the oil over medium-low heat for 2 minutes. • Add the tomatoes,

season with salt, and cook for 4–5 minutes. • Mix in the tuna, stir, and turn off the heat immediately. • Drain the pasta well and place in a heated serving dish. Toss vigorously with the sauce and serve hot.

Serves: 4 · Prep: 10 min. · Cooking: 15 min. · Level: 1

MACCHERONI ALLA SICILIANA
Sicilian-style macaroni

☞ This simple dish is traditionally served during Lent. There are many versions from the various regions of Sicily.

- 2 whole cloves garlic, lightly crushed
- 1/3 cup extra-virgin olive oil
- 10 anchovy fillets
- 1 tablespoon finely chopped parsley
- 1 lb canned tomatoes, skinned and coarsely chopped
- 1 lb macaroni
  salt to taste
- 1/4 cup fine dry bread crumbs, toasted in a hot oven

Wine: a dry white (Alcamo)

Sauté the garlic in the oil in a large, heavy-bottomed saucepan until it starts to color, then remove and discard. • Add the anchovies, crushing them with a fork so that they dissolve in the flavored oil. • Add the parsley and tomatoes. Simmer over a low heat for 15–20 minutes. • Cook the macaroni in a large pot of salted, boiling water until *al dente*. Drain, add to the sauce and toss briefly. • Place in a heated serving dish. Sprinkle with the bread crumbs and serve hot.

Serves: 4 · Prep: 10 min. · Cooking: 20 min. · Level: 1

SPAGHETTI CON LE SEPPIE
Spaghetti with cuttlefish

- 8 cuttlefish
- 2 onions, finely chopped
- 2 cloves garlic, finely chopped
- 1/2 cup extra-virgin olive oil
- 8 oz peeled and chopped canned tomatoes
  salt and freshly ground black pepper to taste
- 1 lb spaghetti

Wine: a dry white (Bianchello del Metauro)

Clean the cuttlefish as explained in the recipe for Seafood salad on page 97. Take care not to break the internal ink sac. The ink can be added later (when tossing the pasta with the sauce) or discarded. • Cut the cuttlefish crosswise into thin half circles. • Put the onion and garlic in a large skillet with the oil and sauté over medium heat until they begin to change color. Add the cuttlefish and tomatoes. Season with salt and pepper. Turn the heat down low, cover, and simmer for about 45 minutes, or until the cuttlefish are tender. • Add the ink, if using, and stir over medium heat for 2–3 minutes. • Cook the spaghetti in a large pot of salted, boiling water until *al dente*. Drain well and place in a heated serving dish. Toss with the sauce and serve hot.

Serves: 4 · Prep: 20 min. · Cooking: 1 hr · Level: 2

Spaghetti with cuttlefish

Spaghetti with black truffles

Simmer for 15 minutes, then drain, reserving the water to cook the pasta. • Squeeze the fennel to remove excess moisture and chop coarsely. • Remove any scales from the sardines and gently pull off their heads (the viscera will come away with the heads). Use kitchen scissors to cut down their bellies and lay them out flat. • Sauté the onion in the oil, then add the anchovies, crushing them with a fork so that they dissolve in the oil. • Add the sardines, raisins, pine nuts, and almonds. Season with salt and pepper. • Cook over medium heat for 10 minutes, then add the fennel and saffron. Stir gently to avoid breaking up the fish. Reduce the heat, cover, and simmer for 10 more minutes. • Bring the fennel-flavored water to a boil, add the pasta, and cook until *al dente*. Drain and mix with the sardines and sauce. • Place in an oiled ovenproof dish and sprinkle with the bread crumbs. • Bake in a preheated oven at 425°F for 6–10 minutes. • Serve hot.

Serves: 4 · Prep: 30 min. · Cooking: 50 min. · Level: 3

SPAGHETTI ALLA NORCINA
Spaghetti with black truffles

☞ This dish is a specialty of Umbria, in central Italy, an area famous for its black truffles. The truffle season goes from Christmas until March; at other times of the year canned truffles can be used.

- 1   lb spaghetti
- 5   oz black truffles
- 1/3 cup extra-virgin olive oil
- 2   cloves garlic, cut in half and lightly crushed
- 4   anchovy fillets
      salt and freshly ground black pepper to taste

Wine: a dry white (Orvieto Classico)

Cook the spaghetti in a large pan of salted, boiling water until *al dente*. • Wash the truffles in warm water, scrubbing the surfaces carefully. Dry well and grate finely. • Heat the oil in a small, heavy-bottomed saucepan until fairly hot. Remove from heat and add the truffles. Mix well. • Return to very low heat and add the garlic and anchovies. Squash the anchovies with the back of a fork so that they dissolve in the oil. Stir until the oil is well-flavored with the garlic. Take care that the garlic doesn't burn and that the oil never boils. Remove from heat. Taste and season with salt and pepper, if needed. • Drain the pasta and place in a heated serving dish. Pour the truffle sauce over the top, toss well, and serve.

Serves: 4 · Prep: 15 min. · Cooking: 15 min. · Level: 1

ZITI CON LE SARDE
Ziti with sardines

- 3   quarts water
- 1   tablespoon salt
- 8   oz fennel, cleaned and cut in quarters
- 12 oz fresh or thawed frozen sardines
- 1   medium onion, finely chopped
- 1/3 cup extra-virgin olive oil
- 4–6 anchovy fillets
- 2   tablespoons small, seedless white raisins
- 3   tablespoons pine nuts
- 1/4 cup toasted almonds, chopped
      freshly ground black pepper to taste
- 1/4 teaspoon saffron, dissolved in 2 tablespoons hot water
- 1   lb ziti pasta
- 2/3 cup fine dry bread crumbs, toasted in a hot oven

Wine: a full-bodied white (Partinico)

Bring the water to a boil in a large saucepan and add the salt and fennel.

SPAGHETTI AI MOLLUSCHI
Spaghetti with shellfish

- 12 oz mussels, in shell
- 1 1/4 lb clams, in shell
- 1   lb spaghetti
- 1/3 cup extra-virgin olive oil
- 1/4 cup finely chopped parsley
- 6   cloves garlic, finely chopped
- 1   dried chile, crumbled
      salt to taste

Wine: a dry white (Bianco di Menfi)

Scrub the beards off the mussels and soak them with the clams in a large bowl of cold water for 1 hour. • Place the shellfish in a large skillet over medium high heat until they are all open. Discard any that have not opened. • Extract the mollusks from the shells and set aside in a covered bowl so they do not dry out too much. • Sieve 1/2 cup of their liquid into a large bowl and set aside. • Cook the spaghetti in a large pot of salted water until *al dente*. • Meanwhile, heat the oil in a skillet and sauté the parsley, garlic, and chile for 5 minutes over low heat. Add the mollusks and cook for 5 more minutes. • Moisten with the strained liquid, season with salt, and cook for 2 minutes. • Drain the spaghetti and place in the skillet with the sauce. Toss well and serve.

Serves: 4 · Prep: 35 min. + 1 hr to soak shellfish · Cooking: 20 min. · Level: 2

SPAGHETTI AGLI SCAMPI
Spaghetti with saltwater crayfish

1	lb saltwater crayfish
2	cloves garlic, finely chopped
1	tablespoon finely chopped parsley
1/3	cup extra-virgin olive oil
	salt to taste
1/2	cup dry white wine
1	lb spaghetti

Wine: a dry white (Frascati)

Clean the saltwater crayfish, without removing the shells. Open them in half lengthwise and set aside in a small bowl. • Sauté the garlic and parsley in the oil in a large skillet for 2–3 minutes over a low heat. Increase the heat slightly and add the saltwater crayfish. Season with salt and mix well. • Add the wine, allow to evaporate, and cook for 8 minutes. Turn off the heat and cover the pan. • Cook the spaghetti in a large pot of salted, boiling water until *al dente*. • Drain well and return to the pan. Add the saltwater crayfish sauce and toss for 2 minutes over medium heat. • Place in a heated serving dish and serve.

Serves: 4 · Prep: 20 min. · Cooking: 15 min. · Level: 1

SPAGHETTI MARE E MONTI
Sea and mountain spaghetti

1	lb mussels, in shell
1	lb clams, in shell
1/3	cup finely chopped parsley
3	cloves garlic, finely chopped
1/3	cup extra-virgin olive oil
2 1/2	oz dried porcini mushrooms, soaked in warm water for 20 minutes and coarsely chopped
1	underripe tomato, chopped
	salt to taste
1	lb spaghetti

Wine: a dry white (Cortese dell'Alto Monferrato)

Scrub the beards off the mussels and soak them with the clams in a large bowl of cold water for 1 hour. • Place the shellfish in a large skillet over high heat. Shake the pan and stir with a wooden spoon until they are all open. Discard any that have

Spaghetti with clams

not opened. • Extract the mollusks from their shells and place them in a bowl. • Strain the liquid into another bowl. • In a large skillet, sauté the parsley and garlic in the oil for 5 minutes. Add the porcini mushrooms. Cook for 10 minutes then add the tomato. After 10 more minutes, add the mollusks. Taste the sauce and add more salt if necessary. • Pour in the shellfish liquid and cook for 5 minutes.• Meanwhile, cook the spaghetti in a large pot of salted, boiling water until *al dente*. • Drain, and add to the pan with the sauce. Toss over high heat for 2–3 minutes. • Place in a heated serving dish and serve.

Serves: 4 · Prep: 30 min. + 1 hr to soak shellfish · Cooking: 40 min. · Level: 2

SPAGHETTI ALLE VONGOLE
Spaghetti with clams

1 1/2	lb clams, in shell
1/3	cup extra-virgin olive oil
1/3	cup dry white wine
3	cloves garlic, finely chopped
1/2	teaspoon crushed red pepper flakes
6	ripe tomatoes, peeled and chopped
	salt and freshly ground black pepper to taste
2	tablespoons finely chopped parsley
1	lb spaghetti

Wine: a dry white (Tocai)

Soak the clams in cold water for 1 hour. • Heat 2 tablespoons of the oil in a large skillet with the clams and wine. Cook until all the clams are open. Remove the clams, discarding any that have not opened, and set aside. Strain the cooking liquid into a bowl and set aside. • In the same pan, sauté the garlic and pepper flakes in the remaining oil until the garlic is pale gold. • Add the tomatoes and cook for 5 minutes. • Pour in the clam liquid. Season with salt and pepper. Cook for 15 more minutes. • Add the clams and parsley, and cook for 2–3 minutes. • Cook the spaghetti in a large pot of salted, boiling water until *al dente*. Drain and place in the skillet with the sauce. Toss for 1–2 minutes over high heat and serve.

Serves: 4 · Prep: 10 min. + 1 hr to soak the clams · Cooking: 30 min. · Level: 1

PENNE CON ASPARAGI E PROSCIUTTO COTTO
Penne with asparagus, cream, and ham

- 1 lb penne pasta
- 1¹/₂ lb fresh asparagus
- ¹/₄ cup butter
- 8 oz ham, chopped
- 1 cup light cream
- 1 tablespoon all-purpose flour
  salt and freshly ground black pepper to taste
- ¹/₂ cup freshly grated Parmesan cheese

Wine: a dry white (Bianco di Pitigliano)

Cook the penne in a large pot of salted, boiling water until *al dente*. • Trim the tough parts off the asparagus and cook in a pot of lightly salted, boiling water until the tips are almost tender. Drain well. Chop the stalks into short lengths and leave the tips whole. • Heat the butter and ham in a small, heavy-bottomed saucepan. Cook for 2–3 minutes. • Stir in the cream and flour, then add the asparagus. Stir gently over medium heat for 3–4 minutes, or until the cream thickens. Season with salt and pepper. • Drain the pasta and place in a heated serving dish. Add the sauce and toss well. Sprinkle with the Parmesan and serve hot.

Serves: 4 · Prep: 10 min. · Cooking: 15 min. · Level: 1

PENNE IN SALSA ESTIVA
Penne with summertime sauce

- 1 lb penne pasta
- 10 large ripe tomatoes
- 2 cloves garlic, finely chopped
- ¹/₄ cup extra-virgin olive oil
  salt to taste
- 6 oz Mozzarella cheese, diced
- 1 tablespoon capers, preserved in vinegar, drained
- 12 fresh basil leaves, torn

Wine: a dry white (Albana di Romagna)

Cook the penne in a large pot of salted, boiling water until *al dente*. • Peel the tomatoes and chop into bite-sized chunks. Drain off the extra liquid they produce. Place them in a serving bowl. Add the garlic and oil and season with salt. • Drain the pasta well and toss with the tomato sauce. Sprinkle with the Mozzarella, capers, and basil and serve.

Serves: 4 · Prep: 5 min. · Cooking: 12 min. · Level: 1

PENNE CON POMODORI SECCHI
Penne with dried tomatoes

- ¹/₄ cup extra-virgin olive oil
- 1 small onion, finely chopped
- 1 stalk celery, finely chopped
- 8 oz sun-dried tomatoes, finely chopped
- 12 oz peeled and chopped fresh tomatoes
  salt and freshly ground black pepper to taste
- 1 lb penne pasta

Wine: a dry rosé (Sangiovese di Aprilia)

Heat the oil in a large skillet and sauté the onion and celery until soft. • Add the dried tomatoes and cook for 5 minutes. • Add the fresh tomatoes and cook for about 20 minutes. Season with salt and pepper. • Cook the penne in a large pot of salted, boiling water until *al dente*. • Drain the pasta and add to the skillet with the sauce. Toss over high heat for 1–2 minutes, and serve.

Serves: 4 · Prep: 10 min. · Cooking: 30 min. · Level: 1

PENNE ALL'ARRABBIATA
Penne with spicy tomato sauce

- 2 oz diced pancetta
- 4 cloves garlic, finely chopped
- 1 stalk celery, finely chopped
- 1 medium onion, finely chopped
- ¹/₃ cup extra-virgin olive oil
- 1¹/₂ lb peeled and chopped fresh or canned tomatoes
- 6 fresh basil leaves, torn
- 3 tablespoons finely chopped parsley
- ¹/₂ teaspoon crushed red pepper flakes
  salt and freshly ground black pepper to taste
- 1 lb penne pasta

Wine: a dry rosé (Lagrein Rosato)

Sauté the pancetta, garlic, celery, and onion in the oil in a large skillet for 5 minutes. • Add the tomatoes, basil, parsley, and pepper flakes. Season with salt and pepper. • Simmer over medium heat for about 20 minutes, or until the tomatoes and oil begin to separate. • Cook the penne in a large pot of salted, boiling water until *al dente*. Drain and toss with the sauce in the skillet over high heat for 2–3 minutes. Place in a heated serving dish and serve.

Serves: 4 · Prep: 15 min. · Cooking: 30 min. · Level: 1

Spaghetti with seafood sauce

SPAGHETTI ALLO SCOGLIO
Spaghetti with seafood sauce

10	oz each mussels and clams, in shell
10	oz squid, cleaned (see page 200)
10	oz cuttlefish, cleaned (see recipe for Seafood salad on page 97 for how to clean)
10	oz shrimp tails
$\frac{1}{2}$	cup extra-virgin olive oil
2	cloves garlic, finely chopped
3	tablespoons finely chopped parsley
1	teaspoon crushed pepper flakes
$\frac{1}{2}$	cup dry white wine
	salt and freshly ground black pepper to taste
1	lb spaghetti

Wine: a dry white (Alicante)

Scrub the beards off the mussels and soak them with the clams in a bowl of cold water for 1 hour. • Chop the squid and cuttlefish into bite-sized chunks. Do not peel the shrimp. • Put 3 tablespoons of the oil in a large skillet, add the mussels and clams, and cook over medium heat until they open. Discard any that have not opened. • Extract the mollusks from their shells. Leave just a few in their shells to make the finished dish more attractive. • Heat two-thirds of the remaining oil in a large skillet and sauté the garlic, parsley, and pepper flakes for 2 minutes over medium heat. • Add the squid and cuttlefish. Season with salt and pepper, cook briefly, then add the wine. • Cook for 12 minutes, then add the shrimp tails. • After 5 minutes add the clams and mussels. Mix well and cook for 2 minutes more. Turn off the heat, cover, and set aside. • Meanwhile, cook the spaghetti in a large pan of salted, boiling water until *al dente*. Drain, and add to the pan with the seafood sauce. Toss for 1–2 minutes over high heat. • Place in a heated serving dish and serve.

Serves: 4 · Prep: 25 min. + 1 hr to soak the shellfish · Cooking 25 min. · Level: 2

PENNE AGLI ZUCCHINI CRUDI
Penne with raw zucchini and mint

- 6   very fresh small zucchini
- 1   teaspoon lemon juice
      salt and freshly ground black pepper to taste
- 1/4   cup extra-virgin olive oil
- 6   fresh mint leaves
- 1   lb penne pasta
- 3   oz fresh Pecorino cheese, cubed

Wine: a light, dry red (Sangiovese di Romagna)

Cut the zucchini in julienne strips and place in a bowl (large enough to hold the pasta as well). Add the lemon juice, salt, pepper, oil, and mint leaves. Stir well and let sit for about 20 minutes. • Cook the pasta in a large pan of salted, boiling water until *al dente*. Drain well and place in the bowl with the zucchini. • Toss well, add the Pecorino cheese, toss again, and serve.

Serves: 4 · Prep: 10 min.· Cooking 12 min. · Level: 1

PENNE CON I CARCIOFI
Penne with artichokes

- 6   artichokes
      juice of 1 lemon
- 1/4   cup extra-virgin olive oil
- 2   cloves garlic, finely chopped
      salt and freshly ground black pepper to taste
- 2   tablespoons finely chopped parsley
- 1/2   cup freshly grated Pecorino cheese
- 1   lb penne pasta

Wine: a dry white (Bianco di Castel del Monte)

Trim the artichoke stems, discard the tough outer leaves, and trim the tops. Cut in half lengthwise and scrape any fuzzy choke away with a knife. Cut into wedges. Place in a bowl of cold water with the lemon juice. Soak for 15 minutes, then drain and pat dry with paper towels. • Heat the oil in a skillet and sauté the garlic until it begins to change color. Add the artichokes and cook over medium-low heat for about 25 minutes, or until the artichokes are tender. Add water if the oil has all been absorbed. Season with salt and pepper. • Meanwhile, cook the penne in a large pot of salted, boiling water until *al dente*. Drain well and add to the pan with the artichokes. • Toss over high heat for 2–3 minutes. Sprinkle with the parsley and Pecorino, and serve.

Serves: 4 · Prep: 30 min. · Cooking: 30 min. · Level: 1

RIGATONI CON I PEPERONI
Rigatoni with bell peppers

- 3   medium bell peppers, mixed colors
- 1   large onion, finely chopped
- 2   cloves garlic, finely chopped
- 1/2   cup extra-virgin olive oil
- 1 1/2   cups peeled and chopped fresh tomatoes
- 10   basil leaves, torn
- 3   tablespoons boiling water
      salt and freshly ground black pepper to taste
- 2   tablespoons vinegar
- 6   anchovy fillets
- 1   lb rigatoni pasta

Wine: a dry white (Erbaluce di Caliso)

Cut the bell peppers in half, remove the stalks and seeds, and cut into strips about 1/4 inch wide. • Sauté the bell peppers, onion, and garlic in the oil in a large skillet for 8–10 minutes. Add the tomatoes, basil, and boiling water. Season with salt and pepper. Simmer over medium heat for about 20 minutes, or until the bell peppers are tender. • Stir in the vinegar and anchovies, and cook over high heat for 2–3 minutes until the vinegar evaporates. Remove from heat. • Meanwhile, cook the pasta in a large pot of salted, boiling water until *al dente*. Drain well and place in a heated serving dish. • Pour the sauce over the top and toss well. Serve hot.

Serves: 4 · Prep: 10 min. · Cooking: 35 min. · Level: 1

PENNETTE ALLA POLPA DI GRANCHIO
Penne with crab, brandy, and orange

- 1   lb penne pasta
- 12   oz fresh or frozen crab meat
- 2   cloves garlic, finely chopped
- 2   tablespoons finely chopped parsley
- 1/2   cup extra-virgin olive oil
- 1   tablespoon orange zest, finely chopped
- 1/3   cup brandy
- 1/2   cup freshly squeezed orange juice
      salt and freshly ground black pepper to taste
- 1/2   cup light cream

Wine: a dry white (Riesling del Collio)

Cook the pasta in a large pot of salted, boiling water until *al dente*. • Chop the crab coarsely. • In a large skillet, sauté the garlic and parsley in the oil over medium-low heat for 2–3 minutes. • Add the crab and orange zest. Mix well and cook for 1 minute. Pour in the brandy and cook until it has evaporated. Add the orange juice. • Season with salt and pepper and cook until the liquid has evaporated. • After about 10 minutes add the cream. • Drain the pasta and place in the skillet. Toss with the sauce over high heat for 2–3 minutes.

Serves: 4 · Prep: 20 min. · Cooking: 15 min. Level: 2

Riagtoni with bell peppers

PENNE E RICOTTA
Penne with fresh Ricotta cheese

- 1 lb penne pasta
- 1 cup whole milk, heated
- 12 oz very fresh Ricotta cheese
- 1 tablespoon sugar
- 1 teaspoon ground cinnamon
  salt and freshly ground white pepper to taste
- 1 tablespoon finely chopped fresh marjoram

Wine: a dry white (Bianco di Melissa)

Cook the penne in a large pot of salted, boiling water until *al dente*. • Combine the warm milk with the Ricotta, sugar, cinnamon, salt, pepper, and marjoram. Beat with a fork until smooth and creamy. • Drain the pasta well and place in a heated serving dish. Toss with the sauce and serve hot.

Serves: 4 · Prep: 5 min. · Cooking: 12 min. · Level: 1

FUSILLI ALLA NAPOLETANA
Neapolitan-style fusilli

- ½ cup extra-virgin olive oil
- 14 oz peeled and chopped ripe tomatoes
- 1 tablespoon finely chopped fresh oregano
  salt and freshly ground black pepper to taste
- 1 lb fusilli pasta
- 8 oz Mozzarella cheese, diced
- ½ cup freshly grated Pecorino cheese

Wine: a dry red (Rosso di Capri)

Cook the oil, tomatoes, oregano, salt, and pepper in a small, heavy-bottomed pan over medium heat for about 25 minutes, stirring frequently. • Remove from heat when the tomatoes begin to separate from the oil. • Meanwhile, cook the fusilli in a large pot of salted, boiling water until *al dente*. Drain well, toss with the sauce, and place in a heated serving dish. Sprinkle with the Mozzarella and Pecorino and toss well. Serve hot.

Serves: 4 · Prep: 10 min. · Cooking: 25 min. · Level: 1

PENNE DELL'IMPERATORE
Penne with shrimp and crayfish

- 3 tablespoons butter
- 1 small onion, finely chopped
- 10 oz shrimp, shelled, cleaned, and coarsely chopped
- 6 saltwater crayfish, cleaned and shelled, 2 cut in ¼-inch pieces and 4 left whole
- 1 cup light cream
  salt and freshly ground black pepper to taste
- ⅓ cup finely chopped parsley

Wine: a dry rosé (Settesoli di Sicilia)

Rigatoni with zucchini

Melt the butter in a large skillet over low heat. Add the onion and cook for 15 minutes, stirring and turning frequently and pressing down with a fork. If the pan dries out, add a few tablespoons of water. • Add the shrimp and crayfish and cook for 5 minutes over low heat. • Pour in the cream and season with salt and pepper. Cook over medium heat for 5 minutes. • Cook the penne in a large pan of salted, boiling water until *al dente*. Drain, and add to the sauce. • Cook for 2 minutes, sprinkle with parsley, and serve directly from the skillet so the pasta does not cool too much.

Serves: 4 · Prep: 20 min. · Cooking: 30 min. · Level: 2

RIGATONI CON GLI ZUCCHINI
Rigatoni with zucchini

- 1 lb rigatoni pasta
- 3 tablespoons butter
- 3 tablespoons extra-virgin olive oil
- 2 cloves garlic, finely chopped
- 6 zucchini, sliced in thin wheels
- 1 teaspoon crushed red pepper flakes
  salt and freshly ground black pepper to taste
- 3 tablespoons finely chopped parsley
- ½ cup freshly grated Parmesan cheese

Wine: a dry white (Orvieto Classico)

Cook the rigatoni in a large pot of salted, boiling water until *al dente*. • In a large skillet, sauté the garlic in the butter and oil until it starts to change color. Add the zucchini and pepper flakes. Sauté over high heat until the zucchini begin to turn golden brown. • Lower heat, cover the pan with a lid, and simmer until the zucchini are just tender. Season with salt and pepper. • Drain the pasta and place in a heated serving dish. • Add the zucchini, parsley, and Parmesan, and toss well. Serve hot.

Serves: 4 · Prep: 10 min. · Cooking: 25 min. · Level: 1

PENNE CON PEPERONI ARROSTITI
Penne with roast bell peppers

- 4 medium yellow and red bell peppers
  salt to taste
- 3 cloves garlic, thinly sliced
- ¼ cup extra-virgin olive oil
- 1 lb penne pasta
- 8 fresh basil leaves, torn

Wine: a dry white (Greco di Tufo)

Put the bell peppers whole under the broiler at high heat, giving them quarter turns until their skins blacken. This will take about 20 minutes. When the peppers are black all over, wrap them in foil and set aside for 10 minutes. Unwrap and remove the skins. • Cut the bell peppers in half and discard the stalks, seeds, and pulpy inner core. Rinse under cold running water. • Slice into strips about 1 x 2 inches. • Sauté the garlic in a small saucepan with the oil for 3–5 minutes. Add the bell peppers. • Cook the penne in a large pan of salted, boiling water until *al dente*. Drain, and place in a heated serving dish. Add the bell peppers and basil, toss well, and serve.

Serves: 4 · Prep: 25 min. · Cooking: 25 min. · Level: 1

Penne with cantaloupe, cream,
and Parmesan cheese

partially cover the skillet, and cook for 10 minutes. • Add the shrimp and parsley. Check the seasoning, adding more salt if necessary. Cook for 5 more minutes. If the sauce is too dry, add a few tablespoons of water from the pasta pot. • Cook the penne in a large pot of boiling salted water until *al dente*. Drain well and place in a heated serving dish. • Cover with the fish and vegetable sauce, toss well, and serve.

Serves: 4 · Prep: 30 min. · Cooking: 25 min. · Level: 2

RIGATONI AL CAVOLFIORE
Rigatoni in spicy cauliflower sauce

1	small cauliflower, about 1 lb
1	medium onion
2	tablespoons extra-virgin olive oil
2	tablespoons butter
3	cloves garlic, finely chopped
1/2	teaspoon crushed red pepper flakes
	salt and freshly ground black pepper to taste
1	lb rigatoni pasta

Wine: a dry white (Bianco di Custoza)

Divide the cauliflower into florets and dice the stalk into 1/2-inch cubes. Cook in boiling water until half cooked (about 7 minutes). Drain (reserving the cooking water to cook the pasta), and set aside. • In a large skillet, sauté the onion in the oil and butter until soft. Add the garlic and pepper flakes and sauté until the garlic begins to color. • Add the cauliflower and cook over medium-low heat for 10 more minutes, or until the cauliflower is tender. Season with salt and pepper. • Cook the pasta in a large pot of salted, boiling water until *al dente*. Drain well and place in the skillet. Toss the pasta and sauce together over medium heat for 2–3 minutes. Serve hot.

Serves: 4 · Prep: 5 min. · Cooking: 25 min. · Level: 1

PENNE CON MELONE
Penne with cantaloupe, cream, and Parmesan cheese

1	lb penne pasta
1	small clove garlic, very finely chopped
1	tablespoon extra-virgin olive oil
1	cup heavy cream
1/2	cup Marsala wine
1	small, ripe cantaloupe, about 3/4 lb, peeled and chopped in small cubes
	salt and freshly ground black pepper to taste
1/2	cup freshly grated Parmesan cheese

Wine: a light, dry white (Piave Pinot Grigio)

Cook the pasta in a large pot of salted, boiling water until *al dente*. • In a heavy-bottomed saucepan, sauté the garlic in the oil for 2–3 minutes. Pour in the cream and Marsala, then add the cantaloupe. Simmer for 8–10 minutes. Season with salt and pepper. • Drain the pasta, toss with the sauce, and place in a heated serving dish. Sprinkle with the Parmesan, toss well, and serve.

Serves: 4 · Prep: 10 min. · Cooking: 30 min. · Level: 1

PENNE CON PESCE E VERDURE
Penne with seafood and vegetable sauce

14	oz squid
7	oz white fish fillets
10	oz shrimp, shelled
1	large yellow bell pepper, diced
1	large zucchini, cut in wheels
1	large yellow onion, coarsely chopped
1/3	cup extra-virgin olive oil
	salt and freshly ground black pepper to taste
1/2	cup dry white wine
2	tablespoons finely chopped parsley
1	lb penne pasta

Wine: a dry white (Elba Bianco)

Clean the squid as shown on page 200. • Roughly chop the fish with a sharp knife. Set aside in a covered bowl. • Wash the shrimp and set aside in another bowl. Keep the shrimp separate from the other seafood because it has a different cooking time. • Sauté the onion in the oil in a large skillet over medium heat until soft. • Add the bell pepper and zucchini, and sauté for 5–7 minutes. • Stir in the squid and white fish, season with salt and pepper, and cook for 5 more minutes. • Pour in the wine,

PENNE AL SALMONE
Penne with smoked salmon

2	stalks celery heart, 2 tomatoes, sliced
1/4	cup vinegar
1	cup extra-virgin olive oil
	salt to taste
5	oz smoked salmon, thinly sliced
1	clove garlic, peeled but whole
1/2	cup freshly grated Parmesan cheese
1	lb penne pasta

Wine: a dry white (Amelia Trebbiano)

Put the celery, tomatoes, vinegar, oil, salt, and smoked salmon in a large bowl. • Spear the garlic clove with a fork and use it to stir the ingredients in the bowl. The garlic will flavor the mixture. • Cook the penne in a large pot of salted, boiling water until *al dente*. Drain and place in the bowl. Add the Parmesan, toss well, and serve.

Serves: 4 · Prep: 10 min. · Cooking: 12 min. · Level: 1

PENNE CON LE VERDURE
Penne with vegetable sauce

1	large onion, coarsely chopped
1/3	cup extra-virgin olive oil
1	large eggplant, cut in bite-sized pieces
3	bell peppers, preferably of mixed colors, cut in bite-sized pieces
2	large zucchini, cut in wheels
2	(15 oz) cans peeled and chopped tomatoes
1/2	teaspoon crushed red pepper flakes
	salt to taste
1	lb penne pasta
8	basil leaves, torn
1/2	cup freshly grated Parmesan cheese

Wine: a dry white (Bianco di Ischia)

In a large skillet, sauté the onion in the oil over medium heat until soft. Add the eggplant, bell peppers, and zucchini. Sauté for 7–8 minutes. Add the tomatoes and pepper flakes. Season with salt and cook for 20 minutes. • Meanwhile, cook the pasta in a large pot of salted, boiling water until *al dente*. Drain and add to the skillet. Toss over high heat for 2–3 minutes. Add the basil and Parmesan. Place in a heated serving dish and serve.

Serves: 4 · Prep: 10 min. · Cooking: 35 min. · Level: 1

RIGATONI INTEGRALI CON CACIOTTA
Whole-wheat rigatoni with cheese

1	lb whole-wheat rigatoni pasta
2	potatoes, cut in 1/4-inch cubes
4	oz Caciotta (or fresh Pecorino) cheese
1/2	cup whole milk
1/4	cup butter
	salt and freshly ground black pepper to taste
1/2	cup freshly grated Parmesan cheese

Wine: a dry red (Chianti Classico)

Cook the rigatoni and potatoes in a large pot of salted, boiling water. • Place the cheese, milk, and butter in the top of a

Fusilli with mushrooms

double boiler and cook until the cheese has melted. Season with salt and pepper. • Drain the pasta and potatoes when the pasta is cooked *al dente*. • Pour the cheese sauce over the pasta. Sprinkle with the Parmesan, toss well, and serve.

Serves: 4 · Prep: 10 min. · Cooking: 20 min. · Level: 1

FUSILLI CON I FUNGHI
Fusilli with mushrooms

1	lb white mushrooms
3	cloves garlic, finely chopped
1/4	cup extra-virgin olive oil
3	tablespoons finely chopped parsley
	salt and freshly ground black pepper to taste
1	lb fusilli pasta

Wine: a dry white (Bianco di Custoza)

Rinse the mushrooms under cold running water. Trim the stems and slice the stems and caps coarsely. • In a large skillet, sauté two-thirds of the garlic in half the oil over medium heat until it begins to color. • Add the mushrooms and half the parsley, season with salt and pepper, and cook for 10–15 minutes, or until the mushrooms are tender. • Meanwhile, cook the fusilli in a large pot of salted, boiling water until *al dente*. Drain well and add to the skillet with the sauce. • Sprinkle with the remaining garlic and parsley and drizzle with the remaining oil. Toss for 1–2 minutes, then serve.

Serves: 4 · Prep: 10 min. · Cooking: 40 min. · Level: 1

Cook the fusilli in a large pot of salted, boiling water until *al dente*. • Heat the oil in a large skillet and sauté the garlic for about 3 minutes. Add the oregano and sauté 3 minutes more. Add the tuna. • Season with salt and cook for 5 more minutes (the tuna does not need to cook, but just to blend in with the other flavors). • Drain the pasta, toss with the sauce, and serve.

Serves: 4 · Prep: 5 min. · Cooking: 15 min. · Level: 1

PENNE ALLA VENEZIANA
Penne Venetian-style

1   onion, thinly sliced
2   tablespoons finely chopped parsley
3   tablespoons extra-virgin olive oil
4   oz pancetta, diced
14 oz fresh or frozen peas
1   cup Beef stock (see recipe, page 105)
    salt and freshly ground black pepper to taste
1/3 cup butter
10 oz white mushrooms, sliced
1   lb penne pasta
1   cup freshly grated Parmesan cheese

Wine: a dry white (Roero Arneis)

In a large skillet, sauté the onion and parsley in the oil until soft. • Add the pancetta and sauté until lightly browned and crisp. Add the peas. Cook and stir for 5 more minutes. • Pour in the stock and simmer over low heat for 20 minutes. • Season with salt and pepper and remove from heat. • Heat half the butter with a pinch of salt in a separate skillet. Add the mushrooms and stir until the moisture they produce has evaporated. Cook for 10–15 minutes, or until the mushrooms are tender. • Meanwhile, cook the pasta in a large pot of salted, boiling water until *al dente*. Drain well and add to the skillet with the pancetta. Stir in the mushrooms and the remaining butter. • Sprinkle with the Parmesan, toss well, and serve.

Serves: 4 · Prep: 10 min. · Cooking: 35 min. · Level: 2

Macaroni with onion sauce

FUSILLI AL GAMBERO ROSSO
Fusilli with jumbo shrimp

1   lb fusilli pasta
1/4 cup extra-virgin olive oil
1/4 cup finely chopped parsley
4   cloves garlic, finely chopped
14   oz jumbo shrimp, cleaned, 4 oz left whole
     and 10 oz coarsely chopped
     salt to taste
2   tablespoons butter

Wine: a dry white (Torbato di Alghero)

Cook the fusilli in a large pot of salted, boiling water until *al dente*. • Heat the oil in a large skillet. Sauté the parsley and garlic until the garlic begins to color. • Add all the shrimp, season with salt, and cook for 5 minutes. • Drain the pasta and place in the skillet. • Toss over high heat for 2 minutes. Add the butter, toss again, and serve.

Serves: 4 · Prep: 20 min. · Cooking: 15 min. · Level: 2

MACCHERONI INTEGRALI CON LE CIPOLLE
Whole-wheat macaroni with onion sauce

5   large onions, thinly sliced
1/4 cup butter
1/4 cup extra-virgin olive oil
     salt and freshly ground black pepper to taste

1   cup dry white wine
2   tablespoons finely chopped parsley
1/2 cup freshly grated Parmesan cheese
1   lb macaroni

Wine: a dry white (Orvieto)

Sauté the onions in a skillet with the butter and oil over medium heat until they begin to change color. Season with salt and pepper. • Turn the heat down to low, cover, and simmer for about 40 minutes, or until the onions are very soft. • Uncover and add the wine. Turn the heat up to medium and stir until the wine evaporates. Remove from heat. • Cook the pasta in a large pot of salted, boiling water until *al dente*. Drain well and place in a heated serving dish. • Pour the onion sauce over the top. Add the parsley and Parmesan and toss well. Serve hot.

Serves: 4 · Prep: 5 min. · Cooking: 45 min. · Level: 1

FUSILLI TONNO E ORIGANO
Fusilli with tuna and oregano

1   lb fusilli pasta
2   cloves garlic, minced
1/2 cup extra-virgin olive oil
1   tablespoon oregano
8   oz tuna packed in oil
     salt to taste

Wine: a dry white (Pinot Bianco)

FARFALLE ALLA RUSSA
Farfalle with vodka and caviar

- 1 lb farfalle pasta
- 1/4 cup butter
- 1/4 cup vodka
  juice of 1 1/2 lemons
- 4 oz smoked salmon, crumbled
- 4 teaspoons caviar
- 1/4 cup light cream
  salt and freshly ground black pepper to taste

Wine: a dry white (Soave)

Cook the farfalle in a large pot of salted, boiling water until *al dente*. • In a large skillet, melt the butter over low heat and add the vodka and lemon juice. • Stir in the salmon and caviar. Cook over medium-low heat for 2–3 minutes. Add the cream, and season with salt and pepper. Remove from heat. • Drain the pasta well and add to the skillet with the salmon. • Toss well over medium heat and serve.

Serves: 4 · Prep: 5 · Cooking: 15 min. · Level: 1

MALLOREDDUS
Sardinian gnocchi with Italian sausages and Pecorino cheese

☞ Malloreddus ("little bulls"), or *gnocchi sardi*, as they are also known, are a specialty of Sardinia. They are made with a mixture of bran flour and saffron. They are now available in specialty stores in dried form.

- 12 oz Italian pork sausages, skinned and crumbled
- 1 large onion, finely chopped
- 3 cloves garlic, finely chopped
- 8 basil leaves, torn

Farfalle with vodka and caviar

- 2 tablespoons extra-virgin olive oil
- 1 1/4 lb peeled and chopped tomatoes
  salt and freshly ground black pepper to taste
- 1 lb Sardinian gnocchi
- 1/2 cup freshly grated Pecorino cheese

Wine: a dry red (Cannonau)

In a large skillet, sauté the sausages, onion, garlic, and basil in the oil in a skillet over medium heat until the onion is soft. • Add the tomatoes and season with salt and pepper. Simmer for 15–20 minutes, or until the sauce has reduced. • Meanwhile, cook the pasta in a large pot of salted, boiling water until *al dente*. Drain well and place in a heated serving dish. Pour in the sauce and sprinkle with the Pecorino. Toss well and serve.

Serve: 4 · Prep: 5 min. · Cooking: 30 min. · Level: 1

MALLOREDDUS CON BOTTARGA
Sardinian gnocchi with mullet roe

☞ This is another classic Sardinian dish. Bottarga is the roe (eggs) of either mullet or tuna, although the mullet roe is considered to be of higher quality. It is made by salting the fishs' ovary sacs and then drying them in the sun.

- 1 lb Sardinian gnocchi
- 2 cloves garlic, finely chopped
- 2 tablespoons finely chopped parsley
- 3/4 cup extra-virgin olive oil
- 1 1/4 oz freshly grated dried mullet roe
  freshly ground black pepper to taste

Wine: a dry white (Alghero Vermentino)

Cook the gnocchi in a large pan of salted, boiling water until it is *al dente*. • Drain well and toss quickly in a large skillet with the garlic,

parsley, and oil. • Sprinkle with the mullet roe, season with pepper, and serve.

Serves: 4 · Prep: 5 min. · Cooking: 15 min. · Level: 1

FARFALLE PICCANTI
Farfalle in spicy tomato sauce with Mozzarella cheese

- 1 clove garlic, cut in half
- 1 teaspoon crushed red pepper flakes
- 2 tablespoons extra-virgin olive oil
- 1 1/2 lb cherry tomatoes, cut in half
  salt and freshly ground black pepper to taste
- 1 tablespoon capers
- 5 basil leaves
- 1 lb farfalle pasta
- 4 oz Mozzarella cheese, diced

Wine: a dry white (Frascati Superiore)

In a large skillet, sauté the garlic and pepper flakes in the oil. Add the tomatoes, and season with salt and pepper. Cover and cook over low heat for 15 minutes. • Add the capers and basil and cook for 10 minutes more. • Meanwhile, cook the pasta in a large pot of salted, boiling water until *al dente*. Drain, and toss with the sauce and Mozzarella. Let sit for 2 minutes before serving.

Serves: 6 · Prep: 15 min. · Cooking: 30 min. · Level: 1

FUSILLI CON PISELLI E PROSCIUTTO
Fusilli with ham, peas, and Parmesan

- 1 1/4 cups fresh or frozen peas
- 1/4 cup butter
- 8 oz ham, diced
- 3 tablespoons light cream
- 2 tablespoons finely chopped parsley
  salt and freshly ground black pepper to taste
- 1/4 cup freshly grated Parmesan cheese
- 1 lb fusilli pasta

Wine: a dry red (Barbera di Monferrato)

Boil the peas in a small pot of lightly salted water for 4–5 minutes. • Drain and place in a large skillet with the butter and ham. Sauté over medium-low heat for 10 minutes. • Stir in half the cream and cook until the sauce thickens. • Add the parsley and season with salt and pepper. • Meanwhile, cook the pasta in a large pot of salted, boiling water until *al dente*. Drain well and place in the skillet with the sauce. Add the remaining cream and Parmesan. Toss well and serve hot.

Serves: 4 · Prep: 5 min. · Cooking: 20 min. · Level: 1

This pasta is a specialty of Apulia and neighboring regions in the south of Italy. The name – *orecchiette* – means "little ears" in Italian and refers to the pasta's shell-like shape. It is made with bran flour and water and has ridges which help it to hold the sauce with which it is served.

ORECCHIETTE CON I BROCCOLI
Orecchiette pasta with broccoli

- 1   lb fresh broccoli
- 2   cloves of garlic, finely chopped
- ¼   cup extra-virgin olive oil
- 1   hot red chile, thinly sliced
      salt to taste
- 1   lb orecchiette pasta
- 1¾ cups freshly grated Pecorino cheese

Wine: a dry red (San Severo Rosso)

Trim the stem of the broccoli and dice into small cubes. Divide the broccoli heads into small florets. Boil the stem and florets in a large pot of salted water for about 8 minutes, or until tender. • Drain the broccoli well, reserving the water to cook the pasta. • In a large skillet, sauté the garlic in the oil until it is pale golden brown. • Add the broccoli and chile, season with salt, and cook over low heat for 5 more minutes. • Remove from heat. • Meanwhile, bring the water used to cook the broccoli back to the boil, add the pasta, and cook until *al dente* (about 20 minutes). • Drain well, and add to the broccoli in the skillet. • Toss over high heat for 1–2 minutes. Remove from heat, sprinkle with the Pecorino, and serve.

Serves: 4 · Prep: 15 min. · Cooking: 40 min. · Level: 1

ORECCHIETTE CON LE BIETOLE
Orecchiette with Swiss chard

- 1 lb orecchiette pasta
- 1 lb fresh Swiss chard
- 3 cloves garlic, finely chopped
- 2 anchovy fillets, crumbled
- ½ cup extra-virgin olive oil
- 1 teaspoon crushed red pepper flakes
  salt and freshly ground black pepper to taste
- ½ cup freshly grated Pecorino cheese

Wine: a dry red (Cirò)

Cook the orecchiette in a large pot of salted, boiling water until *al dente*. • Cook the chard in a pot of salted, boiling water for 8–10 minutes. Drain well and squeeze out extra moisture. Chop finely. • Combine the garlic and anchovies in a large skillet with the oil. Sauté until the garlic turns gold. Add the chard and pepper flakes. Season with salt and pepper. • Drain the pasta well and place in the skillet with the sauce. Toss for 1–2 minutes over high heat. Sprinkle with the Pecorino and serve.

Serves: 4 · Prep: 10 min. · Cooking: 15 min. · Level: 1

PENNE CON CARCIOFI CRUDI
Penne with raw artichokes

- 8 small, fresh artichokes
  juice of 1 lemon
  salt and freshly ground black pepper to taste
- ¼ cup extra-virgin olive oil
- 1 lb penne pasta
- 4 oz Parmesan cheese, in flakes

Wine: a light, dry white (Cinque Terre)

Trim the artichoke stems, discard the tough outer leaves, and trim the tops. Cut in half lengthwise and scrape any fuzzy choke away with a knife. Cut in very thin slices. Soak in a bowl of cold water with the lemon juice for 15 minutes. • Drain and pat dry with paper towels. Place in a large serving bowl. Season with salt and pepper and drizzle with the oil. • Meanwhile, cook the pasta in a large pan of salted, boiling water until *al dente*. • Drain well and place in the bowl with the sauce. Toss well, sprinkle with the Parmesan, and serve.

Serves: 4 · Prep: 20 min. · Cooking: 15 min. · Level: 1

Orecchiette pasta with broccoli

RIGATONI INTEGRALI CON PECORINO
Whole-wheat rigatoni with Pecorino cheese

- 1 lb whole-wheat rigatoni pasta
- 3 medium potatoes, diced
- 4 oz Pecorino cheese, chopped
- ½ cup whole milk
- ¼ cup butter
  salt and freshly ground black pepper to taste
- ½ cup freshly grated Parmesan cheese

Wine: a dry red (Chianti Classico)

Cook the rigatoni and potatoes in a large pan of salted, boiling water until the pasta is *al dente*. • Place the Pecorino, milk, and butter in the top of a double boiler and cook until the cheese has melted. Season with salt and pepper. • Drain the pasta and potatoes and place in a heated serving dish. • Pour the cheese sauce over the pasta, sprinkle with the Parmesan, mix well, and serve.

Serves: 4 · Prep: 5 min. · Cooking: 25 min. · Level: 1

FARFALLE CON RADICCHIO E CAPRINO
Farfalle with radicchio and Caprino cheese

- 1 lb farfalle pasta
- 1 onion, thinly sliced
- ¼ cup extra-virgin olive oil
- 1 large head radicchio, cut in strips
  salt and freshly ground black pepper to taste
- ¼ cup light beer
- 4 oz soft fresh Caprino (or other soft, fresh cheese, such as Robiola, Philadelphia, or Stracchino)
- 2 tablespoons milk

Wine: a dry red (Colli Berici Merlot)

Cook the pasta in a large pan of salted, boiling water until it is *al dente*. • In a large skillet, sauté the onion in 3 tablespoons of the oil until soft. • Add the radicchio and season with salt and pepper. Sauté for a few minutes, then add the beer. When the beer has evaporated, add the Caprino and stir well, softening the mixture with the milk. • Drain the pasta well and add to the pan with the sauce. Toss for 2–3 minutes over medium heat. Drizzle with the remaining oil and serve.

Serves: 4 · Prep: 5 min. · Cooking: 15 min. · Level: 1

Bigoli in anchovy and onion sauce

BIGOLI CON L'ANATRA
Bigoli with duck sauce

☞ Bigoli are a type of thick spaghetti made at home with whole-wheat flour. You will need an electric or hand-cranked pasta machine to make them. Other types of whole-wheat pasta are also good with this sauce.

3¹/₂	cups whole-wheat flour
	salt to taste
4	eggs
¹/₄	cup cold water
1	young duck, with its liver and heart
1	onion, finely chopped
1	stalk celery, finely chopped
1	carrot, finely chopped
¹/₄	cup extra-virgin olive oil
5	tablespoons butter
2–3	fresh sage leaves, torn
	salt and freshly ground black pepper to taste
¹/₂	cup freshly grated Parmesan cheese

Wine: a dry red (Colli Euganei Cabernet)

Sift the flour and salt into a mound on a pastry slab or into a large mixing bowl. Make a well in the center and break the eggs into it. Stir with a fork, gradually incorporating the flour and adding water a little at a time, as needed. The dough should be smooth and elastic. Cover the bowl with a damp cloth and leave to stand for 30 minutes. • Make the thick spaghetti-shaped bigoli using an electric or hand-cranked pasta machine. • Wash and dry the duck. Place in a large, oval flameproof casserole, add enough water to cover, a pinch of salt, and the onion, celery, and carrot. Bring to a boil and cook gently for 1 hour. • While the duck is cooking, chop the liver and heart coarsely and sauté in the oil

and butter over high heat. When lightly browned, add the sage leaves, salt, and a generous grinding of pepper. • Remove the duck from the casserole and strain the stock. • Remove the meat from the duck and chop coarsely. • Cook the pasta in a large pot of the stock and boiling water for 5–7 minutes. Drain and place in the skillet with the fried liver. Add the duck meat and Parmesan. Toss carefully and serve.

Serves: 6 · Prep: 40 min. + 30 min. to rest · Cooking: 1¹/₄ hrs · Level: 3

BIGOLI IN SALSA
Bigoli in anchovy and onion sauce

☞ This dish was traditionally served on days of abstinence and fasting, such as Christmas Eve, Ash Wednesday, and Good Friday. Nowadays it has become a gourmet dish.

1	quantity bigoli (whole-wheat spaghetti – see preceding recipe)
6	oz salted anchovies
¹/₄	cup extra-virgin olive oil
4	large white onions, finely sliced
	salt and freshly ground black pepper to taste
2	tablespoons finely chopped parsley

Wine: a dry red (Colli Berici Cabernet)

Prepare the bigoli and spread them out on a floured board or work surface to dry for about 30 minutes. • Rinse the anchovies thoroughly, remove the bones, and chop the flesh coarsely. • Heat the oil in a large skillet and add the onions. Cook gently until tender, adding a spoonful or two of water, if necessary, to prevent them from browning. • Increase the heat and add the anchovies. Use a fork to break them up so that they dissolve

in the oil. Season with salt and pepper and remove from heat. • Cook the bigoli in a large pot of salted, boiling water for 5–7 minutes. Drain and place in a heated serving dish. Stir into the onion and anchovy mixture. Sprinkle with the parsley and serve.

Serves: 6 · Prep: 30 min. + 30 min. to rest · Cooking: 20 min. · Level: 2

TAGLIOLINI AL MASCARPONE
Tagliolini with Mascarpone cheese

1	cup fresh Mascarpone cheese
1	clove garlic, very finely chopped
	salt and freshly ground black pepper to taste
¹/₂	cup freshly grated Parmesan cheese
1	quantity Tagliolini pasta (see recipe, page 124)

Wine: a dry white (Verdicchio)

Prepare the pasta. • Warm the Mascarpone in a saucepan over very low heat. Remove from heat and stir in the garlic. Season with salt. • Cook the tagliolini in a large pot of salted, boiling water until *al dente*. Drain and toss with the sauce. Sprinkle with the Parmesan and pepper. Serve hot.

Serves: 4 · Prep: 5 min. + time to make the pasta · Cooking: 5 min. · Level: 2

FETTUCCINE AL SOFFRITTO
Fettucine in aromatic vegetable sauce

1	quantity Fettuccine pasta (see recipe, page 124)
¹/₄	cup extra-virgin olive oil
2	stalks celery, 2 carrots, 2 large onions, small bunch parsley, 2 cloves garlic, all finely chopped
1	cup dry white wine
2	drained canned tomatoes, coarsely chopped
	salt and freshly ground black pepper to taste
1	cup freshly grated Parmesan cheese

Wine: a dry rosé (Cirò Rosé Superiore)

Prepare the pasta. • Heat the oil in a large, heavy-bottomed saucepan. Add the celery, carrots, onions, parsley, and garlic and sauté for 10 minutes until light golden brown. • Pour in the wine and cook until it has evaporated. Add the tomatoes and simmer for 10 minutes, adding a little hot water to moisten when necessary. The mixture should be just thick enough to form a light, coating sauce for the pasta. Season with salt and pepper. • Cook the fettucine in a large pot of salted, boiling water until *al dente*. Drain well, place in the pan, and toss carefully with the Parmesan. Serve hot.

Serves: 4 · Prep: 15 min. · Cooking: 30 min. · Level: 1

PAGLIA E FIENO CON PISELLI E FUNGHI
Paglia e fieno with peas and mushrooms

1	quantity Paglia e fieno pasta (see recipe, page 124)
1	cup diced pancetta
1/2	cup diced prosciutto
1	onion, 1 stalk celery, 1 carrot, all finely chopped
1/4	cup butter
11/4	lb peeled and chopped tomatoes
12	oz white mushrooms
	pinch of nutmeg
	salt and freshly ground black pepper to taste
1	cup dry white wine
14	oz fresh or frozen peas
1	cup Beef stock (see recipe, page 105)
1	cup freshly grated Parmesan cheese

Wine: a dry red (Chianti dei Colli Fiorentini)

Prepare the pasta. • In a large skillet, sauté the pancetta, prosciutto, onion, celery, and carrot with half the butter over medium heat until the onion is soft. • Add the tomatoes, mushrooms, nutmeg, salt, and pepper. Cook for 15 minutes. • Pour in the wine and when it has evaporated, add the peas. Simmer until the peas and mushrooms are tender, stirring in the beef stock as needed to keep the sauce liquid. • Cook the paglia e fieno in a large pot of salted, boiling water until *al*

dente. Drain well and place in a heated serving dish. Toss carefully with the remaining butter. • Place the pasta, sauce, and Parmesan separately on the table so that everyone can help themselves to as much cheese and sauce as they like.

Serves: 4 · Prep: 30 min. + time to make the pasta · Cooking: 45 min. · Level: 2

TAGLIOLINI AL CURRY
Tagliolini with curry sauce

1	quantity Tagliolini pasta (see recipe, page 124)
1	quantity Béchamel sauce (see recipe, page 16)
1	cup heavy cream
2	tablespoons curry powder
	salt and freshly ground black pepper to taste
1	tablespoon butter
1/2	cup freshly grated Parmesan cheese

Prepare the pasta and the béchamel sauce. • Stir the cream and curry powder into the béchamel and cook for 2–3 more minutes. Season with salt and pepper. • Cook the tagliolini in a large pot of salted, boiling water until *al dente*. Drain well and place in a heated serving dish. • Toss carefully with the butter and curry sauce. Sprinkle with Parmesan and serve.

Serves: 4 · Prep: 10 min. + time to make the pasta · Cooking: 10 min. · Level: 2

FETTUCCINE ALL'ALFREDO
Fettuccine with butter and cream

1	quantity Fettuccine pasta (see recipe, page 124)
1/3	cup butter
11/4	cups heavy cream
1/2	cup freshly grated Parmesan cheese
	pinch of nutmeg
	salt and freshly ground black pepper to taste

Prepare the pasta. • Place the butter and cream in a heavy-bottomed pan and cook over high heat for 2 minutes. Remove from heat. • Cook the fettuccine in a large pot of salted, boiling water until *al dente*. Drain well and place in the pan with the cream. Add the Parmesan, nutmeg, salt, and pepper, and toss carefully over medium heat for 1 minute. • Serve hot.

Serves: 4 · Prep: 5 min. + time to make the pasta · Cooking: 10 min. · Level: 1

PAGLIA E FIENO CON TARTUFI
Paglia e fieno with cream and truffles

☞ Plain fettuccine and green spinach fettuccine are often served together as *paglia e fieno*, which means "straw and hay."

1	quantity Paglia e fieno pasta (see recipe, page 124)
1/4	cup butter
1	white truffle, in shavings
1	cup light cream
	salt and freshly ground black pepper to taste
1/3	cup freshly grated Parmesan cheese

Wine: a dry white (Cortese dell'Alto Monferrato)

Prepare the plain and spinach fettuccine. • Melt the butter in a heavy-bottomed pan and cook the truffle for 1 minute over low heat. Increase the heat and add the cream, season with salt and pepper, and simmer for 4–5 minutes, or until the cream reduces. • Cook the pasta in a large pot of salted, boiling water until *al dente*. Drain, and add to the pan with the truffle sauce. • Sprinkle with the Parmesan and toss carefully over medium heat for 1–2 minutes. Serve hot.

Serves: 4 · Prep: 5 min. + time to make the pasta · Cooking: 10 · Level: 2

Paglia e fieno with cream and truffles

Spinach tagliatelle with butter and rosemary sauce

TAGLIATELLE ALLE VONGOLE E PANNA

Tagliatelle with clams and cream

- 1 quantity Tagliatelle pasta (see recipe, page 124)
- 2 lb clams, in shell
- 2 cloves garlic, finely chopped
- 1/4 cup extra-virgin olive oil
- 1/2 teaspoon crushed red pepper flakes (optional)
- 3 bay leaves
- 1 cup light cream
- 3 large tomatoes, chopped
    salt to taste

Wine: a dry white (Pinot Bianco)

Prepare the pasta. • Soak the clams in a large bowl of cold water for 1 hour. • Drain the clams and cook in a large skillet over high heat until they open. Discard any that do not open. Remove from the skillet and set aside with their strained juice. • Sauté the garlic in the skillet with the oil, pepper flakes, if using, and bay leaves. When the garlic begins to color, add the clams and their cooking juices, the cream, tomatoes,

and salt. Simmer over medium heat for about 10 minutes, or until the sauce has reduced. • Cook the tagliatelle in a large pot of salted, boiling water until *al dente*. Drain well and place in the skillet with the clams. Toss quickly over medium-high heat, remove the bay leaves, and serve.

Serves: 4 · Prep: 10 min. + time to make the pasta + 1 hr to soak the clams · Cooking: 15 min. · Level: 2

TAGLIATELLE VERDI CON BURRO E ROSMARINO

Spinach tagliatelle with butter and rosemary sauce

- 1 quantity Spinach tagliatelle pasta (see recipe, page 124)
- 1 quantity Butter and rosemary sauce (see recipe, page 14)

Wine: a dry white (Pinot Grigio dei Colli Piacentini)

Prepare the pasta and the sauce. • Cook the pasta in a large pot of salted, boiling water until *al dente*. Drain well and place in a heated serving dish. • Pour the sauce over the top, toss carefully, and serve.

Serves: 4 · Prep: 5 min. + time to make the pasta · Cooking: 5 min. · Level: 2

TAGLIATELLE VERDI PRIMAVERILI

Flavors of spring spinach tagliatelle

- 1 quantity Spinach tagliatelle pasta (see recipe, page 124)
- 1 1/4 cups fresh or frozen peas
- 4 oz Gorgonzola cheese
- 1 1/3 cups light cream
    salt and freshly ground black pepper to taste
- 2 tablespoons finely chopped parsley
- 1/2 cup freshly grated Parmesan cheese

Wine: a light, dry white (Soave)

Prepare the pasta. • Cook the peas in a pot of salted, boiling water. Drain well and set aside. • Place the Gorgonzola, diced into 1/2-inch squares, with the cream in a large heavy-bottomed pan over low heat. Stir until the cheese has melted. • Add the peas, and season with salt and pepper. • Cook the pasta in a large pot of salted, boiling water until *al dente*. Drain well and place in the pan with the sauce. • Add the parsley and Parmesan. Toss carefully and serve.

Serves: 4 · Prep: 10 min. + time to make the pasta · Cooking: 15 min. · Level: 2

TAGLIATELLE IN INTINGOLO DI NOCI

Tagliatelle with walnut sauce

- 1 quantity Tagliatelle pasta (see recipe, page 124)
- 1/3 cup pine nuts
- 1 lb walnuts, in their shells
- 2 cloves garlic
- 1 cup finely chopped parsley
- 1/2 cup extra-virgin olive oil
    salt to taste

Wine: a light, dry red (Bonarda dei Colli Piacentini)

Prepare the pasta. • Roast the pine nuts in the oven at 350°F for 5–10 minutes, or until light gold. • Shell the walnuts and chop finely in a food processor with the pine nuts, garlic, parsley, and oil. Season with salt. • Cook the pasta in a large pot of salted, boiling water until *al dente*. Drain and place in a heated serving dish. Cover with the sauce, toss carefully, and serve.

Serves: 4 · Prep: 15 min. + time to make the pasta · Cooking: 10 min. · Level: 2

TAGLIATELLE AL PROSCIUTTO COTTO

Tagliatelle with ham

- 1 quantity Tagliatelle pasta (see recipe, page 124)
- 1 medium onion, finely chopped
- 1/3 cup butter

8 oz ham, in ½-inch cubes, fat trimmed and reserved
1 cup dry white wine
  salt and freshly ground black pepper to taste
¼ cup freshly grated Parmesan cheese

Wine: a light, dry red (Sangiovese di Romagna)

Prepare the pasta. • In a large skillet, sauté the onion and fat from the ham with the butter until the onion is soft. • Add the ham meat and sauté for 2–3 minutes. Pour in the wine and simmer until it evaporates. Season with salt and pepper. • Cook the tagliatelle in a large pot of salted boiling water until *al dente*. Drain well and place in a heated serving dish. Pour the sauce over the top and toss carefully. Sprinkle with the Parmesan and serve hot.

Serves: 4 · Prep: 5 min. + time to make the pasta · Cooking: 10 min. · Level: 2

TAGLIATELLE ALLA PANCETTA
Tagliatelle with crispy-fried pancetta

1 quantity Tagliatelle pasta (see recipe, page 124)
1 cup diced pancetta
¼ cup butter
2 cloves garlic, finely chopped
½ cup freshly grated Parmesan cheese
  freshly ground black pepper to taste

Wine: a dry red (Freisa di Chieri)

Prepare the pasta. • Sauté the pancetta, butter, and garlic in a large skillet until the pancetta is crisp. • Cook the tagliatelle in a large pot of salted, boiling water until *al dente*. Drain and place in the skillet with the pancetta. Toss carefully over medium heat. • Sprinkle with the Parmesan, season with pepper, and serve.

Serves: 4 · Prep: 5 min. + time to make the pasta · Cooking: 10 min. · Level: 2

TAGLIOLINI CON CARCIOFI
Tagliolini with artichokes and eggs

1 quantity Tagliolini pasta (see recipe, page 124)
3 tablespoons finely chopped onion
⅓ cup extra-virgin olive oil
16 frozen artichoke hearts, thawed
  salt and freshly ground black pepper to taste
½ cup water
3 very fresh large eggs
½ cup freshly grated Pecorino cheese

Wine: a dry white (Bianco di Donnafugata)

Prepare the pasta. • In a large skillet, sauté the onion in the oil until soft. • Cut the artichokes in thin wedges and add to the skillet. Season with salt and pepper. Sauté

Tagliatelle with walnut sauce

for 2–3 minutes. • Pour in the water, cover, and cook for 20 minutes, or until the artichokes are tender. • Cook the pasta in a large pot of salted, boiling water until *al dente*. • Break the eggs into a large, heated serving dish, beat with a fork and add half the cheese. • Drain the pasta and toss with the egg, which will harden as it cooks. Toss with the artichokes, sprinkle with the remaining cheese, and serve.

Serves: 4 · Prep: 15 min. + time to make the pasta · Cooking: 30 min. · Level: 2

TAGLIATELLE AL SUGO D'ANATRA
Tagliatelle with duck sauce

1 duck, cleaned and gutted, about 2 lb
3 tablespoons extra-virgin olive oil
  salt and freshly ground black pepper to taste
  sprigs of fresh rosemary and sage
1 cup dry white wine
1 quantity Tagliatelle pasta (see recipe, page 124)
2 cloves garlic, 1 medium onion, 1 carrot, 1 stalk celery, all finely chopped
¼ cup tomato paste, dissolved in 1 cup water

1 bay leaf
⅓ cup freshly grated Parmesan cheese

Wine: a dry rosé (Rosato di Grave del Friuli)

Wash the duck and pat dry with paper towels. Sprinkle with the oil, salt, pepper, rosemary, and sage. Roast in a preheated oven at 375°F for 1 hour. Turn the duck and baste it with the wine during cooking. Remove from the oven and set aside. • While the duck is cooking, prepare the pasta. • Sauté the garlic, onion, carrot, and celery in the gravy from the roast duck until the onion is soft. Add the tomato paste and water. Season with salt and pepper. Simmer over medium-low heat for 15 minutes. • Bone the duck and chop the meat coarsely. Add to the pan with the bay leaf and cook for 45 more minutes, adding water if necessary. Remove the bay leaf. • Cook the tagliatelle in a large pot of salted, boiling water until *al dente*. Drain and place in a heated serving dish. Cover with the sauce, sprinkle with the Parmesan, toss carefully, and serve.

Serves: 4 · Prep: 20 min. + time to make the pasta · Cooking: 2½ hrs · Level: 3

PAPPARDELLE ALLA SICILIANA
Sicilian-style pappardelle

- 1   quantity Pappardelle pasta (see recipe, page 124)
- 6   oz ground lean pork
- 6   oz ground lean veal
- $^{1}/_{4}$ cup extra-virgin olive oil
- 2   tablespoons tomato paste
- $^{1}/_{2}$ cup dry white or dry red wine
- 8   oz peeled and chopped fresh or canned tomatoes
-     salt and freshly ground black pepper to taste
- $2^{1}/_{2}$ oz Ricotta salata cheese
- 8   oz fresh Ricotta cheese
- $^{1}/_{2}$ cup freshly grated Pecorino cheese

Wine: a dry white (Corvo di Salaparuta)

Prepare the pasta. • In a large skillet, sauté the meat in the oil over medium heat, using a fork to break up the lumps. • When the meat is browned, add the tomato paste mixed with the wine. Cook for 4–5 minutes, then add the tomatoes and season with salt and pepper. Simmer over low heat for 40 minutes. • Cook the pappardelle in a large pot of salted, boiling water until *al dente*. • While the pasta is cooking, use a fork to break the Ricotta salata into small, crumbly pieces. • When the pasta is nearly done, mix the fresh Ricotta with 2 tablespoons of the cooking water in a large, heated serving dish. • Drain the pasta and toss carefully with the fresh Ricotta and meat sauce. • Sprinkle with the Ricotta salata and Pecorino and serve.

Serves: 4 · Prep: 10 min. + time to make the pasta · Cooking: 50 min. · Level: 2

PAPPARDELLE SULLA LEPRE
Pappardelle with wild hare sauce

☞ This is a classic Tuscan dish. The traditional recipe calls for wild hare, but if this is not available, use the same amount of rabbit in its place.

- 1   quantity Pappardelle pasta (see recipe, page 124)
- 3   tablespoons parsley, 2 tablespoons fresh rosemary, 1 large onion, 1 large carrot, 1 stalk celery, all finely chopped
- $^{1}/_{3}$ cup extra-virgin olive oil
- $1^{1}/_{4}$ lb boneless wild hare meat, with liver, coarsely chopped
- 3   cups red wine
- 4   cups boiling water
- $^{1}/_{2}$ cup milk
- 2   tablespoons tomato paste
-     salt and freshly ground black pepper to taste
- $^{1}/_{4}$ cup freshly grated Parmesan cheese

Wine: a dry red (Chianti)

Prepare the pasta. • In a heavy-bottomed pan, sauté the parsley, rosemary, onion, carrot, and celery with the oil over medium heat. When the onion and garlic begin to color, add the hare meat and cook for 15–20 minutes, or until the meat is well browned, stirring frequently. Add the wine and stir until it has evaporated. • Pour in the water, milk, and tomato paste. Season with salt and pepper. Simmer over low heat for about $1^{1}/_{2}$ hours. • Add the hare liver and, if necessary, more water. Cook for 30 more minutes, or until the hare is very tender. • Cook the pappardelle in a large pot of salted, boiling water until *al dente*. Drain well and place in a heated serving dish. Toss carefully with the sauce and sprinkle with Parmesan. Serve hot.

Serves: 4 · Prep: 20 min. + time to make the pasta · Cooking: $2^{1}/_{2}$ hrs · Level: 2

TAGLIATELLE CON SUGO DI SALSICCIA E PECORINO
Tagliatelle with sausage and Pecorino cheese

- 1   quantity Tagliatelle pasta (see recipe, page 124)
- 1   large leek, cleaned and thinly sliced
- $^{1}/_{4}$ cup extra-virgin olive oil
-     salt to taste
- 1   lb canned tomatoes
- 20   fresh basil leaves, torn
- 14   oz Italian pork sausages, skinned and crumbled
- 1   cup freshly grated Pecorino cheese

Wine: a dry red (Biferno Rosso)

Prepare the pasta. • In a large skillet, sauté the leek with the oil and a pinch of salt until soft. • Add the tomatoes and half the basil. Season with salt and cook over medium-low heat for about 30 minutes. • Remove from heat and press through a sieve. Beat with a hand-held electric beater until smooth, then add the remaining basil. • Sauté the sausages in a skillet with a little water. • Cook the tagliatelle in a large pot of salted, boiling water until *al dente*. Drain well and place in the skillet with the tomato sauce. Add the sausages and toss carefully. Sprinkle with the Pecorino and serve.

Serves: 4 · Prep: 20 min. + time to make the pasta · Cooking: 40 min. · Level: 2

Tagliatelle with olives and mushrooms

TAGLIATELLE CON FUNGHI E OLIVE
Tagliatelle with olives and mushrooms

- 1 quantity Tagliatelle pasta (see recipe, page 124)
- 2 cloves garlic, finely chopped
- 3 tablespoons finely chopped parsley
- 1/2 cup extra-virgin olive oil
- 12 oz coarsely chopped mushrooms
- 1 cup coarsely chopped black olives
- 8 mint leaves, torn
  salt and freshly ground black pepper to taste
- 1/3 cup boiling water

Wine: a dry, sparkling red (Lambrusco)

Prepare the pasta. • Combine the garlic and parsley in a skillet with the oil and sauté until the garlic begins to color. Add the mushrooms and cook until the liquid they produce has evaporated. • Add the olives, mint, salt, pepper, and boiling water. Simmer for 5 minutes. • Cook the tagliatelle in a large pot of salted, boiling water until *al dente*. Drain and place in a heated serving dish. Toss carefully with the sauce and serve.

Serves: 4 · Prep: 10 min. + time to make the pasta · Cooking: 20 min. · Level: 2

FETTUCCINE ALLA ROMANA
Fresh pasta Roman-style

- 1 quantity Fettuccine pasta (see recipe, page 124)
- 2 tablespoons dried porcini mushrooms
- 3 tablespoons coarsely chopped pork fat
- 1 small onion, finely chopped
- 1 clove garlic, finely chopped
- 1 lb fresh or canned peeled and chopped tomatoes
  salt and freshly ground black pepper to taste
- 1/4 cup butter
- 8 oz trimmed, diced chicken livers
- 1/4 cup dry white wine
- 1/2 cup Beef stock (see recipe, page 105)
- 1/4 cup freshly grated Pecorino cheese

Wine: a dry red (Sangiovese)

Prepare the pasta. • Place the mushrooms in a small bowl of warm water and leave to soften for 15 minutes. • Melt the pork fat in a skillet over medium heat and sauté the onion and garlic. • Drain the mushrooms and chop finely. Add to the skillet with the tomatoes. Season with salt and pepper. Cook for about 15 minutes, or until the sauce reduces. • Melt half the butter in a small, heavy-bottomed pan and cook the chicken livers over medium heat for 4–5 minutes. Pour in the wine and cook until it evaporates. • Add the stock, then cover and cook over low heat for about 15 minutes, or until the chicken livers are well-cooked. • Add the chicken livers to the tomato sauce. • Cook the fettuccine in a large pot of salted, boiling water until *al dente*. Drain and place in a heated serving dish. Add the sauce and toss carefully for 1–2 minutes. • Sprinkle with the Pecorino and serve.

Serves: 4 · Prep: 20 min. + time to make the pasta · Cooking: 30 min. · Level: 2

FETTUCCINE AL POMODORO
Fettuccine with butter and tomato sauce

- 1 quantity Fettuccine pasta (see recipe, page 124)
- 3 cloves garlic, finely chopped
- 3 tablespoons finely chopped parsley
- 1/2 cup butter
- 2 lb peeled and chopped tomatoes
  salt and freshly ground black pepper to taste
- 8 fresh basil leaves, torn

Wine: a dry rosé (Castel del Monte)

Prepare the pasta. • Sauté the garlic and parsley with the butter in a skillet. When the garlic begins to color, add the tomatoes and season with salt and pepper. Simmer over medium-low heat for about 30 minutes. • Cook the fettuccine in a large pot of salted, boiling water until *al dente*. Drain well and place in a heated serving dish. • Toss carefully with the tomato sauce and basil. Serve hot.

Serves: 4 · Prep: 5 min. + time to make the pasta · Cooking: 35 min. · Level: 2

Sausage ravioli with butter and sage

RAVIOLI CON SALSICCIA ALLA SALVIA
Sausage ravioli with butter and sage

- 1 quantity Pasta dough (see recipe, page 124)
- 8 oz fresh spinach
- 1 1/4 lb fresh Swiss chard
- 8 oz Italian pork sausages, skinned and crumbled
- 8 oz fresh Ricotta cheese
- 2 eggs
- 1/2 cup freshly grated Parmesan cheese
- 1 teaspoon fresh marjoram
  salt to taste
- 1 quantity Butter and sage sauce (see recipe, page 14)

Wine: a dry rosé (San Severo Rosato)

Make the pasta dough. • Cook the spinach and chard in a pot of salted water for 8–10 minutes, or until tender. Squeeze out excess moisture and chop finely. • Mix the sausages, Ricotta, eggs, half the Parmesan, and the marjoram with the spinach and chard in a mixing bowl. Combine thoroughly and season with salt. • Prepare the ravioli as shown on page 125. • Cook in a large pot of salted, boiling water until the sealed edges of the ravioli are *al dente*. • While the ravioli are cooking, prepare the sauce. • Drain the ravioli and place in a heated serving dish. Pour the sauce over the ravioli and sprinkle with the remaining Parmesan. Serve hot.

Serves: 4 · Prep: 20 min. + time to make the pasta · Cooking: 15 min. · Level: 3

TAGLIATELLE CON PROSCIUTTO E PISELLI
Tagliatelle with prosciutto and peas

- 1 quantity Tagliatelle pasta (see recipe, page 124)
- 2 cups fresh or frozen peas
- 1/4 cup butter
- 1 small onion, finely chopped
- 4 oz prosciutto, cut in one thick slice and diced
  salt and freshly ground black pepper to taste
- 1/3 cup freshly grated Parmesan cheese

Wine: a dry white (Est! Est!! Est!!!)

Prepare the tagliatelle. • Cook the peas in a small pot of lightly salted water until just cooked. Drain and set aside. • Melt the butter in a skillet and sauté the onion and prosciutto for 5 minutes. • Add the peas and season with salt and pepper. Cook for 5 minutes. • Cook the tagliatelle in a large pot of salted, boiling water until *al dente*. • Drain and place in a heated serving dish. Toss carefully with the sauce, sprinkle with the Parmesan, and serve.

Serves: 4 · Prep: 10 min. + time to make the pasta · Cooking: 20 min. · Level: 2

GARGANELLI CON RAGÙ E PISELLINI
Garganelli with meat sauce and peas

☞ Garganelli are a specialty of Emilia-Romagna. They are quite complicated to make at home and although we have included all the instructions here, you may prefer to buy them ready made.

- 1 quantity Pasta dough (see recipe, page 124)
- 2 tablespoons freshly grated Parmesan cheese
  pinch of nutmeg
  salt to taste
- 1 quantity Bolognese meat sauce (see recipe, page 19)
- 3/4 cup fresh or frozen peas

Wine: a young, dry red (Rubicone Sangiovese)

Prepare the pasta dough, incorporating the Parmesan, nutmeg, and salt with the eggs. Shape the dough into a ball and set aside to rest for 1 hour, wrapped in plastic wrap. • Prepare the meat sauce, adding the peas 10 minutes before the sauce is done. • Roll out the dough until very thin. Use a smooth-edged pastry wheel or a knife to cut the pasta sheet into 2 1/2 inch squares. • To shape the garganelli, place a large comb flat on the work surface, teeth facing away from you. Place a pasta square diagonally on the largest teeth with a corner pointing

toward you; put a pencil across this corner, parallel with the comb, and roll up the square onto it, pushing down on the comb's teeth as you roll it away from you. Slide the garganello off the pencil. • Add the garganelli to a large saucepan of salted, boiling water and cook gently for 5 minutes or less. • Drain well, then toss carefully with the meat sauce and serve.

Serves: 4 · Prep: 45 min. + time to make the pasta and the meat sauce · Cooking: 10 min. · Level: 3

PICI AL RAGÙ
Homemade Tuscan pasta with meat sauce

☞ *Pici* are a specialty of the area around Mount Amiata, in southern Tuscany. They are made with just flour, water, and salt. Originally peasant food, they are now served in restaurants all over Tuscany and Umbria. Try them with meat or tomato sauce and a glass of red wine.

- 2 1/2 cups durum wheat (semolina) flour
  pinch of salt
- 1 cup hot water
- 1 medium onion, finely chopped
- 1 medium carrot, finely chopped
- 1 small stalk celery, finely chopped
- 2 tablespoons finely chopped parsley
- 1/3 cup extra-virgin olive oil
- 10 oz ground lean beef
- 1 fresh Italian pork sausage, skinned
- 1 oz dried porcini mushrooms, soaked for 20 minutes in warm water, drained, and coarsely chopped
- 1/2 cup full-bodied dry red wine
- 1 (15 oz) can Italian tomatoes, chopped
  salt and freshly ground black pepper to taste
- 1 cup Beef stock (see recipe, page 105)
- 1 cup freshly grated Parmesan cheese

Wine: a dry red (Rosso di Montalcino)

Sift the flour and salt into a large mixing bowl and make a well in the center. Gradually add just enough of the water to make a very firm dough, working it in by hand until the dough is smooth and elastic. • On a floured work surface, roll the dough out to about 3/4 inch thick and cut into strips. • Roll each strip between

your floured palms, slowly drawing it out until it is very thin and resembles an untidy spaghetti. • Spread the *pici* out on a lightly floured clean cloth. • Sauté the onion, carrot, celery, and parsley in the oil in a heavy-bottomed saucepan for 5 minutes. • Add the beef and sausage meat, squashing any lumps that form with a fork. • Cook and stir for 5 minutes then add the mushrooms. • Add the wine and cook over higher heat, uncovered, for 5 minutes. • Add the tomatoes, salt, and pepper. • Reduce the heat, cover, and simmer for at least 45 minutes, adding stock as required. • Bring a large saucepan of salted water to a boil, add the pasta and cook until *al dente*. • Drain well and place in a heated serving dish. Add the meat sauce, and toss carefully • Sprinkle with Parmesan and serve hot.

Serves: 4 · Prep: 50 min. · Cooking: 1 hr · Level: 3

PICI AL POMODORO
Homemade Tuscan pasta with tomato sauce

☞ If you like spicy food, try adding a finely chopped chile pepper to the tomato sauce.

- 1 quantity Homemade Tuscan pasta (see preceding recipe)
- 1 quantity Simple tomato sauce (see recipe, page 18)
- 1 cup freshly grated Pecorino cheese

Wine: a light, dry red (Chianti dei Colli Senese)

Prepare the pasta. • Prepare the sauce. • Bring a large saucepan of salted water to a boil, add the pasta and cook until *al dente*. • Drain well and place in a heated serving dish, add the tomato sauce, and toss carefully • Sprinkle with Parmesan and serve hot.

Serves: 4 · Prep: 50 min. · Cooking: 10 min. · Level: 3

Tagliatelle with prosciutto and peas

Maltagliati with lamb sauce and Pecorino

MALTAGLIATI AL RAGÙ DI PECORA
Maltagliati with lamb sauce and Pecorino

☞ *Maltagliati*, which means "badly cut," are usually served in boiling pasta soups, but they can also be served with sauces.

1 quantity Maltagliati pasta (see recipe, page 124)
4 cloves garlic, finely chopped
1/3 cup extra-virgin olive oil
1 lb ground lamb
5 oz ground lean pork
2 bay leaves
1 1/2 lb peeled and chopped tomatoes
8 fresh basil leaves
1 tablespoon finely chopped parsley
   salt and freshly ground black pepper to taste
1/2 cup freshly grated Pecorino cheese

Wine: a dry red (Rosso di Montalcino)

Prepare the pasta. • In a heavy-bottomed pan, sauté the garlic in the oil over medium heat until the garlic starts to color. Add the lamb, pork, and bay leaf and sauté until the meat is browned. • Add the tomatoes, basil, and marjoram. Season with salt and pepper, and simmer over low heat for 1 hour. • Cook the maltagliati in a large pot of salted, boiling water until *al dente*. Drain, place in a heated serving dish, and toss carefully with the sauce. Remove the bay leaf before serving. • Sprinkle with the Pecorino and serve hot.

Serves: 4 · Prep: 15 min. + time to make the pasta · Cooking: 1 1/4 hrs · Level: 2

TORTELLI CON LE BIETE
Tortelli with Swiss chard filling in butter and Parmesan sauce

1 quantity Pasta dough (see recipe, page 124)
1 lb fresh Swiss chard
8 oz fresh Ricotta cheese
5 oz Mascarpone cheese
1/2 cup freshly grated Parmesan cheese
2 eggs
1/4 teaspoon nutmeg
   salt to taste
1 quantity Butter and Parmesan sauce (see recipe, page 14)

Wine: a dry red (Bardolini Chiaretto)

Prepare the pasta dough. • Cook the chard in a pot of salted water for 8–10 minutes, or until tender. Drain well and squeeze out excess moisture. Chop finely and place in a mixing bowl. Add the Ricotta, Mascarpone, Parmesan, eggs, and nutmeg. Mix thoroughly and season with salt. • Prepare the tortelli as shown on page 125. • Cook the tortelli in a large pot of salted, boiling water until the sealed edges of the pasta are *al dente*. • Drain well and place in a heated serving dish. Cover with the sauce, toss carefully, and serve.

Serves: 4 · Prep: 45 min. + time to make the pasta · Cooking: 10–15 min. · Level: 3

RAVIOLI DI PESCE CON SALSA DI VERDURE
Fish ravioli with vegetable sauce

1 quantity Pasta dough (see recipe, page 124)
3/4 cup butter
14 oz bass fillets
12 oz fresh Swiss chard
2 oz fresh Ricotta cheese
2 eggs
1 cup freshly grated Parmesan cheese
1/4 teaspoon nutmeg
   salt to taste
2 1/2 tablespoons dried mushrooms
1 stalk celery, 1 medium onion, 1 tablespoon parsley, all finely chopped
4 ripe tomatoes, peeled and chopped
1 cup water
   salt to taste
1/4 cup pine nuts, toasted and finely chopped

Wine: a dry white (Orvieto Classico)

Prepare the pasta dough. • Melt 1/4 cup of butter in a skillet. Add the fish fillets and cook over medium heat for 5 minutes, or until tender. Chop the cooked fish very finely. • Cook the Swiss chard in a pot of salted water for 8–10 minutes, or until tender. Squeeze out excess moisture and chop finely. • Combine the fish and chard in a bowl with the Ricotta, eggs, half the Parmesan, and nutmeg. Season with salt and mix well. • Prepare the ravioli as shown on page 125. • Put the mushrooms in a small bowl of warm water and leave for 20 minutes. • Drain well and chop finely. • Put the celery, onion, parsley, and remaining butter in the pan used to cook the fish. Add the tomatoes and water, and cook over medium-low heat for 20 minutes. Season with salt and add the pine nuts. • Cook the ravioli in a large pot of salted, boiling water until the sealed edges of the pasta are *al dente*. Drain and place in a heated serving dish. • Pour the sauce over the top, sprinkle with the remaining Parmesan, and serve.

Serves: 4 · Prep: 30 min. + time to make the pasta · Cooking: 40 min. · Level: 3

RAVIOLI DI RICOTTA ALLA SALVIA
Ricotta ravioli with butter and sage

1	quantity Pasta dough (see recipe, page 124)
1³/₄	cups fresh Ricotta cheese
2	eggs
¹/₄	teaspoon nutmeg
¹/₂	cup freshly grated Parmesan cheese
	salt to taste
1	quantity Butter and sage sauce (see recipe, page 14)

Wine: a dry white (Trebbiano di Romagna)

Prepare the pasta dough. • Place the Ricotta in a mixing bowl and add the eggs, nutmeg, half the Parmesan, and salt. Mix well. • Prepare the ravioli as shown on page 125. • Cook the ravioli in a large pot of salted, boiling water until the pasta around the sealed edges is *al dente*. • While the ravioli are cooking, prepare the sauce. • Drain the ravioli and place in a heated serving dish. • Cover with the sage sauce and the remaining Parmesan. Toss carefully and serve.

Serves: 4 · Prep: 10 min. + time to make the pasta · Cooking: 10 min. · Level: 3

RAVIOLI ALLE ZUCCHINE
Ravioli with zucchini filling in butter and rosemary sauce

1	quantity Pasta dough (see recipe, page 124)
2	medium zucchini
1	cup crushed amaretti cookies (macaroons)
²/₃	cup fresh Ricotta cheese
1	cup freshly grated Parmesan cheese
¹/₄	teaspoon nutmeg
	salt to taste
1	clove garlic, finely chopped
¹/₂	cup butter
2	tablespoons finely chopped rosemary

Wine: a dry white (Cortese dell'Alto Monferrato)

Prepare the pasta dough. • Cook the zucchini in a pot of salted, boiling water until tender. Drain, place in a bowl, and mash with a fork. Add the amaretti, Ricotta, two-thirds of the Parmesan, and nutmeg. Season with salt. Mix well to form a thick cream. If the filling is too liquid, add dry bread crumbs; if it is too thick,

Spinach ravioli with herbs and Ricotta cheese filling in tomato sauce

add a little milk. • Prepare the ravioli as shown on page 125. • Cook the ravioli in a large pot of salted, boiling water until the sealed edges of the pasta are *al dente*. Drain well and place in a heated serving dish. • Place the garlic in a small saucepan with the butter and rosemary and cook for 3–4 minutes over medium heat, stirring frequently. • Pour the sauce over the ravioli, sprinkle with the remaining Parmesan, and serve.

Serves: 4 · Prep: 30 min. + time needed to make the pasta · Cooking: 10 min. · Level: 3

RAVIOLI VERDI AL POMODORO
Spinach ravioli with herbs and Ricotta cheese filling in tomato sauce

1	quantity Spinach pasta dough (see recipe, page 124)
1	cup fresh Ricotta cheese
4	cups parsley and 5 cups fresh basil, finely chopped
2	eggs
¹/₄	teaspoon nutmeg
	salt to taste
¹/₄	cup freshly grated Parmesan cheese
1	quantity Tomato and butter sauce (see recipe, page 18)

Prepare the spinach pasta dough. • Place the Ricotta in a mixing bowl. Add the parsley, basil, eggs, nutmeg, and salt. Mix well. • Prepare the Tomato and butter sauce. • Prepare the ravioli as shown on page 125. • Cook the ravioli in a large pot of salted, boiling water until the sealed edges of the pasta are *al dente*. Drain well and place in a heated serving dish. • Pour the tomato sauce over the ravioli and toss carefully. Sprinkle with the Parmesan and serve hot.

Serves: 4 · Prep: 30 min. + time to make the pasta and the sauce · Cooking: 10 min. · Level: 3

TORTELLI DI ZUCCA
Tortelli with pumpkin

2³/₄ lb fresh pumpkin
1³/₄ cups freshly grated Parmesan cheese
1 egg
pinch of nutmeg
¹/₂ cup fine dry bread crumbs
salt to taste
1 quantity Pasta dough
(see recipe, page 124)
¹/₂ cup butter, melted

*Wine: a dry sparkling red
(Lambrusco di Sorbara)*

Without peeling the pumpkin, scrape away the seeds and fibers and cut it in slices 1¹/₂ inches thick. • Bake in a preheated oven at 400°F until tender. • Remove the flesh from the skin. Mash and place in a mixing bowl while still hot. • Stir in three-quarters of the Parmesan, the egg, nutmeg, bread crumbs, and salt. • Cover the bowl with plastic wrap and leave to stand for 2 hours. • Prepare the pasta dough. • Prepare the tortelli as shown on page 125. • Cook the tortelli in a large pot of salted, boiling water until the sealed edges of the pasta are *al dente*. • Drain well. Drizzle with the butter and sprinkle with the remaining Parmesan. Serve hot.

Serves: 4 · Prep: 1 hr + time to make the pasta · Cooking: 30 min. · Level: 3

TORTELLI ALLA MUGELLANA
Potato tortelli with meat sauce

☞ These tortelli are also very good served with Butter and Parmesan sauce (see recipe, page 14).

1 quantity Bolognese meat sauce (see recipe, page 19)
1 quantity Pasta dough (see recipe, page 124)
1³/₄ lb russet potatoes, peeled
1 large fresh egg
1 cup freshly grated Parmesan cheese
2 tablespoons butter
pinch of nutmeg
salt and freshly ground black pepper to taste

Wine: a dry white (Pomino Il Benefizio)

Prepare the meat sauce. • Prepare the pasta dough. • Cook the potatoes in a pot of salted, boiling water for 25 minutes, or until tender. Drain, slip off their skins, and mash. Place in a large mixing bowl with the egg, half the Parmesan, the butter, nutmeg, salt, and pepper. Mix well and set

Potato tortelli with meat sauce

aside. • Prepare the tortelli as shown on page 125. • Cook the tortelli in a large pot of salted, boiling water until the sealed edges of the pasta are *al dente*. Drain and place in a heated serving dish. Pour the meat sauce over the top. Sprinkle with the remaining Parmesan and serve.

Serves: 4 · Prep: 30 min. + time to make the pasta and the sauce · Cooking: 35 min. · Level: 3

TORTELLINI ALLA PANNA
Tortellini with cream sauce

1 quantity Pasta dough (see recipe, page 124)
2 oz boneless lean pork, coarsely chopped
2 oz chicken breast, coarsely chopped
¹/₂ cup butter
2 oz prosciutto, finely chopped
4 oz Mortadella, finely chopped
2 eggs
³/₄ cup freshly grated Parmesan cheese
¹/₄ teaspoon nutmeg
salt and freshly ground black pepper to taste
¹/₂ cup heavy cream
1 small truffle, white or black, in shavings

Wine: a dry white (Pinot Grigio di Breganze)

Prepare the pasta dough. • In a large skillet, sauté the pork and chicken with 2 tablespoons of butter over medium heat for about 5 minutes. Remove from the pan and chop finely in a food processor. • Sauté the prosciutto and Mortadella in the same pan for 2–3 minutes. • Combine the pork, chicken, prosciutto, and Mortadella

in a mixing bowl. Add the eggs, ¹/₂ cup of Parmesan, nutmeg, salt, and pepper. Mix well and set aside. • Prepare the tortellini as shown on page 125. • Cook the tortellini in a large pot of salted, boiling water until the sealed edges of the pasta are *al dente*. • To make the sauce, melt the remaining butter in a saucepan over low heat. Stir in the cream and cook for 2–3 minutes. • When the tortellini are cooked, drain well and place in the pan with the cream. Add the remaining Parmesan, the truffle, salt, and pepper, and toss gently over medium-low heat for 2–3 minutes. Serve hot.

Serves: 4 · Prep: 25 min. + time to make the pasta · Cooking: 10 min. · Level: 3

TORTELLINI ALLA BOSCAIOLA
Tortellini with woodsmen-style sauce

1 quantity Pasta dough (see recipe, page 124)
1 quantity filling (see preceding recipe)
2 cups fresh or frozen peas
14 oz coarsely chopped mushrooms
2 cloves garlic, finely chopped
3 tablespoons finely chopped parsley
¹/₄ cup extra-virgin olive oil
2 (15 oz) cans tomatoes, chopped
salt and freshly ground black pepper to taste

Wine: a dry red (Sangiovese)

Prepare the pasta dough. • Make the tortellini filling and set aside. • Cook the peas in boiling water. Drain and set aside.

• Put the mushrooms, garlic, and parsley in a large skillet with the oil and cook for 5 minutes, or until the mushroom liquid has evaporated. Add the tomatoes and simmer for about 20 minutes. Add the peas and season with salt and pepper. Cook for 3–4 more minutes. • While the sauce is cooking, prepare the tortellini as shown on page 125. • Cook in a large pot of salted, boiling water until the sealed edges of the pasta are *al dente*. Drain well and place in the skillet with the sauce. Toss gently and serve.

Serves: 4 · Prep: 25 min. + time to make the pasta · Cooking: 35 min. · Level: 3

TORTELLI D'ALPEGGIO
Tortelloni with beef, spinach, and rosemary filling in cheese sauce

1	quantity Pasta dough (see recipe, page 124)
1	tablespoon finely chopped fresh rosemary
3/4	cup butter
10	oz lean beef
2	tablespoons dry white wine
8	oz fresh or frozen spinach
1	whole egg and 1 egg yolk
1/4	cup freshly grated Parmesan cheese
	pinch of nutmeg
	salt and freshly ground black pepper to taste
8	oz Fontina cheese, diced
1/2	teaspoon nutmeg

Wine: a dry rosé (Rosato Grave del Friuli)

Prepare the pasta dough. • Put the rosemary in a skillet with 1/4 cup of butter and sauté for 2–3 minutes. Add the beef and wine, and simmer over medium-low heat for 2 hours. When the beef is very tender, remove from the skillet and chop finely in a food processor. • Cook the spinach in a pot of salted water for 8–10 minutes, or until tender. Squeeze out excess moisture and chop finely. • Combine the beef and spinach in a bowl and add the eggs, Parmesan, and nutmeg. Season with salt and pepper. Mix well with a fork and set aside for 1 hour. • Prepare the tortelli as shown on page 125. • Cook the tortelli in a large pot of salted, boiling water until the sealed edges of the pasta are *al dente*. Drain and place in a heated serving dish. • Put the Fontina cheese, remaining butter, and nutmeg in a small saucepan over very low

heat and cook until the cheese has melted. • Pour over the tortelli and serve.

Serves: 4 · Prep: 25 min. + time to make the pasta · Cooking: 2 1/4 hrs. · Level: 3

AGNOLOTTI CON BURRO E SALVIA
Agnolotti with butter and sage sauce

1	quantity Pasta dough (see recipe, page 124)
2	tablespoons butter
3	tablespoons cooking juices from roast meat
1/2	cup finely chopped Savoy cabbage
1	small leek, white part only, finely chopped
2	oz Italian sausage meat
2	oz each lean roast beef and pork
1	egg
1/3	cup freshly grated Parmesan cheese
	pinch of nutmeg
	salt and freshly ground white pepper to taste
1	quantity Butter and sage sauce (see recipe, page 14)

Wine: a dry red (Dolcetto d'Asti)

Prepare the pasta dough. • Melt the butter in a saucepan and add the meat juices, cabbage, leek, and sausage meat. Cook for 5–6 minutes, stirring frequently and moistening, if necessary, with a little water. • Chop finely in a food processor together with the roast beef and pork. • Place in a mixing bowl and add the egg, half the Parmesan, the nutmeg, salt, and pepper. Mix well and set aside. • Prepare the agnolotti as shown on page 125. • Spread the agnolotti out in a single layer on a lightly floured clean cloth and leave to dry in a cool place for at least 4 hours. • Cook the agnolotti in a large pot of salted, boiling water until the sealed edges of the pasta are *al dente*. • Drain and place in a heated serving dish. • Prepare the butter and sage sauce and drizzle over the agnolotti. Sprinkle with the remaining Parmesan and serve.

Serves: 4 · Prep: 30 min. + time to make the pasta · Cooking: 10 min. · Level: 3

AGNOLOTTI CON SUGO DI CARNE
Agnolotti with meat sauce

1	quantity Pasta dough (see recipe, page 124)
1	quantity filling (see preceding recipe)
1	quantity Bolognese meat sauce (see recipe, page 19)
1/4	cup freshly grated Parmesan cheese
1	white truffle, in shavings (optional)

Wine: a dry red (Grignolino)

Prepare the pasta dough. • Prepare the agnolotti filling. • Prepare the agnolotti as shown on page 125. • Prepare the meat sauce. • Cook the agnolotti in a large pot of salted, boiling water until the pasta round the sealed edges is *al dente*. Drain well and place on a heated serving dish. • Cover with the meat sauce. Sprinkle with the Parmesan and, if using, shavings of white truffle. Serve hot.

Serves: 4 · Prep: 30 min. + time to make the pasta and the meat sauce · Cooking: 15 min. · Level: 3

RAVIOLI CON LE BARBABIETOLE
Ravioli with red beet filling

☞ This meatless ravioli, often served during Lent, is a specialty of Cortina d'Ampezzo, in northern Italy. Try replacing the Ricotta with 1/2 cup boiled, mashed potatoes.

1	quantity Pasta dough (see recipe, page 124)
2	lb boiled beets
1 3/4	cups butter
	salt to taste
4	oz fresh Ricotta cheese
1/2	cup fine dry bread crumbs (to be used if necessary)
4	teaspoons poppy seeds
1/2	cup freshly grated Parmesan cheese

Wine: a dry, aromatic white (Lison Pramaggiore Chardonnay)

Prepare the pasta dough. • Chop the beets and sauté in half the butter and a pinch of salt over high heat. • Remove from heat, stir in the Ricotta, adding some bread crumbs if the mixture is too moist. • Prepare the ravioli as shown on page 125. • Cook the ravioli in a large pot of salted, boiling water until the sealed edges of the pasta are *al dente*. • Drain well. Place in a serving dish, dot with the remaining butter, and sprinkle with the poppy seeds. • Sprinkle with the Parmesan and serve.

Serves: 6 · Prep: 1 hr · Cooking: 20 min. + time to make the pasta · Level: 3

FUSILLI GRATINATI AL FORNO
Fusilli baked with tomatoes and cheese

- 2 cloves garlic, finely chopped
- 1 large onion, finely chopped
- 2 tablespoons finely chopped parsley
- 1/4 cup extra-virgin olive oil
- 1 1/2 lb peeled and chopped fresh tomatoes
  salt and freshly ground black pepper to taste
- 1 lb fusilli pasta
- 1 1/2 cups diced pancetta
- 8 oz Mozzarella cheese, diced
- 1 cup freshly grated Pecorino cheese

Wine: a dry red (Rosso di Montalcino)

In a large skillet, sauté the garlic, onion, and parsley with the oil until soft. Add the tomatoes, salt, and pepper and simmer over low heat for 25 minutes. • Cook the fusilli in a large pot of salted, boiling water for half the time indicated on the package. Drain well. • Place a layer of pasta in a greased baking dish. Cover with layers of pancetta, tomato mixture, Mozzarella, and Pecorino. Repeat these layers until all the ingredients are in the dish, reserving a little of both cheeses to sprinkle on top. • Bake in a preheated oven at 350°F for 30 minutes. Serve hot.

Serves: 4 · Prep: 20 min. · Cooking: 1 hr · Level: 1

RIGATONI GIGANTI RIPIENI
Filled rigatoni giganti

- 1 quantity Bolognese meat sauce (see recipe, page 19)
- 1 lb rigatoni giganti pasta (large rigatoni)
- 1 1/4 cups chopped white mushrooms
- 1/4 cup butter
- 10 oz ground beef
- 1 egg
- 1/2 tablespoon all-purpose flour
- 1/4 cup dry white wine
- 1 tablespoon tomato paste, dissolved in 1 cup hot water
  salt and freshly ground black pepper to taste
- 1/2 cup freshly grated Parmesan cheese

Wine: a dry red (Barbera di Monferrato)

Prepare the meat sauce. • Cook the rigatoni in a large pot of salted, boiling water for half the time indicated on the package. Drain well and place on paper towels. • In a heavy-bottomed pan, sauté the mushrooms in half the butter over medium-low heat for 10 minutes, or until tender. • Add the beef, half the meat sauce, the egg, flour, and wine. Mix well. Add all but 1 tablespoon of the tomato and water mixture. Season with salt and pepper. Cover, and cook over medium-low heat for about 15 minutes, stirring frequently. Remove from heat. • Fill a piping bag with the mixture and stuff the rigatoni. • Grease an ovenproof dish with butter and fill with the rigatoni. Mix the remaining tomato mixture and meat sauce together and pour over the top. Sprinkle with the Parmesan and dot with the remaining butter. • Bake in a preheated oven at 350°F for 15 minutes, or until the crust is golden brown.

Serves: 4 · Prep: 35 min. + time to make the sauce · Cooking: 15 · Level: 2

TAGLIATELLE ALLA BURANELLA
Tagliatelle Venetian-style

- 1 lb Tagliatelle (see recipe, page 124)
- 1 1/4 lb shrimp, with heads
- 1 clove garlic, finely chopped
- 1 small onion, finely chopped
- 3 tablespoons extra-virgin olive oil
- 1/2 cup butter
- 1/2 cup dry white wine
- 1/3 cup all-purpose flour
- 1 cup hot milk
  salt to taste
- 1 cup freshly grated Parmesan cheese
- 2 tablespoons finely chopped parsley

Wine: a dry white (Pinot Grigio di Breganze)

Prepare the pasta. • Cook the shrimp in 4 cups of boiling water for 10 minutes. Remove with a slotted ladle. Use a pair of sharply pointed scissors to cut down the center of their backs. Pull the sides of the shell apart and take out the flesh, keeping it as intact as possible, and set aside. • Return the shells and heads to the stock and continue boiling until it has reduced by two-thirds. • In a skillet, sauté the garlic and onion very gently in the oil and half the butter. • Add the shrimp flesh. Sprinkle with the wine and cook until it has evaporated. Season with salt. Remove from heat. • Melt the remaining butter in a small saucepan. Add the flour and stir to prevent lumps forming as you add first the hot milk and then the strained hot shrimp stock. Cook and stir for 10 minutes, or until the sauce has a thick, glossy texture. • Cook the tagliatelle in a large pot of salted, boiling water until *al dente*. • Drain and add to the skillet. Pour in the sauce and stir carefully while cooking briefly over low heat. Place in a heated serving dish. • Sprinkle with the Parmesan and parsley, and bake in a preheated oven at 400°F for 25 minutes, or until a golden brown crust has formed on top. • Serve hot.

Serves: 6 · Prep: 30 min. + time to make the pasta · Cooking: 1 hr · Level: 3

CANNELLONI AL FORNO
Filled spinach cannelloni in tomato and béchamel sauce

- 1/2 quantity Tomato and butter sauce (see recipe, page 18)
- 1 lb fresh spinach
- 1/4 cup butter
  salt and freshly ground black pepper to taste
- 1 1/4 cups fresh Ricotta cheese
- 1 cup freshly grated Parmesan cheese
- 2 eggs
- 1 quantity Béchamel sauce (see recipe, page 16)
- 12 store-bought spinach cannelloni

Wine: a dry red (Chianti Classico)

Prepare the tomato sauce. • Cook the spinach in a pot of salted water for 8–10 minutes, or until tender. Drain, squeeze out excess moisture, and chop finely. • Put half the butter in a skillet with the spinach. Season with salt and pepper. Cook briefly over high heat until the spinach has absorbed the butter. • Place in a bowl and mix well with the Ricotta, half the Parmesan, and the eggs. • Prepare the béchamel sauce. • Cook the cannelloni in a large pot of salted, boiling water for half the time indicated on the package. Drain, and pass the colander with the pasta under cold running water to stop the cooking process. Dry the cannelloni with paper towels and stuff with the Ricotta and spinach mixture. • Line the bottom of an ovenproof dish with a layer of béchamel and place the cannelloni in a single layer on it. Cover with alternate spoonfuls of béchamel and tomato sauce. Sprinkle with the remaining Parmesan and dot with the remaining butter. • Bake in a preheated oven at 400°F for 20 minutes, or until golden brown on top. Serve hot.

Serves: 4–6 · Prep: 40 min. · Cooking: 20 min. · Level: 2

Homemade buckwheat pasta baked with cabbage, potato, and cheese

Pizzoccheri are a specialty of Valtellina, in Lombardy. They are quite complicated to make, but well worth the effort. Factory-made, dried pizzoccheri are now available in specialty stores.

PIZZOCCHERI
Homemade buckwheat pasta baked with cabbage, potato, and cheese

2$^1/_2$	cups buckwheat flour
1$^1/_2$	cups all-purpose flour
3	eggs
$^1/_2$	cup milk
1	teaspoon salt
8	oz potatoes
6	oz Savoy cabbage
6	oz Fontina cheese
$^2/_3$	cup butter
2	cloves garlic, finely chopped
4	leaves fresh sage
	freshly ground black pepper to taste
1	cup freshly grated Parmesan cheese

Wine: a dry red (Valtellina Rosso)

Combine the flours in a large mixing bowl. Add the eggs, milk, and salt and stir to obtain a firm dough. • Place on a lightly floured work surface and knead until smooth. Set aside for 30 minutes. • Roll the pasta out until about $^1/_8$ inch thick. Roll the sheet of pasta loosely and cut into strips $^1/_2$ inch wide and 3 inches long. • Chop the potatoes in $^1/_2$-inch cubes and chop the cabbage into strips. • Bring a large saucepan of lightly salted water to the boil and cook the potatoes and cabbage. Put the potatoes in 5 minutes before the cabbage. • When the potatoes are almost cooked, add the pasta. • When the vegetables and pasta are cooked, drain carefully. • Slice the Fontina thinly. • Melt the butter with the garlic and sage in a small saucepan. Cook for 2 minutes. • Butter an ovenproof dish. • Place a layer of pasta in the bottom of the dish and cover with a layer of potato and cabbage. Drizzle with a little butter, sprinkle with pepper and Parmesan, and cover with slices of Fontina. Repeat this layering process two or three times until all the ingredients are in the dish. Finish with a layer of Parmesan. • Bake in a preheated oven at 350°F for 25 minutes, or until golden brown on top. Serve hot.

Serves: 6 · Prep: 1 hr · Cooking 40 min. · Level: 2

Baked shrimp and salmon penne

PASTICCIO DI FETTUCCINE VERDI AL PROSCIUTTO

Baked spinach fettuccine with ham, cream, and eggs

- 1 quantity Spinach fettuccine pasta (see recipe, page 124)
- 1/4 cup butter
- 4 eggs, separated
- 8 oz ham, finely chopped
- 2 tablespoons finely chopped parsley
  pinch of nutmeg
  salt and freshly ground black pepper to taste
- 1 cup heavy cream
- 1/2 cup freshly grated Parmesan cheese

Wine: a dry red (Chianti Classico)

Prepare the pasta. • Melt the butter in a saucepan over low heat. Add the egg yolks, ham, and parsley, and stir with a wooden spoon for 2–3 minutes. Add the nutmeg and season with salt and pepper. Remove from heat. • Whip the cream until stiff. In a separate bowl, beat the egg whites until stiff. Gently stir the whipped cream into the egg whites and add to the ham mixture. • Cook the pasta in a large pot of salted, boiling water for 2–3 minutes. Drain well and dry on a clean dish towel. • Grease an ovenproof dish with butter and add the pasta. Cover with the ham mixture. Sprinkle with the Parmesan cheese. Bake in a preheated oven at 350°F for about 50 minutes. Serve hot.

Serves: 4 · Prep: 15 min. + time to make the pasta · Cooking: 1 hr · Level: 2

POMODORI CON PASTA AL FORNO

Baked tomatoes with pasta

- 12 medium tomatoes, with stalks still attached
- 12 basil leaves
- 8 oz small, tubular pasta
- 2 tablespoons finely chopped parsley
- 1/3 cup extra-virgin olive oil
  salt and freshly ground black pepper to taste

Wine: a dry white (Orvieto Classico)

Rinse the tomatoes and dry well. Cut a "hat" off the top of each and set aside. Use a teaspoon to hollow out the pulp and place it in a bowl. • Place a basil leaf in the bottom of each hollow shell. • Cook the pasta in a medium pot of salted, boiling water for half the time indicated on the package. Drain well. • Combine the pasta with the tomato pulp. Add the parsley and 3 tablespoons of the oil. Season with salt and pepper. • Stuff the hollow tomatoes with the mixture. • Grease an ovenproof dish with the remaining oil and arrange the tomatoes carefully inside. Put a "hat" back on each tomato. • Bake in a preheated oven at 350°F for about 40 minutes.

Serves: 4 · Prep: 20 min. · Cooking: 45 min. · Level: 1

PENNE AL CARTOCCIO

Baked shrimp and salmon penne

- 1 medium onion, finely chopped
- 2 tablespoons extra-virgin olive oil
- 1/4 cup butter
- 3 1/2 oz shrimp, shelled and coarsely chopped
- 3 1/2 oz smoked salmon, coarsely chopped
- 1/3 cup light cream
- 3 tablespoons tomato purée
  salt and freshly ground black pepper to taste
- 1 lb penne pasta
- 3 tablespoons finely chopped parsley

Wine: a dry white (Capannelle Bianco)

In a large skillet, sauté the onion in the oil and half the butter over medium heat for 5 minutes. • Add the shrimp and salmon. • Mix the cream and tomato purée in a small bowl and add to the skillet. Season with salt and pepper, mix, and cook, uncovered, for 5 more minutes. • Cook the penne in a large pot of salted, boiling water for half the time indicated on the package. Drain and place in a bowl. • Add the sauce and sprinkle with the parsley. • Butter a sheet of waxed paper or foil 13 x 23 inches and place the penne and their sauce in the center. • Dot with the remaining butter, seal the parcel with a second sheet of waxed paper or foil, and bake in a preheated oven at 400°F for 15 minutes. • When cooked, arrange on a heated serving dish. Serve at once, opening the parcel on the table.

Serves: 4 · Prep: 20 min. · Cooking: 35 min. · Level: 2

PASTICCIO DI RADICCHIO

Ruote with radicchio

☞ Radicchio is a variety of chicory native to Italy. Its colorful leaves have a slightly bitter flavor that blends beautifully with fresh or dried pasta.

- 6 heads radicchio
- 1/4 cup butter
  salt and freshly ground black pepper to taste
- 1 1/4 cups heavy cream
- 1 quantity Béchamel sauce (see recipe, page 16)
- 1 lb ruote (wheels) or other short pasta shape
- 1 cup freshly grated Parmesan cheese

Wine: a light, dry white (Soave Classico)

Rinse the radicchio heads thoroughly under cold running water. Dry, and slice lengthwise in quarters. Place in an ovenproof dish greased with the butter. Season with salt and pepper, and pour the cream over the top. Bake in a preheated oven at 350°F for 15 minutes. • Prepare the béchamel sauce. • Cook the pasta in a large pot of salted, boiling water for half the time indicated on the package. • Mix the pasta with the béchamel, and place in the ovenproof dish with the radicchio. Mix well. Sprinkle with the Parmesan and bake in a preheated oven at 400°F for 20 minutes, or until a golden crust has formed on top. • Serve hot, straight from the ovenproof dish.

Serves: 6 · Prep: 10 min. · Cooking: 35 min. · Level: 1

MACCHERONI AL FORNO
Baked macaroni with Ricotta cheese

- 1¼ lb firm ripe tomatoes
- 6 fresh basil leaves
- ¼ cup extra-virgin olive oil
- 2 cloves garlic, finely chopped
   salt and freshly ground black pepper to taste
- 1 cup fresh Ricotta cheese
- 1 lb macaroni or other short pasta
- 8 oz spicy Italian salami, thinly sliced
- 8 oz smoked Provolone cheese, thinly sliced
- ½ cup freshly grated Parmesan cheese

Wine: a light, dry red (Gutturnio)

Blanch the tomatoes in a large pan of boiling water for 1 minute, then place under cold running water. Peel, cut in half, and squeeze out as many of the seeds as possible. Chop coarsely. • Place in a saucepan over medium heat with the basil, half the oil, the garlic, salt, and pepper. Cover and cook for 30 minutes, stirring occasionally. • Press the Ricotta through a sieve. • Cook the pasta in a large pot of salted, boiling water for half the time

indicated on the package. Drain well and place in a bowl with the Ricotta. Mix well. • Place a layer of pasta and Ricotta in the bottom of a greased ovenproof dish and cover with a layer of tomatoes, followed by layers of salami and Provolone. Repeat until all the ingredients are in the dish. • Drizzle with the remaining oil, sprinkle with the Parmesan, and bake in a preheated oven at 350°F for 5–10 minutes. • Set aside for 20 minutes before serving.

Serves: 6 · Prep: 40 min. · Cooking: 40 min. · Level: 1

TIELLA DI PASTA CALABRESE
Calabrian baked pasta

- 3 lb firm ripe tomatoes
- 10 fresh basil leaves, torn
   salt and freshly ground black pepper to taste
- 1 lb potatoes
- ½ cup extra-virgin olive oil
- 1 lb penne pasta (or other short pasta)
- 12 oz black olives, pitted and thinly sliced
- 1 large onion, thinly sliced
- 1 cup freshly grated Pecorino cheese
- 1 tablespoon finely chopped fresh oregano
- ½ cup fine dry bread crumbs

Wine: a dry white (Cirò Bianco)

Blanch the tomatoes in a large pan of boiling water for 1 minute, then place under cold running water. Peel and chop finely. Place in a bowl with the basil and season with salt and pepper. • Peel the potatoes and cut in ¼-inch thick slices.

Grease an ovenproof dish with a little of the oil. Place a layer of tomato on the bottom and cover with a layer of raw pasta, followed by layers of potatoes, olives, onion, oil, cheese, and oregano. • Sprinkle with the bread crumbs and drizzle with the remaining oil. • Bake in a preheated oven at 350°F for 1 hour. • Serve hot.

Serves: 4 · Prep: 15 min. · Cooking: 1 hr · Level: 1

RIGATONI CON UVETTA AL FORNO
Baked rigatoni with raisins

- 1 lb rigatoni pasta
- ¼ cup extra-virgin olive oil
- ½ cup raisins (soaked in warm water for 10 minutes)
- ½ cup pine nuts
   salt and freshly ground black pepper to taste
- ½ cup freshly grated Parmesan cheese

Wine: a light, dry red (Gutturnio)

Cook the rigatoni in a large pot of salted, boiling water until *al dente*. Drain well and place in a bowl with 3 tablespoons of the oil. Toss well. • Drain the raisins and add with the pine nuts to the pasta. Mix well. • Grease a rimmed baking sheet with the remaining oil and spread the pasta out on it. Sprinkle with the Parmesan, salt, and pepper. • Bake in a preheated oven at 350°F for 5–10 minutes. Serve hot or at room temperature.

Serves: 4 · Prep: 10 min. · Cooking: 20 min. · Level: 1

Calabrian baked pasta

Rigatoni baked in pastry with meat sauce, béchamel, and truffles

CANNELLONI ALLA BARBAROUX
Baked crêpes with béchamel sauce

2	tablespoons butter
1	tablespoon extra-virgin olive oil
5	oz ham, chopped
1	lb lean veal, cut in two pieces
1	tablespoon each finely chopped fresh rosemary and sage
1/2	cup dry white wine
2	eggs
1/4	cup freshly grated Parmesan cheese
	salt and freshly ground white pepper to taste
	pinch of nutmeg
1 1/2	quantities Crêpes (see recipe, page 185)
1	quantity Béchamel sauce (see recipe, page 16)

Wine: a dry, full-bodied red (Grignolino del Monferrato Casalese)

Heat the butter and oil in a heavy-bottomed pan just large enough to hold the meat. Sauté the ham for 2 minutes, then add the veal. Add the rosemary and sage, and pour in a little of the wine. Cook over medium-low heat for about 2 hours, adding more wine as required to keep the pan moist. The meat should be very well cooked. • Finely chop the meat and other ingredients in the pan in a food processor. • Place in a mixing bowl and add the Parmesan, eggs, salt, pepper, and nutmeg. • Prepare the crêpes. • Spread some of the filling onto each crêpe and roll them up, not too tightly. • Place the filled crêpes in a fairly shallow ovenproof dish, greased with butter. • Prepare the béchamel sauce and pour it over the stuffed crêpes. • Bake in a preheated oven at 400°F until the surface is light, golden brown. • Serve hot.

Serves: 4 · Prep: 30 min. · Cooking: 2 1/2 hrs · Level: 2

TIMBALLO DI RIGATONI AL TARTUFO
Rigatoni baked in pastry with meat sauce, béchamel, and truffles

1	quantity Bolognese meat sauce (see recipe, page 19)
1	quantity Béchamel sauce (see recipe, page 16)
1	quantity Plain pastry (see recipe, page 49)
1	lb rigatoni pasta
2	tablespoons butter
2	tablespoons fine dry bread crumbs
1	whole white truffle, in shavings
1	cup freshly grated Parmesan cheese

Wine: a dry red (Barbera di Monferrato)

Prepare the meat and béchamel sauces. • Prepare the pastry. • Cook the rigatoni in a large pot of salted, boiling water for half the time indicated on the package. Drain well and mix with half the meat sauce. • Grease a 12-inch ovenproof baking dish with the butter and sprinkle with the bread crumbs. • Roll the dough out to about 1/8 inch thick and line the baking dish. • Cover the bottom with a layer of béchamel, followed by layers of pasta and meat sauce. Sprinkle with the truffle. Repeat until all the ingredients are in the baking dish. The last layer should be of béchamel. Sprinkle with the Parmesan. • Bake in a preheated oven at 350°F for about 30 minutes. Serve hot.

Serves: 6 · Prep: 30 min. + time to make the pastry and the sauces · Cooking: 30 min. · Level: 3

STRUDEL DI SPINACI AL FORNO
Baked spinach and ricotta roll

1	quantity Pasta dough (see recipe, page 124)
1 3/4	lb fresh or frozen spinach
14	oz fresh Ricotta cheese
1 1/4	cups freshly grated Parmesan cheese
1/4	teaspoon nutmeg
	salt to taste
1	quantity Béchamel sauce (see recipe, page 16)

Wine: a dry red (Collio Merlot)

Prepare the pasta dough. • Cook the spinach in a pot of salted water for 8–10 minutes, or until tender. Drain, squeeze out excess moisture and chop finely. • Put the spinach in a bowl and add the Ricotta, 1/4 cup of Parmesan, and nutmeg. Combine thoroughly and season with salt. • Lightly flour a clean work surface and roll the pasta dough out until it is very thin. Cut the dough into a 12 x 16-inch rectangle. • Spread the spinach and Ricotta mixture evenly over the top and roll it up. Seal the ends by squeezing the dough together. Wrap the roll tightly in cheesecloth, tying the ends with string. • Bring a large pot of salted water to a boil. The pot should be wide enough so that the roll can lie flat. Immerse the roll carefully into the boiling water and simmer for about 20 minutes. Remove from the pot and set aside. • While the roll is cooking, prepare the béchamel sauce. • Unwrap the spinach roll and cut into slices about 1/2 inch thick. Cover the bottom of an ovenproof dish with the béchamel and top with slices of spinach roll. • Sprinkle with the remaining Parmesan. Bake in a preheated oven at 350°F for about 15 minutes, or until a golden crust forms on top. Serve hot.

Serves: 6 · Prep: 1 hr + time to make the pasta · Cooking: 45 min. · Level: 3

PASTA AL FORNO ALLA SICILIANA
Baked pasta, Sicilian-style

12	oz ground beef
4	cloves, crushed
2	bay leaves, broken
1	cup dry red wine
1	large eggplant
2	tablespoons coarse sea salt
14	oz anellini (or other tiny pasta shapes)
1	cup extra-virgin olive oil
1	medium onion, finely chopped
1	cup finely chopped parsley
8	oz fresh or canned tomatoes
8	shelled walnuts, chopped
	pinch of cinnamon
	salt and freshly ground white pepper to taste
¼	cup butter
1	cup fine dry bread crumbs
½	cup freshly grated Pecorino cheese

Wine: a dry red (Etna Rosso)

Combine the meat with the cloves, bay leaves, and wine in a bowl and marinate for 2 hours. • Slice the eggplant thinly and place on a slanted cutting board. Sprinkle with the coarse salt and set aside for 1 hour. • Cook the pasta in a large pot of salted, boiling water for half the time indicated on the package. Drain well and set aside. • Rinse the eggplant and dry with paper towels. Heat ¾ cup of oil in a skillet and fry the eggplant until golden brown. Drain on paper towels, then chop coarsely. • Sauté the onion and parsley in the remaining oil until soft. Drain the wine from the meat and add to the skillet with the onion. Mix well and add the tomatoes, walnuts, eggplant, cinnamon, salt, and pepper. Cook for 5 minutes, then add the pasta. • Use the butter to grease a deep ovenproof dish and sprinkle with 2 tablespoons of the bread crumbs. • Place the pasta mixture in the dish and sprinkle with the remaining bread crumbs and cheese. Melt the remaining butter and drizzle over the top. • Bake in a preheated oven at 350°F for 30 minutes, or until the surface is light, golden brown. •

Baked pasta and eggplant

Remove from the oven and let stand for 10 minutes before serving.

Serves: 6 · Prep: 30 min. + 2 hrs to marinate · Cooking: 40 min. · Level: 2

TIMBALLO DI PASTA E MELANZANE
Baked pasta and eggplant

1	lb eggplant
2	tablespoons coarse sea salt
1	lb firm ripe tomatoes
2	cups oil, for frying
1	lb rigatoni pasta
	salt and freshly ground white pepper to taste
4	cloves garlic, peeled and lightly crushed (but whole)
1	cup extra-virgin olive oil
¼	cup butter
12	leaves fresh basil, finely chopped
1	cup fine dry bread crumbs
1	cup freshly grated Pecorino cheese

Wine: a light, dry red (Gutturnio)

Slice the eggplant thinly and place on a slanted cutting board. Sprinkle with the coarse salt and set aside for 1 hour. • Blanch the tomatoes in a large pan of boiling water for 1 minute, then place under cold running water. Peel and cut in half. Squeeze out as many of the seeds as possible and cut in quarters or eighths. • Heat the frying oil in a skillet and fry the eggplant until golden brown. Drain on paper towels. • Cook the pasta in a large pot of salted, boiling water for half the time indicated on the package. Drain well and set aside. • Sauté the garlic in the olive oil until it turns pale gold, then remove. • Add the tomatoes and basil, season with salt and pepper, and cook over medium heat for 10 minutes. • Use the butter to grease a deep-sided ovenproof dish. • Combine the pasta with half the tomatoes and place a layer of this mixture in the dish. Cover with a layer of eggplant. Repeat this process until the eggplant and pasta mixture are used up. Finish with a layer of eggplant. Sprinkle with the bread crumbs and cheese. • Bake in a preheated oven at 375°F for 20 minutes, or until the top is golden brown. • Serve hot or warm.

Serves: 6 · Prep: 40 min. + 1 hr for the eggplants · Cooking: 30 min. · Level: 2

LASAGNE AL FORNO
Lasagne with Bolognese meat sauce

1 · quantity Bolognese meat sauce (see recipe, page 19)
1 · quantity Lasagne (see recipe, page 124)
2 · tablespoons butter, chopped
1 · cup freshly grated Parmesan cheese
1 · quantity Béchamel sauce (see recipe, page 16)

Wine: a dry red (Sangiovese di Romagna)

Prepare the meat sauce. • Make the pasta dough and prepare the lasagne. • Cook the lasagne 4–5 sheets at a time in a large pot of salted, boiling water for about 2 minutes. Remove with a slotted spoon, and plunge into a bowl of cold water to stop the cooking process. Remove quickly, and rinse gently under cold running water. Lay the sheets out separately on clean dishcloths and pat dry. • Prepare the béchamel and combine with the meat sauce. • Smear the bottom of a large oval baking dish with butter to stop the lasagne from sticking. Line with a single layer of cooked lasagne sheets. Cover with a thin layer of meat and béchamel sauce. Sprinkle with a little Parmesan, followed by another layer of lasagne. Repeat until there are at least 6 layers. Leave enough sauce to spread a thin layer on top. Sprinkle with Parmesan and add the butter. • Bake in a preheated oven at 400°F for 15–20 minutes, until a crust has formed on the top. Serve hot.

Serves: 6 · Prep: 30 min. + time to make the pasta and the sauce · Cooking: 25 min. · Level: 3

LASAGNE DI NOCI
Walnut lasagne

1 · quantity Lasagne (see recipe, page 124)
1/3 · cup pine nuts
1 · lb walnuts, in their shells
2 · cloves garlic
1 · cup parsley
1/2 · cup extra-virgin olive oil
  · salt to taste
1 · quantity Béchamel sauce (see recipe, page 16)
1 · cup freshly grated Parmesan cheese

Wine: a dry white (Orvieto Classico)

Prepare the pasta. • Roast the pine nuts in the oven at 350°F for 5–10 minutes, or until lightly browned. Set aside to cool. • Shell the walnuts and combine in a food processor with the pine nuts, garlic, parsley, and oil. Chop finely. Season with salt. • Prepare the béchamel sauce. •

Continue in exactly the same way as for *Lasagne with Bolognese meat sauce* (see first recipe on this page).

Serves: 6 · Prep: 30 min. + time to make the pasta and the sauce · Cooking: 25 min. · Level: 3

LASAGNE DI PESCE
Fish lasagne

1 · quantity Lasagne (see recipe, page 124)
1 · quantity Fish sauce (see recipe, page 19)
1 · quantity Béchamel sauce (see recipe, page 16)
1/2 · cup freshly grated Parmesan cheese

Wine: a dry white (Parrina Bianco)

Prepare the pasta. • Prepare the fish sauce. • Prepare the béchamel sauce. • Continue in exactly the same way as for *Lasagne with Bolognese meat sauce* (see first recipe on this page).

Serves: 6 · Prep: 30 min. + time to make the pasta and the sauce · Cooking: 25 min. · Level: 3

LASAGNE VERDI AL PESTO
Spinach lasagne with basil sauce

1 · quantity Genoese basil sauce: (see recipe, page 21)
1 · quantity Spinach lasagne (see recipe, page 124)
2 · tablespoons butter, chopped
1 · cup freshly grated Parmesan cheese
1 · quantity Béchamel sauce (see recipe, page 16)

Wine: a dry red (Cabernet di Grace del Friuli)

Prepare the basil sauce. • Make the pasta dough and prepare the lasagne. • Continue in exactly the same way as for *Lasagne with Bolognese meat sauce* (see first recipe on this page).

Serves: 6 · Prep: 30 min. + time to make the pasta and the sauce · Cooking: 25 min. · Level: 3

LASAGNE AI FUNGHI
Lasagne with Italian mushroom sauce

1 · quantity Italian mushroom sauce: (see recipe, page 20)
1 · quantity Lasagne (see recipe, page 124)
2 · tablespoons butter, chopped
1 · cup freshly grated Parmesan cheese
1 · quantity Béchamel sauce (see recipe, page 16)

Wine: a dry rosé (Carmignano Rosato)

Prepare the mushroom sauce. • Make the pasta dough and prepare the lasagne. • Continue in exactly the same way as for *Lasagne with Bolognese meat sauce* (see first recipe on this page).

Serves: 6 · Prep: 30 min. + time to make the pasta and the sauce · Cooking: 25 min. · Level: 3

Neapolitan Carnival lasagne

There are many different recipes for lasagne, ranging from the classic Bolognese and Neapolitan versions, to those with vegetable and fish fillings. Carnival lasagne, a very hearty dish, is served in the south during Carnival time in the weeks leading up to Lent.

LASAGNE DI CARNEVALE
Neapolitan Carnival lasagne

1 · quantity Lasagne (see recipe, page 124)
1 · onion, finely chopped
10 · oz beef loin, in 1 piece
1/3 · cup butter
  · salt and freshly ground black pepper to taste
1 · (15 oz) can Italian tomatoes, chopped
1/2 · cup Beef stock (see recipe, page 105)
2 · tablespoons finely chopped parsley
1 · egg
1 · cup freshly grated Parmesan cheese
1 · cup oil, for frying
  · butter for the baking dish
4 · oz salami, cut in cubes
10 · oz Mozzarella cheese, cut in cubes
4 · oz ham, cut in cubes

Wine: a dry red (Cerasuolo di Vittoria)

Prepare the pasta. • Cook the lasagne as explained in the recipe for *Lasagne with Bolognese meat sauce* on this page. • Sauté the onion and beef in a skillet with the butter until lightly browned. Season with salt and pepper and add the tomatoes. Simmer over medium-low heat for 1 hour, adding stock gradually to the skillet to keep it moist. • When the meat is cooked, remove from the skillet and chop finely in a food processor. Reserve the sauce. • Transfer the chopped meat to a mixing bowl and add the parsley, egg, and half the Parmesan. Shape the mixture into small meatballs. • Heat the oil in a large skillet and fry the meatballs for 8–10 minutes, or until nicely browned. Drain on paper towels. • Butter an ovenproof dish and cover the bottom with a layer of lasagne, followed by layers of salami, Mozzarella, ham, Parmesan, meatballs, and sauce. Repeat until all the ingredients are in the dish. Finish with a layer of Parmesan. • Bake in a preheated oven at 350°F for 20 minutes, or until golden brown. • Set aside for a few minutes before serving.

Serves: 4 · Prep: 15 min. + time to make the pasta · Cooking: 2 1/2 hrs · Level: 3

Until quite recently Italy could be divided into two distinct gastronomical areas – the central and southern regions, where pasta was the staple food, and the north, where rice was more common. Although this division has faded, most of the tempting recipes for rice and risotto in this chapter come from the north. Many recipes call for homemade stock; if you are too busy to prepare stock, use boiling water and a bouillon cube in its place.

RICE

RISOTTO ALLA SBIRRAGLIA
Risotto with chicken

☞ This nourishing risotto takes its name from the Austrian soldiers (called *shirri*) who occupied northern Italy in the 19th century.

- ¹/₄ cup butter
- 2 tablespoons extra-virgin olive oil
- 1 stalk celery, 1 onion, 1 carrot, finely chopped
- 1 chicken (about 1¹/₂ lb), cleaned, cut in 8 pieces
  salt and freshly ground white pepper to taste
- 1 cup dry white wine
- 2 cups short-grain rice (preferably Italian arborio)
- 2 chicken livers, cleaned and finely chopped
- 6 cups Chicken stock (see recipe, page 104)
- ¹/₃ cup freshly grated Parmesan cheese

Wine: a dry white (Bianco da Pitigliano)

Melt 3 tablespoons of butter with the oil in a heavy-bottomed saucepan and sauté the celery, onion, and carrot for 2 minutes. • Sprinkle the chicken with salt and pepper and add to the pan. Increase the heat and brown all over. • After 8–10 minutes, sprinkle with a little wine. Cover and cook, gradually adding the wine, for 25–30 minutes. When the chicken is tender, remove and set aside in a warm oven. • Put the rice and chicken livers in the pan with the cooking juices and cook over high heat for 2 minutes. • Stir in ¹/₂ cup of the stock. Cook, stirring often, until the stock is absorbed. Continue adding the stock, ¹/₂ cup at a time, stirring often until each addition is absorbed, until the rice is tender, 15–18 minutes. • Stir in the remaining butter and Parmesan. Transfer the risotto to a heated serving dish. Arrange the chicken on top and serve.

Serves: 4 · Prep: 10 min. · Cooking: 1 hr · Level: 2

◁ Neapolitan rice pie (see recipe, page 178)
▷ Risotto with chicken

RISO CON BURRO E SALVIA
Rice with butter and sage

- 2 cups short-grain rice
- 1/4 cup butter
- 2 cloves garlic, cut in half
- 6 sage leaves (fresh or dried), whole or crumbled
- 1/3 cup freshly grated Parmesan cheese

Wine: an aromatic white (Trebbiano dei Colli Martani)

Cook the rice in 2 quarts of salted, boiling water for about 13–15 minutes. • When the rice is almost ready, melt the butter in a heavy-bottomed saucepan over low heat with the garlic and sage. Remove the garlic after 1 minute. The butter should be dark golden brown. • Drain the rice thoroughly and transfer to a heated serving dish. • Sprinkle with the Parmesan and drizzle with the hot butter and sage. Toss well and serve hot.

Serves: 4 · Prep: 5 min. · Cooking: 15 min. · Level: 1

RISOTTO ALLA PARMIGIANA
Parmesan risotto

☞ This is a classic recipe. In Piedmont, 2 tablespoons of tomato paste are sometimes added after the wine to make a lovely pink, or rosé, risotto.

- 1/4 cup butter
- 1 onion, finely chopped
- 2 cups short-grain rice (preferably Italian arborio)
- 1/2 cup dry white wine
- 6 cups Beef stock (see recipe, page 105)
- 1/4 cup freshly grated Parmesan cheese
   pinch of nutmeg (optional)
   salt and freshly ground white pepper to taste

Wine: a dry white (Pinot Bianco di Breganze)

Melt half the butter in a large, heavy-bottomed saucepan. Add the onion and sauté over medium heat until soft. • Add the rice, increase the heat, and stir for 2 minutes. • Pour in the wine, and stir until absorbed. • Stir in 1/2 cup of the stock. Cook, stirring often, until the stock is absorbed. Continue adding the stock, 1/2 cup at a time, stirring often until each addition is absorbed, until the rice is tender, 15–18 minutes. • Add the Parmesan and nutmeg, if liked, when the rice is almost cooked. • Season with salt and pepper, add the remaining butter, and mix well. Serve hot.

Serves: 4 · Prep: 5 min. · Cooking: 25 min. · Level: 2

RISO ALL'UOVO CON PANNA
Rice with egg, cream, and Parmesan

- 2 1/4 cups short-grain rice
- 3 fresh egg yolks
- 1/2 cup light cream
- 1/3 cup freshly grated Parmesan cheese
   freshly ground white pepper to taste
- 2 tablespoons butter

Wine: a dry white (Bianco dei Colli del Trasimeno)

Cook the rice in 2 quarts of salted, boiling water for about 13–15 minutes. • When the rice is almost ready, beat the egg yolks, cream, Parmesan, and a pinch of pepper in a bowl. • Drain the rice and transfer to a heated serving dish. • Pour the sauce over the hot rice, and dot with the butter. Stir quickly and serve.

Serves: 4 · Prep: 2 min · Cooking: 13–15 min. · Level: 1

RISO ALLA FONTINA
Rice with Fontina cheese

☞ This dish comes from Piedmont and Valle d'Aosta, in northwestern Italy, where it was traditionally served at wedding banquets.

- 2 cups short-grain rice (preferably Italian arborio)
- 1/3 cup butter
- 6 oz Fontina cheese, cubed
   freshly ground white pepper to taste (optional)

Wine: a dry white (Torgiano Bianco)

Cook the rice in 2 quarts of salted, boiling water for about 13–15 minutes. • When the rice is almost ready, heat the butter in a saucepan until golden brown. • Drain the rice over the serving bowl to warm the bowl. Don't drain the rice too thoroughly. Discard the water in the bowl. • Add the rice, alternating with spoonfuls of the cheese. Drizzle with the butter, stir well, and serve immediately, passing the pepper separately.

Serves: 4 · Prep: 5 min. · Cooking: 13–15 min. Level: 1

RISOTTO CON MOZZARELLA
Mozzarella cheese risotto

- 2 tablespoons butter
- 1/2 onion, finely chopped
- 2 cups short-grain rice (preferably Italian arborio)
- 1/2 cup dry white wine
- 4 cups Chicken stock (see recipe, page 104)
- 2/3 cup light cream
- 10 oz Mozzarella cheese, cubed
- 1/3 cup freshly grated Parmesan cheese
   salt and freshly ground white pepper to taste

Wine: an aromatic white (Sauvignon dell'Alto Adige)

Melt the butter in a large, heavy-bottomed saucepan. Add the onion and sauté until soft. • Add the rice and cook for 2 minutes, stirring constantly. • Pour in the wine and when this has been absorbed, begin stirring in the stock, 1/2 cup at a time, cooking and stirring until each addition has been absorbed, until two-thirds have been used. • Add half the cream, stir well, and then add the other half. • After 2–3 minutes add the Mozzarella and Parmesan. Stir in more stock, as required, until the rice is cooked. • Season with salt and pepper and serve.

Serves: 4 · Prep: 5 min. · Cooking: 20 min. · Level: 1

Rice with egg, cream, and Parmesan

RISOTTO AL GORGONZOLA
Risotto with Gorgonzola cheese

- 2 tablespoons butter
- ½ small onion, finely chopped
- 2 cups short-grain rice (preferably Italian arborio)
- ⅔ cup dry white wine
- 6 cups Beef stock (see recipe, page 105)
- 10 oz Gorgonzola cheese, chopped salt and freshly ground white pepper to taste
- ⅓ cup freshly grated Parmesan cheese

Wine: a dry white (Roero Arneis)

Melt the butter in a large, heavy-bottomed saucepan. • Add the onion and sauté until soft. • Add the rice and cook, stirring constantly, for 2 minutes. • Pour in the wine and when it has been absorbed, stir in ½ cup of the stock. Cook, stirring often, until the stock is absorbed. Continue adding the stock, ½ cup at a time, stirring often until each addition is absorbed, until the rice is tender, 15–18 minutes. • About 3–4 minutes before the rice is ready, add the Gorgonzola and mix well. Season with salt and pepper. • Add the Parmesan and serve.

Serves: 4 · Prep: 10 min. · Cooking: 25 min. · Level: 1

RISO CON FORMAGGI E SALSICCE
Baked rice with cheese and sausage

- 2 cups short-grain rice (preferably Italian arborio) salt to taste
- ¼ cup butter
- 5 leaves fresh sage, or 1 sprig rosemary
- 1 clove garlic (optional) pinch of nutmeg (optional)
- 2 oz each of Emmental, smoked Scamorza, and Fontina cheese, chopped
- 1 cup freshly grated Parmesan cheese
- 5 oz Italian pork sausages, skinned and crumbled
- 2 tablespoons bread crumbs

Wine: a light, dry red (Cabernet Franc del Trentino)

Cook the rice in 2 quarts of salted, boiling water for 13–15 minutes, or until tender. • Melt two-thirds of the butter in a small saucepan and add the sage, garlic, and nutmeg, if using. Sauté until golden brown. • When the rice is cooked, drain well and transfer to a bowl. • Stir in the Emmental, Scamorza, Fontina, half the Parmesan, and the sausage. • Remove the sage and garlic from the butter and pour it over the rice. Stir rapidly. • Transfer the mixture to a

buttered ovenproof dish. Smooth the surface, sprinkle with the bread crumbs and remaining Parmesan, and dot with the remaining butter. • Bake in a preheated oven at 400°F for 30 minutes, or until a golden crust has formed. Serve hot.

Serves: 4 · Prep: 15 min. · Cooking: 45 min. · Level: 1

RISOTTO AL VINO
Risotto with wine

- ¼ cup butter
- ½ small onion, finely chopped
- 1 stalk celery, finely chopped
- 1 small carrot, scraped and finely chopped
- 2 cups short-grain rice (preferably Italian arborio)
- 1¼ cups dry, full-bodied red wine
- 5 cups Beef stock (see recipe, page 105)
- ⅓ cup freshly grated Parmesan cheese salt and freshly ground black pepper to taste

Wine: a light, dry red (Gutturnio)

Melt 3 tablespoons of butter in a large, heavy-bottomed saucepan. Add the onion, celery, and carrot, and sauté over low heat for 5 minutes. • Increase the heat slightly, add the rice, and cook for 2 minutes,

stirring continuously. • Gradually stir in the wine. • When the wine has been absorbed, add ½ cup of the stock. Cook, stirring often, until the stock is absorbed. Continue adding the stock, ½ cup at a time, stirring often until each addition is absorbed, until the rice is tender, 15–18 minutes. • Season with salt and pepper. Add the remaining butter and the Parmesan just before serving.

Serves: 4 · Prep: 10 min. · Cooking: 25 min. · Level: 1

RISOTTO ALLO CHAMPAGNE
Risotto with champagne

- ¼ cup butter
- 1 small onion, finely chopped
- 2 cups short-grain rice (preferably Italian arborio)
- 2 cups dry spumante or champagne
- 4 cups Chicken stock (see recipe, page 104) salt and freshly ground black pepper to taste
- ⅓ cup freshly grated Parmesan cheese

Wine: a dry Italian champagne (Berlucchi)

Melt three-quarters of the butter in a large, heavy-bottomed saucepan. Add the onion and sauté over medium heat until soft. • Increase the heat slightly, add the rice, and cook for 2 minutes, stirring constantly. • Gradually stir in the champagne. • When it has been absorbed, add ½ cup of the stock. Cook, stirring often, until the stock is absorbed. Continue adding the stock, ½ cup at a time, stirring often until each addition is absorbed, until the rice is tender, 15–18 minutes. Season with salt and pepper. Add the remaining butter and the Parmesan just before serving.

Serves: 4 · Prep: 10 min. · Cooking: 25 min. · Level: 1

Risotto with wine

Orange risotto with Fontina cheese

RISOTTO ALLA PIEMONTESE
Piedmont-style risotto

☞ Serve this risotto topped with Piedmontese cheese fondue (see recipe, page 89).

- ¼ cup butter
- 2 tablespoons finely chopped onion
- 2 cups short-grain rice (preferably Italian arborio)
- ½ cup dry white wine
- 5 cups Beef stock (see recipe, page 105)
- ¾ cup freshly grated Parmesan cheese
  salt and freshly ground white pepper to taste
- 3 tablespoons cooking juices from roast meat or poultry
  shavings of fresh white truffles (optional)

Wine: a dry, fruity white (Langhe Riesling Renano)

Melt half the butter in a heavy-bottomed saucepan. Add the onion, cover and cook over low heat until soft. • Add the rice and cook, stirring constantly, for 3–4 minutes. • Pour in the wine, and when it has been absorbed, stir in ½ cup of the stock. Cook, stirring often, until the stock is absorbed. Continue adding the stock, ½ cup at a time, stirring often until each addition is absorbed, until the rice is tender, 15–18 minutes.• Stir in half the Parmesan and season with salt and pepper. • Turn off the heat, cover tightly and leave to stand for 2 minutes to finish cooking. • Dot with the remaining butter, sprinkle with the remaining cheese, and stir quickly but gently. Add the roast meat juices and stir once more. • Sprinkle with shavings of truffle, if using, and serve at once.

Serves: 4 · Prep: 5 min. · Cooking: 25 min. · Level: 1

RISOTTO CON ARANCIA E FONTINA
Orange risotto with Fontina cheese

- 2 large unwaxed oranges
- 1 small onion, finely chopped
- ½ cup butter
- 2 cups short-grain rice (preferably Italian arborio)
- ½ cup dry white wine
- 6 cups Chicken stock (see recipe, page 104)
- 4 oz Fontina cheese, diced
  salt and freshly ground white pepper to taste

Wine: a dry white (Ischia Bianco)

Peel the oranges, taking care to use only the outermost, orange layer. Chop the peel in tiny dice. Squeeze the juice and set aside. • In a heavy-bottomed pan, sauté the onion in three-quarters of the butter until soft. • Add the rice and cook for 2 minutes, stirring constantly. • Pour in the wine, and when it has been absorbed, stir in ½ cup of the stock. Cook, stirring often, until the stock is absorbed. Continue adding the stock, ½ cup at a time, stirring often until each addition is absorbed, until the rice is tender, 15–18 minutes. Stir in the Fontina cheese 5 minutes before the rice is cooked. • Just before removing from heat, season with salt and pepper and pour in the orange juice. Stir well and serve.

Serves: 4 · Prep: 10 min. · Cooking: 20 min. · Level: 1

RISOTTO CON ALLORO
Bay leaf risotto

- ¼ cup extra-virgin olive oil
- 1 small onion, finely chopped
- 2 cups short-grain rice (preferably Italian arborio)
- 6 bay leaves
- 2 cups dry white wine
  pinch of nutmeg
- 4 cups Beef stock (see recipe, page 105)
  salt to taste

Wine: a dry white (Orvieto)

Heat the oil in a large, heavy-bottomed saucepan and sauté the onion until soft. • Add the rice and bay leaves. Stir for 2 minutes and then begin adding the wine, a little at a time. • When the wine has been absorbed, add the nutmeg. Stir in ½ cup of the stock. Cook, stirring often, until the stock is absorbed. Continue adding the stock, ½ cup at a time, stirring often until each addition is absorbed, until the rice is tender, 15–18 minutes. Season with salt and pepper and serve hot.

Serves: 4 · Prep: 5 min. · Cooking: 20 min. · Level: 1

RISOTTO AL LIMONE
Lemon risotto

☞ The distinctive flavor of this risotto does not combine well with wine. Serve with ice-cold, sparkling mineral water with slices of lemon.

- 1 small onion, finely chopped
- ¼ cup extra-virgin olive oil
- 2 cups short-grain rice (preferably Italian arborio)
- ½ cup dry white wine
- 6 cups Beef stock (see recipe, page 105)
  grated zest and juice of 2 lemons
  salt and freshly ground white pepper to taste
- 2 tablespoons finely chopped parsley

In a large heavy-bottomed saucepan, sauté the onion in the oil over medium heat until soft. • Increase the heat slightly, add the rice, and cook for 2 minutes, stirring constantly. • Pour in the wine, and when it has been absorbed, stir in ¹/₂ cup of the stock. Cook, stirring often, until the stock is absorbed. Continue adding the stock, ¹/₂ cup at a time, stirring often until each addition is absorbed, until the rice is tender, 15–18 minutes. • After about 10 minutes, stir in the lemon zest. • Cook for about 5 more minutes, or until the rice is cooked. • Season with salt and pepper. Add the lemon juice and parsley, stir well, and serve.

Serves: 4 · Prep: 10 min. · Cooking: 25 min. · Level: 1

RISOTTO CON ASPARAGI
Asparagus risotto

1³/₄	lb asparagus
¹/₄	cup butter
1	small onion, finely chopped
2	cups short-grain rice (preferably Italian arborio)
¹/₂	cup dry white wine
6	cups Chicken stock (see recipe, page 104)
¹/₃	cup freshly grated Parmesan cheese
	salt and freshly ground white pepper to taste

Wine: a dry white (Sauvignon dell'Alto Adige)

Rinse the asparagus and trim the white part off the stalks. Cut the green tips in 2 or 3 pieces. • Melt three-quarters of the butter in a deep, heavy-bottomed saucepan. Add the onion and sauté for 1 minute. Add the asparagus and sauté for 5 minutes. • Add the rice and pour in the wine. Stir well. • When the wine has been absorbed, stir in ¹/₂ cup of the stock. Cook, stirring often, until the stock is absorbed. Continue adding the stock, ¹/₂ cup at a time, stirring often until each addition is absorbed, until the rice is tender, 15–18 minutes. • Add the remaining butter and the Parmesan. Mix well. • Season with salt and pepper and serve.

Serves: 4 · Prep: 15 min. · Cooking: 25 min. · Level: 2

RISOTTO CON SPINACI
Spinach risotto

¹/₄	cup butter
1	small onion, finely chopped
1	stalk celery, finely chopped
1	leek, (white part only), sliced
8	oz fresh spinach (or 6 oz frozen), cooked, squeezed dry, and finely chopped
2	cups short-grain rice (preferably Italian arborio)
6	cups Beef stock (see recipe, page 105)
	salt and freshly ground white pepper to taste

Tomato risotto

	pinch of nutmeg (optional)
¹/₃	cup freshly grated Parmesan cheese

Wine: a dry white (Riesling Renano)

Melt two-thirds of the butter in a large, heavy-bottomed saucepan. Add the onion, celery, and leek and sauté for 3–4 minutes over low heat. • Add the spinach, stir well and sauté for 2 minutes. • Add the rice and after 1 minute stir in ¹/₂ cup of the stock. Cook, stirring often, until the stock is absorbed. Continue adding the stock, ¹/₂ cup at a time, stirring often until each addition is absorbed, until the rice is tender, 15–18 minutes. • Season with salt, pepper, and nutmeg, if using. • Add the remaining butter and the Parmesan, mix well, and serve.

Serves: 4 · Prep: 20 min. · Cooking: 25 min. · Level: 1

RISOTTO AL POMODORO
Tomato risotto

1	medium onion
¹/₃	cup butter
2	tablespoons extra-virgin olive oil
2	cloves garlic, finely chopped
6	fresh basil leaves
2	cups short-grain rice (preferably Italian arborio)
1	lb firm ripe tomatoes, peeled and chopped
	pinch of sugar
	salt and freshly ground black pepper to taste
5	cups Beef stock (see recipe, page 105)
¹/₄	cup freshly grated Parmesan cheese

Wine: a dry white (Trebbiano)

Melt half the butter with the oil in a large, heavy-bottomed saucepan. Add the onion, garlic, and basil and sauté over medium heat for 5 minutes, or until the onion is soft. • Add the tomatoes, sugar, salt, and pepper and cook for 5 more minutes. • Add the rice and cook for 2 minutes, stirring constantly. Stir in ¹/₂ cup of the stock. Cook, stirring often, until the stock is absorbed. Continue adding the stock, ¹/₂ cup at a time, stirring often until each addition is absorbed, until the rice is tender, 15–18 minutes. • When the rice is cooked, stir in the remaining butter and the cheese, and serve.

Serves: 4 · Prep: 15 min. · Cooking: 25 min. · Level: 2

RISOTTO ALLA MILANESE
Milanese-style risotto

¼	cup butter
2	tablespoons finely chopped ox-bone marrow
1	small onion, finely chopped
2	cups short-grain rice (preferably Italian arborio)
½	cup white or red wine (optional)
6	cups Beef stock (see recipe, page 105)
½	teaspoon powdered saffron
½	cup freshly grated Parmesan cheese salt to taste

Wine: a dry red (Rosso della Riviera del Garda Bresciano)

Melt half the butter with the marrow in a large, heavy-bottomed saucepan. • Add the onion and sauté over medium heat until soft. • Add the rice and cook for 2–3 minutes, stirring constantly. • Pour in the wine, and when it has been absorbed, stir in ½ cup of the stock. Cook, stirring often, until the stock is absorbed. Continue adding the stock, ½ cup at a time, stirring often until each addition is absorbed, until the rice is tender, 15–18 minutes. • Add the saffron and half the Parmesan just before the rice is ready. Season with salt. • Add the remaining butter and mix well. • Serve with the remaining Parmesan passed separately.

Serves: 4 · Prep: 10 min. · Cooking: 25 min. · Level: 1

RISOTTO 'AL SALTO'
Milanese-style risotto, the day after

☞ Make a double quantity of Milanese-style risotto and serve this dish the day after.

¼	cup butter
1	quantity Milanese-style risotto (see recipe, above)
¼	cup freshly grated Parmesan cheese

Wine: a dry red (Cabernet Sauvignon dei Colli Bolognesi)

Melt a quarter of the butter in each of two 10-inch skillets. • Divide the rice into two portions and flatten each one out to obtain two round cakes about 1 inch thick. • Cook them in the skillets over high heat for about 5 minutes, or until a crisp crust forms. • Turn them with the help of a plate and slip them back into the skillets in which you have melted the remaining butter. • When both sides are crisp and deep gold, sprinkle with the Parmesan. Cut in half and serve.

Serves: 4 · Prep: 5 min. · Cooking: 15 min. · Level: 1

RISOTTO AI CARCIOFI
Artichoke risotto

6	artichokes
	juice of 1 lemon
3	tablespoons butter
1	small onion, finely chopped
2	cups short-grain rice (preferably Italian arborio)
6	cups Vegetable stock (see recipe, page 104)
	salt and freshly ground black pepper to taste
2	tablespoons finely chopped parsley
1/2	cup freshly grated Pecorino cheese

Wine: a dry white (Vernaccia di San Gimignano)

Trim the artichokes stems, cut off the tops, and discard the tough outer leaves. Cut in half and remove the fuzzy chokes. Soak in a bowl of cold water with the lemon juice for 10 minutes. • Melt the butter in a large, heavy-bottomed saucepan. Add the onion and sauté until soft. • Drain the artichokes, slice thinly, and add to the onion. Sauté for 5 more minutes. • Add the rice and cook for 2 minutes. Increase the heat slightly. Stir in 1/2 cup of the stock. Cook, stirring often, until the stock is absorbed. Continue adding the stock, 1/2 cup at a time, stirring often until each addition is absorbed, until the rice is tender, 15–18 minutes. Season with salt and pepper. • Add the parsley and Pecorino, stir well, and serve.

Serves: 4 · Prep: 20 min. · Cooking: 30 min. · Level: 1

RISO CON CARCIOFI E PISELLI
Rice with artichokes and peas

6	baby artichokes (or 12 frozen artichoke hearts, thawed)
1	lemon
1	medium onion, thinly sliced
1/4	cup extra-virgin olive oil
1–2	cloves garlic, finely chopped
4	anchovy fillets
1	cup peas, fresh or frozen
	salt and freshly ground black pepper to taste
	about 1/2 cup water
2	cups short-grain rice (preferably Italian arborio)
1/2	cup freshly grated Pecorino cheese

Wine: a light, dry white (Verdicchio dei Castelli di Jesi)

If using fresh artichokes, clean them as described in the preceding recipe. Rub all the cut surfaces with lemon juice to prevent discoloration. Cut into quarters lengthwise. • If using thawed artichoke hearts, cut them in halves or quarters. • Sauté the onion in the oil. Add the garlic,

Milanese-style risotto, the day after

cook for 1 minute and then add the anchovies, crushing them with a fork so that they dissolve in the oil. • Add the artichokes and peas. Season with salt and pepper and moisten with half the water. Cook until the water has been absorbed. • Add the rice and stir for 1 minute, then add the remaining water. Stir in 1/2 cup of the stock. Cook, stirring often, until the stock is absorbed. Continue adding the stock, 1/2 cup at a time, stirring often until each addition is absorbed, until the rice is tender, 15–18 minutes. • Sprinkle with the cheese and serve.

Serves: 4 · Prep: 10 min. · Cooking: 25 min. · Level: 1

RISOTTO CON FINOCCHI
Fennel risotto

4	medium fennel bulbs, cleaned
1/4	cup butter
3	tablespoons extra-virgin olive oil
1	small onion, finely chopped
1	small stalk celery, finely chopped
2	cups short-grain rice (preferably Italian arborio)
6	cups Beef stock (see recipe page 105)
	salt and freshly ground white pepper to taste
1/2	cup freshly grated Parmesan cheese

Wine: a light, dry white (Soave Classico)

Cut the fennel bulbs vertically into slices about 1/8 inch thick. • Melt half the butter with the oil in a large, heavy-bottomed saucepan and sauté the onion, celery, and fennel for 5–7 minutes. • Add the rice and cook for 2 minutes, stirring constantly. Increase the heat slightly. Stir in 1/2 cup of the stock. Cook, stirring often, until the stock is absorbed. Continue adding the stock, 1/2 cup at a time, stirring often until each addition is absorbed, until the rice is tender, 15–18 minutes. • Add the remaining butter and the Parmesan. Season with salt and pepper, mix well, and serve.

Serves: 4 · Prep: 15 min. · Cooking: 25 min. · Level: 1

RISO AL PESTO E PISELLI
Rice with peas and Genoese basil sauce

- 1 quantity Genoese basil sauce (see recipe, page 21)
  salt and freshly ground black pepper to taste
- 2 cups short-grain rice
- 14 oz fresh or frozen peas
- 1/4 cup butter
- 4 oz pancetta, diced
- 1 large onion, finely chopped
- 1 tablespoon each finely chopped parsley and thyme
- 1/3 cup freshly grated Parmesan cheese

Wine: a dry white (Sylvaner dell'Alto Adige)

Prepare the Genoese basil sauce. • Bring a large pot of salted water to the boil and add the rice and peas. Cook for 13–15 minutes, or until the rice is tender. • Heat half the butter in a large skillet and sauté the pancetta and onion over medium heat for 5 minutes, or until the onion is soft. • Lower heat and add the parsley and thyme. Cook for 2–3 more minutes. • Drain the rice and peas and add to the skillet together with 2 tablespoons of the cooking water. Stir until well mixed. • Stir in the remaining butter, the basil sauce, Parmesan, and pepper. Serve hot.

Serves: 4 · Prep: 15 min. · Cooking: 25 min. · Level: 1

RISOTTO AI FUNGHI
Mushroom risotto

- 1 oz dried porcini mushrooms
- 1 cup warm water
- 1/4 cup extra-virgin olive oil
- 1 small onion, finely chopped
- 1/2 cup dry white wine
- 2 cups short-grain rice (preferably Italian arborio)
- 6 cups Vegetable stock (see recipe, page 104)
- 2 tablespoons finely chopped parsley
  salt and freshly ground black pepper to taste

Wine: a dry rosé (San Secero Rosato)

Soak the mushrooms in the water for 20 minutes. Drain, reserving the water, and chop coarsely. • Heat the oil in a large, heavy-bottomed saucepan over medium heat. Add the onion and sauté until soft. • Add the mushrooms and sauté for 2–3 minutes. • Add the rice and stir for 2 minutes, stirring constantly. • Pour in the wine, and when it has been absorbed, stir in the mushroom water. • Stir in 1/2 cup of the stock. Cook, stirring often, until the stock is absorbed. Continue adding the stock, 1/2 cup at a time, stirring often until each addition is absorbed, until the rice is tender, 15–18 minutes. • Season with salt and pepper. Add the parsley, mix well, and serve.

Serves: 4 · Prep: 30 min. · Cooking: 25 min. · Level: 1

RISOTTO CON MELANZANE
Eggplant risotto

- 2 large eggplants
- 2 tablespoons coarse sea salt
- 3 cloves garlic, finely chopped
- 2 tablespoons finely chopped parsley
- 1/3 cup extra-virgin olive oil
- 2 cups short-grain rice
- 5 cups Beef stock (see recipe, page 105)
  salt and freshly ground black pepper to taste

Rinse the eggplants and cut them into cubes. Sprinkle with the coarse salt and place on a slanted cutting board for 1 hour so the bitter liquid they produce can run off. • Sauté the garlic and parsley in the oil in a heavy-bottomed pan. • Add the eggplant and cook over medium heat until the eggplants are soft. • Add the rice and cook for 2 minutes, stirring constantly • Stir in 1/2 cup of the stock. Cook, stirring often, until the stock is absorbed. Continue adding the stock, 1/2 cup at a time, stirring often until each addition is absorbed, until the rice is tender, 15–18 minutes. • Season with salt and pepper and serve hot.

Serves: 4 · Prep: 10 min. + 1 hr for the eggplants · Cooking: 25 min. · Level 1

RISOTTO CON LENTICCHIE
Creamy lentil risotto

- 3 tablespoons butter
- 3 tablespoons extra-virgin olive oil
- 1 onion, finely chopped
- 1 clove garlic, finely chopped
- 2 cups short-grain rice (preferably Italian arborio)
- 6 cups Beef stock (see recipe, page 105)
- 1 1/2 cups cooked lentils, drained
- 1/3 cup freshly grated Parmesan cheese
  salt and freshly ground white or black pepper to taste

Wine: a dry red (Rosso Conero)

Heat the butter and oil in a large, heavy-bottomed saucepan. Add the onion and garlic and sauté for 5 minutes over low heat. • Increase the heat slightly and pour in the rice. Cook for 2 minutes, stirring constantly. • Stir in 1/2 cup of the stock. Cook, stirring often, until the stock is absorbed. Continue adding the stock, 1/2 cup at a time, stirring often until each addition is absorbed, until the rice is tender, 15–18 minutes. After about 10 minutes, add the lentils and continue cooking. • Add the Parmesan and season with salt and pepper. • Mix until creamy, and serve.

Serves: 4 · Prep: 10 min. · Cooking: 25 min. · Level: 1

RISO ALLA SICILIANA
Sicilian-style rice

- 2 cups short-grain rice
- 1 small onion, thinly sliced
- 5 tablespoons extra-virgin olive oil
- 2 anchovy fillets
- 1/2 cup dry white wine
- 1 tablespoon white wine vinegar
- 5 peeled and chopped tomatoes
  juice of 2 lemons
- 1/4 teaspoon crushed red pepper flakes
- 1 teaspoon finely chopped fresh marjoram

6 fresh basil leaves
8 large, fleshy black olives, pitted and cut into quarters

Wine: a young, dry rosé (Rosato di Gioa del Colle)

Bring 2 quarts of salted water to a boil in a large saucepan. Add the rice and cook for 13–15 minutes, or until just tender. • Meanwhile, sauté the onion in the oil, then add the anchovies, crushing them with a fork until they dissolve. • Add the wine and vinegar and cook, uncovered, until the liquid has evaporated. • Add the tomatoes, lemon juice, red pepper flakes, marjoram, basil, and olives, and cook over medium heat for 7–8 minutes, stirring frequently. • Drain the rice and transfer to a heated serving dish. Pour the sauce over the top and serve.

Serves: 4 · Prep: 15 min. · Cooking: 20 min. · Level: 1

RISOTTO DELLE CINQUE TERRE
Risotto Cinque Terre-style

☞ This recipe comes from the beautiful coastal villages in southern Liguria known as the Cinque Terre (Five Towns).

1/3 cup butter
6 leaves basil, finely chopped
2 cloves garlic, finely chopped
12 oz ripe tomatoes, peeled and chopped
 salt and freshly ground black pepper to taste
1 oz pine nuts
1/4 cup extra-virgin olive oil
2 cups short-grain rice (preferably Italian arborio)
1 cup dry white wine
4 cups of Beef stock (see recipe, page 105)
1/2 cup freshly grated Pecorino cheese

Wine: a dry white (Cinque Terre)

Heat half the butter in a heavy-bottomed pan and sauté the basil and garlic for 3–4 minutes. Add the tomatoes and season with salt and pepper. Cook for 15 minutes over low heat. • Brown the pine nuts in the oil in a large skillet over medium-high heat. Stir in the rice and cook for 2 minutes in the oil so that it absorbs the flavor of the nuts. Add the wine, and stir until it has evaporated. • Stir in 1/2 cup of the stock. Cook, stirring often, until the stock is absorbed. Continue adding the

stock, 1/2 cup at a time, stirring often until each addition is absorbed, until the rice is tender, 15–18 minutes. Add the tomato sauce about half way through the cooking time. • Stir in the remaining butter and the Pecorino just before removing from heat. Serve hot.

Serves: 4 · Prep: 15 min. · Cooking 35 min. · Level: 1

RISO ARROSTO
Roasted rice

1 onion, finely chopped
5 oz Italian pork sausages, skinned and crumbled
7 oz mushrooms (cultivated or wild), sliced
2 artichokes, cleaned and thinly sliced
1/4 cup fresh or frozen peas
1/4 cup extra-virgin olive oil
 salt and freshly ground black pepper, to taste
1 cup Beef stock (see recipe, page 105)
2 cups short-grain rice (preferably Italian arborio)
1/3 cup freshly grated Pecorino cheese

Wine: a dry white (Vermentino)

Sauté the onion, sausage, mushrooms, artichokes, and peas in a large, heavy-bottomed pan in 3 tablespoons of the oil. Season with salt and pepper. • Add the stock, cover, and cook for about 10 minutes. • In the meantime, cook the rice in a large pot of salted, boiling for 7–8 minutes. • Drain partially (leave some moisture). Transfer to the saucepan with the sauce and stir. Add the cheese and mix well. • Transfer to an ovenproof dish greased with

the remaining oil. Bake in a preheated oven at 400°F for about 20 minutes. The rice will have a light golden crust when ready.

Serves: 4 · Prep: 35 min. ·Cooking: 50 min. · Level: 1

PANISSA
Risotto with beans

☞ This hearty winter dish comes from Piedmont, in the north. If fresh beans are unavailable, use dry beans. Soak them in cold water for 10–12 hours, then cook slowly for about 1 1/2 hours.

8 oz fresh cranberry or red kidney beans, shelled
5 cups Vegetable stock (see recipe, page 104)
1/3 cup finely chopped salt pork
1/3 cup finely chopped lean pancetta
1 small onion, finely chopped
2 cups short-grain rice (preferably Italian arborio)
1 cup full-bodied red wine
 salt and freshly ground white or black pepper to taste

Wine: a dry red (Barbera)

Cook the beans in the stock in a covered pot over low heat for 50 minutes. • Place the salt pork and pancetta in a heavy-bottomed saucepan over low heat. When the fat has melted a little, add the onion and sauté for 5 minutes. • Pour in the rice and stir for 2 minutes. • Add the wine, 1/2 cup at a time. When it has been absorbed, begin adding, one ladle at a time, the hot beans and their stock. • Stir constantly until each addition is absorbed, until the rice is cooked, about 15–18 minutes. • Season with salt and pepper and serve hot.

Serves: 4 · Prep: 30 min. · Cooking: 1 1/4 hrs · Level: 1

Risotto Cinque Terre-style

RISOTTO CON MELANZANE AL FORNO
Baked eggplant risotto

- 2 large eggplants
- 2 tablespoons coarse sea salt
- 1 medium onion, thinly sliced
- ½ cup extra-virgin olive oil
- 2 tablespoons finely chopped parsley
- 6 fresh basil leaves, torn
- 1 lb peeled and chopped fresh or canned tomatoes
  salt and freshly ground black pepper to taste
- 2 tablespoons finely chopped onion
- 2 cups short-grain rice (preferably Italian arborio)
- 3 cups Beef stock (see recipe, page 105)
- 1 cup freshly grated Caciocavallo cheese
  a little all-purpose white flour
- 1 cup oil, for frying
- 10 fresh basil leaves

Wine: a young, dry rosé (Etna Rosato)

Slice the eggplants thinly lengthwise and place them in a colander, sprinkling each layer with coarse salt. Leave to stand for 1 hour, then rinse well and dry on paper towels. • In a heavy-bottomed saucepan, sauté the sliced onion in half the oil for 2–3 minutes, then add the parsley, basil, tomatoes, salt, and pepper. • Simmer over low heat for 20–25 minutes, then set aside. • For the risotto, sauté the second measure of onion in the remaining oil until soft. Add the rice and stir for 2 minutes. • Stir in ½ cup of the stock. Cook, stirring often, until the stock is absorbed. Continue adding the stock, ½ cup at a time, stirring often until each addition is absorbed, until the rice is tender, 15–18 minutes. • Meanwhile, coat the eggplants lightly with flour and fry in hot oil until golden brown on both sides. Remove from the pan and drain on paper towels. • Line the bottom of an oiled casserole with one-third of the eggplant and cover with half the risotto, half the remaining cheese, and half the sauce. Sprinkle half the basil over the sauce and cover with half the remaining eggplant, followed by the remaining rice, sauce, and basil. Top with eggplant and cheese. • Bake in a preheated oven at 425°F for 10 minutes. Serve hot.

Serves: 4–6 · Prep: 20 min. + 1 hr for the eggplants · Cooking: 40 min. · Level: 2

RISOTTO CON PANCETTA E PROSCIUTTO
Risotto with pancetta and prosciutto

- ½ cup butter
- 1 onion, finely chopped
- 2 oz lean pancetta, diced
- 2 cups short-grain rice (preferably Italian arborio)
- ½ cup dry white wine
- 6 cups Beef stock (see recipe, page 105)
  salt and freshly ground black pepper to taste
- 4 oz prosciutto, diced
- ½ cup light cream
- ⅓ cup freshly grated Parmesan cheese

Wine: a light, dry red (Lagrein Rosato)

Melt the butter in a large, heavy-bottomed saucepan. Add the onion and pancetta and sauté over low heat until the onion is soft. • Add the rice and cook for 2 minutes, stirring continuously. • Increase the heat slightly, pour in the wine, and cook until it has been absorbed. Stir in ½ cup of the stock. Cook, stirring often, until the stock is absorbed. Continue adding the stock, ½ cup at a time, stirring often until each addition is absorbed, until the rice is tender, 15–18 minutes. • When the rice is almost cooked, stir in the salt, pepper, prosciutto, cream, and cheese, mixing carefully to combine the ingredients well. • Serve hot.

Serves: 4 · Prep: 10 min. · Cooking: 25–30 min. · Level: 1

RISOTTO ALLA ZUCCA
Pumpkin risotto

- 2 lb orange-fleshed squash or pumpkin
- ½ cup butter
- ¼ cup extra-virgin olive oil
- 2 cups short-grain rice (preferably Italian arborio)
- ½ cup dry white wine
  salt and freshly ground black pepper to taste
- 4 cups Beef stock (see recipe, page 105)
- 1 cup freshly grated Parmesan cheese

Wine: a dry white (Pinot Grigio)

Peel the pumpkin and remove the seeds and fibrous matter. Slice thinly. • Heat half the butter with the oil in a heavy-bottomed saucepan. Add the pumpkin, then cover tightly and cook slowly until almost tender. • Add the rice, stirring well to flavor the grains. Pour in the wine and stir until the wine has evaporated. Season with salt and pepper. • Stir in ½ cup of the stock. Cook, stirring often, until the stock is absorbed. Continue adding the stock, ½ cup at a time, stirring often until each addition is absorbed, until the rice is tender, 15–18 minutes. • Remove from heat, stir in the remaining butter and the Parmesan, and serve.

Serves: 6 · Prep: 10 min. · Cooking: 40 min. · Level: 1

RISO CON I FEGATINI
Rice with chicken liver sauce

- 2 cups short-grain rice
- 1 onion, finely chopped
- ¼ cup butter
- 8 chicken livers, chopped
- 1 oz pine nuts
  salt and freshly ground black pepper to taste
- ⅓ cup dry Marsala wine
- ⅓ cup dry white wine

Wine: a light, dry red (Merlot dei Colli Berici)

Pour the rice into 2 quarts of salted, boiling water, stir well, and cook for 13–15 minutes. • Sauté the onion in the butter in a heavy-bottomed pan until soft. • Turn the heat up, and add the chicken livers, pine nuts, salt, and pepper. Stir for 1–2 minutes to brown, then add half the Marsala and wine. Stir again before adding the rest. • Cook for 6–7 minutes, stirring occasionally. • When the rice is cooked, drain thoroughly and transfer to a serving dish. • Pour the chicken liver sauce over the top and serve.

Serves: 4 · Prep: 10 min. · Cooking: 15 min. · Level: 1

RISO INTEGRALE AL POMODORO
Brown rice with tomato sauce

☞ Serve this dish hot during the winter months. In summer, cook the rice and prepare the sauce ahead of time. Allow both to cool, then toss and serve at room temperature.

- 2 cups brown rice
- 1 quantity Simple tomato sauce (see recipe, page 18)

Wine: a dry red (Merlot del Piave)

Cook the rice in 2 quarts of salted, boiling water, stirring once or twice. It will be cooked in about 45 minutes. • Prepare the tomato sauce. • When the rice is done, drain thoroughly, and transfer to a large bowl. • Add the tomato sauce, toss carefully, and serve.

Serves: 4 · Prep: 20 min. · Cooking: 45 min. · Level: 1

◄ Baked eggplant risotto

and then. • Place the rice in a skillet with half the remaining butter and stir for 2 minutes. • Add stock, ½ cup at a time, stirring often until each addition is absorbed. Add the eggs and Parmesan and cook for 2 more minutes. • Grease a bombe mold or deep ovenproof dish with the remaining butter. Sprinkle with half the bread crumbs. • Use two-thirds of the rice mixture to line the mold, pressing firmly to make sure it stays in place. Arrange the pieces of chicken in the middle of the mold. Cover with the remaining rice and sprinkle with the remaining bread crumbs. • Bake in a preheated oven at 350°F for 30 minutes. • Remove from the oven and leave to stand for 10 minutes. Turn out carefully onto a heated plate and serve.

Serves: 4 · Prep: 10 min. · Cooking: 50 min. · Level: 2

Risotto with pears

RISOTTO CON LE QUAGLIE
Risotto with quail

4	quail, ready to be cooked
	salt and freshly ground white pepper to taste
4	leaves sage
4	slices pancetta or salt pork
3	tablespoons butter
2	tablespoons extra-virgin olive oil
3	tablespoons brandy
2	cups short-grain rice (preferably Italian arborio)
6	cups Beef stock (see recipe, page 105)
⅓	cup freshly grated Parmesan cheese

Wine: a dry white (Cortese di Gavi)

Season the quail inside and out with salt and pepper. Put the sage leaves inside. • Wrap the quail breasts with slices of pancetta or salt pork secured with two or three twists of kitchen string. • In a large, heavy-bottomed saucepan melt half the butter together with the oil. Add the quail and brown well on all sides over medium heat. This will take about 6–7 minutes. • Sprinkle the birds with the brandy and when this has evaporated, lower the heat, partially cover and cook, adding a spoonful of stock occasionally. The birds will be cooked in about 15 minutes. • Remove the quail and set aside in a warm oven. • Add the rice to the juices left in the saucepan and stir well for 2 minutes. • Stir in ½ cup of the stock. Cook, stirring often, until the stock is absorbed.

Continue adding the stock, ½ cup at a time, stirring often until each addition is absorbed, until the rice is tender, 15–18 minutes. • Just before serving, stir in the remaining butter and the cheese. • Serve the rice with the quail arranged on top. Remove the thread but leave the salt pork or pancetta in place.

Serves: 4 · Prep: 15 min. · Cooking: 40 min. · Level: 2

BOMBA DI RISO AL POLLO
Baked risotto with chicken

1	onion, finely chopped
½	cup butter
2	fresh sage leaves
8	chicken pieces
½	cup dry white wine
	salt and freshly ground black pepper to taste
1	tablespoon tomato paste dissolved in ½ cup water
2½	cups short-grain rice (preferably Italian arborio)
4	cups Chicken stock (see recipe, page 104)
2	eggs
½	cup freshly grated Parmesan cheese
½	cup fine bread crumbs

Wine: a dry white (Trebbiano di Capriano del Colle)

Sauté the onion in half the butter in a large skillet until soft. • Add the sage leaves and chicken and sauté until nicely browned. • Pour in the wine and cook, uncovered, until the wine has reduced. Season with salt and pepper. • Stir in the tomato paste and water. Cover and simmer over a low heat for about 20 minutes, stirring now

RISOTTO CON LE PERE
Risotto with pears

4	medium pears
1	onion, finely chopped
2	tablespoons butter
2	cups short-grain rice (preferably Italian arborio)
1	cup dry white wine
6	cups Vegetable stock (see recipe, page 104)
	salt and freshly ground black pepper to taste
3	oz Fontina cheese, diced
¼	cup Williams pear liqueur

Wine: a dry, lightly sparkling red (Lambrusco Reggiano)

Peel, core, and cube the pears. • Sauté the onion in the butter in a heavy-bottomed pan until soft. • Stir in the rice and cook for 2 minutes, then add the wine. • When the wine has all been absorbed, add a ladleful of boiling stock and the pears. • Continue adding stock, ½ cup at a time, stirring often until each addition is absorbed, until the rice is tender, 15–18 minutes. Season with salt and pepper. • Add the Fontina and liqueur shortly before serving. • Stir well and serve.

Serves: 4 · Prep: 10 · Cooking: 20 min. · Level: 1

RISOTTO CON LE ZUCCHINE
Zucchini risotto

- 2 tablespoons extra-virgin olive oil
- 2 oz pancetta, diced
- 2 cloves garlic, finely chopped
- 1 lb zucchini, diced
- 2 cups short-grain rice (preferably Italian arborio)
- 1 cup dry white wine
- 6 cups Vegetable stock (see recipe, page 104)
- 1/2 cup freshly grated Parmesan cheese
- 2 tablespoons finely chopped parsley

Wine: a dry white (Orvieto)

Heat the oil in a large skillet and sauté the pancetta for 5 minutes. Add the garlic and zucchini and sauté for 7–8 minutes, or until the zucchini are pale golden brown. • Stir in the rice and cook for 2 minutes, then add the wine. • When the wine has been absorbed, stir in 1/2 cup of the stock. Cook, stirring often, until the stock is absorbed. Continue adding the stock, 1/2 cup at a time, stirring often until each addition is absorbed, until the rice is tender, 15–18 minutes. • Season with salt and pepper. • Add the Parmesan and parsley just before removing from heat. Stir well and serve.

Serves: 4 · Prep: 10 min. · Cooking: 25 min. · Level: 1

RISOTTO CON LE UVETTE
Raisin risotto

- 1 cup raisins
- 1/2 cup grappa
- 2 tablespoons extra-virgin olive oil
- 2 cloves garlic, finely chopped
- 1 onion, finely chopped
- 2 cups short-grain rice (preferably Italian arborio)
- 6 cups Beef stock (see recipe, page 105)
- 1/2 cup freshly grated Parmesan cheese

Wine: an aromatic white (Pinot Bianco di Breganze)

Place the raisins in a small bowl and cover with the grappa. Leave to soak for about 15 minutes. • Heat the oil in a large skillet and sauté the garlic and onion until soft. • Stir in the rice and cook for 2 minutes. Stir in 1/2 cup of the stock. Cook, stirring often, until the stock is absorbed. Continue adding the stock, 1/2 cup at a time, stirring often until each addition is absorbed, until the rice is tender, 15–18 minutes. • Drain the raisins and add to the risotto about 3 minutes before the rice is cooked. Season with salt and pepper. • Stir well, sprinkle with the Parmesan, and serve.

Serves: 4 · Prep: 20 min. · Cooking: 20 min. · Level: 1

RISOTTO AI PEPERONI
Bell pepper risotto

- 14 oz bell peppers, mixed colors
- 1 medium onion, finely chopped
- 1 tablespoon extra-virgin olive oil
- 1/4 cup butter
- 12 oz peeled and chopped fresh tomatoes
- 1 teaspoon dried oregano
  salt and freshly ground black pepper to taste
- 2 cups short-grain rice (preferably Italian arborio)
- 4 cups Beef stock (see recipe, page 105)
- 1/4 cup freshly grated Parmesan cheese

Wine: a dry white (Pinot Bianco di Latisana)

Clean the bell peppers, removing the seeds and core. Slice each one in 4–6 pieces and place under the broiler until the skins are blackened. Remove the skins and rinse the bell peppers. Cut in thin strips. • In a heavy-bottomed saucepan, sauté half the onion in the oil and half the butter until soft. • Add the tomatoes, bell peppers, oregano, salt, and pepper, and cook over low heat until the sauce reduces. • Sauté the remaining onion in a large skillet with half the remaining butter. Add the rice and stir in 1/2 cup of the stock. Cook, stirring often, until the stock is absorbed. Continue adding the stock, 1/2 cup at a time, stirring often until each addition is absorbed, until the rice is tender, 15–18 minutes. • Add the bell pepper sauce to the rice about half way through the cooking time. Stir in the Parmesan just before serving.

Serves: 4 · Prep: 30 min. · Cooking: 1 hr · Level: 1

RISOTTO AL POMODORO E FUNGHI
Tomato and mushroom risotto

- 2/3 oz dried porcini mushrooms
- 1 small onion, finely chopped
- 1/3 cup extra-virgin olive oil
- 12 oz peeled and chopped canned tomatoes
- 2 cups short-grain rice (preferably Italian arborio)
- 5 cups boiling water
  salt and freshly ground black pepper to taste
- 1/3 cup freshly grated Parmesan cheese

Wine: a dry white (Pigato di Albenga)

Soak the mushrooms in a bowl of warm water for 20 minutes. Drain and chop coarsely. • In a heavy-bottomed pan, sauté the onion in the oil until soft. Add the mushrooms and, after 2 minutes, the tomatoes. • Cook for 10 minutes, covered, then add the rice and stir well. • When all the liquid has been absorbed, begin adding boiling water, 1/2 cup at a time, stirring often until each addition is absorbed, until the rice is tender, about 15–18 minutes. • Season with salt and pepper and serve, passing the Parmesan separately.

Serves: 4 · Prep: 30 min. · Cooking: 35 min. · Level: 1

Bell pepper risotto

Strawberry risotto

RISOTTO ALLE FRAGOLE
Strawberry risotto

1 small onion, cut in 4 or 6 pieces
2 tablespoons extra-virgin olive oil
2 cups short-grain rice (preferably Italian arborio)
¼ cup dry white wine
4 cups Vegetable stock (see recipe, page 104)
12 oz strawberries
2 tablespoons butter
1 tablespoon freshly grated Parmesan cheese
2 tablespoons light cream.

Wine: a dry white (Verduzzo Friulano di Aquileia)

Sauté the onion in the oil in a large skillet over medium heat until soft. Discard the onion. • Add the rice and cook for 2 minutes, stirring constantly. Pour in the wine and cook until it evaporates. Stir in ½ cup of the stock. Cook, stirring often, until the stock is absorbed. Continue adding the stock, ½ cup at a time, stirring often until each addition is absorbed, until the rice is tender, 15–18 minutes. • Meanwhile, wash, clean, and slice the strawberries, reserving 6 whole ones. Add the sliced strawberries to the rice 5 minutes before the end of cooking time. • When the rice is cooked, remove from heat and stir in the butter, Parmesan, and cream. Garnish with the whole strawberries and serve.

Serves: 4 · Prep: 10 min. · Cooking: 20 min. · Level: 2

TIMBALLO DEL PAPA
Pope's pie

¼ cup butter
1 medium onion, finely chopped
10 oz chicken livers, cleaned and chopped
¼ cup dry white wine
2 cups chopped canned tomatoes
    salt and freshly ground black pepper to taste
2 cups short-grain rice (preferably Italian arborio)
4 cups Beef stock (see recipe, page 105)
⅓ cup freshly grated Parmesan cheese

Wine: a dry red (Cerveteri Rosso)

Heat two-thirds of the butter in a large skillet and sauté the onion until soft. • Add the chicken livers and sauté until brown. • Pour in the wine and cook until it evaporates. Add the tomatoes and cook for 15 minutes, or until the sauce reduces. Season with salt and pepper. • Add the rice. Stir in ½ cup of the stock. Cook, stirring often, until the stock is absorbed. Continue adding the stock, ½ cup at a time, stirring often until each addition is absorbed, until the rice is tender, 15–18 minutes. • Remove the skillet from heat and stir in the Parmesan. • Grease the sides of a ring mold with the remaining butter. Transfer the risotto to the mold and press down well. • Bake in a preheated oven at 400°F for 10 minutes. • Turn the baked mold out onto a heated platter and serve.

Serves: 4 · Prep: 15 min. · Cooking: 40 min. · Level: 2

SARTÙ
Neapolitan rice pie

☞ This very elaborate baked rice dish comes from Naples.

2 oz dried porcini mushrooms
1 small onion, finely chopped
3 tablespoons extra-virgin olive oil
2 tablespoons tomato paste
6 cups Beef stock (see recipe, page 105)
8 oz fresh or frozen peas
    salt and freshly ground black pepper to taste
1 Italian pork sausage
12 oz ground beef
3 eggs
½ cup fine dry bread crumbs
½ cup freshly grated Parmesan cheese
½ cup all-purpose flour
2½ cups short-grain rice
7 oz lard
8 oz Mozzarella cheese, sliced
7 oz chicken livers, cleaned and chopped

Wine: a light, dry red (Solopaca Rosso)

Soak the mushrooms in warm water for 20 minutes, then squeeze out excess water, and chop finely. • In a large earthenware pan, sauté the onion in the oil until soft. Add the tomato paste diluted in 1 cup of the stock, together with the mushrooms and peas. Season with salt and pepper. Cook for 5 minutes, then add the sausage. Cook for 20 minutes, then slice the sausage and remove the sauce from heat. • Combine the beef in a mixing bowl with salt, pepper, 1 egg, 2 tablespoons of bread crumbs, and 1 tablespoon of Parmesan cheese. Mix well. Shape into small meatballs and roll in the flour. • Heat the frying oil in a skillet and fry the meatballs in small batches until golden brown. Drain on paper towels. • Heat half the mushroom sauce in a heavy-bottomed pan. When hot, add the rice. Stir in ½ cup of the stock. Cook, stirring often, until the stock is absorbed. Continue adding the stock, ½ cup at a time, stirring often until each addition is absorbed, until the rice is tender, 15–18 minutes. • When the rice is cooked, stir in 2 oz lard, ¼ cup Parmesan, and the remaining eggs. Mix well and set aside to cool. • Add 2 oz of lard and the meatballs to the other half of the sauce. Simmer in a saucepan over low heat. • Heat the remaining lard in a small skillet and sauté the chicken livers, adding a little stock if they dry out. Remove from heat and season with salt. • Grease a 3-quart mold with butter and sprinkle with 3 tablespoons of bread crumbs. • Place almost all the rice in the mold and use a spoon to press it against the sides. Fill the center with layers of meatballs, sauce, chicken livers, Mozzarella, sausage, and the remaining Parmesan. When all the ingredients are in the mold, cover with the remaining rice. Sprinkle with the remaining bread crumbs. • Bake the mold in a preheated oven at 325°F for 30 minutes. Let the pie rest in the mold for 5 minutes before turning out onto a serving dish. Serve hot.

Serves 8 · Prep: 30 min. · Cooking: 1½ hrs · Level: 3

RISOTTO ALLE ROSE ROSSE
Risotto with red roses

☞ The Italian poet Gabriele D'Annunzio served this romantic dish when he entertained the actress Eleonora Duse in his villa at Settignano in the hills above Florence.

4 red roses, freshly opened buds
½ cup butter
2 cups short-grain rice (preferably Italian arborio)
    pinch of nutmeg
    freshly ground black pepper to taste
½ cup dry wine (preferably rosé, otherwise white)
2 cups Beef stock (see recipe, page 105)
⅓ cup light cream
4 oz Emmental cheese
    few drops rose water

Check that the roses are perfectly clean, with no insects in among the petals. Pull off the petals, reserving 8 of the best to use as a garnish. (Keep these in a bowl of cold water). Divide the remaining petals, reserving the more brightly colored ones. • Melt half the butter in a large skillet and

Risotto with red roses

add the less highly-colored petals. When they have wilted, pour in the rice and cook for 2 minutes, stirring constantly. • Season with the nutmeg and pepper. Pour in the wine and cook until it evaporates. Stir in ½ cup of the stock. Cook, stirring often, until the stock is absorbed. Continue adding the stock, ½ cup at a time, stirring often until each addition is absorbed, until the rice is tender, 15–18 minutes. • When the rice is about half cooked, add the reserved brightly colored rose petals. When the rice is tender, fold in the cream and remaining butter. Add the cheese and rose water. Transfer to a serving dish and garnish with the 8 reserved petals. Serve immediately.

Serves 4 · Prep: 20 min. · Cooking: 20 min. · Level: 2

RISO CON SCAMPETTI
Risotto with saltwater crayfish

¼ cup extra-virgin olive oil
⅓ cup finely chopped parsley
4 cloves garlic, finely chopped
24 saltwater crayfish, 8 left whole + 16 shelled and chopped
½ cup dry white wine
¼ cup puréed tomatoes
    salt to taste
2 cups short-grain rice (preferably Italian arborio)
2 cups Fish stock (see recipe, page 104)
⅓ cup light cream

Wine: a dry white (Sauvignon di Albarola)

Heat the oil in a heavy-bottomed saucepan and sauté the parsley and garlic for 5 minutes. • Add the whole and chopped crayfish and cook for 5 minutes. • Sprinkle with the wine and cook until it has evaporated. • Add the tomatoes, season with salt, and cook for 5 minutes. • Add the rice and cook, stirring constantly for 2 minutes. Stir in ½ cup of the stock. Cook, stirring often, until the stock is absorbed. Continue adding the stock, ½ cup at a time, stirring often until each addition is absorbed, until the rice is tender, 15–18 minutes. • When the rice is cooked, stir in the cream. Transfer to a heated serving dish and serve.

Serves: 4 · Prep: 30 min. · Cooking: 35 min. · Level: 2

scallion and the onion until soft. • Add the asparagus and season with salt and pepper. Cook for 2 minutes, add the rice, and cook for 2 more minutes. • Stir in ¹/₂ cup of the stock. Cook, stirring often, until the stock is absorbed. Continue adding the stock, ¹/₂ cup at a time, stirring often until each addition is absorbed, until the rice is tender, 15–18 minutes. • Sauté the remaining scallion in the oil in a skillet for 3 minutes, then add the crayfish. Season with salt and pepper and cook for 2 minutes. • Add the wine and allow to evaporate. Turn off the heat, cover the pan, and set aside. • Add the crayfish and remaining butter to the risotto 3 minutes before the rice is cooked. • Serve hot.

Serves: 4 · Prep: 10 min. · Cooking: 35 min. · Level: 1

RISOTTO ALLE VONGOLE
Clam risotto

- 2 lb clams, in shell
- ¹/₄ cup extra-virgin olive oil
- 4 cloves garlic, finely chopped
- ¹/₃ cup finely chopped parsley
- ¹/₄ cup chopped basil
- 1 medium onion, finely chopped
- 1 cup peeled and chopped fresh tomatoes
- 2 cups simmering water
  salt to taste
- 2 cups short-grain rice (preferably Italian arborio)

Wine: a dry white (Pomino Bianco)

Soak the clams in a large bowl of cold water for 1 hour. • Drain and place the clams in a large skillet over high heat. Stir with a wooden spoon until all the clams are open. Discard any that have not opened. • Turn off the heat, extract the clams from the shells and place in a large bowl. • Sieve the clam liquid into a bowl. • Heat the oil in a large skillet over medium heat and sauté the garlic, parsley, and basil for 2 minutes. Add the onion and sauté until soft. • Add the tomatoes and cook for 5 more minutes. • Pour in the sieved clam water, season with salt, and after 5 minutes, add the rice. • Cook and stir, adding ¹/₂ cup simmering water at a time, stirring frequently until each addition is absorbed, until the rice is almost cooked, 12–15 minutes. • Add the clams and cook for for 2–3 more minutes. • Serve hot.

Serves: 4 · Prep: 30 min. + 1 hr to soak clams · Cooking: 50 min. · Level: 1

Saltwater crayfish and asparagus risotto

RISOTTO CON SCAMPI
Risotto with jumbo shrimp

- 1 clove garlic, peeled but whole
- 1 bay leaf
- 1 lb jumbo shrimp, in their shells
- ¹/₃ cup butter
- ¹/₄ cup extra-virgin olive oil
- 1 shallot, finely chopped
- 2 cups short-grain rice (preferably Italian arborio)
- ¹/₂ cup dry white wine
  salt and freshly ground black pepper to taste
- 1 cup freshly grated Parmesan cheese

Wine: a dry, fruity white (Breganze Vespaiolo Superiore)

Bring 6 cups of water to a boil in a pan with the garlic and bay leaf. Boil for 10 minutes. • Add the shrimp and simmer for 10 minutes. Remove the shrimp with a slotted ladle and peel them, reserving the flesh. • Return the shells and heads to the water and boil for 20 minutes. Strain the stock and reserve. • Heat half the butter and the oil in a skillet. Sauté the shallot gently without coloring. Add the rice and stir for 1–2 minutes. • Sprinkle with the wine and cook until it evaporates. Season with salt and pepper. • Add the shrimp, then stir in ¹/₂ cup of the stock. Cook, stirring often, until the stock is absorbed. Continue adding the stock, ¹/₂ cup at a time, stirring often until each addition is absorbed, until the rice is tender, 15–18 minutes. • Remove from heat, stir in the remaining butter, add the Parmesan, and serve.

Serves: 4 · Prep: 50 min. · Cooking: 30 min. · Level: 1

RISOTTO CON SCAMPI ED ASPARAGI
Saltwater crayfish and asparagus risotto

- 1¹/₄ lb large asparagus spears
- ¹/₄ cup butter
- 2 scallions, chopped
- 1 small onion, thinly sliced
  salt and freshly ground black pepper to taste
- 2 cups short-grain rice (preferably Italian arborio)
- 2 cups Fish stock (see recipe, page 104)
- 3 tablespoons extra-virgin olive oil
- 10 oz saltwater crayfish, shelled and chopped in half
- ¹/₂ cup dry white wine

Wine: a dry white (Cortese di Gavi)

Rinse the asparagus, cut off the tough ends, and chop into pieces about 1 inch long. • Melt half the butter in a skillet and sauté 1

RISOTTO COL BRANZINO
Risotto with sea bass

- 1 sea bass, about 1³/₄ lb, gutted
- 1 tablespoon black peppercorns
- 1 clove garlic, peeled but whole
- 1 bay leaf
- 2 shallots, finely chopped
- ¹/₄ cup extra-virgin olive oil
- ¹/₄ cup butter
- 2¹/₂ cups short-grain rice (preferably Italian arborio)
- ¹/₂ cup dry white wine
- 1 cup freshly grated Parmesan cheese
  salt to taste

Wine: a dry white (Pinot Bianco)

Place the fish in a large saucepan with the peppercorns and enough cold water to cover. Bring to a boil and simmer for 10 minutes, or until cooked. • Drain the fish and remove its head, bones, and skin. Break the flesh up into small pieces. • Return the head, bones, and skin to the saucepan. Add the garlic and bay leaf and boil until the liquid has reduced by about a half. • Sauté the shallots in the oil and half the butter in a large skillet. Add the pieces of fish and the rice. • Pour in a little of the strained fish stock and continue cooking and adding stock ¹/₂ a cup at a time, stirring often until each addition is absorbed, until the rice is almost done. • Add the wine, let it evaporate, then remove from heat. • Stir in the remaining butter and sprinkle with the Parmesan. Serve hot.

Serves: 4 · Prep: 30 min. · Cooking: 40 min. · Level: 1

RISOTTO AI TOTANI
Squid risotto

- 14 oz squid
- ¹/₄ cup extra-virgin olive oil
- 1 onion, finely chopped
  salt and freshly ground black pepper to taste
- 1 cup dry white wine
- 2 cups short-grain rice (preferably Italian arborio)
- 12 oz peeled and chopped fresh tomatoes
- 4 cups simmering water
- 2 tablespoons butter
- 3 tablespoons finely chopped parsley

Wine: a dry white (Cerveteri Bianco)

Clean the squid as shown on page 200, and cut into thin strips. • Sauté the onion in the oil until soft. • Add the squid, season with salt and pepper, and stir well. Cover the pan and cook for 10 minutes. • Pour in the wine

Squid risotto

and cook until it evaporates. • Add the rice to the sauce and cook for 2 minutes. Add the tomatoes and ¹/₂ cup of simmering water. Cook, stirring often, until the water is absorbed. Continue adding water ¹/₂ cup at a time, stirring often until each addition is absorbed, and until the rice is cooked, 15–18 minutes. • Turn off the heat, add the butter, mix well, and allow to stand for a few minutes. • Sprinkle with parsley and serve.

Serves: 4 · Prep: 20 min. · Cooking: 50 min. · Level: 2

RISOTTO CON LE COZZE
Mussel risotto

- 3¹/₂ lb mussels, in shell
- 2 cloves garlic, 1 of which finely chopped
- ¹/₂ cup extra-virgin olive oil
- 1 small onion, finely chopped
- 2 cups short-grain rice (preferably Italian arborio)
- ¹/₂ cup dry white wine
- 4 cups simmering water
  salt and freshly ground black pepper to taste
- 2 tablespoons finely chopped parsley

Wine: a dry white (Tocai Isonzo)

Soak the mussels in a large bowl of water for 1 hour. • Put the mussels and the whole garlic clove in a large skillet. Place over high heat and stir with a wooden spoon until the mussels are open. Discard any that have not opened. • Set aside a dozen of the largest, in their shells, to use as a garnish. • Take the remaining mussels out of their shells and put them in a bowl. • Strain the liquid left in the pan through a fine sieve and set it aside. • Sauté the onion and chopped garlic in the oil in the same skillet until soft. • Add the rice and cook, stirring continuously, for 2 minutes. • Increase heat slightly and pour in the wine. When all the wine has been absorbed, begin slowly adding the mussel liquid and then simmering water, ¹/₂ cup at a time, stirring frequently until each addition is absorbed and the rice is cooked, 15–18 minutes. • Add the mussels and stir well. Sprinkle with the parsley and season with salt and pepper. • Garnish with the whole mussels. Serve hot.

Serves: 4 · Prep: 20 min. + 1 hr to soak mussels · Cooking: 20 min. · Level: 1

POLENTA, GNOCCHI & CRÊPES

Creamy golden polenta is made with cornmeal and comes from northern Italy. The Italian word "gnocchi" is used for small dumplings made from potatoes, cornmeal, or other ingredients, that are baked or boiled and served in a variety of sauces. Crêpes, now famous as a French dish, were introduced to that cuisine by the Florentine, Catherine dei Medici, when she married the future king of France in the 16th century.

GNOCCHI DI POLENTA
Polenta gnocchi

- 4 cups whole milk
- 2½ cups coarse-grain cornmeal
  salt and freshly ground white pepper to taste
  pinch of nutmeg
- ⅔ cup butter
- 1 cup freshly grated Parmesan cheese
- 3 egg yolks, beaten with 1 tablespoon milk
- ½ cup ham, coarsely chopped

Wine: a dry red (Chianti dei Colli Senesi)

Bring the milk to a boil in a large, heavy-bottomed saucepan. • Pour in the cornmeal while stirring continuously with a long-handled wooden spoon to prevent lumps forming. Season with salt, pepper, and nutmeg. Add one-third of the butter. Stir energetically for about 30 minutes. • Remove from heat and add 2 tablespoons of the Parmesan, the egg yolks and milk, and ham. • Dampen a clean work surface and pour the polenta onto it. Spread to about ½ inch thick. Leave to cool for 1 hour. • Use a cookie cutter or glass about 2½ inches in diameter to cut out disks. • Grease a rectangular ovenproof dish with butter and arrange the disks in overlapping layers. • Heat the remaining butter and pour over the top. Sprinkle with the remaining Parmesan and bake in a preheated oven at 400°F for about 10 minutes, or until the topping is golden brown. • Serve hot.

Serves: 4 · Preparation: 10 min. + 1 hr to cool · Cooking: 45 min. · Level: 1

◁ *Potato gnocchi with butter and sage sauce (see recipe, page 187)*
▷ *Polenta gnocchi*

MAKING POLENTA, GNOCCHI, AND CRÊPES

Crêpes are easy and quick to make. Gnocchi and polenta both take a little longer to prepare, but are not especially difficult. When buying cornmeal for polenta, look for the newer polenta brands, many of which can be cooked in 8–10 minutes.

POLENTA BIANCA
White polenta

2½ quarts cold water
2 tablespoons coarse sea salt
2¾ cups white cornmeal

Prepare the polenta following the method for Basic polenta (below). • When cooked, spread out in a layer about 2 inches thick. Cover with a damp cloth and leave to cool. • Cut in slices about ½ inch thick and roast on a charcoal grill or in a sizzling grill pan. • The slices can also be fried in oil. • Serve hot or cold.

Serves: 4 · Prep: 5 min. · Cooking: 50 min. · Level: 2

Basic polenta

5 pints cold water
2 tablespoons coarse sea salt
3½ cups coarse-grain yellow cornmeal

Serves: 4 · Prep: 5 min. · Cooking: 45 min. · Level: 2

1 Bring the water and salt to a boil in a heavy-bottomed pan large enough to hold 4 quarts.

2 Add the cornmeal gradually, stirring continuously so that no lumps form. Polenta should always be perfectly smooth.

3 To cook, stir the polenta over high heat by moving a long, wooden spoon in a circular motion. At a certain point the polenta will begin to draw away from the sides of the pot on which a thin crust will form. The polenta should be stirred almost continuously for the 40–45 minutes it takes to cook. Quantities and method are the same when using an electric polenta cauldron. Stir the cornmeal into the boiling water gradually, then turn on the mixer. Leave for 40–45 minutes.

4 Pour the cooked polenta onto a serving platter and serve hot with sauce, or leave to cool to make fried or baked polenta crostini.

Basic polenta

Potato gnocchi

1½ lb boiling potatoes
2 eggs (optional)
2 cups all-purpose flour

Serves: 6 · Prep: 30 min. + 2 hrs to rest before cooking · Cooking: 35 min. · Level: 2

1 Cook the potatoes in their skins in a pot of salted, boiling water for about 25 minutes, or until tender. Drain and peel while still hot.

2 Place the potatoes in a bowl and mash until smooth.

3 Transfer to a floured work surface and stir in the eggs, if using, and most of the flour. Mix well, adding more flour as required, until the mixture is soft and smooth, but just slightly sticky.

4 Take a piece of the dough and roll it into a long sausage about ½ inch in diameter.

5 Cut into pieces about 1 inch in length. To give the gnocchi their special grooves, use a gnocchi groover, or twist the gnocchi around the tines of a fork.

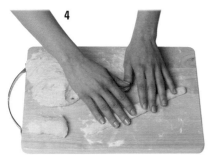

COOKING INSTRUCTIONS

Set a large pot of salted water to boil. The gnocchi should be cooked in batches. Lower the first batch (20–24 gnocchi) gently into the boiling water. After a few minutes they will rise to the surface. Leave them to bob about for 1–2 minutes, then scoop out with a slotted spoon. Place on a heated serving dish. Repeat until all the gnocchi are cooked.

Crêpes

3 eggs
¾ cup all-purpose flour
pinch of salt
1½ cups milk
¼ cup butter

Makes: about 12 crêpes · Prep: 20 min. · Cooking: 35 min. · Level: 2

1 Beat the eggs in a mixing bowl with a whisk. Sift the flour and salt into another bowl and pour the milk in gradually, stirring all the time so that no lumps form. Pour into the eggs and beat until smooth. Cover with plastic wrap and chill in the refrigerator for 30 minutes.

2 Beat the batter again before using. Melt 1 tablespoon of the butter in an 8-inch skillet. Place a ladleful of batter in the skillet. Rotate the skillet so that it covers the bottom in an even layer.

3 Place over medium heat and cook until the underside is golden brown.

4 Use a wooden spatula to flip the crêpe. Brown on the other side, then slide the crêpe onto a plate. Add a little more butter, and prepare another crêpe. Continue until all the batter is used up. Pile the crêpes up in a warm place until ready to use.

GNOCCHI AL POMODORO
Potato gnocchi with tomato sauce

☞ Tomato and butter sauce goes beautifully with soft, fresh potato gnocchi. If you like spicy dishes, add a finely chopped hot chile or 1 teaspoon of red pepper flakes to the sauce.

1   quantity Potato gnocchi (see recipe, page 185)
1   quantity Tomato and butter sauce (see recipe, page 18)
1   cup freshly grated Parmesan cheese
      freshly ground black pepper to taste (optional)

Wine: a dry red (Barbera dei Colli Bolognesi)

Prepare the potato gnocchi. • Prepare the tomato sauce. • Cook the gnocchi in a large pot of salted, boiling water following the instructions on page 185. • Place the gnocchi in a heated serving dish and pour the tomato sauce over the top. Sprinkle with the Parmesan and toss gently. If liked, season with pepper. Serve hot.

Serves: 6 · Prep: 5 min. + time to make the gnocchi and sauce · Cooking: 20 min. · Level: 2

GNOCCHI AI QUATTRO FORMAGGI
Potato gnocchi with four-cheese sauce

1   quantity Potato gnocchi (see recipe, page 185)
½   quantity Béchamel sauce (see recipe, page 16)
8   oz Fontina cheese, freshly grated
4   oz Gorgonzola cheese, coarsely chopped
4   oz Mascarpone cheese
1   cup freshly grated Parmesan cheese
      salt and freshly ground black pepper to taste

Wine: a dry sparkling red (Lambrusco di Sorbara)

Prepare the potato gnocchi. • Prepare the béchamel sauce. • When the béchamel is ready, add the four cheeses and stir over low heat until they have melted and the sauce is smooth and creamy. Season with salt and pepper. • Cook the gnocchi in a large pot of salted, boiling water following the instructions on page 185. • Place the gnocchi in a heated serving dish and pour the cheese sauce over the top. Toss gently and serve hot.

Serves: 6 · Prep: 20 min. + time to make the gnocchi · Cooking: 30 min. · Level: 2

GNOCCHI DI PATATE AL RAGÙ
Potato gnocchi with Bolognese meat sauce

1   quantity Potato gnocchi (see recipe, page 185)
1   quantity Bolognese meat sauce (see recipe, page 19)
1   cup freshly grated Parmesan cheese

Wine: a dry red (Sangiovese di Romagna)

Prepare the potato gnocchi. • Prepare the meat sauce. • Cook the gnocchi in a large pot of salted, boiling water following the instructions on page 185. • Place the gnocchi in a heated serving dish and pour the meat sauce over the top. Sprinkle with the Parmesan and toss gently. Serve hot.

Serves: 6 · Prep: 5 min. + time to make the gnocchi and sauce · Cooking: 20 min. · Level: 2

GNOCCHI AL GORGONZOLA E POMODORO
Potato gnocchi with Gorgonzola cheese and tomato sauce

1   quantity Potato gnocchi (see recipe, page 185)
¼   cup butter
8   oz Gorgonzola cheese, chopped
12 oz peeled and chopped fresh or canned tomatoes
      salt and freshly ground black pepper to taste
½   cup freshly grated Parmesan cheese

Wine: a dry white (Gavi)

Prepare the potato gnocchi. • Melt the butter in a heavy-bottomed saucepan and add the Gorgonzola. Stir over very low heat until the Gorgonzola has melted. • Mash the tomatoes thoroughly with a fork and add them to the butter and cheese. Stir well and leave over very low heat. • Cook the gnocchi in a large pot of salted, boiling water following the instructions on page 185. • Place the gnocchi on a heated serving dish and pour the cheese and tomato sauce over the top. Toss gently and serve hot.

Serves: 6 · Prep: 10 min. + time to make the gnocchi · Cooking: 25 min. · Level: 2

GNOCCHI DI CUNEO
Potato gnocchi with Parmesan and butter

☞ These potato gnocchi come from Cuneo, in Piedmont, where they are served on feast days. Unlike classic potato gnocchi, they are not rolled into sausages and cut into short lengths, but dropped directly into the boiling water for cooking.

1½ lb boiling potatoes
3   eggs, separated
1¼ cups all-purpose flour
      salt and freshly ground white pepper to taste
      pinch of nutmeg
1   quantity Butter and Parmesan sauce
      (see recipe, page 14)

Wine: a light, dry red (Donnas della Valle d'Aosta)

Boil the potatoes in their skins for about 25 minutes, or until tender. Drain and peel. Mash the potatoes and place in a mixing bowl while still hot. • Beat the egg whites in a large mixing bowl until stiff. Gently fold in the yolks, flour, salt, pepper, nutmeg, and, finally, the potatoes. Mix gently but thoroughly. • Bring a large pot of salted water to a boil and drop small rounded tablespoonfuls of the potato mixture into the boiling water. When the gnocchi bob up to the surface, they are done. Use a slotted ladle or spoon to take them out and place them on a heated serving dish. Cook the gnocchi in small batches until they are all ready. • Prepare the butter and Parmesan sauce. • Pour the sauce over the gnocchi and toss gently. • Serve hot.

Serves: 4 · Prep: 15 min. · Cooking: 45 min. · Level: 2

TIMBALLO DI GNOCCHI
Potato gnocchi baked in a pastry casing

- 1 quantity Potato gnocchi (see recipe, page 185)
- 2 cups all-purpose flour
- 2 egg yolks
  zest of 1 lemon, finely grated
  pinch of salt
- ¹/₂ cup butter, melted
- 1 quantity Béchamel sauce (see recipe, page 16)
- ³/₄ cup freshly grated Parmesan cheese

Wine: a dry red (Chianti delle Colline Pisane)

Prepare the potato gnocchi. • Sift the flour into a mixing bowl with the eggs, lemon zest, and salt. Add the butter and mix until the dough is moist and firm. Roll it into a ball, cover with plastic wrap, and chill in the refrigerator for 1 hour. • Roll the dough out until it is about ¹/₂ inch thick. Grease the bottom and sides of a deep-sided 10-inch ovenproof dish or springform pan and line with the dough. Prick well with a fork so that it doesn't swell while in the oven. Fill with pie weights or dried beans. • Bake in a preheated oven at 400°F for about 20 minutes, or until the pastry is golden brown. • Cook the potato gnocchi in a large pot of salted, boiling water following the instructions on page 185. • Prepare the béchamel sauce. • Combine the cooked gnocchi and the béchamel and mix gently. Carefully spoon into the baking dish with the pastry. • Sprinkle with the Parmesan cheese. Return to the oven and bake for 10 minutes more. • Remove from the oven and slip the pastry casing containing the gnocchi out of the baking dish. • Serve hot.

Serves: 6 · Prep: 20 min. + time to make the gnocchi and the pastry · Cooking: 1 hr · Level: 3

GNOCCHI ALLA BAVA
Baked potato gnocchi with cheese

☞ This special dish is perfect for dinner parties because it can be prepared ahead of time and popped into the oven as your guests come in the door. Any of the spinach gnocchi dishes on pages 188–189 can also be prepared in this way.

- 1 quantity Potato gnocchi (see recipe, page 185)
- ¹/₂ cup butter
- 1 clove garlic, finely chopped
- 8 oz Fontina cheese, thinly sliced
- ¹/₂ cup freshly grated Parmesan cheese

Wine: a dry red (Grignolino)

Prepare the potato gnocchi and cook them in a large pot of salted, boiling water following the instructions on page 185. • Drain the gnocchi well and place in a greased baking dish. • Melt half the butter over low heat with the garlic. Pour over the gnocchi. • Cover with the slices of Fontina. Dot with the remaining butter and sprinkle with the Parmesan. • Bake in a preheated oven at 400°F for 10 minutes, or until the top is golden brown. Serve hot.

Serves: 4 · Prep: 25 min. + time to make the gnocchi · Cooking: 40 min. · Level: 2

GNOCCHI CON BURRO E SALVIA
Potato gnocchi with butter and sage sauce

- 1 quantity Potato gnocchi (see recipe, page 185)
- 1 quantity Butter and sage sauce (see recipe, page 14)
- ¹/₂ cup freshly grated Parmesan cheese

Wine: a dry white (Rosso Piceno)

Prepare the potato gnocchi and cook them in a large pot of salted, boiling water following the instructions on page 185. • • Drain the gnocchi well and place them in a heated serving dish. • Prepare the butter and sage sauce and pour over the gnocchi. Sprinkle with the Parmesan and serve hot.

Serves: 6 · Prep: 5 min. + time to make the gnocchi · Cooking: 25 min. · Level: 2

Potato gnocchi with Gorgonzola cheese and tomato sauce

Cook the potatoes in their skins in a pot of salted, boiling water for 25 minutes, or until tender. Drain and peel while hot. • Cook the spinach in a pot of salted, boiling, water for 8–10 minutes, or until tender. Drain and squeeze out excess moisture. • Purée the potatoes and spinach together in a food processor. • Place the mixture on a lightly floured work surface and gradually work the eggs and flour into it. Add the nutmeg. Season with salt and pepper. Knead the mixture until smooth. • To prepare and cook the gnocchi, follow the instructions for potato gnocchi on page 185. • While the gnocchi are cooking, prepare the butter and sage sauce. • Pour the sauce over the gnocchi and toss gently. Sprinkle with Parmesan and serve hot.

Serves: 4–6 · Prep: 20 min. · Cooking: 50 min. · Level: 2

GNOCCHI DI PATATE E SPINACI CON POMODORO AL FORNO
Baked potato and spinach gnocchi

- 1 quantity potato and spinach gnocchi (see preceding recipe)
- 1 quantity Tomato and butter sauce (see recipe, page 14)
- ³/₄ cup freshly grated Parmesan cheese

Wine: a medium red (Merlot di Aprilia)

Prepare the tomato sauce. • Prepare and cook the potato and spinach gnocchi following the instructions in the preceding recipe. • Place the cooked gnocchi in a greased ovenproof dish and pour the tomato sauce over the top. Sprinkle with the Parmesan and bake in a preheated oven at 400°F for 10 minutes, or until the topping is golden brown. Serve hot.

Serves: 4–6 · Prep: 20 min. · Cooking: 1 hr · Level: 2

GNOCCHI ALLA ROMANA
Roman-style gnocchi

- 4 cups milk
- 1²/₃ cups semolina
- 3 egg yolks
  salt and freshly ground white pepper to taste
- ½ cup butter
- ½ cup freshly grated Parmesan cheese
- ½ cup freshly grated Gruyère cheese

Wine: a medium red (Merlot di Aprilia)

Fried gnocchi

GNOCCHI FRITTI
Fried gnocchi

- 1 egg and 5 egg yolks
- 1 tablespoon sugar
- 1 cup potato flour
- 2 cups whole milk
- 1 cup butter
  pinch each of nutmeg, cinnamon, and salt
- ¹/₄ cup all-purpose flour
- 1 cup fine dry bread crumbs
- ¹/₂ cup freshly grated Parmesan cheese

Wine: a dry red (Collio Merlot)

Beat the egg yolks in a bowl with the sugar until smooth. • Place the potato flour in a heavy-bottomed saucepan. Gradually stir in the milk. Add the egg mixture, 2 tablespoons of the butter, the nutmeg, cinnamon, and salt. Mix well with a wooden spoon. • Place the pan over medium heat and, stirring constantly, bring to a boil. Boil for 10 minutes, stirring all the time. Remove from heat. • Turn the gnocchi batter out onto a flat work surface. Using a spatula dipped in cold water, spread it out to a thickness of about ¹/₂ inch and leave to cool for 30 minutes. • Cut the batter into ¹/₂ inch cubes or roll into marble-sized balls. Beat the remaining egg in a bowl with a fork. Dust the gnocchi with flour, drop them into the beaten egg, then roll them in the bread crumbs. • Heat the remaining butter in a 12-inch skillet and fry the gnocchi until golden brown. • Place on a heated serving dish, sprinkle with Parmesan, and serve.

Serves: 4 · Prep: 50 min. · Cooking: 40 min. · Level: 2

GNOCCHI DI PATATE E SPINACI AL BURRO E SALVIA
Potato and spinach gnocchi in butter and sage sauce

- 1 lb boiling potatoes
- 1 lb fresh spinach
- 2 eggs
- ³/₄ cup all-purpose flour
  pinch of nutmeg
  salt and freshly ground black pepper to taste
- 1 quantity Butter and sage sauce (see recipe, page 14)
- ¹/₃ cup freshly grated Parmesan cheese

Wine: a dry rosé (Lagrein Rosato)

Bring the milk to a boil in a heavy-bottomed saucepan. Add the semolina very gradually just as the milk is beginning to boil. Cook and stir over low heat for 15–20 minutes, or until the mixture is thick and comes away from the sides of the pan. • Remove from heat and leave to cool for 2–3 minutes. • Add the egg yolks, salt, and 2 tablespoons each of butter, Parmesan, and Gruyère. Mix well. • Wet a clean work surface with cold water and turn the gnocchi batter out onto it. Using a spatula dipped in cold water, spread it out to a thickness of about ½ inch. Leave to cool. • Use a cookie cutter or glass about 1½ inches in diameter to cut the gnocchi into disks. • Grease a rectangular baking dish with butter and place a row of gnocchi at one end. Lean the next row of gnocchi on the bottoms of the first, roof-tile fashion. Repeat until the baking dish is full. • Melt the remaining butter and pour over the gnocchi. Sprinkle with the remaining Parmesan and Gruyère. • Bake in a preheated oven at 400°F for about 20 minutes, or until a golden crust forms on top. Serve hot.

Serves: 4 · Prep: 25 min. · Cooking: 45 min. · Level: 2

IGNUDI
Parmesan and spinach gnocchi

☞ *Ignudi* in Italian means "naked" and refers to the fact that these gnocchi are similar to the stuffing used for ravioli. They are nude because they lack their pasta wrappings. In Tuscany they sometimes appear on the menu as *Strozzaprete*, or "priest chokers," although the origin of this name is not known!

1½ lb fresh spinach
½ cup soft Ricotta cheese
1 egg and 1 yolk
1 cup freshly grated Parmesan cheese
  pinch of nutmeg
  salt and freshly ground black pepper to taste
1 quantity Butter and Parmesan sauce
  (see recipe, page 14)

Wine: a dry red (Chianti Classico)

Cook the spinach in a pot of boiling, salted water for 8–10 minutes, or until tender. Drain well and squeeze out any excess moisture. Chop finely. • Mix the spinach with the Ricotta, eggs, nutmeg, and all but 2 tablespoons of the Parmesan. Season

Spinach gnocchi with tomato sauce

with salt and pepper. • Shape the mixture into walnut-sized balls. • Bring a large pot of salted water to a boil and cook the gnocchi in small batches. They are cooked when they rise to the surface. Remove with a slotted spoon and place in a serving dish. • Prepare the sauce and pour over the gnocchi. Sprinkle with the remaining Parmesan and serve hot.

Serves: 4 · Prep: 20 min. · Cooking: 20 min. · Level: 2

GNOCCHI DI SPINACI AL POMODORO
Spinach gnocchi with tomato sauce

1 quantity Tomato and butter sauce
  (see recipe, page 18)
1 small onion, sliced in thin rings
¼ cup butter
1½ lb fresh spinach
¾ cup fresh Ricotta cheese
3 eggs
  pinch of nutmeg
1½ cups freshly grated Parmesan cheese
  salt and freshly ground black pepper to taste
2½ cups all-purpose flour

Wine: a dry red (Lambrusco)

Prepare the tomato and butter sauce. • Sauté the onion and butter in a saucepan over medium heat until pale gold. Remove the onion with a fork, leaving as much butter as possible in the pan. • Cook the spinach in a pot of salted, boiling water for 8–10 minutes, or until tender. Drain and squeeze out excess moisture. Chop finely. • Add the spinach to the pan with the butter and sauté for 10 minutes. Remove from heat. • When the spinach is cool, place in a bowl with the Ricotta, eggs, nutmeg, and all but 3 tablespoons of the Parmesan. Season with salt and pepper and mix well. • Stir in the flour gradually until the mixture is firm. Shape into walnut-size balls and place on a lightly floured plate. • Bring a large pot of salted water to a boil and cook the gnocchi in small batches. They are cooked when they rise to the surface. Remove with a slotted spoon and place in the pan with the sauce. Stir carefully. Sprinkle with the remaining Parmesan and serve hot.

Serves: 6 · Prep: 45 min. · Cooking: 25 min. · Level: 2

Pumpkin gnocchi

Wine: a light, dry red (Rosso dell'Oltrepò Pavese)

Prepare the tomato sauce. • Prepare the polenta. Use a little less cornmeal than usual (or a little more water) so that the polenta is soft and creamy. • When the polenta is half cooked, add the pancetta, cheese, and pieces of butter. • When the polenta is ready, transfer to individual soup plates and spoon the tomato sauce over the top. • Serve hot.

Serves: 4 · Prep: 15 min. · Cooking: 50 min. · Level: 1

GNOCCHI DI ZUCCA
Pumpkin gnocchi

☞ This recipe comes from the delta of the Po River, in northern Italy. For a wonderful sweet version, sprinkle with 2 tablespoons of sugar and 1 teaspoon of ground cinnamon just before serving.

3 lb piece of pumpkin
3¹/₂ cups all-purpose flour
2 eggs
pinch of salt
¹/₂ cup butter
¹/₂ cup freshly grated Parmesan cheese

Wine: a light, dry white (Gambellara Tocai Bianco)

Peel the pumpkin and scrape away the seeds and fibrous matter. Cut the flesh into fairly large cubes. Place on a baking sheet and bake in a preheated oven at 400°F for 20 minutes. • Place in a bowl while still hot and mash with a potato masher until smooth. Leave to cool for 10–15 minutes. • Stir in the flour, eggs, and salt. Combine very thoroughly until the mixture is smooth and firm, adding a little more flour if necessary. • Bring a large pot of salted water to a boil. Shape the dough into balls about the size of a walnut. Drop them into the water a few at a time and cook for 2–3 minutes. Remove with a slotted spoon and transfer to a heated serving dish. Repeat until all the gnocchi dough is used up. • Drizzle with melted butter, sprinkle with Parmesan, and serve.

Serves: 6 · Prep: 15 min. · Cooking: 35 min. · Level: 1

POLENTA AL GORGONZOLA
Creamy Gorgonzola cheese polenta

1 quantity Basic polenta (see recipe, page 184)
¹/₄ cup butter, chopped
12 oz Gorgonzola cheese, chopped
¹/₄ cup heavy cream

Wine: a dry white (Tocai Friuliano del Collio)

Prepare the polenta. • When the polenta is cooked, stir in the butter, half the Gorgonzola, and the cream. The polenta should be soft and creamy. • Pour it into individual soup plates, and sprinkle with the remaining Gorgonzola. Serve hot.

Serves: 4–6 · Prep: 5 min. · Cooking: 50 min. · Level: 1

POLENTA D'OROPA
Polenta with Fontina and Parmesan cheese

5 cups boiling water
5 cups hot milk
1 tablespoon coarse sea salt
2¹/₄ cups coarse-grain cornmeal
14 oz Fontina cheese, cut in slivers
¹/₃ cup butter
freshly ground black pepper to taste
¹/₂ cup freshly grated Parmesan cheese

Wine: a dry red (Gamay della Valle d'Aosta)

Use the first four ingredients to prepare the polenta as explained on page 184. These quantities will make a rather soft polenta. • After the polenta has been cooking for about 30 minutes, add the Fontina and cook for 15 more minutes, stirring energetically. • A few minutes before the polenta is cooked, slowly melt the butter in a small saucepan until it starts to bubble. • Pour the polenta into a large serving dish, dust with pepper and sprinkle with the Parmesan. Drizzle the butter over the top and serve.

Serves: 4 · Prep: 10 min. · Cooking: 50 min. · Level: 1

POLENTA CON PANNA E PARMIGIANO
Polenta with cream and Parmesan

1 quantity Basic polenta (see recipe, page 184)
1¹/₂ cups heavy cream
1 cup freshly grated Parmesan cheese

Wine: a light, dry red (Lambrusco di Sorbara)

Prepare the polenta. Use a little less cornmeal than usual (or a little more water) so that the polenta is soft and creamy. • When the polenta is cooked, pour it into small individual soup bowls. Pour a little of the cream over the top, sprinkle with the Parmesan, and serve.

Serves: 6 · Prep: 5 min. · Cooking: 40 min. · Level: 1

POLENTA CON PANCETTA E PECORINO
Polenta with pancetta, tomato, and Pecorino cheese

1 quantity Tomato and butter sauce (see recipe, page 18)
1 quantity Basic polenta (see recipe, page 184)
³/₄ cup diced pancetta

POLENTA E FAGIOLI
Polenta and beans

- 1 1/3 cups dried cranberry, borlotti, or pinto beans
- 1/2 cup diced pancetta
- 1/2 onion, finely chopped
- 1 tablespoon finely chopped fresh sage or rosemary
  salt and freshly ground black pepper to taste
- 2 1/4 cups coarse-grain yellow cornmeal

Wine: a dry red (Colli Berici Cabernet)

Soak the beans overnight in a large bowl of water. • Sauté the pancetta and onion in a large, heavy-bottomed saucepan. • Add the strained beans, sage or rosemary, and sufficient cold water to cover the beans (about 5 cups). Bring to a boil, then cover and simmer gently for 1 hour. • When the beans are nearly done, add salt and pepper to taste and gradually stir in the cornmeal. • Cook slowly for 45 minutes, stirring continuously, and adding a little warm water now and then if necessary. The polenta should be fairly soft, not stiff. • Turn out onto a board or platter and serve.

Serves: 6 · Prep: 20 min. + 12 hrs to soak the beans · Cooking: 1 3/4 hrs · Level: 1

GNOCCHI DI POLENTA AL RAGÙ
Baked polenta gnocchi with Bolognese meat sauce

- 1 quantity Basic polenta (see recipe, page 184)
- 1/4 cup butter
- 1 quantity Bolognese meat sauce (see recipe, page 19)
- 1 1/4 cups freshly grated Parmesan cheese

Wine: a dry red (Carmignano Rosso)

Prepare the polenta. • When the polenta is almost cooked, stir in the butter. The polenta should be thick, smooth, and reasonably firm in texture. • Using a tablespoon, scoop up oval gnocchi, dipping the spoon in cold water to prevent the polenta from sticking. Don't worry if the gnocchi look rather untidy. • Place a layer of gnocchi in a fairly deep, greased ovenproof dish, spoon some meat sauce over the top, and cover with another layer of polenta gnocchi. Continue in this way, finishing with a layer of meat sauce. • Sprinkle with the Parmesan and bake in a preheated oven at 400°F for 8–10 minutes, or until the topping is golden brown. • Serve hot.

Serves: 4 · Prep: 5 min. + time for the meat sauce · Cooking: 50 min. · Level: 1

POLENTA PASTICCIATA IN SALSA DI FORMAGGIO
Baked polenta in cheese sauce

- 1 quantity Basic polenta (see recipe, page 184)
- 2 tablespoons butter
- 1 tablespoon all-purpose flour
- 1 cup milk
  pinch of nutmeg
- 6 oz Gorgonzola cheese, chopped
- 6 oz Emmental (or Gruyère, or similar) cheese, thinly sliced
- 1/2 cup freshly grated Parmesan cheese
- 1 tablespoon butter

Wine: a dry red (Barbacarlo Oltrepò Pavese)

Prepare the polenta. Set aside to cool for at least 3 hours. • Melt the butter in a saucepan. When it stops foaming, add the flour and cook over low heat for 1–2 minutes, stirring continuously. • Begin adding the milk, a little at a time, stirring continuously until the sauce is smooth. • Season with a little nutmeg. • Turn up the heat and add the Gorgonzola, Emmental, and Parmesan, a handful at a time, stirring constantly until smooth. • Use the butter to grease an ovenproof baking dish large enough to hold the polenta and sauce in a layer about 2 inches thick. • Cut the polenta into 3/4 inch cubes. • Cover the bottom of the dish with half the polenta and pour half the sauce over the top. Put the remaining polenta on top and cover with the remaining sauce. • Bake in a preheated oven at 400°F for 25–30 minutes, or until the top is golden brown.

Serves: 4 · Prep: 20 min. + time to make and cool the polenta · Cooking: 30 min. · Level: 1

POLENTA CONDITA
Polenta and salt pork

- 1 quantity Basic polenta (see recipe, page 184)
- 4 oz salt pork, finely chopped
- 1 small onion, finely chopped
- 2 cloves garlic, finely chopped
- 1 cup fresh cream
- 1/2 cup freshly grated Parmesan cheese
- 2 tablespoons finely chopped parsley

Wine: a dry red (Grignolino)

Prepare the polenta. • When the polenta is almost cooked, melt the salt pork in a small skillet and sauté the onion and garlic until pale gold. • Pour a layer of cooked polenta into a heated serving dish. Pour in a little of the cream and sprinkle with a little of the Parmesan. Repeat these layers until the polenta, cream, and Parmesan are all in the dish. Finish with a layer of Parmesan. • Pour the hot salt pork mixture over the top, sprinkle with the parsley, and serve.

Serves: 4–6 · Prep: 5 min. · Cooking: 40 min. · Level: 1

Baked polenta in cheese sauce

Fried mushroom polenta

POLENTA DORATA CON FUNGHI
Fried mushroom polenta

- 1 quantity Basic polenta (see recipe, page 184)
- 1 lb porcini (or other wild) mushrooms
- 1/3 cup extra-virgin olive oil
- 1 onion
- 2 tablespoons finely chopped parsley
- 6 fresh sage leaves, finely chopped
- 2 cups oil, for frying

Wine: a dry red (Valcalepio Rosso)

Prepare the polenta. • While the polenta is cooking, clean the mushrooms, rinse under cold running water, and chop coarsely. • Heat the oil in a large skillet and sauté the onion until soft. • Add the mushrooms, parsley, and sage and cook over medium heat for 10 minutes, stirring frequently. • Add the mushroom mixture to the polenta just before the polenta is cooked. • Dampen a clean work surface and spread the mixture out in a layer about 1/2 inch thick. Leave to cool. • Cut the polenta in slices about 2 x 4 inches. • Heat

the oil in a large skillet until very hot and fry the slices of polenta in batches until golden brown on both sides. Drain on paper towels. Serve hot.

Serves: 4 · Prep: 5 min. · Cooking: 1 hr · Level: 2

POLENTA CON SALSICCIA
Polenta with Italian sausages

- 9 cups boiling water
- 1 tablespoon coarse sea salt
- 2 1/4 cups coarse-grain cornmeal
- 1 tablespoon extra-virgin olive oil
- 12 oz fresh Italian pork sausage, skinned and crumbled
- 1/2 cup salt pork, finely chopped
- 1 tablespoon rosemary leaves, finely chopped
- 2 cloves garlic, finely chopped
- 1/2 cup freshly grated Parmesan cheese

Wine: a light, dry red (Bonarda dei Colli Piacentini)

Use the first three ingredients to prepare the polenta as explained on page 184. These quantities will make a very soft polenta that will cook in about 35 minutes. • Use the oil to grease an ovenproof baking dish large enough to contain the polenta in a 1-inch layer. • Using a fork, carefully mix the sausage, salt pork,

rosemary, and garlic together in a bowl. • When the polenta is cooked, place in the baking dish and smooth with a spatula. • Spread with the sausage mixture, gently pushing it into the polenta with your fingertips. • Bake in a preheated oven at 400°F for 15 minutes. • Sprinkle with the Parmesan just before serving.

Serves: 4 · Prep: 15 min. · Cooking: 50 min. · Level: 1

POLENTA CON PORRI
Polenta with leeks

- 1 quantity Basic polenta (see recipe, page 184)
- 1 lb leeks, (white part only)
- 3 tablespoons butter
     salt and freshly ground white pepper to taste
- 1 1/2 cups light cream
- 1/4 cup milk

Wine: a dry white (Pinot Bianco)

Prepare the polenta. • Cut the leeks into 1/8 inch thick slices. • Melt the butter in a heavy-bottomed saucepan over medium heat, add the leeks, cover and cook for 5 minutes, or until the leeks have wilted. • Season with salt and pepper. Add the cream and milk and cook for 20–25 minutes. • When the polenta is done (it should be very thick, almost stiff), turn it out onto a heated serving dish. • Serve hot with the leek sauce passed separately.

Serves: 4 · Prep: 15 · Cooking: 1 hr · Level: 1

POLENTA ALLA PIZZAIOLA
Polenta with pizza topping

☞ This dish is ideal for children (you may prefer to leave out the anchovies if your children are not used to them). It can also be prepared ahead of time. Reheat about 20 minutes before serving.

- 9 cups boiling water
- 1 tablespoon coarse sea salt
- 2 3/4 cups coarse-grain cornmeal
- 1 quantity Simple tomato sauce (see recipe, page 18)
- 1/3 cup extra-virgin olive oil
- 8 oz Scamorza (or Parmesan) cheese, diced
- 6 anchovy fillets, crumbled (optional)

Wine: a light, dry red (Rosso Conero)

Use the first three ingredients to prepare the polenta as explained on page 184. Cook for 40 minutes; it should be fairly solid but not too hard. • Prepare the tomato sauce. • When the sauce is cooked, add 2 tablespoons of the oil. • Oil an ovenproof baking dish large enough to contain a layer of polenta about 1¼ inches thick with 2 tablespoons of the oil. • When the polenta is ready, transfer it to the dish and level with a spatula. • Spoon the sauce over the top. Arrange the Scamorza evenly on top, add the anchovies, if using, and drizzle with the remaining oil. • Cook in a preheated oven at 400°F for about 15 minutes. • If the dish was prepared ahead of time, preheat the oven to 350°F and cook at that temperature for the first 10–15 minutes, then increase to 400°F for the last 5–10 minutes, otherwise a tough crust will form on the Scamorza.

Serves: 4 · Prep: 10 min. · Cooking: 1 hr · Level: 2

POLENTA CON I FUNGHI
Polenta with mushroom sauce

- 1 quantity Basic polenta (see recipe, page 184)
- 1 lb wild or cultivated mushrooms
- ¼ cup extra-virgin olive oil
- 2 cloves garlic, finely chopped
- 2 tablespoons finely chopped parsley
- 3 large tomatoes, peeled and chopped
     salt and freshly ground white pepper to taste

Wine: a dry white (Cinque Terre)

Prepare the polenta. • Trim the stems of the mushrooms, rinse under cold running water, and pat dry with paper towels. Slice thinly. • Heat the oil in a skillet over medium heat and sauté the garlic for 2–3 minutes. • Add the parsley and mushrooms and cook over high heat for 2–3 minutes. • Add the tomatoes and simmer over medium heat for 15–20 minutes, stirring frequently. • Place the polenta in a serving dish and pour the mushroom sauce over the top. • Serve hot.

Serves: 4 · Prep: 10 min. · Cooking: 45 min. · Level: 2

POLENTA TARAGNA
Buckwheat polenta with cheese

- 7 cups water
- 1 tablespoon coarse sea salt
- 3 cups buckwheat flour
- 1 cup butter
- 8 oz Fontina, Asiago, or Fontal cheese (or a mixture of the three), cut in slivers

Wine: a dry red (Valcalepio Rosso)

Bring the water and salt to a boil. • Sift in the buckwheat flour, stirring with a

Polenta with Italian sausages

whisk, and add half the butter. • Cook, stirring frequently, as for basic polenta (see page 184), for 40 minutes. The buckwheat polenta will be rather soft. • Add the cheese and continue stirring over fairly low heat. • After a couple of minutes add the remaining butter. • After another 5–8 minutes the polenta will be ready. • Serve hot.

Serves: 4 · Prep: 5 min. · Cooking: 50 min. · Level: 2

POLENTA CON LA LUGANEGA
Polenta with luganega sausage

☞ Luganega is a long fresh pork sausage from northern Italy. If not available, replace with another type of fresh Italian pork sausage.

- 1 quantity Basic polenta (see recipe, page 184)
- 1 lb luganega (or very fresh Italian pork sausage)
- 2 tablespoons butter
- 1 tablespoon extra-virgin olive oil
- 1 small sprig rosemary
- ⅔ cup dry red wine

Wine: a dry red (Raboso del Piave)

Prepare the polenta. • About 20 minutes before the polenta is cooked, pierce holes about 1 inch apart in the casing of the luganega with a toothpick, so that the fat can drain during cooking. • Roll the luganega up in a flat spiral, piercing it horizontally with two long thin wooden or metal skewers, placed crosswise, so it will keep its shape. • Melt the butter in a skillet. Add the oil and rosemary, and then carefully add the sausage. Brown for 3–4 minutes over medium heat, then turn so it will brown on the other side. • Increase the heat and pour the wine into the pan; as soon as it is hot, lower the heat and cover the pan. • Simmer for about 10 minutes, turning the luganega again after the first 5 minutes. • When cooked, remove the skewers and cut the sausage into pieces about 2 inches long. • Place the polenta in a serving dish with the pieces of sausage on top. • Discard the rosemary from the pan and drizzle the juices over the polenta. • Serve hot.

Serves: 4 · Prep: 5 min. · Cooking: 50 min. · Level: 2

POLENTA INTEGRALE
Whole-wheat polenta

- 6½ cups water
- 1 tablespoon coarse sea salt
- 1¼ cups coarse-grain yellow cornmeal
- 1¼ cups buckwheat flour
- ½ cup butter
- 3½ oz salted anchovies, rinsed and boned
- 10 oz fresh Toma (or Fontina) cheese

Wine: a dry, full-bodied red (Gattinara)

Bring the water to a boil with the coarse salt. Sprinkle in the cornmeal and the buckwheat flour, stirring continuously with a whisk to prevent lumps forming. • Cook over medium heat, stirring almost continuously for about 40 minutes. • When the polenta is ready (it should be stiff), turn it out onto a platter or cutting board and let it cool for at least 30 minutes. • Melt three-quarters of the butter in a small saucepan. • Use the remaining butter to grease a fairly deep ovenproof dish. • Cut the polenta into pieces about ¾ inch thick. Place a layer of polenta pieces (use about one-third) in the greased dish and sprinkle with one-third of the anchovies, sliced cheese, and melted butter. Repeat the operation, using half the remaining polenta, all the remaining anchovies and cheese, and about half the remaining melted butter. • Cover with a final layer of polenta and drizzle the remaining butter over the top. • Bake in a preheated oven at 400°F for 20 minutes, or until golden brown on top.

Serves: 4 · Prep: 25 min. + 30 min. to rest · Cooking: 1 hr · Level: 1

POLENTA PASTICCIATA CON SALSA AL POMODORO
Baked polenta with simple tomato sauce

☞ For a slightly heavier dish, replace the Simple tomato sauce with one quantity of Tomato meat sauce (see recipe, page 18).

- 1 quantity Basic polenta (see recipe, page 184)
- 1 quantity Simple tomato sauce (see recipe, page 18)
- 1 tablespoon extra-virgin olive oil
- 10 oz mild Provolone cheese, diced freshly ground black pepper to taste

Wine: a light, dry red (San Colombano)

Prepare the polenta and set aside to cool. • Prepare the tomato sauce. • Use the oil to grease an ovenproof baking dish about 8 inches in diameter and about 3 inches deep. • Cut the polenta into ¼-inch slices and use them to line the dish. Scatter one-third of the Provolone on top. Dust with pepper and drizzle with one-third of the tomato sauce. • Repeat this procedure twice, finishing with a layer of sauce. • Bake in a preheated oven at 400°F for 25 minutes. • Serve hot.

Serves: 4 · Prep: 20 min. · Cooking: 1 hr · Level: 1

POLENTA PASTICCIATA CON SALSICCIA E BÉCHAMEL
Baked polenta with sausages

- 1 quantity Basic polenta (see recipe, page 184)
- 1 oz dried porcini mushrooms
- 3 tablespoons butter
- 1 small onion, finely chopped
- 4 oz Italian pork sausage, skinned and crumbled salt and freshly ground black pepper to taste
- 1 quantity Béchamel sauce (see recipe, page 16)
- ¾ cup freshly grated Parmesan cheese
- 4 oz Gruyère cheese (or similar), cut in slivers

Wine: a dry red (Bonarda Oltrepò Pavese)

Prepare the polenta and set aside to cool. • Soak the mushrooms in 1 cup of warm water for 30 minutes. Drain (reserving the liquid), squeeze out excess moisture, and chop coarsely. • Strain the water in which the mushrooms were soaked and set aside. • In a skillet, melt two-thirds of the butter and sauté the onion for a few minutes over low heat; add the sausage, and the mushrooms with their water. • Cover and cook over medium heat for 30 minutes, stirring occasionally. Season with salt and pepper. (This sauce can be prepared ahead of time). • Prepare the béchamel sauce. • Use the remaining butter to grease an ovenproof baking dish about 8 inches in diameter and 3 inches deep. Cut the polenta into ¼-inch slices and use them to line the dish. Cover with one-third of the mushroom sauce, dust with one-third of the Parmesan, arrange one-third of the Gruyère on top, and cover with one-third of the béchamel sauce. Repeat this procedure twice. • Bake in a preheated oven at 400°F for 25 minutes, or until the top is golden brown. • Serve hot.

Serves: 4 · Prep: 30 min. · Cooking: 1 hr · Level: 2

Potato polenta with spareribs

POLENTA DI PATATE CON ROSTICCIANA

Potato polenta with spareribs

2¼	lb potatoes, boiled and peeled, still hot
½	cup coarse-grain yellow cornmeal
½	cup buckwheat flour
1	cup boiling water
3	tablespoons butter
3	tablespoons extra-virgin olive oil
2	onions, thinly sliced
	salt and freshly ground black pepper to taste
6	oz fresh Asiago (or Fontina) cheese, in slivers
2	lb spareribs

Wine: a dry red (Merlot)

Mash the potatoes and transfer to the pot where the polenta is to be cooked. • Add the cornmeal and buckwheat flour, mix well, and continue to mix while adding the water. • Cook over medium-high heat, stirring energetically. • Melt the butter and oil over medium heat in a small saucepan. Add the onion and sauté until soft. • Add the onion mixture to the polenta, which will have been cooking for about 10 minutes by this time. Stir continuously. • After 20 more minutes, add a little salt, a generous pinch of pepper, and the cheese. Stir for 10 more minutes. • Meanwhile, season the spareribs generously with salt and pepper and place them under a hot broiler. Broil until deep golden brown. • When the polenta is ready, turn it out onto a heated serving platter and top with the spareribs. Serve immediately.

Serves: 4 · Prep: 30 min. · Cooking: 50 min. · Level: 1

Roman crêpes with meat sauce

POLENTA PASTICCIATA AL FORMAGGIO
Baked polenta with cheese

- 1 quantity Basic polenta (see recipe, page 184)
- 1/3 cup butter
- 1 cup freshly grated Parmesan cheese
- 6 oz Gruyère cheese, cut in slivers

Wine: a dry red (Donnaz)

Prepare the polenta. When cooked, turn out onto a platter to cool. • Cut the polenta into 1/4-inch thick slices, about 1 1/2 inches long. • Grease an ovenproof baking dish deep enough for three layers of polenta. Cover the bottom with slices of polenta, sprinkle with one-third of the Parmesan, one-third of the Gruyère, and dot with one-third of the butter. • Repeat this procedure twice. • Bake in a preheated oven at 400°F for 25–30 minutes, or until a golden crust has formed. • Serve hot.

Serves: 4 · Prep: 10 min. · Cooking: 1 1/4 hrs · Level: 1

POLENTA AL FORNO
Baked polenta with Taleggio cheese

☞ Taleggio cheese comes from Lombardy. It should be creamy, fragrant, and well ripened. If you can't get Taleggio, use the same quantity of Fontina cheese in its place.

- 6 1/2 cups boiling water
- 3 cups milk
- 1 tablespoon coarse sea salt
- 2 3/4 cups coarse-grain cornmeal

- 1/4 cup butter
- 2/3 cup Parmesan cheese, shredded
- 12 oz Taleggio cheese, thinly sliced

Wine: a dry white (Roero Arneis)

Use the first four ingredients to prepare the polenta as explained on page 184. These quantities will make a rather soft polenta that will cook in about 40 minutes. • Use a little of the butter to grease an ovenproof baking dish about 10 inches in diameter and 3 inches deep. • When the polenta is ready, pour one-third into the dish, sprinkle with one-third of the Parmesan, one-third of the Taleggio, and one-third of the remaining butter. Repeat these layers twice. • Bake in a preheated oven at 400°F for about 15 minutes, or until golden brown. • Serve hot.

Serves: 4 · Prep: 10 min. · Cooking: 1 hr · Level: 1

PIZZACCE DI RIETI
Roman crêpes with meat sauce

- 1 quantity meat sauce (choose from *Tomato meat sauce*, see recipe, page 18; *False meat sauce*, see recipe, page 18, or *Bolognese meat sauce*, see recipe, page 19)
- 1 quantity Roman crêpes (see recipe, below)
- 1 1/4 cups freshly grated Pecorino romano cheese
  pinch of white pepper or paprika (optional)

Wine: a dry red (Velletri Rosso Secco)

Prepare the meat sauce. • Prepare the crêpes. • Roll the crêpes loosely and arrange them in an ovenproof baking dish. Spoon the sauce over the top and sprinkle with the Pecorino. Season with pepper or paprika, if liked. • Bake in a preheated oven at 400°F for 10 minutes, or until the cheese is light, golden brown. • Serve hot.

Serves: 4 · Prep: 5 min. + time to make the meat sauce and crêpes · Cooking: 10 min. · Level: 2

PIZZACCE
Roman crêpes with Pecorino cheese

- 3 eggs
  pinch of salt
- 1 1/4 cups all-purpose flour
- 1/2 cup milk, warm
- 1/4 cup butter or extra-virgin olive oil
- 1 cup freshly grated Pecorino romano cheese

Wine: a dry white (Orvieto Classico)

Beat the eggs with the salt. • Sift in the flour, then add the milk and stir until smooth. The mixture should be about the same consistency as pancake batter. If necessary, add more milk or flour. • Heat the butter or oil in a small skillet until very hot. Add 2 tablespoons of batter and twirl the pan so that it spreads evenly across the bottom. Cook until brown, then flip to brown the other side. Repeat until all the batter is used up. • Sprinkle the crêpes with Pecorino and serve hot.

Serves: 4 · Prep: 5 min. · Cooking: 25 min. · Level: 1

CRÊPES AI QUATTRO FORMAGGI
Four-cheese crêpes

- 1 quantity Crêpes (see recipe, page 185)
- 1 quantity Béchamel sauce (see recipe, page 16)
- 1/2 cup freshly grated Parmesan cheese
- 2 1/2 oz Gruyère cheese, freshly grated
- 2 1/2 oz Fontina cheese, freshly grated
- 2 1/2 oz Gorgonzola cheese, diced
  freshly ground black pepper to taste
- 2 tablespoons butter, chopped

Wine: a young, dry red (Roero)

Prepare the crêpes. • Prepare the béchamel sauce. • Add half the Parmesan, and all the Gruyère, Fontina, and Gorgonzola to the béchamel. Cook over low heat until the cheeses have melted into the sauce. • Spread 2–3 tablespoons of the cheese mixture on each crêpe. Roll them up loosely and place in a lightly buttered ovenproof dish. • Cover with the remaining cheese sauce and sprinkle with the remaining Parmesan. Grind a little black pepper over the top and dot with the pieces of butter. • Bake in a preheated oven at 350°F for 15 minutes, or until the topping is golden brown. • Serve hot.

Serves: 6 · Prep: 20 min. + 1 hr for the crêpes · Cooking: 20 min. · Level: 2

CRÊPES CON BIETOLINA E CAPRINO
Crêpes with Swiss chard and Caprino

- 1 quantity Crêpes (see recipe, page 185)
- 1½ lb fresh Swiss chard
  salt and freshly ground black pepper to taste
- 2 cloves garlic, cut in half
- 2 tablespoons butter
- 1 quantity Béchamel sauce (see recipe, page 16)
- 8 oz fresh Caprino cheese
  pinch of nutmeg
- ½ cup Gruyère cheese, freshly grated

Wine: a semisweet sparkling red (Brachetto d'Acqui)

Prepare the crêpes and set aside. • Cook the Swiss chard in a little salted, boiling water for 5 minutes. Drain, squeeze, and chop finely. • Sauté the garlic with the butter in a skillet until pale gold, then discard the garlic. • In the same skillet, sauté the chard with a pinch of salt for 5 minutes. • Prepare the béchamel. • Spread the Caprino on the crêpes and dust with a little nutmeg. • Place 2 tablespoons of Swiss chard on half of each crêpe. • Fold each crêpe in half and then in half again to form a triangle. • Grease an ovenproof dish and arrange the crêpes overlapping inside. • Pour the béchamel sauce over the top and sprinkle with the Gruyère. • Bake in a preheated oven at 350°F for 20–25 minutes. • Serve hot.

Serves: 6 · Prep: 30 min. + 1 hr for the crêpes · Cooking: 25 min. · Level: 2

CRESPELLE CON POLLO
Baked crêpes with chicken filling

☞ This is a good way to use up leftover roast chicken or the meat from a chicken used to make stock.

- 1 quantity Simple tomato sauce (see recipe, page 18)
- 1 quantity Crêpes (see recipe, page 185)
- ¼ cup butter
- 1 clove garlic, finely chopped
- 12 oz boiled or roast chicken meat, finely chopped
- ¾ cup freshly grated Parmesan cheese
- 2 tablespoons finely chopped parsley
- 2 eggs
  salt and freshly ground black pepper to taste

Wine: a light, dry white (Gavi)

Prepare the tomato sauce. • Prepare the crêpes • Melt the butter in a large skillet and add the garlic and chicken. Sauté over medium-high heat for 5 minutes, then add half the Parmesan, the parsley, and eggs. Cook for 2–3 minutes more, then remove from heat. Season with salt and pepper. • Spread 2–3 tablespoons of the filling on each crêpe. Roll them up loosely and place in a greased ovenproof dish. Pour the tomato sauce over the top and sprinkle with the remaining Parmesan. • Bake in a preheated oven at 400°F for 10 minutes, or until the topping is golden brown. Serve hot.

Serves: 4 · Prep: 20 min. + 1 hr for the crêpes · Cooking: 30 min. · Level: 2

CRESPELLE ALLA FIORENTINA
Florentine-style crêpes

- 1 quantity Crêpes (see recipe, page 185)
- 1 clove garlic, finely chopped
- ½ cup extra-virgin olive oil
- 1 lb spinach, boiled and chopped
  salt and freshly ground black pepper to taste
  pinch of nutmeg
- 4 oz fresh Ricotta cheese
- ½ cup freshly grated Parmesan cheese
- ½ cup all-purpose flour
- 2 cups milk

Wine: a light, dry white (Malvasia Istriana)

Prepare the crêpes • Sauté the garlic in half the oil. Add the spinach, salt, pepper, and a pinch of nutmeg. Remove from heat and mix with the Ricotta and half the Parmesan. • To make the sauce, heat the remaining oil, and add the flour, stirring constantly. Add the milk gradually, still stirring, until the mixture boils and thickens. Add a pinch each of salt, pepper, and nutmeg, and the remaining Parmesan. • Spread 2–3 tablespoons of the filling on each crêpe. Roll them up loosely and place in a lightly buttered ovenproof dish. Pour the sauce over the top. Bake in a preheated oven at 400°F until the top is golden. Serve hot.

Serves: 4 · Prep: 20 min. + 1 hr for the crêpes · Cooking: 20 min. · Level: 2

Crêpes with Swiss chard and Caprino

FISH & SEAFOOD

The Italian peninsula juts out into the Mediterranean Sea, and its many thousands of miles of coastline are plied by individual and commercial fishermen every day. Fish markets and seafood restaurants abound and seafood is an important part of the diet. Traditions linger too, and modern Italians, both practicing Catholics and non-believers, still expect to find fish on the menu on Fridays.

PALLE DI TONNO E RICOTTA
Fried tuna balls

12	oz fresh Ricotta cheese
10	oz canned tuna, drained
2	tablespoons finely chopped parsley + sprigs to garnish
1/4	cup freshly grated Parmesan cheese salt to taste
1	egg
1/2	cup all-purpose flour
2	cups oil, for frying

Wine: a dry white (Greco di Bianco)

Place the Ricotta in a large mixing bowl and mash well with a fork. • Use the fork to mash the tuna, breaking it into flakes. Add to the mixing bowl with the chopped parsley, Parmesan, salt, and egg. Mix until evenly blended. • Scoop up spoonfuls of the mixture with a dessert spoon and shape them into balls about the size of a golf ball. Roll the balls in the flour. • Heat the oil in a large skillet until very hot and fry the balls in batches of 6–8 for about 5 minutes each, turning constantly, until golden brown all over. • Remove from the skillet with a slotted spoon and drain on paper towels. • Garnish with the sprigs of parsley, sprinkle with extra salt, if liked, and serve immediately.

Serves: 4 · Prep: 15 min. · Cooking: 15 min. · Level: 2

◄ Roast grouper with potatoes (see recipe, page 214)
➤ Fried tuna balls

CLEANING FISH & SEAFOOD

Increasingly, the fish we buy is cleaned industrially and arrives at fish counters ready to cook. Even when it is fresh and whole, many fish stores and supermarkets have qualified people on hand to scale, gut, and fillet your fish before your eyes. However, there are times when you may have to do it yourself.

Cleaning octopus

Most of the octopus sold in North America and elsewhere today is already cleaned. If you do buy one that isn't, proceed as follows:

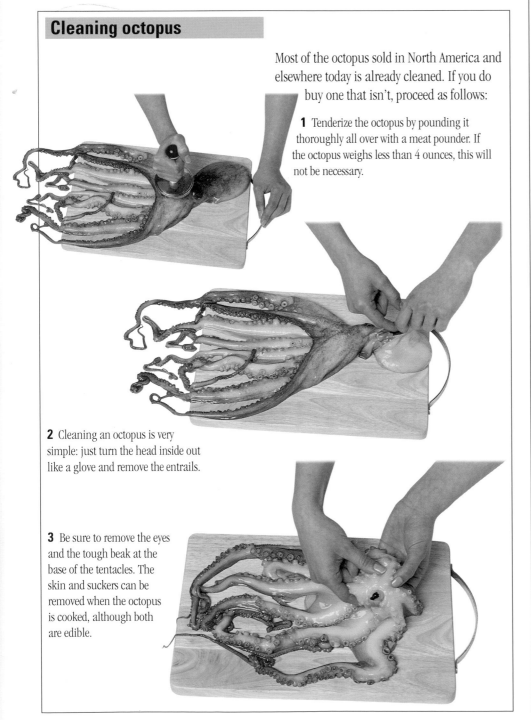

1 Tenderize the octopus by pounding it thoroughly all over with a meat pounder. If the octopus weighs less than 4 ounces, this will not be necessary.

2 Cleaning an octopus is very simple: just turn the head inside out like a glove and remove the entrails.

3 Be sure to remove the eyes and the tough beak at the base of the tentacles. The skin and suckers can be removed when the octopus is cooked, although both are edible.

Cleaning squid

Squid can be cleaned several hours ahead of use and stored in the refrigerator until you are ready to cook it.

1 Rinse the squid and lay it out on a clean work surface ready to begin.

2 Grasp the squid's head and pull it away. Most of the innards and the translucent quill will come away with it. Scrape the rest out with a blunt knife.

3 Cut the tentacles at the hard ball, or beak, just behind the squid's eyes. Discard the head.

4 Use your fingers to remove the mottled skin. It will come away easily in 2 or 3 pieces.

Cleaning whole fish

1 REMOVING THE FINS: Fins can be cut off with a pair of sharp, kitchen scissors. Pull the fin away from the body and snip it off.

2 SCALING: Use a fish scaler, spoon, or the back of a knife. Wet the fish, grip it firmly by the tail, and scrape upward from the tail with short strokes. Scaling can be messy; you may prefer to do it outside.

3 GUTTING: Use sharp kitchen scissors, or a small, sharp knife, and cut the fish, beginning at its vent, or anal opening, up to the gill openings.

4 (at left) Pull out the guts with your fingers, then scrape out the kidneys attached to the backbone. Discard the guts and rinse the fish.

5 (at right) GILLING: If serving a fish whole, or cooking in stock, you must cut out the bitter-tasting gills. To remove, lift the gill covers and cut the gills out with kitchen scissors or a knife.

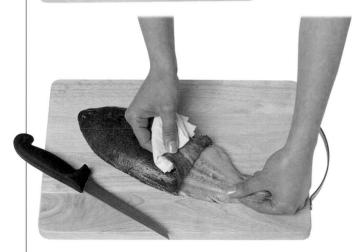

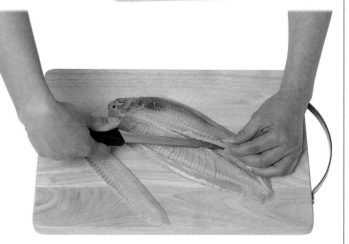

6 SKINNING: Make a small cut just above the tail. Lift the skin away from the flesh and pull upward from the tail. If the fish is fresh, the skin will come away easily. In many cases, skin should be left on the fish during cooking. It will help hold the delicate flesh together during cooking and is easy to remove when cooked.

7 FILLETING: Using the point of a sharp knife, feel for the central bone and run the knife along it for the length of the fish. Peel back the meat, pulling it gently away from the ribs.

Cleaning fresh anchovies and sardines

To remove the head, grasp it firmly and snap it off. As you pull it away, most of the innards will come away with it. Use a finger to remove any remaining entrails. Remove the backbone by grasping it between thumb and forefinger and carefully pulling it out of the fish.

ANGUILLA BRASATA
Stewed eel

☞ Eels are farmed in Italy, near the lagoons on the east coast from Venice southward, where they previously occurred naturally. Ask your fish vendor to skin the eel and cut its head off for you. If you must do it yourself, rub wood ash or coarse salt all over the skin to make it easier to hold.

- 2 lb eel
- 2 large onions, finely chopped
- 2 cloves garlic, finely chopped
- 2 tablespoons extra-virgin olive oil
- 2 tablespoons white wine vinegar
- 2 tablespoons tomato paste, diluted in 1 cup water
  salt and freshly ground black pepper to taste

Wine: a light, dry sparkling red (Lambrusco Mantovano)

Skin the eel. Cut off its head, and then draw it. • Sauté the onion and garlic in the oil until soft. • Add the vinegar, followed by the tomato paste diluted with water. Season with salt and pepper. Add the eel and cook over low heat for 30 minutes. Do not stir the eel while it cooks as the flesh breaks up very easily – simply shake the pan from side to side now and then to prevent it sticking. • Serve very hot.

Serves: 4 · Prep: 20 min. · Cooking: 35 min. · Level: 1

BACCALÀ CON PEPERONI
Salt cod with bell peppers

☞ Salt cod and stockfish, typically northern European dishes, are popular all over Italy. They were adopted centuries ago after trading contacts were established with Holland and Scandinavia. Be sure to buy salt cod or stockfish that is pre-soaked and ready to cook. To prepare it for cooking, remove the bones, rinse briefly, and pat dry with paper towels or a clean cloth.

- 1½ lb pre-soaked salt cod
- 2 cups oil, for frying
- ¾ cup all-purpose flour
- 1 large onion, finely chopped
- ¼ cup extra-virgin olive oil
- 1 (15 oz) can tomatoes
  salt and freshly ground black pepper to taste
- 3 large bell peppers, mixed colors

Wine: a dry white (Velletri Bianco)

Prepare the salt cod as explained above and cut it into bite-sized pieces. • Heat the frying oil in a large skillet until very hot. Flour the salt cod and fry in the oil until nicely browned and well cooked. Drain on paper towels and set aside in a warm oven. • Sauté the onion in the extra-virgin olive oil in a deep-sided skillet until soft. • Add the tomatoes and cook over medium heat for 15 minutes, or until the sauce reduces. Season with salt and pepper. • Clean the bell peppers, removing the seeds and cores. Cut into quarters and place under the broiler until the skin blackens. Remove the blackened skin with your fingers. Rinse the bell peppers and pat them dry. Cut into thin strips. • Add the bell peppers and salt cod to the skillet with the tomato sauce. Cook together for 5 minutes, then serve.

Serves: 4 · Prep: 15 min. · Cooking: 30 min. · Level: 1

BACCALÀ ALLA VICENTINA
Stockfish Vicenza-style

- 2 lb pre-soaked stockfish
- 1 lb onions, finely chopped
- 2 cloves garlic, finely chopped
- 1 cup extra-virgin olive oil
- 8 anchovy fillets
- 2 tablespoons finely chopped parsley
- ¾ cup all-purpose flour
- 1 cup freshly grated Parmesan cheese
  salt and freshly ground black pepper to taste
- 2½ cups milk

Wine: a dry white (Bianco di Breganze)

Remove the skin from the fish without breaking up the flesh. Carefully remove all the bones. • Sauté the onions and garlic in scant ½ cup of the oil. Add the anchovies and then the parsley. • Taking care to keep the fish in one piece, open out the sides a little and spoon the onion and anchovy mixture into the cavity. Sprinkle with a little of the flour and half the Parmesan, and season with salt and pepper. Gently press the fish closed again. • Slice across the length of the fish, cutting it into stuffed steaks about 2 inches wide. Coat these with the remaining flour and Parmesan. • Place the steaks snugly next to one another in a heavy-bottomed flameproof casserole just large enough to hold them in one layer. Pour the milk and remaining oil over the top. • Cook over low heat for at least 4 hours; they must not be stirred—just shake the casserole gently at intervals to prevent the fish from sticking. • Serve hot, or reheat the next day.

Serves: 6 · Prep: 30 min. · Cooking: 4¼ hrs · Level: 2

BACCALÀ ALLA CAPPUCCINA
Baked stockfish, old-fashioned style

☞ Another version of this recipe calls for the same quantity of stockfish, which is poached for 10 minutes, then flaked and mixed with extra-virgin olive oil, finely chopped garlic and parsley, salt, and pepper.

- 1½ lb pre-soaked stockfish or dried cod
- ¾ cup all-purpose flour
- 1 large red onion, finely chopped
- ½ cup extra-virgin olive oil
- 2 tablespoons butter
- 2 bay leaves
- 4 anchovy fillets
- 2 oz seedless white raisins, pre-soaked
- 2 oz pine nuts
- 2 teaspoons sugar
  pinch of cinnamon
  pinch of nutmeg
  salt and freshly ground black pepper to taste
- 1 cup fresh bread crumbs

Wine: a dry white (Colli Berici Chardonnay)

Cut the stockfish or dried cod into fairly small pieces and remove all the bones. Coat lightly with flour. • Sauté the onion in the oil and butter in a flameproof casserole until tender. • Add the fish and pour in sufficient water to cover it. Add the bay leaves, anchovies, white raisins, pine nuts, sugar, cinnamon, and nutmeg. • Simmer over medium heat until the fish has absorbed almost all the liquid. Season with salt and pepper. • Sprinkle with the bread crumbs and bake in a preheated oven at 350°F until a golden brown crust has formed on top. • Serve hot.

Serves: 6 · Prep: 20 min. · Cooking: 40 min. · Level: 2

BACCALÀ CON PATATE
Baked salt cod with potatoes

- ¼ cup extra-virgin olive oil
- 1½ lb pre-soaked salt cod, cut into pieces
- 1½ lb potatoes, cut into fairly large cubes
- 2 tablespoons finely chopped parsley
- 2 medium onions, thinly sliced
- 2 cloves garlic, finely chopped
- 1 teaspoon dried oregano
  salt and freshly ground black pepper to taste
- ¼ cup fine dry bread crumbs

Wine: a dry white (Trebbiano d'Abruzzo)

Grease a large shallow ovenproof dish with 2 tablespoons of the oil. • Arrange the pieces of cod in the dish in a single layer and cover with the potatoes. • Sprinkle with the parsley, onion, garlic, oregano, a little salt, and a generous sprinkling of pepper. Sprinkle with the bread crumbs and drizzle with the remaining oil. • Bake in a preheated oven at 350°F for 45 minutes, or until the potatoes and fish are tender.

Serves: 4 · Prep: 15 min. · Cooking: 45 min. · Level: 1

BACCALÀ ALLA FIORENTINA
Salt cod, Florentine-style

- 2   lb salt cod, pre-soaked
- 2   tablespoons all-purpose flour
- 1/3 cup extra-virgin olive oil
- 1   small onion, thinly sliced
- 2   cloves garlic, whole
- 1   (15 oz) can tomatoes, drained
      salt and freshly ground
      black pepper to taste
- 1/4 cup dry white wine
- 2   tablespoons finely chopped parsley

Wine: a dry white (Bianco Vergine di Valdichiana)

Cut the salt cod into bite-sized pieces. Rinse well under cold running water and dry with paper towels. • Sprinkle with flour, shaking off any excess. • Heat half the oil in a large skillet over medium heat and sauté the onion and garlic for about 5 minutes, or until soft. • Discard the garlic. Add the tomatoes to the skillet and season with salt and pepper. Cook for 15 minutes, or until the sauce reduces. • Meanwhile, in another skillet, heat the remaining oil and fry the pieces of salt cod over medium heat until crisp and nicely browned. Drizzle with the wine while frying. Drain on paper towels. • Clean the oil from the skillet and put the salt cod back into it. Pour the tomato sauce over the top, sprinkle with the parsley, and cover. Cook over medium-low heat for 5 more minutes, then serve.

Serves:4 · Prep: 15 min. · Cooking: 25 min. · Level: 1

PURÉE DI STOCCAFISSO
Stockfish cream

- 2   lb pre-soaked stockfish
- 1   cup extra-virgin olive oil
      salt and freshly ground black pepper to taste
- 2   cloves garlic, finely chopped
- 2   tablespoons finely chopped parsley

Wine: a dry white (Est! Est!! Est!!! di Montefiascone)

Put the stockfish in a large saucepan with enough cold water to cover and place over

medium heat. When it comes to a boil, turn off the heat. • Leave to stand in the water for 20 minutes and then drain. Remove the skin and take care to remove not only the large bones but all the very small ones as well. • Break up into small pieces and transfer to a large mixing bowl. Beat vigorously and continuously with a balloon whisk as you gradually add the oil in a steady trickle. • Keep stirring or beating in the same direction and adding oil until the fish will absorb no more. The mixture should be light and fluffy like a mousse. Add a little salt, if needed, and season generously with pepper. Stir in the garlic and parsley. • Serve at room temperature.

Serves: 6 · Prep: 10 min. + 20 min. to stand · Cooking: 10 min. · Level: 3

STOCCAFISSO ALLA SICILIANA
Stockfish Sicilian-style

- 1 1/2 lb pre-soaked stockfish, bones and fins removed
- 1/2 cup extra-virgin olive oil
- 1   medium onion, finely chopped
- 1   whole clove garlic, lightly crushed
- 2   tablespoons all-purpose flour
      salt and freshly ground black pepper to taste
- 14 oz fresh or canned tomatoes, peeled and chopped

Stockfish cream

- 1 1/4 lb potatoes, peeled and sliced about 1/4 inch thick
- 2   slightly underripe pears, peeled, cored, and sliced
- 5   oz green olives, pitted
- 2   small, tender stalks celery, sliced
- 2   tablespoons capers
- 3   tablespoons pine nuts
- 3   tablespoons seedless white raisins, soaked and drained

Wine: a dry white (Alcamo)

Rinse the stockfish and dry with paper towels. Cut into pieces roughly 3 inches square. • Pour the oil into a flameproof casserole dish and sauté the onion and garlic. Do not let them color. • Coat the pieces of stockfish lightly with flour and cook for a few minutes over a slightly higher heat, turning them once. • Season with a little salt and pepper. • Add the tomatoes and sufficient hot water to just cover the fish. • Cover the casserole and simmer over medium heat for 45 minutes. • Add the potatoes, pears, olives, celery, capers, pine nuts, and raisins. • Stir carefully, cover, and cook for another 40 minutes. • There should be plenty of liquid left when the fish is cooked. If not, moisten with hot water as necessary.

Serves: 4 · Prep: 10 min. · Cooking: 1 1/2 hrs · Level: 2

Mussel stew

juices in the skillet. • Sauté two-thirds of the onion in the skillet until soft. • Place the clams in a large skillet over high heat until they are all open. Discard any that do not open. • Strain the juices the clams produce while cooking and reserve. Take the clams out of their shells and add to the skillet with the onion and half the butter. Cook over low heat for 10 minutes, stirring often. • Remove the clams with a slotted spoon and set aside. Pour the stock and cooking juices from the clams into the skillet and cook for 5 minutes. • Heat the milk and pour over the toasted bread. • Butter an ovenproof dish and cover the bottom with a layer of clams. Cover with a layer of bread and pork, and season with salt and pepper. Repeat until all the clams, bread, and pork are in the dish. Cover with slices of potato and sprinkle with the parsley. • Pour the stock and cooking juices over the top. Sprinkle with the bread crumbs and bake in a preheated oven at 350° for 1 hour. Serve hot.

Serves: 4 · Prep: 20 min. + 1 hr to soak clams · Cooking: 1¹/₂ hrs · Level: 1

CANNOLICCHI AL VINO BIANCO
Razor clams in white wine

2 lb razor clams, in shell
¹/₄ cup extra-virgin olive oil
6 cloves garlic, finely chopped
¹/₄ cup finely chopped parsley
4 plum tomatoes, peeled and chopped
salt to taste
¹/₂ cup dry white wine

Wine: a dry white (Sangioveto di Coltibuono)

Soak the clams in cold water for 1 hour, then rinse thoroughly in cold running water. • Place the clams in a large skillet over medium-high heat for about 10 minutes, or until they are all open. Discard any that have not opened. • Lay a piece of muslin over a bowl and filter the cooking juices through it. • Wash the skillet in which the razor clams were steamed, pour in the oil and sauté the garlic and parsley for 5 minutes over medium heat. • Add the tomatoes and razor clams and season with

salt. Pour in the wine and cook for 10 minutes. • Serve hot.

Serves: 4 · Prep: 20 min. + 1 hr to soak clams · Cooking: 25 min. · Level: 1

VONGOLE AL FORNO CON PATATE
Baked clams with potatoes

2¹/₂ lb large clams, in shell
2 tablespoons extra-virgin olive oil
6 oz finely ground lean pork
1¹/₂ medium onions, finely chopped
¹/₄ cup butter
¹/₂ cup Beef stock (see recipe, page 105)
¹/₂ cup milk
8 thin slices firm-textured bread, toasted
salt and freshly ground black pepper to taste
4 medium potatoes, boiled and sliced
1 tablespoon finely chopped parsley
¹/₂ cup fine dry bread crumbs

Wine: a dry rosé (Cerasuolo d'Abruzzo)

Soak the clams in cold water for 1 hour, then rinse thoroughly in cold running water. • Heat the oil in a medium skillet and cook the pork over medium heat for 10 minutes. Remove the pork with a slotted spoon and set aside, leaving the cooking

ZUPPA DI COZZE
Mussel stew

3 lb fresh mussels in shell
¹/₄ cup extra-virgin olive oil
4 medium tomatoes, peeled and chopped
3 tablespoons finely chopped parsley
3 cloves garlic, finely chopped
salt and freshly ground black pepper to taste
4 large, thick slices of bread, toasted and, if liked, rubbed with garlic

Wine: a dry white (Greco di Tufo)

Scrub the mussels well to remove their beards and rinse thoroughly under cold running water. Soak in cold water for 1 hour. • Heat the oil in a large, deep-sided skillet and add the tomatoes, 2 tablespoons of parsley, and 2 cloves of garlic. Sauté over medium-high heat for 2–3 minutes. Add the mussels and cook until they are all open. Discard any that do not open. • Sprinkle with the remaining parsley and garlic. Season with salt and pepper and cook for 4–5 minutes more. • Arrange the toasted bread in individual serving dishes and spoon the mussels and the cooking juices over the top. Serve hot.

Serves: 4 · Prep: 10 min. + 1 hr to soak clams · Cooking: 5 min. · Level: 1

VONGOLE ALLA NAPOLETANA
Clams sautéed in tomatoes

- 2 lb clams, in shell
- 1/4 cup extra-virgin olive oil
- 4 cloves garlic, finely chopped
- 1 (15 oz) can Italian tomatoes
- 2 tablespoons finely chopped parsley
  salt and freshly ground black pepper to taste

Wine: a dry white (Capri Bianco)

Soak the clams in cold water for 1 hour, then rinse thoroughly in cold running water. • Heat half the oil in a large skillet and sauté the garlic until it begins to color. Add the clams and cook over medium high heat until they are all open. Discard any that have not opened. • Remove the clams and juices from the skillet and set aside to cool. • Heat the remaining oil in the same skillet and add the tomatoes and parsley. Season with salt and pepper. Cook over medium heat for 10–15 minutes, or until the sauce reduces. • Meanwhile, discard the half of each clam shell that does not contain a clam. • Return the clams to the skillet with the sauce and cook for 4–5 minutes more. • Serve hot.

Serves: 4 · Prep: 15 min. + 1 hr to soak clams · Cooking: 20 min. · Level: 1

SCAMPI ALLA GRIGLIA
Broiled or barbecued shrimp

- 2 lb large shrimp
- 1/2 cup extra-virgin olive oil
  salt and freshly ground black pepper to taste
- 1 teaspoon red pepper flakes (optional)
- 2 tablespoons finely chopped parsley
- 2 cloves garlic, finely chopped
  juice of 1 lemon

Wine: a dry white (Bianco d'Italia)

Use a sharp knife to open the shrimps up a little along their backs. • Lay them out on a large plate and drizzle with the oil. Season with salt, pepper, and red pepper flakes, if using. • Place the shrimp under the broiler, in a very hot grill pan, or over the glowing embers of a barbecue. • Cook for 2–3 minutes on each side. •

Clams with white wine

Place on a serving platter and sprinkle with the parsley, garlic, and lemon juice. Serve hot.

Serves: 4 · Prep: 10 min. · Cooking: 5 min. · Level: 1

VONGOLE AL VINO BIANCO
Clams with white wine

- 4 lb fresh clams, in shell
- 3/4 cup extra-virgin olive oil
- 2 medium onions, finely chopped
- 1 cup dry white wine
- 1/4 cup boiling water
  salt and freshly ground black pepper to taste
- 2 tablespoons finely chopped parsley
- 1 clove garlic, finely chopped (optional)

Wine: a dry white (Tocai Friuliano del Collio)

Soak the clams in cold water for 1 hour, then rinse thoroughly in cold running water. • Heat the oil in a large skillet and sauté the onions until light gold. • Add the clams, followed by the wine and then the water. Season with salt and pepper. Cover tightly and simmer over low heat for 15

minutes. • By this time the clams should have opened. Discard any that have not opened. • Sprinkle with parsley and garlic, if using, and serve.

Serves: 6 · Prep: 20 min. + 1 hr to soak clams · Cooking: 15 min. · Level: 1

SCAMPI PICCANTI IN PADELLA
Spicy braised shrimp with orange

- 2 lb large shrimp
- 1/2 cup extra-virgin olive oil
- 4 cloves garlic, finely chopped
  zest of 1 orange (orange part only), finely chopped
- 1–2 spicy chile peppers, finely chopped
  salt and freshly ground black pepper to taste
- 2 tablespoons finely chopped parsley

Wine: a dry white (Bianco d'Italia)

Peel the shrimp. • Heat the oil in a large skillet and add 3 cloves of garlic, the orange zest, and chile peppers. Sauté over medium-high heat until the garlic is light gold. • Add the shrimps and cook for about 2 minutes on each side. • Sprinkle with salt and pepper and add the parsley and remaining garlic. Remove from heat and serve.

Serves: 4 · Prep: 10 min. · Cooking: 5 min. · Level: 1

Fried calamari and shrimp

season with salt and pepper. Sprinkle with the parsley and bread crumbs. • Bake in a preheated oven at 350°F for 15 minutes. • Serve hot or at room temperature.

Serves: 4 · Prep: 15 min. · Cooking: 15 min. · Level: 1

GAMBERETTI E CALAMARI FRITTI
Fried calamari and shrimp

1	lb fresh or frozen (thawed) calamari rings
3/4	lb small shrimp tails
2	cups oil, for frying
1	cup all-purpose flour
	salt to taste

Wine: a dry white (Vermentino)

Rinse the calamari rings and shrimp under cold running water and dry well with paper towels. • Heat the oil in a large skillet until very hot. • Dredge the calamari and shrimp in the flour and fry in batches until pale golden brown. Scoop out the first batch and drain on paper towels. Clean the oil by scooping out any pieces of fish and fry the next batch. • When all the calamari and squid are fried, sprinkle with salt, and serve immediately.

Serves: 6 · Prep: 20 min. · Cooking: 20–30 min. · Level: 2

SARDE ALLA SICILIANA
Sicilian-style stuffed sardine rolls

1 3/4	lb fresh or frozen (thawed) large sardines
1/2	cup extra-virgin olive oil
1 3/4	cups fresh bread crumbs
10	anchovy fillets
3	tablespoons seedless white raisins, soaked and drained
3	tablespoons pine nuts
1	tablespoon capers
6	large black olives, pitted and chopped
1	tablespoon finely chopped parsley
1	tablespoon lemon juice
	finely grated zest of 1/2 lemon
1	teaspoon sugar
	salt and freshly ground black pepper to taste
2	bay leaves

Wine: a dry white (Bianco di Donnafugata)

Scale the sardines and remove the heads and viscera. Use kitchen scissors to slit them along their bellies, remove the bones, and open them out flat. Rinse and dry with paper towels. • Heat 1/4 cup of the oil in a large skillet over medium heat and add two-thirds of the bread crumbs. Stir for 1–2 minutes, then set aside in a mixing bowl. • Pour 1 tablespoon of fresh oil into the skillet and add the anchovies, crushing them with a fork over a low heat so that they turn into a paste. • Stir into the bread crumbs, followed by the raisins, pine nuts, capers, olives, parsley, lemon juice and zest, sugar, a little salt and a generous sprinkling of pepper. Mix well. •

Lay the sardines out flat, skin side downward, and spread some of the mixture on each. • Roll the sardines up, starting at the head end, and place in an oiled ovenproof dish. Pack them closely together, tail downward, and wedge a bay leaf between each one. • Sprinkle with the remaining bread crumbs and drizzle with the remaining oil. • Bake in a preheated oven at 400°F for 20–25 minutes. • Serve hot or at room temperature.

Serves: 4 · Prep: 30 min. · Cooking: 25 min. · Level: 2

SARDE AL FORNO
Baked fresh sardines

☞ Sardines are common in the Mediterranean and are widely used in all its cuisines. Excellent Atlantic or Spanish sardines are sold fresh in American markets. Their delicious, rich, yet muted flavor makes them ideal for baking or broiling.

1 1/2	lb fresh large sardines, filleted
1/4	cup extra-virgin olive oil
	juice of 1 lemon
	salt and freshly ground black pepper to taste
1/4	cup finely chopped parsley
1/2	cup fine dry bread crumbs

Wine: a dry white (Trebbiano di Romagna)

If the sardines are not already cleaned and filleted, see the instructions on page 201. • Place the fillets in a large ovenproof dish. Drizzle with the oil and lemon juice and

SARDONI ALLA GRECA
Baked sardine fillets

☞ Despite its Italian name ("alla greca," means Greek style), this is a Venetian dish.

2	lb fresh large sardines, filleted
	salt to taste
1/2	cup extra-virgin olive oil
2	tablespoons finely chopped parsley
1	clove garlic, finely chopped
1/2	cup white wine vinegar
	juice of 2 lemons

Wine: a dry white (Croara)

If the sardines are not already cleaned and filleted, see the instructions on page 201. • Roll up each fillet, starting with the broader, head end, and arrange them snugly in a single layer in a lightly oiled ovenproof dish. • Sprinkle with salt, oil, parsley, and garlic. • Drizzle with the vinegar and lemon juice and bake in a preheated oven at 400°F for 20 minutes. • Serve hot or at room temperature.

Serves: 6 · Prep: 20 min. · Cooking: 20 min. · Level: 1

SARDELLE IN SAOR
Venetian-style sardines

- 2 lb fresh large sardines, cleaned and gutted
- 1 cup all-purpose flour
- 2 cups oil, for frying
  salt to taste
- 1/2 cup extra-virgin olive oil
- 1 3/4 lb white onions, thinly sliced
- 1 1/4 cups white wine vinegar

Wine: a dry white (Sauvignon dei Colli Berici)

If the sardines are not already cleaned, see the instructions on page 201. • Rinse the sardines in cold running water and dry with paper towels. Dust lightly with flour. • Heat the frying oil to very hot in a large skillet and fry the sardines, a few at a time, until golden brown. Drain on paper towels and sprinkle lightly with salt. • Remove the skillet from heat and carefully pour off the oil. • Heat the olive oil in the same skillet and sauté the onions until pale golden brown. Pour in the vinegar, cook until well reduced, then remove from heat. • Place the sardines in layers in a deep dish, alternating with the onions. Finish with a layer of onions and pour the vinegar mixture over the top. • Refrigerate the dish for 24 hours before serving.

Serves: 6 · Prep: 20 min. + 24 hrs to marinate · Cooking: 20 min. · Level: 1

ACCIUGHE ALLA MENTA
Anchovies with mint

☞ Anchovies have a slightly more delicate flavor than sardines. This dish can be prepared ahead of time and chilled in the refrigerator.

- 1 cup all-purpose flour
- 2 lb fresh small anchovies, heads cut off
- 2 cups oil, for frying
  salt to taste
- 2 tablespoons extra-virgin olive oil
- 2 cloves garlic, finely chopped
- 1/2 cup white wine vinegar
- 2 tablespoons coarsely chopped mint

Wine: a dry white (Cervaro della Sala)

Place the flour in a large dish and flour the anchovies. • Heat the frying oil to very hot in a large skillet and fry the anchovies in batches until golden brown. Drain on paper towels. Sprinkle lightly with salt. • Remove the skillet from heat and carefully pour off the oil. • Heat the olive oil in the same skillet and sauté the garlic

for 2 minutes. Pour in the vinegar and cook for 5 minutes more. Add the mint and remove from heat. • Place the anchovies in a large serving dish and pour the vinegar and mint liquid over the top. Refrigerate for at least 3 hours before serving.

Serves: 4 · Prep: 20 min. + 3 hrs to marinate · Cooking: 20 min. · Level: 1

GRIGLIATA MISTA DI PESCE
Mixed grilled seafood

☞ Grill the seafood outdoors on your barbecue. Be sure to buy only the freshest fish; the best way to tell if it is fresh is by smelling it. Very fresh fish and seafood has almost no odor.

- 4 fillets fresh sole, about 5 oz each
- 8 large fresh shrimp tails
- 4 fillets monkfish
- 8 medium squid, cleaned
- 1/4 cup extra-virgin olive oil
- 1/4 cup fine dry bread crumbs
- 2 tablespoons finely chopped parsley
  salt and freshly ground black pepper to taste
- 1 lemon, cut in wedges

Wine: a dry white (Soave Classico Superiore)

If the seafood is not already cleaned and prepared, see the instructions on pages 200–201. Rinse carefully in cold running water and dry with paper towels. • Place the sole, shrimp, monkfish, and squid on a large tray and drizzle with half the oil. Sprinkle with the bread crumbs. • Grill over the glowing embers of a barbecue for

10 minutes, basting often with a basting brush dipped in the remaining oil. Turn the seafood and cook the other sides, basting frequently. • When the fish is tender and well cooked, place on a large heated serving platter. Sprinkle with the parsley, season with salt and pepper, and arrange the lemon wedges around the edges.

Serves: 4 · Prep: 20 min. · Cooking: 20 min. · Level: 2

POLPI DI SANTA LUCIA
Baby octopus, Neapolitan-style

- 1 1/2 lb baby octopus, cleaned
- 1/4 cup extra-virgin olive oil
- 1/2 cup dry white wine
  salt and freshly ground black pepper to taste
- 4 large ripe tomatoes, peeled and chopped
- 2 tablespoons finely chopped parsley
- 2 cloves garlic, finely chopped

Wine: a dry white (Bianco d'Ischia)

If the baby octopuses are not already cleaned, see the instructions on page 200. Rinse well under cold running water and dry with paper towels. • Heat the oil in a large skillet and sauté the octopuses for 5 minutes over high heat. • Pour in the wine and cook until it evaporates. Season with salt and pepper and add the tomatoes. Cover the pan and cook over low heat for about 1 1/2 hours. • Sprinkle with the parsley and garlic just before serving.

Serves: 4 · Prep: 20 min. · Cooking: 1 3/4 hrs · Level: 1

Anchovies with mint

Plaice rolls with peas

CANNOLI DI PLATESSA CON PISELLI
Plaice rolls with peas

- 4 plaice or flounder fillets, about 8 oz each
- 1/4 cup extra-virgin olive oil
- 1 onion, finely chopped
- 2 cloves garlic, finely chopped
- 6 basil leaves, torn
- 2 bay leaves
- 4 large tomatoes, peeled and finely chopped
  salt and freshly ground black pepper to taste
- 1 lb fresh or frozen peas
- 1/4 cup all-purpose flour
- 2 tablespoons butter
- 4 sage leaves, chopped

Wine: a dry white (Traminer Aromatico)

Wash the plaice under cold running water and dry with paper towels. Cut each fillet in half lengthwise. • Heat the oil in a large skillet and sauté the onion, garlic, basil, and bay leaves. After about 5 minutes, add the tomatoes and season with salt and pepper. Cover and cook for 5 minutes. • Add the peas to the skillet and cook for 15 minutes. • While the peas are cooking, roll up the plaice fillets, securing them with wooden toothpicks. Sprinkle with flour. • Melt the butter in a skillet with the sage. Add the rolled-up plaice fillets and brown gently for 5 minutes. • Remove from heat and transfer to the pan with the peas. Add a little water if necessary. Season with salt and pepper. Cover the skillet and cook over low heat for 10 minutes. Serve hot.

Serves: 4 · Prep: 15 min. · Cooking: 40 min. · Level: 2

CALAMARI PICCANTI
Spicy calamari stew

☞ Calamari, also known as squid or inkfish, is delicious, inexpensive, and very low in fat. It is also versatile and easy to cook. The chile in this recipe enhances the sweet, nutty flavor of the calamari.

- 1 1/2 lb calamari, cleaned
- 1/4 cup extra-virgin olive oil
- 1/2 small onion, finely chopped
- 2 cloves garlic, finely chopped
- 2 tablespoons finely chopped parsley
- 2 tender stalks celery, trimmed and very thinly sliced
- 1/2 cup dry white wine
- 4 small tomatoes, peeled and coarsely chopped
- 10 green olives, pitted and coarsely chopped
- 1 tablespoon capers

- 1 dried chile pepper, seeded and crumbled
  salt to taste

Wine: a dry white (Erbaluce di Caluso)

If the calamari are not already cleaned, see the instructions on page 200. Chop coarsely with a sharp knife. • Heat the oil in a large skillet and sauté the onion, garlic, parsley, and celery until soft. • Add the calamari and cook for 2–3 minutes, then pour in the wine. Cover and simmer over low heat for 15–20 minutes. If the skillet becomes dry during cooking, add more wine or a few tablespoons of water. • Stir in the tomatoes, olives, capers, chile pepper, and salt. • Cover and simmer gently for 30 more minutes, or until the calamari is very tender. • Serve hot or at room temperature.

Serves: 4 · Prep: 20 min. · Cooking: 1 hr · Level: 1

SEPPIE RIPIENE AL POMODORO
Filled squid in tomato sauce

- 1 lb small squid, tentacles removed
- 1 cup soft white bread, crusts removed
- 1 cup milk
- 2 tablespoons finely chopped parsley
- 2 cloves garlic, finely chopped
- 1/4 cup freshly grated Parmesan cheese
- 1 egg, beaten
- 2 sage leaves, finely chopped
- 1 small sprig rosemary, finely chopped
- 1 bay leaf, finely chopped
- 1 tablespoon lemon juice
- 1/4 cup extra-virgin olive oil
  salt and freshly ground black pepper to taste
- 1 quantity Simple tomato sauce (see recipe, page 18)
- 1/2 cup dry white wine

Wine: a dry white (Pomino Bianco)

If the squid are not already cleaned, see the instructions on page 200. • Soften the bread in the milk and drain, squeezing out excess moisture. • Finely chop one squid and place in a bowl with the bread, parsley, garlic, Parmesan, and egg, and mix well with a fork. • Stuff the squid with the mixture and secure the openings with toothpicks. • Place in large ovenproof dish in a single layer. Sprinkle with the sage, rosemary, bay leaf, the remaining garlic, lemon juice, oil, and a little salt. Set aside for 1 hour. • Prepare the tomato sauce. • Bake the squid in a preheated oven at 400° for 10 minutes. • Pour in the wine and season with salt and pepper. Add the tomato sauce and return to the oven at 300°F for 20 minutes. Serve hot.

Serves: 4 · Prep: 20 min. + 1 hr to rest and to make the sauce · Cooking: 30 min. · Level: 2

SEPPIE IN ZIMINO
Squid with spinach

- 1¼ lb small squid
- 1¼ lb fresh spinach
- ¼ cup extra-virgin olive oil
- 1 small onion, finely chopped
- 2 cloves garlic, finely chopped
- 1 small carrot, finely chopped
- 1 small stalk celery, finely chopped
- 2 tablespoons finely chopped parsley
- 2 dried chile peppers, crumbled
  salt and freshly ground black pepper to taste
- ½ cup dry white wine
- 1 (15 oz) can Italian tomatoes, chopped

Wine: a dry rosé (Rosato di Nardò)

If the squid are not already cleaned, see the instructions on page 200. Chop coarsely with a sharp knife. • Wash the spinach under cold running water and boil in a little salted water for about 10 minutes. Drain well, squeeze out excess moisture, and chop coarsely. • Heat the oil in a large skillet and sauté the onion, garlic, carrot, celery, parsley, and chile peppers for 4–5 minutes. • Add the squid, season with salt and pepper, and pour in the wine. Cook uncovered for 5 minutes to reduce. • Add the spinach and cook for 3–4 minutes, then add the tomatoes. Season with salt and pepper, mix well, cover, and leave to simmer for 30 minutes, stirring occasionally. • Serve hot or at room temperature.

Serves: 4 · Prep: 25 min. · Cooking: 1 hr · Level: 2

SEPPIE COL NERO
Squid cooked in its ink

- 2 lb small squid
- ½ cup extra-virgin olive oil
- 1 small onion, finely chopped
- 2 cloves garlic, finely chopped
- 1 cup dry white wine
  salt and freshly ground black pepper to taste

Wine: a dry white (Riesling Renano di Aquileia)

If the squid are not already cleaned, see the instructions on page 200. Be sure to reserve the ink sacs. • Cut the bodies into ½-inch wide strips. Open 4 or 5 of the ink sacs and pour the ink into a cup. • Heat the oil in a large skillet and sauté the

Filled squid in tomato sauce

onion and garlic until pale golden brown. • Add the squid and cook for a few minutes. Drizzle with the wine and cook until it has evaporated. • Dilute the ink with 2–3 tablespoons of hot water and add to the saucepan. Stir briefly, then cover and simmer over low heat for 40 minutes. • Stir gently from time to time and moisten with 2–3 tablespoons of hot water if necessary. • Add salt and pepper when the squid are done. • Serve hot.

Serves: 4 · Prep: 25 min. · Cooking: 50 min. · Level: 1

SEPPIE RIPIENE AL FORNO
Baked stuffed squid

- 1½ lb medium squid
- ¼ cup extra-virgin olive oil
- 3 cloves garlic, finely chopped
- 1 tablespoon finely chopped parsley
- 6 oz ground pork
  salt and freshly ground black pepper to taste
- 1 cup dry white wine
- 2 eggs, beaten
- ¼ cup freshly grated Parmesan cheese
- 1 tablespoon freshly grated Pecorino cheese
- 2 tablespoons fine dry bread crumbs
- 10 oz firm, ripe tomatoes, peeled, seeded, and diced

Wine: a dry white (Isonzo Traminer Aromatico)

If the squid are not already cleaned, see the instructions on page 200. Chop the tentacles coarsely and leave the bodies whole. • Heat half the oil in a large skillet and sauté half the garlic and parsley over medium heat until soft. • Add the pork and tentacles and cook for 5 minutes over medium heat, stirring frequently. Season with salt and pepper, pour in the wine, and allow to evaporate. • Remove from heat, add the eggs, Parmesan, Pecorino, and bread crumbs, and mix well. • Stuff the squid with this mixture, securing with toothpicks. • Heat the remaining oil in the same skillet and sauté the remaining parsley and garlic with the stuffed squid for 5 minutes. • Add the tomatoes, and check the seasoning. • Transfer to an oveproof dish and bake in a preheated oven at 375°F for 30 minutes. • Serve hot.

Serves: 4 · Prep: 30 min. · Cooking: 1 hr · Level: 2

TORTA DI PESCE
Sweet and sour seafood pasta pie

☞ This unusual sweet and sour dish comes from the coastal town of Gaeta in southern Lazio, where centuries of trade with the Middle East have left their mark on the local cuisine.

- 1/2 oz fresh yeast or 1 (1/4 oz) package active dried yeast
- 1 teaspoon sugar
- 3/4 cup warm water
- 3 cups + 2 tablespoons all-purpose flour
- 1 teaspoon salt
- 1/2 cup extra-virgin olive oil
- 3 cloves garlic, finely chopped
- 1 lb squid, coarsely chopped
- 4 ripe tomatoes, peeled and diced
- 1 1/2 cups pitted black olives
- 1/4 cup golden raisins
- 1/4 cup pine nuts
- 1/4 cup capers
  salt and freshly ground black pepper to taste

Wine: a dry, fruity white (Cerveteri Bianco)

Use the first 3 ingredients to prepare the yeast mixture as explained on page 24. • Sift the flour into a large mixing bowl with the salt. Make a well in the center and pour in the yeast liquid, 3 tablespoons of oil, and most of the remaining water. • Stir with a wooden spoon until the flour has been absorbed. Add a little more warm water if necessary. • Place the dough on a floured work surface and knead until soft and elastic. • Shape into a ball and place in a large bowl. Cover with a large clean cloth and leave to rise in a warm place for 1 hour. • Heat the oil in a large skillet and sauté the garlic for 2–3 minutes. Add the squid and cook over medium heat, stirring frequently, for 15 minutes. • Stir in the remaining ingredients and cook for 5 more minutes. Season with salt and pepper. • Knead the dough briefly on a lightly floured surface. Divide into two portions, one almost twice as large as the other. Roll the larger piece of dough out to about 1/8 inch thick. Use it to line a 10-inch springform pan. Leave enough dough to slightly overlap the edges. • Fill the pan with the squid mixture. • Roll out the smaller piece of dough to the same thickness as the first and use it to cover the springform pan. Fold the overlapping dough over the top to seal. • Bake in a preheated oven at 400°F for 30 minutes. • Serve hot.

Serves: 4 · Prep: 25 min. + 1 hr for the dough to rise · Cooking: 1 hr · Level: 2

TONNO ALLA GRIGLIA
Grilled tuna steaks

☞ Fresh tuna steaks are especially suitable for the barbecue. If the weather is not right for outdoor grilling, cook them in a heavy, ridged grill pan or under the broiler.

- 4 tuna steaks, about 8 oz each
- 1/2 cup extra-virgin olive oil
- 2 tablespoons finely chopped fresh oregano
- 2 tablespoons lemon juice
  salt and freshly ground black pepper to taste

Wine: a dry white (Cirò Bianco)

Rinse the tuna steaks and dry on paper towels. • Mix the oil, oregano, lemon juice, salt, and pepper together in a bowl and pour over the steaks. Set aside to marinate for 30 minutes. • Take the steaks out of the marinade just before they are to be cooked. • Heat the broiler, grill pan, or barbecue to very hot and cook the steaks for 4–5 minutes each side. While they are cooking, especially if you are barbecuing them, baste often with the marinade.

Serves: 4 · Prep: 5 min. + 30 min. to marinate · Cooking: 8–10 min. · Level: 2

PESCE SPADA ALLA SICILIANA
Sicilian-style swordfish

- 1 cup extra-virgin olive oil
- 1/3 cup hot water
- 1/2 cup lemon juice
- 2 tablespoons finely chopped parsley
- 2 cloves garlic, finely chopped
- 2 tablespoons finely chopped fresh oregano
  salt and freshly ground black pepper to taste
- 6 steaks or slices swordfish, about 8 oz each

Wine: a dry white (Donnafugata Bianco)

Pour half the oil into a small blender and gradually add the hot water and lemon juice, processing continuously. • Pour into a small heatproof bowl. Stir in the parsley, garlic, oregano, salt, and pepper. • Place the bowl in a pan of boiling water for 3–4 minutes to heat. • Coat the swordfish steaks with the remaining oil and broil or barbecue for 4–5 minutes on each side. • Serve hot, with the heated sauce passed separately.

Serves: 6 · Prep: 10 min. · Cooking: 8–10 min. · Level: 1

TONNO CON POMODORO
Fresh tuna with tomatoes and oregano

- 1 lb fresh or canned tomatoes, peeled and chopped
- 2 cloves garlic, finely chopped
- 1 tablespoon capers
- 2 tablespoons finely chopped fresh oregano
  salt and freshly ground black pepper to taste
- 4 slices fresh tuna, about 6 oz each
- 1/2 cup extra-virgin olive oil

Wine: a dry white (Pinot Bianco Trentino)

Put the tomatoes in a mixing bowl with the garlic, capers, oregano, a pinch of salt, and a generous sprinkling of pepper. • Rinse the tuna and dry with paper towels. • Pour half the oil into a wide ovenproof dish and arrange the tuna slices in a single layer. • Cover with the tomato mixture and drizzle with the remaining oil. Cook in a preheated oven at 350°F for 30 minutes. Serve hot.

Serves: 4 · Prep: 10 min. · Cooking: 30 min. · Level: 1

PESCE SPADA CON RUCOLA
Swordfish steaks with arugula and basil sauce

- 4 steaks swordfish, cut 1/2 inch thick, about 8 oz each
  salt and freshly ground black pepper to taste
- 1/2 cup extra-virgin olive oil
- 2 cloves garlic, finely chopped
- 1 tablespoon finely chopped parsley
- 12 basil leaves, torn
- 1 bunch arugula (rocket), coarsely chopped
  juice of 1 lemon

Wine: a dry white (Ischia Bianco)

Rinse and dry the swordfish steaks without removing the skins. Place on a plate and sprinkle with salt and pepper. Drizzle with the oil, coating both sides, and set aside. • Heat a grill pan (or broiler or barbecue). Cook the swordfish steaks for 15 minutes, turning twice. • Put the garlic, parsley, basil, arugula, and remaining oil in a small bowl, add a pinch of salt, a grinding of pepper, and the lemon juice, and whisk with a fork until thoroughly emulsified. • When the steaks are done, place them on a heated serving platter. Spoon the sauce over the top and serve.

Serves: 4 · Prep: 10 min. · Cooking: 15 min. · Level: 1

SOGLIOLE ALLA MUGNAIA
Sole meunière

- 1 cup all-purpose flour
- 6 sole fillets, about 8 oz each
- 2 tablespoons butter
- 1/4 cup extra-virgin olive oil
  salt and freshly ground black pepper to taste
  juice of 2 lemons
- 1/2 cup dry white wine
- 2 tablespoons finely chopped parsley

Wine: a dry white (Alghero Bianco)

Lightly flour the sole fillets. • Heat the butter with the oil in a large skillet (you may need two skillets to cook them all at once) and fry the fillets for 3 minutes each side, turning carefully with a pancake turner as they can break easily. • Season lightly with salt and pepper. • Add the lemon juice and wine and cook for 3 more minutes. • Turn the sole in the cooking juices, sprinkle with parsley, and transfer to a heated serving platter. • Pour the cooking juices over the top and serve hot.

Serves: 6 · Prep: 25 min. · Cooking: 12 min. · Level: 2

PESCE SPADA CON RISO
Swordfish steaks with rice

- 2 tablespoons butter
- 1 small onion, finely chopped
- 1 1/2 cups short-grain white rice
- 1 bouillon cube
- 4 swordfish steaks, about 8 oz each
  salt and freshly ground black pepper to taste
- 1 tablespoon finely chopped fresh oregano
- 1 tablespoon capers
- 2 tablespoons finely chopped parsley
- 1/4 cup extra-virgin olive oil

Wine: a dry white (Vernaccia di San Gimignano)

Put the butter and onion in an ovenproof dish and place in a preheated oven at 300°F for about 10 minutes, stirring often. Add the rice, enough boiling water to cover the rice by 2 inches, and the bouillon cube. Cover and cook for 15 minutes, stirring frequently. • Rinse the swordfish and dry well. Cook in a grill pan (or under the broiler or on a barbecue) over high heat for 4–5 minutes on each side. Remove from heat, season with salt and pepper, and transfer to a serving platter. • Sprinkle with the oregano and capers. Keep hot. • Mix the parsley and oil into the rice and arrange on the platter with the fish. • Serve hot.

Serves: 4 · Prep: 15 min. · Cooking: 35 min. · Level: 2

Swordfish steaks with rice

Fried swordfish steaks with herbs

and add the egg. Mix well, then add the butter, Parmesan, garlic, parsley, nutmeg, and salt. • Take up tablespoonfuls of the mixture with a spoon and roll into croquettes. Roll in the bread crumbs and set on a tray or plate. • Heat the oil to very hot in a large skillet. Fry the croquettes in small batches until golden brown. • Scoop out with a slotted spoon and drain on paper towels. When all the croquettes are cooked, transfer to a heated serving platter and serve.

Serves: 4 · Prep: 20 min. · Cooking: 30 min. · Level: 1

PESCE SPADA ALLA GRIGLIA
Swordfish with lemon and herb sauce

1/2	cup extra-virgin olive oil
1/4	cup hot water
1/3	cup lemon juice
2	tablespoons finely chopped parsley
1	clove garlic, finely chopped
2	teaspoons dried oregano
	salt and freshly ground black pepper to taste
4	swordfish steaks, about 8 oz each

Wine: a dry white (Bianco Alcamo)

Place half the oil in a small, heatproof bowl and gradually beat in the water and lemon juice with a whisk, adding a little at a time. • Stir in the parsley, garlic, oregano, salt, and pepper. • Place the bowl in a pan of boiling water to heat for 3–4 minutes before serving. • Coat the swordfish steaks with the remaining oil and broil or barbecue for 4–5 minutes on each side. • Serve immediately, with the oil and herbs passed separately.

Serves: 4 · Prep: 10 min. · Cooking: 8–10 min. · Level: 1

PESCE SPADA ALLE ERBE
Fried swordfish steaks with herbs

6	swordfish steaks, about 8 oz each
2/3	cup extra-virgin olive oil
1/2	cup all-purpose flour
2	cloves garlic, finely chopped
1/4	cup finely chopped parsley
1	tablespoon finely chopped fresh oregano
1	tablespoon finely chopped fresh thyme
1	dried chile pepper, crumbled
	salt and freshly ground black pepper to taste

Wine: a dry white (Bianco dell'Etna)

Rinse the swordfish steaks and dry them carefully with paper towels. • Heat 1/4 cup oil in a large skillet over high heat. • Flour the swordfish steaks and when the oil is hot, fry them for 15 minutes, or until golden brown on both sides. Remove from the skillet and drain on paper towels. • Mix the remaining oil with the garlic, parsley, oregano, thyme, and chile pepper in a small pan. Season with salt and pepper and cook over medium heat for 15 minutes. • Pour the sauce over the swordfish steaks and serve hot.

Serves: 6 · Prep: 15 min. · Cooking: 30 min. · Level: 2

CROCCHETTE DI PESCE
Fish croquettes

1 1/4	lb cod, hake, or grouper, scaled and gutted
	salt to taste
1	fresh egg
2	tablespoons butter, at room temperature
1/4	cup freshly grated Parmesan cheese
2	cloves garlic, finely chopped
1/4	cup finely chopped parsley
1	teaspoon nutmeg
1/4	cup bread crumbs
2	cups oil, for frying

Wine: a dry white (Nuragus di Cagliari)

If the fish are not already scaled and gutted, see the instructions on page 201. Rinse the cleaned fish in cold running water. • Fill a large pan with water and bring to a boil. Add salt and simmer the fish for 10 minutes. Drain and transfer to a plate. Remove the heads, skin, and all the bones. • Put the fish in a large bowl, mash it coarsely with a fork,

TRIGLIE ALL'ERBA CIPOLLINA
Mullet with scallions

8	mullet, about 1 1/4 lb, cleaned and gutted
1/4	cup extra-virgin olive oil
1	clove garlic, finely chopped
1	(15 oz) can Italian tomatoes
	salt and freshly ground black pepper to taste
1/4	cup finely chopped scallions

Wine: a dry white (Vermentino di Gallura)

If the mullet are not already scaled and gutted, see the instructions on page 201. Rinse the cleaned fish in cold running water and dry with paper towels. • Heat the oil in a large, heavy-bottomed saucepan and sauté the garlic until pale gold. Add the tomatoes, season with salt and pepper, and cook over medium-low heat for 30 minutes. • Add the mullet to the pan and sprinkle with the scallions. Spoon the tomato sauce over the fish and cook for about 15 minutes. • Serve hot.

Serves: 4 · Prep: 15 min. · Cooking: 45 min. · Level: 1

TRIGLIE ALLA LIVORNESE
Mullet Leghorn-style

8	mullet, about 1 1/4 lb, cleaned and gutted
	salt and freshly ground black pepper to taste
1/4	cup all-purpose flour
1/4	cup extra-virgin olive oil
2	cloves garlic, finely chopped
1	stalk celery, finely chopped
2	tablespoons finely chopped parsley
12	oz peeled and chopped fresh or canned tomatoes

Wine: a dry rosé (Cirò Rosato)

If the mullet are not already scaled and gutted, see the instructions on page 201.

Rinse the cleaned fish in cold running water and dry with paper towels. • Sprinkle the fish with salt and pepper and dredge in the flour. • Heat half the oil in a large, heavy-bottomed saucepan and cook the fish for 5 minutes on each side. Remove from the pan and set aside in a warm oven. • Clean the skillet and heat the remaining oil in it. Sauté the garlic, celery, and half the parsley for 4–5 minutes, then add the tomatoes. Cook over medium heat for 15 minutes. • Place the mullet on a heated serving dish and spoon the tomato sauce over the top. Sprinkle with the remaining parsley and serve.

Serves: 4 · Prep: 15 min. · Cooking: 35 min. · Level: 1

PLATESSA AL FORNO SEMPLICE
Baked plaice with capers

1¼ lb plaice or flounder fillets
¼ cup extra-virgin olive oil
  salt and freshly ground white pepper to taste
2 tablespoons capers
16 cherry tomatoes, cut in half

Wine: a dry white (Gavi di Gavi)

Rinse the fillets under cold running water and dry with paper towels. • Grease a large ovenproof dish with half the oil. Place the fillets in the dish and sprinkle with salt, pepper, capers, and the cherry tomatoes. Drizzle with the remaining oil. • Bake in a preheated oven at 350°F for about 15 minutes. • Serve hot.

Serves: 6 · Prep: 20 min. · Cooking: 35 min. · Level: 1

CERNIA CON IL PESTO
Grouper with Genoese basil sauce

2 quantities Genoese basil sauce (see recipe, page 21)
4 large grouper steaks, about 8 oz each
2 large tomatoes
4 anchovy fillets
2 tablespoons extra-virgin olive oil
  salt and freshly ground black pepper to taste

Wine: a dry white (Gavi di Gavi)

Prepare the basil sauce. • Rinse the grouper steaks under cold running water and dry with paper towels. • Heat a broiler to very hot and broil the grouper on both

sides until cooked. Place in a warm oven. • Peel the tomatoes and chop finely. Crush the anchovies with the back of a fork. • Heat the oil in a heavy-bottomed saucepan and add the tomatoes and anchovies. Cook over medium heat for 10 minutes. • Add the basil sauce to the pan and heat, without letting it boil. • Pour the sauce over the grouper steaks and serve at once.

Serves: 4 · Prep: 10 min. · Cooking: 20 min. · Level: 1

ORATA ALLA PUGLIESE
Gilthead Puglia-style

☞ Gilthead is a delicately-flavored fish found in the Mediterranean and the temperate areas of the Atlantic Ocean. If not available, replace with another mild, sweet fish with firm texture.

1 gilthead, about 2 lb, cleaned, gutted, and filleted
½ cup extra-virgin olive oil
  juice of 1 large lemon
1 tablespoon each finely chopped parsley, thyme, sage, bay leaves
4 cloves garlic, finely chopped
  salt and freshly ground white pepper to taste
4 slices firm-textured bread, toasted

Wine: a dry white (Trebbiano d'Aprilia)

If the fish is not already scaled and gutted, see the instructions on page 201. Rinse the cleaned fish in cold running water and dry with paper towels. • Place the fillets in a deep-sided dish and pour in the oil and lemon juice. Sprinkle with the parsley, thyme, sage, bay leaves, garlic, salt, and pepper. Marinate for 1 hour. • Broil the fillets on both sides until cooked, basting

Baked plaice with capers

frequently with the marinade. • Arrange the toast on a heated serving platter and cover with the fillets. Spoon a little of the marinade over the top and serve hot.

Serves: 4 · Prep: 10 min. + 1 hr to marinate · Cooking: 10 min. · Level: 1

SOGLIOLE ALL'ARANCIA
Sole fillets with oranges

1½ lb sole fillets
2 large oranges
⅓ cup butter
  salt and freshly ground black pepper to taste
2 tablespoons all-purpose flour
¼ cup finely chopped parsley

Wine: a dry white (Orvieto Classico)

Rinse the sole fillets in cold running water and dry with paper towels. • Peel the oranges with a very sharp knife, removing all the white part under the peel. Slice in very thin rounds, discarding any seeds. • Heat half the butter in a skillet large enough to hold the sole in a single layer. • Season the sole with salt and pepper and dust with the flour. Add to the skillet with the butter and cook until nicely browned on both sides. • Heat the remaining butter in a small, heavy-bottomed saucepan until golden brown. • Place the cooked sole on a large heated serving platter and cover with the slices of orange. Sprinkle with the parsley and pour the hot butter over the top. Serve at once.

Serves: 4 · Prep: 10 min. · Cooking: 10 min. · Level: 1

Salt-baked porgy

ORATA AL SALE
Salt-baked porgy

☞ Many different kinds of fish can be cooked in this way. Try striped bass, red snapper, rockfish, tilefish, or grouper.

- 2 whole porgy, about 2 lb each, gutted
- 5 lb coarse sea salt

Wine: a dry white (Bianco Pisano San Thorpé)

Rinse the gutted fish without removing the scales, gills, or fins. Dry with paper towels. • Put half the salt into the bottom of a (preferably earthenware) roasting pan into which the fish will fit snugly. Put the fish on top and cover with the remaining salt. The fish should be completely covered – adjust the quantity of salt as required. • Bake in a preheated oven at 400°F for 30 minutes. • Serve the fish directly from the roasting pan, breaking the crust at the table. Peel off the skin, spoon the fish off the bone, and serve hot.

Serves: 6 · Prep: 10 min. · Cooking: 30 min · Level: 1

CERNIA ARROSTO CON PATATE
Roast grouper with potatoes

- 1 grouper, about 2¹/₂ lb
- 2 cloves garlic, peeled and cut in half
- ¼ cup fresh rosemary leaves
- 6 sage leaves
  salt and freshly ground black pepper to taste
- 1 lemon, thickly sliced
- 2 lb potatoes
- ¾ cup extra-virgin olive oil

Wine: a dry white (Vermentino di Gallura)

If the grouper is not already cleaned, see the instructions on page 201. Rinse the fish in cold running water and dry with paper towels. • Fill the cavity with the garlic, half the rosemary and sage, the salt, pepper, and lemon slices. • Peel the potatoes and cut them into bite-sized chunks. Don't leave them too large, they must cook in the same time the fish takes to cook. • Pour half oil into the bottom of a roasting pan and add the potatoes and the remaining rosemary and sage. Roll the potatoes in the oil. • Place the fish in the pan, making sure that it touches the

bottom (not on the potatoes). Arrange the potatoes around the fish. Drizzle with the remaining oil and bake in a preheated oven at 400°F for 30 minutes. Turn the potatoes every 10 minutes during the roasting time and baste them and the fish with the oil, so that they brown evenly. • When cooked, place the fish on a serving platter with the potatoes and serve.

Serves: 4 · Prep: 20 min. · Cooking: 30 min. · Level: 1

CERNIA AI FUNGHI
Grouper with mushrooms

- 1 grouper, about 5 lb, cleaned and gutted
- 2 tablespoons extra-virgin olive oil
- ¹/₃ cup butter, cut into small pieces
- ¹/₂ cup all-purpose flour
  salt and freshly ground black pepper to taste
- 1 cup dry white wine
- 1 lb white mushrooms, thinly sliced

Wine: a dry rosé (Taburno Rosato)

If the grouper is not already cleaned, see the instructions on page 201. Rinse the fish in cold running water and dry with paper towels. • Place the oil and one-third of the butter in an oval ovenproof dish. Coat the fish lightly all over with flour and place in the dish. Season with salt and pepper. Dot the surface of the fish with one-third of the remaining butter. • Bake in a preheated oven at 400°F for 10 minutes. • Take the dish out of the oven, drizzle the fish with the wine, then return to the oven for 15 minutes. • Meanwhile, sauté the mushrooms over medium heat in the remaining butter for 15 minutes. Season with salt and pepper and remove from heat. • Take the fish out of the oven and transfer to a heated serving platter. Add its cooking liquid to the mushrooms and their juices and reduce over medium heat for 5 minutes. • Spoon the mushrooms and liquid over the fish and serve.

Serves: 6 · Prep: 20 min. · Cooking: 35 min. · Level: 1

PALOMBO FRITTO
Fried dogfish steaks

- 4 dogfish steaks, about ³/₄ inch thick
  salt and freshly ground black pepper to taste
- 3 tablespoons all-purpose flour
- ¹/₃ cup extra-virgin olive oil
- 1 medium onion, very thinly sliced

2 cloves garlic, coarsely chopped
1 large fresh tomato, peeled and chopped
2 tablespoons pine nuts
2 tablespoons seedless white raisins, soaked and drained
2 tablespoons finely chopped parsley

Wine: a dry white (Alcamo)

Sprinkle the steaks with salt and pepper and coat them lightly with flour. • Heat the oil in a large skillet until very hot and fry the steaks over medium-high heat, browning well on both sides. Remove from the skillet and set aside. • In the same oil, sauté the onion and garlic until soft. Add the tomato and cook for 10 minutes over low heat, then add the pine nuts, raisins, and parsley. • Stir well and return the steaks to the pan. Cover and simmer over low heat for 10–15 minutes, turning once. • Remove from heat and set aside to cool for at least 2–3 hours so that the fish can absorb all the flavors. • Serve at room temperature.

Serves 4 · Prep: 10 min. + 2–3 hrs to rest · Cooking: 30 min · Level: 1

MERLUZZO CON ACCIUGHE
Baked hake, Sicilian-style

1 hake, about 3 lb, cleaned and gutted
8 anchovy fillets
1/3 cup extra-virgin olive oil
1/4 cup fine dry bread crumbs
1 tablespoon finely chopped parsley
1/2 tablespoon very finely chopped rosemary leaves
  salt and freshly ground black pepper to taste
1 lemon, cut in wedges

Wine: a dry white (Verdicchio dei Castelli di Jesi)

If the hake is not already cleaned, see the instructions on page 201. Rinse the fish in cold running water and dry with paper towels. • Place the anchovies in a small saucepan with 2 tablespoons of oil over low heat. Crush them with a fork until they dissolve in the oil. • Spread half this mixture inside the hake and the remainder over the outside. • Mix the bread crumbs, parsley, rosemary, salt, and pepper and coat the fish all over. • Grease an ovenproof dish or roasting pan with 2 tablespoons of the oil and place the fish in it. Drizzle with the remaining oil and bake in a preheated oven at 375°F for 25 minutes. • Serve hot, garnished with lemon.

Serves 4 · Prep: 20 min · Cooking: 25 min · Level: 1

Poached salmon with three sauces

TROTE FARCITE AL PROSCIUTTO
Fresh trout with prosciutto

4 trout, about 8 oz each, cleaned and gutted
1/4 cup freshly grated Parmesan cheese
1 dried chili pepper, crumbled
1/4 cup finely chopped parsley
1 tablespoon white wine vinegar
  salt and freshly ground black pepper to taste
8 thin slices prosciutto
1/4 cup extra-virgin olive oil

Wine: a dry white (Pinot Grigio dell'Isonzo)

If the trout are not already cleaned, see the instructions on page 201. Rinse the fish in cold running water and dry with paper towels. • Combine the Parmesan, chili pepper, parsley, vinegar, salt, and pepper in a small bowl. Mix well and then use it to stuff the trout. • Wrap each trout in 2 slices of prosciutto. Heat the oil in a skillet large enough to hold the trout in a single layer. Add the trout, cover, and cook over very low heat for about 1 hour.

Serves: 4 · Prep: 10 min. · Cooking: 1 hr · Level: 1

SALMONE BOLLITO ALLE SALSE
Poached salmon with three sauces

☞ Try the salmon with other sauces too. *Pine nut* (see recipe, page 20) and *Tarragon* (see recipe, page 21) are also good.

1 quantity Mayonnaise (see recipe, page 16)
1 quantity Caper sauce (see recipe, page 16)
1 quantity Walnut sauce (see recipe, page 20)
1 salmon, about 4 lb, gutted
1 leek, thickly sliced
1 carrot, thickly sliced
1 stalk celery, thickly sliced
1 bunch parsley
10 peppercorns
2 teaspoons salt

Wine: a dry white (Pinot Grigio dell'Isonzo)

Prepare the sauces • Fill a pan just large enough to hold the salmon with cold water and add the leek, carrot, celery, parsley, peppercorns, salt, and salmon. Simmer gently for about 25 minutes. • When the fish is done, transfer to a large heated plate and remove the head, skin, and backbone. • Place on a heated serving platter and serve with the sauces.

Serves: 4 · Prep: 10 min. · Cooking: 55 min. · Level: 1

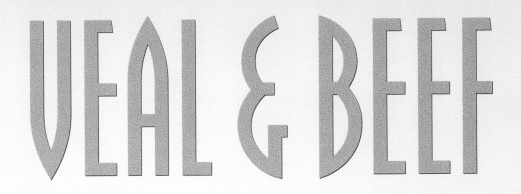
VEAL & BEEF

A traditional Italian meal begins with an appetizer, followed by a pasta, rice, or soup dish, and then a main course featuring meat, usually served with a salad or vegetable dish. Even busy young people who eat a sandwich on the run at lunch, will revert to tradition when entertaining or at a family meal. Versatile veal and beef are among the most popular meats because they suit almost all palates.

POLPETTE AL POMODORO
Meatballs in tomato sauce

- 2 tablespoons finely chopped onion
- 1/4 cup extra-virgin olive oil
- 14 oz peeled and chopped fresh or canned tomatoes
- 6 fresh basil leaves
  salt and freshly ground black pepper to taste
- 1 cup dry bread crumbs
- 1/4 cup milk
- 14 oz ground beef or veal
- 1 cup freshly grated Pecorino cheese
- 2 eggs, beaten
- 2 tablespoons finely chopped parsley
- 2 cloves garlic, finely chopped

Wine: a light, dry red (Montepulciano d'Abruzzo)

Sauté the onion in the oil in a large, heavy-bottomed saucepan. Add the tomatoes, basil, salt, and pepper. • Cook over medium heat for 10 minutes. • Place the bread crumbs in a large mixing bowl with the milk. Stir in the meat, Pecorino, eggs, parsley, and garlic. Season with salt and pepper and mix well. • Shape into meatballs and add to the tomato sauce. Simmer for 15–20 minutes, turning carefully once or twice. • Serve hot.

Serves: 4 · Prep: 15 min. · Cooking: 30 min. · Level: 1

◄ Roast veal with lemon sauce (see recipe, page 228)
➤ Meatballs in tomato sauce

Tenderloin beef with balsamic vinegar

FILETTO ALL'ACETO BALSAMICO
Tenderloin beef with balsamic vinegar

- 2 tablespoons butter
- 1/2 shallot, finely chopped
- 1 1/4 lb tenderloin beef, cut in 4 slices
- 1/2 cup balsamic vinegar
  salt and freshly ground black pepper to taste
- 1 tablespoon cornstarch

Wine: a dry, fruity red (Teroldego Rotaliano)

Melt the butter in a heavy-bottomed pan over high heat. When it is foaming, add the shallot and then the meat. Cook for about 4 minutes each side. • Pour in the balsamic vinegar and season with salt and pepper. Cook for 1–2 minutes more. • Set the meat aside in a warm oven on a heated serving dish. • Return the cooking juices to heat and cook until they foam, then stir in the cornstarch. • Pour the sauce over the meat and serve hot.

Serves: 4 · Prep: 10 min. · Cooking: 10 min. · Level: 1

CARPACCIO COTTO ALLA RUCOLA
Seared tenderloin with arugula

- 2 bunches arugula
- 1 lb tenderloin, thinly sliced
  salt and freshly ground black pepper to taste
- 1/4 cup extra-virgin olive oil
  juice of 1/2 lemon

Wine: a dry, aromatic white (Chardonnay di Latisana)

Wash and dry the arugula and chop coarsely. • Heat a large nonstick skillet over medium-high heat. Cook the slices of meat, 2 or 3 at a time, by dropping them into the skillet and turning them immediately. They will only take a minute or two to cook. • When all the meat is cooked, arrange the slices on a heated serving dish, sprinkle with salt and pepper, and cover with the arugula. Sprinkle lightly with salt and pepper again and drizzle with the oil and lemon juice. • Serve hot.

Serves: 4 · Prep: 10 min. · Cooking: 20 min. · Level: 1

BISTECCA ALLA FIORENTINA
Florentine beef steak

☞ This dish is the ultimate treat for steak-lovers. In Italy, the steak is cut from Tuscan-bred Chianina beef and hung for at least 6 days. It is cooked over the embers of a charcoal or wood-burning grill and eaten so rare that the meat nearest the bone is only just warm. Small wonder that it was outlawed for several months in 2001 when the mad-cow disease scare was at its peak!

- 1 3/4—2 1/4 lb T-bone steak at least 1 1/2 in thick
  salt and freshly ground black pepper to taste

Wine: a dry, full-bodied red (Brunello di Montalcino)

Season the steak with pepper. • Place on a grill about 4 inches above the glowing embers. • After 4–5 minutes the steak will come away easily from the grill. Sprinkle the seared surface with a little salt, turn and cook the other side, sprinkling with more salt and pepper. • It should be well-browned on the outside, juicy inside. • Serve at once.

Serves: 2 · Prep: 1 min. · Cooking: 10 min. · Level: 1

FILETTI AL PEPE VERDE
Beef fillets with green pepper

- 2 tablespoons soft green peppercorns (in liquid)
- 4 beef fillets, cut 1 inch thick
- 2 tablespoons butter
- 1/4 cup extra-virgin olive oil
  salt to taste
- 1/2 cup cognac (or brandy)
- 2 tablespoons heavy cream

Wine: a dry white (Vernaccia di San Gimignano)

Mash the peppercorns with a fork. Press the crushed peppercorns so that they stick to both sides of the fillets. • Heat the butter and oil in a heavy-bottomed pan. Sprinkle the fillets with salt and add to the pan. • Pour in the cognac and cook until it evaporates. • Add the cream and cook for about 5 minutes more, turning the meat at least once. If the sauce is too liquid, remove the fillets and set them aside. Turn up the heat and cook the sauce until it reduces sufficiently. • Arrange the fillets on a heated serving dish and spoon the sauce over the top. • Serve hot.

Serves: 4 · Prep: 10 min. · Cooking: 10 min. · Level: 1

SCALOPPINE ALLA PIZZAIOLA
Veal scaloppine with pizza topping

☞ Veal scaloppine, popular in Italy and well known abroad, can be served in many different ways. Cut from topside, and then lightly pounded, they should weigh about 2 oz each and shouldn't be more than ¼ inch thick. Because they are cooked so quickly, they must be cut from the best quality veal.

1	lb small, thinly sliced veal scaloppine
1¼	cups all-purpose flour
⅓	cup extra-virgin olive oil
	salt and freshly ground black pepper to taste
2	cloves garlic, finely chopped
1	tablespoon coarsely chopped capers
½	quantity Simple tomato sauce (see recipe, page 18)
4	oz Mozzarella cheese, thinly sliced
2	tablespoons finely chopped parsley

Wine: a dry red (Sangiovese di Maremma)

Remove any small pieces of fat from the scaloppine. • Cover with parchment paper and pound lightly. Dredge in the flour, then shake thoroughly. • Heat the oil in a large skillet and brown the scaloppine on both sides. • Season with salt and pepper and sprinkle with the garlic and capers. Cover each slice with a little tomato sauce and cook for 6 minutes. Cover each veal slice with Mozzarella and cook for 4 minutes more. • Sprinkle with the parsley and serve hot.

Serves: 4 · Prep: 25 min. · Cooking: 15 min. · Level: 1

SCALOPPINE AL PARMIGIANO E POMODORO FRESCO
Veal scaloppine with cherry tomatoes

1	lb small, thinly sliced veal scaloppine
½	cup all-purpose flour
¼	cup extra-virgin olive oil
2	tablespoons butter
	salt and freshly ground black pepper to taste
½	cup dry white wine
2	shallots, coarsely chopped
10	oz cherry tomatoes, cut in half
4	oz Parmesan cheese, shredded
2	tablespoons finely chopped parsley
12	leaves fresh basil, torn

Wine: a dry white (Pinot Bianco)

Remove any small pieces of fat from the meat. • Cover with parchment paper and pound lightly. • Dredge in the flour, then shake well to remove excess. • Heat the oil and butter in a large skillet over

Seared beef with asparagus

medium heat. Add the scaloppine and season with salt and pepper. Brown on both sides. • Pour in the wine and cook until it evaporates. • Remove the slices of meat and set aside in a warm oven. • Add the shallots to the skillet and lightly brown. • Add the tomatoes, salt, and pepper, and cook for 5 minutes. • Add the scaloppine and sprinkle with the Parmesan, parsley, and basil. • Turn off the heat, cover, and leave to stand for a few minutes. • Serve hot.

Serves: 4 · Prep: 25 min. · Cooking: 25 min. · Level: 1

CARPACCIO COTTO CON ASPARAGI
Seared beef with asparagus

12	oz asparagus
1	shallot, chopped
⅓	cup extra-virgin olive oil
	salt and freshly ground black pepper to taste
¼	cup dry white wine
¾	cup Beef stock (see recipe, page 105)
1¼	lb prime beef fillet or tenderloin, thinly sliced

Wine: a dry white (Vermentino di Argiolas)

Wash the asparagus, trim the tough parts off the bottom of the stalks, and cut into ½-inch long pieces. Leave the tips whole. • Sauté the shallot in the oil over medium heat. • When the shallot is soft, add the asparagus and season with salt and pepper. • Pour in the wine and cook until it evaporates. • Add half the stock and cook for 10–15 minutes. Add more stock during cooking if the sauce becomes too dry. • Remove from heat when the asparagus is cooked but still crunchy. • Heat a large nonstick skillet over medium-high heat. Cook the slices of meat, 2 or 3 at a time, by dropping them into the skillet and turning them immediately. They will only take a minute or two to cook. • Arrange the cooked meat on four heated dinner plates, and season with salt and pepper • Spoon the asparagus and its sauce over the top and serve hot.

Serves: 4 · Prep: 15 min. · Cooking: 25 min. · Level: 1

SCALOPPINE AL LIMONE
Veal scaloppine in lemon sauce

- 1 lb small, thinly sliced veal scaloppine
- 1/2 cup all-purpose flour
- 3 tablespoons butter
- 2 tablespoons extra-virgin olive oil
  salt and freshly ground black pepper to taste
- 1/2 cup Beef stock (see recipe, page 105)
  juice of 1 lemon
- 1 tablespoon finely chopped parsley

Wine: a dry white (Pinot Bianco)

Remove any small pieces of fat from the meat. • Cover with parchment paper, and pound lightly. • Dredge the scaloppine in the flour, shaking off any excess.• Sauté the veal in the butter and oil in a heavy-bottomed pan over high heat, turning often until both sides are evenly browned. Season with salt and pepper. • Lower the heat to medium and continue cooking, adding a little stock to moisten. • When the veal is cooked, after about 12 minutes, turn off the heat and pour the lemon juice over the top. • Sprinkle with the parsley and serve hot.

Serves: 4 · Prep: 15 min. · Cooking: 12 min. · Level: 1

SCALOPPINE AL MARSALA
Veal scaloppine in Marsala wine

- 1 lb small, thinly sliced veal scaloppine
- 1/2 cup all-purpose flour
- 1/4 cup extra-virgin olive oil
  salt and freshly ground black pepper to taste
- 1/2 cup Beef stock (see recipe, page 105)
- 2 tablespoons finely chopped marjoram

Wine: a dry, fulled-bodied red (Cirò Rosso)

Veal scaloppine in Marsala wine

Remove any small pieces of fat from the meat. • Cover with parchment paper, and pound lightly. • Dredge the scaloppine in the flour, shaking off any excess.• Sauté the veal in the oil in a heavy-bottomed pan over high heat, turning often until both sides are evenly browned. Season with salt and pepper. • Lower the heat to medium and continue cooking, adding a little stock to moisten. • The veal will be cooked after about 12 minutes. Transfer to a heated serving dish and set aside in a warm oven. • Add the Marsala wine and the marjoram to the juices left in the pan, and reduce over medium-high heat. Pour the Marsala sauce over the veal and serve immediately.

Serves: 4 · Prep: 15 min. · Cooking: 12 min. · Level: 1

COTOLETTE ALLA BOLOGNESE
Bolognese cutlets

☞ For an extra special dish, sprinkle shavings of raw white truffle on top of the melted cheese just before serving.

- 4–8 veal cutlets, about 1 lb total
- 1 egg
  pinch of salt
- 1 cup fine dry bread crumbs
- 1/2 cup butter
- 6 thin slices of prosciutto
- 1 cup Parmesan cheese, in small shavings
- 1 cup sieved tomatoes (passata)
- 1/2 cup Beef stock (see recipe, page 105)

Wine: a light, dry red (Barbera dei Colli Bolognesi)

Beat the veal lightly with a meat pounder. • Beat the egg in a shallow dish with the salt.

• Dip the cutlets into the egg and then coat with the bread crumbs, pressing so they stick. • Fry the cutlets in the butter until they are golden brown on both sides. • Arrange the veal in a single layer in a very wide skillet or flameproof casserole. Place a slice of prosciutto on each and cover with the Parmesan shavings. • Mix the sieved tomatoes with the meat stock and pour into the dish or pan. Cover and simmer for about 15 minutes, until the cheese has melted. • Serve hot.

Serves: 4 · Prep: 20 min. · Cooking: 25 min. · Level: 1

COTOLETTE ALLA FONTINA
Veal cutlets with Fontina cheese

- 4 veal cutlets with bone, about 6–7 oz each
- 4 oz Fontina cheese, thinly sliced
  wafer-thin slices of fresh truffle (optional)
  salt and freshly ground black pepper to taste
- 1 tablespoon all-purpose flour
- 1 egg, lightly beaten
- 1/2 cup fine, dry bread crumbs
- 1/3 cup butter

Wine: a dry, full-bodied red (Barbaresco)

Use a very sharp, pointed knife to cut horizontally into the meat of the cutlets toward the bone to form a pocket. • Place a quarter of the Fontina inside each pocket, together with a few slivers of truffle, if using. • Beat the edges of the pockets lightly to make the cut edges stick together, enclosing the contents. • Sprinkle the cutlets with a little salt and pepper and coat with flour. Dip them into the egg and then coat with bread crumbs. • Heat about two-thirds of the butter over high heat in a large, nonstick skillet until it stops foaming. Add the cutlets and fry until golden brown on both sides. Add the remaining butter as you turn them. • Serve hot.

Serves: 4 · Prep: 10 min. · Cooking: 15 min. · Level: 1

COTOLETTE ALLA PARMIGIANA
Cutlets with Parmesan cheese

- 4 veal cutlets,about 6–7 oz each
- 1 egg
  salt to taste
- 1/3 cup butter
- 1 cup Parmesan cheese, in small shavings
- 1/2 cup Beef stock (see recipe, page 105)

Wine: a light, dry red (Rosso di Breganze)

Beat the veal lightly with a meat pounder. •
Lightly beat the egg and a pinch of salt
together, then dip the cutlets in the mixture. •
Heat the butter in a skillet and fry the cutlets
until light golden brown on both sides. •
Arrange in a single layer in a fireproof
casserole that has been greased with butter.
Cover with a layer of the Parmesan shavings.
Add the stock, then cover and cook over
low heat until the cheese has
melted. • Serve very hot.

Serves: 4 · Prep: 15 min. ·
Cooking: 25 min. · Level: 1

Veal cutlets with anchovy sauce

FARSUMAGRU
Stuffed beef roll

☞ This long roll, with its rich, hidden filling, is
a classic Sicilian dish.

4   oz ground lean beef or veal
8   oz Italian sausage meat
1   egg
½   cup freshly grated Pecorino cheese
2   tablespoons finely chopped parsley
2   tablespoons finely chopped onion
2   cloves garlic, finely chopped
    salt and freshly ground black pepper to taste
1   thick slice lean beef from top round, rib, chuck, or
    sirloin, about 1½ lb
4   oz prosciutto, thinly sliced
½   cup diced pancetta
3   hard-boiled eggs, shelled
4   oz mature Provolone cheese, cut into narrow strips
¼   cup extra-virgin olive oil
½   cup dry red wine
1   tablespoon tomato paste, diluted in 1 cup hot water

Wine: a dry red (Corvo Rosso)

Mix the ground beef and sausage meat in a
large mixing bowl. • Add the raw egg,
Pecorino, parsley, onion, garlic, salt, and
pepper, and mix well. • Place the slice of
beef flat between 2 sheets of parchment
paper and beat carefully until it is about ¼
inch thick. • Lay the meat out flat and
cover with the prosciutto and pancetta.
Spread the ground meat mixture over the
top, leaving a narrow border around the
edge. • Slice the pointed ends off the hard-
boiled eggs and place the eggs "nose to
tail" down the middle. • Lay the Provolone
cheese on either side of the eggs. •
Carefully roll up, bringing one long side
over the eggs. Tie with kitchen string •
Heat the oil in a large, flameproof
casserole and brown the meat roll all over.

• Pour the wine over the top and cook,
uncovered, until it has evaporated. • Add
the diluted tomato paste. • Cover and
simmer over a very low heat for about 1
hour, turning several times. • Just before
serving, remove the string and transfer to a
heated serving dish. • Carve slices about ¾
inch thick. Spoon some of the cooking
liquid over the top and serve hot.

Serves: 6 · Prep: 30 min. · Cooking: 1¼ hrs · Level: 2

ROLLATA DI VITELLO
Stuffed veal roll

1   piece boned breast of veal, about 1 lb
4   oz fatty Italian prosciutto, sliced
2   tablespoons finely chopped fresh rosemary leaves
4   fresh sage leaves, finely chopped
2   cloves garlic, finely chopped
    salt and freshly ground white pepper to taste
¼   cup butter
¾   cup dry white wine
½   cup Beef stock (see recipe, page 105)

Wine: a dry white (Franciacorta Bianco)

Lay the veal out between 2 sheets of
parchment paper and beat carefully until it
is about ½ inch thick. • Spread the
prosciutto over the veal and sprinkle with
the rosemary, sage, garlic, salt, and pepper.
• Roll up the veal carefully and tie with
kitchen string. Do not salt the outside. •
Heat the butter in a large fireproof
casserole. When it has stopped foaming,
add the meat and brown over high heat for
6–7 minutes. • Add one-third of the wine,
then reduce the heat a little and cover. •
Turn the meat at frequent intervals adding
more wine as the liquid evaporates. Add a

little stock, if necessary, when you have
used up all the wine. • After 45 minutes,
the veal roll will be cooked. Turn off the
heat and leave to rest in the casserole for
6–8 minutes. • Remove the string and
carve the roll into slices about ½ inch
thick. • Serve hot or at room temperature.

Serves: 4 · Prep: 15 min. · Cooking: 1 hr · Level: 1

COTOLETTE CON ACCIUGATA
Veal cutlets with anchovy sauce

4–8   veal cutlets, about 1 lb total
2   eggs
    salt to taste
½   cup all-purpose flour
2   cups fine dry bread crumbs
½   cup oil, for frying
½   cup butter
8   anchovy fillets

Wine: a dry rosé (Rosato di Leverano)

Beat the veal lightly with a meat pounder. •
Make little cuts around the edges to stop
them from curling up during cooking. •
Coat the cutlets with flour, shaking off any
excess. • Beat the eggs in a bowl with the
salt. Dip the cutlets in the egg, then coat
with bread crumbs, pressing so they stick.
• Heat the oil in a large skillet until very hot
and fry the cutlets until golden brown on
both sides. • Drain on paper towels. •
Prepare the anchovy sauce by melting the
butter in a small, heavy-bottomed saucepan
over low heat. Stir in the anchovies, crushing
them with a fork until they dissolve. When
smooth, spoon over the cutlets. • Serve hot.

Serves: 4 · Prep: 20 min. · Cooking: 10 min. · Level: 1

Loin of veal with leeks

add the leeks and cook for 5 minutes, stirring frequently. Sprinkle with salt and pepper to taste. • Pour in the milk so that it covers the meat and cook for about 1 hour, or until the milk evaporates. • Remove the meat, slice, and transfer to a heated serving dish. • Chop the leek sauce in a food processor until smooth. Reheat and spoon it over the meat. • Serve hot.

Serves: 6 · Prep: 20 min. · Cooking: 1 hr · Level: 1

INVOLTINI AI CARCIOFI
Artichoke rolls

12	thin slices of veal, about 1 lb total
4	eggs
2	tablespoons finely chopped parsley
2	cloves garlic, finely chopped
	salt and freshly ground black pepper to taste
1/2	cup extra-virgin olive oil
2	medium artichokes
	juice of 1/2 lemon
4	oz Mortadella slices, cut in half (12 pieces)
1/4	cup all-purpose flour
1/2	cup dry white wine
1/2	cup Beef stock (see recipe, page 105)

Wine: a dry rosé (Alezio Rosato)

Remove any small pieces of fat from the veal and pound lightly. • Beat the eggs in a small bowl with the parsley, garlic, and salt. • Heat 2 tablespoons of oil in a small skillet, pour in the egg mixture and cook until firm on both sides. Set aside to cool. • To clean the artichokes, remove the tough outer leaves and trim the stalk and tips. Only the tender inner heart should remain. Wash well in cold water and lemon juice. Cut each artichoke into 6 wedges. • Heat 2 tablespoons of oil in a skillet over medium heat and cook the artichokes for 7–8 minutes. Season with salt and pepper and set aside. • Lay the slices of veal flat and place a piece of mortadella on each. • Cut the cooked egg into 12 pieces. Place a piece of egg and a wedge of artichoke on the Mortadella. • Roll the veal up and secure with a toothpick. • Dredge in the flour. Heat the remaining oil in a skillet and brown the rolls well all over. Season with salt and pepper. • Pour in the wine and cook for 20 minutes, adding stock if the pan becomes too dry. • Serve hot.

Serves: 4 · Prep: 25 min. · Cooking: 20 min · Level: 2

VITELLO AL LATTE FARCITO
Stuffed veal roll

1	slice of veal, preferably rump, about 1 1/2-lb
	salt and freshly ground black pepper
4	oz prosciutto, thinly sliced
4	oz Fontina cheese, sliced
1 1/4	cups Parmesan cheese, shredded
1/4	cup extra-virgin olive oil
2	cups whole milk

Wine: a dry white (Müller Thurgau)

Remove any small pieces of fat from the meat. Cover with parchment paper and lightly pound. • Season with salt and pepper, cover with slices of prosciutto and Fontina, and sprinkle with Parmesan. • Roll the veal up tightly (with the grain of the meat running parallel to the length of the roll, so that it will be easier to slice) and tie firmly with kitchen string. • Heat the oil over medium heat in a heavy-bottomed saucepan just large enough to contain the roll. • Brown the roll all over and sprinkle with salt and pepper. • Pour in the milk (which should cover the roll), partially cover the saucepan, and continue cooking over medium heat until the milk reduces. This will take about 1 hour. Turn the meat from time to time during cooking. • Transfer to a serving dish, slice and serve hot or at room temperature. If serving at room temperature, reheat the sauce, and spoon over the sliced roll.

Serves: 6 · Prep: 20 min. · Cooking: 1 1/4 hrs · Level: 2

VITELLO AI PORRI
Loin of veal with leeks

2	lb veal loin
	salt and freshly ground black pepper to taste
1/3	cup extra-virgin olive oil
2	tablespoons butter
4	leeks, sliced
1	quart whole milk

Wine: a dry red (Sangiovese di Romagna)

Tie the veal firmly with kitchen string. Season with salt and pepper. • Sauté the meat with the oil and butter in a heavy-bottomed saucepan just large enough to contain the veal. • When brown all over,

INVOLTINI CON IL PARMIGIANO
Parmesan veal rolls

☞ Neat slices of veal cut from the fillet or taken from a boned leg of veal and trimmed to the same size are best for this specialty from Emilia Romagna. A large slice of veal can be used to make a single roll, which will need to cook for about 30 minutes.

½	cup butter
2	tablespoons finely chopped parsley
2	cloves garlic, finely chopped
1	cup fine dry bread crumbs
1¼	cups freshly grated Parmesan cheese
2	eggs
	salt and freshly ground black pepper to taste
12	thin slices of veal, about 1 lb total
1	small onion, finely chopped
2	tablespoons tomato paste diluted in
½	cup water

Wine: a dry white (Colli di Parma Sauvignon)

Melt half the butter and mix well with the parsley, garlic, bread crumbs, Parmesan, eggs, salt, and pepper in a bowl. • Spread this mixture on the slices of veal. Roll each slice up, securing with kitchen thread or toothpicks. • Sauté the onion in the remaining butter in a large skillet. • Add the diluted tomato paste, and season with salt and pepper. • Place the veal rolls in the pan in a single layer. Cover and cook over low heat for about 15 minutes, turning them frequently. • Serve hot.

Serves: 4 · Prep: 20 min. · Cooking: 15 min. · Level: 1

POLPETTE DI MANZO CON LE MELE
Beef croquettes with apple

2	medium apples (Granny Smith are ideal)
1¼	lb finely ground lean beef
2	eggs, beaten
½	cup freshly grated Parmesan cheese
2	cloves garlic, finely chopped
	salt and freshly ground black pepper to taste
1	cup all-purpose flour
½	cup butter
2	tablespoons sugar
¼	cup dry white wine

Wine: a dry red (Dolcetto d'Alba)

Rinse the apples and grate them into a mixing bowl. • Add the beef, eggs, Parmesan, garlic, salt, and pepper and mix well. • Form the mixture into oblong croquettes and dredge them in the flour. • Heat the butter in a large skillet and fry the croquettes until golden brown. •

Hamburger with mustard sauce

Dissolve the sugar in the wine and drizzle spoonfuls over the croquettes. • Serve hot when the wine has all been absorbed.

Serves: 4 · Prep: 10 min. · Cooking: 15 min. · Level: 1

HAMBURGER ALLA SALSA DI SENAPE
Hamburger with mustard sauce

1	large onion, finely chopped
¼	cup extra-virgin olive oil
4	hamburgers made with 1 lb lean beef
	salt and freshly ground black pepper to taste
½	cup dry white wine
½	cup Beef stock (see recipe, page 105)
2	tablespoons hot mustard

Wine: a dry red (Cabernet dei Colli Orientali del Friuli)

Sauté the onion in the oil in a heavy-bottomed pan over medium heat until soft. • Add the hamburgers and season with salt and pepper. Pour in the wine and cook until it evaporates, turning the hamburgers frequently. • Gradually add the stock and cook for 10–15 minutes.

• Transfer the meat to a heated serving dish. • Stir the mustard into the sauce left in the pan. Mix well. • Spoon the mustard sauce over the hamburgers and serve hot.

Serves: 4 · Prep: 10 min. · Cooking: 20 min. · Level: 1

POLPETTE DI VITELLO AL LIMONE
Veal croquettes with lemon

1	lb finely ground lean veal
4	eggs
½	cup freshly grated Parmesan cheese
	juice of 1 lemon
	salt and freshly ground white pepper to taste
2	cups oil, for frying

Wine: a dry red (Dolcetto d'Alba)

Mix the veal, eggs, Parmesan, lemon juice, salt, and pepper until smooth. • Heat the oil in a large skillet until very hot and fry tablespoonfuls of the mixture until golden brown all over. • Drain on paper towels. Drizzle with the remaining lemon juice and serve hot.

Serves: 4 · Prep: 10 min. · Cooking: 20 min. · Level: 1

BOLLITO MISTO
Mixed boiled meats

- 2 medium onions, peeled, stuck with 4–6 cloves
- 3 stalks celery, trimmed and washed
- 3 medium carrots, peeled
- 20 black peppercorns
- 3 tablespoons coarse salt
- 6 quarts boiling water
- 3½ lb boneless beef cuts from brisket, bottom round, or rump roast
- 2 lb boneless veal cuts from breast or shoulder
- ½ oven-ready chicken
- 1¼ lb calf's tongue
- 1 cotechino sausage, about 1½ lb

Place 1 onion, 2 stalks celery, 2 carrots, 15 peppercorns, and 2 tablespoons of salt in the boiling water. • Add the beef and when the water has returned to a boil, reduce heat a little and cover. Simmer for 1 hour, then add the veal and chicken. • Cook for 2 more hours, topping up with boiling water if necessary. Test the meats with a thin skewer: if they are not tender, simmer for 30 more minutes or longer. • Meanwhile, in a separate pot, cook the calf's tongue with the remaining onion, celery, carrot, peppercorns, and salt. This will take about 2 hours. Time it so that it is ready at the same time as the other meats. • Soak the cotechino sausage in cold water for 1 hour. Prick the skin with a needle and place in a saucepan with enough cold water to cover. Bring to a boil over very low heat and simmer gently. The sausage will take about 3 hours to cook. • All the meats should, ideally, be ready at the same time, but they will not spoil if kept in their cooking liquid until everything is done. • Slice the cotechino sausage, but leave the other meats whole. Arrange on heated serving platters. Serve hot or at room temperature.

Serves: 10 · Prep: 10 min. · Cooking: 4 hrs · Level: 2

SALTIMBOCCA ALLA ROMANA
Veal cutlets with prosciutto and sage

☞ This is a classic Roman dish. Translated literally, its Italian name means "leaps into your mouth!" It is especially good when served with a side dish of spinach, lightly boiled and then sautéed briefly in garlic and butter.

- 14 oz veal, preferably rump, cut in 8 slices
- 1/4 cup all-purpose flour
- 4 oz prosciutto, cut in 8 thin slices
- 8 leaves fresh sage
- 2 tablespoons butter
- 3 tablespoons extra-virgin olive oil
  salt and freshly ground black pepper to taste
- 1/2 cup dry white wine

Wine: a dry red (Cerveteri Rosso)

Cover the veal with parchment paper and pound lightly. • Dredge the slices in the flour and shake off any excess. • Place a slice of prosciutto on each, top with a sage leaf, and secure with a toothpick. • Melt the butter and oil in a large skillet. Add the veal slices, with the prosciutto and sage facing downward. Brown on both sides over high heat. • Season with salt and pepper (taste first, the prosciutto is already salty and you may not need much more). • Pour in the wine and cook for 5–6 minutes more. • Serve hot.

Serves: 4 · Prep: 15 min. · Cooking: 12 min. · Level: 1

POLPETTE DI LESSO E PATATE
Meat and potato croquettes

- 2 large potatoes, boiled and peeled
- 14 oz boiled brisket or chuck
- 1–2 eggs
- 2 tablespoons finely chopped parsley
- 2 cloves garlic, finely chopped
  salt and freshly ground black pepper to taste
- 2 cups fine dry bread crumbs
- 2 cups oil, for frying

Wine: a dry rosé (Rosé Antinori)

Place the potatoes in a mixing bowl and mash well. • Chop the boiled meat in a food processor, then add to the bowl with the potatoes. • Stir in one egg, the parsley, and garlic. Season with salt and pepper and mix well. The mixture should be quite dense, but if it is too dry, add the other egg. • Shape the mixture into croquettes, and roll them in bread crumbs. • Heat the oil in a skillet until very hot and fry the croquettes until golden brown all over. • Drain on paper towels. Sprinkle with salt and serve hot.

Serves: 4 · Prep: 25 min. · Cooking: 25 min. · Level: 2

TAPILON
Ground beef with tomato sauce

☞ This dish used to be made with donkey meat, cut into tiny pieces. Nowadays ground beef is used in its place.

- 2 large cloves garlic, finely chopped
- 1 tablespoon finely chopped rosemary leaves
- 1/4 cup extra-virgin olive oil
- 3 tablespoons butter
- 1 1/4 lb lean ground beef
  salt and freshly ground black pepper to taste
- 1 bay leaf
- 1 1/4 cups dry, full-bodied red wine

Wine: a dry, full-bodied red (Gattinara)

Sauté the garlic and rosemary in the oil and butter over medium heat for 2 minutes. • Add the beef, breaking it up with a fork. Cook for 5–7 minutes, stirring frequently, until all the meat changes color and its liquid has evaporated. Season with salt and pepper. • Add the bay leaf and half the wine and simmer gently over low heat for 40 minutes. Stir now and then during cooking and gradually add the remaining wine. • Remove the bay leaf and serve hot.

Serves: 4 · Prep: 5 min. · Cooking: 50 min. · Level: 1

◁ Mixed boiled meats
▷ Ground beef
with tomato sauce

POLPETTONE CON I FUNGHI
Meat loaf with mushrooms

- 6 oz white bread, crusts removed
- 2 cups milk
- 1¹/₄ lb lean ground veal
- 2 eggs
- ¹/₄ cup freshly grated Pecorino cheese
- 2 oz prosciutto, finely chopped
  salt and freshly ground black pepper to taste
- 2 tablespoons fine dry bread crumbs
- 2 tablespoons all-purpose flour
- ¹/₄ cup extra-virgin oil
- ¹/₂ cup dry white wine
- 4 large ripe tomatoes, peeled and chopped
- 8 oz white mushrooms, cleaned and coarsely copped
- 1 clove garlic, finely chopped
- 2 tablespoons parsley, finely chopped

Wine: a dry red (Bardolino)

Soak the bread in the milk for 5 minutes.
Squeeze well and place the bread in a
mixing bowl. Add the veal, eggs, Pecorino,
prosciutto, salt, and pepper. • Shape the
mixture into a meat loaf and roll carefully
first in the bread crumbs then in the flour. •
Heat the oil in a large, heavy bottomed pan
over medium heat and brown the loaf on all
sides. • Pour in the wine and cook for 5
minutes. • Add the tomatoes, mushrooms,
garlic, and parsley. Stir well and transfer to
an ovenproof dish or roasting pan. Bake in
a preheated oven at 350°F for about 45
minutes. Serve hot or at room temperature.

Serves: 6 · Prep: 20 min. · Cooking: 1 hr · Level: 1

POLPETTONE IN SALSA PICCANTE
Meat loaf with spicy tomato sauce

- 1 lb lean ground veal
- 1 egg
- 1 thick slice Mortadella, finely chopped
  pinch of freshly ground nutmeg
- 2 tablespoons bread soaked in milk and squeezed
- 1 clove garlic, finely chopped
- 2 tablespoons parsley, finely chopped
  salt and freshly ground black pepper to taste
- ¹/₄ cup all-purpose flour
- ¹/₂ cup extra-virgin olive oil
- 1 tablespoon butter
- ¹/₂ onion, 1 carrot, 1 stalk celery, finely chopped
- ¹/₂ teaspoon red pepper flakes
- 1 (15 oz) can Italian tomatoes
- 1 cup Beef stock (see recipe, page 105)

Wine: a dry red (Brusco dei Barbi)

Mix the veal with the egg, Mortadella,
nutmeg, bread, garlic, and parsley in a

Meat loaf with mushrooms

bowl. Season with salt and pepper. •
Shape the mixture into a meat loaf. • Roll
the loaf carefully in the flour. • Heat half
of the oil in a large, heavy bottomed pan
over medium heat and brown the loaf on
all sides. • After 10 minutes, drain the
meat loaf from the cooking oil and set
aside. • Heat the butter and the remaining
oil in a skillet. Add the onion, carrot,
celery, and parsley and sauté for 4–5
minutes. • Add the pepper flakes and
tomatoes and cook for 5 minutes. • Place
the meat loaf in the pan and season with
salt and pepper. • Partially cover and
simmer over low heat for 1 hour. Stir
frequently, so that the meat does not stick
to the bottom. • If the sauce is too dense,
add a little stock. • Set aside to cool. Slice
when almost cold. • Arrange on a serving
dish. Heat the sauce just before serving
and spoon over the top.

Serves: 6 · Prep: 30 min. · Cooking: 1¼ hrs · Level: 1

MANZO AI CAPPERI E ACCIUGHE
Sirloin with capers and anchovies

2½ lb sirloin
⅓ cup extra-virgin olive oil
1 onion, 1 carrot, 1 stalk celery, coarsely chopped
   salt and freshly ground black pepper to taste
½ cup dry white wine
1 heaped tablespoon capers
2 anchovy fillets
½ cup Beef stock (see recipe, page 105)

Wine: a dry red (Aprilia Merlot)

Brown the sirloin in the oil in a large,
heavy-bottomed pan over high heat. • Add
the onion, carrot, and celery, and sprinkle
with salt and pepper (be sure not to add
too much salt, as anchovies can be quite
salty). Stir well and cook for 4–5 minutes.
• Pour in the wine, cover the pan, and
cook for about 30 minutes, turning the
meat often. • When the meat is tender, set
aside on a chopping board, ready to be
sliced. • Remove the pan from heat and
add the capers and anchovies to the
vegetables. Chop finely in a food
processor. • Slice the sirloin and arrange
on a heated serving dish. Reheat the sauce
and spoon it over the meat. Serve hot.

Serves: 6 · Prep: 20 min. · Cooking: 40 min. · Level: 2

FRANCESINA
Boiled beef with leeks

☞ This is a delicious way of using up beef
leftover from making stock. The traditional recipe
uses onions, but leeks are also good. Try both!

4 large leeks, thinly sliced
¼ cup extra-virgin olive oil
1 cup Beef stock (see recipe, page 105)
1½ lb leftover boiled beef (brisket, rump roast or bottom
   round, or silverside)
   salt and freshly ground black pepper to taste
1 (15 oz) can Italian tomatoes, sieved

Wine: a dry red (Chianti Classico)

Sauté the leeks in the oil in a large skillet
over medium heat for 5 minutes. • Add half
the stock, partially cover, and cook for 10
minutes. • Chop the meat into small pieces
or thin slices. Add to the leeks, season with
salt and pepper, and stir for 3–4 minutes. •
Add the tomatoes and a little more salt. Stir
well, cover, and simmer over low heat for 15
minutes. If necessary, moisten with some of
the remaining stock. • Serve hot.

Serves: 4 · Prep: 15 min. · Cooking 35 min. · Level: 1

INVOLTINI ALLA BARESE
Bari-style beef rolls

12 thin slices of veal, weighing about 1 lb total
3 cloves garlic, finely chopped
2 tablespoons finely chopped parsley
8 oz Pecorino cheese, cut in cubes
1 medium onion, finely chopped
2 tablespoons extra-virgin olive oil
2 bay leaves
   salt and freshly ground black pepper to taste
1 (15 oz) can Italian tomatoes

Wine: a dry red (Chianti Classico)

Lay the slices of veal out flat. Sprinkle with
the garlic and parsley followed by the
cheese. • Roll the veal up and secure with a
toothpick. • Sauté the onion in the oil with
the bay leaves until soft. • Add the veal rolls
and cook over medium heat for about 5
minutes. Season with salt and pepper. •
Pour in the tomatoes, partly cover the

skillet, and cook until the tomatoes reduce
and the meat is tender (20–30 minutes). •
Remove the bay leaves and serve hot.

Serves: 4 · Prep: 15 min. · Cooking: 30 min. · Level: 2

ROAST-BEEF CON MOSTARDA
Spicy roast beef

½ cup extra-virgin olive oil
2½ lb boneless beef roast
   salt and freshly ground black pepper to taste
1 cup mustard
½ cup brandy

Wine: a dry red (Lessona)

Heat the oil in a deep-sided, heavy-
bottomed pan. • Sprinkle the beef with a
generous coating of pepper and add to
the pan. • Brown the meat evenly on all
sides over high heat. • After about 10
minutes, turn the heat down and smother
the beef with the mustard and brandy.
Cook for 15 minutes more. • Sprinkle the
meat with salt only after it is cooked; if it
is added before it will be less tender. •
Slice thinly, arrange on a warm serving
dish, and serve hot.

Serves: 6 · Prep: 5 min. · Cooking: 25 min. · Level: 1

POLPETTINE SEMPLICI
Plain beef meatballs

14 oz ground lean beef
1 egg
1 tablespoon bread, soaked in milk and squeezed dry
   salt and freshly ground black pepper to taste
2 cups fine dry bread crumbs
⅓ cup extra-virgin olive oil
½ cup Beef stock (see recipe, page 105)
½ cup whole milk

Wine: a light, dry red (Chianti delle Colline Pisane)

In a mixing bowl, combine the beef, egg,
soaked bread, salt, and pepper. Mix well
until firm. • Take egg-sized pieces of the
mixture and shape them into oval
meatballs. Coat them in bread crumbs and
then flatten them a little. • Heat the oil
until very hot in a large skillet over
medium heat. Fry the meatballs in batches
until golden brown all over. • Pour in the
stock and cook until it evaporates. •
Season with salt and pepper. • Add the
milk and cook until it reduces, so that the
sauce is a dense cream. • Serve hot.

Serves: 4 · Prep: 20 min. · Cooking: 25 min. · Level: 1

ARROSTO DI VITELLO AL LIMONE
Roast veal with lemon sauce

- 1½ lb veal, preferably rump
  salt to taste
- 2 tablespoons butter
- 1 tablespoon all-purpose flour
- 1 cup Beef stock (see recipe, page 105)
- 2 tablespoons finely chopped parsley
  juice of 2 lemons

Wine: a dry red (Chianti dei Colli Fiorentini)

Tie the veal with kitchen string. Heat half the butter in a heavy-bottomed saucepan. Sprinkle the meat with salt and brown well in the butter. • Stir in the flour and stock. Cover the pan and cook over medium-low heat for about 1½ hours. • About 15 minutes before the veal is cooked, heat the remaining butter in a small skillet. Add the parsley and lemon juice and cook over low heat. • Slice the veal on a heated serving platter and spoon the sauce over the top. Serve hot or at room temperature.

Serves: 4 · Prep: 15 min. · Cooking: 1¾ hrs · Level: 2

MANZO GLASSATO CON CHAMPIGNONS
Glazed topside with mushrooms

- 2½ lb slice of beef, preferably rump, rolled, and tied with kitchen string
  salt and freshly ground black pepper to taste
- ½ cup extra-virgin olive oil
- 3 cloves garlic, 1 whole, 2 finely chopped

Tuscan-style braised beef

- 1 sprig sage
- 1 sprig rosemary
- 1 cup dry white wine
- 1 cup Beef stock (see recipe, page 105)
- 1½ lb white mushrooms
- 1 tablespoon finely chopped parsley
- 2 tablespoons all-purpose flour

Wine: a dry red (Chianti dei Colli Fiorentini)

Sprinkle the meat with salt and pepper. Transfer to a roasting pan and drizzle with two-thirds of the oil. Add the whole clove of garlic and the sage and rosemary. • Roast in a preheated oven at 400°F for 15 minutes, or until the meat is brown all over. Pour half the wine over the top and continue roasting for about 1 hour, basting from time to time. If the meat becomes too dry, add a little stock. • In the meantime, rinse the mushrooms under cold running water. Cut off and discard the stalks. Peel the mushroom caps and cut into large strips. If the mushrooms are small, leave them whole. • Heat the remaining oil in a skillet over medium heat and sauté the chopped garlic and parsley for 2–3 minutes. • Add the mushrooms and sprinkle with salt and pepper. Stir well and cook for 5–7 minutes. • Pour in the remaining wine and cook until it evaporates. Add the remaining stock and cook over medium

heat for 20–25 minutes, until the liquid reduces, stirring frequently. The mushrooms should be tender, but not mushy. • When the meat is cooked, transfer to a heated serving dish and set aside in a warm oven. • Discard the garlic, rosemary, and sage from the cooking juices. Place the sauce over high heat, and stir in the flour. Stir until it thickens, then spoon over the meat. • Arrange the mushrooms around the meat and serve hot.

Serves: 6 · Prep: 25 min. · Cooking: 1½ hrs · Level: 2

BRASATO AL BAROLO
Beef braised in red wine

- 2 ½-inch thick slices pork fat
- 2 lb beef, chuck, boneless rump roast, or silverside
  salt and freshly ground black pepper to taste
- 1–2 tablespoons all-purpose flour
- ¼ cup extra-virgin olive oil
- 3 tablespoons butter
- ½ tablespoon finely chopped fresh rosemary leaves
- 4 sage leaves, 1 clove garlic, 1 teaspoon parsley, all finely chopped
- 1 onion, 1 carrot, 1 stalk celery, coarsely chopped
- 2 bay leaves
- 1–2 cloves
  pinch of nutmeg
- 2–3 tablespoons boiling water
- 1 bottle Barolo wine

Wine: a dry, full-bodied red (Barolo)

Wrap the pork fat around the beef and tie with kitchen string. Sprinkle with salt and pepper, then coat lightly with flour. • Heat the oil and butter in a fireproof casserole large enough to hold the meat snugly. When the oil and butter are sizzling, add the beef and brown all over. This will take about 10 minutes. • Remove the meat from the casserole and set aside. • Add the rosemary, sage, garlic, parsley, onion, carrot, and celery to the butter, oil, and juices left in the casserole. Sauté gently over medium heat for 5 minutes. • Add the meat, bay leaves, cloves, and nutmeg, and moisten with the boiling water. Cook for 1 minute. • Add 1 cup of the Barolo wine. Reduce heat to low and cover the casserole tightly. • Discard the bay leaves and cloves just before serving. Remove the beef and keep hot. • Taste the cooking liquid, and add a little salt if necessary, then strain through a fine sieve. • Slice the beef about ½ inch thick. Transfer to a heated serving dish and cover with the sauce. • Serve hot.

Serves: 6 · Prep: 20 min. · Cooking: 4 hrs · Level: 1

Tuscan black pepper stew

STRACOTTO TOSCANO
Tuscan-style braised beef

☞ In this traditional Tuscan recipe, the beef is braised slowly in red wine and stock. After 3 hours the meat is extremely tender.

- 1 clove garlic, finely chopped
- 1 tablespoon rosemary, finely chopped
   salt and freshly ground black pepper to taste
- 2 lb beef (rump or sirloin)
- ⅓ cup extra-virgin olive oil
- 2 onions, 2 carrots, 1 stalk celery, coarsely chopped
- 1 tablespoon parsley finely chopped
- 3 sage leaves, torn
- 2 bay leaves
- 1 cup dry red wine
- 14 oz peeled and chopped canned tomatoes
- 2 cups Beef stock (see recipe, page 105)

Wine: a dry red (Vino Nobile di Montepulciano)

Mix the garlic and rosemary with a generous quantity of salt and pepper. Using a sharp knife, make several slits in the meat and fill with the herb mixture. • Tie the meat loosely with kitchen string. • Heat the oil in a heavy-bottomed pan over medium-high heat and brown the meat well all over. • Add the onions, carrots, celery, parsley, sage, and bay leaves and sauté for 5 minutes. • Season with salt and pepper and pour in the wine. When the wine has evaporated, add the tomatoes, cover the pan, and simmer over medium-low heat for 2½–3 hours. Turn the meat from time to time, adding the stock gradually so that the sauce doesn't dry out. • When the meat is cooked, transfer to a heated serving dish

and cut in slices. Spoon the sauce over the top and serve hot.

Serves: 4–6 · Prep: 25 min. · Cooking: 3 hrs · Level: 1

CARBONADE DELLA VAL D'AOSTA
Beef casserole from Val d'Aosta

☞ This dish used to be made with salted beef. Nowadays fresh beef is always used. It is traditionally served with freshly made polenta (see recipe, page 184), but is equally good with potato purée or rice.

- 1½ lb lean braising beef
- 2 tablespoons all-purpose flour
- ¼ cup butter
- 2 large onions, peeled and sliced
   salt and freshly ground black pepper to taste
- 1¾ cups full-bodied, dry red wine

Wine: a dry red (Valle d'Aosta Chambave Rosso)

Cut the meat into very thin slices, and coat lightly with flour. • Melt the butter in a fireproof casserole. Add the beef slices and brown all over, turning them frequently for 2 minutes over high heat. • Remove the meat from the casserole with a slotted spoon and set aside. • Add the onions to the butter and juices left in the casserole and sauté over medium heat until soft. • Add the meat and stir. Season with salt and pepper and moisten with ¼

of the wine. Simmer gently over low heat, uncovered, for 45–50 minutes, adding more wine at 10-minute intervals. • When cooked, there should be plenty of rich, dark liquid and the onion should have almost completely dissolved. • Serve hot.

Serves: 4 · Prep: 15 min. · Cooking: 1 hr · Level: 1

PEPOSO
Tuscan black pepper stew

- 3½ lb muscle from veal shanks, cut in bite-sized pieces
- 4 cloves garlic, finely chopped
- 1¼ lb tomatoes, peeled and chopped
   pinch of salt
- ¼ cup freshly ground black pepper
- 1 quart cold water
- 1½ cups full-bodied, dry red wine

Wine: a dry red (Chianti Classico)

Place the meat in a large, heavy-bottomed saucepan (preferably earthenware) with the garlic, tomatoes, salt, and pepper and add just enough of the water to cover the meat. • Cook over medium heat for 2 hours, adding extra water if the sauce becomes too dry. Stir from time to time. • After 2 hours, pour in the wine and cook for 1 hour more, or until the meat is very tender. • Serve hot.

Serves: 6 · Prep: 10 min. · Cooking: 3 hrs · Level: 1

Beef stew with mushrooms

STUFATINO
Roman beef stew

☞ To lighten the dish, add 1 cup of coarsely chopped, lightly boiled celery stalks to the pot 5 minutes before serving.

- 2 tablespoons extra-virgin olive oil
- ¼ cup pancetta
- 1 large onion, finely chopped
- 2 cloves garlic, finely chopped
- 1 stalk celery, finely chopped
- 1 lb boneless beef chuck, cut into bite-sized pieces
  salt and freshly ground black pepper to taste
- ½ cup dry white wine
- 2 large ripe tomatoes, peeled and diced
- 1 tablespoon marjoram (or parsley), finely chopped

Wine: a dry red (Cerveteri Rosso)

Heat the oil in a large, heavy-bottomed pan and sauté the pancetta and onion. When the onion turns pale gold, add the garlic and celery, and sauté for 5 more minutes. • Add the beef and season with salt and pepper. Stir continually until the meat is lightly browned all over. • Pour in the wine and cook until it evaporates. Add the tomatoes and cook for another 10 minutes, stirring frequently. • Add enough cold water to cover the meat. Cover and cook over a low heat for at least 2 hours. The sauce should be thick and dark in color. • Remove from the heat and stir in the marjoram or parsley just before serving. • Serve hot.

Serves: 4 · Prep: 10 min. · Cooking: 2¼ hrs · Level: 1

STUFATO DI MANZO AI FUNGHI
Beef stew with mushrooms

- 1 clove garlic, finely chopped
- 1 onion, finely chopped
- ¼ cup extra-virgin olive oil
- 1¼ lb boneless beef chuck, cut into bite-sized pieces
  salt and freshly ground black pepper to taste
- ½ cup dry white wine
- ½ quantity Simple tomato sauce (see recipe, page 18)
- 1¼ lb white mushrooms
- 2 tablespoons finely chopped parsley
- 1 cup Beef stock (see recipe, page 105)

Wine: a dry red (Vino Nobile di Montepulciano)

Sauté the garlic and onion in the oil in a heavy-bottomed pan over medium heat. • Add the meat when the onion is translucent. Season with salt and pepper and simmer in the liquid produced by the meat. • When this liquid has reduced, pour in the wine and cook until it has evaporated. • Add the tomato sauce, stir well, and simmer gently over medium-low heat. • In the meantime, clean and wash the mushrooms. Cut the caps into thick strips and the stalks into chunks. • Add the mushrooms and parsley to the stew after about 40 minutes. Partially cover the pan and simmer until cooked, stirring frequently. Add a little stock if the sauce dries out too much. • Serve hot.

Serves: 4 · Prep: 25 min. · Cooking: 1¼ hrs · Level: 1

SPEZZATINO AL LATTE
Veal stew with milk and parsley

- 2 lb lean veal, cut into bite-sized pieces
- ¼ cup extra-virgin olive oil
- 2 cloves garlic, finely chopped
- 2 tablespoons parsley, finely chopped
  salt and freshly ground black pepper to taste
- 1 cup milk
- ½ cup Beef stock (see recipe, page 105)

Wine: a light, dry red (Bonarda dell'Oltrepò Pavese)

Remove any pieces of fat from the veal. • Heat the oil in a large, heavy-bottomed pan over medium heat and sauté the garlic and parsley for 2–3 minutes. • Add the meat and cook in its juices until it reduces. Season with salt and pepper. • Pour in the milk and stock. The meat should be almost, but not completely, covered. Reduce the heat and partially cover the pan, so that the liquid gradually evaporates. Cook slowly, stirring frequently since the milk tends to stick, until the liquid completely reduces, forming a dense sauce. • Transfer to a heated serving dish and serve hot.

Serves: 6 · Prep: 15 min. · Cooking: 1 hr · Level: 1

SPEZZATINO RUSTICO
Beef stew with potatoes

- 1/3 cup extra-virgin olive oil
- 1 clove garlic, 1 onion, 1 carrot, 1 stalk celery, all finely chopped
- 4 large tomatoes, peeled and chopped
- 1 tablespoon chopped, mixed herbs (sage, parsley, oregano, rosemary, thyme)
- 1½ lb beef chuck with muscle, cut into bite-sized pieces salt and freshly ground black pepper to taste
- 1 cup red wine
- 2 cups Beef stock (see recipe, page 105)
- 1¼ lb potatoes, peeled and cut into bite-sized chunks

Wine: a dry red (Carmignano Rosso)

Heat the oil in a large, heavy-bottomed pan. Add the garlic, onion, carrot, celery, tomatoes, and mixed herbs and sauté for 5 minutes. • Remove any little pieces of fat from the meat. Add to the pan, season with salt and pepper, and cook until brown. • Pour in the wine and cook until it evaporates. • Cover the pan and simmer for about 1 hour, gradually adding the stock. Stir frequently, to stop the meat from sticking to the pan. • Add the potatoes about 30 minutes before the meat is cooked. • Serve hot.

Serves: 6 · Prep: 25 min. · Cooking: 1¼ hrs · Level: 1

SPEZZATINO ALLA PANNA
Veal stew with fresh cream

- 1¼ lb veal, shank or shoulder, cut into bite-sized pieces salt and freshly ground white pepper to taste
- ¼ cup butter
- 2 tablespoons all-purpose flour
- 1½ cups heavy cream

Wine: a dry rosé (Rosé di Fontanarossa)

Season the meat lightly with a little salt and pepper. • Heat a quarter of the butter in a fireproof casserole until it stops foaming. Add the veal and brown, stirring frequently for 10–15 minutes over medium heat. • While the meat is browning, melt the remaining butter in a small saucepan. Add the flour and stir with a wooden spoon while cooking over medium heat for 2 minutes, or until it starts to color. Add the flour mixture to the meat and cook for a few minutes, stirring constantly. • Pour in the cream and cover the pan. Simmer over low heat for at least 1 hour, stirring now and then. • If the liquid reduces too much, add 2 tablespoons of milk or water. There

Beef stew with potatoes

should be plenty of sauce. • Taste and add more salt if necessary. Serve hot.

Serves: 4 · Prep: 5 min. · Cooking: 1½ hrs · Level: 1

OSSIBUCHI CON GREMOLADA
Braised veal shanks with lemon sauce

☞ This is a classic Milanese dish. The special sauce, made with lemon peel, garlic, and parsley, is added just before removing from heat. It lightens and freshens the dish. If liked, serve with Milanese-style risotto (see recipe, page 172).

- 6 veal hind shanks, cut in 1½-inch thick slices
- 1/3 cup all-purpose flour salt and freshly ground black pepper to taste
- ¼ cup extra-virgin olive oil
- 3 tablespoons butter
- 1 carrot, 1 onion, 1 stalk celery, all finely chopped
- 4 sage leaves, torn
- 1 cup dry white wine
- 1 cup Beef stock (see recipe, page 105)
- ¼ cup peeled and diced tomatoes zest of 1 lemon, finely chopped
- 1 clove garlic, finely chopped
- 1 tablespoon finely chopped parsley

Wine: a dry red (Chianti Classico Ruffino)

Make 4–5 incisions around the edge of each shank to stop them curling up during cooking. Dredge in the flour and sprinkle with salt and pepper. • Heat the oil in a large, heavy-bottomed saucepan over medium-high heat and cook the shanks briefly on both sides. Remove and set aside. • Melt the butter in the pan and sauté the carrot, onion, celery, and sage until soft. Add the meat and cook for a few minutes. • Pour in the wine. When the wine has evaporated, add the stock and tomatoes, and season with salt and pepper to taste. • Cover and simmer over low heat for 1½ hours, adding extra beef stock if necessary. • When cooked, stir in the lemon peel, garlic, and parsley. • Transfer to a heated serving dish and serve hot.

Serves: 4–6 · Prep: 25 min. · Cooking: 1¾ hrs · Level: 2

Cold veal with tuna sauce

VITELLO TONNATO
Cold veal with tuna sauce

☞ This dish requires careful preparation, but the end result is well worth the effort. Be sure to cool the veal in its cooking water so that it doesn't become tough. The sauce should be spooned over the cool meat and left for several hours before serving so that the veal and tuna sauce are fully blended.

2   lb lean veal roast, preferably rump
1   carrot
1   stalk celery
1   bay leaf
1   onion skewered with 2 cloves
    salt and freshly ground black pepper to taste
1   quantity Mayonnaise (see recipe, page 16)
6   oz tuna, packed in oil
2   tablespoons capers, plus some to garnish
    juice of 1 lemon, plus ½ lemon to garnish
¼   cup extra-virgin olive oil

Wine: a dry, sparkling white (Prosecco di Conegliano)

Remove any fat from the meat and tie firmly with kitchen string. • Put the meat, carrot, celery, bay leaf, and onion skewered with cloves in a pot with just enough boiling water to cover the meat. Season with salt, cover, and simmer for 2 hours. Leave the veal to cool in its cooking water. • Prepare the mayonnaise. • Drain the oil from the tuna and place the fish in a food processor with the mayonnaise, capers, lemon juice, oil, salt, and pepper. Mix until smooth. • Slice the veal thinly, transfer to a serving dish and smother with the sauce. Garnish with capers and slices of lemon. • Cover and refrigerate for at least 6 hours. • Serve at room temperature.

Serves: 4 · Prep: 25 min. + 6 hrs to chill · Cooking: 2 hrs · Level: 2

SPIEDINI DI CARNE E VERDURE
Mixed meat and vegetable skewers

☞ There are many variations on the traditional recipe for mixed meat and vegetable skewers. The basic dish calls for bite-sized chunks of two or three different meats alternated with cherry tomatoes, baby onions, bell peppers, and bread. Always place the bread next to the meat, so that it absorbs the cooking juices. The crisp pieces of roasted bread are one of the best parts of this dish. The skewers are also very good when cooked over a barbecue.

10 oz pork
12 oz boned veal shoulder or shank
1   lb chicken breast
1   yellow and 1 red bell pepper
10 oz baby onions
20 cherry tomatoes
5   slices crusty bread
3   fresh Italian pork sausages
10 leaves fresh sage
    salt and freshly ground black pepper to taste
¼   cup extra-virgin olive oil
½   cup Beef stock (see recipe, page 105)

Remove any fat from the meat. • Chop the meat, vegetables, and bread into large cubes or squares. Slice the sausages thickly. • Thread the cubes onto wooden skewers, alternating pieces of meat, sausage, vegetables, bread, and sage leaves. • Arrange the skewers in a roasting dish and season with salt and pepper. Drizzle with the oil. • Bake in a preheated oven at 400°F for 30 minutes, turning occasionally and adding beef stock to moisten, if required. • When the meat is well browned, remove from the oven and serve hot.

Serves: 6 · Prep: 1 hr · Cooking: 30 min. · Level: 2

SPIEDINI IN SALSA
Beef skewers in herb sauce

1¾ cups dry white wine
¾   cup white wine vinegar
6   large white onions, finely chopped
1   tablespoon finely chopped marjoram
1¼ lb veal, shank or shoulder, cut into bite-sized pieces
½   cup butter
    salt and freshly ground white pepper to taste
2   tablespoons finely chopped parsley
1   red bell pepper
15 baby onions
    olive oil for basting

Wine: a dry white (Franciacorta Bianco)

Place 1¼ cups of the wine in a bowl with the vinegar, onions, and marjoram. Add the meat and marinate in the refrigerator for 4 hours. • Remove the meat from the marinade and drain well. • Heat the butter in a skillet and pour in the marinade. Season with salt and pepper. • Bring to the boil, then add the remaining wine and the parsley. Simmer for 5 minutes until the sauce reduces a little. • Preheat the broiler or prepare a grill. Clean the bell pepper and chop into 1 inch squares. Clean the onions. • Thread the meat and vegetables onto skewers and broil or grill until meat is cooked through. Turn frequently, basting with olive oil as required. Serve hot.

Serves: 4 · Prep: 5 min. · Cooking: 30 min. · Level: 1

FEGATO ALLA VENEZIANA
Venetian-style liver

☞ This is a classic recipe from Venice. The slight sweetness of the onion balances the liver's hint of bitterness, combining to make a superb dish. Serve with potato purée.

1½ lb white onions, thinly sliced
¼   cup butter
2   tablespoons extra-virgin olive oil
1½ lb calf's liver, cut into thin strips
    salt and freshly ground black pepper to taste
2   tablespoons finely chopped parsley

Wine: a dry, lightly sparkling red (Raboso Veronese)

Place the onions, butter, and oil in a very large skillet over low heat. Let them sweat gently for 15 minutes, then add the liver. • Cook over a high heat, stirring and turning constantly for 5 minutes at most. Sprinkle with salt just before removing from the heat (or the liver will become tough). • Season with pepper, sprinkle with the parsley, and serve hot.

Serves: 6 · Prep: 15 min. · Cooking: 20 min. · Level: 1

FEGATO ALL'ACETO BALSAMICO
Calf's liver with balsamic vinegar

☞ Pig's liver can be used instead of calf's liver. In the original recipe, lard was used for frying instead of butter.

14 oz calf's liver, very thinly sliced
½   cup all-purpose flour
2   eggs, lightly beaten
1   cup fine, dry bread crumbs
    salt and freshly ground black pepper to taste
¼   cup butter
2   tablespoons balsamic vinegar

Wine: a dry red (Colli Piacentini Barbera)

Coat the slices of liver with flour. Dip in the beaten egg and then coat with bread crumbs. Sprinkle lightly with salt and pepper. • Heat the butter in a wide skillet.

Add the the liver and cook until golden brown on both sides. • Drain very briefly on paper towels to absorb excess fat. • Drizzle with balsamic vinegar and serve hot.

Serves: 4 · Prep: 10 min. · Cooking: 15 min. · Level: 1

FEGATO ALLA SALVIA
Calf's liver with sage

1¼ lb calf's liver, thinly sliced
½   cup all-purpose flour
¼   cup extra-virgin olive oil
3   cloves garlic
6   fresh sage leaves
    salt and freshly ground black pepper to taste

Wine: a dry red (Vino Rosso di Montepulciano)

Lightly flour the liver, shaking off any excess. • Heat the oil with the garlic and sage over moderate heat in a large nonstick skillet. When the oil starts to sizzle around the garlic, raise the heat to moderately high, add the liver and cook quickly to ensure tenderness, turning once. • Sprinkle with a little salt and pepper when well-browned and remove from the heat. • Serve hot.

Serves: 4 · Prep: 5 min. · Cooking: 10 min. · Level: 1

ROGNONI TRIFOLATI ALLA SALVIA
Truffled kidneys

1   lb calf's kidneys
2   cups cold water
1   cup vinegar
¼   cup extra-virgin olive oil
1   tablespoon butter
2   cloves garlic, finely chopped
1   tablespoon finely chopped parsley
5   sage leaves
    salt and freshly ground black pepper to taste
½   cup red wine

Slice the kidneys in two lengthways, and remove the fatty parts and sinews. Cut into thin slices and set aside in a bowl with the

cold water and vinegar for about 1 hour. • Heat the oil and butter in a heavy-bottomed pan over medium-high heat. Add the garlic, parsley and sage and sauté for 2–3 minutes. • Add the drained kidneys. Season with salt and pepper and pour in the wine. • Cook for 5 minutes only, or the kidneys will become tough. • Serve hot with the cooking juices.

Serves: 4 · Prep: 15 min. + 1 hr to marinate · Cooking: 8 min. · Level:1

TRIPPA ALLA FIORENTINA
Florentine-style tripe

2   lb ready-to-cook calf's honeycomb tripe
1   large onion, finely chopped
1   large carrot, finely chopped
1   stick celery, finely chopped
¼   cup extra-virgin olive oil
    salt and freshly ground black pepper to taste
½   cup dry white wine
1   (15 oz) can Italian tomatoes, sieved
1   cup freshly grated Parmesan cheese

Wine: a dry red (Chianti dei Colli Fiorentini)

Rinse the tripe thoroughly under cold running water, drain, dry with a clean cloth and cut into thin strips with kitchen scissors or a very sharp knife. • Sauté the onion, carrot, and celery in the oil in a heavy-bottomed casserole for 5 minutes. • Add the tripe and season with salt and pepper. Continue cooking for 3–4 minutes, stirring. • Add the wine and cook over high heat, uncovered, for 5–6 minutes to reduce. • Mix in the tomatoes, check the seasoning, cover and simmer for 30 minutes, stirring occasionally. If necessary, reduce the amount of liquid by cooking uncovered over a higher heat for a few minutes. • Sprinkle with the cheese and serve.

Serves: 4 · Prep: 20 min. · Cooking: 45 min. · Level: 1

Venetian-style liver

PORK & LAMB

Pork is a staple in the Italian diet. Salami, prosciutto, ham, sausages, and many other deli meats are all pork products. Although less popular than veal and beef as a meat dish, it is still served often. Lamb also has a strong tradition in Italy, especially from Tuscany southward and on the islands of Sicily and Sardinia. Many of the recipes in this section come from Lazio, where lamb (known in the local dialect as abbacchio) is the most common meat.

ABBACCHIO ALLA ROMANA
Pan-roasted lamb

☞ Succulent, pan-roasted lamb is a classic Roman dish. The fresh herbs, garlic, and vinegar meld with the flavor of the meat as it slowly cooks. The salty anchovies added right at the end provide the finishing touch.

- 3   cloves garlic, finely chopped
- 2   tablespoons finely chopped rosemary leaves
- 10   fresh sage leaves
- 1/4   cup extra-virgin olive oil
- 2   lb tender young shoulder of lamb, cut into 8 pieces, with the bone left in
  salt and freshly ground black pepper to taste
- 1   tablespoon all-purpose flour
- 1/2   cup white wine vinegar
- 1/4   cup cold water
- 6   anchovy fillets

Wine: a light, dry red (Montescudaio Rosso)

Sauté the garlic, rosemary, and sage in the oil in a large, deep-sided skillet. Add the lamb and season with salt and pepper. • Stir in the flour, vinegar, and water. Turn the lamb so that it is well coated with the sauce. Cover and cook over low heat for 1 hour, adding extra water if the cooking liquid reduces too much. • Put 2 tablespoons of the cooking liquid in a small bowl and dissolve the anchovy fillets in it. • Pour into the skillet and stir well. Cook for another 2–3 minutes, then remove from heat and serve.

Serves: 4 · Prep: 10 min. · Cooking: 1¼ hrs · Level: 1

◁ Roast spareribs, Tuscan-style
(see recipe, page 238)
▷ Pan-roasted lamb

COSCIOTTO DI MAIALE AL CHIANTI
Roast pork with Chianti wine

4–5	lb roasting pork, with bone
	salt and freshly ground black pepper to taste
1	teaspoon ground cinnamon
1/4	cup all-purpose flour
2	onions, coarsely chopped
4	bay leaves
1/4	cup extra-virgin olive oil
1	cup Chianti wine
4	oz raisins
6	oz green olives

Wine: a dry red (Chianti Classico)

Sprinkle the pork with salt, pepper, and cinnamon, then dust with the flour. • Place in a roasting pan with the onions and bay leaves and drizzle with the oil. • Bake in a preheated oven at 350°F. • After 30 minutes, drizzle with half the wine and return to the oven. • Soak the raisins in a small bowl of tepid water for 15 minutes. Drain well. • After another 30 minutes, drizzle the pork with the remaining wine, and sprinkle with the raisins and olives. Return to the oven and cook for 1 more hour. Serve hot.

Serves: 6 ·Prep: 10 min. · Cooking: 2 hrs · Level: 1

SALAME AL VINO ROSSO
Salami cooked in red wine

1 1/4	lb salami (in one piece)
2	tablespoons cold water
2	tablespoons red wine vinegar
1	cup red wine
8	oz peeled and chopped fresh or canned tomatoes
14	oz canned garbanzo beans
	salt and freshly ground pepper to taste

Wine: a light, dry red (Freisa di Cheri)

Cut the salami into slices about 1/2 inch thick. • Heat the water in a deep-sided skillet and add the salami. Cook over medium heat, adding first the vinegar then, a little at a time, the wine. • When the wine has evaporated, heat the tomatoes in a saucepan and pour them into the skillet. Add the garbanzo beans and season with salt and pepper. (Taste before adding salt; the sauce may already be salty because of the salami.) • Simmer for 10 minutes, then serve hot.

Serves: 6 · Prep: 10 min. · Cooking: 20 min. · Level: 1

Roast pork with Chianti wine

MAIALE CON LE PRUGNE
Pan-roasted pork loin with prunes

18	dried prunes, pitted
1/2	cup brandy
1 1/2	lb boneless pork loin
	salt and freshly ground black pepper to taste
6	sprigs rosemary
1/4	cup extra-virgin olive oil
3/4	cup dry white wine
1	cup Beef stock (see recipe, page 105)

Wine: a dry red (Cabernet di Breganze)

Cut half the prunes in quarters and marinate in a bowl with the brandy and enough water to cover for 30 minutes. • Drain the prunes well. Use a sharp knife to make incisions in the pork. Fill with a little salt, pepper, and the soaked prunes. • Loosely bind the rosemary to the pork with kitchen string. Sprinkle with salt and pepper. • Heat the oil in a roasting pan over medium heat. When hot, add the pork and brown on all sides. • Transfer to a preheated oven at 350°F and cook for 30 minutes. • Remove from the oven and baste the meat with the wine. Add the remaining prunes, tucking them under the kitchen string used to bind the rosemary. Cook for 30 minutes more, adding stock if the pan dries out. • When cooked, transfer to a heated serving dish and slice thickly. Spoon the cooking juices and prunes over the top. Serve hot.

Serves: 4 · Prep: 10 min. + 30 min. to marinate · Cooking: 1 hr · Level: 1

MAIALE STUFATO AL VINO ROSSO
Pork stewed in red wine

☞ This dish is traditionally served with polenta.

3	lb mixed cuts of pork (spareribs, boned neck, boneless shanks)
3	Italian pork sausages
1/3	cup extra-virgin olive oil
2	onions, finely chopped
1	carrot, diced
1	stalk celery, finely chopped
3	cloves garlic, finely chopped
2	tablespoons finely chopped parsley
2	bay leaves
	salt and freshly ground black pepper to taste
3/4	cup full-bodied red wine
1	(15 oz) can Italian tomatoes
1	cup Beef stock (see recipe, page 105)

Wine: a dry, full-bodied red (Vino Rosso di Montalcino)

Chop each sparerib into 3 pieces. Cut the neck, shanks, and sausages into bite-sized pieces. • Heat the oil in a large, heavy-bottomed saucepan over medium-high heat. Add the onion, carrot, celery, parsley, and bay leaves, and sauté for 3–4 minutes. • Add the pork, season with salt and pepper, and brown all over. • Pour in the wine and cook until it has evaporated. • Stir in the tomatoes. • Cover and simmer gently over low heat for about 1 1/4 hours. Add the stock gradually as the sauce dries out. Turn the meat from time to time. • Serve hot.

Serves: 6 · Prep: 25 min. · Cooking: 1 1/2 hrs · Level: 2

MAIALE ARROSTO
Pan-roasted pork with potatoes

2 1/2	lb pork loin rib roast
3	cloves garlic, cut in half
3	twigs fresh rosemary
6	fresh sage leaves
4	oz smoked pancetta (bacon), diced
	salt and freshly ground black pepper to taste
1/2	cup extra-virgin olive oil
2	cups Beef stock (see recipe, page 105)
3	lb potatoes
2	cloves garlic, unpeeled

Wine: a dry, full-bodied red (Vino Nobile di Montepulciano)

Detach the loin from the ribs. Use a sharp knife to make 6 incisions in the loin. Fill with the garlic. Sprinkle the pork with the rosemary, sage, and pancetta and season with salt and pepper. • Tie the ribs to the loin with kitchen string. • Heat the oil in a heavy-bottomed pan over medium heat. Add the meat and brown all over, then add a ladleful of stock. • Cover and continue cooking, adding the stock gradually to keep the pan moist. • Peel the potatoes and cut them into bite-sized pieces. • When the pork has been cooking for 30 minutes, add the potatoes and unpeeled cloves of garlic. • When cooked, untie the ribs and arrange the meat and potatoes in a heated serving dish. Spoon the cooking juices over the top and serve hot.

Serves: 6 · Prep: 20 min. · Cooking: 1 1/2 hrs · Level: 1

ROSTICCIANA
Roast spareribs, Tuscan-style

- 5 lb spareribs
  salt and freshly ground black pepper to taste
- 2 tablespoons fresh rosemary leaves
- ¼ cup extra-virgin olive oil
- 4 cloves garlic, peeled and cut in half

Wine: a dry, full-bodied red (Chianti Classico Riserva)

Place the spareribs in a large roasting pan. Season with salt and pepper, sprinkle with the rosemary, and drizzle with the oil. Use a sharp knife to make 8 incisions in the meaty parts of the spareribs and fill each one with a piece of garlic. • Roast the spareribs in a preheated oven at 350°F for about 45–50 minutes. The exact cooking time will depend on how much meat is on the spareribs • Serve hot.

Serves: 6 · Prep: 10 min. · Cooking: 50 min. · Level: 1

MAIALE AL VINO E LATTE
Marinated pork braised in milk

- 3½ lb pork loin roast
- 4¼ cups white wine
  salt and freshly ground black pepper to taste
- ½ cup butter
- 4¼ cups milk
- 6 fresh sage leaves
- 2 sprigs fresh rosemary
  pinch of nutmeg

Wine: a dry, full-bodied red (Piave Cabernet Sauvignon)

Tie the pork with kitchen string as if for roasting. Place in a deep bowl and pour in

enough wine to cover it. Place in the refrigerator to marinate for 12 hours. • Take the pork out of the wine and dry with paper towels. Season with salt and pepper and place in a heavy-bottomed pan with the butter. Brown well over high heat. • Add the milk, sage leaves, and rosemary. Cover the pan and cook over low heat for 2 hours. When the pork has 20 minutes cooking time left, turn up the heat and cook, uncovered, to reduce the liquid. • Slice the pork and arrange on a serving dish. Spoon some of the cooking liquid over it and serve.

Serves: 6 · Prep: 20 min. + 12 hrs to marinate · Cooking: 2 hrs · Level: 1

MAIALE ARROSTO AL PANE E LATTE
Pan-roasted pork with milk and bread

☞ Cook veal and turkey roasts this way too. Milk gives a delicate flavor to many types of meat.

- ½ cup all-purpose flour
- 2 lb pork loin roast
- ¼ cup butter
  salt and freshly ground black pepper to taste
- 3 cups milk
- 1 cup cream
- 8 slices firm-textured bread

Wine: a dry red (Riviera del Garda)

Lightly flour the meat. Place in a heavy-bottomed pan with 3 tablespoons of butter. Cook until browned. • Season with salt and pepper and add 1 tablespoon of milk. Cover

the pan and cook over medium heat, gradually adding the remaining milk. Cook for 1½ hours, turning the pork from time to time. • Add the cream 30 minutes before the meat is cooked. • After about 2 hours, when the roast is well-cooked and the sauce thick, transfer it to a cutting board and slice. • Add the remaining butter to the pan and cook until thick. Spread on the bread and arrange the slices around the meat on a heated serving dish. Pour the remaining sauce over the meat and serve hot.

Serves: 4 · Prep: 10 min. · Cooking: 2 hrs · Level: 1

SALSICCE CON L'UVA
Sausages with grapes

- 30 large white grapes
- 8 large Italian pork sausages, about 2 lb
- 2 tablespoons extra-virgin olive oil
- 1 clove garlic, finely chopped

Wine: a light, dry red (Pinot Nero dei Colli Piacentini)

Rinse the grapes under cold running water and dry with paper towels. • Place the sausages in a large skillet with the oil and garlic. Prick them with a fork, and sauté over medium-high heat for 10 minutes. • Add the grapes and cook for 10–15 more minutes, or until the grapes have reduced to about half their original volume. • Serve hot.

Serves: 4 · Prep: 5 min. · Cooking: 25 min. · Level: 1

MAIALE ALLA REGGIANA
Pan-roasted pork with milk and juniper

- 3½ lb loin of pork
- 1 cup extra-virgin olive oil
- 2 tablespoons white wine vinegar
- 2 cloves garlic, peeled and lightly crushed
- 1 sprig rosemary
- 10 juniper berries
- 4¼ cups whole milk (enough to cover the meat)
  salt and freshly ground black pepper to taste

Wine: a lightly sparkling, dry red (Colli Piacentini Bonarda)

Tie the meat with kitchen string so that it will keep its shape as it cooks. • Place in a casserole or heavy-bottomed pan just large enough to accommodate the meat. Pour the oil and vinegar into the casserole, then add the garlic, rosemary, juniper berries, and meat. Marinate in the refrigerator for 24 hours, turning frequently. • Pour in enough milk to cover the

Sausages with flowering turnip tops

meat, season with salt and pepper, and cook over low heat for 1 hour. At the end of this time the milk will have been completely absorbed. • Turn up the heat and brown the meat all over. • Carve into chops and serve. This dish is equally good served hot or at room temperature.

Serves: 6 · Prep: 15 min. + 24 hrs to marinate · Cooking: 1 hr · Level: 2

BISTECCHE DI MAIALE AL CAVOLO NERO
Pork cutlets with Tuscan kale

☞ *Cavolo nero*, known as Tuscan kale or black cabbage in English, is a tall leafy member of the cabbage family. It is a specialty of Tuscany. If it is not available, replace with the same quantity of Swiss chard. The Swiss chard does not need to be boiled for 30 minutes before chopping; 8–10 minutes will be enough.

1	lb Tuscan kale (or Swiss chard)
1	onion, finely chopped
1	clove garlic, finely chopped
1/4	cup extra-virgin olive oil
4	pork cutlets, about 1 1/4 lb
	salt and freshly ground black pepper to taste
3/4	cup red wine

Wine: a dry red (Velletri Rosso)

Rinse the kale, remove the tough stalks, and cook in a pot of salted, boiling water for 30 minutes. • Drain well and chop finely. • Sauté the onion and garlic in the oil in a heavy-bottomed pan until soft. • Add the cutlets, sprinkle with salt and pepper, and brown on both sides. • Pour in the wine and cook for 15–20 minutes, or until the cutlets are tender. • When the meat is cooked, remove from the pan and set aside. Add the Tuscan kale to the cooking juices in the pan. Cook over medium heat for 10 minutes, stirring frequently. • Return the cutlets to the pan and reheat. • Serve hot.

Serves: 4 · Prep: 15 min. · Cooking: 1 hr · Level: 1

MAIALE ARROSTO ALLE MELE
Roast pork with apple

6	Golden Delicious apples
2	cups dry white wine
2	pork fillets, about 1 lb each
	salt and freshly ground black pepper to taste
1/4	cup extra-virgin olive oil

Wine: a dry red (Freisa)

Pan-roasted pork with milk and bread

Cut the apples in half and remove the cores. Place in a bowl, cover with the wine, and set aside to marinate for at least 2 hours. • Season the pork with salt and pepper and place in a baking dish with the oil. • Bake in a preheated oven at 400°F. After 10 minutes, pour about half the wine used to marinate the apples over the pork. Turn the pork and cook for another 20 minutes. • Arrange the apples around the pork in the baking pan and add more wine if the pan is dry. Cook for 30 minutes more. • Slice the pork and transfer to a serving dish. Arrange the apples around the pork and serve hot.

Serves: 4 · Prep: 5 min. + 2 hrs to marinate · Cooking: 1 hr · Level: 1

SALSICCE E FAGIOLI ALL'UCCELLETTO
Sausages and beans in tomato sauce

1/4	cup extra-virgin olive oil
2	cloves garlic, finely chopped
6	leaves sage
1	lb cannellini or white kidney beans, precooked
14	oz peeled and diced fresh or canned tomatoes
	salt and freshly ground black pepper to taste
8	large Italian pork sausages

Wine: a dry red (Chianti dei Colli Fiorentini)

Heat the oil in a heavy-bottomed pan and sauté the garlic and sage. • Add the beans and cook for a few minutes so that they absorb the seasoning. • Add the tomatoes and season with salt and pepper. • Prick the sausages with a fork and add to the beans. Cover and cook over medium-low heat for about 20 minutes, stirring frequently. • Serve hot.

Serves: 4 · Prep: 5 min. · Cooking: 25 min. · Level: 1

SALSICCE CON BROCCOLETTI
Sausages with flowering turnip tops

☞ Flowering turnip tops, known as "broccoletti" in Italian, are a common winter vegetable. If they are not available, replace with the same amount of broccoli.

2	cloves garlic, finely chopped
1	fresh red chile pepper, thinly sliced
2	tablespoons extra-virgin olive oil
8	large Italian pork sausages
1 1/4	lb flowering turnip tops (or broccoli, if preferred)
	salt and freshly ground black pepper to taste

Wine: a dry white (Orvieto)

Sauté the garlic and chile pepper in the oil in a large skillet over medium heat until pale gold. • Add the sausages and brown all over, pricking well with a fork to let some of the fat run out. • Clean and wash the flowering turnip tops and add to the skillet. Season with salt and pepper. Cook for 20 minutes, or until the greens are tender, but not overcooked. Add a little water during cooking if the skillet dries out too much. • Serve hot.

Serves: 4 · Prep: 5 min. · Cooking: 25 min. · Level: 1

Pork skewers

SPIEDINI DI MAIALE
Pork skewers

☞ For an even tastier dish, chop 2 large pork sausages in 8 pieces and thread them onto the skewers as well.

 2 lb boned leg or shoulder of pork
16 button mushrooms
16 cherry tomatoes
10 oz pancetta, sliced
16 leaves fresh basil
   salt and freshly ground black pepper to taste
1/4 cup extra-virgin olive oil

Wine: a light, dry red (Merlot dei Colli Bolognesi)

Chop the pork into bite-sized pieces. • Wash the mushrooms and tomatoes and pat dry with paper towels. • Thread 8 skewers with the pork and other ingredients. • Sprinkle with salt and pepper and cook over a barbecue or under the broiler or grill until the meat and vegetable are cooked. Drizzle with extra-virgin olive oil as required during cooking. • Serve hot.

Serves: 4 · Prep: 5 min. · Cooking: 15–20 min. · Level: 1

PROSCIUTTO AL CALVADOS
Ham with Calvados

 1 ham, weighing about 2¼ lb
   salt and freshly ground black pepper to taste
1/3 cup extra-virgin olive oil
1/4 cup honey
   juice of 1 orange
 6 apples, peeled and cut in segments
1/2 cup Calvados liqueur (made with distilled apples)
 2 lb potatoes
 2 tablespoons butter

Wine: a dry red (Chianti Classico - Brolio)

Trim the ham of any small pieces of fat or skin. Season with pepper and bake with the oil in a preheated oven at 425°F. • After 15 minutes, dilute the honey in the orange juice and brush the meat with this mixture. Reduce oven temperature to 375°F. • After 15 minutes turn the ham over, brush with the honey mixture again, and return to the oven. • Repeat this process twice more, before you finish cooking. This should take about 1 hour. • In the meantime, halfway through cooking add the apples to the ham and pour half the Calvados over them. •

Wash the potatoes and boil them in their skins in a large pan of boiling, salted water. • When the ham is cooked, transfer to a heavy-bottomed pan with the cooking juices and apples. Place over high heat, pour in the remaining Calvados, and cook until the liqueur has evaporated. • When the potatoes are cooked, drain, peel, and mash them. • Mash the apples cooked with the ham, season with salt and butter, and combine with the potatoes. If the mixture is too liquid, add a little flour. Place over low heat, stirring frequently, until thick. • Slice the ham and transfer to a heated serving dish. • Serve hot with the potato and apple purée.

Serves: 6 · Prep: 10 min. · Cooking: 1¼ hrs · Level: 2

MAIALE AL GINEPRO
Pork loin with juniper berries

2½ lb pork loin
 2 shallots, sliced
 1 onion, finely chopped
15 juniper berries
 4 bay leaves
   salt and freshly ground black pepper to taste
1/3 cup extra-virgin olive oil
1/2 cup dry white wine
 4 oz pancetta, sliced

Wine: a light, dry red (Barbera dei Colli Piacentini)

Place the pork loin in a bowl with the shallot, onion, juniper berries, bay leaves, salt, pepper, 3 tablespoons of oil, and the wine. Marinate for 2 hours. • Drain the pork and wrap in the pancetta. Tie with kitchen string. Transfer to a baking dish. • Strain the vegetables and herbs used in the marinade and add to the pork. • Add the remaining oil and place in a preheated oven at 375°F. • Cook for 1½ hours, moistening from time to time with the marinade and turning the pork over every so often. • Slice the pork. Strain the cooking juices and spoon over the meat. Serve hot.

Serves: 6 · Prep: 25 min. + 2 hrs to marinate · Cooking: 1½ hrs · Level: 2

PUCCIA
Pork casserole with polenta

☞ This hearty winter dish comes from the town of Alba, in Piedmont.

 1 lb loin of pork, cut into 1¼-inch cubes
1¼ lb Savoy cabbage, cut into thin strips

1 small onion, thickly sliced
1 small carrot, 1 stalk celery, sliced
  pinch of salt
1½ cups coarse-grain yellow cornmeal
⅓ cup butter, cut into small pieces
¼ cup freshly grated Parmesan cheese

Wine: a dry, full-bodied red (Dolcetto d'Alba Superiore)

Place the pork in a casserole with the cabbage, onion, carrot, and celery. Add the salt and ½ cup hot water. Cover tightly and bring quickly to the boil. • Reduce heat to medium and simmer for 30 minutes. • While the pork and vegetables are cooking, bring 5¼ cups of salted water to a boil in a large, heavy bottomed saucepan. Sprinkle in the cornmeal while stirring continuously with a large balloon whisk to prevent lumps forming. Continue cooking over medium heat, stirring almost continuously for 20–25 minutes. • Add the meat, vegetables, and their cooking liquid to this very soft polenta and stir well. • Simmer for 20–25 minutes more, stirring frequently and adding a little boiling water as necessary to keep the polenta moist and soft. • Stir in the butter and Parmesan. Serve hot.

Serves: 4 · Prep: 10 min. · Cooking: 1 hr · Level: 1

STINCHI DI MAIALE CON VERDURE
Roast pork shanks with vegetables

3 pork shanks, about 3 lb
¼ cup all-purpose flour
  salt and freshly ground black pepper to taste
⅓ cup extra-virgin olive oil
¾ cup dry white wine
4 large carrots, peeled and cut in wheels
6 stalks celery, coarsely chopped
4 medium onions, coarsely chopped
4 large potatoes, peeled and diced
4 large zucchini, diced
2 cups Beef stock (see recipe, page 105)

Wine: a full-bodied, dry red (Nobile di Montepulciano)

Remove any remaining hairs from the shanks. Rinse under cold running water and pat dry with paper towels. • Roll in the flour and sprinkle with salt and pepper. • Heat ¼ cup of oil in a large, heavy-bottomed pan, add the shanks and cook over high heat until golden brown. • Transfer the shanks and their cooking juices to a roasting pan. Place in a

Roast suckling pig with vegetables

preheated oven at 400°F. • Cook for 20 minutes. Add the wine and cook for 40 minutes more, adding a little stock if the pan becomes too dry. • Meanwhile, heat the remaining oil in a heavy-bottomed pan and sauté the vegetables over high heat for 5–7 minutes. • When the shanks have been in the oven for about 1 hour, add the vegetables and their cooking juices. • Return to the oven and cook for 1 hour more, basting with stock as required to stop the pan from drying out. • When cooked, arrange the meat and vegetables on a heated serving dish and serve hot.

Serves: 6 · Prep: 50 min. · Cooking: 2 hrs · Level: 2

MAIALINO AL FORNO
Roast suckling pig with vegetables

2 onions, 2 carrots, 2 stalks celery, 2 zucchini, 3 potatoes, all diced
1 leek, sliced
⅓ cup extra-virgin olive oil
  pinch of salt
½ suckling pig, about 4½ lb
10 black peppercorns
2 bay leaves
1 cup dry white wine
1 tablespoon garlic and parsley, finely chopped

Wine: a dry, full-bodied red (Barolo)

Sauté the vegetables in a large, heavy-bottomed pan with 2 tablespoons of oil over high heat for 5–6 minutes. • Sprinkle with salt and stir thoroughly. Remove from heat and set aside. • Add the remaining oil to the same pan and brown the pork. • Transfer the meat and any liquid it has produced to a roasting pan. Sprinkle with a little more salt and the peppercorns. Add the bay leaves and turn the meat in its juices. • Cook in a preheated oven at 400°F for 1½ hours, basting frequently and gradually adding the wine. • After about 1 hour, add the vegetables and sprinkle with the garlic and parsley. • Arrange on a heated serving dish with the vegetables and serve hot.

Serves: 6 · Prep: 10 min. · Cooking: 1¾ hrs · Level: 2

Cotechino sausage wrapped in beef

COTECHINO IN CAMICIA
Cotechino sausage wrapped in beef

- 1 large, thin slice of beef, cut from the rump, about 8 oz
- 1 large cotechino sausage
- 1 small onion, 1 stalk celery, 1 small carrot, all coarsely chopped
- 2 tablespoons butter
- 1/2 cup dry red wine
- 2 oz dried porcini mushrooms, soaked in warm water, drained, and chopped
- 2 cups water

Wine: a dry red (Colli Piacentini Gutturnio)

Use a meat pounder to flatten the slice of beef. • Skin the cotechino sausage. Wrap it up in the slice of beef, enveloping it completely. Tie the resulting roll securely but not too tightly with kitchen string. • Sauté the onion, celery, and carrot in the butter for a few minutes. • Add the meat and sausage roll, and brown well all over. • Pour in the wine and cook until it has evaporated. • Add the mushrooms and the water they were soaked in. • Simmer gently for 1 1/2 hours. • Untie the string and serve. Slice, moistening with the cooking juices.

Serves: 4 · Prep: 25 min. · Cooking: 1 1/2 hrs · Level: 2

COTECHINO CON I FAGIOLI
Cotechino sausage with beans

- 1 large cotechino sausage, about 2 lb
- 14 oz dried red kidney beans, soaked for 12 hours
- 1 onion
- 1 small bunch parsley
- 1/4 cup extra-virgin olive oil
  salt and freshly ground black pepper to taste

Wine: a dry red (Pinot Nero dei Colli Piacentini)

Prick the sausage all over with a large needle. Place in a pot with enough cold water to cover and simmer gently for 3 1/2 hours. • About 1 1/2 hours before the cotechino sausage is cooked, place the beans in a saucepan of water with the onion and parsley and cook until tender. • Drain the cotechino when cooked and slice thickly. Drain the beans, discarding the onion and parsley, and return to the saucepan. Add the cotechino and the oil. Season well with salt and pepper. Stir over medium heat for 5 minutes then serve.

Serves: 6 · Prep: 15 min. · Cooking: 3 hrs · Level: 1

ZAMPONE CON LE LENTICCHIE
Zampone sausage with lentils

☞ In Italy, zampone is served with lentils on New Year's day because it is believed that it will bring good luck throughout the new year.

- 1 zampone, about 2 lb (or 1 1/2 lb cotechino)
- 2 1/2 cups lentils, precooked
- 1 carrot, 1 stalk celery, 1 small onion, all finely chopped
- 1/4 cup extra-virgin olive oil
  salt and freshly ground black pepper to taste
- 8 oz canned tomatoes
- 2 cups Beef stock (see recipe, page 105)

Wine: a dry red (Gutturnio)

Place the sausage in a pot with enough lightly salted cold water to cover completely. Cover and simmer gently for 3 hours. Be careful not to puncture the skin during cooking. • In the meantime prepare the lentils. Sauté the carrot, celery, and onion with the oil in a skillet over medium-high heat. • When the vegetables are light golden, add the lentils and sauté for 2–3 minutes more. Season with salt and pepper and add the tomatoes. • Cook for a few minutes, then pour in the stock. Cover and cook for 40 minutes. • Spoon the lentils onto a heated serving dish. Slice the sausage thickly and arrange the slices on the lentils. • Serve hot.

Serves: 6 · Prep: 15 min. + time to soak · Cooking: 3 hrs · Level: 1

ZAMPONE CON IL CAVOLO ACIDO
Zampone sausage with cabbage

- 1 zampone, about 2 lb
- 1 cabbage, about 1 lb
- 1/2 cup extra-virgin olive oil
- 1/2 cup white wine vinegar
- 2 cloves garlic, finely chopped
- 1 cooking apple, peeled and thinly sliced
- 1 bay leaf and 5 juniper berries
  salt and freshly ground black pepper to taste

Wine: a dry red (Pinot Nero)

Cook the sausage following the method for *Zampone sausage with lentils* (this page). • About 1 1/2 hours before the sausage is cooked, cut the cabbage in thin strips. Rinse well under cold running water. • Place in a heavy-bottomed saucepan and cook over low heat. After about 30 minutes, drain any liquid from the pan and pour in the oil and vinegar. Add the garlic, apple, bay leaf, and juniper berries. Season with salt and pepper. Cover and cook for 30 minutes, or until very tender. • Slice the cooked sausage and serve on a heated serving dish with the cabbage.

Serves: 6 · Prep: 15 min. · Cooking: 3 hrs · Level: 1

COTECHINO ALLO SPUMANTE
Cotechino sausage with sparkling wine

- 2 tablespoons butter
- 2 lb sauerkraut
- 1 large cotechino sausage
- 1/2 cup diced pancetta
- 1 bottle dry sparkling wine

Wine: a dry sparkling white (Berlucchi)

Grease the bottom of a large flameproof dish with the butter and cover with the sauerkraut. Arrange the cotecchino and pancetta on top. • Place over medium heat and pour in half the wine. When the sauerkraut becomes dry, pour in the remaining wine. • The dish will take about 50 minutes to cook. Slice the cotechino and arrange on top of the sauerkraut on a heated serving dish. • Serve hot.

Serves: 4 · Prep: 25 min. · Cooking: 50 min. · Level: 2

Zampone and cotechino are large sausages made with a mixture of pork, salt, pepper, nutmeg, cloves, and other seasonings, wrapped in pig's trotter for zampone, and in rind from pig snout and jowl for cotechino. They are regional dishes from the city of Modena in Emilia-Romagna. Cotechino should be soaked in cold water for at least 1 hour before cooking. Zampone will require at least 4 hours soaking. Nowadays, some brands of both sausages are precooked and do not require soaking. Read the instructions on the package when you buy the sausage.

ZAMPONE CON PURÉE DI PATATE
Zampone sausage with potatoes

1	zampone, about 2 lb (or 1½ lb cotechino)
1½	lb potatoes, peeled
½	cup whole milk
1	tablespoons butter
	salt and freshly ground black pepper to taste
	pinch of nutmeg

Wine: a dry red (Pinot Nero dei Colli Piacentini)

Cook the sausage following the method for *Zampone sausage with lentils* (facing page). • About 30 minutes before the sausage is cooked, boil the potatoes in a large pot of salted water for 25 minutes, or until tender. Mash the potatoes and stir in the milk and butter. Season with nutmeg, salt, and pepper. • Slice the cooked sausage and serve on a heated serving dish with the potatoes.

Serves: 6 · Prep: 15 min. · Cooking: 3 hrs · Level: 1

ZAMPONE CON GLI SPINACI
Zampone sausage with spinach

1	zampone, about 2 lb (or 1½ lb cotechino)
2	lb spinach
¼	cup butter
	salt and freshly ground black pepper to taste

Wine: a light, dry red (Lambrusco di Sorbara)

Cook the sausage following the method for *Zampone sausage with lentils* (facing page). • About 20 minutes before the sausage is cooked, boil the spinach in salted water for 8–10 minutes, or until tender. Drain well. Add the butter and chop finely in a food processor. Season with salt and pepper. • Slice the sausage and serve hot with the spinach.

Serves: 6 · Prep: 15 min. · Cooking: 3 hrs · Level: 1

Zampone sausage with potatoes

AGNELLO ALLE ERBE AROMATICHE
Roast leg of lamb with aromatic herbs

☞ Use the same ingredients and method to prepare roast legs of turkey. Turkey has a less distinctive flavor than lamb and the herbs will enhance it (whereas they tend to mellow and blend with the stronger taste of the lamb).

- 4 slices sandwich bread
- 3 cloves garlic
- 6 leaves sage
- 1 sprig each rosemary, thyme, and marjoram
- 1 large bunch parsley
  salt and freshly ground black pepper to taste
- 2 tablespoons butter
- 2 lb leg of lamb
- ¼ cup extra-virgin olive oil
- ⅔ cup dry white wine

Wine: a dry red (Rosso di Franciacorta)

Trim the crusts off the bread and mix in a food processor with the garlic and aromatic herbs (leaves only). Season with salt and a generous grinding of pepper. • Put the butter in a roasting pan and place in a preheated oven at 375°F for a few minutes, until the butter melts. • Place the lamb in the roasting pan, drizzle with the oil, and scatter with the chopped herbs and bread. • Return to the oven and cook for 1½ hours, basting from time to time with the wine. • Transfer to a heated serving dish and serve hot.

Serves: 4 · Prep: 10 min. · Cooking: 1¾ hrs · Level: 1

AGNELLO ALLE OLIVE
Lamb with olives

☞ In Sicily this dish is often made with kid, or baby goat's meat (sometimes marketed in the U.S. as chevron). Both the delicate flavor of kid and the stronger taste of lamb work well with the olives.

- 2 lb lamb, cut into fairly small pieces
- ¼ cup extra-virgin olive oil
  salt and freshly ground black pepper to taste
- 8 oz large black olives, pitted and cut into quarters
- 1¼ cups dry red wine

Wine: a dry, full-bodied red (Etna Rosso)

Place the lamb in an ovenproof earthenware casserole. Drizzle with the oil and season with salt and a generous sprinkling of pepper. Sprinkle with the olives and moisten with half the wine. • Cover and cook in a preheated oven at 350°F for about 1 hour or until the meat is very tender, basting at frequent intervals with a little more wine.

Serves: 4 · Prep: 10 min. · Cooking: 1 hr · Level 2

AGNELLO AL LATTE E BRANDY
Lamb stewed in butter, brandy, rosemary, and milk

- 2½ lb lamb shoulder and leg, cut into bite–sized pieces
- 1 cup all-purpose flour
- 3 tablespoons butter
- ½ cup diced pancetta
- 1 tablespoon finely chopped rosemary
  salt and freshly ground black pepper to taste
- ½ cup brandy
- 2 cups milk

Wine: a dry red (Carmignano Rosso)

Dredge the lamb in the flour and then shake off any excess. • Melt the butter in a large, heavy-bottomed pan and sauté the pancetta for 2–3 minutes over medium heat. • Add the lamb, rosemary, salt and pepper. • Sauté for 4–5 minutes, then pour in the brandy. Stir continuously until the brandy has evaporated. • Add the milk, partially cover the pan, and cook over medium-low heat, stirring often, for about 1 hour, or until the milk has reduced to a dense sauce. • Serve hot.

Serves: 6 · Prep: 15 min. · Cooking: 1¼ hrs · Level: 2

AGNELLO ALL'AGRO
Lamb in butter, oil, and white wine

- 2½ lb lamb, leg or shoulder, cut into bite-sized pieces
- 2 tablespoons butter
- 2 tablespoons extra-virgin olive oil
  salt and freshly ground black pepper to taste
- ½ cup dry white wine
  juice of 2 lemons

Wine: a robust, dry white (Donnafugata)

Sauté the lamb in the butter and oil over high heat in a large, heavy-bottomed pan. • Season with salt and pepper, mix well, and pour in half the wine and lemon juice. • Reduce the heat to medium-low, partially cover the pan and cook for about 1½ hours. Gradually stir in the remaining wine and lemon juice as the sauce reduces. • Serve hot.

Serves: 6 · Prep: 10 min. · Cooking: 1¾ hrs · Level: 1

AGNELLO CON I PISELLI
Lamb stew with rosemary, garlic, and peas

- ⅓ cup extra-virgin olive oil
- 4 cloves garlic, finely chopped
- 1 tablespoon finely chopped rosemary
- ½ cup diced pancetta
- 2½ lb lamb shoulder, cut into pieces, with bone
  salt and freshly ground black pepper to taste
- ½ cup dry white wine
- 4 tomatoes, peeled and chopped
- 1 lb fresh or frozen shelled peas

Wine: a dry red (Barolo)

Heat the oil in a large skillet and sauté the garlic, rosemary, and pancetta over medium heat for 4–5 minutes. • Add the lamb and season with salt and pepper. • Pour in the wine and cook until it has evaporated. • Stir in the tomatoes, lower the heat and partially cover the pan. Cook for about 50 minutes, stirring from time to time. • Remove the lamb from the pan, and set aside in a warm place. Add the peas to the pan and sauté briefly in the sauce. • Add the lamb again and cook for 30 minutes more. • Serve hot.

Serves: 6 · Prep: 10 min. · Cooking: 1½ hrs · Level: 2

ABBACCHIO AL FORNO
Roast lamb with rosemary and garlic

☞ Roast baby lamb with potatoes is a traditional dish at Easter in most parts of Italy.

-   shoulder of baby lamb (with some loin attached), weighing about 2¼ lb
- 3 cloves garlic, peeled and cut in half
- 4–6 sprigs fresh rosemary
- ¼ cup extra-virgin olive oil
  salt and freshly ground black pepper to taste
- 2 lb roasting potatoes

Wine: a dry red (Cerveteri Rosso)

Place the lamb in an ovenproof dish large enough to hold the lamb and the potatoes. • Use the point of a sharp knife to make small incisions in the meat and push the pieces of garlic in. Close the meat around it, so that its flavor will permeate the meat during cooking. • Run your hand backward up two of the rosemary sprigs and sprinkle the leaves over the lamb. Tuck the remaining sprigs in around the meat. Drizzle with the oil. Sprinkle with salt and pepper to taste. • Place in a preheated oven at 350°F. • Peel the potatoes and cut into large bite-sized chunks. Arrange them around the meat after it has been in the oven for about 20 minutes. The meat should take about 1 hour to cook, while the potatoes will need only about 40 minutes. Baste the meat with the cooking juices 2 or 3 times during roasting and turn the potatoes so that they are evenly browned. • Serve hot.

Serves: 4 · Prep: 10 min. · Cooking: 1 hr · Level 1

Roast lamb with rosemary and garlic

sprinkle with coarse sea salt and leave to drain for about 2 hours. • Heat the oil in a heavy-bottomed pan and sauté the lamb over medium-high heat until golden brown. Season with salt and pepper. • Add the onion and cook for 10 minutes, stirring continually so that it doesn't stick. • Add the eggplant, marjoram, and thyme and cook for 5 minutes. • Pour in the tomato sauce and mix well. • Cover the pan partially and cook over medium-low heat for about 1 hour, adding the stock gradually as the sauce dries out. • Serve hot.

Serves: 4 · Prep: 20 min. + 2 hrs for the eggplants · Cooking: 1¼ hrs · Level: 2

AGNELLO E CARCIOFI IN FRICASSEA
Lamb and artichoke fricassée

1¼	lb lamb (boneless leg and shoulder), cut into bite-sized pieces
	salt and freshly ground black pepper to taste
½	cup extra-virgin olive oil
	juice of 2 lemons
4	artichokes
2	cloves garlic, finely chopped
¾	cup dry white wine
¾	cup Beef stock (see recipe, page 105)
1	egg
1	tablespoon finely chopped parsley

Wine: a dry white (Malvasia secca del Carso)

Place the lamb in a bowl with salt, pepper, ¼ cup of oil and the juice of half a lemon. Marinate for 2 hours. • Clean the artichokes by discarding the tough outer leaves and cut off the tips. Cut the tender inner heart into segments and place them in a bowl of cold water with the remaining lemon juice. • Heat the remaining oil in a skillet over medium heat. Add the garlic and artichokes, sauté for 5–6 minutes, then set aside. • Drain the lamb, and sauté in a heavy-bottomed pan with half the remaining oil. • When the lamb is well browned, pour in the wine and cook until it evaporates. • Transfer the lamb to the skillet with the artichokes and season with salt. • Partially cover and cook over medium heat for 1 hour, adding stock from time to time as the sauce reduces, and stirring frequently. • When the lamb is cooked, beat the egg with a little salt and the

Lamb and potato casserole

AGNELLO AL FORMAGGIO
Braised lamb with cheese

☞ This recipe comes from Sicily, where a little of the local cheese is often added to the cooking juices for extra flavor.

2	large scallions or 1 small onion, thinly sliced
2½	tablespoons extra-virgin olive oil
2½	tablespoons finely chopped fresh pork fat
2	lb lamb (from the shoulder or leg), diced
1	cup dry red or dry white wine
1	tablespoon finely chopped parsley
2	cloves garlic, lightly crushed
	salt and freshly ground black pepper to taste
1	cup Beef stock (see recipe, page 105)
1¾	lb small new potatoes or large potatoes, diced
¾	cup coarsely grated Pecorino cheese

Wine: a dry, full-bodied red (Etna rosso)

Sauté the scallions or onion briefly in the oil over a very low heat in a large flameproof casserole. • Add the pork fat and stir until it has melted. Add the lamb and brown all over. • Pour in the wine and cook, uncovered, over medium heat until it has evaporated. • Stir in the parsley, garlic, salt, and pepper and then add most of the stock. Cover and cook over a low heat for 45 minutes. • Add the potatoes and more stock, if the lamb is too dry. • Cover and cook for 30 minutes, or until the potatoes and meat are tender. • Sprinkle with the cheese, stir briefly, and turn off the heat. • Leave to stand for 4–5 minutes before serving.

Serves: 4–5 · Prep: 15 min. · Cooking: 1½ hrs · Level: 2

AGNELLO CON LE MELANZANE
Lamb stew with eggplant

2	large eggplants
2	tablespoons coarse sea salt
¼	cup extra-virgin olive oil
2	lb lamb shoulder, cut in 2 in pieces with bone
	salt and freshly ground black pepper to taste
1	onion, coarsely chopped
1	teaspoon each finely chopped marjoram and thyme
1	quantity Simple tomato sauce (see recipe, page 18)
1¼	cups Beef stock (see recipe, page 105)

Wine: a dry red (Barbaresco)

Rinse the eggplants under cold running water and, without peeling them, cut into bite-sized pieces. Place in a colander,

remaining lemon juice. Pour the egg mixture over the stew and turn off the heat. Stir continuously so that the egg sets. • Add the parsley and serve hot.

Serves: 4 · Prep: 25 min. + 2 hrs to marinate · Cooking: 1¼ hrs · Level: 1

AGNELLO IN AGRODOLCE
Sweet and sour lamb

- 1 large onion, finely chopped
- ¼ cup extra-virgin olive oil
- 2 lb lamb shoulder, boned and cut in 2-inch cubes
  salt and freshly ground black pepper to taste
- 4 oz canned tomatoes, peeled and chopped
- 6 basil leaves, torn
- ½ cup white wine vinegar
- 2 tablespoons sugar

Wine: a light, dry red (Torgiano Rosso)

Sauté the onion in the oil in a large skillet until soft. • Add the lamb and season with salt and pepper. Cook over medium heat for about 15 minutes. • Stir in the tomatoes and basil and cook for 10 more minutes, or until the lamb is tender. • Pour in the vinegar and cook for 2–3 minutes, then add the sugar. Stir until the sugar has melted. • Serve hot.

Serves: 4 · Prep: 10 min. · Cooking: 25 min. · Level: 1

AGNELLO CON LE PATATE
Lamb and potato casserole

- 2 lb lamb, cut into bite-sized pieces
- 1½ lb yellow, waxy potatoes, thickly sliced or in wedges
- 4 large tomatoes, quartered or cut into 6 pieces
- 1 medium onion, sliced
- ¼ cup extra-virgin olive oil
  salt and freshly ground black pepper to taste
  leaves from a small sprig of fresh rosemary
- 1 teaspoon oregano

Wine: a dry, full-bodied red (Etna Rosso)

Place the lamb, potatoes, tomatoes, and onion in an ovenproof casserole. • Drizzle with the oil and season with a little salt and plenty of pepper. Sprinkle with the rosemary and oregano. • Cover and cook in a preheated oven at 400°F for about 1 hour or until the meat is very tender. Baste at frequent intervals with a little hot water. • Serve hot.

Serves: 4 · Prep: 15 min. · Cooking: 1 hr · Level: 2

Hot and spicy lamb and tomato stew

AGNELLO AL POMODORO
Hot and spicy lamb and tomato stew

- ¼ cup extra-virgin olive oil
- 1 onion, 1 carrot, 1 stalk celery, coarsely chopped
- 2 cloves garlic, finely chopped
- 2 tablespoons finely chopped parsley
- 1 teaspoon crushed red pepper flakes
- 1 cup diced pancetta
- 2¼ lb lamb, shoulder or leg, cut in bite-sized pieces
  salt and freshly ground black pepper to taste
- ⅔ cup dry white wine
- 1 lb ripe tomatoes, peeled and chopped

Wine: a dry rosé (Cirò)

Heat the oil in a large, heavy-bottomed pan, preferably earthenware and sauté the onion, carrot, celery, garlic, parsley, pepper flakes, and pancetta over medium-high heat. • When the pancetta and onion are light golden brown, add the lamb and cook with the vegetable mixture, stirring continuously for 7–8 minutes. • Season with salt and pepper and add the wine. Cook until the wine has evaporated. • Add the tomatoes, then lower the heat to medium and partially cover. Cook for about 1 hour, adding a little hot water if the sauce reduces too much. • Serve hot.

Serves: 4–6 · Prep: 15 min. · Cooking: 1¼ hrs · Level: 1

COSTOLETTE D'AGNELLO FRITTE
Breaded and fried lamb chops

- 8 lamb chops
  salt to taste
- ½ cup all-purpose flour
- 1 egg, lightly beaten
- 2 cups bread crumbs
- 1 cup oil, for frying

Wine: a dry, full-bodied red (Carmignano Rosso)

Sprinkle the chops with salt, roll in the flour, and shake to remove excess. • Dip in the egg and coat well with the bread crumbs. • Heat the oil in a heavy-bottomed pan, until hot but not smoking, and fry the chops until golden brown all over. • Drain on paper towels and serve very hot.

Serves: 4 · Prep: 10 min. · Cooking: 10 min. · Level: 1

Grilled lamb chops

peppers, removing the seeds and cores. Dice into 1-inch squares. • Heat the remaining oil in the pan used to cook the lamb, and add the pancetta, garlic, and onion. Sauté until the onion is soft, then add the bell peppers. Cook for 5 more minutes, then pour in the wine. • When the wine has evaporated, partially cover the pan and cook until the bell peppers are soft. • Add the lamb and parsley, season with pepper and cook until the lamb is reheated. • Serve hot.

Serves: 4 · Prep: 15 min. · Cooking: 40 min. · Level: 1

AGNELLO IN AGRODOLCE
Sweet and sour lamb, Puglia-style

- 1/4 cup extra-virgin olive oil
- 1 large onion, finely chopped
- 2 lb lamb, cut into bite-sized pieces
- 4 large tomatoes, peeled and chopped
- 1/2 cup milk
   salt and freshly ground black pepper to taste
- 1/4 cup granulated sugar
- 1/2 cup white wine vinegar

Wine: a dry red (Casteller)

Heat the oil in a heavy-bottomed saucepan over medium-high heat and sauté the onion until soft. • Add the lamb and cook until well browned all over. • Add the tomatoes and milk. Season with salt and pepper. Lower heat to medium-low and cook for about 1 hour, or until the lamb is very tender. • When the lamb is almost done, add the sugar and vinegar. Cook for 10 more minutes, then serve.

Serves: 4 · Prep: 10 min. · Cooking: 1 1/4 hrs · Level: 1

COSTOLETTE ALLA PARMIGIANA
Fried lambchops with Parmesan cheese

- 1 egg
- 1 tablespoon lemon juice
   salt and freshly ground black pepper to taste
- 8 large lamb chops
- 1 cup freshly grated Parmesan cheese
- 1/4 cup butter
- 2 tablespoons extra-virgin olive oil

Wine: a dry red (Gutturnio)

Beat the egg with the lemon juice, salt, and pepper. • Dip the chops in the egg then in the Parmesan. Press the cheese and egg mixture against the chops to make it stick.

COSTOLETTE A SCOTTADITO
Grilled lamb chops

☞ These chops are even more delicious when cooked over a barbecue. Their Italian name "scottadito," means "finger burners" and refers to the fact that they are best eaten with your fingers.

- 2 lb lamb chops
- 2 tablespoons extra-virgin olive oil
   salt and freshly ground black pepper to taste

Wine: a dry red (Merlot d'Aprilia)

Place the chops on a large plate and drizzle with the oil, if using. Sprinkle with salt and a generous grinding of pepper. • Arrange the chops under in a grill pan and place over high heat. Turn frequently until well-cooked. If you don't have a grill pan, arrange the chops on a broiler rack and place under the broiler. Turn frequently until they are done. • Serve very hot.

Serves: 4 · Prep: 5 min. · Cooking: 15 min. · Level: 1

COSTOLETTE D'AGNELLO PICCANTI
Lamb chops with mustard sauce

- 2 lb lamb chops
- 1/2 cup extra-virgin olive oil
- 4 cloves garlic, finely chopped
   pinch dried oregano
   salt and freshly ground black pepper to taste
- 8 anchovy fillets
- 1 tablespoon hot mustard
- 1 tablespoon finely chopped parsley
- 2 tablespoons lemon juice

Wine: a dry red (Chianti di Montalbano)

Place the chops in a deep-sided dish just large enough to hold them. Add the oil, garlic, oregano, salt, and pepper. Set aside for 1 hour to marinate. • Crush the anchovy fillets in a bowl with a fork, then combine with the marinade. Stir in the mustard, parsley, and lemon juice, and mix well. • Arrange the chops on a broiler rack and place under the broiler. Turn frequently, basting with the sauce, until cooked. • Serve hot.

Serves: 6 · Prep: 15 min. + 1 hr to marinate· Cooking: 15 min. · Level: 1

AGNELLO CON I PEPERONI
Lamb and bell pepper stew

- 1/2 cup extra-virgin olive oil
- 2 lb lamb shoulder, boned and cut in 2-inch cubes
   salt and freshly ground black pepper to taste
- 3 large bell peppers (preferably mixed red, yellow, and green)
- 1/2 cup diced pancetta
- 2 cloves garlic, finely chopped
- 1 large onion, coarsely chopped
- 1/2 cup dry white wine
- 2 tablespoons finely chopped parsley

Wine: a light, dry red (Rosso Piceno)

Heat half the oil in a large, heavy-bottomed pan and sauté the lamb over medium heat until browned all over. Season with salt. Remove the lamb from the pan and set aside in a warm place • Clean the bell

- Heat the butter and oil in a large skillet until very hot. Fry the lamb chops until golden brown. • Serve immediately.

Serves: 4 · Prep: 10 min. · Cooking: 30 min. · Level: 2

AGNELLO CON CARCIOFI
Lamb with artichokes

- 4 large artichokes
  juice of 1 lemon
- 2 oz prosciutto, finely chopped
- 2 cloves garlic, finely chopped
  small bunch of parsley or marjoram, finely chopped
- 2 tablespoons extra-virgin olive oil
- 2 lb lamb chops
- 1 small onion, finely chopped
- 1/2 cup dry white wine
- 1 tablespoon tomato paste
  salt and freshly ground black pepper to taste

Wine: a light, dry red (Torgiano Rosso)

Clean the artichokes by stripping off the tough outer leaves and trimming the tops and stalks, so that only the tender hearts remain. Cut them in quarters and place in a bowl of cold water with the lemon juice. • Finely chop the prosciutto, garlic, and parsley together and transfer to a large skillet with the oil. Sauté for 3–4 minutes, then add the lamb chops and onion. Season with salt and pepper. • When the onion is soft, pour in the wine and cook until it has evaporated. • Add the tomato paste and the drained artichokes. Cover, and cook over medium-low heat for about 15–20 minutes, or until the lamb and artichokes are tender. • Serve hot.

Serves: 4 · Prep: 15 min. · Cooking: 40 min. · Level: 2

AGNELLO CON ZUCCHINI
Lamb with dried tomatoes and zucchini

- 1/4 cup extra-virgin olive oil
- 2 lb lamb shoulder, boned and cut in 2-inch cubes
  salt to taste
- 2 cloves garlic, finely chopped
- 4 oz sun-dried tomatoes, finely chopped
- 1 teaspoon oregano
- 4 large zucchini, cut in wheels

Wine: a light, dry red (Rosso Piceno)

Heat the oil in a large, heavy-bottomed pan and sauté the lamb over medium heat until browned all over. Season with salt. • Add the garlic and sauté for 2–3 minutes more. • Stir in the tomatoes and oregano and cook for 10 more minutes. • Meanwhile, cook the zucchini in a pot of salted, boiling water for about 7 minutes. They should be cooked but still quite firm. • Drain the zucchini and add to the lamb, together with 2–3 tablespoons of their cooking water. Stir well until the liquid has been absorbed. • Serve hot.

Serves: 4 · Prep: 10 min. · Cooking: 35 min. · Level: 1

SPEZZATINO D'AGNELLO PRIMAVERA
Lamb stew with spring vegetables

- 1 1/4 lb lamb, cut into bite-sized pieces
  salt and freshly ground black pepper to taste
- 1/4 cup butter
- 2 tablespoons all-purpose flour
- 4 cups Beef stock (see recipe, page 105)
- 1 bay leaf
- 1 clove garlic, finely chopped
- 4 medium carrots, cut in wheels
- 1 tablespoon each finely chopped parsley and thyme
- 8 oz small new potatoes, scrubbed
- 4 oz fresh or frozen peas
- 4 oz small white onions, cleaned

Wine: a dry white (Vernaccia di San Gimignano)

Sprinkle the lamb with salt and pepper. • Heat the butter in a large, heavy-bottomed saucepan over high heat. Add the lamb and cook, stirring constantly, for 10 minutes. • Add the flour and cook for 3–4 minutes, stirring constantly. Add the stock, bay leaf, carrots, parsley, and thyme. Cover and cook over low heat for about 1 hour. • Drain half the cooking juices and place them in another heavy-bottomed saucepan with the potatoes, peas, and onions. Cover and cook over low heat for 25 minutes, or until very tender. • Remove the bay leaf from the meat and place in a heated serving dish. Arrange the vegetables on the same dish and serve hot.

Serves: 4 · Prep: 15 min. · Cooking: 1 3/4 hrs · Level: 1

AGNELLO AL LIMONE
Braised lamb with lemon

☞ This dish comes from Sicily. In the traditional recipe, kid (baby goat) is used instead of lamb.

- 2 oz rendered pork fat or finely chopped fresh pork fat
- 2 lb lamb, cut into bite-sized pieces
  salt and freshly ground black pepper to taste
- 1 3/4 cups hot Beef stock (see recipe, page 105)
  juice of 2 lemons

Wine: a dry white (Corvo Bianco)

Melt the pork fat over low heat in an ovenproof earthenware casserole. Add the meat and season with salt and pepper. • Moisten with some of the hot stock. Cover and cook in a preheated oven at 350°F for about 1 hour or until the meat is very tender, basting at frequent intervals with a little more hot stock. • Drizzle with the lemon juice and serve hot.

Serves: 4 · Prep: 10 min. · Cooking: 1 hr · Level: 2

Lamb with dried tomatoes and zucchini

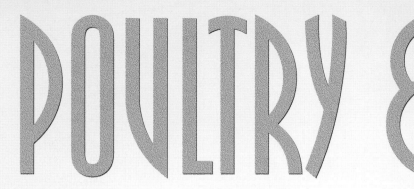

POULTRY & GAME

Versatile chicken appears in some form or another on every Italian menu. Duck, turkey, and rabbit are raised for food and are available in every supermarket. Wild game meats, such as venison, hare, and wild boar, are generally reserved for special occasions.

POLLO FRITTO
Fried chicken

1	roasting chicken, about 3 lb
	salt and freshly ground black pepper to taste
	juice of 3 lemons
2	cups oil, for frying
2	cloves garlic, peeled but whole
½	cup all-purpose flour
2	eggs, beaten

Wine: a light, dry red (Barbera d'Asti)

Rinse the chicken inside and out and dry with paper towels. Cut into 8 pieces • Sprinkle with salt and pepper. Place in a deep bowl just large enough to hold the chicken and drizzle with the lemon juice. Place in the refrigerator for 2 hours to marinate. • Heat the oil and garlic in a large skillet until very hot. Remove the garlic when it turns light gold. • Squeeze the pieces of marinated chicken to remove as much lemon juice as possible. Dip them in the flour and then in the egg. Fry until deep golden brown. • Drain on paper towels. Sprinkle with a little more salt, if liked, and serve hot.

Serves: 4 · Prep: 15 min. + 2 hrs to marinate · Cooking: 20 min. · Level: 1

◄ Braised mixed poultry and game (see recipe, page 265)
⬈ Fried chicken

POLLO ARROSTO AL LIMONE
Roast chicken with lemon and herbs

1 roasting chicken, about 3 lb
2 tablespoons coarsely chopped fresh sage
2 tablespoons coarsely chopped fresh rosemary
2 tablespoons coarsely chopped fresh thyme
4 cloves garlic, finely chopped
  salt and freshly ground black pepper to taste
¼ cup extra-virgin olive oil
1 lemon

Wine: a light, dry red (Franciacorta Rosso)

Rinse the chicken under cold running water and dry with paper towels. • Combine the sage, rosemary, thyme, garlic, salt, pepper, and half the oil in a bowl. Rub the oil mixture all over the chicken, inside and out. • Wash the lemon thoroughly, prick several times with a fork and insert in the abdominal cavity of the chicken. • Place the chicken in a roasting pan and pour the remaining oil over the top. Bake in a preheated oven at 400°F for about 1 hour. • Turn the chicken every 15 minutes and baste with the oil and cooking juices. When cooked, the skin should be crisp and the flesh tender. • Transfer to a heated serving dish and serve hot.

Serves: 4 · Prep: 10 min. · Cooking: 1 hr · Level: 1

POLLO AI FUNGHI
Chicken with mushrooms

1 chicken, about 2½ lb
1 lb white mushrooms
2 tablespoons butter
¼ cup extra-virgin olive oil
2 cloves garlic, finely chopped
2 sprigs fresh thyme
  salt and freshly ground black pepper to taste
2 tablespoons finely chopped parsley
½ cup dry white wine
1 white onion, coarsely chopped
¾ cup milk

Wine: a dry white (Riesling Renano dei Colli Berici)

Rinse the chicken under cold running water and dry with paper towels. Cut into 8–10 pieces. • Clean the mushrooms, rinse well, and pat dry carefully with paper towels. Dice the caps and stems into fairly large cubes. • Melt half the butter in a large skillet over medium heat. Add 1 tablespoon of oil and sauté the garlic briefly. • Add the mushrooms and thyme. Sprinkle with salt and pepper and cook for a few minutes. Sprinkle with the parsley, remove from heat, and set aside. • Place the remaining butter and oil in another large skillet over medium heat. Add the chicken and brown well. Season with salt and pepper. • Pour in the wine and cook over high heat until it evaporates. • Add the onion and cook until soft. • Pour in the milk and reduce the heat. Add salt and pepper to taste, cover the pan, and cook for 25 minutes, stirring frequently. • Remove the lid; if the sauce is too liquid, raise the heat until it reduces a little. • Add the mushrooms, stir well, and cook over medium-low heat for 10 minutes. • Transfer to a heated serving dish.

Serves: 4–6 · Prep: 30 min. · Cooking: 1 hr · Level: 2

POLLO ALLA DIAVOLA
Barbecued chicken

☞ This dish's Italian name (*alla diavola* means "the devil's way") is a reference to the way the chicken is barbecued over hot embers, just as some people believe sinners will be "barbecued" when they get to hell.

2 spring chickens, about 1½ lb each, cleaned
  salt and freshly ground black pepper to taste
½ cup extra-virgin olive oil

Wine: a dry, full-bodied red (Nobile di Montepulciano)

Rinse the chickens under cold running water and dry with paper towels. • Place the chickens on their backs and, using a sharp knife, cut down the middle so that they can be opened out like a book but are still in one piece. • Sprinkle the chickens generously with salt and pepper. Heat 2 tablespoons of the oil in a skillet and brown the chickens on both sides over high heat. This will take 8–10 minutes. • Place the chickens on the barbecue (or under the broiler) and drizzle with a little more of the oil. Cook until tender (about 30 minutes), turning often and basting with oil as required. Sprinkle with more salt and pepper, if liked. • Serve hot.

Serves: 4–6 · Prep: 10 min. · Cooking: 40 min. · Level: 1

FILETTI DI POLLO AL FORMAGGIO
Chicken breast with cheese sauce

- 1/4 cup extra-virgin olive oil
- 1 lb boneless chicken breast, sliced in fillets
  salt and freshly ground black pepper to taste
- 6 oz Fontina cheese, sliced
- 2 oz ham, finely chopped
- 3/4 cup whole milk

Wine: a dry white (Cirò Bianco)

Heat the oil in a large skillet over medium heat and add the chicken. Sauté until golden brown on both sides. Season with salt and pepper. • Cover each fillet with slices of cheese and a sprinkling of ham. Carefully pour the milk over the top. • Continue cooking until the cheese has melted and the milk has reduced to a creamy sauce. • Serve hot.

Serves: 4 · Prep: 10 min. · Cooking: 20 min. · Level: 1

POLLO ALLA MARENGO
Napoleon's chicken

☞ On June 14, 1800, Napoleon Bonaparte won a narrow victory over Austrian troops at Marengo, in northern Italy. According to legend, the great French general's cook invented this dish on the evening of the battle to celebrate.

- 1 chicken, about 3 lb, cut into 6–8 pieces
- 2 tablespoons butter
- 2 tablespoons extra-virgin olive oil
  salt and freshly ground black pepper to taste
  pinch of nutmeg
- 1/2 cup dry white wine
- 1 tablespoon all-purpose flour
- 3/4 cup Beef stock (see recipe, page 105)
  juice of 1/2 lemon

Wine: a dry red (Grignolino d'Asti)

Wash the chicken under cold running water and dry with paper towels. • Heat the butter and oil in a large skillet. Add the chicken and sauté until light gold. Season with the salt, pepper, and nutmeg. • Combine the wine and flour in a small bowl and mix well. • Discard most of the liquid in the pan and add the wine mixture. Cover and cook over medium-low heat for about 50 minutes, or until the chicken is tender. Add stock as required during cooking to keep the chicken moist. • Arrange the chicken on a serving dish and drizzle with the lemon juice. • Serve hot.

Serves: 4–6 · Prep: 15 min. · Cooking: 1 hr · Level: 1

POLLO E PEPERONI
Chicken with bell peppers

- 1 chicken, about 2 1/2 lb
- 3 cloves garlic, finely chopped
- 1/2 cup extra-virgin olive oil
- 14 oz peeled and chopped canned or fresh tomatoes
  salt and freshly ground black pepper to taste
- 1 lb bell peppers, mixed colors
- 1 cup dry white wine

Wine: a light, dry red (Velletri Rosso)

Rinse the chicken under cold running water and dry with paper towels. Cut into 8 pieces. • Sauté the garlic in 2 tablespoons of the oil for 2–3 minutes, then add the tomatoes. Season with salt and pepper and cook over medium heat for 15 minutes, or until the sauce reduces. • Clean the bell peppers, removing the seeds and core. Cut in quarters and place under the broiler until the skin blackens. Peel the blackened skin away with your fingers. Rinse the peppers and dry with paper towels. Cut into thin strips. • Sauté the chicken in the remaining oil. Season with salt and pepper, then pour in the wine. Cook over medium heat for 15 minutes. • Add the tomato sauce and bell peppers and cook for 10 minutes more. •

Serves: 4 · Prep: 10 min. · Cooking: 45 min. · Level: 2

POLLO IN PADELLA CON VERDURE
Braised chicken and vegetables

- 1 chicken, about 3 lb
- 2 medium onions, finely chopped
- 2 cloves garlic, finely chopped
- 1/4 cup extra-virgin olive oil
- 1/2 cup dry white wine
- 14 oz potatoes, peeled and coarsely chopped
- 4 large carrots, peeled and coarsely chopped
- 4 stalks celery, cut in 1-inch lengths
- 2 tablespoons finely chopped parsley
  salt and freshly ground black pepper to taste
- 2/3 cup Chicken stock (see recipe, page 104)

Wine: a dry rosé (Teroldego Rotaliano Rosato)

Rinse the chicken under cold running water and dry with paper towels. Cut into 8 pieces. • Sauté the onion and garlic in the oil in a large skillet until soft. • Add the chicken and brown well. • Pour in the wine and cook until it evaporates. Add the potatoes, carrots, celery, and parsley and season with salt and pepper. • Pour in enough stock to moisten the dish. Cover and cook over medium heat for 25–30 minutes, stirring frequently. Add more stock as required during cooking. • When the chicken is cooked and the vegetables tender, remove from heat and serve.

Serves: 4 · Prep: 10 min. · Cooking: 45 min. · Level: 1

Chicken with bell peppers

POLLO ALLE OLIVE NERE
Braised chicken with black olives

- 1 chicken, about 2¹/₂ lb
- ¹/₄ cup butter
- 2 cloves garlic, peeled and lightly crushed
  salt and freshly ground black pepper to taste
- ¹/₂ cup dry white wine
- 2 tablespoons white wine vinegar
- 1 cup black olives, pitted and chopped
- 6 anchovy fillets (optional)

Wine: a light, dry red (Nebbiolo d'Alba)

Rinse the chicken under cold running water. Dry well and cut into 8 pieces. • Heat the butter with the garlic in a large skillet. Remove the garlic when lightly browned. Add the chicken pieces and sauté until golden brown all over. • Season with salt and pepper and pour in the wine and vinegar. Cook until the liquids have almost evaporated. • Add the olives and anchovies, if using, partially cover the skillet, and cook over medium heat for about 40 minutes, or until the chicken is tender. • Transfer to a heated serving dish and serve hot.

Serves: · 4 Prep: 30 min. · Cooking: 50 min. · Level: 1

POLLO IN TECIA CON POMODORI
Braised chicken with tomatoes

- 1 large chicken, about 4 lb
- 1 small onion, finely chopped
- 1 small stalk celery, finely chopped
- 1 small carrot, finely chopped
- ¹/₄ cup butter
- 2 tablespoons extra-virgin olive oil
- 1 cup all-purpose flour
- 1 cup dry white wine
- 3 cloves
  pinch of cinnamon
- 1 (15 oz) can Italian tomatoes, sieved
  salt and freshly ground black pepper to taste
- 1 tablespoon finely chopped parsley

Wine: a light, dry white (Piave Chardonnay)

Rinse the chicken under cold running water and dry with paper towels. Cut into 6 large pieces. • Sauté the onion, celery, and carrot briefly in a large skillet in the butter and oil. • Lightly flour the chicken pieces and add to the skillet. Fry over medium-high heat until lightly browned all over. • Add the wine and cook until it evaporates. Add the cloves, cinnamon, and tomatoes and season with salt and pepper. • Cook over medium heat for about 30 minutes, adding a little hot water if necessary. • Sprinkle with the parsley, stir well, and serve hot.

Serves: 6 · Prep: 20 min. · Cooking: 45 min. · Level: 1

POLLO ALLA CACCIATORA
Hunter's chicken

- 1 chicken, about 4 lb
- 1 medium onion, thinly sliced
- ¹/₂ cup extra-virgin olive oil
- 4 oz fresh pork fat, finely chopped
- 1 cup dry white wine
- 8 oz ripe tomatoes, blanched, peeled and diced
  salt and freshly ground black pepper to taste

Wine: a light, dry red (Barbera dei Colli Piacentini)

Rinse the chicken under cold running water and dry with paper towels. Cut into 8–12 small pieces. • Sauté the onion in the oil in a large skillet until soft. Remove the onion from the skillet and set it aside. • Add the pork fat to the flavored oil, followed by the chicken pieces. Cook over slightly higher heat for about 10 minutes, turning frequently. • Pour in the wine and cook until it evaporates. • Add the tomatoes and the reserved onion. Season with salt and pepper. • Cook for about 30 minutes, stirring at intervals, until the chicken is tender. • Serve very hot.

Serves: 6 · Prep: 20 min. · Cooking: 1 hr · Level: 1

POLLO ARROSTO CON FINOCCHIO
Roast chicken with fennel seeds

- 1 chicken, about 3 lb
- ¹/₂ cup finely chopped pancetta
- 2 cloves garlic, finely chopped
- 1 tablespoon finely chopped fresh sage leaves
- 1 tablespoon finely chopped fresh rosemary leaves
- 2 tablespoons finely chopped parsley
- 1 teaspoon fennel seeds
  salt and freshly ground black pepper to taste
- ¹/₃ cup extra-virgin olive oil

Wine: a light, dry red (Cabernet dei Colli Orientali del Friuli)

Rinse the chicken inside and out and dry with paper towels. • In a small mixing bowl, combine the pancetta, garlic, sage, rosemary, parsley, and fennel seeds with a generous pinch each of salt and pepper. Place in the chicken cavity. Use a trussing needle and thread to sew up the opening. • Pour half the olive oil into a roasting pan, place the chicken in it and drizzle with the remaining oil. Sprinkle with salt and pepper. • Roast for 1 hour, or until the juices run clear when a knife is inserted deep into the thigh. • Serve hot.

Serves: 4: · Prep: 20 min. · Cooking: 1 hr · Level: 1

Braised chicken with black olives

GALANTINA DI POLLO
Chicken galantine

- 10 oz lean ground beef
- 5 oz lean ground pork
- 5 oz ground turkey breast
- 5 oz ground suckling veal
- 4 oz ground Mortadella
- 1/2 cup shelled pistachios
- 1 egg
- 1 oz black truffle, finely sliced (optional)
  salt and freshly ground black pepper to taste
- 1 chicken, about 4 lb, boneless
- 1 onion, cut in half
- 1 carrot, cut in 3
- 1 stalk celery, cut in 3
- 2 sprigs parsley
- 8 black peppercorns
- 1 chicken bouillon cube
- 2 packets (1/4 oz each) unflavored gelatin
  juice of 1/2 lemon

Wine: a light, dry red (Merlot del Piave)

Put the beef, pork, turkey, veal, and Mortadella in a large bowl and mix well. Add the pistachios, egg, and truffle, if using. Sprinkle with salt and pepper and mix until well blended. • Stuff the chicken with the mixture and sew up the neck and stomach cavity openings with a trussing needle and string. • Mold the stuffed chicken into a rectangular shape. Wrap in a piece of cheesecloth and tie with kitchen string. • Place a large saucepan of salted water over medium heat. Add the onion, carrot, celery, parsley, peppercorns, and bouillon cube. • When the water is boiling, carefully immerse the stuffed chicken and simmer over low heat for 1 1/2 hours. • Remove from the heat and drain the stock (this can frozen for later use as stock or served as a light soup). • Unwrap the chicken and place it between two flat dishes or trays with a heavy weight on top (for example, a cast-iron skillet or a heavy book). Set aside to drain. • When cool, chill in the refrigerator for at least 12 hours. • A few hours before serving, prepare the gelatin by following the instructions on the package and adding the lemon juice in place of other fruit juice. • Slice the chicken thinly and arrange on a serving dish. Dice the gelatin and sprinkle over the top just before serving.

Serves: 6–8 · Prep: 40 min. + 12 hrs to chill · Cooking: 1 1/2 hrs · Level: 3

POLLO IN FRICASSEA
Fricasséd chicken with parsley and lemon

- 2 chickens, about 1 1/2 lb each
- 2 tablespoons butter
- 3 tablespoons extra-virgin olive oil
- 2 tablespoons all-purpose flour
- 1 1/2 cups Chicken stock (see recipe, page 104)
- 1 carrot, cut in half lengthwise
- 1 stalk celery, cut in half lengthwise
- 4 sprigs parsley
- 1 onion, cut in quarters
  salt and freshly ground black pepper to taste
- 3 egg yolks, lightly beaten
  juice of 1 lemon
- 2 tablespoons finely chopped parsley

Wine: a light, dry red (Chianti dei Colli Senesi)

Rinse the chicken under cold running water. Dry well and cut each chicken into 6 pieces. • Heat the butter and oil in a large, heavy-bottomed pan. Add the flour and cook over medium heat, stirring occasionally, until it turns reddish-brown. • Add 2/3 cup of the stock and, stirring constantly, bring the mixture to a boil. • Tie the pieces of carrot, celery, and the sprigs of parsley together and add to the pan with the onion. Cook for 5 minutes, then add the chicken pieces. • Season with salt and pepper, then cover the pot and cook for about 30 minutes, or until the chicken is tender. Add more stock during cooking if the pan becomes dry. • When the chicken is cooked, remove and discard the pieces of onion and the bunch of carrot, celery, and parsley. • Add the egg yolks, lemon juice, and parsley. Stir well and serve immediately.

Serves: 4 · Prep: 20 min. · Cooking: 35 min. · Level: 2

POLLO ALLA SALVIA
Braised chicken with sage

- 1 chicken, about 2 1/2 lb
- 2 tablespoons butter
- 2 tablespoons extra-virgin olive oil
- 2 cloves garlic, finely chopped
  salt and freshly ground black pepper to taste
- 1/2 cup dry white wine
- 1/2 cup diced pancetta
- 8 leaves fresh sage

Wine: a light, dry red (Chianti dei Colli Senesi)

Rinse the chicken under cold running water. Dry well and cut into 8 pieces. • Heat the butter and oil in a large skillet and sauté the garlic until light gold. • Add the chicken pieces and sauté until golden brown all over. • Season with salt and pepper and pour in the wine. Cook until the wine has almost evaporated. • Add the pancetta and sage, partially cover the skillet, and cook over medium heat for about 40 minutes, or until the chicken is tender. • Transfer to a heated serving dish and serve hot.

Serves: 4 · Prep: 30 min. · Cooking: 50 min. · Level: 1

Braised chicken with sage

SPEZZATINO DI POLLO
Chicken stew with vinegar and rosemary

- 1   cup all-purpose flour
- 4   skinless, boneless chicken breast halves, about 2 lb total weight, cut into bite-sized pieces
- 1/4   cup butter + 1 tablespoon
- 2   twigs fresh rosemary
- 1/4   cup diced lean pancetta
    salt and freshly ground black pepper to taste
- 1/2   cup white wine vinegar
- 6   anchovy fillets
- 4   cloves garlic, finely chopped

Wine: a dry white (Riesling Renano dei Colli Berici)

Lightly flour the chicken pieces. • Heat 1/4 cup butter with the rosemary in a large skillet. When the butter turns deep gold, remove the rosemary and add the chicken and pancetta. Sauté until the chicken is lightly browned. Remove the chicken and pancetta (leaving as much of the butter as possible in the skillet) and set aside in a warm oven. Sprinkle with salt and pepper. • Pour the vinegar into the skillet and mix well. Add the anchovies and stir until they dissolve. Stir in the garlic and remaining butter and cook until the mixture thickens. • Add the chicken and pancetta and cook for 10–15 minutes more. • Place on a heated platter and serve.

Serves: · 4–6 · Prep: 10 min. · Cooking: 30 min. · Level: 1

POLLO ALLA MELA
Roast chicken wrapped in smoked pancetta with apple stuffing

☞ Smoked pancetta is very similar to bacon, so use that if preferred.

- 2   chickens, about 3 lb total weight, cleaned
    salt and freshly ground black pepper to taste
- 4   tart apples, such as Granny Smith, Cortland, or Empire, peeled, cored, and coarsely chopped
- 6   prunes, soaked in warm water for 5 minutes, then pitted and chopped
- 2   cups fresh, soft bread crumbs
- 2   eggs, lightly beaten
- 1   teaspoon dried oregano
- 8–12   strips bacon or smoked pancetta

Wine: a dry, full-bodied red (Nobile di Montepulciano)

Rinse the chickens under cold running water and dry with paper towels. • Sprinkle the insides of the chickens with salt. Place the apples in a bowl and add the prunes, bread crumbs, eggs, oregano, and pepper. Mix well and use the mixture to stuff the chickens. • Wrap the chickens in the bacon and roast in a preheated oven at 400°F for 15 minutes. • Turn the heat down to 375°F and cook for another 45 minutes, or until the chickens are tender. • Place the chickens in a serving dish and bring to the table still wrapped in the bacon. Unwrap, slice, and include some of the bacon with each serving.

Serves: 6 · Prep: 10 min. · Cooking: 1 hr · Level: 2

PETTI DI POLLO AL BRANDY
Chicken breasts with orange brandy

- 1/4   cup butter
- 4   skinless, boneless chicken breasts, about 1 1/2 lb total weight
- 2   cloves garlic, peeled and cut in half
    salt to taste
- 1   cup dry white wine
- 2   onions, finely chopped
- 1/2   cup brandy
- 1/2   cup heavy cream
- 1/2   small dried red chili pepper, crumbled

Wine: a light, dry red (Franciacorta Rosso)

Place half the butter in a large skillet and add the chicken breasts and garlic. Sprinkle with salt and cook for 5 minutes, turning the chicken breasts frequently. • Remove the garlic and pour in a little of the wine. Turn the chicken breasts in the wine. Add wine as required and cook until the chicken breasts are tender. • Meanwhile, place the remaining butter in a small, skillet and sauté the onion over medium heat until soft. Pour in the brandy, followed by the cream and chili pepper. Cook for 4–5 minutes, stirring all the time. • Arrange the chicken breasts in a heated serving dish and pour the sauce over the top. Serve at once.

Serves: 4 · Prep: 10 min. · Cooking: 30 min. · Level: 1

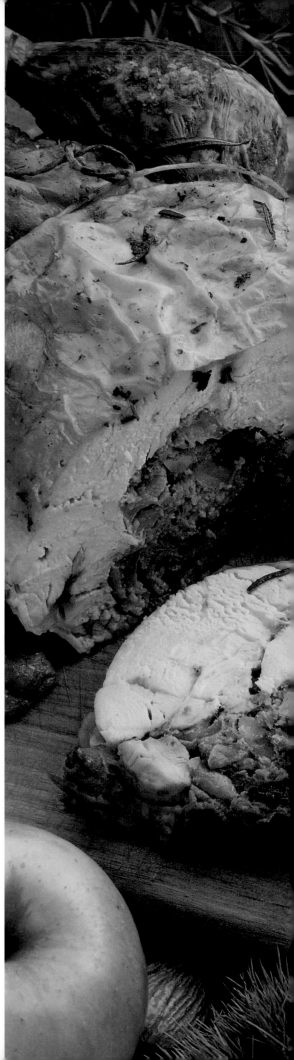

TACCHINO NATALIZIO
Stuffed roast turkey, Lombardy-style

- 1 small turkey, boneless, about 8 lb, with liver
- 4 oz ground beef
- 6 oz Italian sausages, peeled and crumbled
- 1 egg
- 2 apples (such as Golden Delicious), peeled, cored, and diced
- 12 chestnuts, boiled in chicken stock until soft, peeled and cut in half
- 12 prunes, soaked in warm water for 5 minutes, then pitted and chopped
    salt and freshly ground black pepper to taste
    pinch of nutmeg
- 1/2 cup brandy
- 2 tablespoons butter
- 8 strips salt pork
- 6 twigs fresh rosemary
- 12 leaves fresh sage
- 1/2 cup white wine
- 1/2 cup Beef stock (see recipe, page 105)

Wine: a dry, full-bodied red (Nobile di Montepulciano)

Ask your butcher to remove the bones from the turkey through an incision in the neck. • Finely chop the turkey liver and place in a bowl with the beef, sausages, egg, apples, chestnuts, prunes, salt, pepper, nutmeg, and brandy. Mix well. • Stuff the turkey with the mixture and close the incision with a trussing needle and kitchen thread. • Butter a cast-iron pot that will hold the turkey snugly. Cover the bottom of the pot with the strips of salt pork, add the turkey, and place the rosemary and sage on top. • Place over medium heat for 30 minutes, turning often so that the turkey is evenly browned. • Drain the fat and discard. Pour in the wine and cook until it evaporates. • Add a ladleful of stock, cover and cook in a preheated oven at 400°F for 3 hours. Baste the turkey with the cooking juices (and a little extra stock, if the pan dries out) during cooking. • The turkey should be very tender and with a crisp, golden skin.

Serves: 8 · Prep: 30 min. · Cooking: 3 1/2 hrs · Level: 3

Savoy cabbage turkey loaf

POLPETTONE DI TACCHINO
Savoy cabbage turkey loaf

- 1¼ lb ground turkey breast
- 8 oz Italian pork sausage, skinned and crumbled
- ¼ cup finely chopped pancetta
- 1 cup freshly grated Parmesan cheese
- 1 egg + 1 yolk
- ½ cup fresh, soft bread crumbs
  pinch of nutmeg
  salt and freshly ground black pepper to taste
- 10 leaves Savoy cabbage
- 1 small onion, finely chopped
- 14 oz peeled and chopped tomatoes
- ½ cup extra-virgin olive oil
- ½ cup dry white wine
- ½ cup Beef stock (see recipe, page 105)

Wine: a dry red (Chianti Classico)

Put the turkey, sausage, pancetta, Parmesan, eggs, bread, nutmeg, salt, and pepper in a large bowl and mix well. • Parboil the cabbage leaves in a large pan of lightly salted water for 4 minutes. Drain well and dry with paper towels. • Arrange the cabbage leaves on a work surface in a rectangle; they should be overlapping so that there is no space between the leaves. • Place the stuffing mixture in the middle of the leaves and shape into a loaf. • Wrap the cabbage leaves around the loaf, taking care not to tear them. Tie with a few twists of kitchen string. • Carefully transfer the turkey loaf to an ovenproof dish. Mix the onions, tomatoes, and oil together and pour over the top. • Bake in a preheated oven at 400°F for 1¼ hours, basting frequently with the wine and stock. • Slice the turkey loaf and serve.

Serves: 6 · Prep: 20 min. · Cooking: 1¼ hrs · Level: 2

TACCHINO RIPIENO DI RISO
Turkey stuffed with rice and Parmesan

- 2 large red bell peppers, broiled (see recipe, page 85)
- 1 young, tender turkey, about 4 lb, boneless
  salt and freshly ground black pepper to taste
  pinch of nutmeg
- 1 cup short-grain white rice
- ⅔ cup butter
- 8 oz chicken livers, finely chopped
- 1 onion
- 1 stalk celery
- 4 cloves
- 12 whole black peppercorns
- ½ cup dry white wine
- 2 tablespoons all-purpose flour
  juice of 1 lemon
- ½ cup heavy cream
- 1 cup freshly grated Parmesan cheese

Wine: a dry, full-bodied red (Barolo)

Prepare the bell peppers. When peeled, cut into small squares. • Rinse the turkey under cold running water and dry with paper towels. Rub the insides with salt, pepper, and nutmeg. • Cook the rice in a large pot of salted, boiling water until tender. Drain and place in a bowl. • Place half the butter in a small skillet and cook the chicken livers for 5 minutes. Stir the chicken livers into the rice then add the bell peppers. Mix well and use this mixture to stuff the turkey. Sew up the turkey using a trussing needle and kitchen thread. • Place all but 1 tablespoon of the remaining butter in a cast-iron pot that will hold the turkey snugly. Add the onion, celery, cloves, peppercorns, and salt and sauté until soft. • Put the turkey in the pot and cook over medium heat, turning often until evenly browned. Pour in the wine and continue cooking until the turkey is tender, about 2½ hours. • Remove the turkey from the pot and set aside in a warm oven. Stir the remaining butter and the flour into the cooking juices. Add the lemon juice then the cream. Cook for 2–3 minutes. Pour the sauce over the turkey, sprinkle with the Parmesan, and place in a preheated oven at 375°F for 10 minutes to brown. Serve hot.

Serves: 6 · Prep: 25 min. · Cooking: 3¼ hrs · Level: 2

TACCHINO AL PROSCIUTTO
Turkey with prosciutto

- 1 young, tender turkey, about 4 lb, boneless
- 4 oz thinly sliced prosciutto, with fat, chopped
- 4 cloves, crushed
- 1 tablespoon finely chopped rosemary
- 1 tablespoon finely chopped sage
  salt and freshly ground black pepper to taste
- ¼ cup water
- 2 tablespoons butter
- 1 cup cream

Wine: a light, dry red (Rosso Piceno)

Rinse the turkey under cold running water and dry with paper towels. • Sprinkle with the prosciutto, cloves, rosemary, sage, salt, and pepper, and rub the turkey all over. Wrap in ovenproof parchment paper and drizzle with the water. • Bake in a preheated oven at 375°F for about 3 hours. • Unwrap the turkey and cut in strips. • Heat the butter in a skillet and add the turkey. Pour in the cream, season with salt and pepper, and cook over medium heat for 10 minutes, or until most of the cream is absorbed. Serve hot.

Serves: 6 · Prep: 25 min. · Cooking: 3¼ hrs · Level: 2

PETTI DI TACCHINO GRIGLIATI
Marinated broiled turkey breasts

2	lb boneless turkey breasts
²/₃	cup extra-virgin olive oil
¼	cup white wine vinegar
4	cloves, crushed
2	cloves garlic, finely chopped
2	tablespoons finely chopped marjoram
	salt and freshly ground black pepper to taste

Wine: a light, dry red (Montepulciano d'Abruzzo)

Rinse the turkey well under cold running water and dry with paper towels. Cut into 6 or 12 pieces. • Place the turkey in a bowl. Mix the oil, vinegar, cloves, garlic, marjoram, salt, and pepper together and pour over the turkey. Marinate in the refrigerator for at least 3 hours. • Cook the breasts under a broiler or over the hot embers of a barbecue. Baste with the marinade as they cook to stop them from drying out. Serve hot.

Serves: 6 · Prep: 10 min. + 3 hrs to marinate · Cooking: 15 min. · Level: 1

ANATRA AGLI AROMI
Roast duck with herbs

1	large onion
2	bay leaves
	mixed sprigs fresh herbs: sage, rosemary, thyme, marjoram
1	duck, about 2 lb
	salt to taste
¼	cup extra-virgin olive oil
1	chicken bouillon cube, crumbled
1	tablespoon pink peppercorns
½	cup dry white wine
½	cup white wine vinegar

Wine: a dry red (Barbaresco)

Peel and wash the onion, leaving it whole. Tie the bay leaf and mixed herbs together in a bunch. • Rinse the duck under cold running water and dry with paper towels. • Place in a roasting pan and sprinkle with the salt and oil. Add the onion, herbs, bouillon cube, and

Roast turkey with pomegranate

pink pepper, and bake in a preheated oven at 400°F. • After about 10 minutes, pour the wine and vinegar over the top and cook for about 50 minutes more, basting from time to time. • Cut the duck into small pieces and arrange on a heated serving dish with the onion and herbs. • Serve hot.

Serves 4 · Prep: 10 min. · Cooking: 1 hr · Level: 1

TACCHINO ALLA MELAGRANA
Roast turkey with pomegranate

1	young, tender turkey, about 4 lb, with liver
	salt and freshly ground black pepper to taste
¼	cup butter
²/₃	cup extra-virgin olive oil
4	fresh sage leaves, finely chopped
3	whole ripe pomegranates

Wine: a dry red (Valpolicella Amarone)

Rinse the turkey under cold running water and dry with paper towels. Sprinkle the cavity with a little salt and place half the butter inside. Tie up the turkey so that the

legs and wings sit snugly against its sides. • Place the turkey in a fairly deep roasting pan or ovenproof dish. Smear with the remaining butter, drizzle with ½ cup of oil, and sprinkle with the sage. • Roast in a preheated oven at 350°F for 3 hours. Baste with its own juices at intervals as it cooks. • Place the seeds of 2 of the pomegranates in a blender and process to obtain a smooth juice. • After the turkey has been in the oven for 1½ hours, drizzle with half the pomegranate juice. • Rinse and trim the liver. Chop coarsely and fry in 1 tablespoon of the oil over high heat. Add the remaining pomegranate juice, season with salt and pepper, and remove from heat. • When the turkey is done, cut it into at least 8 pieces. Place in an ovenproof dish and pour the liver and pomegranate sauce over the top. Sprinkle with the seeds of the remaining pomegranate and roast in a preheated oven at 450°F for 10 minutes before serving.

Serves: 6 · Prep: 20 min. · Cooking: 3¼ hrs · Level: 2

Roast-duck, Venetian-style

ANATRA ALL'ARANCIA
Roast duck with orange sauce

☞ Despite French claims to this recipe, it comes from the Florentine court of the Medici during the Renaissance and was taken to France by Catherine de' Medici in the 16th century when she married Henry II, future king of France.

- 1 duck, about 3 lb
- 2 cloves garlic, whole
- 1 sprig rosemary
  salt and freshly ground black pepper to taste
- 3 oranges
- 1/4 cup extra-virgin olive oil
- 1 onion, coarsely chopped
- 1 carrot, coarsely chopped
- 1 stalk celery, coarsely chopped
- 1/2 cup dry white wine
- 1/2 cup cold water
- 1/2 cup superfine sugar
- 1 1/2 tablespoons cold water

Wine: a dry red (Vino Nobile di Montepulciano)

Rinse the duck under cold running water and dry with paper towels. Put the garlic, rosemary, salt, pepper, and the coarsely chopped zest of 1 orange into the cavity. •

Pour half the oil into a large roasting pan, add the duck and sprinkle with more pepper. Arrange the onion, carrot, and celery around the duck and drizzle with the remaining oil. Roast in a preheated oven at 375°F for about 1 1/2 hours. • Ten minutes into the roasting time, pour the wine over the duck. • Meanwhile, peel the zest off the remaining oranges and cut into very thin strips. Place in a small saucepan with the 1/2 cup water, bring to a boil and drain. Repeat the process. This removes bitterness from the zest. • In a small, nonstick saucepan heat the sugar and the 1 1/2 tablespoons water over medium heat until the sugar caramelizes to pale golden brown. Add the zest, stir over low heat for 2 minutes and set aside. • Thirty minutes into the roasting time, squeeze the juice from the oranges and pour over the duck. • When the duck is done (test by inserting a sharp knife into the thigh, if the juices run clear the duck is ready), remove the garlic, rosemary, and zest from the cavity. • Carve into 8–10

portions, leaving all the flesh on the bone, and transfer to a casserole with the cooking juices and vegetables. Add the caramelized orange zest and place over medium heat for 5 minutes, turning the portions over to coat them. • Serve hot.

Serves: 4 · Prep: 25 min. · Cooking: 1 1/2 hrs · Level: 2

ANATRA DEL REDENTORE
Roast duck, Venetian-style

- 1 duck, about 4 1/2 lb, boneless
- 4 oz ground pork
- 4 oz chicken livers, finely chopped
- 2 tablespoons finely chopped parsley
- 4 amaretti cookies (macaroons)
- 1 cup fresh bread crumbs mixed with 2 tablespoons Marsala wine
- 2 tablespoons extra-virgin olive oil
- 1 egg
- 2 tablespoons freshly grated Parmesan cheese
- 1 oz salt pork, finely chopped
- 2 tablespoons finely chopped rosemary
  salt and freshly ground black pepper to taste
- 1 cup dry red wine
- 1/2 quantity *Salsa peverada* (see recipe for *Guinea fowl in Venetian sauce*, page 262, and follow the instructions for the sauce)

Wine: a dry, full-bodied red (Lison Pramaggiore Cabernet)

Rinse the duck under cold running water and dry with paper towels. • Combine the pork, chicken livers, parsley, amaretti cookies, bread crumbs and Marsala, half the oil, the egg, and Parmesan together in a bowl. Mix well and use to stuff the duck. Sew up the duck with a trussing needle and kitchen thread and place in a roasting pan. Bind the duck with a few twists of kitchen string. • Combine the salt pork and rosemary in a small bowl with the remaining oil and sprinkle over the duck. Season with salt and pepper. • Place in a preheated oven at 400°F and cook for 1 3/4 hours. Baste with the wine at frequent intervals during cooking. • Prepare the *Salsa peverada* while the duck is cooking. • Place the duck on a heated serving dish and cut into 1/4 inch slices. Pour the sauce over the top and serve.

Serves: 4 · Prep: 20 min. · Cooking: 1 3/4 hrs · Level: 2

ANATRA CON POLPETTE DI SEDANO
Duck with celery balls

- 1 duck, about 4 lb, cleaned
- 2 cloves garlic, 1 onion, 1 carrot, all finely chopped
- 1 tablespoon finely chopped parsley

3/4 cup extra-virgin olive oil
    salt and freshly ground black pepper to taste
1/2 cup dry, full-bodied red wine
1 (15 oz) can Italian tomatoes
2 cups Beef stock (see recipe, page 105)
4 large stalks celery, with leaves
3/4 cup all-purpose flour
1 egg, beaten
1 cup oil, for frying

Wine: a dry red (Santa Cristina)

Rinse the duck under cold running water and dry with paper towels. Cut into 8 to 10 pieces. • Sauté the garlic, onion, carrot, and parsley in the oil in a heavy-bottomed pan over medium heat. • After about 5 minutes, add the duck. Season with salt and pepper and cook until the duck is brown. • Pour in the wine and cook until it evaporates. • Stir in the tomatoes, partially cover the pan, and simmer for about 1 1/2 hours. Stir frequently, gradually adding the stock as the sauce reduces. • In the meantime, wash the celery stalks and cut into large pieces. Boil in a little salted water for 20–25 minutes. Drain well, squeeze out excess moisture and coarsely chop. • Shape the celery into small balls, and dip in the flour, then the egg. • Heat the frying oil in a large skillet until very hot. Fry the celery balls in small batches until golden brown. Drain and set aside on paper towels. • Add the celery balls to the duck during the last 15 minutes of cooking. Take care when stirring or the balls may break. • Serve hot.

Serves: 4 · Prep: 40 min. · Cooking: 1 1/2 hrs · Level: 2

PETTO D'ANATRA IN AGRODOLCE
Sweet and sour duck

6 duck breasts, about 2 1/2 lb total weight
    salt and freshly ground black pepper to taste
1/2 cup butter
1/2 teaspoon each fennel, anise, cumin, coriander, cinnamon bark (use whole dried seeds and cinnamon bark and grind them together in a pestle)
1 tablespoon sesame seeds, crushed
1 teaspoon finely chopped fresh ginger root
1 tablespoon honey
3 1/2 cups red wine vinegar
1 1/4 cups homemade Beef stock (see recipe, page 105)

Wine: a dry red (Lison Pramaggiore Cabernet)

Rinse the duck breasts under cold running water and dry on paper towels. Season with salt and pepper. • Melt one-third of the butter in a skillet and sauté

Braised duck with green olives

the duck breasts over medium heat for 5–6 minutes each side. Take them out and keep warm. • Spoon off and discard some of the excess fat from the surface of the juices in the skillet. Stir in the spices, sesame seeds, and ginger root. • Add the honey and, after a minute or two, the vinegar. Cook until the vinegar has evaporated, then add the beef stock. • Reduce this sauce over high heat to half its original volume. Remove from heat, then stir in the remaining butter and beat lightly with a fork. • Carve the duck breasts into strips about 1 inch wide and arrange on a serving dish. Spoon the sauce over the top and serve.

Serves: 6 · Prep: 20 min. · Cooking: 35 min. · Level: 1

ANATRA ALLE OLIVE
Braised duck with green olives

1 duck, about 3 lb
2 tablespoons butter
2 tablespoons extra-virgin olive oil

1 bay leaf
1 clove garlic, finely chopped
1 small carrot
1 stalk celery, finely chopped
1 small onion, finely chopped
2 tablespoons finely chopped parsley
    salt and freshly ground black pepper to taste
1 1/2 cups boiling Beef stock (see recipe, page 105)
20 giant green olives, pitted, 10 coarsely chopped and 10 whole
4 large ripe tomatoes, peeled and chopped

Wine: a dry, full-bodied red (Grave del Friuli)

Rinse the duck under cold running water and dry with paper towels. • Place the butter and oil in a large skillet and add the bay leaf, garlic, carrot, celery, parsley, salt, and pepper and sauté until the vegetables are soft. • Add the duck and cook, turning frequently, until brown all over. Season with salt and pepper. • Pour in the stock, and add the olives and tomatoes. • Cover and cook over medium-low heat for 45 minutes. Remove the lid and cook for 15 more minutes, or until the liquid has reduced and the duck is tender. Serve hot.

Serves: 4 · Prep: 20 min. · Cooking: 1 1/4 hrs · Level: 1

Roast pheasant

pheasant to the sauce, turning once or twice to moisten and reheat. • Transfer to a heated serving dish. Spoon the sauce over the pheasant and garnish with the shavings of truffles. • Serve hot.

Serves: 4 · Prep: 15 min. · Cooking: 1 hr · Level:1

FARAONA IN PEVERADA
Guinea fowl in Venetian sauce

1	oven-ready guinea fowl, about 2$^1/_2$ lb
2	tablespoons butter
$^1/_2$	cup extra-virgin olive oil
2	oz pancetta, cut into small dice
	salt and freshly ground black pepper to taste
$^1/_2$	cup dry white wine
7	oz chicken livers
1	small fresh Italian sausage, crumbled
4	anchovy fillets
	zest and juice of 1 lemon
1	clove garlic
2	tablespoons finely chopped parsley
2	tablespoons white wine vinegar

Wine: a dry red (Marzemino del Trentino)

Rinse the guinea fowl under cold running water and dry with paper towels. Cut into 6 pieces. • Melt the butter in a flameproof casserole and add half the oil, the pancetta, and guinea fowl. Brown all over on high heat. • Season with salt and pepper. Drizzle with the wine and turn down the heat to low. Cover and cook for 1 hour, turning the pieces at intervals. • Chop the livers together with the sausage, anchovy fillets, lemon zest, and garlic. Sauté these ingredients gently in the remaining oil, then add the parsley and lemon juice. • Drizzle with the vinegar and add a pinch of salt. Season generously with pepper and remove from heat. • Serve the guinea fowl on a heated serving dish with the sauce spooned over the top.

Serves: 4 · Prep: 20 min. · Cooking: 1$^1/_4$ hrs · Level: 1

PICCIONE RIPIENO AI FEGATINI
Roast squab pigeon with sausage stuffing

4	squab pigeons, with their livers
2	chicken livers
2	Italian pork sausages
	salt and freshly ground black pepper to taste
8	leaves sage
$^1/_4$	cup extra-virgin olive oil

Wine: a dry red (Colli Piacentini Bonarda)

Clean the pigeons, discarding all internal organs except the livers. Wash the pigeons under cold running water and dry with

FAGIANO ARROSTO
Roast pheasant

2	young roasting pheasants
8	slices unrolled pancetta
$^1/_4$	cup butter, melted
	salt and freshly ground white pepper to taste
$^1/_4$	cup cold water

Wine: a dry red (Savuto)

Rinse the pheasants under cold running water and dry with paper towels. • Wrap each bird in half the pancetta and secure them with kitchen string. Smear with the butter and sprinkle with salt and pepper (not too much salt, as the pancetta is already salty). • Place in a roasting pan. Bake at 400°F for about 40 minutes, basting occasionally with the cooking juices. • Remove the pancetta and return the pheasants to the oven for 10 minutes so that they become crisp and golden. • Chop the pancetta and place on a heated serving dish. • Put the pheasants on the pancetta. • Place the roasting pan over medium heat and pour in the water. Cook for 2–3 minutes then pour over the pheasants. • Serve hot.

Serves: 4–6 · Prep: 10 min. · Cooking: 1 hr · Level: 1

FAGIANO ARROSTO TARTUFATO
Pan roasted truffled pheasant

1	roasting pheasant, about 2$^1/_2$ lb
	salt and freshly ground white pepper to taste
4	juniper berries, lightly crushed
4	slices unrolled pancetta
2	tablespoons butter
2	tablespoons coarsely chopped onion
1	stalk celery, coarsely chopped
4	fresh sage leaves
1	small sprig fresh rosemary
$^2/_3$	cup dry white wine
$^1/_4$	cup light cream
1	fresh truffle, in wafer-thin slices

Wine: a dry, full-bodied red (Barbera d'Alba)

Rinse the pheasant under cold running water and dry with paper towels. • Season with salt and pepper and place the juniper berries inside the cavity. • Wrap the slices of pancetta around the breast of the bird and secure them with kitchen string. Tie the legs and wings snugly against the bird's body so that it keeps its shape as it cooks. • Heat the butter in a saucepan just large enough to contain the pheasant. Brown the bird all over for 5 minutes, turning frequently. • Add the onion, celery, sage, and rosemary. Pour in the wine. Cover and reduce heat to low. Cook for 40–45 minutes. • Remove the pheasant when it is done and keep hot. • Strain the cooking liquid and return it to the saucepan. Pour in the cream and simmer for 2–3 minutes, adding salt to taste. • Remove the string, pancetta, and juniper berries from the pheasant and carve it into 4 or more pieces. • Add the pieces of

paper towels. • Finely chop the pigeon livers with the chicken livers and sausages. Place the mixture in a bowl. Season with salt and pepper and mix well. • Fill each pigeon with the stuffing and close them up with toothpicks. • Fix 2 leaves of sage to each pigeon with a toothpick. • Sprinkle the birds with salt and pepper and transfer to a roasting pan. Drizzle with the oil and roast in a preheated oven at 375°F for 45 minutes. • Serve hot.

Serves: 4 · Prep: 25 min. · Cooking: 45 min. · Level: 1

QUAGLIETTE BARDATE
Quails wrapped with pancetta

6	quails, cleaned
	salt and freshly ground black pepper to taste
12	slices pancetta
1/4	cup extra-virgin olive oil
1	carrot, 1 stalk celery, finely chopped
2	oz prosciutto, finely chopped
1	bay leaf
2	juniper berries
1	scallion, coarsely chopped
1/2	cup dry white wine
1	cup Beef stock (see recipe, page 105)

Wine: a dry red (Brunello di Montalcino)

Rinse the quails under cold running water and dry with paper towels • Sprinkle lightly with salt and pepper. Wrap each bird in 2 slices of pancetta and tie with kitchen string. • Transfer to a baking dish with the oil, carrot, celery, and prosciutto. Add the bay leaf and juniper berries and scatter the scallion over the top. • Bake in a preheated oven at 400°F for about 45 minutes. • Pour the wine over the quails during cooking. When the wine is finished, continue with the stock. • Serve the quails hot with the sauce spooned over the top.

Serves: 6 · Prep: 30 min. · Cooking: 45 min. · Level: 1

STUFATO DI CONIGLIO AI PINOLI E OLIVE VERDI
Rabbit stew with pine nuts and green olives

1	rabbit, about 2 1/2 lb, cut in 8–10 pieces
1/4	cup extra-virgin olive oil
1	clove garlic, finely chopped
	salt and freshly ground black pepper to taste
1/2	cup dry white wine
3/4	cup Beef stock (see recipe, page 105)
4	oz green olives, pitted
1/3	cup pine nuts

Wine: a dry white (Trebbiano d'Abruzzo)

Rinse the rabbit under cold running water and dry with paper towels. • Heat the oil in a large, heavy-bottomed pan over medium heat and sauté the garlic for 2 minutes. • Add the rabbit, sprinkle with salt and pepper, and cook until the meat is white. • Pour in the wine and cook until it has evaporated. • Reduce the heat to low, partially cover and cook for 40 minutes, adding the stock gradually as the meat dries out. You may not need to add it all. • Add the olives and pine nuts and cook for 15 minutes more. The rabbit should be very tender. • Serve hot.

Serves: 6 · Prep: 10 min. · Cooking: 1 hr · Level: 1

FAGIANO ALLE OLIVE NERE
Pheasant with black olives

1	pheasant, about 2lb
	salt and freshly ground black pepper to taste
1/4	cup all-purpose flour
1	large white onion, sliced
1/4	cup extra-virgin olive oil
2/3	cup dry white wine
1	(15 oz) can tomatoes
2/3	cup Beef stock (see recipe, page 105)
4	oz black olives

Wine: a dry red (Barolo)

Clean and sear the pheasant to eliminate any remaining plumage. • Season with salt and pepper inside and out. Sprinkle with flour, and shake to remove any excess. • Sauté the onion in the oil in a large, heavy-bottomed pan. • Add the pheasant and sauté for a few minutes. • Pour in the wine and cook until it evaporates. • Stir in the tomatoes and season with salt. Partially cover and cook over medium heat for about 45 minutes. Gradually add the stock as the sauce reduces. • Add the olives, stir well, and cook for 15 minutes more. • Remove the pheasant from the pan and cut into pieces. Return to the sauce to reheat over medium heat. • Arrange on a heated serving dish. Serve hot.

Serves: 4 · Prep: 15 min. · Cooking: 1 1/4 hrs Level: 1

CONIGLIO CON LE OLIVE
Rabbit stew with black olives

1	rabbit, about 3 lb, cleaned
1/3	cup extra-virgin olive oil
1	large white onion, coarsely chopped
2	cloves garlic, finely chopped
1	tablespoon finely chopped rosemary
1 1/2	cups red wine
	salt and freshly ground black pepper to taste
3	large tomatoes, peeled and chopped
4	oz black olives, pitted

Wine: a dry red (Rossese di Dolceacqua)

Rinse the rabbit under cold running water and dry with paper towels. Chop into 8–10 pieces. • Heat the oil in a flameproof terra-cotta pan over medium-high heat and sauté the onion, garlic, and rosemary for 2–3 minutes. • Add the rabbit and cook until the meat is white. • Pour in the wine and season with salt and pepper. Cover and turn heat down to low. After 30 minutes, add the tomatoes and olives and cook for 1 hour, or until the rabbit is very tender. • Serve hot.

Serves: 4 · Prep: 15 min. · Cooking: 1 1/4 hrs · Level: 1

Rabbit stew with black olives

CONIGLIO IN FRICASSEA
Rabbit fricassée

- 1 rabbit, about 2¹/₂ lb, cleaned
- 2 tablespoons all-purpose flour
- 1 onion, thinly sliced
- 2 tablespoons butter
- ¹/₄ cup extra-virgin olive oil
- ¹/₂ cup dry white wine
  salt and freshly ground black pepper to taste
- 1 cup Beef stock (see recipe, page 105)
- 2 egg yolks
  juice of 1 lemon
- 2 tablespoons finely chopped parsley

Wine: a dry white (Galestro)

Rinse the rabbit under cold running water and pat dry with paper towels. • Cut into small pieces, roll in the flour, shaking off any excess. • Sauté the onion in the butter and oil over medium-high heat in a large, heavy-bottomed pan until soft. • Add the rabbit and cook on all sides until the meat is white. • Pour in the wine and cook until it evaporates. Season with salt and pepper. • Reduce the heat, partially cover, and cook for about 40 minutes, adding the stock gradually as the sauce reduces. • When the rabbit is cooked, beat the egg yolks in a bowl with the lemon juice and parsley. Pour the mixture over the rabbit and turn off the heat. Stir quickly so that the eggs cook. • Serve hot.

Serves: 4 · Prep: 15 min. · Cooking: 1 hr · Level: 1

CONIGLIO ALL'ISCHITANA
Ischia-style rabbit

- 1 rabbit, about 3 lb, cleaned, with liver
  juice of 1 lemon
- 4 cloves garlic, finely chopped
- ³/₄ cup extra-virgin olive oil

- ³/₄ cup dry white wine
- 1¹/₂ lb tomatoes, peeled and chopped
  salt and freshly ground black pepper to taste
- 6–8 sprigs fresh rosemary

Wine: a light, dry white (Biferno Bianco)

Rinse the rabbit under cold running water and dry with paper towels. Cut into about 8 pieces. • Wash the liver in a little cold water mixed with the lemon juice. • Sauté the garlic in the oil for 2–3 minutes. Add the rabbit and sauté until lightly browned. • Pour in the wine and cook until it has evaporated. • Add the tomatoes and season with salt and pepper. Cook over medium heat for about 20 minutes. • Chop the liver coarsely and add to the pan with the rosemary. Cook over high heat for 5 minutes then serve.

Serves: 4 · Prep: 15 min. · Cooking: 30 min. · Level: 1

CAPRIOLO STUFATO
Marinated venison stew

- 2 cloves garlic, finely chopped
- 1 medium onion, finely chopped
- 1 carrot, cut in wheels
- 1 stalk celery, sliced
- 1 tablespoon finely chopped parsley
- 1 tablespoon finely chopped thyme
- 10 black peppercorns
- ¹/₄ cup extra-virgin olive oil
  salt and freshly ground black pepper to taste
- ³/₄ cup dry white wine
- ¹/₂ cup white vinegar
- 2 lb venison, cut into pieces
- 5 oz diced pancetta
- ¹/₄ cup butter
- 2 cups Beef stock (see recipe, page 105)

Wine: a dry red (Gattinara)

Marinated venison stew

Sauté the garlic, onion, carrot, celery, parsley, thyme, and peppercorns in the oil over medium-high heat. • Sprinkle with salt and pour in the wine and vinegar. Cook for 20 minutes. • Remove from heat and set aside to cool for 20 minutes. Purée in a food processor. Place in a bowl with the venison. Stir well and place in the refrigerator to marinate for 24 hours. • Drain the venison, reserving the marinade. • Sauté the pancetta in the butter in a large, heavy-bottomed pan for a few minutes. • Add the venison, season with salt and pepper. Partially cover and cook over low heat for about 2¹/₂ hours, stirring frequently, and gradually adding the marinade and the stock. • Serve hot.

Serves: 6 · Prep: 30 min. + 24 hrs to marinate · Cooking: 2¹/₂ hrs · Level: 2

LEPRE STUFATA AL VINO ROSSO
Hare and red wine stew

- 1 hare, about 4¹/₂ lb, cleaned and cut in pieces
- 2 cups dry red wine
- 1 stalk celery, 1 carrot, 1 onion, coarsely chopped
- 1 twig rosemary, 2 leaves sage, 3 bay leaves, tied together in a bunch
- 2 cloves garlic, whole
- 1 teaspoon juniper berries
- ¹/₄ cup extra-virgin olive oil
- 2 tablespoons butter
- ¹/₄ cup all-purpose flour
  salt and freshly ground black pepper to taste
- ¹/₄ cup tomato paste
- 14 oz tomatoes, peeled and chopped
- ¹/₂ cup boiling water

Wine: a dry red (Taurasi)

Place the hare in a large bowl with the red wine, celery, carrot, onion, rosemary, sage, bay leaves, garlic, and juniper berries. Place in the refrigerator to marinate for at least 8 hours. • Drain the hare, and set the marinade aside for cooking. Finely chop the celery, carrot, onion, and garlic. Set the bunch of herbs aside. • Heat the oil and butter over medium heat in a heavy-bottomed pan. Add the vegetables and sauté until soft. • In the meantime, lightly flour the pieces of hare and add them to the vegetables. Add the bunch of herbs and sauté for 5–10 minutes. • Pour in the wine marinade and cook until it has evaporated. Season with salt and pepper to taste. • Add the tomato paste, tomatoes, and water. Partially cover and cook for about 1¹/₂ hours, or until the hare is very tender.

Stir from time to time. • Discard the bunch of herbs. • Serve hot.

Serves: 8 · Prep: 40 min. + 8 hrs to marinate · Cooking: 2 hrs · Level: 2

ROTOLO DI CONIGLIO
Crispy, rolled roast rabbit

2½	lb boneless rabbit
	salt and freshly ground black pepper to taste
2	tablespoons combination of finely chopped aromatic herbs (thyme, sage, rosemary)
2	cloves garlic, finely chopped
1	teaspoon fennel seeds
¼	cup extra-virgin olive oil
½	cup dry white wine

Wine: a dry white (Rosso di Gallura)

Open the rabbit out into a single flat slice and lightly beat with a meat pounder. • Season with salt and pepper and sprinkle with the herbs, garlic, and fennel seeds. • Roll the rabbit up and tie with kitchen string. • Transfer to an ovenproof dish with the oil and bake in a preheated oven at 400°F for 1 hour. Turn the rabbit at intervals and baste with the wine so that the meat does not become too dry. • Slice the roast rabbit and serve hot.

Serves: 6 · Prep: 15 min. · Cooking: 1 hr · Level: 1

CINGHIALE STUFATO
Wild boar in red wine and tomato sauce

2¾	lb wild boar, cut in pieces
1	onion, sliced
1	carrot, thickly sliced
1	stalk celery, thickly sliced
1	clove garlic, cut in half
2	cloves
2	bay leaves
	salt and freshly ground black pepper to taste
1	cup robust red wine
½	quantity Basic tomato sauce (see recipe, page 18)
¼	cup extra-virgin olive oil

Wine: a dry red (Barbaresco)

Place the wild boar in a large bowl with the onion, carrot, celery, garlic, cloves, bay leaves, salt, and pepper. Cover with the wine and place in the refrigerator to marinate for 24 hours. Prepare the tomato sauce. • Drain the marinade from the wild boar. Reserve the liquid, discard the cloves and bay leaves, and coarsely chop the vegetables. • Heat the oil in a large, heavy-bottomed pan over medium heat and sauté the vegetables for 5–7 minutes. • Add the meat and sauté until brown. • Stir in the tomato sauce, then add the liquid from

the marinade. Partially cover the pan and cook over medium-low heat for 2 hours, stirring from time to time. • Serve hot.

Serves: 6 · Prep: 30 min. · Cooking: 2¼ hrs + 24 hrs to marinate · Level: 2

SCOTTIGLIA
Braised mixed poultry and game

¼	cup extra-virgin olive oil
2	cloves garlic, peeled and cut in half
1	onion, finely chopped
6	leaves basil, torn
2	tablespoons finely chopped parsley
2½	lb mixed poultry and game (chicken, rabbit, wild boar, squab pigeon, hare), cut in pieces
	salt and freshly ground black pepper to taste
1	cup full-bodied red wine
1	cup Beef stock (see recipe, page 105)
1¼	lb tomatoes, peeled and chopped
6	slices Bruschetta (see recipe, page 76)

Wine: a dry, full-bodied red (Sassicaia)

Heat the oil in a large, heavy-bottomed pan and add the garlic. Cook until the garlic turns golden brown, then discard. • Add the onion and sauté until soft. Add the basil and parsley. • Add the meat and sauté until well browned. Season with salt and pepper. • Pour in a little wine and cook until it evaporates. When all the wine has been been absorbed, add the tomatoes. Partially cover and cook over medium-low heat for 2 hours. Stir at frequent intervals, adding stock to keep the stew moist. • Prepare the bruschetta and place in heated serving bowls. Pour in the stew and serve hot.

Serves: 6 · Prep: 30 min. · Cooking: 2¼ hrs · Level: 2

CINGHIALE AI PORRI
Wild boar with leeks

2¼	lb wild boar, cut in pieces
3	cups dry white wine
4	cloves
2	bay leaves
	salt and freshly ground black pepper to taste
¼	cup extra-virgin olive oil
4	oz prosciutto, chopped
4	leeks, in thin slices
2	cups Beef stock (see recipe, page 105)
¼	cup white vinegar
1	tablespoon pine nuts
1	tablespoon all-purpose flour

Wine: a dry red (Carmignano Rosso)

Place the wild boar in a large bowl with the wine, cloves, and bay leaves. Sprinkle with salt and pepper and place in the refrigerator to marinate for 24 hours. • Drain the marinade and set the liquid aside for cooking. Discard the cloves and bay leaves. • Heat the oil in a large, heavy-bottomed pan over medium heat and sauté the prosciutto for 2 minutes. • Add the leeks and a ladleful of stock and cook until the leeks begin to soften. • Add the meat and brown all over. • Pour in the liquid from the marinade, partially cover the pan, and cook for 2½ hours, adding stock so the meat doesn't dry out. • When the meat is tender, add the vinegar and pine nuts and stir well. Dissolve the flour in 2 tablespoons of cold water and stir into the sauce until it thickens. • Serve hot.

Serves: 6 · Prep: 15 min. + 24 hrs to marinate · Cooking: 2¾ hrs · Level: 2

Wild boar in red wine and tomato sauce

VEGETABLES

The Mediterranean sun ripens a dazzling array of flavorful vegetables. Not surprisingly, vegetables feature in every Italian meal. They are baked, sautéed, stuffed, boiled, grilled, roasted, stewed, and fried into every dish imaginable.

CIPOLLINE BRASATE AL VINO
Baby onions with herbs and white wine

1¾ lb white baby onions, peeled
2 tablespoons extra-virgin olive oil
3 tablespoons butter
    salt and freshly ground black pepper to taste
2 cups dry white wine
3 bay leaves
1 tablespoon each finely chopped thyme, marjoram, and mint

Wine: a dry white (Orvieto Classico)

Place the onions, oil, and butter in a large skillet. Sauté over high heat for about 10 minutes, stirring with a wooden spoon so that the onions brown evenly. Season with salt and pepper. • Add the wine, bay leaves, and herbs. Partially cover and cook for 15 more minutes. • Uncover and cook until the sauce thickens. • Serve hot or at room temperature.

Serves: 4 · Prep: 10 min. · Cooking: 30 min. · Level: 1

◁ Stuffed mushrooms (see recipe page 280)
△ Baby onions with herbs and white wine

LENTICCHIE STUFATE CON SALSICCIA
Lentil and sausage stew

- 1³/₄ cups lentils, soaked in cold water overnight
- ¹/₂ cup extra-virgin olive oil
- 1 medium onion, 1 large carrot, 2 stalks celery, finely chopped together
- ¹/₂ cup diced pancetta
- 1 cup white wine
- 2 tablespoons tomato paste, diluted in
- 2 tablespoons hot water
- 1 teaspoon crushed red pepper flakes
- 1 beef bouillon cube
  salt and freshly ground black pepper to taste
- 6 Italian sausages, pricked with a fork to eliminate fat during cooking

Wine: a dry red (Barbaresco)

Place the soaked lentils in a pot and cover with cold water. Add salt and simmer for 30 minutes, then drain. • Heat the oil in a large skillet and sauté the onion, carrot, celery, and pancetta until pale golden brown. • Add the lentils and stir for 2–3 minutes. • Pour in the white wine and cook until it has evaporated. Add the diluted tomato paste, pepper flakes, and the bouillon cube. Season with salt and pepper, and pour in enough boiling water to cover the lentils. Cook for 40 minutes over low heat. • In the meantime, brown the sausages in a skillet with 2 tablespoons of cold water. Drain the excess fat and add the sausages to the lentils when they have been cooking for about 20 minutes. • The lentils should be tender and the stew slightly liquid; if it is too liquid, stir over high heat until it reduces. • Serve hot.

Serves: 4 · Prep: 10 min. · Cooking: 1¹/₂ hrs · Level: 1

Sweet Sicilian fava beans and peas

FAVE IN UMIDO
Fava bean stew

- 1 lb freshly hulled fava beans (about 5 lb of fresh bean pods)
- ¹/₄ cup extra-virgin olive oil
- 1 cup diced pancetta
- 2 cloves garlic, finely chopped
- 1 onion, thinly sliced
- 1¹/₂ tablespoons finely chopped parsley
  salt and freshly ground black pepper to taste
- 1 cup boiling Chicken or Vegetable stock (see recipes, page 104)

Wine: a light, dry red (Rosso di Cori)

Place the beans in a bowl and cover with cold water to prevent their skins from toughening. • Heat the oil in a large skillet and sauté the pancetta, garlic, and onion for 5–6 minutes over medium heat. • Drain the beans and add to the skillet with the parsley, salt, pepper, and stock. Cover and simmer over medium-low heat for 25 minutes, or until the beans are tender. • If the stew is too liquid, stir over high heat until it reduces sufficiently. • Serve hot.

Serves: 4 · Prep: 15 min. · Cooking: 30 min. · Level: 1

FRITTEDDA
Sweet Sicilian fava beans and peas

- 4 artichokes
  juice of 1 lemon
- ¹/₄ cup extra-virgin olive oil
- 1 small onion, finely chopped
- 1 lb freshly hulled fava beans,
- 1 lb freshly hulled peas
  pinch of nutmeg
  salt and freshly ground black pepper to taste
- 1 tablespoon finely chopped mint
- 1 teaspoon sugar
- 1 teaspoon white wine vinegar

Wine: a dry white (Ciclopi Bianco)

To clean the artichokes, remove all the tough outer leaves and trim the tops and stalks. Cut them in half and remove the fuzzy inner choke. Cut the tender hearts in thin wedges and soak in a bowl of cold water with the lemon juice for 10 minutes. • Heat the oil in a skillet over medium heat and sauté the onion for 3–4 minutes. • Drain the artichokes and add to the pan. Cook for 5 minutes, then add the beans, peas, and nutmeg. Season with salt and pepper and cook over medium-low heat for 25 minutes, or until tender. • Stir in the mint, sugar, and vinegar a few minutes before the beans and peas are done. • Serve at room temperature.

Serves: 4–6 · Prep: 15 min. · Cooking: 30 min. · Level: 1

FAGIOLI IN SALSA
Beans with anchovy sauce

☞ This anchovy sauce is delicious with cannellini, cranberry, or borlotti beans.

- 2 cups dry beans, soaked overnight
  salt and freshly ground black pepper to taste
- 1 clove garlic, peeled
- 2 tablespoons finely chopped parsley
- ¹/₄ cup extra-virgin olive oil
- 12 anchovy fillets
- 1 cup red wine vinegar

Wine: a dry red (Chianti Rufina)

Drain the soaked beans and place in a saucepan with enough cold water to cover. Bring to a boil and simmer gently over low heat for at least 2 hours; add salt only just before they are done or their skins will toughen. • In a heavy-bottomed saucepan, sauté the garlic and parsley in the oil. Discard the garlic when it starts to color. Add the anchovies and cook gently until they have dissolved in the oil. • Add the vinegar and a generous grinding of pepper and simmer, uncovered, for 10 minutes. • Drain the beans when cooked and place in a serving dish. Drizzle with the vinegar dressing and leave to stand at room temperature for 1 hour before serving.

Serves: 4 · Prep: 10 min. + 1 hr to flavor · Cooking: 2¹/₄ hrs · Level: 1

BAGGIANATA PIEMONTESE
Green beans, Piedmontese-style

- 1 lb ripe tomatoes
- 2 tablespoons lard (or butter)
- 1 clove garlic, finely chopped
- 8 leaves fresh basil, finely chopped
- 2 tablespoons finely chopped parsley
- 2 lb green beans, trimmed
- 1/2 cup dry red wine
  salt and freshly ground black pepper to taste

Wine: a young, dry red (Barbera d'Asti)

Plunge the tomatoes into a pot of boiling water for 1 minute. Drain and place in cold water. Peel and cut in half. Squeeze out as many seeds as possible and chop coarsely. • Melt the lard in a large skillet and add the garlic, basil, and parsley. Sauté over medium-high heat for 5 minutes. • Add the green beans, tomatoes, and wine, and season with salt and pepper. Cover and cook over medium-low heat for about 40 minutes, or until the beans are tender. • Serve hot or at room temperature.

Serves: 4 · Prep: 15 min. · Cooking: 45 min. · Level: 1

FAGIOLI ALL'UCCELLETTO
Tuscan-style kidney beans

- 4 cloves garlic, finely chopped
- 2/3 cups extra-virgin olive oil
- 1 (15 oz) can tomatoes, coarsely chopped
- 8 leaves fresh sage
  salt and freshly ground black pepper to taste
- 1 (15 oz) can white kidney beans (or soaked and pre-cooked dry beans)

Wine: a light, dry red (Chianti Novello)

Sauté the garlic in the oil and as soon as it begins to color, add the tomatoes, sage, salt, and pepper. • Simmer over medium heat for 10 minutes. • When the sauce has reduced a little, add the beans and cook for about 15 more minutes. • Serve hot.

Serves: 4 · Prep: 10 min. · Cooking: 25 min. · Level: 1

SFORMATO DI FAGIOLINI
Green bean mold

- 14 oz fresh green beans
- 2 tablespoons extra-virgin olive oil
- 1/4 cup butter
- 1/2 onion, finely chopped

Green beans, Piedmontese-style

- 1 stalk celery, finely chopped
- 1 tablespoon finely chopped parsley
- 1/2 bouillon cube dissolved in 1/2 cup boiling water
- 1/4 cup freshly grated Parmesan cheese
  salt and freshly ground black pepper to taste
- 1/2 quantity Béchamel sauce (see recipe, page 16)
- 2 eggs, beaten
- 2 tablespoons bread crumbs
- 1 quantity Simple tomato sauce (see recipe, page 18)

Wine: a dry white (Bianco di Custoza)

Clean and wash the beans and cook for 10 minutes in salted, boiling water. Drain and pass under cold running water. Dry well with paper towels. • Heat the oil and half the butter in a skillet. Add the onion, celery, and parsley, and when the onion begins to color, add the beans. Sauté until the beans have absorbed the seasoning. • Add the bouillon. • Cover the pan and simmer for about 20 minutes. • Prepare the béchamel sauce and stir in the Parmesan and a generous grinding of pepper. • Drain the beans and transfer to a bowl. Add half the béchamel sauce and the eggs. Mix well. • Butter a mold and sprinkle with the bread crumbs. Fill with the beans and cover with the remaining béchamel sauce. • Place a large container of cold water in a preheated oven at 350°F. Place the mold pan in the water-filled container and cook for 40 minutes. •

Invert the mold onto a serving dish. Pour the tomato sauce over the top and serve.

Serves: 4 · Prep: 20 min. · Cooking: 1 1/4 hrs · Level: 2

FAGIOLATA
Bean casserole

☞ If fresh borlotti beans are not available, use 1 1/2 cups dry borlotti beans soaked in cold water overnight.

- 1 1/2 lb freshly hulled borlotti beans
- 12 oz fresh pork rind, cut into 1-inch squares
- 1 large onion, peeled and sliced
- 2 tablespoons tomato paste
- 1/4 cup extra-virgin olive oil
- 1 tablespoon finely chopped rosemary leaves
- 2 cloves
- 1 cup finely chopped Savoy cabbage
  salt and freshly ground black pepper to taste

Wine: a dry red (Nebbiolo)

Place the beans, pork rind, and onion in a fireproof earthenware casserole or heavy-bottomed saucepan with just enough cold water to cover. • Bring to a boil over high heat, then simmer gently over low heat for 1 1/2 hours, stirring now and then. • The liquid will reduce considerably, but the beans should remain very moist. Add a little boiling water if necessary. • Add the tomato paste, oil, rosemary, cloves, and cabbage. Season with salt and pepper. Cook for 30 more minutes. • Serve hot.

Serves: 4 · Prep: 15 min. · Cooking: 2 hrs · Level: 1

Pea mousse

Bring 2 quarts of salted water to a boil in a pan and cook the peas and onion for 10–15 minutes. • Drain well and set aside to cool. • Place the Caprino, peas, onion, and oil in a blender and blend until the mixture is creamy. Season with salt and pepper. • Line a 1-quart pudding mold with plastic wrap and pour the mixture in, pressing with a spoon to eliminate pockets of air. Knock the mold against the work bench to eliminate air bubbles. • Chill in the refrigerator for at least 2 hours. • Invert onto a round serving dish and, if liked, garnish with the cherry tomatoes and parsley.

Serves: 4 · Prep: 2¹/₂ hrs · Cooking: 15 min. · Level: 2

TACCOLE IN SALSA DEL POVR'OM
Sugar snap peas in Poor man's sauce

    1 quantity Poor man's sauce (see recipe, page 15)
    1 lb sugar snap peas

Wine: a dry white (Pinot Grigio)

Prepare the sauce. • Rinse the sugar snap peas and string them, if necessary. • Place in a saucepan of salted, boiling water and cook for 8–10 minutes, or until tender. • Drain the sugar snap peas and arrange on a preheated serving platter. • Cover with the sauce and serve hot.

Serves: 4 · Prep: 10 min. · Cooking: 20 min. · Level: 1

TACCOLE ALLA PANNA
Sugar snap peas with cream

☞ These tender little peas, also called snow peas or mange-tout, are eaten whole, pods and all. If not available, substitute with fresh young ordinary peas in their pods.

    1 lb sugar snap peas
       pinch of salt
    ¹/₄ cup butter
    ¹/₃ cup heavy cream
    ¹/₂ cup freshly grated Parmesan cheese

Wine: a dry rosé (Mosaico)

Rinse the sugar snap peas and string them, if necessary. • Place in a saucepan of salted, boiling water and cook for 8–10 minutes, or until tender. • When they have about 2 minutes cooking time left, heat the butter in a small saucepan until it turns

golden brown. • Drain the peas and place in a heated serving dish. Cover with the cream and sprinkle with the Parmesan. Pour the hot butter over the top and serve.

Serves: 4 · Prep: 5 min. · Cooking: 10 min. · Level: 1

PISELLINI AL PROSCIUTTO
Spring peas with prosciutto

    1 small onion, finely chopped
    ¹/₂ cup lard (or butter)
    1¹/₂ lb fresh or frozen peas
    ¹/₂ cup Beef stock (see recipe, page 105)
       salt and freshly ground black pepper to taste
    3 oz prosciutto, cut in one thick slice, then diced

Wine: a dry white (Frascati Novello)

Sauté the onion in the lard over medium heat until pale gold. • Add the peas and stock. Season with salt and pepper and cook for 10 minutes, or until the peas are tender. • Add the prosciutto 2 minutes before the peas are cooked. • Serve hot.

Serves: 4 · Prep: 5 min. · Cooking: 10 min. · Level: 1

MOUSSE DI PISELLI
Pea mousse

    1 lb fresh or frozen peas
    1 medium onion, cut in half
    2 cups Caprino cheese
    3 tablespoons extra-virgin olive oil
       salt and freshly ground black pepper to taste
    8 cherry tomatoes, cut in quarters (optional)
    8 tiny sprigs parsley (optional)

Wine: a dry red (Cabernet Sauvignon)

SPINACI AL BURRO
Spinach with butter

    2 lb fresh or 1¹/₂ lb frozen spinach (thawed)
    ¹/₄ cup butter
       salt and freshly ground black pepper to taste
    ¹/₄ cup freshly grated Parmesan cheese

Wine: a dry white (Bianco di Custoza)

If using fresh spinach, rinse well under cold running water. • Cook the spinach in a pot of salted, boiling water for 8–10 minutes, or until tender. Drain, squeeze out excess moisture, and chop coarsely. • Heat the butter in a large skillet and add the spinach. Season with salt and pepper. Cook over medium-high heat for 3–4 minutes, tossing continually, so that the spinach absorbs the butter and seasoning. • Sprinkle with the Parmesan and serve.

Serves: 6 · Prep: 10 min. · Cooking: 15 min. · Level: 1

SPINACI ALLA PIEMONTESE
Spinach with butter and anchovies

    1¹/₂ lb fresh or 1 lb frozen spinach
    ¹/₄ cup butter
    4 anchovy fillets, crumbled
    ¹/₂ clove garlic, finely chopped
       salt and freshly ground white pepper to taste
       slices of bread fried in olive oil

Wine: a light, dry white (Cortese di Gavi)

If using fresh spinach, rinse well under cold running water. • Cook the spinach in a pot of salted, boiling water for 8–10 minutes, or until tender. Drain, squeeze out excess moisture, and chop in a food processor. • Melt the butter in a saucepan, then add the anchovies and garlic. Stir the anchovies into the butter until they dissolve. • Add the spinach and season with salt and pepper. • Cook for 6–7 minutes over low heat, stirring frequently. • Place in a preheated serving dish with the fried bread.

Serves: 4 · Prep: 10 min. · Cooking: 10 min. · Level: 1

SOUFFLÉ DI SPINACI
Spinach soufflé

- 1¹/₂   lb fresh spinach
- ¹/₃   cup butter
- ¹/₄   cup freshly grated Parmesan cheese
- 3   eggs, separated
    salt to taste
- 3   tablespoons fine dry bread crumbs
- 8   anchovy fillets

Wine: a dry red (Torgiano Rosso)

Rinse the spinach under cold running water. Do not drain. Cook over medium heat with just the water left clinging to the leaves. • Chop finely in a food processor. • Place in a small skillet with ¹/₄ cup of butter over medium heat and cook until all the butter has been absorbed . • In a mixing bowl, combine the spinach with the Parmesan and egg yolks. Mix until smooth. • Beat the egg whites with a pinch of salt until very stiff. Fold them into the spinach mixture. • Butter an 8-inch soufflé mold

with 1 tablespoon of butter and sprinkle with the bread crumbs. • Place half the spinach mixture in the mold and cover with the anchovy fillets. Cover with the remaining spinach. • Chop the remaining butter and scatter over the top of the soufflé. • Bake in a preheated oven at 350°F for 30 minutes. Serve immediately.

Serves: 4 · Prep: 15 min. · Cooking: 40 min. · Level: 2

SFORMATO DI SPINACI
Spinach mold

- 1¹/₂   lb fresh or 1 lb frozen spinach (thawed)
    salt and freshly ground black pepper to taste
- ¹/₄   cup fresh cream
- 1   quantity Béchamel sauce (see recipe, page 16)
- ¹/₃   cup freshly grated Parmesan cheese
- ¹/₄   teaspoon nutmeg
- 2   eggs, separated
    butter and flour to grease and dust the mold

Wine: a dry white (Pinot Bianco dei Colli Euganei)

If using fresh spinach, rinse well under cold running water. • Cook the spinach in a pot of salted, boiling water for 8–10 minutes, or until tender. Drain, squeeze out excess moisture, and chop in a food processor. • Put the spinach in a saucepan with the cream and stir over medium heat until all the moisture has been absorbed. Remove from heat. • Prepare the béchamel sauce. Set aside to cool for 5 minutes. • Combine the béchamel with the

spinach purée and add the Parmesan, nutmeg, and egg yolks. Season with salt and pepper. • Beat the egg whites until stiff and carefully fold them into the spinach mixture. • Grease a 12-inch ring mold with the butter and dust with flour. Pour the mixture into the mold. • Place the mold in a larger container filled with water and cook in a preheated oven at 350°F for about 45 minutes. • Invert onto a plate while still hot. Serve hot or at room temperature.

Serves: 4 · Prep: 20 min. · Cooking: 1 hr · Level: 2

CAROTE CARAMELLATE
Carrots in butter sauce

- 2   lb carrots, scraped
- ¹/₃   cup butter, chopped
    salt and freshly ground black pepper to taste
- 2   tablespoons superfine sugar
- ¹/₄   cup finely chopped parsley

Wine: a dry red (Barbaresco)

Rinse the carrots under cold running water. Cut into sticks about 2 inches long. • Place in a large sauté pan and cover with cold water. Add half the butter. • Cook over high heat until the water evaporates. • Season with salt and pepper, add the remaining butter and sprinkle with the sugar. Sauté the carrots until well-coated with butter. • Add the parsley, mix well, and serve hot.

Serves: 6 · Prep: 10 min. · Cooking: 25 min. · Level: 1

Spinach soufflé

Spinach sautéed with garlic and oil

SPINACI CON AGLIO E OLIO
Spinach sautéed with garlic and oil

- 2 lb fresh or 1¹/₂ lb frozen spinach (thawed)
- 2 large cloves garlic, finely chopped
- ¹/₄ cup extra-virgin olive oil
  salt to taste

Wine: a dry white (Bianco di Custoza)

If using fresh spinach, rinse well under cold running water. • Cook the spinach in a pot of salted, boiling water for 8–10 minutes, or until tender. Drain, squeeze out excess moisture, and chop coarsely. • Sauté the garlic in the oil over high heat for 2–3 minutes. • Add the spinach and cook over medium-high heat for 3–4 minutes, tossing continually, so that the spinach absorbs the flavors of the garlic and oil. • Serve hot or at room temperature.

Serves: 6 · Prep: 10 min. · Cooking: 15 min. · Level: 1

CIPOLLE FARCITE DI RISO
Onions stuffed with rice and marjoram

- 1¹/₂ cups short-grain white rice
- 8 large onions
- 3 eggs, beaten
- 2 tablespoons finely chopped fresh marjoram
- ¹/₂ cup freshly grated Parmesan cheese
- 1 cup freshly grated Pecorino romano cheese
- 4 oz pitted black olives (3 oz coarsely chopped and 1 oz cut in half)
  salt and freshly ground black pepper to taste
- ¹/₄ cup extra-virgin olive oil
- 1 cup dry white wine
- 1 cup Vegetable stock (see recipe, page 104)
- 2 tablespoons butter

Wine: a light, dry red (Lambrusco Mantovano)

Cook the rice in a large pot of salted, boiling water for 15 minutes, or until tender. Drain well. • Peel the onions, trim the bottoms, and slice off the tops. Cook for 7–8 minutes in a pot of salted, boiling water. Set aside on paper towels to cool. • Hollow out the onions with a sharp knife leaving a ¹/₂-inch thick shell. Set the pulp aside. • Combine the eggs in a bowl with the rice, the marjoram, Parmesan, half the Pecorino, chopped olives, salt, and pepper. Mix well. • Spoon the filling into the onions and sprinkle with the remaining Pecorino. • In a bowl, mix ¹/₄

cup of onion pulp, the halved olives, 1 tablespoon of olive oil, salt, and pepper, and pour into an ovenproof dish. • Arrange the stuffed onions on top and drizzle with the remaining oil, the wine, and stock. Dot each onion with butter and bake in a preheated oven at 350°F for 35 minutes. • Serve hot.

Serves: 4 · Prep: 25 min. · Cooking: 1 hr · Level: 2

SPIEDINI DI CIPOLLINE E ALLORO
Onion skewers with bay leaves

- 28 baby onions, peeled
- 12 bay leaves, cut in half
- ¹/₄ cup extra-virgin olive oil
  salt and freshly ground black pepper to taste

Wine: a dry red (Pinot Nero)

Cook the onions in a pot of salted, boiling water for 5 minutes. • Drain well and dry with paper towels. Thread the onions onto 4 skewers (7 onions each, with a half bay leaf between each onion). Skewer the onions horizontally so that they will lie flat during cooking. • Drizzle with the oil and cook in a hot grill pan or under a broiler, turning often. Cook for about 15 minutes, or until the onions are golden brown. • Sprinkle with salt and pepper. Serve hot or at room temperature.

Serves: 4 · Prep: 10 min. · Cooking: 20 min. · Level: 1

CIPOLLE E PATATE AL FORNO
Baked onions with potato and cheese

- 3 lb potatoes
- 8 medium white onions, thickly sliced
- 1 tablespoon extra-virgin olive oil
- ¹/₂ cup butter
- 1 cup dry white wine
- ¹/₂ cup Vegetable stock (see recipe, page 104)
  salt and freshly ground black pepper to taste
- 1¹/₄ cups milk
- 3 eggs, beaten to a foam
- 1 cup freshly grated Parmesan cheese
- 1 cup freshly grated Gruyère cheese
- 2 tablespoons fine dry bread crumbs

Wine: a dry red (Refosco)

Boil the potatoes in their skins in a pot of salted water for about 25 minutes. Drain and cover to keep warm. • Place the onions, oil, half the butter, the wine, stock, salt, and pepper in a saucepan. Cover and simmer for about 30 minutes, or until the onions are very soft. • Peel the potatoes and mash until smooth. • Heat the milk in a saucepan and add the potatoes and all but 1 tablespoon of the remaining butter. Stir until smooth. Remove from heat and let cool for 10 minutes. • Combine the potato mixture with the eggs, salt, and pepper. Stir in two-thirds of the Parmesan, mixing well. • Butter an ovenproof dish and spread half the potato mixture on the bottom in an even layer. • Drain the cooked onions and spread over the potatoes. Sprinkle with the Gruyère and cover with the remaining potatoes. • Sprinkle with bread crumbs and remaining Parmesan. • Bake in a preheated oven at 350°F for 25 minutes. • Serve hot.

Serves: 4 · Prep: 30 min. · Cooking: 1 hr · Level: 1

CIPOLLE RIPIENE
Onions stuffed with Parmesan, peach brandy, and amaretti cookies

- 8   medium white onions
- 4   oz fresh Italian sausages, crumbled
- 8   oz ground beef
- ¼   cup butter
- 1   cup freshly grated Parmesan cheese
- 1   large egg
- 1   tablespoon peach brandy
- 4   amaretti cookies (macaroons), crushed
     salt and freshly ground white pepper to taste
- ¼   cup fine dry bread crumbs
- ¼   cup boiling water

Wine: a medium or dry, lightly sparkling red (Barbera del Monferrato Frizzante or Barbera del Monferrato Vivace)

Peel the onions and boil for 10–15 minutes in salted water. Drain and set aside to cool. • Cut the onions in half horizontally and scoop out enough pulp from their centers to form a hollow into

Onions stuffed with Parmesan, peach brandy, and amaretti cookies

which half an egg would fit. • Finely chop the pulp. • Combine the sausage meat and beef in a skillet with half the butter and sauté for 6–7 minutes. • Place in a mixing bowl and add the chopped onion pulp, Parmesan, egg, peach brandy, amaretti cookies, salt, and pepper. Mix well. • Use this mixture to stuff the onions, heaping it up into a smooth mound on each one. • Arrange the onions close together in a single layer in a roasting pan or baking dish greased with butter. • Sprinkle with the bread crumbs and place a sliver of the remaining butter on each one. • Pour the boiling water into the bottom of the dish. • Bake the onions in a preheated oven at 350°F for 40–45 minutes, adding a little more water to prevent them sticking to the dish, if necessary. • Serve hot or at room temperature.

Serves: 4 · Prep: 30 min. · Cooking: 1 hr · Level: 1

CIPOLLE AL FORNO CON FORMAGGIO FRESCO
Baked onions with fresh cheese

- 8   medium white onions
- ¼   cup extra-virgin olive oil
     salt and freshly ground black pepper to taste
- ¾   cup creamy fresh cheese (cream cheese, Caprino Robiola, Mascarpone)

Wine: a dry white (Frascati)

Trim the onions top and bottom, taking a larger slice from the top. • Wrap each onion in a piece of aluminum foil. • Bake in a preheated oven at 350°F for 35 minutes. Pierce an onion through the center with a wooden skewer. If it goes in easily, the onions are done; if the center still feels hard or moist bake for 5–10 more minutes. • Remove from the oven, unwrap the foil, and cut in half horizontally. Drizzle with the oil and sprinkle with salt and pepper. Divide the cheese evenly among the onions and serve.

Serves: 4 · Prep: 10 min. · Cooking: 45 min. · Level: 1

FONDI DI CARCIOFO
Braised artichoke hearts

☞ Artichokes are a common vegetable in Italy. They can be served in many different ways. To clean them, remove all the tough outer leaves and trim the tops and stalks. Cut them in half and remove the fuzzy inner choke. Soak in a bowl of cold water with the juice of 1 lemon for 10 minutes to stop them from discoloring.

- ½ cup extra-virgin olive oil
- 2 tablespoons finely chopped parsley
- 2 cloves garlic, finely chopped
- 12 fresh or frozen raw artichoke hearts
    salt and freshly ground black pepper to taste

Wine: a light, dry white (Soave Classico)

Pour the oil into a large skillet and add the parsley and garlic. Sauté over low heat for 5 minutes. • Add the artichoke hearts, salt, pepper, and sufficient water to cover the hearts. Cover and cook over medium-low heat for 10 minutes. Remove the lid, increase the heat and cook for 10 more minutes to reduce the cooking liquid. • Serve hot or at room temperature.

Serves: 6 · Prep: 15 min. · Cooking: 25 min. · Level: 1

CARCIOFI CON PISELLI
Artichokes with peas

- 8 medium artichokes
    juice of 1 lemon
- 1 onion, finely chopped
- 2 tablespoons extra-virgin olive oil
- 2 oz prosciutto, chopped (optional)
    salt and freshly ground black pepper to taste
- 12 oz fresh or frozen peas

Wine: a dry white (Marino)

Clean the artichokes as explained above. Soak in a bowl of cold water with the lemon juice. • Sauté the onion in the oil in a large skillet until pale gold. Add the prosciutto. • Drain the artichokes and add them to the skillet. Cook for 10 minutes. • Season with salt and pepper and add the peas. Cover and cook over medium heat for about 15 minutes, or until the peas and artichokes are both tender. Add a little cold water as necessary to keep the vegetables moist. • Serve hot or at room temperature.

Serves: 4 · Prep: 10 min. · Cooking: 35 min. · Level: 1

Braised artichoke hearts

STUFATO DI CARCIOFI
Artichoke stew

☞ For a perfect light lunch, serve this stew with a platter of fresh cheeses (Ricotta, Mozzarella, Caprino, Robiola, cream cheese).

8	medium artichokes
	juice of 1 lemon
3	cloves garlic, finely chopped
1/4	cup extra-virgin olive oil
1	cup dry white wine
	salt and freshly ground black pepper to taste
3	tablespoons parsley, finely chopped

Wine: a dry white (Greco di Tufo)

Clean the artichokes as explained on page 274. The stalks can also be used in this dish; peel them with a knife and soak with the artichokes in a bowl of cold water with the lemon juice. • Drain the artichokes and stalks. Cut the artichokes into quarters. • Put the artichokes, stalks, garlic, oil, wine, salt, and pepper in a heavy-bottomed pan. Cover and cook over medium heat for 20 minutes, then uncover and add the parsley. Stir and finish cooking without a lid. • Serve hot or at room temperature.

Serves: 4 · Prep: 20 min. · Cooking: 25 min. · Level : 1

CARCIOFI IN AGRODOLCE
Sweet and sour artichokes

8	very young, fresh artichokes
	juice of 1 lemon
1/2	cup all-purpose flour
1/2	cup extra-virgin olive oil
1/4	cup finely chopped onion
1	tablespoon salted capers, rinsed
12	green olives, pitted and chopped
1	small carrot, diced
2	tender stalks celery, trimmed and thinly sliced
	salt and freshly ground black pepper to taste
1/2	cup hot water
4	medium tomatoes, seeded and chopped
4	anchovy fillets
3	teaspoons sugar
1/4	cup Italian wine vinegar

Wine: a young, dry white (Bianco di Donnafugata)

Clean the artichokes as explained on page 274. Cut each artichoke lengthwise into six wedges and soak in a bowl of cold water with the lemon juice for 10 minutes. • Coat the artichokes lightly with flour and fry in a flameproof casserole over high heat for 2–3 minutes, turning once or twice. • Remove the artichokes, letting the excess

oil drain back into the casserole. • Add the onion, capers, olives, carrot, celery, salt, pepper, and hot water, and simmer over medium heat for about 10 minutes. • Stir in the tomatoes and then add the artichokes and anchovies. Cover and simmer over low heat for 20–25 minutes. • Mix the sugar with the vinegar and stir into the vegetables. Leave to cook for a final 4–5 minutes. • Serve hot or at room temperature.

Serves: 4 · Prep: 15 min. · Cooking: 45 min. · Level: 1

MAMME DI CARCIOFI RIPIENE
Stuffed artichoke hearts

8	large artichokes
	juice of 1 lemon
4	eggs
	salt and freshly ground black pepper to taste
6	oz ground lean pork
1	Italian pork sausage, peeled and crumbled
5	oz prosciutto, chopped
1 1/2	cups freshly grated Parmesan cheese
3	cloves garlic, finely chopped
2	tablespoons finely chopped parsley
2	cups oil, for frying
1/2	cup extra-virgin olive oil
1	(28 oz) can tomatoes, chopped
10	fresh basil leaves

Wine: a dry red (Montepulciano d'Abruzzo)

Clean the artichokes as explained on page 274. Trim the stalks so that the artichokes will stand upright in the pot. Chop the stems coarsely and soak them with the artichokes in a bowl of cold water with the lemon juice. • Season the beaten eggs with salt and pepper. • Add the pork, sausage, prosciutto, Parmesan, garlic, parsley, salt, and pepper and blend well with a fork. • Use a teaspoon to open out the leaves and fill each artichoke with stuffing. • Heat the frying oil in a skillet until hot but not smoking. Hold each artichoke upside down in the oil for about 2 minutes, to

seal in the filling. Roll the artichokes in the oil for 2 more minutes to cook the leaves. Using two forks, remove from the oil and set aside. • Place the olive oil, tomatoes, basil, artichoke stems, salt, and pepper in a skillet and simmer over low heat for 10 minutes. • Add the stuffed artichokes and baste them with the sauce. Cover and simmer for 20 minutes. Uncover and cook for 10 more minutes, or until the sauce has reduced. • Serve hot.

Serves: 4 · Prep: 25 min. · Cooking: 1 hr · Level: 1

CARCIOFI IN FRICASSEA
Artichokes with egg and lemon

8	large artichokes
	juice of 2 lemons
1/4	cup butter
	pinch of salt
1/4	cup hot water
3	egg yolks
2	tablespoons light cream
1/4	cup cold water
2	tablespoons finely chopped parsley
	freshly ground white pepper

Wine: a young, dry white (Monferrato Bianco Vivace)

Clean the artichokes as explained on page 274. • Cut each artichoke in 10–12 thin wedges. Soak in a bowl of cold water with the juice of 1 lemon for 10 minutes. • Melt the butter in a skillet and add the well-drained artichokes. Sprinkle with salt and cook over medium heat. • Stir frequently, adding 1–2 tablespoons of hot water at intervals to keep the artichokes moist. They will take about 15 minutes to cook. Test to make sure they are tender. • Beat the egg yolks, cream, and cold water lightly together in a small bowl with the parsley, salt, and pepper. • Sprinkle the remaining lemon juice over the cooked artichokes and reduce the heat to very low. • Pour the egg mixture over the artichokes and toss well for about 2 minutes. • Serve at once.

Serves: 4 · Prep: 20 min. · Cooking: 20 min. · Level: 1

FINOCCHI ALLA PARMIGIANA
Baked fennel with Parmesan cheese

- 6 large bulbs fennel
- ½ cup butter
- ¼ cup all-purpose flour
- 1 large onion, thinly sliced
- 1¼ cups diced ham
- ¼ cup heavy cream
  salt and freshly ground black pepper to taste
- 1¼ cups freshly grated Parmesan cheese

Wine: a dry white (Soave)

Clean the fennel by removing the tough outer leaves. Trim the stalks and cut each bulb in half. • Cook in salted, boiling water for 8 minutes, or until almost cooked. • Drain, dry with paper towels, and cut each half in 2 or 3 pieces. • Heat half the butter in a skillet over medium heat. Dredge the fennel and onion in the flour and cook in the butter until golden brown. • Add the ham and cream and season with salt and pepper. Cover and let the sauce reduce over low heat for about 15 minutes. • Arrange in layers in a buttered baking dish. Sprinkle with the Parmesan and dot with the remaining butter. • Bake in a preheated oven at 375°F for 20 minutes. • Serve hot.

Serves: 4 · Prep: 15 min. · Cooking: 45 min. · Level: 1

ASPARAGI ALLA PARMIGIANA
Baked asparagus with Parmesan cheese

- 3 lb asparagus
- ½ cup butter
- 1½ cups freshly grated Parmesan cheese
  salt to taste

Wine: a dry white (Colli di Parma Sauvignon)

Trim the tough parts off the asparagus stalks and cut them all to the same length. • Starting halfway up the green stalks, use a sharp knife to scrape off the thin outer skin from the lower half of each stalk. • Place the asparagus upright, tips uppermost, in an asparagus steamer or a deep, narrow saucepan. Pour in sufficient boiling water to come two-thirds of the way up the stalks, leaving the very tender tips out of the water so that they steam cook. Cook for 10–15 minutes (depending on the thickness of the stalks), until tender. • Drain well and arrange in layers in an ovenproof dish greased with butter. Sprinkle flakes of butter

Baked fennel with Parmesan cheese

and some of the Parmesan on each layer, including the top one. Season lightly with salt. • Cook in a preheated oven at 400°F for 10 minutes, or until the cheese has melted. • Serve hot.

Serves: 4 · Prep: 20 min. · Cooking: 30 min. · Level: 1

ASPARAGI CON FONTINA
Asparagus with Fontina cheese

3¹/₂ lb asparagus
¹/₄ cup butter
   salt and freshly ground white pepper to taste
4 oz Fontina cheese, very thinly sliced

Wine: a dry, fruity white (Roero Arneis)

Trim the tough parts off the asparagus stalks, leaving only the tender top part. • Steam the stalks for about 8 minutes. They should be tender but still firm. • Melt the butter in a large skillet. Add the asparagus with tips all facing the same way. • Season lightly with salt and pepper. Cook for 6–7 minutes, shaking the pan gently to turn the asparagus and cook evenly. • Lay the Fontina over the asparagus. Cover the skillet and cook for 2–3 minutes more, or until the cheese has melted. • Serve hot.

Serves: 4 · Prep: 5 min. · Cooking: 20 min. · Level: 1

ASPARAGI AL BRANDY
Asparagus in brandy and cream sauce

2¹/₂ lb fresh asparagus
   salt and freshly ground white pepper to taste
¹/₄ cup butter
¹/₃ cup brandy
2¹/₃ cups fresh cream
2 tablespoons bread crumbs

Wine: a dry white (Corvo Bianco)

Choose a pan large enough to lay the asparagus flat, fill with cold water, and bring to a boil. Add salt and cook the asparagus for 10–15 minutes (depending on the thickness of the stalks). • Drain and cut off the tough white part at the bottoms of the stalks. • Melt the butter in a large skillet and add the asparagus. Season with salt and pepper and cook for 3–4 minutes over medium heat. • Pour in the brandy and cook until it evaporates. Keep the asparagus moving by gently shaking the skillet. • Meanwhile, put the cream and bread crumbs in a saucepan, mix well, and cook over medium heat for 10–15 minutes, or

Asparagus Milan-style

until the sauce is thick and creamy. • Place the asparagus stalks on a heated serving dish and pour the sauce over the top.

Serves: 4 · Prep: 15 min. · Cooking: 25 min. · Level: 1

ASPARAGI ALLO ZABAIONE
Asparagus in sabayon sauce

3 lb fresh asparagus
4 egg yolks
¹/₂ cup dry white wine
2 tablespoons butter, at room temperature
   pinch of salt

Wine: a light, dry white (Langhe Arneis)

Trim the tough parts off the asparagus stalks and rinse under cold running water. • Steam the asparagus for 10–15 minutes (depending on the thickness of the stalks). The stalks should be tender but still firm. • While the asparagus is cooking, use the egg yolks, wine, butter, and salt to make the Sabayon sauce, following the method given on page 311 for Zabaglione. • Pour the sauce over the asparagus tips and serve hot.

Serves: 4 · Prep: 15 min. · Cooking: 25 min. · Level: 1

ASPARAGI ALLA MILANESE
Asparagus Milan-style

2¹/₂ lb fresh asparagus
¹/₄ cup butter
¹/₂ cup freshly grated Parmesan cheese
   salt to taste

Wine: a light, dry white (Lugana)

Trim the tough parts off the asparagus stalks and cut them all to the same length. • Starting halfway up the green stalks, use a sharp knife to scrape off the thin outer skin from the lower half of each stalk. • Place the asparagus upright, tips uppermost, in an asparagus steamer or a

deep, narrow saucepan. Pour in sufficient boiling water to come two-thirds of the way up the stalks, leaving the very tender tips out of the water so that they steam cook. Cook for 10–15 minutes (depending on the thickness of the stalks), until tender. • Drain well and place on a heated serving dish. Sprinkle with the Parmesan. • Heat the butter in a heavy-bottomed pan until pale golden brown. Pour over the asparagus and serve.

Serves: 4 · Prep: 15 min. · Cooking: 25 min. · Level: 1

PORRI GRATINATI AL PROSCIUTTO
Baked leeks with béchamel and ham

2 lb fresh leeks
   salt and freshly ground black pepper to taste
1 quantity Béchamel sauce (see recipe, page 16)
1 tablespoon butter
1 egg yolk
4 oz ham, finely chopped
¹/₂ cup freshly grated Gruyère cheese

Wine: a dry white (Tocai di Lison)

Clean the leeks and chop off the green tops. Cook in salted, boiling water for about 10 minutes, or until tender but still firm. • Prepare the béchamel. • Sauté the leeks for 5 minutes in a large skillet with the butter, salt, and pepper. Place in an ovenproof dish. • Combine the egg yolk and three-quarters of the ham with the béchamel, mix well, and pour over the leeks. Sprinkle with the Gruyère and remaining ham. • Bake in a preheated oven at 350°F for 20 minutes. • Serve hot.

Serves: 4 · Prep: 15 min. · Cooking: 45 min. · Level: 1

Stuffed eggplants

medium heat. • Add the basil, uncover, and cook for 5 more minutes. • Serve hot.

Serves: 4 · Prep: 15 min. + 1 hr to drain eggplants · Cooking: 30 min. · Level: 1

MELANZANE IN OLIO PICCANTE
Spicy grilled eggplants

3	large round eggplants, trimmed
2	tablespoons coarse sea salt
1–2	finely chopped hot chili peppers
	salt and freshly ground black pepper to taste
1	cup extra-virgin olive oil
10	fresh basil leaves, torn

Wine: a dry red (Chianti Nipozzano)

Slice the eggplants in ¹/₂-inch-thick slices, sprinkle with sea salt, and leave to drain as explained in the first recipe on this page. • Heat a grill pan to very hot and place the slices on it. Press them down with a fork so the eggplant adheres to the grill pan. Turn the slices often. • As soon as the pulp is soft, remove from the grill pan and arrange on a serving dish. If you do not have a grill pan, cook the eggplants under a broiler. • Combine the chilies, salt, and pepper in the oil and beat well with a fork. Cover and set aside. • When the eggplants are all cooked, pour the spicy oil over the top and sprinkle with the basil. • Serve at room temperature.

Serves: 4 · Prep: 15 min. + 1 hr to drain eggplants · Cooking: 20 min. · Level: 1

MELANZANE RIPIENE
Stuffed eggplants

4	large round eggplants
2	tablespoons coarse sea salt
4	cloves garlic, finely chopped
¹/₂	cup diced pancetta
14	oz sharp Provolone or Pecorino romano cheese, cut in small cubes
¹/₃	cup extra-virgin olive oil
1	lb peeled and chopped fresh tomatoes
¹/₃	cup freshly grated Parmesan cheese
	freshly ground black pepper to taste

Wine: a dry white (Cerveteri Bianco)

Cut the eggplants in half lengthwise and use a sharp knife to open crosswise slits in the pulp. Sprinkle with sea salt and leave to drain as explained in the first recipe on this page. • Combine the garlic, pancetta, and Provolone or Pecorino cheese in a bowl. • Grease an ovenproof dish with half the oil and place the eggplants in it. Cover with the filling, pushing it into the slits opened

MELANZANE MARINATE
Marinated eggplants

☞ Eggplants have a bitter flavor which can be eliminated by sprinkling with coarse sea salt. Place the sliced or cubed eggplant on a large flat plate. Sprinkle with the salt and cover with another plate. Place a heavy weight on top and leave to drain for 1 hour. Pour off the bitter liquid, rinse the eggplants under cold running water, and dry well with paper towels.

4	large round eggplants
2	tablespoons coarse sea salt
2	cups oil, for frying
4	cloves garlic, thinly sliced
10	fresh sage leaves
	salt to taste
	good-quality wine vinegar (see method for quantity)

Wine: a light, dry red (Lambrusco Grasparossa)

Clean, wash, and dry the eggplants. Slice thinly lengthwise, sprinkle with sea salt, and leave to drain as explained above. • Heat the oil in a large skillet to very hot and fry the eggplant until golden brown on both sides. Drain on paper towels. • Arrange in layers in a deep, serving dish, placing slices of garlic and sage leaves between the layers. • Pour in sufficient wine vinegar to completely cover. Marinate for 24 hours before serving.

Serves: 4–6 · Prep: 20 min. + 1 hr to drain eggplants + 24 hrs to marinate · Cooking: 30 min. · Level: 2

MELANZANE AL POMODORO
Eggplant with tomato and garlic

6	long eggplants
2	tablespoons coarse sea salt
4	cloves garlic, finely chopped
¹/₄	cup extra-virgin olive oil
	salt and freshly ground black pepper to taste
8	medium tomatoes, peeled and diced
8	leaves fresh basil, torn

Wine: a dry red (Valpolicella)

Clean, wash, and dry the eggplants. Cut them into bite-sized chunks, sprinkle with sea salt, and leave to drain as explained in the first recipe on this page. • Sauté the garlic with the oil in a large skillet until it turns gold. • Add the eggplant, season with salt and pepper, stir well and cover. Cook over medium-low heat for 10 minutes. • Add the tomatoes, mix well, and cook for 15 more minutes over

earlier. Cover with the tomato, drizzle with the remaining oil, and sprinkle with the Parmesan. Season with a generous grinding of pepper. • Bake in a preheated oven at 350°F for about 30 minutes. • Serve hot or at room temperature.

Serves: 4 · Prep: 20 min. + 1 hr to drain eggplants · Cooking: 30 min. · Level: 1

MELANZANE CON PECORINO
Fried eggplant with Pecorino cheese

- 4 medium eggplants
- 2 tablespoons coarse sea salt
- 2 eggs
  freshly ground black pepper
- 4 oz hard Pecorino cheese, cut into short thin strips
- 8 anchovy fillets, coarsely chopped
- 20 fresh basil leaves, torn
- 3/4 cup bread crumbs
- 2 cups oil, for frying

Wine: a dry red (Rosso di Donnafugata)

Cut the eggplants across their width in 1/4-inch thick slices, sprinkle with sea salt, and leave to drain as explained in the recipe for Marinated eggplants (page 278). • Beat the eggs lightly with pepper in a shallow bowl. • Select pairs of eggplant slices and fill with a few pieces of cheese, 2–3 anchovy pieces, and some basil. • Press the slices together, dip in the egg, and coat with bread crumbs. • Heat the oil in a large skillet until very hot. Fry the sandwiches until golden on both sides. • Serve hot.

Serves: 4 · Prep: 20 min + 1 hr to drain eggplants · Cooking: 30 min. · Level: 2

PARMIGIANA DI MELANZANE
Baked eggplant with Parmesan cheese

☞ This classic recipe, originally from Sicily, can be served as a main course.

- 2 quantities Simple tomato sauce (see recipe, page 18)
- 3 large round eggplants
- 1 cup all-purpose flour to dredge
- 3 cups oil, for frying
- 4 eggs beaten to a foam, with a pinch of salt
- 12 oz Mozzarella cheese
- 2 1/2 cups freshly grated Parmesan cheese
- 2 tablespoons butter

Wine: a dry red (Solopaca Rosso)

Prepare the tomato sauce. • Peel the eggplants, cut in 1/4-inch-thick slices, sprinkle with sea salt, and leave to drain as explained in the recipe for Marinated eggplants (page 278). • Dredge with flour, shaking to eliminate any excess. • Heat the

Baked eggplant with Parmesan cheese

oil in a large skillet, dip the eggplant slices in the egg mixture and fry until golden brown. • Drain on paper towels. • Place a layer of tomato sauce in an ovenproof dish and cover with a layer of eggplants and a layer of Mozzarella and Parmesan. Repeat until all the ingredients are in the dish. Finish with a layer of tomato sauce and Parmesan. • Dot with butter and bake in a preheated oven at 350°F for 35 minutes. • Serve hot.

Serves: 6 · Prep: 30 min. + 1 hr to drain eggplants · Cooking: 50 min. · Level: 1

CANNOLI DI MELANZANE AL FORNO
Baked stuffed eggplant rolls

- 4 medium eggplants
- 2 tablespoons coarse sea salt
- 5 oz chicken breast, chopped
- 3 oz Mortadella, chopped
- 5 oz prosciutto, chopped
- 1 cup freshly grated Parmesan cheese
- 1 egg + 1 yolk, beaten
- 3 cloves garlic, finely chopped
  salt and freshly ground black pepper to taste
- 2 tablespoons finely chopped parsley

- 2 cups oil, for frying
- 1 medium onion, finely chopped
- 1/4 cup extra-virgin olive oil
- 1 (15 oz) can tomatoes

Wine: a dry red (Chianti Classico)

Cut the eggplants in 1/4-inch-thick slices, sprinkle with sea salt, and leave to drain as explained in the recipe for Marinated eggplants (page 278). • Combine the chicken, Mortadella, prosciutto, Parmesan, eggs, garlic, pepper, and parsley in a bowl and mix well. • Heat the oil in a large skillet until very hot and fry the eggplant slices a few at a time until golden brown. Drain on paper towels. • Carefully fill the slices with the stuffing and roll them up. • Sauté the onion in the olive oil in a large ovenproof skillet for 5 minutes. Add the tomatoes, season with salt and pepper, and cook for 5 more minutes. Add the eggplant rolls, with the seam facing down, and bake in a preheated oven at 350°F for 30 minutes. Baste the eggplant with the sauce during cooking. • Serve hot.

Serves: 4 · Prep: 30 min. + 1 hr to drain eggplants · Cooking: 45 min. · Level: 2

TESTE DI FUNGHI RIPIENE
Stuffed mushrooms

- 12 fresh medium Caesar's mushrooms
- 1 small clove garlic, finely chopped
- 2 thick slices white bread, crusts removed, soaked in warm milk and squeezed dry
  salt and freshly ground black pepper to taste
- 1 whole egg + 1 yolk
- 1½ cups freshly grated Parmesan cheese
- ½ teaspoon dried oregano
- 1 tablespoon each finely chopped parsley and marjoram
- ¼ cup extra-virgin olive oil

Wine: a dry red (Grignolino d'Asti)

Detach the stems from the mushrooms. Rinse the caps and stems under cold running water and dry with paper towels. Peel the caps and leave them whole. • Chop the stems finely. Place in a bowl with the garlic, bread, salt, and pepper and mix well. Add the eggs, Parmesan, oregano, parsley, marjoram, and 1 tablespoon of oil. Mix well. • Use this mixture to stuff the mushrooms, pressing it in carefully with your fingertips. • Oil an ovenproof dish just large enough to hold the mushrooms snugly. Fill with the mushrooms and drizzle with the remaining oil. Bake in a preheated oven at 350°F for 30 minutes. • Serve hot or at room temperature.

Serves: 4 · Prep: 20 min. · Cooking: 30 min. · Level: 2

FUNGHI ALLA GRIGLIA
Grilled wild mushrooms on toast

- 1½ lb whole mushrooms (porcini, shiitake, chanterelle, hedgehog, cremini, or portobello)
- 4 cloves garlic, sliced
- ¼ cup fresh thyme
- ¼ cup extra-virgin olive oil
  salt and freshly ground black pepper to taste
- ½ cup softened butter
- 1 clove garlic, finely chopped
- 1 tablespoon finely chopped scallions
- 2 tablespoons finely chopped parsley
- 4 slices firm-textured bread, toasted

Wine: a dry red (Chianti Classico Aziano)

Trim the mushrooms. Rinse carefully under cold running water and dry with paper towels. • Slice the stems in half lengthwise. Make small slits with a sharp knife in the caps and stems and fill with garlic and thyme. • Mix the oil, salt, and pepper in a small bowl and drizzle over the mushrooms. • Place the butter, garlic, scallions, parsley, salt, and pepper in a

small bowl and mix until smooth. Set aside. • Heat a grill pan to very hot and place the mushrooms in it, beginning with the stems. • Cook for 5–7 minutes, turning often so they don't stick. • Spread the toast with the herb butter, and cover with the mushrooms. • Serve hot.

Serves: 4 · Prep: 10 min. · Cooking: 15 min. · Level: 1

FUNGHI TRIFOLATI
Stewed mushrooms

- 2 lb fresh wild or cultivated mushrooms
- 2 large cloves garlic, finely chopped
- ¼ cup extra-virgin olive oil
  salt and freshly ground black pepper to taste
- 1 tablespoon finely chopped fresh thyme

Wine: a light, dry red (Cabernet Franc del Trentino)

Trim the tough parts off the stems of the mushrooms. Rinse carefully under cold running water. Dry with paper towels. • Cut the stems and caps in thick slices. • Sauté the garlic in a large skillet until pale gold. Add the stems and sauté for 7–8 minutes. • Add the mushroom caps, salt, and pepper and stir carefully. Stir in the thyme and finish cooking over low heat. • Serve hot.

Serves: 4 · Prep: 15 min. · Cooking: 15 min. · Level: 1

FUNGHI MISTI IN FRICASSEA
Braised mushrooms with egg sauce

- ¼ cup extra-virgin olive oil
- 1 medium onion, finely chopped
- 1¾ lb mixed fresh or frozen mushrooms (porcini, white, chanterelle, or Caesar's), washed and trimmed
  salt and freshly ground black pepper to taste
- 3 egg yolks
  juice of 1 lemon
- 2 tablespoons finely chopped parsley

Wine: a young, dry red (Novello Falò)

Heat the oil in a large skillet and sauté the onion until soft. • Cut the larger mushrooms in thick slices and leave the smaller ones whole. • Add the mushrooms to the skillet. Season with salt and pepper, cover, and cook for 15–20 minutes over medium-low heat. • While the mushrooms are cooking, beat the egg yolks in a bowl with the lemon juice and parsley. • Pour the egg sauce over the mushrooms and toss quickly so that the egg doesn't set but becomes a creamy sauce. • Serve hot.

Serves: 4 · Prep: 15 min. · Cooking: 20 min. · Level: 1

This recipe is part of Sicilian culinary history and is still very popular. The same subtle blend of sweet and sour flavors is present in many of the island's dishes.

CAPONATA
Sweet and sour Sicilian vegetables

- 2 lb eggplants, cut into ½-inch cubes
- 2 tablespoons coarse sea salt
- ⅔ cup extra-virgin olive oil
- 4 tender stalks celery, cut into ¾-inch lengths
- 1 large onion, sliced
- 1 lb sieved tomatoes
- 12 fresh basil leaves, torn
- 1 small, firm pear, peeled, cored, and diced
- 1½ tablespoons pickled capers, drained
- 20 green or black olives, pitted and chopped
- 3 tablespoons pine nuts
- 2 tablespoons sugar
- ½ cup white wine vinegar
- 3 tablespoons coarsely chopped roasted almonds

Wine: a dry rosé (Sciacca)

Sprinkle the eggplants with the coarse salt and leave to drain as explained on page 278. • Heat ½ cup of oil in a skillet and sauté the eggplant over medium heat for 10 minutes. Set aside. • Blanch the celery in salted, boiling water for 5 minutes. Drain and set aside. • Sauté the onion in the remaining oil until pale golden brown and add the tomato and half the basil. Cook for 10 minutes and then add the celery, pear, capers, olives, pine nuts, sugar, and vinegar. • Cook for 20 minutes, stirring now and then. • Add the eggplant and the rest of the basil. Cook, stirring occasionally, for another 10 minutes. • Remove from heat, and when the mixture is just warm, transfer to a serving dish. The eggplant should have absorbed most of the moisture. • Chill in the refrigerator for 12 hours or overnight. • Serve at room temperature, adding a few fresh basil leaves and sprinkling with the almonds. • Caponata keeps well for 3–4 days if refrigerated in a tightly closed container.

Serves: 6–8 · Prep: 1 hr + 12 hrs to stand · Cooking: 50 min. · Level: 1

Sweet and sour Sicilian vegetables

FUNGHI CON PINOLI
Mushrooms with pine nuts

- 2 large potatoes, diced
- ¼ cup extra-virgin olive oil
- 1½ lb (fresh or frozen) white mushrooms, coarsely chopped
- 2 cloves garlic, finely chopped
  salt and freshly ground black pepper to taste
- ⅔ cup pine nuts
- ½ cup almond shavings
- 1 tablespoon coarsely chopped mint

Wine: a dry red (Freisa d'Asti)

Fry the potatoes with the oil and garlic in a large skillet. • Add the mushrooms and season with salt and pepper. Cover and cook for 5 minutes. • Uncover and let some of the moisture evaporate. Stir in the pine nuts and almonds and cook for 10 more minutes. • Sprinkle with the mint just before removing from heat. • Serve hot.

Serves: 4 · Prep: 10 min. · Cooking: 25 min. · Level: 1

ZUCCHINE TRIFOLATE
Stewed zucchini

- ¼ cup extra-virgin olive oil
- 2 cloves garlic, finely chopped
- 1 small onion, finely chopped
- 2 tablespoons butter
- 1¾ lb small zucchini, cut into wheels
- 10 cherry tomatoes, cut in half
  salt and freshly ground black pepper to taste
- 2 tablespoons finely chopped parsley

Wine: a light, dry red (Grignolino d'Asti)

Heat the oil in a large skillet and sauté the garlic and onion over medium heat until soft. • Add the butter, zucchini, and tomatoes, and cook over high heat for 5 minutes. • Reduce

Mushrooms with pine nuts

heat to medium-low, cover, and simmer for 5 minutes. • Season with salt and pepper, uncover, and complete cooking. The zucchini should be firm, not mushy. • Remove from heat, add the parsley, toss well, and transfer to a heated serving dish.

Serves: 4 · Prep: 10 min. · Cooking: 15 min. · Level: 1

ZUCCHINE GRIGLIATE ALLE ERBE
Grilled zucchini with garlic and herbs

- 8 large zucchini
- ½ cup extra-virgin olive oil
  salt to taste
- 1 tablespoon finely chopped parsley
- 1 tablespoon finely chopped fresh marjoram
- 2 cloves garlic, finely chopped
  salt and freshly ground black pepper to taste

Wine: a dry rosé (Lagrein Rosato)

Trim the zucchini and cut lengthwise into ¼-inch-thick slices. • Place in a hot grill pan (or under a broiler) and cook the slices for 3–4 minutes on each side. Remove and set aside to cool. • Put the oil in a bowl with the salt, parsley, and marjoram and beat with a fork until well mixed. • Place the zucchini in a small, fairly deep-sided serving dish. Sprinkle with the garlic and season with salt and pepper. • Pour the oil mixture over the zucchini and chill in the refrigerator for at least 2 hours before serving.

Serves: 4 · Prep: 20 min. + 2 hrs to chill · Cooking: 10 min. · Level: 1

CANNOLI DI ZUCCHINE RIPIENE
Grilled zucchini with fresh cheese

- 8 large zucchini
- 14 oz soft, fresh cheese (Caprino, Robiola)
- 1 cup canned tuna, crumbled
  salt and freshly ground black pepper to taste
- 1 tablespoon finely chopped thyme or marjoram
- 1 tablespoons pickled capers, drained
- 10 basil leaves, torn
- 3 tablespoons extra-virgin olive oil

Wine: a dry white (Vespaiolo)

Trim the zucchini and slice them lengthwise in ⅛-inch slices. • Place in a hot grill pan (or under a broiler) and cook for about 4 minutes on each side. Transfer to a plate. • Put the Caprino in a bowl and mash with a fork. Add the tuna and mix well. Season with salt and pepper, add the thyme or marjoram, and mix well. • Place 2 teaspoons of filling on each zucchini slice, add some basil and roll up, fastening with a wooden toothpick. • Place the rolls on a serving dish. Sprinkle with capers and basil leaves, and drizzle with the oil. • Serve at room temperature.

Serves: 4 · Prep: 15 min. · Cooking: 10 min. · Level : 2

ZUCCHINE RIPIENE
Stuffed zucchini

- 8 long zucchini
- 2 tablespoons finely chopped parsley
- 1 clove garlic, finely chopped
- 1 cup fine dry bread crumbs
- 1 cup freshly grated Parmesan cheese
- 1 egg
- 4 oz Mortadella, diced
- 2 tablespoons milk
- 1 large scallion, thinly sliced
- ¼ cup butter
- 2 tablespoons sieved tomatoes
  salt and freshly ground black pepper to taste

Wine: a light, dry white (Colli Bolognesi Bianco Asciutto)

Wash the zucchini. Trim the ends and cut in half lengthwise. • Use a teaspoon to scoop out the center of the zucchini. Chop the flesh finely, then mix it with the parsley, garlic, bread crumbs, Parmesan, egg, Mortadella, and milk in a bowl. • Fill the hollowed-out zucchini with this mixture. • Sauté the scallion in the butter in a large skillet until tender. Add the sieved

tomato, and season with salt and pepper. •
Arrange the zucchini in a single layer in the
skillet with the scallion and tomato
mixture. Pour in sufficient water
to come halfway up the
sides. • Cook over
medium heat for
20 minutes.

*Serves: 4 · Prep: 20 min. ·
Cooking: 30 min. · Level: 1*

Stuffed zucchini

ZUCCHINE E FAGIOLINI AL FORNO
Baked zucchini and green bean pie

10	oz zucchini
8	oz green beans
2/3	cup butter
4	eggs
2/3	cup sugar
2 1/2	cups all-purpose flour
2/3	cup pine nuts
2	teaspoons baking powder
	butter to grease the cake pan

Wine: a dry red (Sangiovese di Romagna)

Cook the zucchini and beans in a pot of
salted, boiling water for 10 minutes. Drain
and cut the zucchini into wheels and the
beans into pieces. Dry on a cotton dishcloth.
• Melt the butter and place in a bowl with
two whole eggs, two yolks, and the sugar.
Beat vigorously for 2 minutes with a whisk
or fork. Stir in the flour, zucchini, beans,
pine nuts, and baking powder. • Beat the
remaining egg whites to stiff peaks and
carefully fold into the mixture. • Grease a 10
x 6 inch cake pan with butter and pour in
the mixture. • Bake in a preheated oven at
350°F for 1 hour. • Remove from the pan
when cool and cut into 1/2-inch thick slices.
• Serve hot or at room temperature.

Serves: 6 · Prep: 30 min. · Cooking: 1 1/4 hrs · Level: 2

ZUCCHINE MARINATE
Marinated zucchini

8	large zucchini
1/4	cup extra-virgin olive oil
1	cup white wine vinegar
	salt and freshly ground black pepper to taste
1	red chili pepper

Wine: a light, dry white (Est! Est!! Est!!!))

Wash the zucchini under cold running
water and trim the ends. Dry well with
paper towels. Cut into wheels. • Heat the

oil in a large skillet and sauté the zucchini
for 7–8 minutes. Transfer to a deep-sided
dish. • Heat the vinegar with the salt and
chili pepper until it begins to boil. Pour
over the zucchini. • Season with a
generous grinding of black pepper and
cover. Chill in the refrigerator for 24
hours. • Serve at room temperature.

*Serves: 6 · Prep: 5 min. + 24 hrs to marinate ·
Cooking: 25 min. · Level: 1*

SFORMATO DI CAROTE E CIPOLLE
Carrot and onion mold

1 1/4	lb carrots, cut in wheels
1/4	cup extra-virgin olive oil
4	medium onions, grated
1	quantity Béchamel sauce (see recipe, page 16)
1/2	cup freshly grated Parmesan cheese
2	eggs, beaten to a foam
2	tablespoons fresh mint, finely chopped
	salt and freshly ground black pepper to taste
	butter and bread crumbs for the mold

Wine: a dry white (Locorotondo)

Sauté 4 oz of the carrots in a skillet with 1
tablespoon of oil over medium heat for 5
minutes. Set aside. • Sauté the onions in the
rest of the oil for 5 minutes. • Add the
remaining carrots, partially cover, and cook
for 20 minutes, or until the carrots are
tender. Chop in a food processor until
smooth. • Prepare the béchamel sauce. Let
cool for 5–10 minutes. • Combine the
béchamel with the Parmesan, eggs, mint,
and carrot and onion mixture. Season with
salt and pepper and mix well. • Grease a
12-inch ring mold with the butter and
sprinkle with bread crumbs. • Line the

mold with the carrot wheels by sticking
them one by one to the butter and bread
crumbs until the entire mold is covered. •
Pour the carrot mixture carefully into the
mold. • Place the mold in a larger pan of
water and cook in a preheated oven at
400°F for 50 minutes. • Let stand for 10
minutes, then invert on a serving dish. •
Serve at room temperature.

Serves: 6 · Prep: 40 min. · Cooking: 1 1/2 hrs · Level: 2

FIORI DI ZUCCA FRITTI
Fried zucchini flowers

14	oz very fresh zucchini flowers
1	cup all-purpose flour
1/2	teaspoon salt
1	tablespoon extra-virgin olive oil
1	tablespoon cold water
1	cup oil, for frying
1–2	tablespoons cold water

Wine: a dry white (Elba Bianco)

Remove the pistil (the bright yellow
center) and calyx (the green leaflets at the
base) from each flower, rinse carefully and
dry gently with paper towels. • Sift the flour
into a mixing bowl, make a well in the
center and add the salt, olive oil, and water.
• Gradually mix into the flour, adding
enough extra water to make a batter of
thick pouring consistency that will cling to
the flowers. • Heat the oil in a large skillet
until very hot. • Dip 4–6 flowers in the
batter and fry until golden brown on both
sides. Drain on paper towels. Fry all the
flowers in the same way. • Serve hot.

Serves: 4 · Prep: 10 min. · Cooking: 25 min. · Level: 2

New potatoes with zucchini and flowers

remaining burnt skin and dry with paper towels. • Cut the bell peppers into strips. • Place in a serving dish and sprinkle with the garlic, capers, basil, mint, parsley, salt, pepper, and oil. • Mix carefully and set aside for at least 1 hour before serving. • Serve at room temperature.

Serves: 4 · Prep: 20 min. + 1 hr to rest · Cooking: 20 min. · Level: 1

PEPERONATA
Mixed bell peppers

☞ Variations on this classic dish are served all over Italy. For a stronger, more distinctive flavor, add 1 medium eggplant, diced but not peeled, 6 oz of pitted black olives, and 1 teaspoon of dried oregano.

- 6 large bell peppers, mixed colors, cleaned and cut into 1/2 inch strips
- 3 large onions, thinly sliced
- 1 lb peeled and chopped fresh or canned tomatoes
- 1/4 cup extra-virgin olive oil
- 3 cloves garlic, finely chopped
  salt and freshly ground black pepper to taste
- 8 leaves fresh basil, torn

Wine: a light, dry red (Merlot di Aquileia)

Place the bell peppers, onions, and tomatoes in a large, heavy-bottomed saucepan. Add the oil and garlic, and season with salt and pepper. Cover and cook over medium heat for about 20 minutes. • Turn the heat up to high and uncover to let some of the liquid evaporate. Cook until the bell peppers are tender. • Garnish with the basil and serve hot or at room temperature.

Serves 6 · Prep: 10 min. · Cooking: 35 min. · Level: 1

PEPERONI IN PADELLA
Bell peppers with capers and vinegar

- 1/4 cup extra-virgin olive oil
- 4 cloves garlic, finely chopped
- 6 large bell peppers, mixed colors, cleaned and cut into 1/2 inch strips
  salt and freshly ground black pepper to taste
- 1/3 cup vinegar
- 2 tablespoons capers

Wine: a dry white (Greco di Tufo)

Heat the oil in a large skillet and sauté the garlic until it begins to color. Add the bell peppers and press them down with the lid. Season with salt and pepper. • Cook over medium heat for about 15 minutes, or until the bell peppers soften. Stir from time to time with a wooden

PATATE, ZUCCHINE E FIORI
New potatoes with zucchini and flowers

- 1/4 cup extra-virgin olive oil
- 1 clove garlic, finely chopped
- 16 small new potatoes, scrubbed and cut in half
- 8 medium zucchini, cut in wheels and short lengths
  salt and freshly ground black pepper to taste
- 1 tablespoon each finely chopped parsley and thyme
- 16 large zucchini flowers

Wine: a dry rosé (Ravello)

Heat the oil in a large skillet and sauté the garlic until light gold. • Add the potatoes, cover, and cook for 15 minutes, stirring frequently. • Add the zucchini and season with salt, pepper, parsley, and thyme. Cook, partially covered, for 10 minutes more. If the zucchini have produced a lot of water, uncover and cook until it evaporates. • Trim the stems of the zucchini flowers just below the bloom, wash carefully, and dry with paper towels. • Add 12 flowers to the zucchini and potatoes and cook for 5 minutes more. • Place in a heated serving dish, garnish with the remaining zucchini flowers, and serve hot.

Serves: 4 · Prep: 15 min. · Cooking: 30 min. · Level: 1

PEPERONI GRIGLIATI ALLE ERBE
Broiled bell peppers with garlic and herbs

- 6 large bell peppers, mixed colors
- 6 cloves garlic, thinly sliced
- 1/4 cup pickled capers, drained
- 20 fresh basil leaves, torn
- 15 mint leaves, whole
- 2 tablespoons finely chopped parsley
  salt and freshly ground black pepper to taste
- 3/4 cup extra-virgin olive oil

Wine: a dry rosé (Rosato di Castel del Monte)

Place the bell peppers whole under the broiler at fairly high heat, giving them quarter turns until their skins scorch and blacken. This will take about 20 minutes. When the peppers are black all over, wrap them in foil (not too tightly) and set aside for 10 minutes. When unwrapped, the skins will peel away easily. • Cut the bell peppers in half lengthwise and discard the stalks, seeds, and pulpy inner core. Rinse under cold running water to get rid of any

fork. • When the bell peppers are tender, turn the heat up to high and pour the vinegar and capers over the top. Mix rapidly, and cook for 2–3 minutes, or until the vinegar evaporates. • Serve hot or at room temperature.

Serves: 4 · Prep: 15 min. · Cooking: 25 min. · Level: 1

POMODORI ALLA GRIGLIA
Broiled tomatoes with Parmesan

8	large ripe tomatoes
	salt to taste
1	teaspoon dried oregano
1/2	cup freshly grated Parmesan
1/2	cup fine dry bread crumbs
1/4	cup extra-virgin olive oil
16	fresh basil leaves, torn

Wine: a dry red (Refosco)

Cut the tomatoes in half and squeeze out as many seeds as possible. Sprinkle lightly with salt and stand the halves upside down in a colander for 20 minutes. • Sprinkle with the oregano. • Heat the broiler to hot and place the tomatoes under it, cut sides down. Cook for about 5 minutes, then turn the tomatoes. Sprinkle with the bread crumbs and Parmesan and drizzle with the oil. Broil for 10 more minutes. • Place a basil leaf on each tomato and serve.

Serves: 4 · Prep: 30 min. · Cooking: 15 min. · Level: 1

PEPERONI AL FORNO
Baked bell peppers

☞ This brightly colored dish is delicious served hot but even better when left to stand at room temperature for 2–3 hours before serving.

6	large bell peppers, mixed colors, cleaned and cut into 1/2-inch strips
20	black olives, pitted and quartered
6	anchovy fillets, coarsely chopped
1/4	cup pine nuts
2	tablespoons capers
12	fresh basil leaves, torn
1/3	cup extra-virgin olive oil
	salt to taste
1/2	cup fine dry bread crumbs

Wine: a light, dry red (Merlot)

Rinse the bell peppers and dry with paper towels. Place in a large mixing bowl and add the olives, anchovies, pine nuts, capers, and basil. • Add 1/4 cup of oil and the salt and toss (as if you were tossing a

Baked stuffed bell peppers

salad). • Grease a large ovenproof dish with the remaining oil and add the bell pepper mixture, pressing down gently. • Sprinkle with the bread crumbs and bake in a preheated oven at 350°F for 35 minutes, or until the peppers are tender.

Serves: 4 · Prep: 15 min. · Cooking: 35 min. · Level: 1

PEPERONI RIPIENI AL FORNO
Baked stuffed bell peppers

4	large plump bell peppers, mixed red and yellow
8	slices day-old bread
	salt and freshly ground black pepper to taste
1/4	cup pickled capers, drained
14	oz black olives, coarsely chopped
4	cloves garlic, finely chopped
1/4	cup finely chopped parsley
10	fresh basil leaves, torn
8	anchovy fillets, crumbled
12	oz peeled and chopped fresh or canned tomatoes
1 1/2	cups freshly grated Parmesan cheese
1	cup freshly grated Pecorino cheese
1/2	cup extra-virgin olive oil
1	tablespoon white wine vinegar

Wine: a dry white (Fiano di Avellino)

Trim the stalks of the bell peppers to about 1 inch. Cut their tops off about 1/2 inch from the top and set aside. Remove the seeds and membranes. • Soak the bread in cold water for 10 minutes. Squeeze out excess moisture, crumble, and place in a bowl. Season with salt and pepper. • Add the capers, olives, garlic, parsley, basil, anchovies, tomatoes, Parmesan, and Pecorino. Add the vinegar and half the oil and mix thoroughly. • Stuff the bell peppers with the filling, replace the tops, and stand them upright in an oiled roasting pan that is at least as tall as they are. Add the remaining oil and 1/2 cup of water. • Cook in a preheated oven at 350°F, basting often with liquid from the bottom of the pan. • After about 35 minutes, pierce a bell pepper with the point of a sharp knife; when done, the bell peppers will be soft. • Spoon the dark stock over the bell peppers and serve hot.

Serves: 4 · Prep: 20 min. · Cooking: 35 min. · Level: 1

Baked pumpkin and potato purée

POMODORI RIPIENI SEMPLICI
Classic baked tomatoes

- 6 medium tomatoes
- 4 cloves garlic, finely chopped
- 1 cup finely chopped parsley
- 1 cup dry bread crumbs
- 1 cup freshly grated Parmesan cheese
- 1/2 cup extra-virgin olive oil
  salt and freshly ground black pepper to taste

Wine: a light, dry red (Bardolino)

Cut the tomatoes in half horizontally and squeeze out as many seeds as possible. Stand the halves upside down in a colander for 20 minutes. • Mix the garlic and parsley in a bowl, add the bread crumbs and Parmesan, and, using a fork, work the oil in little by little. Season with salt and pepper. • Using a teaspoon, push the stuffing into the tomatoes. Press it down with your fingers. • Place the tomatoes in a greased ovenproof dish and bake in a preheated oven at 350°F for 35 minutes. • Serve hot or at room temperature.

Serves: 4 · Prep: 30 min. · Cooking: 35 min. · Level: 1

POMODORI GRATINATI
Stuffed baked tomatoes

- 8 medium ripe tomatoes
  salt and freshly ground black pepper to taste
- 2 medium onions, finely chopped
- 2 cloves garlic, finely chopped
- 2 tablespoons extra-virgin olive oil
- 1/4 cup fine dry bread crumbs
- 12 black olives, pitted and chopped
- 1 tablespoon each pine nuts, raisins, and capers

Wine: a dry white (Corvo)

Rinse the tomatoes under cold running water and dry with paper towels. • Cut the tough pithy core from the top of each tomato. Use a teaspoon to scoop out the pulp and juice and place in a bowl. Sprinkle the whole tomatoes with salt and pepper. • Sauté the onion and garlic in the oil until soft, then add the tomato pulp and juice and cook for 5 minutes until it reduces a little. • Remove from heat and stir in the bread crumbs, olives, pine nuts, raisins, and capers. • Spoon the mixture into the tomatoes and place in an oiled ovenproof dish. • Bake in a preheated oven at 350°F for 30 minutes. • Serve hot or cold.

Serves: 4 · Prep: 10 min. · Cooking: 40 min. · Level: 1

POMODORI RIPIENI AL RISO
Baked tomatoes with rice

- 8 medium tomatoes
- 1 tablespoon very finely chopped onion
- 1/3 cup butter
- 1 cup short-grain white rice
- 1 cup Beef stock (see recipe, page 105)
- 1/2 cup freshly grated Parmesan cheese
  salt and freshly ground black pepper to taste
- 2 eggs
- 1 cup fine dry bread crumbs
- 2 tablespoons butter

Wine: a dry red (Grignolino d'Asti)

Rinse and dry the tomatoes and cut a slice 1/2 inch thick off the stalk end. Set these little "lids" aside. • Scoop out and discard the seeds and the central fleshy parts which divide the seed chambers. • Sauté the onion in 2 tablespoons of butter over low heat until the soft. • Add the rice and cook for 2–3 minutes, stirring continuously. • Pour in about half the stock and stir continuously over until the liquid has been absorbed. • Add 1/2 cup stock at intervals, stirring and cooking until the rice is tender but still fairly firm. This will take about 10–15 minutes. • Remove from heat and stir in the Parmesan. Season with salt and pepper. • Stuff the tomatoes with the rice and cover each one neatly with its lid. • Beat the eggs lightly in a bowl and carefully dip the stuffed tomatoes into the egg. Coat with the bread crumbs. • Use 1 tablespoon of butter to grease an ovenproof dish into which the tomatoes will fit snugly. Place them in a single layer, lid-side uppermost, and top each one with a little of the remaining butter. • Bake in a preheated oven at 400°F for 25–30 minutes. • Serve hot or at room temperature.

Serves: 4 · Prep: 30 min · Cooking: 1 br · Level: 1

FRIZON
Savory onions and tomatoes

- 1 cup extra-virgin olive oil
- 2 lb onions, peeled and sliced
- 1 red bell pepper and 1 yellow bell pepper, cleaned and cut into small pieces
- 1 1/4 lb ripe tomatoes, peeled and chopped
  salt and freshly ground black pepper to taste

Wine: a light, dry white (Colli Piacentini Trebbiano)

Heat the oil in a large, heavy-bottomed saucepan and sauté the onions until soft. • Add the bell peppers and cook for 10 minutes more. • Add the tomatoes and season with salt and pepper. Simmer over low heat for 30 minutes, stirring now and then. • Serve hot or at room temperature.

Serves: 6 · Prep: 15 min. · Cooking: 45 min. · Level: 1

PURÈ DI ZUCCA E PATATE AL FORNO
Baked pumpkin and potato purée

- 1 lb potatoes
- 1 lb pumpkin, peeled
- 1/4 cup butter
- 1/4 cup finely chopped parsley
- 4 eggs, separated
- 1 cup freshly grated Parmesan cheese
  salt and freshly ground black pepper to taste
- 8 oz Mozzarella cheese, thinly sliced
- 1/2 cup fine dry bread crumbs

Wine: a light, dry red (Bardolino)

Cook the potatoes in their skins in salted, boiling water for 25 minutes, or until tender. Drain well and slip off their skins. • Chop the pumpkin into 2-inch cubes and place in a lightly buttered baking dish. Cover with foil and bake in a preheated oven at 350°F for about 20 minutes, or until soft. • Purée the potatoes and pumpkin together in a food processor (or mash with a potato masher). • Place in a mixing bowl and stir in half the butter, the parsley, egg yolks, and half the Parmesan. Season with salt and pepper. Beat the egg whites until stiff and fold them into the mixture. • Grease an ovenproof baking dish with 1 tablespoon of butter and fill with half the potato and pumpkin mixture. Cover with the Mozzarella and then the remaining potato and pumpkin mixture. Sprinkle with the bread crumbs and remaining Parmesan. Dot with the remaining butter and bake in a preheated oven at 350°F for 45 minutes. • Serve hot.

Serves: 6 · Prep: 20 min. · Cooking: 1¼ hrs · Level: 1

SFORMATO DI CAVOLFIORE
Cauliflower mold with black olives

- 2 lb cauliflower head
- 1 quantity Béchamel sauce (see recipe, page 16)
- 1/2 cup freshly grated Parmesan cheese
- 20 black olives, pitted and chopped
- 3 eggs, beaten to a foam
  salt and freshly ground black pepper to taste
- 1/4 teaspoon nutmeg
  butter to grease the mold and bread crumbs

Wine: a dry white (Melissa)

Divide the cauliflower into large florets and trim the stems to about 1/2 inch.

Cauliflour mold with black olives

Cook in a pot of salted, boiling water for 5–7 minutes. Drain and set aside. • Prepare the béchamel sauce. • Mash the cauliflower until smooth. • Combine with the béchamel, Parmesan, olives, eggs, salt, pepper, and nutmeg. • Grease a 12-inch ring mold with a little butter and sprinkle with bread crumbs. Pour the mixture into the mold and place in a larger container filled with water. • Cook in a preheated oven at 350°F for about 45 minutes. • Invert onto a platter while still hot. Serve hot or at room temperature.

Serves: 4 · Prep: 25 min. · Cooking: 55 min. · Level: 2

SEDANO ALLA PRATESE
Baked celery with meat sauce

- 1 quantity Tomato meat sauce (see recipe, page 18)
- 12 large, tender stalks celery
- 1/2 cup chicken livers
- 2 tablespoons butter
- 2 tablespoons extra-virgin olive oil
- 1 onion, finely chopped
- 1 clove garlic, finely chopped
- 6 oz prosciutto, finely chopped
- 8 oz ground lean veal
  salt and freshly ground black pepper to taste
- 1/2 cup dry white wine
- 1/2 cup all-purpose flour
- 2 eggs, beaten
- 3/4 cup fine dry bread crumbs
- 1 cup oil, for frying
- 1 cup freshly grated Parmesan cheese

Wine: a dry red (Chianti dei Colli Fiorentini)

Prepare the tomato meat sauce. • Blanch the celery in a pan of salted, boiling water for 5 minutes. Drain and cool. • Trim any connective tissue and discolored parts from the chicken livers and chop finely. • Heat the butter with the olive oil in a medium skillet. Add the onion and garlic and sauté for 3–4 minutes. • Add the chicken livers and prosciutto, cook for a few minutes then add the veal, breaking up any lumps with a fork. • Season with salt and pepper, stir and cook for 4–5 minutes. • Pour in the wine, cover and cook over low heat for 20 minutes. • Cut the celery stalks into 3 pieces and fill each one with the chicken liver mixture. • Coat the pieces of celery with flour, dip in the egg, and coat with bread crumbs. • Heat the oil in a large skillet until very hot. Fry the celery in small batches until golden brown. Drain on paper towels. • Place a layer of celery sticks in an ovenproof dish, spoon some meat sauce (and any remaining stuffing) over the top and sprinkle with a little Parmesan. Repeat until all the celery, meat sauce, and Parmesan are in the dish. Finish with a layer of cheese. • Bake in a preheated oven at 425°F for 10–15 minutes, or until the Parmesan is golden brown. • Serve hot.

Serves: 4 · Prep: 30 min. + time to make the meat sauce · Cooking: 45 min. · Level: 3

PATATE GRATINATE CON CIPOLLE
Potato gratin with onions and walnuts

- 1 quantity Onion sauce (see recipe, page 15)
- 2 lb boiling potatoes
- ¼ cup butter
- 1 quantity Béchamel sauce (see recipe, page 16)
- 1 cup freshly grated Parmesan cheese
  salt and freshly ground black pepper to taste
- 8 oz fresh Fontina cheese, thinly sliced
- 1 cup shelled walnuts, coarsely chopped
- 1 tablespoon fine dry bread crumbs

Wine: a dry red (Dolcetto D'Alba)

Prepare the onion sauce. • Cook the potatoes in their skins in salted, boiling water for 25 minutes, or until tender. Drain, slip off their skins, and mash with 3 tablespoons of butter until smooth. • Prepare the béchamel sauce and stir in the Parmesan. • Grease an ovenproof dish with the remaining butter and spread with one-third of the potatoes. Cover with half the béchamel, followed by half the Fontina and onions. Sprinkle with half the walnuts. Cover with half the remaining potatoes, then the remaining béchamel, Fontina, and onions. Make a top layer of potatoes and sprinkle with the bread crumbs and remaining walnuts. • Bake in a preheated oven at 350°F for 25 minutes.

Serves: 6 · Prep: 15 min. + time to make the sauce · Cooking: 50 min. · Level: 1

VERDURE FARCITE AL FORNO
Baked stuffed vegetables

- 6 medium zucchini
- 6 medium onions
- 6 medium tomatoes
- 3 large bell peppers, mixed colors
- 3 eggs
- 2 cups fine dry bread crumbs
- ¼ cup finely chopped parsley
- 2 cloves garlic, finely chopped
- ½ cup freshly grated Parmesan cheese
  salt and freshly ground black pepper to taste
- ⅓ cup extra-virgin olive oil

Wine: a dry, aromatic white (Müller Thurgau)

Blanch the zucchini in salted water for 5 minutes. Drain and cool. Cut in half lengthwise and use a teaspoon to remove the pulp. Chop the pulp and set aside. • Peel the onions and blanch in salted water for 5 minutes. Drain, then cut in half horizontally. Hollow them out, leaving ½-inch-thick sides. Chop the pulp and set aside. • Cut the tomatoes in half horizontally and hollow them out. Chop the pulp and set aside. • Cut the bell peppers in half lengthwise and remove the seeds and core. • Beat the eggs in a bowl and add the bread crumbs, parsley, garlic, half the Parmesan, and salt. • Add the tomato, zucchini, and onion pulp and mix well. • Stuff the vegetables and sprinkle with the remaining Parmesan. • Pour the oil into an ovenproof dish into which the vegetables will fit snugly in a single layer. Add the vegetables and bake in a preheated oven at 400°F for about 35 minutes. • Serve hot or at room temperature.

Serves: 6 · Prep: 15 min. · Cooking: 40 min. · Level : 1

INVOLTINI DI CAVOLO SAPORITI
Stuffed cabbage-leaf rolls

- 8 large cabbage leaves
- 8 oz Italian sausages, peeled and crumbled
- ¾ cup dry white wine
- 2 eggs
  salt and freshly ground black pepper to taste
- 1 cup freshly grated Edam cheese
- 1 cup freshly grated Parmesan cheese
- ¼ cup fine dry bread crumbs
- ¼ cup extra-virgin olive oil
- 1 medium onion, finely chopped

Wine: a dry white (Chardonnay)

Wash the cabbage leaves, taking care not to tear them. • Bring a pot of salted water to a boil and, using tongs, blanch each leaf by dipping it into the water for 30 seconds. Lay the leaves on a clean cloth to dry. • Brown the sausage meat in a skillet without oil. Add the wine and let it evaporate. Remove from heat and set to cool on a plate, leaving any fat in the skillet. • Beat the eggs in a bowl. Add the salt, pepper, Edam, Parmesan, bread crumbs, and sausage. Mix until smooth. • Distribute the filling evenly among the cabbage leaves and roll them up, folding in the ends. Tie with kitchen string. • Heat the oil in a skillet over medium heat, add the onion and sauté until soft. • Place the stuffed cabbage leaves in the skillet with the onion, cover, and cook for 5 minutes. Turn with a fork, uncover and cook for 5 more minutes. • Serve hot.

Serves: 4 · Prep: 30 min. · Cooking: 40 min. · Level: 2

PATATE E CAVOLI
Potato and cabbage mix

- 4 large potatoes
  salt and freshly ground black pepper to taste
- ½ medium Savoy cabbage
- 2 tablespoons extra-virgin olive oil
- 1 small onion, finely chopped
- ¼ cup diced pancetta
- 1 clove garlic, finely chopped
- ½ teaspoon crushed red pepper flakes

Wine: a light, dry white (Frascati)

Cook the potatoes in a large pot of salted, boiling water for 25 minutes, or until tender. Drain, peel, and mash. • Boil the cabbage in a pot of salted water for 10 minutes. Drain well and chop coarsely. • Heat the oil in a large skillet and sauté the onion until pale gold. Add the pancetta, garlic, and pepper flakes. Season with salt and pepper, add the potatoes and cabbage and mix well. • Serve hot.

Serves: 4 · Prep: 15 min. · Cooking: 50 min. · Level: 1

SPIEDINI MISTI DI VERDURE
Skewered mixed vegetables

- 2 zucchini
- 12 cherry tomatoes
- 2 medium onions
- 3 small bell peppers, mixed colors
- 3 tablespoons extra-virgin olive oil
  salt and freshly ground black pepper to taste
- ½ teaspoon paprika
  juice of ½ lemon
- 1 tablespoon chopped fresh or 1 teaspoon dried herbs (oregano, mint, or thyme)

Wine: a light dry white (Prosecco di Conegliano)

Cut the zucchini in thick wheels. Cut the cherry tomatoes in half. Cut the onion in 4 wedges, then cut each wedge in half. Cut the bell peppers in 1½-inch squares. • Thread the vegetable pieces on wooden skewers. Set them on a plate. • Place the oil, salt, pepper, paprika, lemon juice, and herbs in a small

bowl and beat with a fork until well mixed. •
Pour over the skewers, cover with
aluminum foil, and marinate in the
refrigerator for 2 hours. • Heat a grill pan
until very hot, drain the skewers, and place
half of them in the grill pan. Cook for about
10 minutes, turning them so that they brown
on all sides. Repeat with the remaining
skewers. • Serve hot.

*Serves: 4 · Prep: 25 min. + 2 hrs to marinate ·
Cooking: 20 min. · Level: 1*

TORTINO DI PATATE
Potato pie

1½	lb firm, waxy potatoes
½	cup butter
8	oz Parmesan cheese, sliced
	salt and freshly ground black pepper to taste
1	cup milk

Wine: a light, dry red (Colli Piacentini Gutturnio Secco)

Boil the potatoes in their skins for about
25 minutes. • Peel while hot and set aside
to cool. • Cut into ½-inch slices and
arrange in layers in a greased ovenproof
dish. Distribute flakes of butter and slices
of Parmesan over each layer, then
sprinkle with salt and pepper. • Pour in
the milk and bake in a preheated oven at
400°F for 25 minutes.

Serves: 4 · Prep: 20 min. · Cooking: 50 min. · Level: 1

CAVOLINI DI BRUXELLES PICCANTI
Hot and spicy Brussels sprouts

2	lb Brussels sprouts
3	cloves garlic, finely chopped
3	tablespoons extra-virgin olive oil
1	cup diced pancetta
1	Italian sausage, peeled and crumbled
1	hot red chili, thinly sliced
	salt to taste
1	bunch chives, coarsely chopped

Wine: a dry red (Sangiovese)

Cook the Brussels sprouts in salted, boiling
water for 7–8 minutes. Drain and set aside.
• In an earthenware pot or skillet, sauté the
garlic in the oil until golden. • Add the
pancetta and sausage. Sauté briefly and stir
in the Brussels sprouts and chilies. • Season
with salt, cover, and cook for 10 minutes. •
Uncover, sprinkle with the chives and cook
for 5 more minutes. • Serve hot.

Serves: 4 · Prep: 10 min. · Cooking: 25 min. · Level: 1

Hot and spicy Brussels sprouts

Swiss chard, Roman-style

with the béchamel and sprinkle with the remaining cheese. Bake in a preheated oven at 350° F for 30 minutes. • Serve hot.

Serves: 4 · Prep: 25 min. · Cooking: 55 min. · Level: 1

VERZE ALLA VENEZIANA
Venetian-style cabbage

- 1 medium Savoy cabbage
- 3¹/₂ oz finely chopped fresh pork fat
- 1 sprig rosemary
- 1 clove garlic, whole but lightly crushed
  salt to taste
- ¹/₂ cup dry white wine

Wine: a light, dry white (Valdadige Pinot Grigio)

Discard the tougher leaves of the cabbage; then take the rest apart leaf by leaf, cutting out the hard ribs and rinsing. Cut the leaves into thin strips. • Chop the pork fat and rosemary leaves together with a heavy kitchen knife. Sauté them briefly in a heavy-bottomed saucepan with the garlic, discarding the latter when it starts to color. • Add the shredded cabbage and a pinch of salt. Cover the pan and cook over low heat, stirring frequently for 1 hour. • Pour in the wine, cover again, and cook for 1 hour more. • Serve hot.

Serves: 6 · Prep: 10 min. · Cooking: 2 hrs · Level: 1

GRATIN DI BELGA E PROSCIUTTO
Baked Belgian endives with ham

- 8 medium heads Belgian endives
- 3 tablespoons extra-virgin olive oil
- ¹/₂ cup water
- 1 quantity Béchamel sauce (see recipe, page 16)
  salt and freshly ground black pepper to taste
- 1 tablespoon butter to grease the pan
- 8 thick slices ham
- ³/₄ cup freshly grated Gruyère cheese

Vino: a dry red (Chianti Castelgreve)

Using a sharp knife, hollow out the base of the endives to remove the bitter part and ensure uniform cooking. • Place the heads in a large pan with the oil, water, and dash of salt. Cover and braise over medium heat for about 40 minutes. Drain well. • Prepare the béchamel sauce. • Wrap each endive in a slice of ham (take care to place the part where the ham overlaps underneath) and arrange the heads in a greased ovenproof dish. • Pour the béchamel over the rolls and sprinkle Gruyère over the top. •

BIETOLA ALLA ROMANA
Swiss chard, Roman-style

- 2 lb Swiss chard
- ¹/₄ cup extra-virgin olive oil
- 2 cloves garlic, finely chopped
- 4 anchovy fillets
- 6 medium tomatoes, peeled and diced
  salt and freshly ground black pepper to taste

Wine: a dry white (Colli Albani)

Clean the chard, cut into 1-inch pieces, and rinse thoroughly under cold running water. • Boil in a pot of lightly salted water for about 10 minutes, or until tender. • Drain well and dry by wringing gently in a clean cotton cloth. • Heat the oil in a large skillet and sauté the garlic for 5 minutes. Discard the garlic. • Add the anchovy fillets to the flavored oil and mash with a fork until they dissolve in the oil. Add the tomatoes and cook for 15 minutes. • Add the chard and stir over medium heat for 5 minutes. • Serve hot.

Serves: 4 · Prep: 25 min. · Cooking: 55 min. · Level: 1

GRATIN DI VERZA E RISO
Baked cabbage, rice, and tomato

- 1 medium Savoy cabbage
- 3 tablespoons extra-virgin olive oil
- 2 onions, finely chopped
- 2 cloves garlic, finely chopped
- 1¹/₃ cups parboiled short-grain white rice
- 1 (15 oz) can Italian tomatoes
- 1 quantity Béchamel sauce (see recipe, page 16)
- 2 cups freshly grated Gruyère cheese
- 1 tablespoon butter

Wine: a dry red (S. Costanza)

Clean the cabbage by discarding the tough outer leaves. Trim the stalk. Cut in half and then into strips. Blanch in salted, boiling water, drain well, and spread on a dishcloth to dry. • Heat the oil in a large skillet and sauté the onion and garlic until soft. • Stir in the rice and season with salt and pepper. • Add the tomatoes and cook for 15 minutes, or until the rice is just tender. • Prepare the béchamel. When ready, stir in half the Gruyère. • Grease an ovenproof dish and fill with alternate layers of cabbage and rice and tomatoes. • Cover

Bake in a preheated oven at 350°F for 25 minutes, or until the topping turns golden brown. • Serve hot.

Serves: 4 · Prep: 40 min. · Cooking: 1 hr · Level: 1

CICORIA IN PADELLA
Spicy chicory with garlic and anchovies

- 1 large head chicory
- 5 cloves garlic, finely chopped
- 1/2 teaspoon crushed red pepper flakes
- 1/4 cup extra-virgin olive oil
  salt to taste
- 8 anchovy fillets, crumbled
- 2 tablespoons capers

Wine: a dry red (Valpolicella)

Trim the head of chicory, remove any yellow or wilted leaves and cut in half . Rinse in cold running water. • Cook in a pan of salted boiling water for 10–15 minutes. • Drain thoroughly without squeezing and cut lengthwise into 1½-inch pieces. • Sauté the garlic with the oil in a large skillet until it begins to color. • Add the chicory and red pepper flakes, and season with a little salt . • Cook over medium heat for about 10 minutes, stirring frequently. • Add the anchovies and capers and stir them in over high heat for 2–3 minutes. • Serve hot.

Serves: 4 · Prep: 10 min. · Cooking: 30 min. · Level: 1

RADICCHIO ALLA TREVIGIANA
Treviso radicchio

☞ This recipe probably shows Treviso radicchio to its best advantage: tender, flavorsome, but still slightly crunchy.

- 6 heads Treviso radicchio or red chicory
- 1/4 cup extra-virgin olive oil
  salt and freshly ground black pepper to taste

Rinse the radicchio heads and drain thoroughly or shake to get rid of all the water. Trim off the end of the stalk and cut each head lengthwise into 4 pieces. • Grease a large skillet with a little of the oil and place the radicchio quarters in it in a single layer. Drizzle with the remaining oil, salt, and pepper, then cook, uncovered, over a gentle heat for 20 minutes, until the radicchio is tender but still crisp. • Serve this vegetable with various meats and with game.

Serves: 6 · Prep: 10 min. · Cooking: 20 min. · Level: 1

Baked potatoes, onions, and tomatoes

TEGLIA DI PATATE E CIPOLLE
Baked potatoes, onions, and tomatoes

- 1³/₄ lb potatoes
- 4 large red onions
- 6 large ripe tomatoes
  salt and freshly ground black pepper to taste
- 1/3 cup extra-virgin olive oil
- 1/2 cup cold water
- 1/3 cup freshly grated Pecorino cheese
- 1 teaspoon dried oregano

Wine: a dry red (Bonarda dell'Oltrepò Pavese)

Peel the potatoes and slice thinly. • Plunge the tomatoes into a pot of boiling water for 1 minute, then transfer to cold water. Slip off their skins. Cut in ¹/₂-inch slices. • Place the potatoes, onions, and tomatoes in a large mixing bowl. Add the Pecorino, salt, pepper, oil, and water and mix carefully. • Place in an ovenproof baking dish and sprinkle with the oregano. Bake in a preheated oven at 350°F for 1 hour. Serve hot or at room temperature.

Serves: 6 · Prep: 15 min. · Cooking: 1 hr · Level: 1

INDIVIA SCAROLA ALLA SICILIANA
Escarole with pine nuts, capers, olives, raisins, and anchovies

- 3 large, fresh heads of escarole
- 1/4 cup extra-virgin olive oil
- 1/3 cup pine nuts
- 1/3 cup raisins soaked for 30 minutes in water
- 12 black olives, pitted and chopped
  salt and freshly ground black pepper to taste
- 1/4 cup capers
- 4 anchovy fillets, finely chopped

Wine: a dry white (Donnafugata)

Use the green leaves of the escarole and set the creamy white hearts aside to use in a salad. • Blanch the leaves in salted, boiling water, drain well, and spread in a colander to dry for about 10 minutes. • Place the oil in a skillet and add the escarole, pine nuts, raisins, olives, salt, and pepper. Sauté over medium heat for 10 minutes. Use a fork and spoon to toss the leaves from time to time as they cook. • Add the capers and anchovy, toss well and cook until any excess water has evaporated. • Serve hot.

Serves: 4 · Prep: 10 min. · Cooking: 25 min. · Level: 1

Salads served as starters pique the appetite for the dishes to come. Served as side dishes, they should be chosen to round out the main course and to refresh the palate. Many of the salads in this chapter are meant to accompany cheese, omelet, meat, or fish dishes. A wine has not been indicated for salads meant to be served as side dishes. Wine should be chosen to complement the main dish.

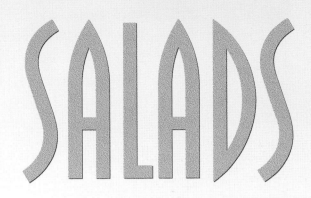

SALADS

INSALATA DI FAGIOLINI CON IL PANE FRITTO

Green bean salad with fried bread

- 1 lb green beans
  salt and freshly ground black pepper to taste
- 2 bunches chives, finely chopped
- 6½ oz pancetta, cut in strips
- ½ cup, plus 1 tablespoon, extra-virgin olive oil
- 5 thick slices firm-textured bread, diced
- 1 large clove garlic, cut in quarters
  juice of 2 lemons
- 1 tablespoon oregano
- 1 tablespoon finely chopped parsley
- 8 scallions, finely chopped
- 2 tablespoons capers

Wine: a dry white (Riesling Italico)

Top and tail the beans, cut in half, rinse well, and cook in a pot of boiling, salted water for 7–8 minutes, or until tender. Drain, dry on a dishcloth, and place in a large salad bowl. • Sauté the pancetta in a small skillet with 1 tablespoon of oil until crisp. Drain and set aside. • Fry the bread in a skillet with ¼ cup of oil and the garlic until golden brown. Drain on paper towels. • In a small bowl, dissolve a pinch of salt in the lemon juice, and add the pepper, oregano, parsley, scallions, and ¼ cup of oil. Dress the salad, sprinkle with the capers, and toss with the diced bread. • Serve at once before the bread becomes soggy.

Serves: 4 · Prep: 20 min. · Cooking: 15 min. · Level: 1

◁ Pear and bell pepper salad (see recipe, page 298)
◣ Green bean salad with fried bread

Artichoke salad

INSALATA DI POMODORI
Tomato and basil salad

- 1 clove garlic
- 6 large tomatoes, firm and ripe
  salt and freshly ground black pepper to taste
- 15 fresh basil leaves, torn
  pinch of dried oregano
- ⅓ cup extra-virgin olive oil

Peel the garlic and rub the insides of a salad bowl with the clove stuck on a fork. • Wash, dry, and slice the tomatoes. Squeeze gently to remove as many seeds as possible. • Sprinkle the slices with a little salt and place on a slightly inclined cutting board for about 10 minutes so the liquid they produce can drain away. • Transfer to a salad bowl and sprinkle with the basil. • In a small bowl, beat the oregano, salt, pepper, and oil with a whisk until well mixed. • Pour over the tomatoes and toss gently. • Cover and set aside for 15 minutes before serving.

Serves: 4 · Prep: 15 min. + 15 min to rest · Level: 1

INSALATA MISTA
Mixed green salad

☞ In Italy, mixed salads are made with a mixture of wild and cultivated salad greens and herbs, depending on the season and what is available. Use only the freshest greens and wash and dry them carefully before use.

- 1 lb mixed fresh salad greens (romaine, leaf lettuce, chicory, dandelion greens, arugula, corn salad, burnet)
- 6 oz young, tender cabbage leaves (optional)
  salt and freshly ground black pepper to taste
- ¼ cup red wine vinegar
- ½ cup extra-virgin olive oil

Wash the salad greens under cold running water, drain, and dry well. • Place the leaves, whole or coarsely torn, in a large salad bowl. Sprinkle with salt and pepper, drizzle with the vinegar, and then the oil. • Toss gently and serve.

Serves: 4–6 · Prep: 10 min. · Level: 1

INSALATA MISTA CON CAPRINI
Mixed salad with Caprino cheese

- 1 lb mixed young fresh salad greens (romaine, leaf lettuce, chicory, dandelion greens, arugula, corn salad, burnet)
- ¼ cup extra-virgin olive oil
- 2 oz pitted black olives
- 1 tablespoon honey
  salt to taste
- 4–8 tiny forms Caprino cheese

Wine: a light, dry white (Tocai Colli Orientali)

Wash the salad greens under cold running water, drain, and dry well. • Place the leaves, whole or coarsely torn, in four serving bowls. • In a blender, mix half the oil with the olives and honey until creamy. • Season the individual salads with salt and drizzle with the remaining olive oil. • Heat the cheese in a preheated oven at 350°F, for 5–10 minutes. • Place 1 or 2 forms of Caprino on top of each salad. Pour the olive cream over the top and serve.

Serves: 4 · Prep: 15 min. · Cooking: 10 min. · Level: 1

INSALATA ALL'ACETO BALSAMICO
Mixed salad with balsamic vinegar

- 1 lb mixed fresh salad greens (romaine, leaf lettuce, chicory, dandelion greens, arugula, corn salad, burnet)
- 4 oz Parmesan cheese, shredded
- ⅓ cup extra-virgin olive oil
  salt and freshly ground black pepper to taste
- 2 tablespoons balsamic vinegar

Wash the salad greens under cold running water, drain, and dry well. Place the leaves, whole or coarsely torn, in a salad bowl. • Add the Parmesan. • Use a whisk to beat the oil, salt, pepper, and balsamic vinegar together in a small bowl until well blended. • Drizzle over the salad and toss gently. Serve at once.

Serves: 4–6 · Prep: 10 min. · Level: 1

INSALATA DI PANCETTA CROCCANTE
Mixed salad with crispy fried pancetta

- 1 lb mixed fresh salad greens (romaine, leaf lettuce, chicory, dandelion greens, arugula, corn salad, burnet)
- 1 cup diced pancetta
- 2 cloves garlic, finely chopped
- 2 tablespoons butter
- 2 tablespoons balsamic vinegar
  salt to taste

Wine: a light, dry white (Colli Piacentini Malvasia)

Wash the salad greens under cold running water, drain, and dry well. Place the leaves, whole or coarsely torn, in a heatproof bowl. • Sauté the pancetta and garlic in the butter until the pancetta is crisp and lightly browned. • Add the balsamic vinegar and a little salt. Remove from heat. • Pour over the salad greens and toss gently. Serve immediately before the salad greens start to wilt.

Serves: 4 · Prep: 15 min. · Cooking: 10 min. · Level: 1

INSALATA DI CARCIOFI
Artichoke salad

- 4 large fresh artichokes
  juice of 2 lemons
- 1 teaspoon salt
  freshly ground black pepper to taste
- ⅓ cup extra-virgin olive oil
- 2 tablespoons finely chopped parsley
- 2 tablespoons finely chopped mint leaves

Wine: a dry sparkling white (Pignoletto Frizzanti)

Clean the artichokes by removing all the tough outer leaves and trimming the tops and stalks. Remove the fuzzy inner choke and cut in thin wedges. Soak in a bowl of cold water with the juice of 1 lemon for 10 minutes to prevent discoloring. • Dissolve the salt in the remaining lemon juice. Add the oil, pepper, parsley, and mint, and beat vigorously with a whisk to emulsify. • Drain the artichokes and dry well. Place them in a salad bowl. Pour the dressing over the top and toss well. • Serve at once.

Serves: 4 · Prep: 10 min. + 10 min. to soak · Level: 1

INSALATA DI ASPARAGI E FUNGHI
Asparagus and mushroom salad

1½	lb asparagus
2	cups arugula
3	cups thinly sliced white mushrooms
	salt and freshly ground black pepper to taste
	peel of 2 lemons, very finely chopped
10	basil leaves, finely chopped
⅓	cup extra-virgin olive oil
¼	cup lemon juice

Wine: a dry, aromatic white (Malvasia Secco dei Colli di Parma)

Trim the tough parts off the asparagus stalks and cook for 7–10 minutes, or until just tender, in a pot of salted, boiling water. Drain well, dry with paper towels, and set aside to cool. • Wash the arugula under cold running water, drain, and dry well. • Place a bed of arugula on a large serving dish and scatter with the mushrooms. Arrange the asparagus on top. • Dissolve a pinch of salt in the lemon juice and add the lemon peel and basil, oil, and pepper and blend thoroughly. • Pour the dressing over the salad and serve.

Serves: 4 · Prep: 20 min. · Cooking: 10 min. · Level: 1

INSALATA CON RISO SELVATICO
Green salad with raspberries and wild rice

1	cup long-grain brown rice
1	cup wild black or red rice
1	lb mixed salad greens (arugula, witloof, dandelion greens, wild endives, succory, leaf lettuce, chicory, corn salad, burnet)
1	tablespoon white wine vinegar
	salt and freshly ground black pepper to taste
½	cup extra-virgin olive oil
1	lb fresh raspberries
15	fresh mint leaves
1	bunch fresh chervil, in sprigs
2	bunches watercress, coarsely chopped
4	carrots, coarsely grated

Cook the different types of rice separately, according to the package directions. • Wash the salad greens under cold running water, drain, and dry well. •

Put the vinegar in a bowl with the salt and pepper. Pour in half the oil and beat well with a whisk. Crush about 15 raspberries and add to the dressing. Blend well. • Place the salad greens on a large platter, add the mint, chervil, and watercress, and toss carefully. • Sprinkle with the carrot and pour half the dressing over the top. Garnish with 20 raspberries. • Drain the rice, shaking thoroughly to remove excess moisture. Place on the platter with the salad greens and toss with the remaining oil. • Garnish with the remaining raspberries. Drizzle with the remaining dressing and serve.

Serves: 4 · Prep: 20 min. · Cooking: 40 min. · Level: 1

INSALATA DI CAROTE
Carrot salad with garlic, lemon, and parsley

☞ For an unorthodox touch, add 2–4 tablespoons of coarsely chopped candied ginger to this vitamin-packed salad.

4–6	large carrots, coarsely grated
1–2	cloves garlic, finely chopped
½	cup finely chopped parsley
	juice of 1 lemon
¼	cup extra-virgin olive oil
	salt and freshly ground black pepper to taste

Place the carrots, garlic, and parsley in a salad bowl. Add the lemon juice, oil, salt, and pepper and mix well. • Chill in the refrigerator for 30 minutes before serving.

Serves: 4 · Prep: 10 min. + 30 min. to chill · Level: 1

Carrot salad with garlic, lemon, and parsley

INSALATA DI SPINACI E MELONE
Spinach with cantaloupe and Parmesan

12	oz dwarf spinach, tender and very fresh
2	carrots, peeled
4	oz corn kernels, or 8 baby corn cobs
4	oz Parmesan cheese, shredded
1	small cantaloupe
4	oz prosciutto
½	teaspoon salt
	juice of 1 lemon
¼	cup extra-virgin olive oil
	freshly ground black pepper to taste

Wine: a dry white (Bianco di Ischia)

Rinse the spinach under cold running water, drain, and dry well. Trim the stems and discard any bruised leaves. Chop very coarsely. • Grate the carrots coarsely or cut in julienne strips. • Place the spinach in a large salad bowl and sprinkle with the carrots and corn. • Cut the cantaloupe in half and use a melon baller to make small balls. Arrange on top of the salad. • Trim any fat from the prosciutto, chop coarsely, and sprinkle over the salad. Sprinkle with the Parmesan. • In a small bowl, dissolve the salt in the lemon juice, add the oil and pepper, and beat vigorously with a whisk until well blended. • Pour the dressing over the salad, toss gently, and serve.

Serves: 4 · Prep: 20 min. · Level: 1

Mixed vegetable and mayonnaise salad

Use a whisk to blend the oil, chives, salt, and pepper. Set aside for 20 minutes. • Wash the salad greens under cold running water, drain, and dry well. Arrange a bed of mixed salad leaves in a large salad bowl. • Wash the apples thoroughly, cut in half, remove the core and cut in thin wedges, without peeling. • Arrange a ring of apple wedges over the salad. • Scatter the radishes over the apples. • Cut the strawberries in half and use to garnish the salad, placing a teaspoon of Ricotta between each strawberry. • Pour the dressing over the top and serve.

Serves: 4 · Prep: 20 min. · Level: 1

INSALATA DI CETRIOLI E CIPOLLA
Cucumber and onion salad

☞ This refreshing summer salad is the ultimate for onion lovers. Serve with a platter of fresh cheeses (Ricotta, Caprino, Robiola, Crescenza, Stracchino) and freshly baked bread.

- 6   medium red onions
     salt and freshly ground black pepper to taste
- 1   tablespoon white wine vinegar
- 1/4   cup extra-virgin olive oil
- 2   medium cucumbers
- 1   tablespoon pickled capers, drained
- 6   leaves fresh basil, torn

Wine: a dry white (Cirò Bianco)

Peel the onions and slice in thin wheels. • Put the onions in a salad bowl, sprinkle with the salt, pepper, vinegar, and oil. Toss well and set aside for 30 minutes. • Peel the cucumbers and slice very thinly. • Add the cucumbers and capers to the onions and toss again. • Sprinkle with the basil and serve.

Serves: 4–6 · Prep: 15 min. + 30 min. to rest · Level: 1

INSALATA DI VERZA
Cabbage and apple salad

- 1/2   medium Savoy cabbage
- 1   small white onion
- 1   Golden Delicious apple
- 2   tablespoons finely chopped parsley
- 1   clove garlic, finely chopped
     salt and freshly ground black pepper to taste
     juice of 1 lemon
- 1/4   cup extra-virgin olive oil

Wine: a dry sparkling white (Prosecco di Conegliano)

Shred the cabbage and slice the onion thinly. • Peel and core the apples, dice, and add to the cabbage. Add the parsley

INSALATA RUSSA
Mixed vegetable and mayonnaise salad

- 1/2   cup Mayonnaise (see recipe, page 16)
- 6   oz green beans
- 2   large carrots
- 2   large potatoes
- 2   tablespoons white wine vinegar
- 6   oz fresh or frozen peas
- 8   pickled gherkins
- 3   hard-boiled eggs
- 1   tablespoon pickled capers, drained
     salt and freshly ground white pepper to taste
- 1/4   cup extra-virgin olive oil

Wine: a dry white (Orvieto Classico)

Prepare the mayonnaise. • Top and tail the beans and chop into 1/4-inch pieces. • Peel the carrots and potatoes and chop them into 1/4-inch cubes. • Add 1 tablespoon of vinegar to a saucepan of boiling water. Add the potatoes and cook for about 5 minutes, or until tender. Drain and set aside to cool. • Add the peas, beans, carrots, and remaining vinegar to another saucepan of salted, boiling water and cook for 5 minutes, or until the vegetables are tender. Drain and set aside to cool. • While the vegetables are cooking, slice the gherkins into 1/4-inch-thick wheels and peel and slice the eggs. • When the vegetables are cool, place them in a large salad bowl and add the gherkins and capers. Season with salt and pepper, drizzle with the oil and mix gently. Add the mayonnaise and garnish with the eggs. • Chill in the refrigerator for 15 minutes before serving.

Serves: 4–6 · Prep: 15 min. + 15 min. to chill · Cooking: 15 min. · Level: 1

INSALATA CON FRAGOLE E MELE
Salad with strawberries and apples

- 1/4   cup extra-virgin olive oil
- 2   tablespoons chopped chives
     salt and freshly ground black pepper to taste
- 12   oz mixed corn salad and green leaf lettuce
- 6   oz endive hearts
- 2   Red Delicious apples
- 10   red radishes, sliced
- 14   oz firm ripe strawberries
- 1 1/2   cups very fresh Ricotta cheese

Wine: a dry white (Soave Classico)

and garlic and toss well. • Season with salt and pepper, drizzle with the lemon juice and oil, and toss gently. • Set aside for 15 minutes before serving.

Serves: 4 · Prep: 5 min. + 15 min. to rest · Level: 1

INSALATA DI RADICCHIO
Radicchio with egg, apples, and cheese

☞ Striking red radicchio is a part of the chicory family. Substitute with the same quantity of tender young spinach leaves if radicchio is unavailable.

- 1 lb red radicchio
  juice of 1 lemon
- 1/4 cup extra-virgin olive oil
- 4 hard-boiled eggs, peeled
- 2 crisp eating apples
- 8 oz Provolone cheese
- 20 large black olives, pitted and chopped
- 2 tablespoons hot mustard
- 1 tablespoon white wine vinegar
  salt and freshly ground black pepper to taste

Wine: a dry white (Vernaccia di San Gimignano)

Clean the radicchio by discarding the outer leaves. Wash under cold running water, drain, and dry well. Chop coarsely and place in a salad bowl. • Season with the lemon juice and half the oil, toss well, and set aside. • Slice the eggs. Peel the apples and dice. • Dice the Provolone. • Add the eggs, apples, Provolone, and olives to the salad bowl. • Mix the mustard, vinegar, remaining oil, salt, and pepper together in a bowl. Beat with a whisk and pour over the salad. • Toss carefully and serve.

Serves: 4–6 · Prep: 15 min. · Level: 1

INSALATA VARIOPINTA
Fairview salad

- 8 oz leaf lettuce
- 8 oz arugula
  salt and freshly ground black pepper to taste
- 4 oz canned peas, well-drained
- 8 oz white mushrooms
- 4 oz Fontina cheese, diced
- 1/2 cup extra-virgin olive oil
- 1 tablespoon mustard
- 2 tablespoons white wine vinegar
- 4 hard-boiled eggs, peeled and sliced
- 2 carrots, grated
- 12 cherry tomatoes, cut in half

Wine: a dry sparkling white (Prosecco di Valdobbiadene)

Wash the salad greens under cold running water, drain, and dry well. Place the leaves, coarsely torn, in a salad bowl. Season with salt and pepper. • Sprinkle the peas over

Tomato, Mozzarella cheese, and mixed raw vegetables

the top. • Clean, wash, peel, dry, and thinly slice the mushrooms. Place them in a bowl with the cheese. • Prepare a dressing by beating the oil, mustard, salt, and vinegar together in a bowl. Pour half of it over the mushrooms and toss well. • Sprinkle the mushroom mixture over the salad and cover with the eggs, carrots, and tomatoes. • Just before serving, drizzle with the remaining dressing and toss again.

Serves: 4–6 · Prep: 20 min. · Level: 1

INSALATA CAPRESE CLASSICA
Tomato and Mozzarella cheese

- 8 large red tomatoes
- 1 lb Mozzarella cheese
- 20 large basil leaves, torn
  salt and freshly ground black pepper to taste
- 1/3 cup extra-virgin olive oil

Wine: a dry white (Müller Thurgau)

Cut the tomatoes in 1/4-inch-thick slices and arrange on a flat serving dish. • Cut the Mozzarella in slices of the same width and

alternate with the tomato. • Sprinkle with basil, salt, and pepper, and drizzle with the oil. • Serve at once.

Serves: 4–6 · Prep: · 10 min. · Level: 1

INSALATA CAPRESE CONDITA
Tomato, Mozzarella cheese, and mixed raw vegetables

- 14 oz Mozzarella cheese
- 4–6 large red tomatoes
- 1 cup mixed raw vegetables (zucchini, carrots, celery, bell peppers, onion), cut in small cubes
- 1 tablespoon pickled capers, drained
  salt and freshly ground black pepper to taste
- 1/4 cup extra-virgin olive oil
- 8 leaves fresh basil, torn

Wine: a dry white (Bianco di Capri)

Cut the Mozzarella in 1/4-inch-thick slices and arrange on a flat serving dish. • Cut the tomatoes in slices of the same width and place over the Mozzarella. • Place the mixed vegetables in a bowl with the capers, salt, pepper, and oil. Toss well and sprinkle over the Mozzarella and tomato. Garnish with the basil and serve.

Serves: 4–6 · Prep: 15 min. · Level: 1

INSALATA AL GORGONZOLA
Winter salad with Gorgonzola dressing

- 2 fennel bulbs
- 2 carrots
- 1 bunch celery
- 1 Granny Smith apple
- 1 clove garlic, finely chopped
   salt and freshly ground black pepper to taste
- 1 tablespoon lemon juice
- 1/4 cup extra-virgin olive oil
- 6 oz Gorgonzola cheese
- 1 tablespoon finely chopped parsley

Wine: a dry white (Tocai di San Martino della Battaglia)

Clean the fennel by discarding the tough outer leaves, then cut the bulbs in half. Wash under cold running water, drain, and dry well. Cut into 1/8-inch-thick slices. • Trim the carrots, scrape, and cut in julienne strips. • Trim the celery, removing the tough outer leaves and stringy filaments. Cut the stalks in thin slices. • Wash the apple and cut in thin wedges. • Place the vegetables in a salad bowl with the garlic and apple and season with salt, pepper, lemon juice, and 2 tablespoons of olive oil. • Dice the Gorgonzola and heat in a heavy-bottomed saucepan with the remaining oil. Melt slowly over very low heat, stirring continuously. • When it is barely lukewarm and has become creamy, pour it over the vegetables. • Sprinkle with the parsley and serve.

Serves: 6 · Prep: 15 min. · Level: 1

INSALATA DI RUCOLA E MELONE
Cantaloupe and arugula salad

- 1 cantaloupe, weighing about 1 lb
- 12 oz arugula
   juice of 1 lemon
- 1/4 cup extra-virgin olive oil
   salt and freshly ground black pepper to taste

Wine: a dry, aromatic white (Roero Arneis)

Wash the arugula under cold running water, drain, and dry well. Coarsely chop and drizzle with the lemon juice and half the oil. Place in a salad bowl. • Use a melon baller to make round balls of cantaloupe. • Add the cantaloupe to the arugula. Drizzle with the remaining oil and season with salt and pepper. Toss carefully and serve.

Serves: 4 · Prep: 15 min. · Level: 1

INSALATA DI ZUCCHINE TENERE
Raw zucchini with Parmesan cheese

- 14 oz very fresh zucchini
- 6 oz Parmesan cheese, shredded
- 1/4 cup extra-virgin olive oil
   juice of 1 lemon
   salt and freshly ground black pepper to taste

Wine: a dry white (Lugana)

Wash the zucchini, trim the ends, and slice very thinly. • Transfer to a serving dish and sprinkle with the cheese. • Beat the oil, lemon juice, salt, and pepper together in a small bowl. Pour over the zucchini and Parmesan and serve.

Serves: 4 · Prep: 10 min. · Level: 1

INSALATA DI PERE E PEPERONI
Pear and bell pepper salad

- 3 medium bell peppers (preferably mixed colors)
- 2 large ripe pears
   juice of 1 small lemon
- 1 clove garlic, finely chopped (optional)
   salt and freshly ground black pepper to taste
- 1 tablespoon finely chopped parsley
- 1/4 cup extra-virgin olive oil

Wine: a dry, sparkling white (Asti Spumante)

Clean the bell peppers by removing the top, seeds, and core. • Rinse under cold running water, drain, and dry well. Cut in short, thin strips. • Rinse the pears. Peel, core, and cut into match-size sticks. Drizzle with the lemon juice.• Put the pear and bell pepper in a salad bowl, and add the garlic, salt, pepper, parsley, and oil. • Toss gently and serve.

Serves: 4–6 · Prep: 15 min. · Level: 1

INSALATA DI CARCIOFI E UOVA
Artichoke and egg salad

☞ This simple salad makes an excellent, light appetizer. For a richer dish, add a few sliced button mushrooms or diced Mozzarella cheese. Dress with the mayonnaise just before serving.

- 4 artichokes
   juice of 1 lemon
- 1 fennel bulb
- 6 hard-boiled eggs
- 2 tablespoons extra-virgin olive oil
   salt and freshly ground black pepper to taste
- 1 tablespoon white wine vinegar
- 1 quantity Mayonnaise (see recipe, page 16)
- 3 tablespoons heavy cream
   parsley, to garnish

Wine: a dry white (Frascati)

Clean the artichokes by removing the tough outer leaves and trimming the tops and stalks. Leave only the tender leaves near the heart. Cut in half and remove any fuzzy choke. Soak in a bowl of cold water with the lemon juice for 10 minutes. • Remove the tough outer leaves from the fennel bulb. • Wash and dry the fennel hearts and cut in thin strips. Cut the artichokes in thin wedges. • Peel the eggs and cut in quarters. • Put all the vegetables in a bowl and season with the oil, salt, pepper, and vinegar. Toss gently. • Prepare the mayonnaise. Using a hand whisk, mix

Winter salad with Gorgonzola dressing

the mayonnaise with the cream. • Transfer the salad to a bowl, arrange the eggs on top, and dress with the mayonnaise. • Garnish with the parsley and serve.

Serves: 6 · Prep: 30 min. · Level: 1

POMODORO AL TONNO
Stuffed tomatoes with tuna and mayonnaise

8	round ripe tomatoes
	salt and freshly ground black pepper to taste
1¼	quantities Mayonnaise (see recipe page 16)
4	hard-boiled eggs
6	anchovy fillets, finely chopped
¼	cup pickled capers (half finely chopped, half left whole)
12	oz tuna, packed in oil, crumbled with a fork
2	tablespoons finely chopped parsley
16	fresh basil leaves, torn

Wine: a dry white (Pinot Grigio)

Rinse the tomatoes under cold running water. Slice the top off each tomato. Use a teaspoon to remove the pulp, taking care not to break the skin. Place upside down in a colander to drain for 10 minutes. • Sprinkle the insides with salt and pepper. • Prepare the mayonnaise. • In a bowl, squash the egg yolks with a fork and add the anchovies, chopped capers, tuna, and parsley. Stir in almost all the mayonnaise. • Chop the egg whites and add them to the mixture. Season with pepper. • Fill the tomatoes with the mixture. Top each tomato with a teaspoon of mayonnaise. Garnish with capers and basil. • Chill in the refrigerator for 1 hour.

Serves: 4 · Prep: 20 min. + 1 hr to chill · Level: 1

INSALATA DI FONTINA, PERE E NOCI
Fontina cheese with pears and walnuts

8	oz Fontina cheese
2	large pears
6	oz walnuts
1	bunch watercress
	bunch of fresh tender spinach leaves
3	tablespoons extra-virgin olive oil
	juice of 1 small lemon
	salt and freshly ground black pepper to taste
1	clove garlic, finely chopped

Wine: a dry or medium, slightly sparkling red (Freisa)

Dice the Fontina • Wash, peel, and core the pears. Cut into small dice. • Shell the walnuts and coarsely chop. • Wash and dry the watercress. • Wash and dry the spinach leaves and arrange in the bottom of a salad bowl. • Add the pears, cheese, watercress, and walnuts. • Put the oil, lemon juice, salt, pepper, and garlic in a small jar. Screw the top down and shake vigorously for 2–3 minutes. Remove the garlic and drizzle the dressing over the salad. • Toss carefully, without disturbing the spinach leaves, and serve.

Serves: 4–6 · Prep : 20 min. · Level: 1

INSALATA DI LENTICCHIE E ODORI
Lentil and herb salad

4	whole cloves
1	large onion
1	lb lentils, soaked in cold water for 12 hours
4	sprigs fresh thyme
4	bay leaves
4	large carrots
	salt and freshly ground black pepper to taste
¼	cup extra-virgin olive oil
2	tablespoons red wine vinegar
4	cloves garlic, finely chopped
2	tablespoons finely chopped parsley

Wine: a dry red (Barbera d'Alba)

Press the cloves into the onion. Cook the lentils with the onion, thyme, bay leaves, and carrots in a large pot of salted water for about 45 minutes. • Check the carrots during cooking and remove as soon as they are soft (after about 15–20 minutes). • Drain the lentils, shaking well to remove excess moisture, and transfer to a salad bowl. Discard the bay leaves, thyme, and cloves. • Cut the onion in thin slices and dice the carrots and add to the lentils. • While still hot, season with oil, vinegar, salt, and pepper, and mix well. • Add the garlic and parsley and mix again. Set aside for 5 minutes. • Serve warm.

Serves: 4 · Prep: 20 min. + 12 hrs to soak the lentils · Cooking: 45 min. · Level: 1

INSALATA ARANCIATA
Orange salad with olives and leeks

☞ This recipe comes from Sicily where fresh oranges are plentiful. It is usually served as a side dish with roast meats.

3	large juicy oranges
2	medium leeks
3	oz black olives, pitted and coarsely chopped
⅓	cup extra-virgin olive oil
2	tablespoons white wine vinegar
	salt and freshly ground black pepper to taste
2	tablespoons finely chopped parsley

Wine: a dry white (Corvo di Salaparuta)

Use a sharp knife to peel the oranges, removing all the white pith. Cut in thick wheels, discarding any seeds, and cut each wheel in half. • Wash the leeks, remove the tough outer leaves, and slice into thin wheels. • Place the oranges, leeks, and olives in a salad bowl. • Beat the oil, vinegar, salt, and pepper together in bowl and pour over the salad. Sprinkle with the parsley and toss well. • Set aside for 20 minutes before serving.

Serves: 4 · Prep: 20 min. + 20 min. to rest · Level: 1

Stuffed tomatoes with tuna and mayonnaise

INSALATA DI FUNGHI
Mushroom salad

6	oz arugula
12	oz button mushrooms
1	cup shelled and chopped walnuts
1	cup Parmesan cheese, shredded
¼	cup extra-virgin olive oil
	salt and freshly ground white pepper to taste
1	clove garlic, finely chopped
	juice of 1 lemon

Wine: a dry, sparkling white (Prosecco di Valdobbiadene)

Wash the arugula under cold running water, drain, and dry well. Place in the bottom of a salad bowl. • Trim the mushrooms and rinse well in cold running water. Dry with paper towels. • Thinly slice the mushrooms and sprinkle over the arugula. • Sprinkle with the walnuts and Parmesan. • Combine the oil, salt, pepper, garlic, and lemon juice in a bowl and beat vigorously with a fork. Pour over the salad. • Toss gently and serve.

Serves: 4 · Prep: 10 min. · Level: 1

INSALATA DI POLLO E AVOCADO
Chicken and avocado salad

1	chicken, about 2 lb, boiled (to boil see recipe for Chicken and bell pepper salad, this page)
1	cup almonds, shelled
2	avocados
	juice of 1 lemon
1	lettuce heart
2	carrots, cut in julienne strips
1	celery heart, coarsely chopped
	salt and freshly ground black pepper to taste
2	quantities Mayonnaise (see recipe, page 16)
3	tablespoons finely chopped parsley

Wine: a light, dry red (Merlot del Piave)

Remove the skin and bones from the chicken and cut the flesh into small pieces. • Blanch the almonds for 2–3 minutes in boiling water, then drain and peel. • Peel and dice the avocados, and sprinkle with lemon juice. • Wash and dry the lettuce. Line a salad bowl with the leaves. • Arrange the chicken in the center and cover with the avocado, almonds, carrots, and celery. Season with salt and pepper. • Chill in the refrigerator for at least 2 hours. • Prepare the mayonnaise and add the parsley. • Just before serving, spoon the mayonnaise over the chicken and mix carefully.

Serves: 4 · Prep: 20 min. · + 2 hrs to chill · Level: 1

INSALATA DI GAMBERI E FAGIOLI
Shrimp and red kidney beans

2	large heads red radicchio
2	chicory hearts
1	lb cooked red kidney beans (pre-soaked and boiled for 1 hour or one 16 oz can)
20	shrimp, shelled
½	cup extra-virgin olive oil
¼	cup white wine vinegar
	grated zest of ½ a lemon
	salt and freshly ground black pepper to taste
4	scallions, finely chopped
1	celery heart, finely chopped
2	tablespoons finely chopped parsley

Wine: a dry white (Bianco di Capri)

Wash the radicchio and chicory under cold running water, drain, and dry well. • Strip the red leaves from the radicchio and arrange in the bottom of a large salad bowl. • Chop the chicory coarsely and sprinkle over the radicchio. • Drain the beans and arrange over the salad. • Heat 2 tablespoons of the oil in a skillet and sauté the shrimp with a little salt over high heat for 2 minutes. • Add the vinegar and lemon zest and cook for 3–4 minutes more. • Place the remaining oil, salt, pepper, scallions, celery, and parsley in a bowl and mix well with a fork. • Divide the shrimp, 4 in each salad bowl, and pour the oil mixture over the top. • Serve at once.

Serves: 4 · Prep: 30 min. · Cooking: 5 min. · Level: 1

POLLO E PEPERONI SOTT'OLIO
Chicken and bell pepper salad

1	chicken, about 2 lb
1	carrot
1	large onion
1	stalk celery
4	sprigs parsley
1	teaspoon salt
	freshly ground black pepper to taste
6	oz bell peppers, preserved in oil
¾	cup pine nuts
10	oz arugula, washed and dried
¼	cup extra-virgin olive oil
2	tablespoons white vinegar

Wine: a light, dry red (Velletri Rosso)

Place the chicken in a large saucepan with the carrot, onion, celery, and salt. Bring to the boil and simmer over medium-low heat for about 1 hour. When cooked, drain and set the chicken aside to cool. (Reserve, or freeze, the stock for later use.) • Remove the skin and bones from the chicken and cut into small pieces. Place in a salad bowl. • Drain the bell peppers and chop coarsely. Add to the chicken together with the pine nuts and arugula. • Sprinkle with salt and pepper and drizzle with the vinegar and oil. Toss carefully and serve.

Serves: 4 · Prep: 20 · Cooking: 1 hr · Level: 2

INSALATA DI PETTO DI POLLO
Simple chicken and celery salad

2	boned chicken breasts, poached in chicken stock
2	celery hearts
¼	cup extra-virgin olive oil
1	tablespoon lemon juice
	salt and freshly ground white pepper to taste
2	anchovy fillets (optional)

Wine: a dry white (Cortese di Gavi)

Use your fingers to tear the chicken breasts into small pieces and place in a salad bowl. • Rinse the celery hearts, dry well, and chop coarsely. Add to the salad bowl. • Combine the oil, lemon juice, salt, pepper, and anchovy, if using, in a small mixing bowl and beat vigorously with a fork until well blended. • Pour over the chicken and celery. • Toss gently and serve.

Serves: 4 · Prep: 10 min. · Level: 2

INSALATA COTTA
Platter of boiled vegetables

☞ Simple and light, this is an Italian classic. If you don't like mayonnaise, dress with extra-virgin olive oil and a little freshly squeezed lemon juice.

5	fennel bulbs
5	artichokes
6	carrots
6	zucchini
6	potatoes
6	beets
1	lb green beans
1	quantity Mayonnaise (see recipe, page 16)

Wine: a light, dry red (Chianti dei Colli Aretini)

Cook the vegetables whole in a large pot of salted, boiling water until tender. Except for the beets, they can all be cooked together, removing the different vegetables as they are ready. • Peel the potatoes and beets after cooking. • When all the vegetables are cooked, drain well and arrange (either sliced or whole) on a large serving dish, divided by types. • Leave to cool. • Prepare the mayonnaise and serve separately.

Serves: 6 · Prep: 25 min. · Cooking: 30 min. · Level: 1

PINZIMONIO
Raw vegetables with oil, salt, and pepper dip

4	artichokes
	juice of 2 lemons
4	carrots (or 8 baby spring carrots)
4	celery hearts
2	large fennel bulbs
12	scallions
12	radishes
1½	cups extra-virgin olive oil
	salt and freshly ground black pepper to taste

Wine: a light dry white (Verzemino)

Wash all the vegetables thoroughly under cold running water. • Artichokes: Remove all but the pale inner leaves by pulling the outer ones down and snapping them off. Cut off the stem and the top third of the remaining leaves. Cut the artichokes in half lengthwise and scrape the fuzzy choke away with a knife. Cut each artichoke in wedges and soak in a bowl of cold water with the juice of 1 lemon for 15 minutes. • Carrots: Scrub with a brush or peel and soak in a bowl of cold water with the remaining lemon juice for 10 minutes. • Celery: Discard the stringy outer stalks and trim off the leafy tops. Keep the inner white stalks and the heart. • Fennel: Slice off the base, trim away the leafy tops, and discard the blemished outer leaves. Divide into 4 or more wedges, depending on size. • Scallions: Remove the roots and trim the tops. • Radishes: Cut the roots off and trim the tops. • For the dip: Whisk the oil with salt and pepper to taste. Pour into 4 small bowls.

Serves: 4 · Prep: 20 min. · Level: 1

Raw vegetables with oil, salt, and pepper dip

Grilled eggplant, bell pepper, and tomato salad

INSALATA GRIGLIATA
Grilled eggplant, bell pepper, and tomato salad

- 4 bell peppers, mixed colors
- 2 large eggplants
- 8 ripe tomatoes
- 3 cloves garlic, finely chopped
   salt and freshly ground black pepper to taste
- 6 fresh basil leaves, torn
- 1/2 cup extra-virgin olive oil

Wine: a dry white (Soave)

Clean the bell peppers by removing the core and seeds. Cut in strips and cook in the grill pan, turning with a fork until tender. Set aside. • Cut the eggplants in 1/2-inch-thick slices with their skins. Cook in the grill pan until tender. Set aside. • Peel the tomatoes, cut them in half, and cook in the grill pan until lightly cooked. • Place the grilled vegetables in a salad bowl. Sprinkle with the garlic, salt, pepper, basil, and oil. • Serve hot or at room temperature.

Serves 6 · Prep: 10 min. · Cooking: 45 min. · Level: 1

INSALATA DI FARRO
Spelt with tomatoes and Mozzarella

- 3 cups spelt
- 24 cherry tomatoes, cut in half
- 8 oz Mozzarella cheese, diced
- 6 scallions, chopped
- 4 small, tender zucchini, cut in julienne strips
- 10 basil leaves, torn
- 1/3 cup capers
   salt and freshly ground black pepper to taste
- 1/3 cup extra-virgin olive oil
- 8 fresh mint leaves to garnish

Wine: a dry white (Galestro)

Cook the spelt in a pot of boiling, salted water. (This will take about 40 minutes. The grain should be tender but still firm.) • Drain and rinse under cold running water. Drain again and dry well. • Transfer to a salad bowl. • Add the tomatoes, Mozzarella, scallions, zucchini, basil, capers, salt, pepper, and oil. Mix well and set aside for 5–10 minutes before serving. Garnish with mint and serve with extra olive oil on the side.

Serves 4 · Prep: 15 min. · Cooking: 40 min. · Level: 1

INSALATA DI BARBABIETOLE
Red beet salad

☞ In Italy, red beets are available precooked in vacuum packs so this salad is quick to prepare. If you have raw beets, cook them for about 30 minutes in lightly salted, boiling water. Peel and proceed as in the recipe.

- 1 lb cooked red beets
- 2 hard-boiled eggs
- 1/4 cup extra-virgin olive oil
- 1 teaspoon spicy mustard
- 2 tablespoons red wine vinegar
   salt and freshly ground black pepper to taste
- 1 tablespoon finely chopped parsley

Chop the red beets into small cubes. Place in a salad bowl. • Peel the eggs and cut in 1/4-inch slices. Arrange on top of the red beets. • Place the oil, mustard, vinegar, salt, and pepper in a small bowl and beat vigorously with a fork. • Drizzle the dressing over the salad, sprinkle with the parsley, and serve.

Serves: 4–6 · Prep: 10 min. · Level: 1

FAGIOLINI CON MAIONESE
Green beans with mayonnaise

- 1 1/2 lb green beans
- 1 quantity Mayonnaise (see recipe, page 16)

Top and tail the beans and rinse under cold running water. Cook in a pot of salted, boiling water for 15 minutes, or until tender. • Drain the beans and set aside to cool. • Prepare the mayonnaise. • Place the beans in a salad bowl and dress with the mayonnaise.

Serves: 4–6 · Prep: 10 min. · Cooking: 15 min. · Level: 1

INSALATA RUSTICA
Hearty peasant salad

- 2–3 large potatoes
- 8 oz green beans
- 1/4 cup extra-virgin olive oil
   juice of 1 lemon
- 10 fresh basil leaves, coarsely chopped
   salt and freshly ground black pepper to taste
- 8 oz canned kidney beans
- 8 oz canned garbanzo beans
- 2 large salad tomatoes, cut in wedges
- 2 scallions, thinly sliced

Wine: a dry white (Pinot Grigio)

Cook the potatoes in their skins in a large pot of salted, boiling water for about 25 minutes, or until tender. • Clean the green beans and add to the potato pot after the potatoes have been cooking for about 10 minutes. Drain well. Slip the potato skins off and slice. • Cut the green beans in half. • Combine the oil, lemon juice, basil, salt, and pepper in a small bowl and beat vigorously with a fork until well blended. • Arrange the potatoes, green beans, kidney beans, garbanzo beans, and tomatoes on a large serving dish. • Top with the scallions and drizzle with the oil and basil dressing.

Serves: · Prep: 15 min. · Cooking: 25 min. · Level: 1

INSALATA DI RISO CON GAMBERETTI

Rice salad with shrimp

1³/₄	lb shrimp, shelled
	juice of 2 lemons
¹/₃	cup extra-virgin olive oil
1¹/₂	cups short-grain white rice
	salt and freshly ground white pepper to taste
	small bunch arugula, washed and coarsely chopped

Wine: a dry white (Pinot Bianco)

Cook the shrimp in plenty of salted, boiling water and the juice of 1 lemon for 5 minutes. • Drain well and set aside to cool. Place in a bowl with all but 1 tablespoon of the oil. • Cook the rice in plenty of salted, boiling water until tender but still firm, about 15 minutes. • Drain and pass briefly under cold running water to stop the cooking process. Drain again and dry well. Transfer to the bowl with the shrimp. • Season with salt and pepper and toss carefully. Add the remaining lemon juice and oil, and the arugula. Toss again and serve.

Serves: 4 · Prep: 30 min. · Cooking: 15 min. · Level: 1

Rich rice salad

INSALATA DI RISO

Basic rice salad

☞ Rice salads are popular in Italy through the summer months. They are convenient because they can be prepared ahead of time and chilled in the refrigerator until 1 hour before serving.

1¹/₂	cups short-grain white rice
¹/₄	cup extra-virgin olive oil
20	cherry or 6 medium salad tomatoes, chopped
1	cucumber, peeled and diced
1	tablespoon pickled capers, drained
10	green or black olives, pitted and chopped
4	oz cheese (Emmenthal, Fontina, Mozzarella), diced
8	leaves basil, torn

Wine: a dry white (Pinot Grigio)

Cook the rice in plenty of salted, boiling water until tender but still firm, about 15 minutes. • Drain and pass under cold running water for 30 seconds to stop the cooking process. Drain again and dry well. Transfer to a large salad bowl. • Toss with the oil. • Add the other ingredients, toss carefully, and serve.

Serves: 4 · Prep: 15 min. · Cooking: 15 min. · Level: 1

INSALATA DI RISO RICCA

Rich rice salad

1¹/₂	cups short-grain white rice
¹/₄	cup extra-virgin olive oil
2	tablespoons lemon juice
	salt and freshly ground white pepper to taste
4	medium tomatoes, diced
2	celery stalks, sliced
6	pickled gherkins, sliced
8	small white pickled onions, quartered
1	tablespoon pickled capers, drained
10	green olives in brine, pitted and quartered
¹/₄	cup golden raisins, rinsed and drained
4	oz Parmesan cheese, shredded

Wine: a dry white (Bianco di Bolgheri)

Cook the rice in plenty of salted, boiling water until tender but still firm, about 15 minutes. • Drain and pass under cold running water for 30 seconds to stop the cooking process. Drain again and dry well. Transfer to a large salad bowl. • Season with oil, lemon juice, and pepper. • Just before serving, add the remaining ingredients and toss well.

Serves: 4 · Prep: 15 min. · Cooking: 15 · Level: 1

Pasta salad with tomato, garlic, and Mozzarella cheese

INSALATA DI SPIRALI

Spiral pasta with eggs, tomato, tuna, Mozzarella, and mayonnaise

- 1   lb spiral pasta
- 1/4 cup extra-virgin olive oil
- 4   hard-boiled eggs
- 3   large ripe tomatoes
- 8   oz tuna, packed in olive oil
- 4   oz Mozzarella cheese
- 2   tablespoons finely chopped parsley
- 1/3 cup Mayonnaise (see recipe, page 16)
     salt to taste

Wine: a dry, fruity red (Nebbiolo d'Alba)

Cook the pasta in a large pot of boiling, salted water until *al dente*. Drain well. Transfer to a large salad bowl and toss well with half the oil. Set aside to cool. • Peel the eggs and cut into quarters lengthwise. Dice the tomatoes. Break the tuna up by lightly pressing with a fork. Dice the Mozzarella. • When the pasta is cool, add the eggs, tomatoes, tuna, Mozzarella, parsley, remaining oil, and mayonnaise. Sprinkle with salt, toss thoroughly, and serve.

Serves: 4 · Prep: 5 min. · Cooking 12 min. · Level: 1

INSALATA DI PENNE CON POMODORI, AGLIO E MOZZARELLA

Pasta salad with tomato, garlic, and Mozzarella cheese

- 1   lb plain, whole wheat, or colored penne pasta
- 1/4 cup extra-virgin olive oil
- 4   large ripe tomatoes
- 2   cloves garlic, finely chopped
- 2   tablespoons finely chopped parsley
     salt and freshly ground black pepper to taste
- 14 oz Mozzarella cheese
- 6   fresh basil leaves

Wine: a dry white (Colonna)

Cook the penne in a large pot of boiling, salted water until *al dente*. Drain well. Transfer to a large salad bowl and toss vigorously with half the oil. Set aside to cool. • Cut the tomatoes into bite-sized pieces and add to the pasta. Combine the garlic and parsley with the remaining oil and salt and add to the salad bowl. • Just before serving, dice the Mozzarella on a cutting board. Sprinkle the cheese over the salad with the torn basil leaves and freshly ground black pepper. Serve cool.

Serves: 4 · Prep: 10 min. · Cooking: 12 min. · Level: 1

INSALATA DI RISO E FAGIOLI

Rice and bean salad

- 10 oz fresh cranberry or red kidney beans, shelled
- 1   small onion
- 2   bay leaves
     salt and freshly ground black pepper to taste
- 4   oz green beans
- 1 3/4 cups short-grain white rice
- 1/3 cup extra-virgin olive oil

Wine: a dry white (Bianco dei Colli Perugini)

Place the beans in a pot with the onion and bay leaves, and add enough cold water to cover by about 2 inches. • Cover and cook over medium-low heat for about 40 minutes, or until tender. • Season with salt just before removing from heat (do not add the salt earlier as the skins of the beans will become tough). • Top and tail the green beans and cut them into 2–3 pieces. • About 15 minutes before the cranberry beans are ready, bring a large saucepan of salted water to a boil and add the rice and green beans. Cook over medium heat, stirring occasionally, until the rice is tender. • Drain the rice and green beans thoroughly and transfer to a salad bowl. • Drain the cranberry beans. Discard the onion and bay leaves, and add the beans to the rice, stirring well. • Season with oil and pepper. • Serve hot or at room temperature.

Serves: 4 · Prep: 10 min. · Cooking: 40 min · Level: 1

INSALATA DI RISO CON TONNO

Rice salad with tuna

- 1 1/2 cups short-grain white rice
- 1/4 cup extra-virgin olive oil
- 2   tablespoons lemon juice
- 2   hard-boiled egg yolks
- 2   anchovy fillets, finely chopped
- 8   oz tuna, preserved in oil, crumbled with a fork
- 1   tablespoon capers
- 12 pitted mild green olives in brine, thinly sliced
     salt and freshly ground white pepper to taste

Wine: a dry, fruity red (Nebbiolo d'Alba)

Cook the rice in plenty of salted, boiling water until tender, about 15 minutes. • Drain and pass under cold running water for 30 seconds to stop the cooking process. Drain again and dry well. Transfer to a salad bowl. • Pour the oil and lemon juice into a large mixing bowl. Add the egg yolk and use a fork to crush it into the oil and lemon juice. • Add the anchovy and beat until well blended. • Add the tuna, capers, and olives, and season with salt and pepper. • Pour over the rice, toss carefully, and serve.

Serves: 4 · Prep: 15 min. · Cooking: 15 min. · Level: 1

INSALATA DI PASTA AI PEPERONI
Roast bell pepper pasta salad

6 large bell peppers (mixed red and yellow)
1/4 cup extra-virgin olive oil
   salt and freshly ground black pepper to taste
2 tablespoons capers
2 anchovy fillets, crumbled
1 tablespoon raisins, soaked in warm water
1 tablespoon pine nuts
1 lb rigatoni (or similar short pasta)

Wine: a dry rosé (Etna Rosato)

Roast the bell peppers under a broiler until the skins are blistered and black all over. Transfer to a brown paper bag, close tightly and leave for 10–15 minutes (this loosens the skins further and makes peeling easier). When cool enough to handle, peel off the skin with your fingers. • Cut the bell peppers in half and remove the stems and seeds. Cut the soft flesh into bite-sized pieces. Arrange on large shallow dish. • Mix the olive oil, salt, pepper, capers, anchovy, raisins, and pine nuts in a small bowl. Spread this mixture over the bell peppers. Leave for about 30 minutes. • Cook the pasta in a large saucepan of salted boiling water until *al dente*. Drain well and place under cold running water to stop the cooking process. Drain again and dry well. Transfer to a serving dish.

Add the bell pepper mixture and toss well. Serve at room temperature.

Serves: 4 · Prep: 30 min. · Cooking 10 min. · Level: 1

INSALATA DI PASTA CON LE VERDURE
Pasta salad with vegetables

1 lb plain, whole wheat, or colored wheel-shaped pasta
1/3 cup extra-virgin olive oil
1 large eggplant
2 large bell peppers, mixed colors
2 scallions
2 tablespoons pickled capers, drained
1 teaspoon dried oregano
2 tablespoons finely chopped parsley
1/4 cup freshly grated Pecorino cheese
   salt and freshly ground black pepper to taste

Wine: a dry white (Frascati)

Cook the pasta in a large pot of boiling, salted water until *al dente*. Drain thoroughly. Transfer to a large salad bowl and toss vigorously with half the oil. Set aside to cool. • Cut the stalk and hard base off the eggplant and peel. Cut crosswise into slices about 1/2 inch thick. Place the slices under the broiler and cook for about 10 minutes, or until tender. Cut the cooked slices into 3/4-inch squares. • Clean the bell peppers, and cut in quarters lengthwise. Slice each quarter into thin strips. • Slice the white, bottom part of the scallions very finely. • When the pasta is cool, combine with the remaining oil, capers, oregano, parsley, eggplant, bell peppers, and Pecorino and toss well. Sprinkle with salt and pepper and serve.

Serves: 4 · Prep: 15 min. · Cooking 15 min. · Level: 1

INSALATA DI PASTA CON RICOTTA E RUCOLA
Pasta salad with Ricotta and arugula

1 lb fusilli pasta
1/3 cup extra-virgin olive oil
3 cloves garlic, finely chopped
4 ripe tomatoes, seeded and diced
2 oz black olives, pitted
1 1/2 cups fresh Ricotta cheese
2 oz arugula, coarsely chopped
2 oz Ricotta salata cheese, shredded

Wine: a medium white (Malvasia Istriana)

Cook the fusilli in a large pot of salted, boiling water until *al dente*. Drain well and transfer to a salad bowl large enough to hold all the ingredients. Toss vigorously with half the oil. Set aside to cool. • Add the remaining oil, garlic, tomatoes, olives, Ricotta, and arugula to the bowl with the pasta. • Toss well. Sprinkle with the Ricotta salata and chill in the refrigerator for 30 minutes before serving.

Serves: 4 · Prep: 10 min. · Cooking 10 min. + 30 min. to chill · Level: 1

Roast bell pepper pasta salad

DESSERTS

The Italian dessert repertoire is truly vast. The problem in this chapter was choosing what could not possibly be left out! We have tried to include most of the classics, such as Cannoli alla Siciliana, Cassata, and some basic gelato recipes. Where possible, we have given modern versions of these, suited to today's cooks in terms of time and method.

CRESPELLE AL MASCARPONE
Crêpes with Mascarpone, raisins, and rum

1	quantity Basic sweet crêpes (see recipe, page 324)
1²/₃	cups Mascarpone cheese
³/₄	cup granulated sugar
3	tablespoons rum
	grated zest of 1 lemon
¹/₃	cup golden raisins
¹/₄	cup confectioners' sugar

Wine: a light, sweet white (Moscatello di Imperia)

Prepare the crêpes. • Combine the Mascarpone, sugar, rum, and lemon zest in a mixing bowl and beat until soft and creamy. Stir in the golden raisins. • Fill the crêpes with this mixture, fold them over, and dust with confectioners' sugar. Serve immediately.

Serves: 6 · Prep: 20 min. + 2 hrs to rest · Cooking: 20 min. · Level: 2

◁ Raspberry charlotte (see recipe, page 315)
▷ Crêpes with Mascarpone, raisins, and rum

MAKING PASTRY AND VANILLA CREAM

The three recipes on this page are used to make many of the dishes in this final section of the book. A few recipes call for short crust pastry (see recipe, page 49). If liked, when using short crust pastry in sweet dishes, add 2 tablespoons of sugar to the flour.

Making vanilla cream

Vanilla cream is used to fill cakes and pies or as a basic ingredient in many desserts. It can be flavored with chocolate and many other ingredients.

- 5 egg yolks
- 2/3 cup granulated sugar
- 1/3 cup all-purpose flour
- 2 cups whole milk
  pinch of salt
- 4 drops vanilla extract

Makes: about 2 cups · Prep: 10 min. · Cooking: 10 min. · Level: 1

1 Whisk the egg yolks and sugar until pale and creamy.

2 Bring the milk to a boil with the salt and vanilla, then stir it into the egg and sugar.

3 Cook over very low heat, stirring constantly, until the cream thickens.

VARIATIONS

- To make hazelnut or almond cream, add 2 tablespoons of ground hazelnuts or almonds to the cream while still hot.
- To make liqueur cream, add one or two tablespoons of rum, cognac, or other liqueur to the cream while still hot.
- To make lemon cream, boil the very finely grated zest of 1 lemon in the milk and omit the vanilla extract.
- To make chocolate cream, melt 4 oz of grated bittersweet chocolate in the milk.

Making sweet plain pastry

- 2 cups all-purpose flour
- 1/3 cup granulated sugar
  pinch of salt
  grated zest of 1–2 lemons (optional)
- 1/2 cup butter, chopped
- 2 egg yolks

Serves: 4–6 · Prep: 10 min. + 30 min. to rest · Cooking: 30 min. · Level: 1

1 Combine the flour with the sugar and salt in a mixing bowl. Add the lemon zest, if using.

2 Add the butter and work it in with your fingertips until the mixture is fine and crumbly — the same texture as bread crumbs.

3 Transfer to a clean work surface and shape into a mound. Make a well in the center, add the egg yolks, and work them into the flour.

4 Knead the pastry briefly until it is smooth and elastic. Do not knead for too long, as this will make it tough and chewy. Wrap in foil and chill in the refrigerator until ready to use.

This crumbly, melt-in-the-mouth pastry is used as a base in many pies and tarts.

This pastry improves with time. Prepare it a day ahead and chill in the refrigerator.

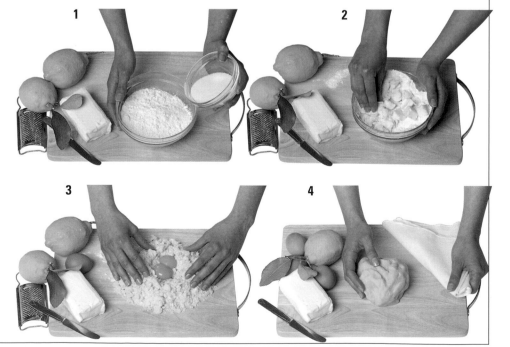

Making puff pastry

Puff pastry is time-consuming to make, but not especially difficult. For a light, flaky pastry, be sure to use high-gluten (strong or bread) flour, which retains more air while the dough is being made, then releases it during cooking. Puff pastry freezes well, so make it in large quantities and freeze in single portions.

4   cups all-purpose flour
    pinch of sugar
    pinch of salt
1   cup (approx) cold water
2   cups butter, at room temperature
1   egg white

1 Place 3 cups of sifted flour on a clean work surface. Make a well in the center. Dissolve the sugar and salt in the water and gradually work in enough of the water to make a smooth dough. Wrap in a clean cloth and chill in the refrigerator for 30 minutes.

1

2 Place the remaining flour on a clean work surface and combine the butter with the egg white. When smooth and well mixed, shape into a rectangle, wrap in a cloth, and chill in the refrigerator for 30 minutes.

3 Remove both doughs from the refrigerator. Unwrap, and place the flour-and-water dough on a lightly floured work surface.

2

3

4

5

6
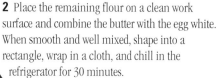

4 Using a well-floured rolling pin, roll the dough out into a large square shape.

5 Place the flour-and-butter mixture in the center of the pastry and fold the edges over it.

6 Roll into a rectangular shape about 1 inch thick. Wrap the dough carefully in a clean cloth and chill in the refrigerator for 20 minutes.

7-8 Roll the dough out into a rectangle about $1/2$ inch thick. Flatten it, using gentle strokes of the rolling-pin. Continue rolling, making sure that the rolling-pin always moves in the same direction, from the center to the edges. Never roll twice in exactly the same place. Fold the dough over on itself to form a slab consisting of three equal folds, then roll it out in the other direction and fold into three again. Refrigerate the dough again for 20 minutes. Repeat the folding, turning, and chilling 4 times. After the last time, the dough can be used in the recipes that follow or frozen for later use.

7
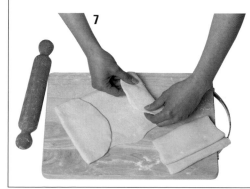

8
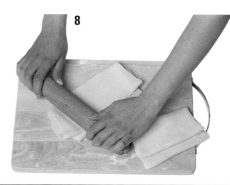

CREMA DI RICOTTA VANIGLIATA
Ricotta vanilla cream

☞ For Chocolate Ricotta cream, add
2 tablespoons of unsweetened cocoa powder.

1¼ lb very fresh Ricotta cheese
1 cup confectioners' sugar
1 teaspoon vanilla extract

Wine: a light, sweet white (Albana di Romagna Dolce)

In a large mixing bowl, combine the Ricotta, confectioners' sugar, and vanilla extract. Mix well to obtain a smooth, light cream. • Chill in the refrigerator for at least 1 hour before serving.

Serves: 4 · Prep: 5 min. + 1 hr to chill · Level: 1

MASCARPONE AL CIOCCOLATO
Chocolate Mascarpone cream

½ quantity Meringues (see recipe, page 345)
¼ cup eggnog
½ cup granulated sugar
14 oz Mascarpone cheese
4 oz bittersweet chocolate, chopped
2½ tablespoons milk

Prepare the meringues. • Beat the eggnog and sugar for 1–2 minutes. • Stir in the Mascarpone and mix well. • Place the milk in a small saucepan with the chocolate over very low heat until the chocolate has melted. Set aside to cool. • Mix the chocolate mixture with half the Mascarpone mixture. • Crumble the meringues in the bottom of 6 ice cream dishes and cover with the plain and chocolate Mascarpone mixtures. • Blend the surfaces of the two mixtures with a knife to give a marbled effect. • Chill in the refrigerator for at least 2 hours before serving.

Serves: 6 · Prep: 30 min. + 2 hrs to chill · Level: 1

CREMA DI AMARETTI
Amaretti cream

zest of 1 lemon, in one piece
1¼ cups milk
4 egg yolks
¾ cup granulated sugar
1 heaped tablespoon cornstarch
4 oz amaretti cookies (macaroons), crushed

Wine: a light, sweet white (Moscato d'Asti Spumante)

Bring the lemon zest and milk to a boil. Discard the lemon zest. • Place the egg yolks and sugar in a heavy-bottomed saucepan and beat until pale and creamy. • Stir the cornstarch and milk into the eggs and sugar and cook over very low heat until the mixture is boiling. • Cook for 3 more minutes, stirring continuously. • Remove from heat and add the amaretti cookies. • Place in a serving bowl and chill in the refrigerator for at least 2 hours before serving.

Serves: 4 · Prep: 15 min. + 2 hrs to chill · Cooking: 20 min. · Level: 1

BIANCOMANGIARE
Lemon cream

½ cup superfine sugar
1 cup all-purpose flour
grated zest of 2 lemons
4¼ cups whole milk

Wine: a sweet dessert wine (Moscato di Noto)

Place the sugar, flour, and zest of 1 lemon in a heavy-bottomed pan. Stir in the milk gradually, making sure that no lumps form. • Place the pan over a medium-low heat and, stirring continuously, bring to the boil. • Boil for 1 minute, then remove from heat. • Pour into a mold and leave to cool. Chill in the refrigerator for at least 2 hours. • Sprinkle with the remaining grated lemon zest and serve.

Serves: 4 · Prep: 15 min. + 2 hrs to chill · Cooking: 10 min. · Level: 1

CREMA CON LIMONCELLO
Limoncello cream with almonds

☞ Limoncello liqueur comes from the breathtakingly beautiful Amalfi coast, south of Naples, where terraces of lemon trees line the azure Mediterranean.

1 quantity Vanilla cream made with 4 egg yolks (see recipe, page 308)
1 cup Limoncello
4 slices candied lemon peel
2 oz flaked almonds

Prepare the vanilla cream. • Stir the Limoncello into the vanilla cream. Place plastic wrap on the surface to prevent a skin forming and set aside to cool. • Spoon into 4 individual bowls and chill for at least 1 hour. • Decorate with the candied peel and almonds and serve.

Serves: 4 · Prep 15 min. + 1 hr to chill · Cooking: 10 min. · Level: 1

CREMA BRUCIATA
Crème brûlée

2 eggs
7 egg yolks
2½ cups sugar
2½ cups light cream
brown sugar for caramelizing

Wine: a light, sweet white (Moscato d'Asti Spumante)

Whisk the eggs and egg yolks with the sugar until pale and creamy. • Warm the cream slightly and beat it into the mixture. • Strain the mixture into 6 ramekins. • Arrange the ramekins in a roasting pan and fill it with 1 to 2 inches of water. Bake in a preheated oven at 350°F for 1 hour. • Leave to cool and then chill

Cooked cream with coffee

in the refrigerator for at least 2 hours. •
Just before serving, sprinkle the ramekins
with brown sugar, place under a hot
broiler and broil until the sugar is
caramelized.

*Serves: 6 · Prep: 10 min. + 2 hrs to chill · Cooking: 1
hr · Level: 2*

PANNA COTTA
Cooked cream

☞ Panna Cotta is delicious served with crushed
fresh berry fruit diluted with a little water and
spooned over the top.

2   cups heavy cream
²⁄₃ cup whole milk
¹⁄₃ cup superfine sugar
2   teaspoons vanilla extract
2–3 tablespoons peach brandy
1   heaped tablespoon unflavored gelatin powder
3¹⁄₂ tablespoons cold water

Wine: a sweet white (Moscato d'Asti)

Heat the cream, milk, sugar, vanilla, and
peach brandy in a saucepan over
medium heat until almost boiling. •
Meanwhile, put the cold water in a bowl
and sprinkle with the gelatin. Leave to
stand for 3 minutes to soften. • Remove
the saucepan from heat and use a whisk
to beat in the gelatin until dissolved. •
Pour the creamy mixture into little molds
or individual glass dishes and set aside to
cool. • Refrigerate for at least 2 hours
before serving.

*Serves: 4 · Prep: 10 min. + 2 hrs to chill · Cooking:
8–10 min. · Level: 1*

PANNA COTTA AL CAFFÉ
Cooked cream with coffee

1   packet unflavored gelatin
²⁄₃ cup strong espresso coffee
5   cups heavy cream
³⁄₄ cup superfine sugar
2   tablespoons confectioners' sugar
     coffee beans to decorate

Wine: a sweet white (Malvasia delle Lipari)

Sprinkle the gelatin over the coffee in a
bowl and leave to soften for 5 minutes. •
Place 4 cups of the cream in a heavy-
bottomed saucepan with the sugar over low
heat and bring to the boil. Remove from
heat. • Stir in the coffee and gelatin and
mix until the gelatin is dissolved. • Pour the
mixture into a 10-inch ring mold. When it
begins to set (not before, otherwise the
gelatin and cream will separate) refrigerate
for at least 5 hours. • Whip the remaining
cream and confectioners' sugar until stiff.
Unmold the cooked cream and decorate
with the coffee beans. • Serve with the
whipped cream in a separate bowl.

*Serves: 6 · Prep: 15 min. + 5 hrs to chill · Cooking:
10 min. · Level: 1*

ZABAIONE
Zabaglione

☞ The Marsala can be replaced with other
strong dessert wines, such as Vin Santo, Port, or
even with sherry.

4   egg yolks
¹⁄₄ cup superfine sugar
¹⁄₂ cup dry Marsala wine

Place the egg yolks and sugar in a saucepan
and whisk until pale and creamy. Gradually
beat in the Marsala, then place the saucepan
in a larger pan of simmering water over very
low heat (or use a double-boiler). Cook,
beating continuously, until the mixture
thickens. The cream must not boil because
it will curdle. If serving cold, cover with
plastic wrap touching the surface to prevent
a skin forming as the mixture cools.

Serves: 4 · Prep: 15 min. · Cooking: 10 min. · Level: 1

BONET
Chocolate egg cream

6   eggs
1   cup superfine sugar
2   tablespoons unsweetened cocoa powder, sifted
2   tablespoons Amaretto di Saronno (almond) liqueur
2   cups milk, very hot
6   crisp amaretti cookies (macaroons), crushed

Wine: a sweet white (Malvasia di Nus)

Whisk the eggs and sugar until pale and
creamy. • Stir in the cocoa and almond
liqueur. • Add the milk gradually, stirring
constantly, then add the amaretti
cookies. • Pour the mixture into a 10-
inch ring mold and place in a roasting
pan half-filled with water. • Bake in a
preheated oven at 350°F for 1 hour. •
Cool for 15 minutes before unmolding
onto a serving dish. Serve at room
temperature (or chill for several hours
in the refrigerator and serve cold).

Serves: 6 · Prep: 30 min. · Cooking: 1 hr · Level: 2

Mascarpone mousse with strawberries

MASCARPONE CON LE FRAGOLE
Mascarpone mousse with strawberries

☞ Rich and creamy Mascarpone cheese is perfect for desserts. If it is not available, use a double or triple cream cheese in its place. Raspberries and other berry fruit also work well in this recipe.

2 tablespoons unflavored gelatin
3 tablespoons cold water
¼ cup strawberry liqueur
1 cup fruity white wine
½ cup confectioners' sugar
1 cup Mascarpone cheese
1¼ cups heavy cream, whipped
2 cups strawberries

Wine: a light, sweet white (Albana di Romagna Dolce)

Sprinkle the gelatin over the water in a small bowl and leave to soften for 5 minutes. Add half this mixture to the liqueur and the other half to the wine. Stir both over medium-low heat to dissolve the gelatin. When cool, refrigerate both mixtures. • Mix the Mascarpone with the liqueur, then fold in the cream and lastly the egg white mixture. • Chill in the refrigerator for at least 4 hours. • Slice the strawberries and arrange in individual dishes (reserving a few to garnish). Pour a little of the jellied wine over the top and fill the dishes with the mousse. Top with the remaining strawberries and serve.

Serves: 4 · Prep: 30 min. + 4 hrs to chill · Level: 1

SOUFFLÉ AL CIOCCOLATO
Chocolate soufflé

☞ Serve this delicious soufflé straight from the oven with a bowl of whipped cream flavored with 1 tablespoon of confectioners' sugar and a few drops of vanilla extract.

8 oz bittersweet chocolate, chopped
¼ cup boiling water
¾ cup granulated sugar
6 eggs, separated
1 tablespoon butter

Melt the chocolate with the water in a heavy-bottomed saucepan over very low heat. Stir continuously with a wooden spoon as it melts. • Remove from heat and stir in the sugar. Add the egg yolks one by one, beating vigorously until they are absorbed into the mixture. • Beat the egg whites until very stiff, then fold them into the chocolate mixture. Butter a 7-inch soufflé and pour the mixture into it. • Bake in a preheated oven at 325°F for 10 minutes, then turn the heat up to 350°F and bake for 20 more minutes.

Serves: 4 · Prep: 30 min. + 4 hrs to chill · Cooking: 15 min. · Level: 1

SPUMONE AL LAMPONE
Raspberry mousse

1 quantity Basic custard (see recipe, page 308)
3 tablespoons Maraschino (cherry liqueur)
1½ cups heavy cream, whipped
4 Meringues (see recipe, page 345), crumbled
2 cups raspberries
¾ cup confectioners' sugar

Wine: a light, sweet white (Moscatello di Imperia)

Prepare the basic custard and set aside to cool. • When cool, stir in the cherry liqueur, followed by the whipped cream and, finally, the meringues. Place in a 10-inch mold and chill in the refrigerator for at least 2 hours. • Place the raspberries (reserving a few to garnish) in a bowl and mash well with a fork. Stir in the confectioners' sugar and chill in the refrigerator for 30 minutes. • Unmold the mousse and turn out onto a serving platter. Spoon the raspberry sauce over the top and serve.

Serves: 6 · Prep: 20 min. + 2 hrs to chill · Level: 1

MOUSSE DI RICOTTA CON ALBICOCCA
Ricotta mousse with apricot sauce

14 oz fresh Ricotta cheese
½ cup confectioners' sugar
4 drops vanilla extract
3 tablespoons eggnog
grated zest of 1 lemon
¾ cup cream, whipped
3 oz white chocolate, grated
1 lb ripe apricots, pitted (or 1 cup apricot jam mixed with ½ cup boiling water)
½ cup brown sugar
juice of ½ lemon

Wine: a light, sweet white (Moscato di Sardegna Spumante)

Combine the Ricotta with the confectioners' sugar and vanilla extract and mix until smooth. • Add the eggnog, lemon zest, and rum and continue to beat until smooth. • Pour the mixture into a mixing bowl and carefully fold in the cream and two-thirds of the chocolate. Chill in the refrigerator for at least 1 hour. • Meanwhile, cook the apricots (reserving 2 to decorate), brown sugar, and lemon juice over medium heat until the mixture thickens. Transfer to a food processor and beat until reduced to a smooth sauce. • Spoon the mousse into individual bowls for serving and pour the apricot sauce over the top. Sprinkle with the remaining chocolate. Slice the reserved apricots and decorate each bowl with a few slices.

Serves: 4–6 · Prep: 20 min. Cooking: 15 min. + 1 hr to chill · Level : 1

CRÈME CARAMEL
Baked caramel custard

- 2 eggs + 3 egg yolks
- 1 cup granulated sugar
- 2²/₃ cups whole milk
- ¹/₈ teaspoon vanilla extract
- 2 tablespoons cold water

Beat all the eggs with ¾ cup of sugar until very pale and creamy. • Heat the milk and vanilla extract to boiling point over medium heat. Remove from heat and pour it into the eggs and sugar. Stir well until the sugar dissolves. • Put the remaining sugar in a small, heavy-bottomed saucepan with the water over very low heat until it turns to caramel. • Pour the caramel into an ovenproof pudding mold. Strain the milk and egg mixture into the same mold. • Place the mold in a roasting pan half-filled with water and bake in a preheated oven at 350°F for 50 minutes. • Leave to cool, then chill for at least 3 hours in the refrigerator before unmolding to serve.

Serves: 4 · Prep: 50 min. + 3 hrs to chill · Cooking: 30 min. · Level: 2

ZUPPA INGLESE
Florentine trifle

☞ Despite its Italian name ("English soup"), the origins of this most Italian of desserts appear to go back to before the 18th century when it became popular with the already-large expatriate English community in Florence.

- 1 quantity Italian sponge cake (see recipe, page 332)
- ¹/₂ quantity Chocolate cream (see recipe, page 308)
- ¹/₂ quantity Vanilla cream (see recipe, page 308)
- ¹/₂ cup Alchermes liqueur
- ¹/₂ cup dark rum
- ¹/₄ cup water
- ¹/₂ cup heavy cream, whipped

Prepare the Italian sponge cake • Prepare the chocolate cream and the vanilla cream (these can be made at the same time; flavoring half of the mixture with chocolate).

Baked caramel custard

Set the vanilla and chocolate creams aside to cool before using. • Mix the Alchermes, rum, and water together in a bowl. • Chop or break the cool sponge into pieces (about 3 x 1 inches). Dip them into the water and liqueur mixture and use one-third of them to line a 2-quart glass bowl or soufflé dish. • Pour the chocolate custard over the top, cover with another layer of dipped sponge and spread the vanilla cream on top. • Finish with the remaining sponge fingers, cover with foil and chill in the refrigerator for about 12 hours. • Just before serving, decorate with the whipped cream and, if liked, a little more grated chocolate.

Serves: 6 · Prep: 30 · + 12 hrs to chill · Level : 2

ZUPPA ALLE CILIEGE
Cherry trifle

- 1 quantity Italian sponge cake (see recipe, page 332)
- ¹/₂ cup granulated sugar
- 3 egg yolks
- ²/₃ cup all-purpose flour
- 3¹/₂ cups warm milk
- 1 cup Maraschino (cherry) liqueur
- ³/₄ cup cherry or plum jelly

Wine: a sweet white (Albana Dolce)

Prepare the Italian sponge cake • Beat the sugar and egg yolks in a heatproof bowl until pale and creamy. • Stir in the flour, adding a little at a time to prevent lumps forming. • Pour in the milk, stirring all the time. • Place the bowl over a saucepan of gently simmering water. Cook, while stirring, until the mixture begins to thicken. • Remove from heat and set aside to cool. • Lightly grease a 10-inch springform cake pan. • Line the bottom with thin slices of sponge cake. Dip a pastry brush in the liqueur and moisten the cake. • Spread with half the custard. Cover with a layer of the jelly, followed by the remaining custard. Cover with a final layer of sponge cake, briefly dipped in the liqueur. Chill in the refrigerator for 3–4 hours. Remove from the springform pan just before serving.

Serves: 4 · Prep: 45 min. + 3–4 hrs to chill · Cooking: 15 min. · Level: 2

Peach and Ricotta pie

ZUCCOTTO
Tuscan ice cream cake

- 1   quantity Italian sponge cake (see recipe, page 332)
- $^1/_2$ cup Cointreau or rum
- $2^1/_4$ cups heavy cream
- $^1/_2$ cup confectioners' sugar
- 5   oz bittersweet chocolate, grated
- 1   oz peeled, finely chopped almonds
- $^1/_4$ cup diced candied orange and citron peel

Wine: a dry, sparkling white (Vernaccia di San Gimignano Spumante)

Cut the sponge cake in half horizontally, then divide it into 8–12 triangular wedges. • Moisten the cake on both sides with Cointreau or rum and use to line a $3^1/_2$ pint mold. • Beat the cream until stiff, adding the sugar when almost ready. Fold in half the chocolate, the almonds, and candied fruit. • Transfer half this mixture to a separate bowl. • Melt the remaining chocolate in a double-boiler (or a bowl over boiling water) and mix gently into one half of the cream. • Spread the white cream over the sponge cake in the mold. Cover with foil and place in the freezer for 10–15 minutes. • Spoon the chocolate cream into the mold, which it should fill completely. • Cover with foil and freeze for at least 4 hours before serving.

Serves: 6–8 min. · Prep: 40 min. · Level: 2

COPPA ALLE CASTAGNE
Candied chestnut cups

- 2   egg yolks
- $^1/_2$ cup superfine sugar
- $^1/_4$ cup all-purpose flour
-     finely grated zest of $^1/_2$ lemon
-     pinch of salt

- 1   cup boiling milk
- 4   slices sponge cake, cut $^1/_2$-inch thick
- $^3/_4$ cup rum
- $^1/_3$ cup crumbled candied chestnuts
- $^1/_2$ cup unsweetened whipped cream
- 4   candied cherries

Wine: a dry, sparkling wine (Asti Spumante Brut)

Place the egg yolks, sugar, flour, lemon peel, and salt in a small saucepan. Mix thoroughly with a wooden spoon until they are pale and creamy. • Add the boiling milk in a very thin stream, stirring continuously. Place over very low heat and continue stirring until the custard thickens; this will take only a few minutes. Do not let it boil or it will curdle. • Remove from heat and leave to cool. Cover with a piece of plastic wrap, resting it on the surface of the custard to prevent a skin forming. • Place a slice of sponge cake in the bottom of four individual serving dishes. Sprinkle with the rum diluted with 2–3 tablespoons of water. • Cover with a thick layer of cool custard. • Sprinkle with the candied chestnuts and top with whipped cream. • Decorate each dish with a candied cherry and serve.

Serves: 4 · Prep: 15 min. · Cooking: 4–5 min. · Level: 1

ZUPPA ALLE PRUGNE
Plum jam trifle

- $^1/_2$ cup superfine sugar
- 3   egg yolks
- $^2/_3$ cup all-purpose flour
- $3^1/_2$ cups warm milk
- 5   oz semisweet chocolate, grated
- 1   quantity Italian sponge cake (see recipe, page 332)
- $^3/_4$ cup Jamaican rum
- $^3/_4$ cup plum jam

Wine: a sweet white (Albana Dolce)

Beat the sugar and egg yolks in a heatproof bowl until they are very pale and creamy. • Sift in the flour, adding a little at a time to prevent lumps forming. • Pour in the milk, stirring all the time. • Place the bowl over a saucepan of gently simmering water or in the top of a double-boiler. Cook, while stirring, until the mixture begins to thicken. • Remove from heat and pour half the mixture into another bowl. • Add the grated chocolate to the custard remaining in the first bowl. Place over the simmering water until the chocolate has melted. Remove from heat. • Lightly grease a 10-inch springform cake pan. • Line the bottom with thin slices of sponge cake. Dip a pastry brush into the rum and moisten the cake. • When the plain custard has cooled, spread it over the cake. Cover with a layer of the jam, followed by the chocolate custard. Cover with a final layer of sponge cake, briefly dipped in the liqueur or rum. Chill in the refrigerator for 4 hours. Turn out onto a plate just before serving.

Serves: 4 · Prep: 45 min. + 4 hrs to chill · Cooking: 15 min. · Level: 1

TORTA DI PESCHE
Peach and Ricotta pie

- $^1/_4$ cup butter
- $^1/_2$ cup sugar
-     pinch of salt
- 2   eggs, separated
- 8   oz Ricotta cheese, sieved
- $^1/_3$ cup cornstarch
-     zest and juice of 1 lemon,
- 2   tablespoons toasted ground almonds
- 3   large yellow peaches, pitted and sliced
- $^1/_4$ cup bread crumbs
- 2   tablespoons confectioners' sugar

Wine: a sweet white (Albana Dolce)

Beat the butter, sugar, and salt together until creamy. • Add the egg yolks one by one, followed by the sieved Ricotta. Mix in the cornstarch, lemon juice and zest, and almonds. • Beat the egg whites until stiff, and fold gently into the mixture. Stir in the peaches and pour the mixture into a greased 8-inch pie pan coated with the bread crumbs. • Bake in a preheated oven at 325°F for about 1 hour. • Dust with the confectioners' sugar and serve warm.

Serves: 4 · Prep: 15 min. · Cooking: 1 hr · Level: 1

Rice cake with pears

ZUPPA DI PESCHE NOCI
Nectarine trifle with cream

- 1 quantity Italian sponge cake (see recipe, page 332)
- 3 lb nectarines (or peaches), stoned
- 1/3 cup granulated sugar
- 1/8 teaspoon vanilla extract
  pinch of ground cinnamon
- 1/4 cup rum
- 2 cups heavy cream, whipped

Prepare the sponge cake. • Chop the nectarines into bite-sized pieces. Put them in a heavy-bottomed saucepan with the sugar, vanilla, and cinnamon and cook over high heat for 5 minutes, or until the fruit is slightly caramelized. • Slice the sponge cake thinly and place a layer in the bottom of a large serving bowl. Brush with rum, cover with a layer of fruit followed by some whipped cream. • Continue in this way until all the ingredients are used up.• Chill in the refrigerator for at least 1 hour before serving.

Serves: 6 · Prep: 30 min. + 1 hr to chill · Cooking: 5–10 min. · Level: 1

TORTA DI RISO CON LE PERE
Rice cake with pears

- 4 cups whole milk
- 1 cup brown sugar
  pinch of salt
- 1 cup short-grain white rice (preferably Italian arborio)
- 3 tablespoons butter
- 4 large pears
  juice of 1/2 lemon
- 2 whole eggs and 2 yolks
- 1/2 cup fine dry bread crumbs

Wine: a light sweet white (Albana di Romagna Dolce)

Bring the milk to the boil. Dissolve half the sugar and salt in the milk. Pour in the rice and cook until the milk has been absorbed. • Remove from heat, stir in the butter and leave to cool. • Peel 3 of the pears, dice them, and cook with the lemon juice and all but 1 tablespoon of the remaining brown sugar until soft. • Add the whole eggs and yolks to the rice one at a time. • Pour half this mixture into the pan and sprinkle with bread crumbs. • Cover with two-thirds of the pear compote, then add another layer of rice followed by the rest of the pear. • Peel the remaining pear, slice it thinly and arrange on top. • Sprinkle with the remaining brown sugar and bake in a preheated oven at 350°F for 45 minutes. Serve warm.

Serves: 6 · Prep: 30 min. · Cooking: 45 min. · Level: 1

CHARLOTTE AI LAMPONI
Raspberry charlotte

- 1 quantity Italian sponge cake (see recipe, page 332)
- 2 1/2 cups heavy cream
- 2 tablespoons confectioners' sugar
- 1 1/2 cups raspberries, chopped
- 6 Meringues (see recipe, page 345), crumbled
- 2/3 cup raspberry syrup
- 2 tablespoons raspberry liqueur

Wine: a light sweet white (Moscato del'Oltrepò Pavese)

Prepare the sponge cake. • Whip the cream, reserving 1/2 cup for decoration. Combine the confectioners' sugar, raspberries (reserve a few to decorate), and 2 crushed meringues; fold in the whipped cream. • Cut the sponge into slices. • Brush a charlotte mold with a little of the syrup and line it with slices of cake. • Pour in half the filling and half the meringues, followed by the rest of the filling and meringues. • Mix the remaining raspberry syrup and liqueur. Dip the remaining sponge cake in this mixture and cover the charlotte with them. Chill in the refrigerator overnight. • Unmold by placing the mold in warm water for a few minutes. • Decorate with the remaining raspberries and cream.

Serves: 6–8 min. · Prep: 40 min. · Level: 1

CHARLOTTE DI MELE
Apple charlotte

- 6 large cooking apples, peeled and cored
- 1/2 cup water
- 1/2 cup granulated sugar
- 1/8 teaspoon vanilla extract
- 10 oz sliced white bread, crusts removed
- 3/4 cup butter, melted
- 1 egg white
- 2 tablespoons white rum
- 1/4 cup confectioners' sugar

Chop the apples and cook in the water until soft. • Add 3 tablespoons of the sugar and the vanilla and continue cooking until the mixture thickens. • Cut the bread slices in half and brush with some of the melted butter. • Line a charlotte mold with some of them, overlapping slightly. • Beat the egg white and remaining sugar and brush over the bread. • Finish with a sprinkling of rum, then pour in the apple purée. • Cover with more bread slices spread with butter and sprinkled with rum. • Bake in a preheated oven at 350°F for 40 minutes. • Sprinkle with confectioners' sugar and serve.

Serves: 8 · Prep: 50 min. · Cooking: 40 min. · Level: 1

Thousand-layer cake

TORTA VENEZIANA
Venetian surprise

☞ This recipe is a Venetian variation on the classic Italian rice cake. The ingredients used reflect the centuries of contact between the city on the lagoon and the Middle East.

- 4¼ cups whole milk
- ½ cup granulated sugar
- 1½ cups Italian short-grain rice
  pinch of salt
- ⅔ cup finely chopped almonds
- ½ cup Muscatel raisins, seeded
- ¼ cup pine nuts
- 10 dates, preferably fresh, finely chopped
- 2 eggs, plus 2 extra egg yolks
- 1 tablespoon rose water
  butter and fine bread crumbs for ring mold

Wine: a sweet, sparkling red (Valpolicella Valpantena Recioto Spumante)

Bring the milk to a boil in a saucepan. • Stir in the sugar, then the rice and salt. Cook for 10 minutes, stirring continuously, then drain off any milk that has not been absorbed and transfer the rice to a bowl. • Stir in the almonds, raisins, pine nuts, dates, whole eggs, and yolks. Mix well, adding the rose water. • Grease a turban ring mold with butter and sprinkle with bread crumbs. • Transfer the rice mixture to the mold. Bake in a preheated oven at 350°F for 30 minutes, or until lightly browned. • Serve warm.

Serves: 6 · Prep: 20 min. · Cooking: 40 min. · Level: 1

BUDINO DI RISO DELL'ARTUSI
Artusi's rice pudding

☞ Food writer Pellegrino Artusi published his famous *The Art of Eating Well* in 1891. Never out of print, it remains Italy's best-selling cookbook. This is one of his classic desserts.

- 1½ cups Italian Arborio (short-grain) rice
- 4 cups whole milk
- ⅛ teaspoon vanilla extract
- ⅓ cup granulated sugar
- ½ cup golden raisins
- 2 tablespoons chopped candied peel
  pinch of salt
- 1 tablespoon butter
- 2 whole eggs and 2 yolks
- 1 cup rum or cognac
  butter and fine bread crumbs for ring mold

Wine: a light, sweet white (Moscato dei Colli Euganei)

Combine the rice, milk, and vanilla in a heavy-bottomed saucepan over medium heat and bring to the boil. • Simmer for 10 minutes, then add the sugar, raisins, peel, salt, and butter. • When the rice is cooked, remove from heat and set aside to cool. • When cool, add the whole eggs and yolks, one at a time, and then the rum. Grease an ovenproof mold with the butter and sprinkle with bread crumbs. Fill with the rice mixture. • Bake in a preheated oven at 350°F for 35 minutes. • Unmold and serve while still warm.

Serves: 6 · Prep: 15 min. · Cooking: 35 min. · Level: 1

RISO AL CIOCCOLATO
Chocolate rice pudding

- 4½ cups whole milk
- ⅓ cup sugar
- 2¼ cups short-grain rice
- 7 oz semisweet chocolate, grated
  pinch of cinnamon
  finely grated zest and juice of 1 orange

Wine: a sweet dessert wine (Moscato di Pantelleria)

Place the milk and sugar in a heavy-bottomed pan over medium-low heat. • When the milk is boiling, add the rice and cook for about 20 minutes, or until the rice is well-cooked and the milk has all been absorbed. • Add three-quarters of the chocolate and the cinnamon and stir until well mixed. • Remove from heat and stir in the orange zest and juice. Pour the rice into a serving bowl and sprinkle with the remaining chocolate. Serve warm.

Serves: 6 · Prep: 5 min. · Cooking: 25 min. · Level: 1

MILLEFOGLIE ALLA CREMA
Thousand-layer cake

- 1 quantity flaky pastry (see recipe, page 308)
- 3 egg yolks
- ¾ cup granulated sugar
- ¼ cup Marsala wine
- ⅔ cup heavy cream
- ½ cup confectioners' sugar
- 2 tablespoons butter
- ⅛ teaspoon vanilla extract
  about 2 tablespoons boiling water
- 1 cup almond shavings

Prepare the flaky pastry. • Roll the pastry out into 4 very thin sheets of equal size. Place on baking sheets, prick well with a fork, and bake in a preheated oven at

380°F for about 20 minutes, or until golden brown. • Beat the egg yolks with the sugar in a saucepan until pale and creamy. • Stir in the Marsala and place the saucepan in a larger pan of simmering water over low heat. Cook, stirring continuously, until the cream is smooth and thick. Remove from heat and pour into a bowl to cool. • Whip the cream and fold it carefully into the cooled egg mixture. • Place 1 sheet of cooled pastry on a large serving platter and cover with one-third of the cream. Cover with another sheet of pastry and layer of cream. Repeat, and cover with the fourth sheet of pastry. • Place the confectioners' sugar in a small bowl with the butter and vanilla extract. Stir in enough boiling water to make a thick glaze. Spread over the top sheet of pastry. Sprinkle with the almonds. • Serve as soon as possible so that the pastry doesn't have time to become soggy.

Serves: 6–8 · Prep: 40 min. · Cooking: 40 min. · Level: 2

BABÀ DI NAPOLI
Neapolitan rum cakes

☞ Serve the babàs as they are or with a bowl of lightly sugared, freshly whipped cream.

1	oz fresh yeast or 2 (¼ oz) packages active dry yeast
¼	cup lukewarm water
5	eggs
3	tablespoons sugar
½	cup extra-virgin olive oil
2	tablespoons butter, melted and cooled,
3	cups all-purpose flour, sifted
	pinch of salt
1⅓	cups granulated sugar
2	cups water
1	lemon, sliced
½	cup rum

Put the yeast in a small bowl with the ½ cup lukewarm water. Stir until dissolved then set aside for 10 minutes. • Beat the eggs and 3 tablespoons of sugar until pale and creamy. • Gradually beat in the oil, butter, and yeast mixture. • Lastly, add the sifted flour and salt. • Knead the dough thoroughly by hand until it is soft and elastic. • Fill the babà molds just under half full, cover, and leave in a warm place to rise. • When the dough has risen to just below the rim of each mold

Neapolitan rum cakes

bake in a preheated oven at 350°F for about 15 minutes. • Meanwhile, boil the 1⅓ cups sugar and the water for 10 minutes, or until the mixture becomes syrupy. • Add the lemon slices and the rum and leave to cool. • When the babàs are cooked, set aside to cool before soaking them in the rum syrup. Leave on a wire rack to drain, then serve.

Serves: 6 · Prep: 20 min. · Cooking: 15 min. · Level: 2

MONTE BIANCO
Mont Blanc

2	cups chestnuts
½	cup unsweetened cocoa powder
⅔	cup confectioners' sugar
2	tablespoons white rum
1¼	cups whipped cream
	candied chestnuts to decorate

Wine: a sweet sparkling white (Asti Spumante)

Place the chestnuts in a saucepan and cover with cold water. Bring to the boil, then cook for about 40 minutes. • Drain and peel the chestnuts, removing the inner skin. Mash them with a potato-masher while still hot, then place in a large bowl and stir in the cocoa powder, sugar, and rum. • Put the purée through a potato-ricer, letting it drop onto the serving dish in a little mound. • Chill in the refrigerator for at least 1 hour. • Cover with whipped cream and decorate with the candied chestnuts just before serving.

Serves: 4–6 · Prep: 40 min. · Cooking: 40 min. · Level: 2

GELATO ALLA CREMA
Basic ice cream

☞ This basic recipe can be flavored with vanilla extract, coffee, chocolate, or many different types of spices, flavorings, and liqueurs to make a wide variety of ice creams. Basic instructions for making ice cream without an ice-cream maker have also been included.

- 4 egg yolks
- 1 scant cup granulated sugar
- 2 cups milk
- 1 cup light or heavy cream

Whisk the egg yolks and sugar until pale and creamy. • Place the milk and cream in a heavy-bottomed saucepan and bring to a boil. Remove from heat and cool slightly. Gradually stir them into the egg and sugar. • Cook this mixture in the top of a double-boiler until it starts to coat the back of a spoon. Make sure it does not come to a boil at any point. • Remove from heat and leave until completely cold. • If you have an ice cream maker, pour the mixture into it and follow the instructions on your machine. • If you don't have an ice cream maker, pour it into a large bowl and place in the freezer. After 3 hours, stir the mixture to make sure it freezes evenly. After another 3 hours, whisk it for a few minutes and return to the freezer for another 3 hours before serving.

Serves: 4 · Prep: 30 min. + 9 hrs to freeze (without ice-cream maker) · Cooking: 15 min. · Level: 2

Chocolate ice cream with raspberries

GELATO AL CIOCCOLATO CON LAMPONI
Chocolate ice-cream with raspberries

- 1 quantity Basic ice cream mixture (see recipe, this page)
- ¼ cup unsweetened cocoa powder
- 1 pint raspberries
  fresh mint leaves for decoration

Prepare the ice cream, dissolving the cocoa powder in the hot milk-and-cream mixture. • When the ice cream is ready, serve in individual ice cream dishes. Garnish each serving with the raspberries and fresh mint leaves.

Serves: 6 · Prep: 30 min. · Freezing: 9 hrs (without ice-cream maker) · Cooking: 15 min. · Level: 2

GELATO AL GIANDUIA
Hazelnut ice-cream

- 1 quantity Basic ice cream mixture (see recipe, this page)
- 2 tablespoons unsweetened cocoa powder
- ¼ cup finely ground hazelnuts
- ½ cup heavy cream
- ¼ cup chocolate chips

Prepare the ice cream, dissolving the cocoa powder and hazelnuts in the hot milk-and-cream mixture. • When the ice cream is ready, serve in individual ice-cream dishes. Whip the cream until stiff and use it to decorate each serving. Sprinkle with the chocolate chips and serve.

Serves: 6 · Prep: 30 min. + 9 hrs to freeze (without ice-cream maker) · Cooking: 15 min. · Level: 2

GELATO AL CROCCANTE
Praline ice-cream

- 1 quantity Basic ice cream mixture (see recipe, this page)
- 3 oz Praline, finely chopped

Prepare the ice cream. • When the ice cream is almost ready, stir in the chopped praline. Transfer to a bowl and place in the freezer until you are ready to serve.

Serves: 6 · Prep: 30 min. + 9 hrs to freeze (without ice-cream maker) · Cooking: 15 min. · Level: 2

GRANITA DI CAFFÈ CON PANNA
Coffee ice with cream

☞ Granita is similar to sorbet, though less well frozen and usually not as sweet. This coffee based recipe is a wonderful way to finish a meal. However, it originally comes from Sicily, where it was served with a brioche at breakfast.

- 1 cup granulated sugar
- ⅔ cup strong black coffee (preferably espresso)
- 2¼ cups water
- 1 cup heavy cream
- 2 tablespoons confectioners' sugar

Dissolve the sugar in the hot, freshly made coffee, then stir in the water. • Transfer the mixture to a large ice tray or bowl and place in the freezer for 3–4 hours. Stir the mixture about once every 20 minutes so that it doesn't become solid but freezes as crystals of ice. • Remove from the freezer about 30 minutes before serving and spoon into individual serving bowls. • Whip the cream with the confectioners' sugar until stiff and spoon in equal portions over the coffee ice.

Serves 6: Prep 10 min + 3–4 hr to cool; Cooking: 10 min. Level:

CREMA DI MELONE ALLA SICILIANA
Sicilian watermelon jelly

5	lb freshly cut watermelon, peeled and seeded
½	cup granulated sugar
½	cup cornstarch
	pinch of ground cinnamon
¼	cup candied pumpkin or candied citron peel, diced
¼	cup bittersweet chocolate, coarsely grated fresh

Wine: a sweet white (Moscato di Siracusa)

Sieve or liquidize the watermelon to obtain about 4½ cups of sieved watermelon flesh. • Place in a large saucepan with the sugar and cornstarch over low heat. Stir frequently until the mixture is boiling, then simmer for 4–5 minutes, stirring continuously. • Remove from heat, add the cinnamon, and set aside to cool. Add the candied pumpkin or citron peel and the chocolate. • Rinse the inside of a 1 quart pudding mold with cold water and fill with the watermelon mixture. • Chill in the refrigerator for several hours, or until completely set. • Turn out onto a serving dish and serve.

Serves: 4. · Prep: 15 min. · Cooking: 7–8 min. · Level: 1

SORBETTO DI LIMONE
Lemon sorbet

☞ Sorbet is a dish of Arabic origin. Originally only lightly frozen, it was served between courses at banquets to refresh the diners' jaded palates. This is the basic recipe with the addition of sliced fresh fruit to round it out and make it more suitable to serve as a dessert.

1	cup granulated sugar
2¼	cups water
	juice of 4 lemons
3	egg whites
	pinch of salt
3	large peaches
4	apricots
2	tablespoons semifine sugar
	juice of 1 lemon

Place the sugar and water in a saucepan and bring to the boil. Boil for 3–4 minutes, then set aside to cool. • Stir in the lemon juice when the mixture is completely cool. • Whisk the egg whites and salt until very stiff in a freezerproof bowl. • Gradually stir in the lemon syrup and place in the freezer. Stir every 30 minutes to make sure it freezes evenly. After three hours whisk the mixture, then return to the freezer for another 30 minutes. Serve in individual dishes together with the thinly sliced fruit sprinkled with sugar and lemon juice.

Serves: 6 · Prep: 20 min. + 3½ hrs to chill · Cooking: 5 min. · Level: 1

GELATO ALLA FRAGOLA
Strawberry ice-cream

☞ This is a basic recipe for fruit-flavored ice cream. For different flavors, replace the strawberries with the same quantity of other types of fruit. They should all be puréed before adding to the ice cream mixture. Classic fruit flavored ice creams include apricot, pineapple, raspberry, kiwi, cantaloupe, peach, cherry, mandarin, and banana.

2	cups whole milk
1	cup light cream
1	scant cup granulated sugar
12	oz strawberries + about 12 extra, cut in half, to garnish

Place the milk and cream in a heavy-bottomed saucepan and bring to the boil. Boil for about 4 minutes. • Dissolve the sugar in this mixture and set aside to cool. • Purée the strawberries, and stir them into the milk and cream mixture. • Follow the instructions for basic ice cream on the previous page to finish. • Serve the ice cream in individual ice cream dishes garnished with the extra fruit.

Serves: 4 · Prep: 20 min. · Cooking: 5 min. · Level: 1

Lemon sorbet with peaches and apricots

Strawberries and cantaloupe with port

and mint leaves and chill in the refrigerator for at least 2 hours. • Add the crushed ice just before serving.

Serves: 6 · Prep: 20 min. + 2 hrs to chill · Level: 1

MACEDONIA DELIZIA
Fresh fruit salad with vanilla cream

1	quantity Vanilla cream (see recipe, page 308)
3	bananas
	juice and finely grated zest of 1 lemon
½	medium pineapple
3	oranges
3	tangerines
½	cup brown sugar

Wine: a sweet dessert white (Albana di Romagna Dolce)

Prepare the vanilla cream. • Slice the bananas and sprinkle with the lemon juice and zest. • Peel the pineapple and cut into bite-sized pieces. • Peel the oranges and tangerines, removing all the white inner membranes. • Drain the bananas and mix with the rest of the fruit. Place in a large serving bowl. • Pour the vanilla cream into another serving bowl. Place the two bowls on the table so that your guests can help themselves to the fruit and cream as liked.

Serves: 6 · Prep: 20 min. · Cooking: 10 min. · Level: 1

CILIEGE AL VINO ROSSO
Cherries in red wine

2	lb cherries, pitted
1¼	cups granulated sugar
2	cups dry, full-bodied, dry red wine
1	cinnamon stick
2	tablespoons orange zest, cut into short, thin strips
¼	cup red currant jelly

Wine: a sweet, lightly sparkling red (Brachetto d'Acqui)

Place the cherries, sugar, wine, cinnamon, and orange strips together in a saucepan. Cook gently, uncovered, over low heat for 25–30 minutes. Stir very carefully from time to time so as not to damage the cherries. • Use a slotted spoon to take the cherries out of the liquid, letting them drain briefly as you do so, and transfer them to a serving dish. • Remove and discard the cinnamon stick. • Add the red currant jelly to the cooking liquid and reduce over medium heat. Then pour over the cherries. • Serve warm with vanilla ice cream, or cold with freshly whipped cream.

Serves: 6 · Prep: 10 min. · Cooking: 30 min. · Level: 1

ALBICOCCHE AL FORNO
Baked cinnamon apricots

1	cup white wine
½	cup brown sugar
1	teaspoon ground cinnamon
12	large apricots
1	tablespoon butter, to grease baking dish
12	amaretti cookies (macaroons), crushed
¼	cup pine nuts
¼	cup raisins

Wine: a sweet dessert white (Albana di Romagna Dolce)

Combine the wine, brown sugar, and cinnamon in a saucepan and cook over high heat for 15 minutes, or until the mixture becomes syrupy. • Rinse the apricots under cold running water and dry with paper towels. Cut them in half and remove the pits. Use a teaspoon to scoop out a little of the flesh. Chop this finely. • Arrange the apricot halves in a lightly buttered baking dish just large enough to hold them all snugly. • Drizzle the syrup over the top, and sprinkle with the amaretti cookies, chopped apricot, and pine nuts, and raisins. • Bake in a preheated 400°F for about 15 minutes. Serve hot or warm.

Serves: 6 · Prep: 30 min. · Cooking: 30 min. · Level: 1

FRAGOLE E MELONE AL PORTO
Strawberries and cantaloupe with port

☞ Serve this refreshing dessert to finish a meal on hot summer evenings.

2	small cantaloupes
1	cup wild strawberries
24	large strawberries
2	cups white port
3	cups sweet sparkling white wine
	juice of 1 lemon
¼	cup superfine sugar
	fresh mint leaves
½	cup crushed ice

Wine: a sweet or dry sparkling white (Asti Spumante)

Scoop the flesh out of the cantaloupes using a melon-baller. • Place the balls of cantaloupe in a salad bowl with the wild strawberries. Slice the large strawberries in half and add to the bowl. • Add the port, sparkling wine, lemon juice, sugar,

SFORMATO DI FRAGOLE
Strawberry mold

- 3 cups strawberries
- 1 cup sugar
- ⅛ teaspoon vanilla extract
- ¼ cup orange-flavored liqueur
- 2 cups whole milk
- 3 egg yolks and 1 whole egg
- 2 tablespoons potato flour
- ¼ cup strawberry jam
- 2 tablespoons water

Wine: a sweet, sparkling white (Asti Spumante)

Clean the strawberries and rinse well under cold running water. Dry well and chop. • Place in a bowl and sprinkle with ¼ cup of the sugar. Drizzle with the vanilla and 3 tablespoons of the orange liqueur. • Heat the milk with the remaining sugar and bring to the boil. • Place the whole egg and yolks in a bowl with the potato flour and mix well. Gradually pour in the hot milk, stirring continuously. • Add the strawberries and mix well. Butter a 10-inch ring mold and fill with the mixture. Bake in a preheated oven at 350°F for about 1 hour. Set aside to cool. • Just before serving, place the jam in a small, heavy-bottomed pan over low heat with the remaining liqueur and the water. Cook for 5 minutes, then pour over the mold and serve.

Serves: 6 · Prep: 20 min. · Cooking: 15 min. · Level: 2

PESCHE AL FORNO
Stuffed baked peaches

- 4 large ripe yellow peaches
- 20 amaretti cookies (macaroons), crushed
- ⅔ cup granulated sugar
- 2 tablespoons butter
- ¼ cup dark rum

Wine: a sweet dessert white (Colli Albani Dolce)

Rinse the peaches under cold running water and dry with paper towels. Cut them in half and remove the pits. Use a teaspoon to make a hollow about the size of a golf ball in each peach half. Place the peach flesh in a bowl and add three-quarters of the amaretti cookies and all but ¼ cup of sugar. Mix well

Stuffed baked peaches

and use to fill the peaches. • Use the butter to grease a baking pan large enough to hold all the peach halves snugly in a single layer. Arrange the peaches in the pan. • Drizzle with the rum and sprinkle with the remaining amaretti cookies and sugar. • Bake in a preheated oven at 350°F for 30 minutes. • Serve hot or at room temperature.

Serves: 4 · Prep: 20 min. · Cooking: 30 min. · Level: 1

ARANCE AL RUM
Oranges with rum

- 6 oranges
- ½ cup dark rum
- ⅓ cup confectioners' sugar
- ⅛ teaspoon vanilla extract

Peel the oranges, removing the white parts. Slice thinly and then cut each slice in half. • Place in a serving bowl and add the rum, confectioners' sugar, and vanilla. • Mix well and chill in the refrigerator for 4 hours before serving.

Serves: 6 · Prep: 10 min. + 4 hrs to chill · Level: 1

MELE E FICHI AL FORNO
Apple and fig bake

- 12 large figs
- 6 Golden Delicious apples
- ½ cup sugar
- 6 egg yolks
- 10 amaretti cookies (macaroons), crumbled
- 2 tablespoons dark rum
- 3 egg whites
  pinch of salt

Rinse the figs and apples and dry well. Clean the figs and peel and core the apples. Cut into segments and arrange on the baking tray lined with nonstick baking paper. Sprinkle with half the sugar and place the baking tray under the broiler for about 10 minutes. Meanwhile, whisk together the egg yolks, the remaining sugar, amaretti cookies, and rum. Beat the egg whites with the salt and fold them in. Arrange the figs and apples in a buttered ovenproof dish and pour the egg mixture over the top. Bake in a preheated 350°F for about 30 minutes. Serve warm.

Serves: 8 · Prep: 30 min. · Cooking: 40 min. · Level: 1

Pears in red wine

Peel the pears, cut them in half, and remove the cores. Drizzle with half the lemon juice to stop the flesh from discoloring. • Place the pears in a saucepan with enough cold water to cover. Add half the sugar, half the remaining lemon juice, and the cinnamon stick. Cook for about 15 minutes, or until tender but still firm. Remove the pears from heat and leave to cool in the syrup. • Meanwhile, place the raspberries (reserving a few as a garnish), remaining sugar, $^1/_4$ cup water, wine, and remaining lemon juice over low heat and cook until the mixture starts to thicken. • Remove from heat and purée in a blender, then push through a fine-meshed sieve to remove the seeds. • Drain the pears thoroughly and slice. Place in individual serving dishes and pour the raspberry sauce over the top. Garnish with the reserved raspberries, sprinkle with the confectioners' sugar, and serve.

Serves: 6 · Prep: 30 min. · Cooking: 1 hr · Level: 2

PESCHE AL VINO ROSSO DOLCE
Peaches in red wine

- 2   lb peaches
- $^1/_4$ cup honey
- 1   cup sweet red wine

Wine: a sweet rosé (Malvasia di Casorzo d'Asti Rosato)

Peel the peaches, remove the pits, and slice thinly. Place in a serving dish. • Dissolve the honey in the wine over very low heat. Pour the wine over the peaches and mix carefully. • Chill in the refrigerator for at least 2 hours before serving.

Serves: 6 · Prep: 20 min. · Level: 1

FRUTTA FRESCA CON FONDUTA AL CIOCCOLATO
Fresh fruit chocolate fondue

- 2   lb fresh fruit (grapes, figs, strawberries, bananas, apples, apricots, plums, peaches, etc)
- 2   cups water (optional)
      juice of 1 lemon (optional)
- 1   lb bittersweet chocolate, chopped
- 1   cup light cream
- $^1/_4$ cup butter

PERE AL BAROLO
Pears in red wine

- 4   large, firm cooking pears
- 1¼   cups brown sugar
- 2   cups dry, full-bodied red wine (preferably Barolo)
- 3   cloves
- 2   pieces lemon zest
- 1   cinnamon stick

Wine: a sweet rosé (Malvasia di Casorzo d'Asti Rosato)

Peel the pears carefully, leaving them whole with the stalk still attached. • Transfer to a deep, fireproof casserole into which they fit snugly, standing upright, stalks uppermost. Sprinkle with half the sugar, then pour in the wine. Add the cloves, lemon zest and cinnamon. • Place in a preheated oven at 350°F and cook for about 1 hour, or until the pears are tender. • Lift the pears carefully out of the wine and place in individual glass dishes. • Reduce the cooking liquid over medium heat until it has thickened to a pouring syrup. Discard the cloves, lemon zest, and cinnamon and pour the syrup over the pears. • Serve at room temperature.

Serves: 4 · Prep: 10 min. · Cooking: 1¼ hrs · Level: 1

ALBICOCCHE ALLO ZABAIONE
Apricots with zabaglione

- 2   cups sweet white wine
- ½   cup brown sugar

- 1   cinnamon stick
- $^1/_2$ cup cold water
- 6   cling peaches, peeled
- 1   quantity Zabaglione (see recipe, page 311)

Wine: a sweet white

Place the wine, sugar, cinnamon stick, and water in a large, heavy-bottomed saucepan and bring to a boil. Boil for 5 minutes. • When the sugar has dissolved, immerse the peaches in this liquid and cook until tender but still firm. Remove from the saucepan and set aside to cool. • Meanwhile, reduce the wine and sugar liquid over high heat until it turns to syrup. Set aside to cool. • Place the peaches in a large serving bowl and pour the syrup over the top. Chill in the refrigerator. • Prepare the zabaglione. When cool spoon it over the peaches. Decorate each dish with ground pistachio nuts and serve.

Serves: 6 · Preparation: 40 min. · Cooking: 30 min. · Level: 2

PERE CON SALSA DI LAMPONI
Cooked pears with raspberry sauce

- 6   large pears
      juice of 2 lemons
- 2   cups sugar
- 1   cinnamon stick
- 1½   cups fresh raspberries (or blueberries)
- ¼   cup water
- ½   cup sweet dessert wine
- ½   cup confectioners' sugar

¼ cup superfine sugar
½ cup each chopped toasted almonds and hazelnuts
½ cup shredded coconut

Rinse and dry the fruit. Cut the larger pieces into bite-sized chunks. • If using apple, pear, or banana, immerse the chunks in water and lemon juice for a few seconds to prevent the flesh from browning, then dry carefully. • Arrange the fruit in a serving dish. • Melt the chocolate in the top of a double-boiler over hot water. Dilute with the cream, add the butter and sugar and mix well. • Pour the chocolate mixture into a fondue bowl and keep warm over the flame. • Place bowls filled with the almonds, hazelnuts, and coconut on the table, so that your guests can dip pieces of fruit into them, after dipping them in the chocolate sauce.

Serves: 8 · Prep: 15 min. · Cooking: 15 min. · Level: 2

FRAGOLE ALLA CARDINALE
Cardinals' strawberry dessert

☞ Many Italian dishes with red toppings are referred to as "*alla cardinale.*" The reference is clearly to the churchmen's red hats.

1¼ lb fresh strawberries
¾ lb fresh raspberries
⅓ cup confectioners' sugar
½ cup almonds, finely chopped

Clean the strawberries and place in 6 individual serving bowls. Crush the raspberries with a fork in a mixing bowl and stir in the confectioners' sugar. Pour the raspberries over the strawberries and sprinkle with the almonds. Chill for 30 minutes before serving.

Serves: 6 · Prep: 10 min. + 30 min. to chill · Level: 1

FRAGOLE AL VINO BIANCO
Strawberries in white wine

☞ Healthy and delicious on their own, these strawberries are excellent when served with vanilla ice cream. Try replacing the wine with the same amount of lemon juice.

1¼ lb fresh strawberries
⅓ cup superfine sugar
½ cup dry white wine

Wine: a light, dry white (Frascati)

Clean the strawberries and rinse under cold running water. Drain well, then pat dry with paper towels. • Transfer the strawberries to a serving dish. Sprinkle with the sugar and drizzle with the wine. • Place in the refrigerator to rest for at least 1 hour before serving.

Serves: 4 · Prep: 5 min. + 1 hr to rest · Level: 1

FRAGOLE AL CIOCCOLATO
Strawberry delight

32 large strawberries, with stems
4 oz bittersweet chocolate
4 oz white chocolate
1 cup sweet white wine

Rinse the strawberries under cold running water and dry carefully with paper towels. • Melt the two types of chocolate in separate pans in the top of a double-boiler. • Dip the strawberries in the white wine and dry with paper towels. • Grasp a strawberry by its stalk, and dip one half of it in the dark chocolate then the other half in the white chocolate. Place on nonstick baking paper until the chocolate is solid. Repeat until all the strawberries are covered in chocolate.

Serves: 6 · Prep: 20 min. + time for the chocolate to cool · Level: 1

FRUTTA ESTIVA IN PADELLA
Sautéed summer fruit

3 large peaches
6 large apricots
4 oz white grapes
3 tablespoons butter
½ cup sugar

1 cup dry white wine
4 oz strawberries
1 cup heavy cream
½ cup toasted almonds, chopped

Dice the peaches and apricots and halve the grapes, removing the seeds. • Place the butter in a small skillet and sauté the fruit. Add the sugar and wine and cook for about 10 minutes, then set aside to cool. • When cold, mix in the strawberries, divide the mixture among the serving-dishes and serve garnished with lightly whipped cream and a sprinkling of chopped, toasted hazelnuts.

Serves: 6 · Prep: 20 min · Cooking: 10 min. · Level: 1

GRIGLIATA DI PRUGNE
Broiled plums with vanilla cream

1 quantity Vanilla cream (see recipe, page 308)
12 large black plums
6 oz amaretti cookies (macaroons), crumbled
¾ cup sliced almonds, toasted
¼ cup sugar

Prepare the vanilla cream. • Rinse the plums and dry well. Cut them in half and pit. • Combine the amaretti cookies with the almonds and sugar. • Place the plums in an ovenproof dish with the cut surfaces upwards. Spoon the vanilla cream over the top and sprinkle with the amaretti mixture. • Place under a very hot broiler for about 10 minutes before serving.

Serves: 6 · Prep: 30 min. · Cooking: 10 min. · Level: 2

Strawberries in white wine

Basic crêpes

until the pumpkin is just tender. Drain well and wrap in a cloth to absorb any excess moisture. • Place in a bowl and add the raisins, sugar, lemon zest, and salt. Sift in the flour and baking powder and mix thoroughly with a wooden spoon. • Scoop out spoonfuls of the mixture and shape them into fritters about the size of a flattened walnut. • Heat the oil to very hot in a large skillet. Fry the fritters in batches, removing them with a slotted spoon when golden brown all over. Drain on paper towels. • Sprinkle with sugar and serve hot.

Serves: 6 · Prep: 30 min. · Cooking: 35 min. · Level: 2

CRESPELLE DI MARRONI CON CIOCCOLATO
Chestnut crêpes with cream

- 1   cup chestnut flour, sifted
- 1   cup all-purpose flour, sifted
- 3   eggs
- 1   tablespoon sugar
- 3   tablespoons butter, melted
- 2   cups milk
- 1   cup heavy cream
- 2   tablespoons confectioners' sugar,
- 1   cup chocolate chips

Combine the two flours in a mixing bowl. Stir in the eggs, sugar, and butter. • Add the milk gradually, beating the mixture with a whisk to prevent lumps from forming. Set the batter aside for 2 hours to rest. • Cook the crêpes following the method on page 185. • Whip the cream with the confectioners' sugar and mix the chocolate chips in gently. Spread the cream on the crêpes, roll them loosely, and serve.

Serves: 4 · Prep: 20 min. + 2 hrs to rest the crêpes · Cooking: 20 min. · Level: 2

FETTE DI MELE FRITTE
Sliced apple fritters

- 2   eggs
- 1   cup all-purpose flour
- ½   cup dry white wine
- 2   tablespoons extra-virgin olive oil
       pinch of salt
- 6   cooking apples
       juice of 1 lemon
- 2   cups oil, for frying
- 1   cup confectioners' sugar

Wine: a sweet white (Cesanese del Piglio Dolce)

CRESPELLE CON I FICHI
Crêpes with figs

- 1   quantity Crêpes (see recipe, page 185)
- 12 black figs
- 2   tablespoons dark rum
- ⅓   cup confectioners' sugar
- 1   cup heavy cream

Prepare the batter for the crêpes. • Rinse the figs and dry well. Cut each fig into 4 pieces. • Place the figs in a skillet and sprinkle with the rum and 2 tablespoons of confectioners' sugar. Cover and cook over low heat for 10 minutes. Remove from heat. • Whip the cream. • Cook the crêpes, spreading some of the fig mixture over each one. Roll them up loosely. • Sprinkle with the remaining confectioners' sugar and serve with the whipped cream passed separately.

Serves: 4 · Prep: 20 min. + 2 hrs to rest the batter · Cooking: 20 min. · Level: 2

CRESPELLE CON LA FRUTTA
Crêpes with fresh fruit

- 1   quantity Crêpes (see recipe, page 185)
- 1   apple
- 1   pear
- 1   banana
- 1   tablespoon sugar
       juice of 1 lemon
- ⅛   teaspoon vanilla extract
- 1   cup confectioners' sugar

Prepare the batter for the crêpes. • Peel the fruit, cut it into thin slices and leave to macerate for 1 hour in the sugar and lemon juice. • When the batter is rested, drain the fruit thoroughly. Stir the vanilla into the batter, then pour the batter into the bowl with the fruit. • Cook the crêpes in the usual way and serve hot, sprinkled with confectioners' sugar.

Serves: 4 · Prep: 20 min. + 2 hrs to rest the batter · Cooking: 15 min. · Level: 2

FRITTELLE DI ZUCCA
Sweet pumpkin fritters

- 6   oz seedless golden raisins
- 1   cup sweet Marsala wine
- 1   pumpkin, about 2½ lb
- ½   cup granulated sugar
       grated zest of 1 lemon
       pinch of salt
- 1¼ cups all-purpose flour
- 1   tablespoon baking powder
- 1   cup oil, for frying

Wine: a sweet white (Malvasia dei Colli Piacentini Dolce)

Soak the raisins in the Marsala for 10 minutes, then drain. • Cut the pumpkin in half and remove the seeds and fibrous matter. Peel, then chop the flesh into large pieces. • Place in a saucepan with enough cold water to cover. Cover the pan and cook over medium heat for about 15 minutes, or

Separate the eggs and beat the yolks in a bowl until smooth. • Add the flour, wine, extra-virgin olive oil, and salt, and mix to obtain a smooth, fairly liquid batter. Cover the bowl and set aside to rest for 1 hour. • Peel and core the apples, leaving them whole. Slice crosswise and drizzle with the lemon juice to stop them turning black. • Heat enough oil to cover the bottom of a large skillet until very hot. • Beat the egg whites until stiff. Stir them into the batter. • Dip the apple slices into the batter and fry in batches until light golden brown on both sides. Don't put too many slices in the pan at once or they will stick together. Repeat until all the apples are used up. Drain the fritters on paper towels. • Sprinkle with confectioners' sugar and serve immediately.

Serves 4–6 · Prep: 10 min. + 1 hr to rest · Cooking: 15 min. · Level: 1

FRITTELLE DI SAN GIUSEPPE
St. Joseph's day fritters

☞ Many Italian foods are associated with festivals. These delicious lemon and egg fritters are served on March 19, St. Joseph's feast day.

1   cup water
    pinch of salt
½   cup butter
¼   cup superfine sugar
    finely grated zest of 1 lemon
2   cups all-purpose flour
8   eggs
1–2 cups olive oil, for frying
1   cup confectioners sugar

Wine: a sweet white (Orvieto Dolce)

Put the water, salt, butter, sugar, and lemon zest in a heavy-bottomed saucepan and bring to the boil. • Add the flour and stir with a wooden spoon. Continue cooking, stirring continuously, until the dough is thick and comes away from the sides of the saucepan. Remove from heat and set aside to cool. • When cool, stir in the eggs one at a time. The dough should be soft, but not runny. • Set aside to rest for at least 1 hour. • Heat the oil in a large skillet until very hot. • Drop teaspoonfuls of the dough into the hot oil

and fry, in batches, until they are plump and golden brown. • Remove the fritters from the oil with a slotted spoon and drain on paper towels. Keep warm. Repeat until all the dough has been used up. • Sprinkle with confectioners' sugar and serve hot.

Serves 4–6 · Prep: 25 min. + 1 hr to rest · Cooking: 25 min. · Level: 1

FRITTELLE DI RISO
Rice fritters

2½   cups white rice
2   cups water
4   cups milk
1½   cups sugar
     grated zest of 1 lemon (or orange)
     pinch of salt
3   egg yolks
2   tablespoons all-purpose flour
⅛   teaspoon vanilla extract
2   cups oil, for frying
1   cup confectioners' sugar

Wine: a sweet or dry dessert wine (Vin Santo)

Place the rice in a saucepan with the water, milk, sugar, lemon zest, and salt and cook over low heat until all the liquid has been absorbed. Set aside to settle for 12 hours or overnight. • Stir in the egg yolks one at a time, mixing well after each addition. Add the flour and vanilla. • Shape the mixture into fritters about the size of a walnut. • Heat the oil in a large skillet until very hot.

Fry the fritters in batches until golden brown all over. Scoop them out of the oil with a slotted spoon, roll them in sugar, and set aside to drain on paper towels. • Serve hot or at room temperature.

Serve 8 · Prep: 20 min. · Cooking: 1 hr · Level: 2

FRITTELLE DOLCI DI RICOTTA
Sweet Ricotta fritters

14   oz Ricotta cheese
3   eggs
⅓   cup granulated sugar
     grated zest of 1 orange
     pinch of salt
     pinch of baking soda
¼   cup raisins, soaked in rum overnight
1½   cups all-purpose flour
2   cups oil, for frying
¾   cup confectioners' sugar

Wine: a dry sparkling white (Prosecco di Conegliano)

Sieve the Ricotta into a mixing bowl. • Add the eggs, sugar, orange zest, salt, baking soda, and drained raisins. Lastly, stir in the sifted flour. Mix until smooth. Leave to rest for 1 hour. • Heat the oil to very hot in a large skillet. Scoop out tablespoonfuls of the batter and fry in batches of 6–8 until golden brown. Drain on paper towels. Sprinkle with the confectioners' sugar and serve hot.

Serves: 6 · Prep: 15 min. + 1 hr to rest · Cooking: 20 min. · Level: 1

Sweet Ricotta fritters

CAKES, PIES & COOKIES

Every town and village in Italy has its own special cakes and cookies, usually served on feast days or religious holidays. Some have become famous. They are produced industrially and exported all over Italy and abroad. Others are well-kept secrets, which can only be tasted by visiting their place of origin. We have included most of the better-known ones in this chapter, alongside some local ones.

RICCIARELLI
Siennese marzipan cookies

1³/₄   cups peeled whole almonds
1   cup granulated sugar
1¹/₄   cups confectioners' sugar + extra for dusting
¹/₄   cup finely chopped candied orange peel
¹/₈   teaspoon almond extract
1   egg white, stiffly beaten

Wine: a sweet or dry dessert wine (Vin Santo)

Spread the almonds on a cookie sheet and bake in a preheated oven at 400°F for 3–4 minutes. Transfer to a food processor and chop finely. • Place in a mixing bowl and stir in both sugars, the orange peel, and almond extract. Mix well, then carefully fold in the egg white. • Shape the mixture into diamond shapes and place on parchment paper, trimming off the excess. • Place on cookie sheets and refrigerate for about 10 hours. • Bake in a preheated oven at 300°F for about 1 hour, reducing the heat if they begin to brown. These cookies should be pale and soft when cooked. • Remove from the oven and dust generously with the extra confectioners' sugar. • Serve when cool.

Serves: 4–6 · Prep: 25 min. + 10 hrs to rest the dough · Cooking: 1 hr · Level: 2

◀ Sicilian cheesecake (see recipe page 335)
▶ Siennese marzipan cookies

Rice cake

TORTA FREGOLOTTA
Almond cake

2¼	cups peeled almonds
1¼	cups granulated sugar
2¾	cups all-purpose flour
	pinch of salt
1	cup butter, cut in small pieces
4	eggs
	butter and flour for the cake pan

Wine: a dry sparkling white (Prosecco di Conegliano)

Whirl the almonds in a food processor with 3 tablespoons of the sugar until very finely chopped. • Transfer to a bowl and mix with the flour, salt, and remaining sugar. • Add the butter and eggs and use your fingertips to obtain a crumbly, bread crumb-like mixture. • Butter a 10-inch springform pan and dust with flour. Add the cake mixture and press down gently with your fingertips. • Bake in a preheated oven at 350°F for 40 minutes. • When cool, break into irregular shapes (it will be too crumbly to cut with a knife).

Serves: 6 · Prep: 20 min. · Cooking: 40 min. · Level: 1

TORTA CON LA CREMA AL CIOCCOLATO
Chocolate cream pie

2	cups all-purpose flour, sifted
1	tablespoon baking powder
½	cup granulated sugar
½	cup butter
2	eggs

	pinch of salt
1	quantity Chocolate cream (see recipe, page 308)
	butter and flour for the cake pan
¼	cup slivered almonds
¼	cup unsweetened cocoa powder

Wine: a dry sparkling red (Freisa d'Asti Spumante)

Use the first 6 ingredients to make a sweet pastry as explained on page 308. • Prepare the chocolate pastry cream. • After chilling, divide the dough into two parts and roll out into two disks large enough to cover a 10-inch springform pan. • Butter and flour the pan and place one pastry disk in the bottom. • Fill with the chocolate pastry cream. Spread it so it is mounded higher in the center of the pan. cover with the other disk of pastry and seal the edges. • Bake in a preheated oven at 350°F for about 40 minutes. • When cool, sprinkle with the almonds and dust with the cocoa powder.

Serves: 6–8 · Prep: 30 min. + 30 min. · to chill · Cooking: 40 min. · Level: 2

TORTA DI GRANO SARACENO AL LIMONE
Buckwheat cake with lemon filling

1	cup butter
1	cup granulated sugar
6	eggs, separated
1¾	cups buckwheat flour
1½	cups almonds, finely chopped
⅛	teaspoon vanilla extract
	pinch of salt
	butter and flour for the cake pan

14	oz lemon jelly (or lemon curd)
1	cup whipping cream
2	tablespoons confectioners' sugar

Wine: a dry sparkling white (Prosecco di Conegliano)

Beat the butter and sugar together until light and creamy, then add the egg yolks one at a time. • Gradually stir in the buckwheat flour, almonds, and vanilla extract, and beat until smooth. • Whip the egg whites and salt until stiff but not dry. • Fold them into the mixture. • Butter and flour a 12-inch cake pan. Pour the mixture into the pan and smooth the top with a rubber spatula. • Bake in a preheated oven at 350°F for about 1 hour. • Take the cake out of the oven. Open the springform pan and place on a rack to cool. • Use a long knife to slice the cake in half to make two disks. Spread the lemon jelly on one disk and cover with the other. • Whip the cream with the confectioners' sugar until stiff. Decorate the top of the cake with the cream and serve.

Serves: 8–10 · Prep: 20 min. · Cooking: 1 hr · Level: 2

TORTA DI RISO
Rice cake

4	cups milk
	salt to taste
1¼	cups short-grain rice
⅓	cup superfine sugar
	finely grated zest of 1 lemon (yellow part only)
¾	cup finely chopped toasted almonds
⅛	teaspoon almond extract
4	eggs, separated
	butter and fine bread crumbs for the cake pan

Wine: a sweet white (Colli Piacentini Malvasia Dolce)

Put the milk and a pinch of salt in a heavy-bottomed saucepan and bring to the boil. • Add the rice and simmer over low heat, stirring frequently, until it is cooked. Remove from the heat. • Stir in the sugar, then the lemon zest. Set aside to cool. • Stir in the almonds, almond extract, and egg yolks. • Whip the egg whites and a pinch of salt until stiff, then fold them into the rice mixture. • Butter a 10-inch springform pan, then sprinkle with the bread crumbs. Spoon in the cake mixture. • Bake in a preheated oven at 350°F for 40 minutes.

Serves: 6–8 · Prep: 45 min. · Cooking: 1 hr · Level: 2

BENSONE
Modena cake

- 3³/₄ cups all-purpose flour
- ¹/₂ cup superfine sugar
- pinch of salt
- finely grated zest of 1 lemon (yellow part only)
- 3 teaspoons baking powder
- ¹/₂ cup butter, chopped in small pieces
- 3 eggs, lightly beaten
- 3 tablespoons milk
- butter and flour for the baking sheet
- ¹/₂ cup decorating sugar

Wine: a semisweet sparkling red (Lambrusco di Sorbara)

Sift the flour into a mixing bowl. • Mix in the sugar, salt, lemon zest, and baking powder. • Turn out onto a pastry board and heap up into a mound. Make a well in the center and add the butter and eggs (reserving 1 tablespoon of beaten egg to glaze the cake). • Work these ingredients together, gradually combining them with the flour, and adding 2–3 tablespoons of milk. Knead the dough only just long enough to make it smooth and homogenous. • Grease a baking sheet and dust with flour. • Shape the dough into a long, thick sausage and place this in an S-shape on the baking sheet. • Brush the surface with the reserved egg and sprinkle with the decorating sugar. Using a sharp, pointed knife, make an incision along the center of the entire length of the cake. • Bake in a preheated oven at 350°F for 40 minutes. • Leave to cool on a cake rack for 10 minutes before serving.

Serves: 6 · Prep: 25 min. · Cooking: 40 min. · Level: 1

TORTA GLASSATA AL LIMONE
Iced lemon cake

- 1 cup butter, softened
- 1¹/₄ cups granulated sugar
- grated zest and juice of 1 lemon
- 4 eggs
- 1¹/₄ cups potato flour
- 2 cups all-purpose flour
- 1 teaspoon baking powder
- butter and flour for the loaf pan
- 1¹/₂ cups confectioners' sugar

Wine: a light, sweet white (Moscato d'Asti)

Beat the butter and sugar together until light and creamy, then add the lemon zest followed by the eggs, one at a time. • Stir in the potato and all-purpose flours, then the baking powder. Butter and flour a 9 x 5-inch loaf pan and pour in the mixture. • Bake in a preheated oven at 350°F for about 1 hour. • Set aside on a cake rack to cool. • Beat the confectioners' sugar with enough lemon juice to make a thick icing. Spread on the cake and serve.

Serves: 6–8 · Prep: 20 min. · Cooking: 60 min. · Level: 1

TORTA SABBIATA
Venetian crumble cake

☞ This crumbly cake is a specialty of the Veneto region in the northeast. Serve it with coffee or tea or a glass of sparkling white wine.

- 1¹/₄ cups butter
- 1¹/₂ cups superfine sugar
- 3 eggs, separated
- 1 cup potato flour
- 1¹/₄ cups all-purpose flour, sifted
- 1 teaspoon baking powder
- pinch of salt
- butter and flour for the cake pan

Wine: a sweet white (Recioto di Soave)

Cut the butter into small pieces and beat vigorously with the sugar in a bowl until it is pale and fluffy. • Beat in the egg yolks, one at a time, making sure each is fully incorporated before adding the next one. • Mix the two types of flour thoroughly with the baking powder. Sift them into the egg, butter, and sugar mixture. Stir until well blended. • Whisk the egg whites with the salt until stiff but not dry and fold into the cake mixture. • Butter and flour a 10-inch springform pan. Pour in the cake mixture and gently smooth the surface level. • Bake in a preheated oven at 350°F for 45 minutes. • Cool before serving.

Serves: 6 · Prep: 30 min. · Cooking: 45 min. · Level: 2

GIRELLA ALL'ALBICOCCA
Apricot roll

- 8 eggs, separated
- 1 cup superfine sugar
- 2 cups all-purpose flour, sifted
- pinch of salt
- ²/₃ cup butter
- ²/₃ cup apricot jam
- ¹/₂ cup confectioners' sugar

Wine: a light, sweet white (Moscato d'Asti)

Beat the egg yolks and sugar in a mixing bowl until pale and creamy. • Gradually stir in the flour. • Beat the egg whites and salt until stiff. Fold into the yolk mixture. • Melt all but 2 tablespoons of the butter (without cooking it) and stir into the mixture. • Use the reserved butter to grease a jelly-roll pan and pour in the mixture. • Bake in a preheated oven at 375°F oven for about 30 minutes, or until light golden brown. • Remove the cake from the pan and spread with the apricot jam. Roll the cake up carefully and sprinkle with the confectioners' sugar.

Serves: 6 · Prep: 15 min. · Cooking: 30 min. · Level: 2

Iced lemon cake

Veronese noodle cake

TORTA VERONESE
Verona noodle cake

- 2¹/₄ cups all-purpose flour
- 3 eggs
  pinch of salt
- 1 cup butter, softened
- 1 cup shelled almonds
- 1 cup granulated sugar
  finely grated zest and the juice of 1 lemon
- 1 cup very sweet fruit liqueur (Cointreau)
  butter and flour for the cake tin

Wine: a light, sweet white (Recioto di Soave)

Sift the flour into a large mixing bowl. Add the eggs, salt, and ¹/₄ cup of softened butter. Mix rapidly to form a smooth, elastic dough. • Transfer to a floured work surface and roll out very thinly. • Grind the almonds in a food processor. Place in a bowl with the sugar and lemon zest and mix well. • Roll the sheet of dough up very loosely and cut it into thin (¹/₈-inch) strips or "noodles." Lay them out on a clean dish cloth for 10 minutes. • Butter and flour a 10-inch springform pan. Cover the bottom with a layer of strips of dough. They should be scattered over the bottom, not carefully arranged. Sprinkle with part of the almond mixture. Repeat this process until all the dough and almond mixture are in the pan, finishing with a layer of noodles. • Melt the remaining butter. Pour the butter and liqueur over the noodles. Cover the cake with aluminum foil and bake in a preheated oven at 400°F for 1 hour. • Remove the cake from the pan, drizzle with the lemon juice, and serve.

Serves: 6 · Prep: 20 min. · Cooking: 1 hr · Level: 2

TORTA DI RICOTTA E PATATE
Ricotta cheese and potato cake

- 4 large potatoes
- 14 oz Ricotta cheese
- 1¹/₂ cups granulated sugar
- ¹/₄ cup butter, melted
- 4 eggs
- 1¹/₃ cups all-purpose flour, sifted
- 2 teaspoons baking powder
- 1 tablespoon grated lemon zest
- ¹/₄ cup confectioners' sugar

Wine: a light, sweet white (Albana di Romagna Dolce)

Boil the potatoes in a pot of salted water for 25 minutes, or until tender. Slip off the skins and mash. • Combine the potatoes with the Ricotta, sugar, butter, and eggs. Stir in the flour, baking powder, and lemon zest until the dough is smooth and well mixed. Butter and flour a 10-inch springform pan and pour in the dough. Bake in a preheated oven at 350°F for about 35 minutes. • When cool, sprinkle with confectioners' sugar and serve.

Serves: 6 · Prep: 15 min. · Cooking: 1 hr · Level: 1

TORTA DI PANE CON UVETTA
Bread and raisin cake

- ¹/₂ cup dark Jamaica rum
- 1 cup seedless white raisins
- 4 cups milk
- ¹/₂ cup butter, cut into pieces
- 1 cup granulated sugar
- 14 oz day-old white bread, cut in small pieces
- 5 eggs
  grated zest of 1 lemon (yellow part only)
  butter and fine dry bread crumbs for the cake pan

Wine: a sweet white (Soave Recioto Dolce)

Put the rum and raisins in a small bowl to soak. • Put the milk in a saucepan and bring to a boil. Remove from heat and stir in the butter and sugar until melted. • Put the bread in a large mixing bowl and pour the milk mixture over the top. Set aside for 30 minutes, or until the bread has absorbed all the milk. • Beat the eggs lightly and add them to the bread and milk. Add the drained raisins and lemon zest and mix well. Butter a 10-inch springform pan and sprinkle it with bread crumbs. Fill with the mixture. • Bake in a preheated oven at 350°F for 30 minutes. • Serve hot or at room temperature.

Serves: 6 · Prep: 20 min. + 30 min. to soak · Cooking: 30 min. · Level: 1

SFORMATO AL CIOCCOLATO
Chocolate ring mold cake

- ¹/₂ cup all-purpose flour
- 1 cup milk
- ²/₃ cup superfine sugar
- ¹/₄ cup butter
- 4 eggs, separated
- ¹/₃ cup unsweetened cocoa powder
  butter and flour for the ring mold

Wine: a dry sparkling white (Frascati Spumante)

Place the flour in a small bowl with 2 tablespoons of milk. Mix until smooth. •

Bring the remaining milk to a boil in a heavy-bottomed pan with the sugar and butter. Stir in the flour mixture and mix well. Remove from heat and set aside to cool. • Beat the egg yolks until creamy. • Whisk the egg whites until stiff. • Sift the cocoa powder into the flour mixture and mix well. • Stir in the egg yolks, then carefully fold in the egg whites. • Butter and flour a 10-inch ring mold and pour in the mixture. • Bake in a preheated oven at 375°F for 25 minutes. • Place on a cake rack to cool, then serve.

Serves: 6 · Prep: 30 min. · Cooking: 25 min. · Level: 2

TORTA AL CIOCCOLATO
Simple chocolate cake

    8   oz semisweet chocolate
    1/2 cup butter
    3/4 cup brown sugar,
    1/4 cup all-purpose flour
    4   egg whites
         pinch of salt
    1   cup heavy cream
    1/8 teaspoon vanilla extract
    1/4 cup confectioners' sugar

Wine: a dry sparkling white (Prosecco di Conegliano)

Melt the chocolate with the butter in the top of a double-boiler (or in a small saucepan placed in a large pan of hot water over low heat). • Remove from heat and stir in the sugar, followed by the flour. • Whisk the egg whites and salt until very stiff. Carefully fold into the chocolate mixture. • Butter and flour a 10-inch springform pan. Fill with the cake mixture and bake in a preheated oven at 300°F for 25 minutes. Set aside on a cake rack to cool. • When cool, whip the cream with the vanilla and confectioners' sugar until stiff. Decorate the cake and serve.

Serves: 6–8 · Prep: 15 min. · Cooking: 25 min. · Level: 1

TORTA MOKA ALLA CREMA
Mocha cream cake

    4   eggs, separated
    1   cup granulated sugar
    1/3 cup milk
    1   cup butter, melted and cooled
    1/4 cup unsweetened cocoa powder
    2   tablespoons instant coffee powder
    2   cups all-purpose flour, sifted
    2   teaspoons baking powder
         pinch of salt
         butter and flour for the pan
    1   quantity Vanilla cream (see recipe, page 308)
    2   tablespoons unflavored gelatin
    2   tablespoons cold water

Mocha cream cake

    1/3 cup strong hot coffee
    1/2 cup heavy cream
    2   tablespoons confectioners' sugar
         coffee beans to garnish (optional)

Wine: a sweet white (Colli Euganei Moscato)

Beat the egg yolks and sugar until pale and creamy. • Stir in the milk, butter, cocoa powder, coffee, flour, and baking powder. Beat until smooth. • Whip the egg whites and salt until stiff and fold them into the mixture. • Butter and flour a 10-inch springform pan and pour in the mixture. Bake in a preheated oven at 350°F for 30 minutes. Place on a cake rack to cool. • Prepare the vanilla cream. • Soften the gelatin in the cold water. Stir into the hot coffee until it dissolves. Combine the coffee mixture with the vanilla cream. • Cut the cake in half and fill with the vanilla cream. • Whip the heavy cream with the confectioners' sugar until stiff. Cover the cake with cream and coffee beans.

Serves: 6–8 · Prep: 30 min. · Cooking: 35 min. · Level: 2

TORTA ALLA PRALINA
Praline cake

    1 1/4 cups granulated sugar
    2   cups toasted almonds
    3   eggs
    1/3   cup butter, melted
    3/4   cup all-purpose flour, sifted
           pinch of salt
           butter and sugar for the ring mold

Wine: a sweet sparkling white (Asti Spumante)

Place the sugar in a small, heavy-bottomed saucepan over low heat and cook until it melts and turns a caramel color. • Pour the caramelized sugar over a sheet of aluminum foil and leave to harden and cool. • When cool, break up and grind in a food processor with the toasted almonds until finely ground. • Beat the eggs in a bowl with the caramel and almond mixture. • Gradually stir in the butter, flour, and salt. Butter a 10-inch ring mold and sprinkle with sugar. Fill with the mixture and bake in a preheated oven at 350°F for about 35 minutes. • Serve at room temperature.

Serves: 6 · Prep: 25 min. · Cooking: 35 min. · Level: 2

PAN DI SPAGNA
Italian sponge cake

☞ This recipe for sponge cake is used as the basis of many other cakes and desserts. It is relatively simple to make and will keep for up to a week in an airtight container. It also freezes well. If potato flour is not available, increase the quantity of all-purpose flour by $1/2$ cup.

- 6 eggs
- 1 cup granulated sugar
- 2 teaspoons grated lemon zest
- 1 cup all-purpose flour, sifted
- $1/2$ cup potato flour, sifted
  pinch of salt

Place the eggs and sugar in the top part of a double boiler (or in a small saucepan placed in a larger pan of simmering water over heat) and whisk until frothy. • Remove from heat, add the lemon zest and continue to whisk until cooled. • Fold in the flours and salt carefully so that the egg mixture does not collapse. • Butter and grease a 10-inch springform pan and fill with the sponge mixture. Bake in a preheated oven at 325°F oven for 40 minutes.

Serves: 6 · Prep: 30 min. · Cooking: 40 min. · Level: 2

TORTA ALLE NOCCIOLE
Hazelnut cake

- $2/3$ cup butter, cut into pieces
- $2/3$ cup granulated sugar
- 4 eggs, separated
- 1 cup all-purpose flour, sifted
- 1 teaspoon baking powder
- 1 cup toasted hazelnuts, finely chopped (leave a few whole to garnish)
- 14 oz semisweet chocolate, half of which grated

- $1/4$ teaspoon vanilla extract
- $1/2$ cup heavy cream
- $1/2$ cup chocolate chips

Wine: a sweet white (Moscato di Pantelleria)

Beat the butter and sugar until creamy. • Stir in the egg yolks, one at a time, and beat until smooth. • Beat in the flour and baking powder. • Stir in the chopped hazelnuts and grated chocolate. • Whip the egg whites and salt until stiff and fold them into the mixture. • Butter and flour a 10-inch springform pan and pour in the mixture. • Bake in a preheated oven at 350°F for about 50 minutes. Set aside to cool on a cake rack. • Melt the remaining chocolate with the vanilla and 2 tablespoons of cream in the top of a double-boiler (or in a small saucepan placed inside a large pan of boiling water over low heat). • Whip the remaining cream and stir in the chocolate chips. • Cut the cake into 2 disks and fill with the whipped cream. • Glaze with the chocolate icing and decorate with the whole hazelnuts.

Serves: 6–8 · Prep: 40 min. · Baking: 50 min. · Level: 3

SCHIACCIATA ALLA FIORENTINA
Florentine sponge cake

☞ This cake comes from Florence, where it is traditionally eaten on the Thursday before Lent. Try it filled with whipped cream too.

- 1 oz fresh yeast or 2 ($1/4$ oz) packages active dry yeast
- 1 cup lukewarm water
- 4 cups all-purpose flour, sifted
- 4 eggs
- $2/3$ cup sugar

- $1/2$ cup butter, melted
  grated zest of 1 orange
  pinch of salt
  butter and flour for the jelly-roll pan
- $1/4$ cup confectioners' sugar

Wine: a sweet or dry dessert wine (Vin Santo)

Dissolve the yeast in a little of the warm water. • Place the flour in a large mixing bowl and pour in the yeast mixture. Mix until the flour has all been absorbed, adding enough of the remaining water to obtain a smooth dough. Transfer to a lightly floured work surface and knead for 5 minutes. Wrap in a clean dishcloth and leave in a warm place to rise for 1 hour. • Knead the dough again, adding the eggs, sugar, butter, orange zest, and salt. • Butter and flour a jelly-roll pan. Spread the dough out in the pan. Leave to rise for another 2 hours. • Bake in a preheated oven at 350°F for 30 minutes. Set aside on a cake rack to cool. • Sprinkle with confectioners' sugar and serve.

Serves: 8 · Prep: 20 min. + 3 hrs to rise · Cooking: 30 min. · Level: 2

PIZZA DOLCE
Sweet pizza

- 1 oz fresh yeast or 2 ($1/4$ oz) packages active dry yeast
- $2/3$ cup lukewarm water
- $3 1/2$ cups all-purpose flour
- 7 eggs
- $2/3$ cup superfine sugar
- 2 oz fresh Ricotta cheese
- $1/2$ cup rum
- $1/2$ cup milk
- 1 teaspoon ground cinnamon
- $1/2$ teaspoon crushed aniseed seeds
  grated zest of 1 lemon
- $1/2$ cup butter, softened
- $1/2$ cup confectioners' sugar

Wine: a sweet dessert wine (Aleatico di Gradoli)

Dissolve the yeast in the water. • Put about a quarter of the flour in a mixing bowl and stir in the yeast mixture. Transfer to a lightly floured work surface and knead to obtain a smooth dough. Form the dough into a ball, then cover with a clean cloth and set aside to rise overnight. • Next morning, separate the eggs and beat 6 yolks with the sugar in a large mixing bowl until pale and creamy. • Whip the 7 egg whites until stiff. • Stir the Ricotta, rum, milk, egg whites, cinnamon, aniseed, and lemon rind into the egg yolk and sugar mixture. • Mix well, then add the risen dough, the remaining flour, and the butter. Turn the mixture out onto a floured work surface and knead for about 10 minutes. Form the dough into a ball, cover with a clean cloth and set aside in a warm place to rise for 2 hours. • Knead again for a few minutes, and form into a ball. Set aside as before to rise for 1 hour. • Butter and flour a 12-inch springform pan and put the dough in it. Beat the remaining egg yolk and brush it over the top. Sprinkle with the confectioners' sugar. • Bake in a preheated oven at 325°F for 40 minutes or until lightly browned. • Place on a cake rack to cool.

Serves: 8–10 · Prep: 30 min. + overnight rising + 3 hrs to rise · Cooking: 40 min. · Level: 3

PANDOLCE GENOVESE
Genoese Christmas bread

- 5 cups all-purpose flour
- 1/2 teaspoon salt
- 1/4 quantity risen dough for White bread (see recipe, page 26)
- 1/2 cup lukewarm water
- 3/4 cup granulated sugar
- 1/4 cup Marsala wine
- 1 teaspoon orange flower water
- 1/3 cup butter, melted
- 1/4 cup pine nuts
- 1/4 cup raisins, soaked in warm water
- 1/4 cup pistachio nuts
- 1/4 cup candied fruit
- 1/4 teaspoon fennel seeds
  butter and flour for the baking sheet

Wine: a semisweet dessert wine (Vin Santo)

Sift half the flour and salt into a mixing bowl. Add the risen bread dough and enough of the water to make a smooth, elastic dough. Shape the dough into a ball and wrap in a clean dish cloth. Set aside to rise in a warm place for 12 hours. • Combine the remaining flour, sugar, Marsala, and orange flower water in a large bowl. Add the melted butter. Mix well, then add the risen dough. Knead well, adding extra warm water if required. The dough should be smooth and puffy. • Work in the pine nuts, raisins, pistachio nuts, candied fruit, and fennel seeds. Knead

for about 15 more minutes. • Shape the dough into a large loaf (or several small rolls) and place on a buttered and floured baking sheet. Set the baking sheet with the dough aside in a warm place for 12 hours. • Use a knife to make a cross in the top of the loaf or rolls, and bake in a preheated oven at 400°F for about 30 minutes.

Serves: 4 · Prep: 25 min. + 24 hrs to rise · Cooking: 30 min. · Level: 3

SCHIACCIATA CON L'UVA
Grape sweet bread

- 1/2 oz fresh yeast or 1 (1/4 oz) package active dried yeast
- 1/3 cup lukewarm water
- 2 cups all-purpose flour
- 1/2 teaspoon salt
- 1/3 cup extra-virgin olive oil
- 2/3 cup superfine sugar
- 2 lb unpeeled seedless red grapes

Wine: a sweet white (Moscadello di Montalcino)

Dissolve the yeast in the water. • Sift the flour and salt into a large mixing bowl, and pour in the yeast liquid. Mix until the flour has all been absorbed. • Transfer to a floured work surface and knead briefly. • Shape the dough into a ball, wrap in a clean cloth and leave to rise for 1 hour. • Knead again, gradually working in three-quarters of the oil, one-third of the sugar and a little more salt. • Shape into a ball, wrap in a cloth and leave to rise for 1 hour. • Divide the dough in half. Grease a jelly-roll pan and press 1 piece of the dough into it. Cover with half the grapes, gently pressing them into the

dough. Sprinkle with half the remaining sugar. Cover with the other layer of dough. • Press the remaining grapes into the top and sprinkle with the remaining sugar. • Leave to rise for 1 hour. Bake in a preheated oven at 375°F for 30 minutes. • Serve warm.

Serves: 6 · Prep: 25 min. + 3 hrs to rise · Cooking: 30 min. · Level: 2

CASTAGNACCIO
Tuscan chestnut cake

☞ This unusual flat cake comes from Tuscany where it is popular in late fall when the new season's chestnuts are in.

- 2 3/4 cups sweet chestnut flour
- 1 1/2 cups water
- 2/3 cup extra-virgin olive oil
  pinch of salt
- 1/2 cup small seedless white raisins, soaked in warm water for 15 minutes, drained and squeezed
- 1/3 cup pine nuts
  a few young, tender rosemary leaves

Wine: a semisweet dessert wine (Vin Santo)

Sift the flour into a mixing bowl, make a well in the center and pour in the water, 1 tablespoon of the oil, and the salt. Stir well to obtain a thick, lump-free, pouring batter. • Stir in the drained raisins and the nuts and then pour into a 9 x 13 inch baking pan greased with 2 tablespoons of the oil. • Sprinkle with the rosemary leaves and drizzle with the remaining oil. • Bake in a preheated oven at 400°F for about 30 minutes, or until a thin crust has formed. • Serve hot or warm.

Serves: 4 · Prep: 15 min. · Cooking: 50 min. · Level: 2

Tuscan chestnut cake

PANDORO
Veronese Christmas cake

- 2½ cups all-purpose flour
- 1 oz fresh yeast or 2 (¼ oz) packages active dry yeast
- 1 egg + 5 extra yolks
- ½ cup superfine sugar
- 1 tablespoon milk, warmed
- 1 cup butter, softened
- grated zest of 1 lemon
- ⅛ teaspoon vanilla extract
- ½ cup light cream
- butter and confectioner's sugar for the mold
- ⅓ cup confectioner's sugar

Wine: a sweet dessert wine (Soave Recioto)

Sift ¼ cup of the flour into a mixing bowl. Crumble in the yeast and add 1 egg yolk and 1 tablespoon of sugar. Mix quickly, adding the milk, to form a soft dough. Shape into a ball. Cover with a cloth and leave to rise for 2 hours at warm room temperature. • Sift half the remaining flour into a mixing bowl. Place the risen ball of dough in the center with half the remaining sugar, 3 egg yolks, and 3 tablespoons of the butter. Combine quickly and thoroughly. Transfer to a floured work surface and knead to a smooth and elastic dough. Place the dough in a lightly floured bowl, cover and leave to rise for 2 hours. • Combine the remaining flour, sugar, egg yolk, and whole egg with the risen dough, kneading energetically. Shape into a ball, cover and leave to rise for 2 hours. • Transfer the dough to a floured work surface and work in the lemon zest, vanilla, and cream. • Roll the dough out into a rectangle. Place the remaining butter in the center and fold over first one-third of the rectangle, then the other to make a 3-layered "sandwich" of dough. Roll out again and repeat. Roll out more gently into a smaller rectangle and leave to rest for 30 minutes. Repeat the last folding and rolling stage and leave to rest for 30 minutes. • Butter a fluted turban mold and dust with confectioners' sugar. Add the dough and leave to rise until it has reached the top of the mold. Bake in a preheated oven at 375°F for 30 minutes, then turn down to 350°F and continue baking for 20 minutes. • Turn out onto a wire rack; dust with the confectioner's sugar and serve.

Serves: 6 · Prep: 30 min. + 7½ hrs to rest · Cooking: 50 min. · Level: 3

Veronese Christmas cake

PANFORTE
Siennese dried fruit and nut cake

- 2 cups peeled whole almonds
- 1 cup shelled walnuts
- 1/2 cup dried figs, finely chopped
- 1 1/4 cups candied peel (orange, citron, and melon), finely chopped
- 1 tablespoon ground spice mixture (cinnamon, cloves, coriander seeds, white peppercorns, and nutmeg)
- 2/3 cup unsweetened cocoa powder
- 1 1/4 cups confectioners' sugar + extra to dust
- 1/3 cup honey
- 2 tablespoons all-purpose flour
  rice paper to line the baking sheet

Wine: a sweet or dry dessert wine (Vin Santo)

Siennese dried fruit and nut cake

Spread the almonds and walnuts out on baking sheets and bake at 400°F for 3–4 minutes. Allow to cool slightly and then chop finely. • Mix the nuts in a large bowl with the figs, candied peel, spices, and cocoa powder. • Dissolve the sugar in the honey in the top of a double boiler (or in a small saucepan placed in a larger one half-filled with boiling water over medium heat). After about 8 minutes, test to see if it forms a thread when you lift a spoonful above the pan. If not, cook for a few minutes more. • Remove from heat and stir in the flour, then the nuts and figs. Line a baking sheet with wax paper and place the mixture on it. Press down until it is about 3/4-inch thick. • Bake in a preheated oven at 350°F for 40 minutes. • Place on a cake rack to cool. Dust with confectioners' sugar and serve. Well-wrapped in foil, it will keep for several weeks.

Serves: 6 · Prep: 30 min. · Cooking: 1 hr · Level: 2

CASSATA SICILIANA
Sicilian cheesecake

☞ This must be one of Italy's best known cakes, and the one most closely associated with Sicily.

- 1 1/4 cups granulated sugar
- 1/2 cup water
- 1 vanilla bean
- 1 1/4 lb Ricotta cheese, sieved
- 6 oz semisweet chocolate, chopped in tiny pieces
- 1 1/4 cups mixed candied fruit
- 2 tablespoons shelled pistachio nuts
- 2 tablespoons Maraschino or Kirsch liqueur
- 1 quantity Sponge cake (see recipe, page 332)
- 2 tablespoons apricot jam
- 2 cups confectioners' sugar
- 2 tablespoons powdered egg whites
- 3 tablespoons water

Wine: a dry sparkling white (Berlucchi)

Boil the sugar, 1/2 cup water, and vanilla bean in a heavy-based saucepan until the mixture turns to syrup. • Set aside to cool. • Beat the Ricotta vigorously, then add the syrup gradually, stirring until the mixture is creamy. • Stir in the chocolate, candied fruit (reserving some to decorate), nuts, and liqueur. • Cut the sponge cake in thin slices and line a 10-inch springform pan with them. Use the apricot jam to bind them together. • Put the Ricotta mixture on top and spread evenly. • Cover with the remaining sponge cake and chill in the refrigerator for 2 hours. • Beat together the confectioners' sugar, powdered egg whites and 3 tablespoons water until smooth. • Coat the cake with the glaze, decorate with the reserved candied fruit and serve.

Serves: 6 · Prep: 2 hrs + 2 hrs to chill · Level: 3

TORTA CANDITA
Sicilian candied fruit cake

- 3 cups all-purpose flour
- 2/3 cup butter, softened
- 1/2 cup granulated sugar
- 1 whole egg + 1 yolk
  pinch of salt
- 1/3 cup dry Marsala wine
- 2/3 cup almonds, toasted
- 1 1/2 cups dried figs
- 4 oz semisweet chocolate
- 1/3 cup pistachio nuts
- 1/3 cup shelled walnuts
  pinch of ground cinnamon
  grated zest of 1 lemon

Wine: a dry Marsala (Marsala Superiore)

Mix the flour, butter, sugar, whole egg, salt, and half the Marsala together in a bowl to form a firm, smooth dough. • Wrap in a clean dish cloth and set aside to rest for 2 hours. • Chop the almonds, figs, chocolate, pistachio nuts, and walnuts together and place in a heavy-bottomed pan with the cinnamon, lemon zest, and remaining Marsala. • Cook over low heat for 10 minutes, stirring frequently. Set aside to cool. • Roll out the dough in a rectangular shape until it is about 1/2-inch thick. • Spread the cooled fruit mixture over the dough and roll up. Join the ends of the roll to form a ring and seal well. • Transfer to an oiled baking sheet and bake in a preheated oven at 400°F for 25 minutes. • Beat the egg yolk with a whisk. • Remove the ring from the oven and brush with the egg yolk. Return to the oven and cook for 5 minutes. • Turn off the oven and leave the ring in the oven until cool.

Serves: 6 · Prep: 30 min. + 2 hrs to rest · Cooking: 45 min. · Level: 2

TORTA CON LA FRUTTA
Fresh fruit cake

- 2 eggs
- 1/4 cup sugar
- 1/2 cup melted butter
  pinch of salt
- 1/4 cup flour, sifted
- 1 teaspoon baking powder
- 2 tablespoons water
- 12 oz mixed fresh fruit (apricots, bananas, peaches, apples, pears, cherries, – whatever is in season), peeled, cored, and chopped into tiny pieces

Wine: a dry sparkling white (Prosecco di Conegliano)

Beat the eggs and sugar until creamy, then add the butter, salt, flour and, lastly, the baking powder and water. • Mix to a smooth cream. • Stir the fruit into the mixture. • Butter and flour an 8-inch springform pan and fill with the mixture. • Bake in a preheated oven at 350°F for 30 minutes.

Serves: 6 · Prep: 10 min. · Cooking: 30 min. · Level: 1

Prepare the Italian sponge cake. • Sieve the Ricotta and mix with ½ cup of the sugar and the yogurt in a mixing bowl. • Whip the cream until stiff and fold it into the mixture. • Lastly, stir in 3 tablespoons of berries. • Place 1 sponge cake in the bottom of a 10-inch springform pan. Cover with the Ricotta mixture. Spread it out evenly and cover with the other sponge cake. • Cook the remaining berries with the rest of the sugar and the lemon juice over medium heat until mushy. • Spread the stewed fruit over the cake and refrigerate for at least 3 hours before serving.

Serves: 6 · Prep: 40 min. + 3 hrs to chill · Level: 1

TORTA GLASSATA AL CIOCCOLATO
Almond cake with chocolate icing

4	eggs, separated
1	cup granulated sugar,
1	cup butter, softened
2	cups all-purpose flour, sifted
1	cup almonds, finely chopped
⅛	teaspoon vanilla extract
1	teaspoon baking powder
	pinch of salt
7	oz bittersweet chocolate
	chocolate shavings to decorate

Wine: a sweet sparkling white (Moscato d'Asti Spumante)

Beat the egg yolks and sugar until pale and creamy. • Stir in the butter, followed by the flour, almonds, vanilla, and baking powder. • Whisk the egg whites and salt until very stiff and fold them into the mixture. • Butter and flour a 9-inch square cake pan and pour in the mixture. Bake in a preheated oven at 350°F for about 40 minutes. • Set aside to cool on a cake rack. • Melt the chocolate in the top of a double-boiler (or in a small saucepan placed inside a large pan of boiling water over low heat). Spread over the cooled cake. Sprinkle with the chocolate shavings. and serve.

Serves: 6–8 · Prep: 20 min. · Cooking: 40 min. · Level: 2

TORTA PIEMONTESE
Chocolate cream cake

4	eggs, separated + 2 egg yolks
1½	cups confectioners' sugar
1¾	cups all-purpose flour, sifted
5	tablespoons unsweetened cocoa powder
¾	cup butter, melted

Yogurt cake with Nutella cream filling

TORTA ALLO YOGURT CON NUTELLA
Yogurt cake with Nutella cream filling

1¼	cups butter
¾	cup granulated sugar
2	eggs
2	cups all-purpose flour, sifted
2	teaspoons baking powder
	grated zest of 1 lemon (yellow part only)
8	oz whole yogurt
	butter and flour for the pan
1	cup Nutella
⅔	cup toasted hazelnuts, coarsely chopped
2	tablespoons all-purpose flour
⅓	cup heavy cream

Wine: a sweet white (Moscato d'Asti)

Beat 1 cup of the butter with ½ cup of the sugar until creamy. • Stir in the eggs, one at a time, and beat until smooth. • Beat in the flour (reserving 2 tablespoons) and baking powder. • Add the lemon zest and all but 2 tablespoons of the yogurt and beat until smooth. Butter and flour a 10-inch springform pan and pour half the mixture into it. • Soften the Nutella by sitting the jar in a pan of hot water. Spread it over the cake mixture in the pan and cover with the rest of the mixture. • In a small mixing bowl, combine the remaining flour, butter, and sugar with the hazelnuts until the mixture resembles coarse bread crumbs. Sprinkle over the cake. • Bake in a preheated oven at 350°F for about 45 minutes. Set aside on a cake rack to cool. • Whip the cream until stiff. Stir in the remaining yogurt. Serve separately with the cake.

Serves: 6–8 · Prep: 20 min. · Cooking: 45 min. · Level: 2

PAN DI SPAGNA, RICOTTA E FRUTTI DI BOSCO
Italian sponge with Ricotta cheese and berry fruit

2	quantities Italian sponge cake (see recipe, page 332)
1	lb Ricotta cheese
1¼	cups granulated sugar
1	cup whole yogurt
1¾	cups heavy cream
1	lb mixed berry fruits (raspberries, strawberries, blueberries, blackberries)
	juice of 1 lemon

Wine: a dry sparkling white (Prosecco di Conegliano)

butter and flour for the pan
$^2/_3$ cup superfine sugar
$3^1/_2$ oz bittersweet chocolate, grated
$^1/_4$ teaspoon vanilla extract
2 cups milk
$^1/_4$ cup toasted, shelled almonds

Wine: a sweet, sparkling wine (Asti Spumante)

Beat 4 egg yolks with the confectioners' sugar in a mixing bowl until pale and creamy. • Stir in 1$^1/_4$ cups of the flour and the cocoa powder and mix well. • Beat the 4 egg whites until stiff and fold them into the mixture. Melt $^1/_4$ cup of butter and stir it into the mixture. • Butter and flour a 9-inch springform pan and pour the cake mixture into it. Bake in a preheated oven at 350°F for 35–40 minutes. • Remove from the oven and place on a cake rack to cool. • Meanwhile, beat the 2 extra egg yolks with the superfine sugar until pale and creamy. • Stir in the remaining flour and butter, the chocolate, vanilla, and, gradually, the milk. • Place over low heat and stir continuously until thick and creamy. The mixture must not boil. When thick, set aside to cool. • When the cake is cool, cut in half horizontally and cover one half with half the chocolate cream. Place the other piece of cake on top and cover with the remaining chocolate cream. • Sprinkle with the almonds and serve.

Serves: 6 · Prep: 30 min. · Cooking: 45 min. · Level: 3

TORTA DI MERINGA CON FRUTTA
Meringue with zabaglione and fruit

6 egg whites
1$^1/_2$ cups confectioners' sugar
pinch of salt
4 drops vanilla extract
butter to grease the pan
1 quantity Zabaglione (see recipe, page 311)
2 bananas
4 kiwi fruit
2 tablespoons superfine sugar

Wine: a sweet white (Moscato di Noto)

Beat the egg whites until stiff, then fold in with confectioners' sugar, salt, and vanilla. • Butter a 9-inch springform pan and pour in the mixture. Bake in a preheated oven at 180°F for 1$^1/_2$ hours. • Prepare the zabaglione. • Peel the

Meringue with zabaglione and fruit

bananas and kiwi fruit and slice thinly. Sprinkle with the sugar. • When the meringue is cooked, place on a cake rack to cool. When cool, pour the zabaglione over the top. Leave to cool and harden. • Arrange the fruit on top and serve.

Serves: 6 · Prep: 10 min. · Cooking: 1$^1/_2$ hrs · Level: 2

SAVOIARDI CREMOSI
Ladyfingers with candied fruit and cream

2 cups whole milk
$^1/_4$ cup superfine sugar
6 oz ladyfingers (preferably Italian Savoiardi), crumbled
4 oz mixed candied fruit, finely chopped
finely grated zest of 1 lemon
3 eggs, separated
butter for the pan

Wine: a medium or sweet dessert wine (Vin Santo)

Place the milk and sugar in a heavy-bottomed saucepan over medium heat and bring to the boil. • Add the ladyfingers and cook for 5 minutes, stirring continuously. Remove from heat

and press through a sieve. Set aside to cool, stirring from time to time. • When the cream is cool, stir in the candied fruit and lemon zest followed, one at a time, by the egg yolks. • Beat the egg whites until stiff and fold them into the mixture. • Butter a 10-inch ring mold and fill with the mixture. Bake in a preheated oven at 350°F for 1 hour. • Remove from the oven and let sit for a few minutes. Unmold and serve immediately.

Serves: 4–6 · Prep: 30 min. · Cooking: 1 hr · Level: 1

TORTA DI MELE
Apple pie

- ¹/₄ cup raisins
- ¹/₂ cup warm water
- 2 tablespoons fine dry bread crumbs
- 3 oz amaretti cookies (macaroons), crumbled
- ¹/₂ cup Marsala wine
- ¹/₄ cup coffee
- 2 eggs
- 1 lb Golden Delicious apples
- 2 tablespoons honey
       finely grated zest of 1 lemon
- 1   teaspoon unsweetened cocoa powder
       butter and flour for the pie pan
- ¹/₂ cup confectioners' sugar

Wine: a dry sparkling white (Prosecco di Conegliano)

Place the raisins in a small bowl with the water and leave to soak for 10 minutes. Drain, and squeeze out excess moisture. • In a large mixing bowl, combine the bread crumbs, amaretti cookies, Marsala, coffee, and eggs. • Peel and core the apples then grate them into the mixing bowl. Stir in the raisins, honey, lemon zest, and cocoa powder. Mix well. • Butter and flour a 10-inch springform pan and bake in a preheated oven at 350°F for about 1 hour. • Place on a cake rack to cool. Sprinkle with the confectioners' sugar and serve.

Serves: 6 · Prep: 30 min. · Cooking: 45 min. · Level: 1

TORTA DI POLENTA E LIMONE
Polenta and lemon cake

- 1 cup butter
- 2¹/₂ cups confectioners' sugar
- 3 eggs + 6 egg yolks
- 2 tablespoons Limoncello (lemon liqueur)
- 1 cup finely ground almonds
- 1³/₄ cups finely ground yellow cornmeal
- 1 cup all-purpose flour
       grated zest of 1 lemon
- 1 teaspoon baking powder
- ¹/₄ teaspoon vanilla extract
       butter and flour for the cake pan

Wine: a sweet dessert wine (Madeira)

Melt the butter over very low heat and set aside to cool. • Beat the butter and sugar until pale and creamy. • Beat in the eggs and yolks one by one. • Stir in the lemon liqueur, almonds, cornmeal, flour, and lemon zest. Beat well, then add the baking powder and vanilla. • Butter and flour a 9¹/₄ x 3¹/₄-inch fluted tube and pour the mixture into it. • Bake in a preheated oven at 375°F for 40 minutes. • Slice when cool to serve.

Serves: 6–8 · Prep: 20 min. · Cooking: 40 min. · Level: 1

TORTA DI POLENTA E NOCCIOLE
Hazelnut polenta cake

- 1¹/₂ cups toasted hazelnuts
- ³/₄ cup granulated sugar
- 2 cups all-purpose flour
- 2 cups finely ground yellow cornmeal
       grated zest of 1 lemon
- ¹/₄ teaspoon vanilla extract
       pinch of salt
- 1 cup butter, cut in small pieces
- 2 egg yolks, beaten
       butter and flour for the cake pan

Wine: a sweet sparkling white (Moscato d'Asti Spumante)

Whirl the hazelnuts in a food processor until finely chopped. • Transfer to a mixing bowl and add the sugar, flour, cornmeal, lemon zest, vanilla, and salt. Add the butter and egg yolks and use your fingertips to obtain a crumbly, bread crumb-like mixture. • Butter and flour a 10-inch cake pan. Pour in the cake mixture and press down with your fingertips. • Bake in a preheated oven at 375°F for 40 minutes. • When cool, break into pieces and serve.

Serves: 6–8 · Prep: 20 min. · Cooking: 40 min. · Level: 1

STRUDEL DI CILIEGE
Cherry strudel

☞ This is a variation of the traditional apple strudel which is made in northeastern Italy. Use this recipe for apple strudel too, by replacing the cherries with 2 lb of cooking apples and ¹/₂ cup raisins.

- 7 tablespoons cold water
- ¹/₄ cup butter
- 2 cups all-purpose flour
       pinch of salt

½ cup granulated sugar
1 egg
1¾ lb cherries
½ teaspoon ground cinnamon
grated zest of 1 lemon
1⅓ cups dry white bread crumbs
⅓ cup butter
⅓ cup apricot jam
superfine sugar for sprinkling
1 cup whipped cream

Wine: a dry sparkling white (Albana di Romagna)

Heat the water and melt the butter in it. Set aside to cool. • Sift the flour onto a work surface. Make a well in the center, and add the salt, 1 tablespoon of the sugar, the egg, and the butter mixture. Knead the ingredients into a smooth soft dough by working vigorously for about 20 minutes. • Roll into a ball, wrap in a floured cloth and set aside under a heated bowl for about 30 minutes. • Pit the cherries and cut in half. • • Mix the remaining sugar with the cinnamon and lemon zest. Place the bread crumbs in a small saucepan with half the butter and cook for 5 minutes. • Roll the dough out on a lightly floured work surface, using a rolling pin to start with, then using your hands to stretch it. Place your fists underneath the dough with your knuckles upward and pull gently outward from the center. The dough should be almost as thin as a sheet of paper. • Brush it with melted butter, then spread with the bread crumbs, followed by the cherries, sugar mixture, and lastly, the apricot jam. • Roll up carefully, sealing the edges well. Slide onto a baking sheet covered in baking paper. Brush with melted butter and bake in a preheated oven at 350°F for about 1 hour. Sprinkle with the superfine sugar and serve hot or warm with the whipped cream in a separate bowl.

Serves: 4–6 · Prep: 30 min. + 30 min. to rest the dough · Cooking: 1 hr

TARTUFI AL CIOCCOLATO
Chocolate truffles

¼ cup butter
¼ cup confectioners' sugar
2 egg yolks
⅓ cup heavy cream
2 tablespoons vanilla sugar
10 oz bittersweet chocolate, grated
¼ cup cocoa powder

Wine: a sweet dessert wine (Moscato di Siracusa)

Beat the butter and confectioners' sugar until creamy, then add the egg yolks one at a time. • Bring the cream to a boil, add the vanilla sugar and stir to dissolve. Pour the boiling cream into the butter mixture, stir in the chocolate and chill in the refrigerator for at least 2 hours. • Shape tablespoonfuls of the mixture into walnut-sized ball and roll in the cocoa powder.

Makes: 30 truffles · Prep: 30 min. + 2 hrs to chill · Level: 1

SPONGATA
Christmas pie

☞ *Spongata* is one of the oldest cakes in Italy. Records show that it was already being served in Emilia-Romagna as a Christmas cake during the 15th century.

1 cup walnuts
1 cup chunky jam
1 cup fine, dry bread crumbs
1¾ cups honey
½ cup water
½ cup seedless golden raisins, soaked in water, well drained
½ cup pine nuts
pinch of ground cinnamon
2½ cups all-purpose flour
½ cup superfine sugar
pinch of salt
finely grated zest of 1 lemon
⅔ cup butter, cut into small pieces
1 whole egg + 2 egg yolks
confectioners' sugar

Wine: a sweet dessert wine (Aleatico di Puglia)

Chop the walnuts finely. • Spread the bread crumbs out on a shallow baking sheet. Place in a medium oven to brown lightly. • Chop the fruit pieces in the jam into very small pieces. • Place the jam, walnuts, and bread crumbs in a mixing bowl. • Pour the honey into a small saucepan with the water and bring slowly to a boil. • Stir into the mixing bowl with the nut and bread crumb mixture. Add the raisins, pine nuts, and cinnamon. Mix well. • Cover the bowl and refrigerate for 2–3 days. • To make the pastry, sift the flour into a mixing bowl. Add the sugar, salt, and lemon zest and mix well. • Turn out onto a pastry board and heap up into a mound. Make a well in the center, add the butter, and use your fingertips to rub it into the flour. The mixture should resemble fine bread crumbs. • Add the egg and yolks and combine, working the pastry dough briefly. Shape it into a ball and cover with plastic wrap. Chill in the refrigerator for 1 hour. • Divide the dough in two portions, one slightly larger than the other. Roll them out into two disks, trimming one to 9½ inches, the other to 11 inches in diameter. • Place a sheet of baking paper on a baking sheet and transfer the smaller disk carefully onto it. • Give the filling a final stir and spoon it onto the pastry dough, spreading it out, but leaving a ½-inch border around the edge. • Cover with the large disk, pressing the border and edges to seal well (trim off any overlapping dough from the larger disk). Bake in a preheated oven at 375°F for 25 minutes. • Leave to cool before sprinkling with sifted confectioners' sugar.

Serves: 6 · Prep: 2 hrs + 2–3 days to rest the filling · Cooking: 25 min. · Level: 3

TORTA DI POLENTA E MELE
Cornmeal and apple pie

2 eggs
1 cup sugar
1 cup finely ground cornmeal
2 cups all-purpose flour
1 teaspoon baking powder
¾ cup extra-virgin oil
¼ cup white wine
1 apple
2 tablespoons superfine sugar
juice of ½ lemon

Wine: a dry sparkling white (Prosecco di Conegliano)

Beat the eggs and sugar until very smooth and creamy. • Stir in the sifted cornmeal and flour, then add the baking powder. • Gradually add the oil, followed by the white wine, and continue beating until the mixture is smooth and creamy. Butter and flour a 9-inch springform pan and pour the mixture into it. • Peel and core the apple and slice it thinly. Sprinkle it with the lemon juice. Arrange the slices over the tart and sprinkle with the brown sugar. • Bake in a preheated oven at 350°F for 50 minutes.

Serves: 6 · Prep: 20 min. · Cooking: 50 min. · Level: 1

2 tablespoons all-purpose flour
12 oz wild strawberries, well-washed and dried

Wine: a light, sweet white (Moscato Giallo del Trentino)

Prepare the pastry. • Butter and flour the pie pan. • Roll out the pastry so that it is large enough to line a fairly shallow 10-inch pie pan. • Prick well with a fork and bake blind in a preheated oven at 350°F for 25 minutes. • Beat the eggs with the sugar until creamy. Stir in the cream and add the ground almonds and flour. • Take the pastry case out of the oven, and sprinkle with the wild strawberries. Cover with the egg and almond mixture and return to the oven for another 35 minutes. • Serve warm.

Serves: 6–8 · Prep: 20 min. + time to make the pastry · Cooking: 1 hr · Level: 1

CROSTATA DI NOCI
Walnut and honey pie

☞ This hearty pie is perfect on cold winter evenings. If liked, replace the white flour in the short crust pastry with the same amount of whole-wheat flour. In this case, add an extra 2 tablespoons of butter to the pastry.

1 quantity Short crust pastry (see recipe, page 49)
  finely grated zest of 1 lemon
20 shelled walnuts
2 tablespoons liquid honey
2 tablespoons butter
  butter and fine dry bread crumbs for the pie pan

Wine: a sweet dessert wine (Moscato di Pantelleria)

Prepare the pastry, incorporating the lemon zest together with the butter. • Peel the walnuts and chop them coarsely. • Heat the honey in a small, heavy-bottomed saucepan over low heat and stir in butter. Add the walnuts and cook over low heat until the mixture caramelizes. • Roll out the pastry so that it is large enough to line a fairly shallow 12-inch pie pan. Grease the pan with butter and sprinkle with the bread crumbs. Line the pan with the pastry, leaving a narrow border of the pastry hanging over the sides. Prick well with a fork. • Spread the honey and walnut mixture evenly over the pastry. Bake in a preheated oven at 350°F for 30 minutes. • Serve warm or at room temperature.

Serves: 6 · Prep: 30 min. + time to make the pastry · Cooking: 30 min. · Level: 2

Apricot pie

CROSTATA DI ALBICOCCHE
Apricot pie

1/2 quantity Sweet plain pastry (see recipe, page 308)
1/2 quantity Italian sponge cake (see recipe, page 332)
1 lb small apricots
  butter and flour for the pan
1/4 cup Maraschino or Kirsch (cherry liqueur)
1/4 cup finely chopped almonds
1/3 cup superfine sugar
1 egg yolk

Wine: a light, sweet white (Moscato d'Asti)

Prepare the pastry. • Prepare the Italian sponge cake. • Rinse the apricots under cold running water and dry well. Remove the pits and cut them in half. • Break off a piece of pastry about the size of a tennis ball and reserve. Roll the rest out so that it is large enough to line a fairly shallow 10-inch pie pan (greased with butter and dusted with flour). Leave a narrow border of the pastry hanging over the sides. Prick well with a fork. • Slice the sponge cake and place pieces over the pastry. Drizzle with the liqueur and sprinkle with the almonds. Arrange the apricot halves, cut side down, on top. Sprinkle with the sugar. • Roll out the remaining pastry into a square sheet. Use a fluted pastry wheel to cut it into 1/4-inch wide strips. Place these over the apricots in a lattice pattern. Fold the overhanging pastry border over the ends of the lattice to form a rolled edging. • Beat the egg yolk with a fork and brush the top of the pie with it. • Bake in a preheated oven at 375°F for 35–40 minutes. • Serve warm.

Serves: 6 · Prep: 10 min. + time to make the pastry and sponge cake · Cooking 35–40 min. · Level: 2

CROSTATA DI FRAGOLINE
Wild strawberry pie

1 quantity Short crust pastry (see recipe, page 49), using the milk instead of water and adding 2 tablespoons granulated sugar
  butter and flour for the pie pan
2 eggs
1/3 cup granulated sugar
1/3 cup light cream
1/3 cup almonds, freshly ground

CROSTATA DI PERE
Pear pie

- 2 lb firm cooking pears
- ³/₄ cup superfine sugar
- 1¹/₄ cups full-bodied dry red wine
  pinch of ground cinnamon
- 2 tablespoons unsweetened cocoa powder
- 12 amaretti cookies, coarsely crushed
- 2 cups all-purpose flour
- 1 cup fine yellow cornmeal
  pinch of salt
- ²/₃ cup butter, at room temperature, cut in tiny flakes
- 3 egg yolks

Wine: a sweet white (Moscato di Strevi Banfi)

Rinse the pears and dry well. Peel them, then cut lengthwise into quarters, and core. Cut each quarter lengthwise into 3 slices. • Place the slices of pear in a saucepan just large enough to hold them. Add ¹/₄ cup of the sugar, the wine, and cinnamon, and cook gently over medium heat for 10 minutes. • Pour off the cooking liquid, then sprinkle the pears with the cocoa powder. Set aside to cool. • To make the pastry, begin by mixing the two types of flour thoroughly in a bowl. Stir in the sugar and salt. • Using a fork, stir in the butter, followed by the egg yolks. Work the ingredients quickly together to form a mixture that resembles fine bread crumbs. Gather these together by hand and combine (do not knead) to form a soft ball of pastry dough which is not in the least elastic. • Use two-thirds of the pastry to line the bottom and sides of an ungreased, fairly shallow 9-inch pie pan. Do this by placing the pastry in the pie pan and gradually working it into a lining of even thickness using your fingertips. • Chill the uncooked pie shell in the refrigerator for 1 hour. • Wrap the remaining pastry dough in plastic wrap and put it a cool place (not in the refrigerator as it still has to be rolled out.) • Take the pie shell out of the refrigerator. Sprinkle evenly with the crumbled amaretti cookies and arrange the pears on top. • Roll out the remaining pastry dough into a round slightly larger than the diameter of the pie pan. Place this on top of the pears, pinching the pastry edges together to seal. Pierce a few little holes in the pie lid with a

Cherry pie

fine skewer. • Bake in a preheated oven at 400°F for about 40 minutes. • Let cool slightly in the pan before transferring to a serving plate. Serve at room temperature.

Serves: 6 · Prep: 30 min. + 1 hr to chill · Cooking: 40 min. · Level: 2

CROSTATA DI CILIEGE
Cherry pie

- 1¹/₂ lb ripe cherries
  juice of 2 lemons
- ²/₃ cup granulated sugar
- 4 cloves
- 1 cinnamon stick
- 1 quantity Plain sweet pastry (see recipe, page 308)
- 1 cup cherry jam
- 2 tablespoons Kirsch (cherry liqueur)
- ²/₃ cup butter
  butter and flour for the pie pan

Wine: a sweet red (Colli di Conegliano Refrontolo Passito Dolce)

Rinse the cherries under cold running water. Dry well, and pit them. Place in a bowl with the lemon juice, sugar, cloves, and cinnamon stick. Stir gently and leave to stand for 2 hours. • Prepare the pastry. • Put the cherry jam in a small heavy-bottomed saucepan with the liqueur and butter. Simmer for 5 minutes, then set aside to cool. • Break off two-thirds of the pastry dough and roll it out so that it is large enough to line a fairly shallow 10-inch pie pan (greased with butter and dusted with flour). Leave a narrow border of the pastry hanging over the sides. • Spread the cherry jam mixture over the bottom of the pastry and cover with the well-drained cherries. • Roll out the remaining pastry into a square sheet. Use a fluted pastry wheel to cut it into ¹/₂-inch wide strips. Place these over the cherries in a lattice pattern. Fold the overhanging pastry border over the ends of the lattice to form a rolled edge. • Bake in a preheated oven at 375°F for 40 minutes. • Serve warm.

Serves: 6 · Prep: 20 min. + 2 hrs to soak · Cooking: 40 min. · Level: 2

Apple charlotte

medium heat until melted. Add the apples and cook with the lemon juice and half the sugar until soft. • Roll out the pastry and use it to line a 10-inch springform pan. • Prick the base with a fork and bake blind in a preheated oven at 350°F for about 30 minutes. • Spread the vanilla cream over the pastry and cover with the cooked apples. • Sprinkle with the remaining sugar and place the pie under the grill until the sugar caramelizes. Serve hot.

Serves: 6 · Prep: 45 min. + time to make the pastry · 40 min. · Level: 2

CROSTATA CON LA MARMELLATA
Blackberry jam pie

☞ I have suggested blackberry jam as a topping, but any jam can be used with equal success.

- 1 quantity Sweet plain pastry (see recipe, page 308) butter and flour for the pie pan
- 1 cup blackberry jam
- 1 egg yolk

Wine: a sweet rosé dessert wine (Lacryma Christi del Vesuvio Rosato Dolce)

Prepare the pastry. • Butter and flour the pie pan. • Break off two-thirds of the pastry dough and roll it out so that it is just large enough to line a fairly shallow 10-inch pie pan. Leave a narrow border of the pastry hanging over the sides. • Spread the blackberry jam evenly over the pastry. • Roll out the remaining pastry into a square sheet. Use a fluted pastry wheel to cut it into $1/2$-inch wide strips. Place these over the jam in a lattice pattern. Fold the overhanging pastry border over the ends of the lattice to form a rolled edge. • Beat the egg yolk and brush the top of the pie with it. • Bake in a preheated oven at 375°F for 30 minutes. • Serve warm.

Serves: 6 · Prep: 20 min. + time to make the pastry · Cooking: 30 min. · Level: 1

CHARLOTTE DI MELE
Apple charlotte

- 4 large cooking apples, peeled and cored
- $1/2$ cup water
- $1/4$ cup superfine sugar
- $1/4$ teaspoon vanilla extract

- 10 oz sliced white bread, crusts removed
- 1 cup butter, melted
- 1 egg white
- $1/4$ cup rum
- $1/2$ cup confectioners' sugar

Slice the apples into bite-sized pieces and cook in the water until soft and mushy. • Add 3 tablespoons of the superfine sugar and the vanilla and continue cooking until the mixture thickens. • Butter a charlotte mold and line it with baking parchment. • Cut the slices of bread in half and brush with some of the melted butter. Line the mold with them, overlapping slightly. • Beat the egg white with the remaining superfine sugar and brush over the bread. • Finish with a light sprinkling of rum, then pour in the apple purée. • Cover with more bread slices spread with butter and sprinkled with rum. • Bake in a preheated oven at 350°F for 40 minutes. • Sprinkle with confectioners' sugar and serve.

Serves: 8 · Prep: 50 min. · Cooking: 40 min. · Level: 2

CROSTATA DI MELE CARAMELLATE
Caramel apple pie

- $2^1/2$ lb Golden Delicious apples
- $1/2$ cup butter
  juice of $1/2$ lemon
- $1^1/4$ cups brown sugar
- 1 quantity Short crust pastry (see recipe, page 49)
- $1/2$ quantity Vanilla cream (see recipe, page 308)

Wine: a dry sparkling white (Prosecco di Conegliano)

Peel, core, and dice the apples. • Place the butter in a saucepan and heat over

CROSTATA DI UVA BIANCA
White grape and almond pie

- 1 quantity Short crust pastry (see recipe, page 49)
- 2 tablespoons granulated sugar
- $1/2$ cup finely ground almonds
- $1^3/4$ lb white grapes
- 2 tablespoons butter
- 2 tablespoons brown sugar
- 2 tablespoons dark rum
- 6 amaretti cookies (macaroons), crumbled
  a lump of butter

Wine: a dry sparkling white (Prosecco di Conegliano)

Prepare the pastry, working 2 tablespoons of granulated sugar and half the ground almonds into the dough. • Rinse the grapes and cut them in half. Place in a heavy-bottomed saucepan and sauté in the butter for 4–5 minutes. • Turn the heat up to high and add the sugar and rum. Stir quickly and remove from heat. • Sprinkle the pastry base with the amaretti cookies, then spoon the grapes and their juice over the top. • Sprinkle with the remaining almonds. Bake in a preheated oven at 350°F for 30 minutes. • Serve warm.

Serves: 6 · Prep: 10 min. + time to make the pastry · Cooking: 30 min. · Level: 1

TORTA AL LIMONE
Lemon pie

- 1 quantity Sweet plain pastry (see recipe, page 308) butter and flour for the pie pan
- 2 eggs + 2 egg whites
  pinch of salt

1 cup granulated sugar
1½ cups ground almonds
⅓ cup butter, melted
finely ground zest and juice of 2 lemons
10 pieces candied lemon peel
confectioner's sugar

Wine: a dry sparkling white (Prosecco di Conegliano)

Prepare the pastry. • Roll the pastry out so that it is large enough to line a fairly shallow 10-inch pie pan. Butter and flour the pan and line it with the pastry. Prick well with a fork. • Whisk the egg whites with the salt until stiff. • Beat the whole eggs with the sugar in a bowl, and add the almonds, egg whites, butter, and the lemon zest and juice. • Spread this mixture evenly over the dough. Bake in a preheated oven at 350°F for 40 minutes. • Decorate the tart with the candied peel and sprinkle with a little confectioners' sugar. • Serve chilled.

Serves: 6 · Prep: 15 min. + time to make the pastry · Cooking: 40 min. · Level: 2

TORTA NERA
Black pie

2 cups all-purpose flour
pinch of salt
¼ cup superfine sugar
2 teaspoons baking powder
½ cup butter, cut in small pieces
2 egg yolks
2 tablespoons Sassolino liqueur or Jamaica rum
For the filling:
1 cup toasted almonds, finely chopped
⅔ cup superfine sugar
⅓ cup unsweetened cocoa powder, sifted
2 egg yolks
⅓ cup strong coffee, cooled
butter and flour for the pan

Wine: a dry sparkling white (Colli Piacentini Malvasia Spumante Secco)

Mix the flour, salt, sugar, and baking powder together in a bowl. • Turn out onto a pastry board and heap up into a mound. Make a well in the center and add the butter. • Rub the butter into the dry ingredients with your fingertips. The resulting mixture will look like fine bread crumbs. • Add the egg yolks and liqueur or rum and combine. Work briefly to make a smooth dough. • To make

the filling, mix the almonds in a bowl with the sugar and cocoa powder. • Stir in the egg yolks and coffee, blending well. • Roll out the pastry so that it is large enough to line a shallow 10-inch springform pan. Butter and flour the pan. Line with pastry. • Pinch all round the edge of the pastry to obtain a fluted effect. • Fill the pie shell with the filling. • Bake in a preheated oven at 350°F for 35 minutes. • Serve warm.

Serves: 4–6 · Prep: 45 min. Cooking: 45 min. · Level: 1

TORTA DI AMARETTI E CIOCCOLATO
Macaroon and chocolate pie

For the pastry:
2¼ cups all-purpose flour
½ cup superfine sugar
½ cup butter, softened
1 whole egg and 1 yolk
1 teaspoon baking powder
4 amaretti cookies (macaroons), crushed
1 tablespoon dark rum
For the custard:
1¼ cups whole milk
shaving of lemon zest
3 egg yolks
3 tablespoons superfine sugar
⅓ cup all-purpose flour
½ teaspoon vanilla extract
pat of butter
For the filling:
15 amaretti cookies (macaroons), crushed
1¾ cups Alchermes liqueur (or light rum mixed with few drops red food coloring)
10 ladyfingers
10 oz semisweet chocolate, coarsely grated

Wine: a dry sparkling white (Prosecco di Conegliano)

To make the pastry, combine the flour, sugar, butter, whole egg and yolk, baking powder, amaretti cookies, and rum together in a bowl. Use your fingers to work these ingredients into a firm dough. • Shape the dough into a ball, wrap in plastic wrap and chill in the refrigerator for 1 hour. • To make the custard, place the milk in a saucepan with the lemon shaving. Bring to a gentle boil. • In a separate bowl, beat the egg yolks with the sugar, then stir in the flour. • Remove the lemon shaving from the hot milk. Then gradually beat the milk into the egg mixture, adding a little at a time. • Return the mixture to the saucepan and cook over medium heat until the custard thickens, stirring continuously. • Add the vanilla and butter and stir well. Remove from heat and leave to cool. • Roll out the pastry dough and use half of it to line an 8-inch springform pan. • Cover with a layer of custard followed by a layer of amaretti cookies and ladyfingers briefly dipped in the liqueur (or red-colored rum), and a layer of chocolate. Repeat this sequence until all the ingredients are in the pan. • Cover with the other half of the pastry dough. • Prick the surface with a fork. Bake in a preheated oven at 350°F for 1 hour. • Serve at room temperature.

Serves: 6 · Prep: 30 min. + 1 hr to chill the pastry · Cooking: 1¼ hrs · Level: 2

Lemon pie

Prato cookies

AMARETTI
Macaroons

☞ These cookies owe their name to bitter almonds (*"amaro"* means "bitter" in Italian). If bitter almonds are not available, add a few drops of almond extract to the sweet almonds.

1½   cups sweet almonds, toasted
3   teaspoons bitter almonds, toasted
10   oz confectioners' sugar
2   egg whites

Wine: a dry sparkling white (Prosecco di Conegliano)

Grind the sweet and bitter almonds together with a little sugar. • Add half the sugar, then one of the egg whites, followed by the remaining sugar and the second white. • Mix by hand to form a smooth paste and roll into small cylinders 1–2 inches in diameter. Cut these into slices about ½ inch thick, form into balls and flatten slightly. • Arrange the cookies on a baking sheet, dust with confectioners' sugar, and bake in a preheated at 425°F for 30 minutes. • Serve cold.

Makes: about 30 cookies · Prep: 20 min. · Cooking: 30 min. · Level: 2

BISCOTTINI DI PRATO
Prato cookies

☞ These crisp almond cookies come from Prato, a town on the outskirts of Florence. They are served with a glass of Vin Santo for dipping and sipping at the end of a hearty meal.

2   cups sweet almonds, unpeeled
4   egg yolks
2¼   cups granulated sugar
4½   cups all-purpose flour
       pinch of salt
       butter and flour for the cookie sheet

Wine: a sweet or dry dessert wine (Vin Santo)

Spread the almonds out in a shallow baking pan and roast at 400°F for 4–5 minutes. • When cool enough to handle, skin and chop finely. • Beat the egg yolks and sugar together in a mixing bowl until pale and fluffy. • Stir in the flour, almonds and salt gradually, using a fork and then combining by hand. • Knead the mixture quickly but thoroughly on a floured work surface. • Shape the dough into long cylinders about ½ inch in diameter. • Transfer to a buttered and floured cookie sheet. Bake in a preheated oven at 375°F for 25 minutes. • Remove from the oven and raise the temperature to 400°F. • Slice the cylinders diagonally into pieces 1½ inches long, and return them to the oven for 10 minutes more, or until pale golden brown.

Serves 6 · Prep: 15 min. · Cooking: 45 min. · Level: 1

MAZARISI
Sicilian pistachio cookies

       butter and potato flour for preparing the molds
8   oz shelled pistachio nuts
1   cup granulated sugar
       pinch of salt
4   eggs, separated
       finely grated zest of 1 medium orange
½   cup potato flour

Wine: a sweet white (Malvasia delle Lipari)

Grease and flour the inside of 10–12 little cake molds (about ½ cup capacity). • To blanch the pistachio nuts, place them in a heatproof bowl and pour boiling water over them. Leave to stand for 1 minute, then drain well. Transfer to a large, clean cloth and rub off their thin, inner skins. • Put the pistachios into a food processor with the sugar and salt, grind finely, and transfer to a mixing bowl. • Whisk the egg whites until stiff but not dry. • Stir the yolks and orange peel into the pistachio and sugar mixture until thoroughly combined. • Gently fold a little at a time into the egg whites, alternating with the potato flour sifted directly into the bowl. • Fill each little mold not more than three-quarters full and bake in a preheated oven at 325°F for 20 minutes. • Turn out of their molds while still hot and leave to cool completely before serving.

Serves: 4–6 · Prep: 45 min. · Cooking: 20 min. · Level: 2

FAVE DOLCI
All Soul's cookies

☞ These cookies are traditionally served in early November to celebrate the Roman Catholic All Soul's feast day.

1   cup whole blanched almonds
⅔   cup superfine sugar
1   cup all-purpose plain flour
¼   cup butter
1   teaspoon ground cinnamon
1   egg
       grated zest of ½ lemon

Wine: a sweet dessert wine (Aleatico di Gradoli)

Spread the almonds in a large baking pan and toast in a preheated oven at 350°F for around 8 minutes, or until the almonds are just beginning to color. Remove from the oven and set aside to cool. • Combine the cooled almonds with half the sugar in a food processor fitted with a steel blade. Process until the almonds are ground to a powder. • Place the almonds and sugar in a mixing bowl and stir in three-quarters of the flour, the butter, cinnamon, egg, and lemon zest. Mix well to obtain a smooth, firm dough. • Use the remaining flour to lightly flour a clean work surface and shape the dough into a long sausage. Slice crosswise to obtain small, oval cookies. Sprinkle with the remaining sugar. • Transfer the cookies to a greased and floured baking sheet and bake in a preheated oven at 300°F for 20 minutes, or until the cookies are light golden brown. • Remove from the sheet and set aside to cool on a wire rack. After a few hours, they will be crisp. Store in an airtight cookie jar.

Serves: 8–10 · Prep: 20 min. · Cooking: 20 min. · Level: 1

BRUTTI MA BUONI
Ugly but good cookies

☞ These cookies may not look very elegant, but their crisp texture and delicious almond flavor make them the perfect snack, or after-dinner treat, to accompany dessert wine or coffee.

3¹/₂ cups toasted almonds
1¹/₂ cups granulated sugar
5 egg whites
  pinch of cinnamon

Wine: a dry sparkling white (Prosecco di Conegliano)

Grind the almonds together with a little of the sugar. • Beat the whites until stiff and fold in the rest of the sugar, the ground almonds, and cinnamon. • Cook this mixture over a very low heat, stirring continuously, until it comes away from the side of the saucepan. Set aside for a few minutes. • Using two teaspoons, space out on the baking sheet in small roughly-shaped heaps. • Bake in a preheated oven at 300°F for 30 minutes. • Cool completely before serving.

Serves: 6–8 · Prep: 4 min. · Cooking: 30 min. · Level: 2

SOGNO AL CIOCCOLATO
Chocolate dream squares

8 oz semisweet chocolate
¹/₂ cup butter
1¹/₄ cups granulated sugar
¹/₄ cup all-purpose flour
4 egg whites
  pinch of salt
1 cup heavy cream

Melt the chocolate and butter in the top of a double-boiler (or in a small saucepan placed in a larger one filled with

simmering water over low heat). • Remove from heat and beat in the sugar, then the flour. • Whisk the egg whites with the salt until very stiff and fold them gently into the cooled chocolate mixture. Butter a shallow 10-inch pie pan and fill with the mixture. Bake in a preheated oven at 300°F for 25 minutes. The cake should have a slight crust, but still be soft inside. Set aside to cool. • Whip the cream until stiff and serve with the cooled cake.

Serves: 6 · Prep: 15 min. · Cooking: 25 min. · Level: 1

CAVALLUCCI
Siennese cookies with spices, honey, and nuts

1 cup granulated sugar
¹/₃ cup honey
3 cups all-purpose flour + ¹/₄ cup extra
¹/₂ cup chopped walnuts
¹/₄ cup finely chopped candied orange and citron peel
1 teaspoon freshly ground anise seeds
1 teaspoon freshly ground coriander seeds
1 tablespoon butter

Wine: a sweet or dry dessert wine (Vin Santo)

In a double boiler or a bowl over simmering water, heat the sugar and honey together. • When a thread of honey forms when a spoonful is lifted above the pan, remove from heat and gently fold in the flour together with the walnuts, candied

peel, and anise and coriander seeds. • Dust your hands with flour and break off pieces of the dough, rolling them into small cylinders. Cut into slices about 1 inch thick and form into curved shapes. • Transfer to a greased and floured cookie sheet and bake in a preheated oven at 320°F for about 1 hour.

Serves: 6 · Prep: 20 min. · Cooking: 1¹/₄ hrs · Level: 2

MERINGA
Meringue

  pinch of salt
3 egg whites
2 cups confectioners' sugar
2 tablespoons superfine sugar, to sprinkle

Combine the salt with the egg whites and beat with an electric whisk. When the egg whites start to stiffen, gradually add half the confectioners' sugar. Decrease the speed of the whisk, and incorporate the remaining sugar. • Continue whisking until the mixture is very stiff, then transfer it to a piping-bag with a plain or fluted nozzle. • Line a baking sheet with paper and squeeze out dollops of the mixture, leaving about 2 inches between each one. • Sprinkle with the sugar. Bake in a preheated oven at 250°F for about 50 minutes.

Serves: 6 · Prep: 20 min. · Cooking: 50 min. · Level: 1

Siennese cookies with spices, honey, and nuts

ANELLI DORATI
Sweet rings

- 3 cups all-purpose flour
- 1 cup superfine sugar
- 1/4 teaspoon vanilla extract
- 1 teaspoon ground cinnamon
  finely grated zest of 1 lemon
- 1 teaspoon baking powder
- 1/4 cup extra-virgin olive oil
- 2 eggs
  butter and flour for the baking sheet(s)

Wine: a sweet white (Orvieto Dolce)

Place the flour, sugar, vanilla, cinnamon, lemon rind, and baking powder in a mixing bowl. Stir in the oil and eggs and mix for about 5–8 minutes with a wooden spoon. Cover with a clean cloth and leave to rest for 1 hour. • Lightly flour a clean work surface and shape pieces of dough into long, thin sausages. Cut into pieces about 4 inches long and pinch the ends of each piece together to form a ring. • Transfer the rings to a buttered and floured baking sheet. • Bake in a preheated oven at 400°F for 25 minutes. • Cool on a wire rack.

Serves: 6 · Prep: 15 min. + 1 hr to rest · Cooking: 25 min. · Level: 1

Sweet rings

ZALETT
Cornmeal, pine nut, and raisin cookies

- 2 cups very fine yellow cornmeal
- 1 3/4 cups all-purpose flour
- 1/2 cup superfine sugar
  pinch of salt
  finely grated zest of 1 lemon
- 2/3 cup butter, cut into small pieces
- 1/4 cup milk
- 1/2 cup seedless golden raisins, soaked in water, then drained and squeezed of excess moisture
- 1/3 cup pine nuts
  butter and flour for the baking sheet(s)
- 1/2 cup confectioners' sugar

Wine: a sweet white (Albana Dolce)

Sift the cornmeal and flour into a mixing bowl. Mix in the sugar, salt, and lemon zest. • Turn out onto a pastry board and heap up into a mound. Make a well in the center and add the butter and the milk. • Gradually mix these ingredients into the flour, adding a little more milk if necessary. The dough should be firm. • Work the dough, incorporating the raisins and pine nuts. • Break off pieces of dough each about the size of a large walnut. Shape them into balls, then flatten slightly. • Place them, well spaced out, on a greased and floured baking sheet. • Bake in a preheated oven at 400°F for 15 minutes. • Cool on a rack. Dust with sifted confectioners' sugar and serve.

Serves: 6 · Prep: 40 min. · Cooking: 15 min. · Level: 1

These little fried cookies are served all over southern Italy at Christmas time. This particular recipe comes from Naples. There is a wonderful story associated with them that shows just how irresistible they are.... A Neapolitan woman left a large dish of homemade Struffoli on the back seat of her car. She was so busy with her Christmas shopping that she forgot to lock the door and a man stole them. He was caught and duly appeared in court charged with theft. Since he had been caught red-handed, things did not look good. But when the judge learned what he had stolen the culprit was absolved since "no one could resist such a prize." The woman was admonished in future to hide her goodies and lock her car. This is a true story!

STRUFFOLI
Neapolitan Christmas fritters

- 3 1/2 cups all-purpose flour, sifted
- 4 eggs
- 2 tablespoons superfine sugar
- 1/2 cup liqueur (Strega or anise)
  pinch of salt
- 2 cups oil, for frying
- 3/4 cup honey
- 1 cup each candied orange and lemon peel, diced
- 1/4 cup sprinkles

Combine the flour with the eggs, sugar, liqueur, and salt in a mixing bowl and beat until smooth and well-mixed. Set aside to rest for 2 hours. • Scoop out tablespoonfuls of the dough and roll them into sticks about the thickness of a pencil. Cut into pieces about 1/2 inch long. • Heat the oil to very hot in a large skillet and fry the fritters in small batches until light golden brown. Scoop the fritters out of the oil with a slotted spoon and drain on paper towels. • Heat the honey in a large, heavy-bottomed saucepan until thoroughly melted. Add the Struffoli and the candied orange and lemon peels. Stir carefully until they are all coated with honey. • Place the Struffoli on a serving dish. Decorate with the sprinkles and serve.

Serves: 10 · Prep: 1 hr · Cooking: 30 min. · Level: 2

Neapolitan Christmas fritters

INDEX

Dry Measures

IMPERIAL	METRIC
½ oz	15 g
1 oz	30 g
2 oz	60 g
3 oz	90 g
3½ oz	100 g
4 oz	125 g
5 oz	155 g
6 oz	185 g
6½ oz	200 g
7 oz	220 g
8 oz (½ lb)	250 g
9 oz	280 g
10 oz	315 g
11 oz	345 g
12 oz (¾ lb)	375 g
13 oz	410 g
14 oz	440 g
15 oz	470 g
16 oz (1 lb)	500 g
24 oz (1½ lb)	750 g
32 oz (2 lb)	1 kg

Liquid Measures

IMPERIAL	METRIC
1 fluid oz	30 ml
2 fluid oz (¼ cup)	60 ml
3 fluid oz	100 ml
4 fluid oz (½ cup)	125 ml
5 fluid oz	150 ml
6 fluid oz	185 ml
8 fluid oz (1 cup)	250 ml
10 fluid oz (½ pint)	300 ml
16 fluid oz	500 ml
24 fluid oz	750 ml
32 fluid oz (1¾ pints/1 quart)	1000 ml (1 liter)

Oven Temperatures

F (FAHRENHEIT)	C (CELSIUS)	GAS MARK
250	120	1
300	150	2
325	160	3
350	180	4
375	190	5
400	200	6
450	230	7

Helpful measures

IMPERIAL	METRIC
⅛ inch	3 mm
¼ inch	6 mm
½ inch	1 cm
¾ inch	2 cm
1 inch	2.5 cm
2 inches	5 cm
2½ inches	6 cm
3 inches	8 cm
4 inches	10 cm
5 inches	13 cm
6 inches	15 cm
7 inches	18 cm
8 inches	20 cm
9 inches	23 cm
10 inches	25 cm
11 inches	28 cm
12 inches	30 cm